AMERICA'S
Favorite
INNS,
B&Bs,
& SMALL HOTELS
1999

U.S.A. and Canada

States, Territories, and Canadian Provinces Covered in This Edition

UNITED STATES

Alabama
Alaska
Arizona
Arkansas
California
Colorado
Connecticut
Delaware
District of Columbia
Florida
Georgia
Hawaii
Idaho
Illinois
Indiana
Iowa
Kansas
Kentucky
Louisiana
Maine
Maryland
Massachusetts
Michigan
Minnesota
Mississippi
Missouri
Montana
Nebraska
Nevada

New Hampshire
New Jersey
New Mexico
New York
North Carolina
North Dakota
Ohio
Oklahoma
Oregon
Pennsylvania
Rhode Island
South Carolina
South Dakota
Tennessee
Texas
Utah
Vermont
Virginia
Washington
West Virginia
Wisconsin
Wyoming

CANADA

Alberta
British Columbia
New Brunswick
Nova Scotia
Ontario
Prince Edward Island
Québec

Also in This Series

America's Favorite Inns, B&Bs, & Small Hotels, New England
America's Wonderful Little Hotels & Inns, The Middle Atlantic
America's Wonderful Little Hotels & Inns, The Midwest
America's Wonderful Little Hotels & Inns, The Rocky Mountains and The Southwest
America's Wonderful Little Hotels & Inns, The South
America's Wonderful Little Hotels & Inns, The West Coast

AMERICA'S
Favorite
INNS,
B&Bs,
& SMALL HOTELS

1999

U.S.A. and Canada

Edited by Sandra W. Soule

Associate Editors:
Nancy P. Barker, Elyse Brown,
Carol Dinmore, Betsy Nolan Sandberg,
Hilary Soule

Contributing Editors:
Suzanne Carmichael, Rose Ciccone,
Gail Davis, Nancy Debevoise, Linda Goldberg,
Betty Norman, Pam Phillips, Joe Schmidt,
Susan Schwemm, Diane Wolf

Editorial Assistants:
Rachel Brown, Tyler Sandberg

St. Martin's Griffin
New York

This book is dedicated to the people who take the time and trouble to write about the hotels and inns they've visited, and to my children—Hilary and Jeffrey—my husband, and my parents.

ISBN 0-312-19435-8

First St. Martin's Griffin Edition: January 1999

10   9   8   7   6   5   4   3   2   1

Maps by David Lindroth © 1998, 1997, 1996, 1995, 1994, 1993, 1992, 1991, 1990, 1989, 1988, 1987 by St. Martin's Press

Contents

Acknowledgments	vii
Introduction	1
Glossary of Architectural and Decorating Terms	19
Key to Abbreviations and Symbols	25

U.S.A.

Alabama	27
Alaska	33
Arizona	43
Arkansas	57
California	65
Colorado	119
Connecticut	138
Delaware	152
District of Columbia	157
Florida	162
Georgia	176
Hawaii	187
Idaho	201
Illinois	209
Indiana	215
Iowa	224
Kansas	229
Kentucky	234
Louisiana	242
Maine	252
Maryland	280
Massachusetts	291
Michigan	324
Minnesota	336
Mississippi	342
Missouri	349
Montana	357
Nebraska	373

CONTENTS

Nevada   375
New Hampshire   379
New Jersey   395
New Mexico   405
New York   419
North Carolina   443
North Dakota   465
Ohio   467
Oklahoma   477
Oregon   481
Pennsylvania   497
Rhode Island   516
South Carolina   523
South Dakota   531
Tennessee   534
Texas   543
Utah   556
Vermont   569
Virginia   598
Washington   618
West Virginia   634
Wisconsin   640
Wyoming   647

Canada   658

Alberta   659
British Columbia   663
New Brunswick   673
Nova Scotia   675
Ontario   683
Prince Edward Island   691
Québec   694

Maps   699
Index of Accommodations   721
Hotel/Inn Report Forms   725

Acknowledgments

I would like again to thank all the people who wrote in such helpful detail about the inns and hotels they visited. To them belong both the dedication and the acknowledgments, for without their support, this guide would not exist. If I have inadvertently misspelled or omitted anyone's name, please accept my sincerest apologies.

I would also like to thank my wonderful colleagues Nancy Barker, Carol Dinmore, Elyse Brown, Betsy Sandberg, Suzanne Carmichael, Rose Ciccone, Nancy Debevoise, Gail Davis, Linda Goldberg, Betty Norman, Pam Phillips, Susan Schwemm, and Diane Wolf; and to faithful respondents Peg Bedini, Maureen Banner, Carol Blodgett, Donna Bocks, Judith Brannen, Sherrill Brown, James and Pamela Burr, Tina Chen, Marjorie Cohen, Dianne Crawford, Judy Dawson, Lynne Derry, Gail DeSciose, Cecille Desroches, Brian Donaldson, Sally Ducot, Lynn Edge, John Felton, Ellie and Robert Freidus, Connie Gardner, Gail Gunning, B. J. Hensley, Lisa Hering, Emily Hochemong, Stephen Holman, Ruth Hurley, Linda Intaschi, Donna Jacobsen, Christopher Johnston, Keith Jurgens, Arleen Keele, Peggy Kontak, Ellis Locher, Bradley Lockner, Bill MacGowan, Myra Malkin, Pat Malone, Julia and Dennis Mallach, Celia McCullough, Mark Mendenhall, Michael and Dina Miller, Carol Moritz, Carolyn Myles, Sybil Nestor, Eileen O'Reilly, Marilyn Parker, Julie Phillips, Adam Platt, Penny Poirier, Jill Reeves, Stephanie Roberts, Leigh Robinson, Glenn Roehrig, Duane Roller, Marion Ruben, Lori Sampson, Conrad & Nancy Schilke, Joe and Sheila Schmidt, B. J. and Larry Schwartzkopf, Robert Sfire, Fritz Shantz and Tara O'Neal, Maggie Sievers, Nancy Sinclair, Mary Jane Skala, Christine Tanguay, Ruth Tilsley, Susan Ulanoff, Wendi Van Exan, Marty Wall and Kip Goldman, Hopie Welliver, Jim and Mary White, Tom Wilbanks, Beryl Williams, Linda Wrigley, Karl Wiegers and Chris Zambito, Susan Woods, and the many others who went far beyond the call of duty in their assistance and support.

Introduction

Reading the Entries

Each entry generally has three parts: a description of the inn or hotel, quotes from guests who have stayed there, and relevant details about rooms, rates, location, and facilities. Please remember that the length of an entry is in no way a reflection of that inn or hotel's quality. Rather, it is an indication of the type of feedback we've received both from guests and from the innkeepers themselves.

Wherever a location is of particular tourist interest, we've tried to include some information about its attractions. In some areas the magnet is not a particular town but rather a compact, distinct region. Travelers choose one place to stay and use it as a base from which to explore the area. But because this guide is organized by town, not by region, the entries are scattered throughout the chapter. When this applies, you will see the name of the region noted under the "Location" heading; check back to the introduction for a description of the region involved. Cross-referencing is also provided to supplement the maps at the back of the book.

The names at the end of the quotations are those who have recommended the hotel or inn. Some writers have requested that we not use their names; you will see initials noted instead. *We never print the names of those who have sent us adverse reports, although their contributions are invaluable indeed.*

Although we have tried to make the listings as accurate and complete as possible, mistakes and inaccuracies invariably creep in. The most significant area of inaccuracy applies to the rates charged by each establishment. In preparing this guide, we asked all the hotels and inns to give us their 1999–2000 rates, ranging from the least expensive room in the off-season to the most expensive peak-season price. Some did so, while others just noted the current rate.

Some of the shorter entries are marked **"Information please"** or **"Also recommended."** These tend to be establishments that are either too large or too small for a full entry, or about which we have insufficient information to complete a full entry.

Please remember that the process of writing and publishing a book takes nearly a year. *You should always double-check the rates when you make your reservations; please don't blame the inn or this guide if the prices are wrong.* On the other hand, given the current level of inflation, you should not encounter anything more than a 5% increase, unless there has been a substantial improvement in the amenities offered or a change of ownership. Please let us know immediately if you find anything more than that!

If you find any errors of omission or commission in any part of the entries, we urgently request your help in correcting them. We recognize that it takes extra time and effort for readers to write us letters or fill in report forms, but this feedback is essential in keeping this publication totally responsive to consumer needs.

The Fifteen Commandments of Vacation Travel

We all know people who come back from a vacation feeling on top of the world, and others who seem vaguely disappointed. Here's how to put yourself in the first category, not the second.

1. Know yourself. A successful vacation is one that works for the person you are, not the person you think you should be. Confirmed couch potatoes who resent having to walk from the far end of the parking lot will not find true fulfillment on a trek through the Himalayas. If privacy is a top priority, a group tour or communal lodge will turn fantasy into frustration. Acknowledge your own comfort levels. How important is it for you to be independent and flexible? Structured and secure? How essential are the creature comforts when it comes to sleeping, eating, and bathing? Would you rather have one week of luxury travel or two weeks of budget food and accommodation? And remember that while your personality doesn't change, your needs do. The type of vacation you plan for a romantic getaway is totally different from a family reunion.

2. Know your travel companions. Adjust your plans to accommodate your travel partners. Whether you are traveling with friends, spouse, children, and/or parents, you'll need to take their age, attention span, agility, and interests into account. If you're traveling with the kids, balance a morning at an art museum with an afternoon at the zoo; if you're spending time with elderly parents, make sure that they can stroll a country lane while you go rock-climbing; if your group includes skiers and nonskiers, pick a resort that has appealing shops and other activities.

3. Plan ahead: anticipation is half the fun. Enjoy the process. The more you know about an area you're going to visit, the more fun you'll have. Skim a guidebook; get a calendar of events; write to the local chambers of commerce and tourist offices; read a novel set in the region; talk to friends (or friends of friends) who have been there recently.

4. Don't bite off more than you can chew. Keep your itinerary in line with the amount of time and money available. Focus on seeing a smaller area well, rather than trying to cover too much ground and seeing nothing but interstate highways. Don't overprogram; allow yourself the luxury of doing nothing.

5. Avoid one-night stands. Plan to stay a minimum of two nights everywhere you go. A vacation made up of one-nighters is a prescription for exhaustion. You will sleep poorly, spend most of your time in transit, and will get only the smallest glimpse of the place you're visiting. If it's worth seeing, it's worth spending a full day in one place.

6. Travel off-season. Unless your vacation dates are dictated by the school calendar, off-season travel offers many advantages: fewer crowds, greater flexibility, and a more relaxed atmosphere. Learn to pick the best dates for off-season travel; typically these are the weeks just before and after the rates change. Off-season travel offers big savings, too; for example, most ski areas are delightful places to visit in summer, and offer savings of 50% or more on accommodations.

7. Book well ahead for peak season travel. If you must travel during peak periods to popular destinations, make reservations well in advance for the key sites to avoid aggravation, extra phone calls, and additional driving time.

8. Take the road less traveled by. Get off the beaten path to leave the crowds behind. Instead of booking a room in the heart of the action, find a quiet inn tucked in the hills or in a neighboring village. If you visit the Grand Canyon in August, at the height of the tourist season, stay at the North Rim, which attracts 90% fewer visitors than the South Rim.

9. Ditch the car. Sure you need a car to get where you're going. But once you're there, get out and walk. You'll see more, learn more, experience more at every level, while avoiding crowds even at the most popular destinations. We promise. Car travel is an isolating experience, even when you're in bumper-to-bumper traffic.

10. Hang loose. The unexpected is inevitable in travel, as in the rest of life. When your plans go astray (and they will), relax and let serendipity surprise you. And keep your sense of humor in good working order. If possible, travel without reservations or a set itinerary.

11. Carpe diem—seize the day. Don't be afraid to follow your impulses. If a special souvenir catches your eye, buy it; don't wait to see if you'll find it again later. If a hiking trail looks too inviting to pass up, don't; that museum will wait for a rainy day.

12. Don't suffer in silence. When things go wrong—an incompetent guide, car troubles, a noisy hotel room—speak up. Politely but firmly express your concern then and there; get your room changed, ask for a refund or discount, whatever. Most people in the travel business would rather have you go away happy than leave grumbling.

13. Remember—being there is more than seeing there. People travel to see the sights—museums and mountains, shops and scenery—but it is making new friends that can make a trip memorable. Leave a door open to the people-to-people experiences that enrich travel immeasurably.

14. Don't leave home to find home. The quickest way to take the wind out of the sails of your trip is to compare things to the way they are at home. Enjoy different styles and cultures for what they are and avoid comparisons and snap judgments.

15. Give yourself permission to disregard all of the above. Nothing is immutable. If you find a pattern that works for you, enjoy it!

Inngoer's Bill of Rights

Although nothing's perfect, as we all know, inngoers are entitled to certain reasonable standards. Of course, the higher the rates, the higher those standards should be. So, please use this Bill of Rights as a kind of checklist in deciding how you think a place stacks up on your own personal rating scale. And, whether an establishment fails, reaches, or exceeds these levels, be sure to let us know. We would also hope that innkeepers will use this list to help evaluate both the strong points and shortcomings of their own establishments, and are grateful to those who have already done so.

The right to suitable cleanliness: An establishment that looks, feels, and smells immaculate, with no musty, smoky, or animal odors.

The right to suitable room furnishings: A firm mattress, soft pillows, fresh linens, and ample blankets; bright lamps and night tables on each side of the bed; comfortable chairs with good reading lights; and adequate storage space.

The right to comfortable, attractive rooms: Guest rooms and common rooms that are as livable as they are attractive. Appealing places where you'd like to read, chat, relax

The right to a decent bathroom: Cleanliness is essential, along with reliable plumbing, ample hot water, good lighting, an accessible electric outlet, space for toiletries, and thirsty towels.

The right to privacy and discretion: Privacy must be respected by the innkeeper and ensured by adequate soundproofing. The right to discretion precludes questions about marital status or sexual preference. No display of proselytizing religious materials.

The right to good, healthful food: Fresh nutritious food, ample in quantity, high in quality, attractively presented, and graciously served in smoke-free surroundings.

The right to comfortable temperatures and noise levels: Rooms should be cool in summer and warm in winter, with windows that open, and quiet, efficient air-conditioning and heating. Double windows, drapes, and landscaping are essential if traffic noise is an issue.

The right to fair value: Prices should be in reasonable relation to the facilities offered and to the cost of equivalent local accommodation.

The right to genuine hospitality: Innkeepers who are glad you've come and who make it their business to make your stay pleasant and memorable; who are readily available without being intrusive.

The right to a caring environment: Welcoming arrivals with refreshments, making dinner reservations, providing information on activities, asking about pet allergies and dietary restrictions, and so on.

The right to personal safety: A location in a reasonably safe neighborhood, with adequate care given to building and parking security.

The right to professionalism: Brochure requests, room reservations, check-ins and -outs handled efficiently and responsibly.

The right to adequate common areas: At least one common room where guests can gather to read, chat, or relax, free of the obligation to buy anything.

The right of people traveling alone to have all the above rights: Singles usually pay just a few dollars less than couples, yet the welcome, services, and rooms they receive can be inferior.

The right to a reasonable cancellation policy: Penalties for a cancellation made fewer than 7-14 days before arrival are relatively standard. Most inns will refund deposits (minus a processing fee) after the deadline only if the room is rebooked.

The right to efficient maintenance: Burnt-out bulbs and worn-out smoke detector batteries are the responsibility of the innkeeper—not the guest. When things go wrong, guests have the right to an apology, a discount, or a refund.

Of course, there is no "perfect" inn or hotel, because people's tastes and needs vary so greatly. But one key phrase does pop up over and over again: "I felt right at home." This is not written in the literal sense— a commercial lodging, no matter how cozy or charming, is never the same as one's home. What is really meant is that guests felt as welcome, as relaxed, as comfortable, as they would in their own home.

What makes for a wonderful stay?

We've tried our best to make sure that all the hotels and inns listed in this guide are as special as our title promises. Inevitably, there will be some disappointments. Sometimes these will be caused by a change in ownership or management that has resulted in lowered standards. Other times unusual circumstances will lead to problems. Quite often, though, problems will occur because there's not a good "fit" between the inn or hotel and the guest. Decide what you're looking for, then find the inn that suits your needs, whether you're looking for a casual environment or a dressy one, a romantic setting or a family-oriented one, a vacation spot or a business person's environment, an isolated country retreat or a convenient in-town location.

We've tried to give you as much information as possible on each hotel or inn listed, and have taken care to indicate the atmosphere each innkeeper is trying to create. After you've read the listing, request a copy of the establishment's brochure, which will give you more information. Finally, feel free to call any inn or hotel where you're planning to stay, and ask as many questions as necessary.

Inn etiquette

A first-rate inn is a joy indeed, but as guests we need to do our part to respect its special qualities. For starters, you'll need to maintain a higher level of consideration for your fellow guests. Century-old Victorians are noted for their nostalgic charms, not their sound-proofing; if you come in late or get up early, remember that voices and footsteps echo off all those gleaming hardwood floors and doors. If you're going to pick a fight with your roommate, pull the covers up over your head or go out for a walk. If you're sharing a bath, don't dawdle, tidy up after yourself, and dry your hair back in your room. If you've admired the Oriental carpets, antique decor, handmade quilts, and the thick fluffy towels, don't leave wet glasses on the furniture, put suitcases on the bed, or use the towels for removing makeup or wiping the snow off your car. After all, innkeepers have rights too!

Hotels, inns ... resorts and motels

As the title indicates, this is a guide to exceptional inns and hotels. Generally, the inns have 5 to 25 rooms, although a few have only 2 rooms and some have over 100. The hotels are more often found in the cities and range in size from about 50 to 200 rooms.

The line between an inn or hotel and a resort is often a fine one. There are times when we all want the extra facilities a resort provides, so we've added a number of reader-recommended facilities. We've also listed a handful of motels. Although they don't strictly fall within the context of this book, we've included them because readers felt they were the best option in a specific situation.

What is a B&B anyway?

There are basically two kinds of B&Bs—the B&B homestay and the B&B inn. The homestay is typically the home of an empty nester, who has a few empty bedrooms to fill, gaining some extra income and pleasant company. B&B inns are run on a more professional basis, independently marketed and subject to state and local licensing. Guests typically have dedicated common areas for their use, and do not share the hosts' living quarters, as in a homestay. We list very few homestays in this guide. Full-service or country inns and lodges are similar to the B&B inn, except that they serve breakfast and dinner on a regular basis, and may be somewhat larger in size; dinner is often offered to the public as well as to house guests. The best of all of these are made special by resident owners bringing the warmth of their personalities to the total experience. A B&B is *not* a motel that serves breakfast.

Rooms

All hotel and inn rooms are not created equal. Although the rooms at a typical chain motel or hotel may be identical, the owners of most of the establishments described in this book pride themselves on the individuality of each guest room. Some, although not all, of these differences are reflected in the rates charged.

More importantly it means that travelers need to express their needs clearly to the innkeepers when making reservations and again when checking in. Some rooms may be quite spacious but may have extremely small private baths or limited closet space. Some antique double beds have rather high footboards—beautiful to look at but torture for six-footers. Most inns are trading their double-size mattresses in for queens and kings; if you prefer an oversize bed, say so. If you want twin beds, be sure to specify this when making reservations and again when you check in; many smaller inns have only one twin-bedded room. If you must have a king-size bed, ask for details; sometimes two twin beds are just pushed together, made up with a king-size fitted sheet.

Some rooms may have gorgeous old bathrooms, with tubs the size of small swimming pools, but if you are a hard-core shower person, that room won't be right for you. More frequently, you'll find a showers but no bathtub, which may be disappointing if you love a long, luxurious soak. If you are traveling on business and simply must have a working-size desk with good lighting, an electric outlet, and a telephone jack for your modem, speak up. Some rooms look terrific inside but don't look out at anything much; others may have the view but not quite as special a decor. Often the largest rooms are at the front of the house, facing a busy highway. Decide what's important to you. Although the owners and staff of the hotels and inns listed here are incredibly hard-working and dedicated people, they can't read your mind. Let your needs be known, and, within the limits of availability, they will try to accommodate you.

Our most frequent complaints center around beds that are too soft and inadequate reading lights. If these are priorities for you (as they are for us), don't be shy about requesting bedboards or additional lamps to remedy the situation. Similarly, if there are other amenities your room is lacking—extra pillows, blankets, or even an easy chair—speak up. Most innkeepers would rather put in an extra five minutes of work than have an unhappy guest.

If you really don't like your room, ask for another as soon as possible, preferably before you've unpacked your bags. The sooner you voice your dissatisfaction, the sooner something can be done to improve the situation. If you don't like the food, ask for something else—since you're the guest, make sure you get treated like one. If things go terribly wrong, don't be shy about asking for your money back, and be *sure* to write us about any problems.

What is a single? A double? A suite? A cottage or cabin?

Unlike the proverbial rose, a single is not a single is not a single. Sometimes it is a room with one twin bed, which really can accommodate only one person. Quite often it is described as a room with a standard-size double bed, in contrast to a double, which has two twin beds. Other hotels call both of the preceding doubles, although doubles often have queen- or even king-size beds instead. Many times the only distinction is made by the number of guests occupying the room; a single will pay slightly less, but there's no difference in the room.

There's almost as much variation when it comes to suites. We define a suite as a bedroom with a separate living room area and often a small kitchen, as well. Unfortunately, the word has been stretched to cover other setups, too. Some so-called suites are only one large room, accommodating a table and separate seating area in addition to the bed, while others are two adjacent bedrooms which share a bath. If you require a suite that has two separate rooms with a door between them, specify this when you make reservations.

Quite a few of our entries have cabins or cottages in addition to rooms in the main building. In general, a cabin is understood to be a somewhat more rustic residence than a cottage, although there's no hard-and-fast rule. Be sure to inquire for details when making reservations.

Making reservations

Unless you are inquiring many months in advance of your visit, it's best to telephone when making reservations. This offers a number of advantages: You will know immediately if space is available on your requested dates; you can find out if that space is suitable to your specific needs. You will have a chance to discuss the pros and cons of the available rooms and will be able to find out about any changes made in recent months—new facilities, recently redecorated rooms, nonsmoking policies, even a change of ownership. It's also a good time to ask the innkeeper about other concerns—Is the neighborhood safe at night? Is there any renovation or construction in progress that might be disturbing? Will a wedding reception or bicycle touring group affect use of the common areas during your visit? If you're reserving a room at a plantation home that is available for public tours, get specifics about the check-in/out times; in many, rooms are not available before 5 P.M. and must be vacated by 9 A.M. sharp. The savvy traveler will always get the best value for his accommodation dollar.

If you expect to be checking in late at night, *be sure to say so;* many inns give doorkeys to their guests, then lock up by 10 P.M.; often special arrangements must be made for late check-ins, and a handful of inns won't accept them at all.

We're often asked about the need for making advance reservations. If you'll be traveling in peak periods, in prime tourist areas, and want to be sure of getting a first-rate room at the best-known inns, reserve at least three to six months ahead. This is especially true if you're traveling with friends or family and will need more than one room. On the other hand, if you like a bit of adventure, and don't want to be stuck with cancellation fees when you change your mind, by all means stick our books in the glove compartment and hit the road. If you're traveling in the off-season, or even midweek in season, you'll have a grand time. But look for a room by late afternoon; never wait until after dinner and expect to find something decent. Some inns offer a discount after 4:00 P.M. for last-minute bookings; it never hurts to ask.

Payment

The vast majority of inns now accept credit cards. A few accept credit cards for the initial deposit but prefer cash, traveler's checks, or personal checks for the balance; others offer the reverse policy. When no credit cards are accepted at all, you can settle your bill with a personal check, traveler's check, or even (!) cash.

When using your credit card to guarantee a reservation, be aware that most inns will charge your card for the amount of the deposit, unlike motels and hotels which don't put through the charge until you've checked in. A few will put a "hold" on your card for the full amount of your entire stay, plus the cost of meals and incidentals that you may (or may not) spend. If you're using your card to reserve a fairly extended trip, you may find that you're well over your credit limit without actually having spent a nickel. We'd suggest inquiring; if the latter is the procedure, either send a check for the deposit or go elsewhere. If you have used American Express, Diners Club, MasterCard, or Visa to guarantee your reservation, these companies guarantee if a room is not available, the hotel is supposed to find you a free room in a comparable hotel, plus transportation and a free phone call.

Rates

All rates quoted are per room, unless otherwise noted as being per person. Rates quoted per person are usually based on double occupancy, unless otherwise stated.

"Room only" rates do not include any meals. In most cases two or three meals a day are served by the hotel restaurant, but are charged separately. Average meal prices are noted when available. In a very few cases no meals are served on the premises at all; rooms in these facilities are usually equipped with kitchenettes.

B&B rates include bed and breakfast. Breakfast, though, can vary from a simple continental breakfast to an expanded continental breakfast to a full breakfast. Afternoon tea and evening refreshments are sometimes included as well.

MAP (Modified American Plan) rates are often listed per person and include breakfast and dinner; a 15% service charge is typically added. Full board rates include three squares a day, and are usually found only at old-fashioned resorts and isolated ranches.

State and local sales taxes are not included in the rates unless otherwise indicated; the percentage varies from state to state, city to city, and can reach 20% in a few urban centers, although 10–15% is more typical.

When inquiring about rates, always ask if any off-season or special package rates are available. Sometimes discounted rates are available *only* on request; seniors and AAA members often qualify for substantial discounts. During the week, when making reservations at city hotels or country inns, it's important to ask if any corporate rates are available. Depending on the establishment, you may or may not be asked for some proof of corporate affiliation (a business card is usually all that's needed), but it's well worth inquiring, since the effort can result in a saving of 15 to 20%, plus an upgrade to a substantially better room.

A number of companies specialize in booking hotel rooms in major cities at substantial discounts. Although you can ask for specific hotels by name, the largest savings are realized by letting the agency make the selection; they may be able to get you a discount of up to 65%. **Hotel Reservations Network** (8140 Walnut Hill Lane, Dallas, TX, 75231; 800–96–HOTEL) offers discount rates in over 20 U.S. cities plus London and Paris; **Quikbook** (381 Park Avenue South, New York, NY, 10016; 800–789–9887) is a similar service with competitive rates. **Express Reservations** (3800 Arapahoe, Boulder, CO, 80303; 800–356–1123) specializes in properties in New York City and Los Angeles. For California, try **San Francisco Reservations** (22 Second Street, Fourth Floor, San Francisco, CA, 94105; 800–677–1500), or **California Reservations** (3 Sumner Street, 94103; 800–576–0003).

Another money-saving trick can be to look for inns in towns a bit off the beaten path. If you stay in a town that neighbors a famous resort or historic community, you will often find that rates are anywhere from $20 to $50 less per night for equivalent accommodation. If you're travelling without reservations, and arrive at a half-empty inn in late afternoon, don't hesitate to ask for a price reduction or free room upgrade. And of course, watch for our ¢ symbol, which indicates places which are a particularly good value.

If an establishment has a specific tipping policy, whether it is "no tipping" or the addition of a set service charge, it is noted under "Rates." When both breakfast and dinner are included in the rates, a 15% service charge against the total bill—not just the room—is standard; a few inns charge 18–20%. A number of B&Bs are also adding on a service charge, a practice which sits poorly with us. If you feel—as many of our readers do—that these fees are a sneaky way of making rates seem lower than they really are, let the innkeeper (and us) know how you feel. When no notation is made, it's generally expected that guests will leave $1–3 a night for the housekeeping staff and 15% for meal service. A number of inns have taken to leaving little cards or envelopes to remind guests to leave a tip for the housekeepers; most readers find this practice objectionable. If you welcome a no-tipping policy and object to solicitation, speak up.

While the vast majority of inns are fairly priced, there are a few whose rates have become exorbitant. Others fail to stay competitive, charging top weekend rates when a nearby luxury hotel is offering a beautiful suite at a lower price. No matter how lovely the breakfast, how thoughtful the innkeepers, there's a limit to the amount one will pay for a room without an in-room telephone, TV, or a full-size private bathroom. One B&B has the nerve to charge $125 for a room with shared bath, then asks you to bring your own pool towels during the summer (it's not listed here!).

Deposits and cancellations

Nearly all innkeepers print their deposit and cancellation policies clearly on their brochures. Deposits generally range from payment of the first night's stay to 50% of the cost of the entire stay. Some inns repeat the cancellation policy when confirming reservations. In general, guests canceling well in advance of the planned arrival (one to four weeks is typical) receive a full refund minus a cancellation fee. After that date, no refunds are offered unless the room is resold to someone else. A few will not refund *even if the room is resold,* so take careful note. If you're making a credit card booking over the phone, be sure to find out what the cancellation policy is. We are uncomfortable with overly strict refund policies, and wish that inns would give a gift certificate, good for a return visit, when guests are forced to cancel on short notice.

Sometimes the shoe may be on the other foot. Even if you were told earlier that the inn at which you really wanted to stay was full, it may be worthwhile to make a call to see if cancellations have opened up any last-minute vacancies.

Minimum stays

Two- and three-night minimum weekend and holiday stays are the rule at many inns during peak periods. We have noted these when possible, although we suspect that the policy may be more common than is always indicated in print. On the other hand, you may just be hitting a slow period, so it never hurts to call at the last minute to see if a one-night reservation would be accepted. Again, cancellations are always a possibility; you can try calling on a Friday or Saturday morning to see if something is available for that night.

Pets

Very few of the inns and hotels listed accept pets. When they do we've noted it under "Extras." On the other hand, most of the inns listed in this book have at least one dog or cat, sometimes more. These pets are usually found in the common areas, sometimes in guest rooms as well. If you are allergic to animals, *we strongly urge that you inquire for details before making reservations.*

Children

Some inns are family-style places and welcome children of all ages; we've marked them with our 🚹 symbol. Others do not feel that they have facilities for the very young and only allow children over a certain age. Still others cultivate an "adults only" atmosphere and discourage anyone under the age of 16. We've noted age requirements under the heading "Restrictions." If special facilities are available to children, these are noted under "Facilities" and "Extras." If an inn does not exclude children yet does not offer any special amenities or rate reductions for them, we would suggest it only for the best-behaved youngsters.

Whatever the policy, you may want to remind your children to follow the same rules of courtesy toward others that we expect of adults. Be aware that the pitter-patter of little feet on an uncarpeted hardwood floor can sound like a herd of stampeding buffalo to those on the floor below. Children used to the indestructible plastics of contemporary homes will need to be reminded (more than once) to be gentle with antique furnishings. Most important, be sensitive to the fact that parents— not innkeepers—are responsible for supervising their children's behavior.

State laws governing discrimination by age are affecting policies at some inns. To our knowledge, both California and Michigan now have such laws on the books. Some inns get around age discrimination by limiting room occupancy to two adults. This discourages families by forcing them to pay for two rooms instead of one. Our own children were very clear on their preferences: although they'd been to many inns that don't encourage guests under the age of 12, they found them "really boring"; on the other hand, they loved every family-oriented place we visited.

Porterage and packing

Only the largest of our listings will have personnel whose sole job is to assist guests with baggage. In the casual atmosphere associated with many inns, it is simply assumed that guests will carry their own bags. If you do need assistance with your luggage, don't hesitate to ask.

If you're planning an extended trip to a number of small inns, we'd suggest packing as lightly as possible, using two small bags rather than one large suitcase. You'll know why if you've ever tried hauling a 50-pound oversize suitcase up a steep and narrow 18th-century staircase. On the other hand, don't forget about the local climate when assembling your wardrobe. In mountainous and desert regions, day- and nighttime temperatures can vary by as much as 40 degrees. Also, bear in mind that Easterners tend to dress more formally than Westerners, so pack accordingly.

Meals

If you have particular dietary restrictions—low-salt, vegetarian, or religious—or allergies—to caffeine, nuts, whatever—be sure to mention these when making reservations and *again* at check-in. If you're allergic to a common breakfast food or beverage, an evening reminder will ensure that you'll be able to enjoy the breakfast that's been prepared for you. Most innkeepers will do their best to accommodate your special needs, but be fair. Don't ask an innkeeper to prepare a special meal, and then, when it's being served, say: "I've decided to go off my diet today. Can I have the luscious peaches-and-cream French toast with bacon that everyone else is eating?"

In preparing each listing, we asked the owners to give us the cost of prix fixe and à la carte meals when available. An "alc dinner" price at the end of the "Rates" section is the figure we were given when we requested the average cost of a three-course dinner with a half bottle of house wine, including tax and tip. Prices listed for prix fixe meals do not include wine and service. Lunch prices, where noted, do not include the cost of any alcoholic beverage. Hotels and inns which serve meals to the public are noted with the ✗ symbol.

Dinner and lunch reservations are always a courtesy and are often essential. Most B&B owners will offer to make reservations for you; this can be especially helpful in getting you a table at a popular restaurant in peak season and/or on weekends. Some of the establishments we list operate restaurants fully open to the public. Others serve dinner primarily to their overnight guests, but they also will serve meals to outsiders; reservations are essential at such inns, usually 24 hours in advance.

A few restaurants require jackets and ties for men at dinner, even in rather isolated areas. Of course, this is more often the case in traditional New England and the Old South than in the West. Unless you're going only to a very casual country lodge, we recommend that men bring these items along and that women have corresponding attire.

Breakfast: Breakfast is served at nearly every inn or hotel listed in this guide, and is usually included in the rates. Whenever possible we describe a typical breakfast, rather than using the terms "continental" or "full" breakfast.

Continental breakfast ranges from coffee and store-bought pastry to a lavish offering of fresh fruit and juices, yogurt and granola, cereals, even cheese and cold meats, homemade muffins and breads, and a choice of decaffeinated or regular coffee, herbal and regular tea. There's almost as much variety in the full breakfasts, which range from the traditional eggs, bacon, and toast, plus juice and coffee, to three-course gourmet extravaganzas.

We've received occasional complaints about breakfasts being too rich in eggs and cream, and too sweet, with no plain rolls or bread. A dietary splurge is fun for a weekend escape, but on a longer trip we'd advise requesting a "healthy breakfast" from your innkeeper. You can be sure that they don't eat their own breakfasts every day! Equally important to many guests are the timing and seating arrangements at breakfast. Some readers enjoy the friendly atmosphere of breakfast served family-style at a set time; this approach often enables innkeepers to serve quite spectacular three-course meals. Other readers much prefer the flexibility and privacy afforded by breakfasts served at tables for two over an extended time period.

Lunch: Very few of the inns and hotels listed here serve lunch. Those that do generally operate a full-service restaurant or are located in isolated mountain settings with no restaurants nearby. Quite a number of B&B inns are happy to make up picnic lunches for an additional fee.

Dinner: Meals served at the inns listed here vary widely from simple home-style family cooking to gourmet cuisine. We are looking for food that is a good, honest example of the type of cooking involved. Ingredients should be fresh and homemade as far as is possible; service and presentation should be pleasant and straightforward. We have no interest in the school of "haute pretentious" where the hyperbolic descriptions found on the menu far exceed the chef's ability.

Drinks

With a very few exceptions (noted under "Restrictions" in each listing), alcoholic beverages may be enjoyed in moderation at all of the inns and hotels listed. Most establishments with a full-service restaurant serving the public as well as overnight guests are licensed to serve beer, wine, and liquor to their customers, although "brown-bagging" or BYOB (bring your own bottle) is occasionally permitted, especially in dry counties. Bed & breakfasts, and inns serving meals primarily to overnight guests, do not typically have liquor licenses, although most will provide guests with setups, i.e., glasses, ice, and mixers, at what is often called a BYO (bring your own) bar.

Overseas visitors will be amazed at the hodgepodge of regulations around the country. Liquor laws are determined in general by each state, but individual counties, or even towns, can prohibit or restrict the sale of alcoholic beverages, even beer.

Smoking

The vast majority of B&Bs and inns prohibit indoor smoking entirely, allowing it only on porches and verandas; a few don't allow smoking anywhere on the grounds. Larger inns and hotels usually do permit smoking, prohibiting it only in some guest rooms, and dining areas. Where prohibitions apply we have noted this under "Restrictions." We suggest that confirmed smokers be courteous or make reservations elsewhere. If there is no comment about smoking under "Restrictions," those allergic to smoke should inquire for details.

Physical limitations and wheelchair accessibility

We've used the well-known symbol & to denote hotels and inns that are wheelchair accessible. Where available, additional information is noted under the "Extras" heading. Unfortunately, what is meant by this symbol varies dramatically. In the case of larger hotels and newer inns, it usually means full access; in historic buildings, access may be limited to the restaurant and public rest rooms only, or to a specific guest room but not the common areas. *Call the inn/hotel directly for full details and to discuss your needs.*

If you do not need a wheelchair but have difficulty with stairs, we urge you to mention this when making reservations; many inns and small hotels have one or two rooms on the ground floor, but very few have elevators. Similarly, if you are visually handicapped, do share this information so that you may be given a room with good lighting and no unexpected steps.

Air-conditioning

Heat is a relative condition, and the perceived need for air-conditioning varies tremendously from one individual to the next. If an inn or hotel has air-conditioning, you'll see this listed under "Rooms." If it's important to you, be sure to ask when making reservations. If air-conditioning is not available, check to see if fans are provided. Remember that top-floor rooms in most inns (usually a converted attic) can be uncomfortably warm even with air-conditioning.

Transportation

A car is more or less essential for visiting most of the inns and hotels listed here, as well as the surrounding sights of interest. Exceptions are those located in the major cities. In some historic towns, a car is the easiest way to get there, but once you've arrived, you'll want to find a place to park the car and forget about it.

If you are traveling by public transportation, check the "Extras" section at the end of each write-up. If the innkeepers are willing to pick you up from the nearest airport, bus, or train station, you'll see it noted here. This service is usually free or available at modest cost. If it's not listed, the innkeeper will direct you to a commercial facility that can help.

Parking

Although not a concern in most cases, parking is a problem in many cities, beach resorts, and historic towns. If you'll be traveling by car, ask the innkeeper for advice when making reservations. If parking is not on-site, stop at the hotel first to drop off your bags, then go park the car. In big cities, if "free parking" is included in the rates, this usually covers only one arrival and departure. Additional "ins and outs" incur substantial extra charges. Be sure to ask.

If on-site parking is available in areas where parking can be a problem, we've noted it under "Facilities." Since it's so rarely a problem in country inns, we haven't included that information in those listings. Regrettably, security has become an issue in most cities. Never leave anything visible inside the car; it's an invitation for break-in and theft.

Christmas travel

Many people love to travel to a country inn or hotel at Christmas. Quite a number of places do stay open through the holidays, but the extent to which the occasion is celebrated varies widely indeed. We know of many inns that decorate beautifully, serve a fabulous meal, and organize all kinds of traditional Christmas activities. But we also know of others, especially in ski areas, that do nothing more than throw a few token ornaments on a tree. Be sure to inquire.

Ranch vacations

Spending time on a ranch can give you a real feel for the West—far more than you could ever experience when driving from one tourist attraction to the next. Many families find a favorite ranch and return year after year, usually for the same week, and eventually become close friends with other guests who do the same. When booking a ranch vacation, it's wise to ask about the percentage of return guests, and to get the names and telephone numbers of some in your area. If the return percentage is low, or the telephone numbers of recent guests are "unavailable," try another ranch. When reading a glossy brochure, make sure that the pictures shown were taken on the ranch, and clearly show its cabins (both interior and exterior), horses, and other facilities, rather than generic Western pictures available anywhere.

While wonderful, ranch vacations are expensive, especially when you're budgeting for a family. When toting up the costs, remember to add on 10–15% for gratuities to the wranglers and staff—this is standard at almost every ranch but is not always mentioned in the rate information. Ranch vacations tend to be more expensive in northern Colorado, but they're also most accessible, since you can fly into Denver, rent a car, and be on a horse within a few hours. Ranches in Idaho, Montana, and Wyoming tend to cost less for comparable facilities, but you may have to pay more to get there. When comparing prices, keep in mind that a ranch with a four-diamond AAA rating, gourmet cuisine, and resort facilities will not be in the same ballpark as a working ranch with comfortable but more basic food, accommodation, and activities. Finally, make sure that you pay for the things you want. A ranch with a full-fledged children's program is likely to cost more than one with a more casual approach. The cost of a ranch which includes unlimited riding will inevitably be higher than one that charges for riding by the hour. If you live and breathe horses, unlimited riding is clearly a better value. If one or two rides is all you have in mind, then the à la carte approach makes better sense. Read the fine print to be sure of exactly what is included. By the way, if you or another member of your family is not too keen on horses, look for a ranch that offers other activities—tennis, water sports, and hiking—or for a ranch that is near a major city or tourist center.

Is innkeeping for me?

Many of our readers fantasize about running their own inn; for some the fantasy will become a reality. Before taking the plunge, it's vital to find out as much as you can about this demanding business. Begin by reading *So You Want to Be an Innkeeper*, by Pat Hardy, Jo Ann Bell, and Mary Davies. Hardy and Bell are co-directors of the Professional Association of Innkeepers, International (PAII—pronounced "pie") which also publishes *Innkeeping Newsletter*, various materials for would-be innkeepers, and coordinates workshops for aspiring innkeepers. For details contact PAII, P.O. Box 90710, Santa Barbara, CA, 93190; 805–569–1853, or visit their Internet Website at www.paii.org. Another good book is *How to Start and Run Your Own Bed & Breakfast Inn* by long-time innkeepers Ripley Hotch and Carl Glassman, covering everything from financing to marketing to day-to-day innkeeping responsibilities ($14.95; Stackpole Books, P.O. Box 1831, Harrisburg, PA, 17105; 800–732–3669). Another excellent source, especially in the East, are consultants Bill Oates and Heide Bredfeldt. Contact them at P.O. Box 1162, Brattleboro, VT, 05301; 802–254–5931 to find out when and where they'll be offering their next prospective innkeepers seminar. Bill and Heide are highly respected pros in this field and have worked with innkeepers facing a wide range of needs and problems; his newsletter, *Innquest*, is written for prospective innkeepers looking to buy property. An equally good alternative is Lodging Resources Workshops, 98 South Fletcher Avenue, Amelia Island, FL, 32034; 888–201–7602. Director Dave Caples owns the Elizabeth Pointe Lodge in Amelia Island, and has been conducting workshops throughout the U.S. since 1992. Last but not least is *Yellow Brick Road*, a well-established newsletter that recently changed its focus to provide "insight for aspiring innkeepers." Subscriptions are $45 annually; single copy, $8. Contact Bobbi Zane, P.O. Box 1600, Julian, CA, 92036; 760–765–1224.

For more information

The best sources of travel information in this country and in Canada are absolutely free; in many cases, you don't even have to supply the cost of a stamp or telephone call. They are the state and provincial tourist offices.

For each state you'll be visiting, request a copy of the official state map, which will show you every little highway and byway and will make exploring much more fun; it will also have information on state parks and major attractions in concise form. Ask also for a calendar of events and for information on topics of particular interest, such as fishing or antiquing, vineyards or crafts; many states have published B&B directories, and some are quite informative. If you're going to an area of particular tourist interest, you might also want to ask the state office to give you the name of the regional tourist board for more detailed information. Most states have toll-free numbers; call 800–555–1212 to get the numbers you need. If there's no toll-free listing, call the information operators for the relevant states, and ask them to check for the number under the state's capital city. Many states have also established Websites on the Internet; use search engines to see what you can find.

You may also want to contact the local chamber of commerce for information on local sights and events of interest or even an area map. You can get the necessary addresses and telephone numbers from the inn or hotel where you'll be staying or from the state tourist office.

If you are one of those people who never travel with fewer than three guidebooks (which includes us), you will find the AAA Tour Guides to be especially helpful. The guides are distributed free on request to members, and cover hotels, restaurants, and sightseeing information. If you're not already an AAA member, *we'd strongly urge you join before your next trip;* in addition to their road service, they offer quality guidebooks and maps, and an excellent discount program at many hotels (including a number listed here).

Guidebooks are published only once every year or two; if you'd like to have a more frequent update, we'd suggest one of the following:

Country Inns/Bed & Breakfasts (P.O. Box 182, South Orange, NJ, 07079; 800–877–5491), $23, 6 issues annually. You know what they say about a picture being worth a thousand words. A must for inngoers.

The Discerning Traveler (504 West Mermaid Lane, Philadelphia, PA, 19118; 800–673–7834 or 215–247–5578), $50, 6 issues annually, $8 single copy. Picks a single destination in the New England, Mid-Atlantic, or Southern states and covers it in real depth—sights, restaurants, lodging, and more. The authors have published three delightful books on the subject as well.

Easy Escapes (P.O. Box 120365, Boston, MA, 02112–0365), $47, 10 issues annually, $6 single copy. Covers inns, hotels, and resorts in the U.S.

and the world; exceptionally honest and forthright. Each issue usually covers one or two destinations in a breezy, informal style.

Harper's Hideaway Report (P.O. Box 300, Whitefish, MT, 59937), $125, 12 issues annually. Covers the best (and most expensive) inns, hotels, resorts in the U.S. and abroad.

The Internet: Those of you with on-line access will want to check out the huge amount of travel information found on the World Wide Web. Start with our own Website, at http://www.inns.com, where you'll find thousands of listings and photographs. From there, take a look at some of the other inn directories, as well as the many sites devoted to state and regional travel information. Of equal interest are the chat rooms and bulletin boards covering bed & breakfasts; you can find them on the Internet as well as on the proprietary services like America Online and the Microsoft Network.

Where is my favorite inn?

In reading through this book, you may find that your favorite inn is not listed, or that a well-known inn has been omitted from this edition. Why? Two reasons, basically: In several cases, establishments have been dropped because our readers had unsatisfactory experiences. Feel free to contact us for details. Other establishments have been omitted because we've had no reader feedback at all. This may mean that readers visiting these hotels and inns had satisfactory experiences but were not sufficiently impressed to write about them, or that readers were pleased but just assumed that someone else would take the trouble. If the latter applies, please, please, do write and let us know of your experiences. We try to visit as many inns as possible ourselves, but it is impossible to visit every place, every year. So please, keep those cards, letters, and telephone calls coming! As an added incentive, we will be sending free copies of the next edition of this book to our most helpful respondents.

Little Inns of Horror

We try awfully hard to list only the most worthy establishments, but sometimes the best-laid plans of mice and travel writers do go astray. Please understand that whenever we receive a complaint about an entry in our guide we feel terrible, and do our best to investigate the situation. Readers occasionally send us complaints about establishments listed in *other* guidebooks; these are quite helpful as warning signals.

The most common complaints we receive—and the least forgivable—are on the issue of dirt. Scummy sinks and bathtubs, cobwebbed windows, littered porches, mildewed carpeting, water-stained ceilings, and grimy linens are all stars of this horror show.

Next in line are problems dealing with the lack of maintenance: peeling paint and wallpaper; sagging, soft, lumpy mattresses; radiators that don't get hot and those that make strange noises; windows that won't open, windows that won't close, windows with no screens, decayed or inoperable window shades; moldy shower curtains, rusty shower stalls, worn-out towels, fluctuating water temperatures, dripping faucets, and showers that only dribble, top the list.

Food complaints come next on this disaster lineup: poorly prepared canned or frozen food when fresh is readily available; meals served on paper, plastic, or worst of all, styrofoam; and insensitivity to dietary needs. Some complaints are received about unhelpful, abrasive, or abusive innkeepers, with a few more about uncaring, inept, or invisible staff. Complaints are most common in full-service inns when the restaurant business preoccupies the owners' attention, leaving overnight guests to suffer. Last but not least are noise headaches: trucks and trains that sound like they're heading for your pillow, and being awakened by the sound of someone snoring—in the next room. More tricky are questions of taste—high Victorian might look elegant to you, funereal to me; my collectibles could be your Salvation Army thriftshop donation. In short, there are more than a few inns and hotels that give new meaning to the phrase "having reservations"; fortunately they're many times outnumbered by the many wonderful places listed in this guide.

Pet peeves

Although we may genuinely like an inn, minor failings can keep it from being truly wonderful. Heading our list of pet peeves is inadequate bedside reading lights and tables. We know that there is not always room for a second table, but a light can always be attached to the wall. For reasons of both safety and comfort, a lamp should be at every bedside. Another reader is irked by inadequate bathroom lighting: "I think it must be an innkeepers' conspiracy to keep me from ever getting my makeup on properly." (SU) Other readers object to overly friendly innkeepers: "The innkeeper chatted with us all during breakfast, and was disappointed that we didn't plan to go in to say goodbye after we loaded up the car. Innkeepers should remember that the guests are customers, not long-lost relatives." (KW) Another common gripe concerns clutter: "Although pretty and interesting, the many collectibles left us no space for our personal belongings." And: "Instructions were posted everywhere—how to operate door locks, showers, heat, air-conditioning, and more." Anything you'd like to add?

Glossary of Architectural and Decorating Terms

We are not architectural experts, and when we started writing guidebooks, we didn't know a dentil from a dependency, a tester from a transom. We've learned a bit more since then, and hope that our primer of terms, prepared by associate editor Nancy Barker, will also be helpful to you.

Adam: building style (1780–1840) featuring a classic box design with a dominant front door and fanlight, accented by an elaborate surround or an entry porch; cornice with decorative moldings incorporating dentil, swag, garland, or stylized geometric design. Three-part Palladian-style windows are common.

antebellum: existing prior to the U.S. Civil War (1861–1865).

19

Arts and Craft movement: considered the first phase of the Modern movement that led to the Prairie style (1900–20) of Frank Lloyd Wright in Chicago, and the Craftsman style (1905–30) of the Greene brothers in Southern California. In the Arts and Craft style, historical precedent for decoration and design was rejected and ornamentation was "modernized" to remove traces of its historic origins. It features low-pitched roofs, wide eave overhangs, and both symmetrical and asymmetrical front façades.

beaded board: simple ornamented board, with a smooth, flat surface alternating with a half-round, rod-like carving (bead) running the length of the board. Common wainscoting or panelling in Victorian-era homes.

carpenter Gothic: *see* country, folk Victorian.

chinoiserie: imitation of Chinese decorative motifs; i.e., simulated Oriental lacquer covering pine or maple furniture. *See* also Chinese Chippendale below.

Chippendale: named for English furniture designer, Thomas Chippendale, of the Queen Anne period (1750–1790); the style varies from the Queen Anne style in ornamentation, with more angular shapes and heavier carving of shells, leaves, scrolls. Chinese Chippendale furniture employs chiefly straight lines, bamboo turnings, and as decoration, fluting and fretwork in a variety of lattice patterns.

Colonial Revival: building style (1880–1955) featuring a classic box design with a dominant front door elaborated with pilasters and either a pediment (Georgian-style) or a fanlight (Adam-style); double-hung windows symmetrically balanced.

corbel: an architectural member that projects from a wall to support a weight and is stepped outward and upward from the vertical surface.

Corinthian: column popular in Greek Revival style for support of porch roofs; the capitals are shaped like inverted bells and decorated with acanthus leaves.

cornice: projecting horizontal carving or molding that crowns a wall or roof.

country, folk Victorian: simple house form (1870–1910) with accents of Victorian (usually Queen Anne or Italianate) design in porch spindlework and cornice details. Also known as carpenter Gothic.

Craftsman: building style (1905–1930) with low-pitched, gabled roof and wide, unenclosed eave overhang; decorative beams or braces added under gables; usually one-story; porches supported by tapered square columns.

dentil: exterior or interior molding characterized by a series of small rectangular blocks projecting like teeth.

dependencies: buildings that are subordinate to the main dwelling; i.e., a detached garage or barn. *See* also garçonnière.

Doric: column popular in Greek Revival style for support of porch roofs; the simplest of the three styles, with a fluted column, no base, and a square capital.

Eastlake: architectural detail on Victorian houses, commonly referred to as "gingerbread." Typically has lacy spandrels and knoblike beads, in exterior and interior design, patterned after the style of Charles Eastlake, an English furniture designer. Eastlake also promoted Gothic and Jacobean Revival styles with their strong rectangular lines; quality workmanship instead of machine manufacture; and the use of varnished oak, glazed tiles, and unharmonized color.

Eclectic movement: architectural tradition (1880–1940) which emphasized relatively pure copies of Early American, Mediterranean, or Native American homes.

eyebrow dormer: a semicircular, narrow window over which the adjoining roofing flows in a continuous wave line; found on Shingle or Richardsonian Romanesque buildings.

faux: literally, French for "false." Refers commonly to woodwork painted to look like marble or another stone.

Federal: *See* Adam.

Franklin stove: metal heating stove which is set out into the room to conserve heat and better distribute it. Named after its inventor Benjamin Franklin; some designs resemble a fireplace when their front doors are open.

four-poster bed: variation on a tester bed but one in which the tall corner posts, of equal height, do not support a canopy. Carving of rice sheaves was a popular design in the Southern states, and signified prosperity.

gambrel roof: a two-slope, barn-style roof, with a lower steeper slope and a flatter upper one.

garçonnière: found on antebellum estates; a dependency housing unmarried male guests and family members.

Georgian: building style (1700–1830) featuring a classic box design with a dominant front door elaborated with pilasters and a pediment, usually with a row of small panes of glass beneath the crown or in a transom; cornices with decorative moldings, usually dentil.

Gothic Revival: building style (1840–1880) with a steeply pitched roof, steep gables with decorated vergeboards, and one-story porch supported by flattened Gothic arches. Windows commonly have pointed-arch shape.

Greek Revival: building style (1825–1860) having a gabled or hipped roof of low pitch; cornice line of main and porch roofs emphasized by a wide band of trim; porches supported by prominent columns (usually Doric).

half-tester bed: a bed with a low footboard and a canopy projecting from the posts at the head of the bed. Pronounced "half tee'stir."

Ionic: column popular in Greek Revival style for support of porch roofs; the caps of the column resemble the rolled ends of a scroll.

Italianate: building style (1840–1885) with two or three stories and a low-pitched roof with widely overhanging eaves supported by decorative brackets; tall, narrow windows arched or curved above with elaborate crowns. Many have a square cupola or tower.

keeping room: in a Colonial-era home, the equivalent of a modern family room; it was usually warm from proximity to kitchen, so infants and the ill were "kept" here.

kiva: stuccoed, corner beehive-shaped fireplace common in adobe homes in Southwestern U.S.

latillas: ceiling of unpeeled, rough sticks, supported by vigas (rough beams); seen in flat-roofed adobe homes.

Lincrusta (or Lincrusta-Walton): an embossed, linoleum-like wall-covering made with linseed oil, developed in 1877 in England by Frederick Walton.

lintel: horizontal beam, supported at both ends, that spans an opening.

mansard roof: having two slopes on all sides, with the lower slope steeper than the upper one.

Mission: building style (1890–1920) with Spanish mission-style parapet; commonly with red tile roof, overhanging, open eaves, and smooth stucco finish. In furniture, the Mission style is best represented by the work of designer Gustav Stickley. Using machine manufacture, he utilized simple, rectangular lines and favored quarter-sawn white oak for the rich texture of the graining.

Palladian window: typically a central window with an arched or semicircular head.

Pueblo Revival: building style (1910 to present) with flat roof, parapet above; corners and edges blunted or rounded; projecting vigas, stepped-back roof lines, and irregular stucco wall surfaces. Influenced by the flat-roofed Spanish Colonial buildings and Native American pueblos; popular in Arizona and New Mexico; common in Santa Fe and Albuquerque.

Pewabic (tile): glazed tiles made in the Detroit, Michigan, area, in the first half of the 1890s, whose unique manufacturing process has been lost.

pocket doors: doors that open by sliding into a recess (pocket) in the wall.

portal (or portale): in Spanish-style homes, the long, narrow porch that opens onto an internal courtyard; it functions as a sheltered passageway between rooms.

post and beam: building style based on the Medieval post-and-girder method, where upper loads are supported by heavy corner posts and cross timbers. In contemporary construction, the posts and beams are often left exposed on the interior.

Prairie: building style (1900–1920) with low-pitched roof and widely overhanging eaves; two stories with one-story wings or porches; façade detailing that emphasizes horizontal lines; massive, square porch supports.

Queen Anne: building style (1880–1910) with a steeply pitched roof of irregular shapes; an asymmetrical façade with one-story porch; patterned shingles, bay windows, single tower. In furniture design the Queen Anne style was prevalent from 1725 to 1750, characterized by a graceful, unadorned curve of the leg (known as cabriole) and repeated curve of the top crest and vase-form back (splat) of a chair.

quoin: wood, stone, or brick materials that form the exterior corner of a building and are distinguishable from the background surface because of texture, color, size, or material.

rice-carved bed: *See* four-poster bed.

Richardsonian Romanesque: building style (1880–1900) with massive masonry walls of rough, squared stonework and round-topped arches over windows, porch supports, or entrances; round tower with conical roof common.

Second Empire: building style (1855–1885) with mansard roof adorned with dormer windows on lower slope; molded cornices above and below lower roof, and decorative brackets beneath eaves.

Shaker: style of furniture which represents the Shaker belief in simplicity. The finely crafted pieces are functional, without ornamentation. Chairs have ladder backs, rush seats, and simple turned legs; tables and cabinets are angular, with smooth surfaces.

Sheraton: named for English furniture designer, Thomas Sheraton, of the Federal period (early 1800s); style marked by straight lines, delicate proportions, wood inlays, and spare use of carving; characteristically tapered legs.

Shingle: building style (1880–1900) with walls and roofing of continuous wood shingles; no decorative detailing at doors, windows, corners, or roof overhang. Irregular, steeply pitched roof line and extensive porches common.

shotgun: simple 19th century house form suited to narrow urban lots, featuring a single-story, front gable building one room wide. Rooms and doorways are in a direct line, front to back; theoretically, a bullet fired through the front door would travel through the house unobstructed.

spandrel: decorative trim that fits the top corners of doorways, porches, or gables; usually triangular in shape.

Santa Fe: *see* Pueblo Revival.

Spanish Colonial: building style (1600–1900) of thick masonry walls, with low pitched or flat roof, interior wooden shutters covering small window openings, and multiple doorways. Pitched roof style often has half-cylindrical tiles; flat style has massive horizontal beams embedded in walls to support heavy roof of earth or mortar. Internal courtyards or cantilevered second-story porches are common.

Stick: building style (1860–1890) with a steeply pitched, gabled roof, usually with decorative trusses at apex; shingle or board walls interrupted by patterns of boards (stickwork) raised from the surface for emphasis.

Territorial: a variation of the Spanish Colonial building style found in New Mexico, western Texas, and Arizona. The flat roof and single story are topped by a protective layer of fired brick to form a decorative crown.

tester bed: a bed with a full canopy (the tester), supported at all four corners by tall posts. Pronounced "tee'stir."

transom: usually refers to a window placed above a doorway.

trompe l'oeil: literally, French for "to trick the eye." Commonly refers to wall paintings that create an optical illusion.

Tudor: building style (1890–1940) with steeply pitched roof, usually cross-gabled; decorative half-timbering; tall, narrow, multi-paned windows; massive chimney crowned with decorative chimney pots.

vergeboard: decorative trim extending from the roof overhang of Tudor, Gothic Revival, or Queen Anne–style houses.

vernacular: style of architecture employing the commonest forms, materials, and decorations of a period or place.

viga(s): exposed (interior) and projecting (exterior) rough-hewn wooden roof beams common in adobe homes in Southwestern U.S.

wainscoting: most commonly, narrow wood paneling found on the lower half of a room's walls.

widow's walk: a railed observation platform built above the roof of a coastal house to permit unobstructed views of the sea. Name derives from the fate of many wives who paced the platform waiting for the return of their husbands from months (or years) at sea. Also called a "captain's walk."

Windsor: style of simple chair, with spindle back, turned legs, and usually a saddle seat. Considered a "country" design, it was popular in 18th and early 19th century towns and rural areas.

Criteria for entries

If this guide to the inns and hotels of the U.S. and Canada had included all the entries appearing in our regional editions, this publication would have totaled over 2,000 pages. So how did we manage to condense the information to about 700 pages? With great difficulty. First of all, in areas of strong traveler appeal, where there are many inns, we included full write-ups on just a handful of places, covering the others more briefly under the **"Also recommended"** heading. That part was relatively easy. Secondly, we did not include the inns in towns well off the beaten path. We felt that for a country-wide guide, attention must be focused on key tourist and business centers. That required some really tough decisions, since it meant excluding many of our favorite places. If you plan any in-depth exploring of a particular region, please consult the appropriate regional edition or our Website at http://www.inns.com for optimal coverage.

Unlike many other guides, inns cannot pay to be listed in this book. All selections are made by the editors, based on guest recommendations and personal visits. Entries are written and compiled by the editors, not the inns. When we update a regional guide, inns that received full entries in the previous edition and that will also appear in the new edition are charged a processing fee to help defray our research costs. There is no fee for new entries, and no fee for listing in our *U.S.A & Canada* edition. If we receive significant complaints or insufficient recommendations about a particular property, we omit their listing. As always, what matters most to us is the feedback we get from you, our readers.

About our Name

We've changed our name from *America's Wonderful Little Hotels & Inns* to *America's Favorite Inns, B&Bs, and Small Hotels*. Why? First, we felt that it better reflects what we're all about. Properties listed here are *your* favorites—if you don't like them, we don't include them. Since the majority of our entries are inns and B&Bs, the new title better reflects their importance. Last but not least, reasons connected with the copyright were also a factor.

Key to Abbreviations and Symbols

For complete information and explanations, please see the Introduction.

¢ Especially good value for overnight accommodation.

Ⓜ Families welcome. Most (but not all) have cribs, baby-sitting, games, play equipment, and reduced rates for children.

✗ Meals served to public; reservations recommended or required.

🎾 Tennis court and swimming pool and/or lake on grounds. Golf usually on grounds or nearby.

♿ Limited or full wheelchair access; call for details.

Rates: Range from least expensive room in low season to most expensive room in peak season.

Room only: No meals included; European Plan (EP).

B&B: Bed and breakfast; includes breakfast, sometimes afternoon/evening refreshment.

MAP: Modified American Plan; includes breakfast and dinner.

Full board: Three meals daily.

Alc lunch: A la carte lunch; average price of entrée plus nonalcoholic drink, tax, tip.

Alc dinner: Average price of three-course dinner, including half bottle of house wine, tax, tip.

Prix fixe dinner: Three- to five-course set dinner, excluding wine, tax, tip unless otherwise noted.

Extras: Noted if available. Always confirm in advance. Pets are not permitted unless specified; if you are allergic, ask for details; *most innkeepers have pets.*

We Want to Hear from You!

As you know, this book is effective only with your help. We really need to know about your experiences and discoveries. If you stayed at an inn or hotel listed here, we want to know how it was. Did it live up to our description? Exceed it? Was it what you expected? Did you like it? Were you disappointed? Delighted? Have you discovered new establishments that we should add to the next edition?

Tear out one of the report forms at the back of this book (or use your own stationery if you prefer) and write today. Or email us at afi@inns.com. *Even if you write only "Fully endorse existing entry" you will have been most helpful.*

Thank You!

Free copy of INNroads newsletter

Want to stay up-to-date on our latest finds? Send a business-size, self-addressed, stamped envelope with 55 cents postage and we'll send you the latest issue, *free!* While you're at it, why not enclose a report on any inns you've recently visited? Use the forms at the back of the book or your own stationery.

Can't Find It Here?

Our regional guides include *two to three times* the number of entries contained here. Pick up a copy of our *New England* (plus Eastern Canada), *Middle Atlantic, South, Midwest* (plus Ontario), *Rocky Mountains & Southwest*, or *West Coast* (plus Western Canada) edition for lots more information on great places to stay. If your bookstore doesn't have a current copy in stock, ask them to order it for you or call 800–288–2131. You can also order copies from our Website at http://www.inns.com.

Important Note on Area Codes

Telephone area codes are changing faster than a two-year-old's attention span. Although we've tried to incorporate all the new ones in our listings, many numbers were still in the "to be decided" state at press time. *If you dial a number listed here and get an announcement that it's not in service, we urge you to call the information operator and see if that region has been assigned a new area code.* Please forgive the inconvenience!

Alabama

The Victoria, Anniston

There's much to see and do in Alabama, from Huntsville's Alabama Space and Rocket Center to historic Mobile, and the gorgeous gardens at Bellingrath. To sample Gulf Coast beaches, drive south from Mobile to Dauphin Island, a scenic sliver of land where you can rent boats, swim, and watch huge ships enter Mobile Bay. In northern Alabama visit Russell Cave National Monument, an enormous limestone cave that was used as a seasonal shelter by people beginning in 6500 B.C. Birmingham, a major commercial center, is also known for the unusual "geologic walkway" carved into a mountain at Red Mountain Museum.

ANNISTON

Textile mills and blast furnaces were built in Anniston after the Civil War to help the region recuperate from the ravages of war. Today it's better known as the home of Fort McClellan; although the fort's Chemical Corps Training Command is off-limits to civilians, those intrigued by peculiar museums can make an appointment to visit the Chemical Corps Museum, tracing the history of chemical warfare. More appealing is Anniston's Museum of Natural History, best known for its bird collection (but the kids will prefer the Egyptian mummies). Anniston is located in northeastern Alabama, one hour's drive east of Birmingham via I-20, and about two hours west of Atlanta, Georgia.

The Victoria ¢ ⋔ ✕
1604 Quintard Avenue, P.O. Box 2213, 36202

Tel: 256–256–0503
800–256–8781
Fax: 256–236–1138
E-mail: victoria@thevictoria.com
URL: http://www.thevictoria.com

Built in 1888 and listed on the National Register of Historic Places, The Victoria wears its name well, with a three-story turret, beautiful stained and etched glass windows, a conservatory, and colonnaded verandas. Restored in 1985 and expanded in 1996, the inn consists of the original building, housing a restaurant and three suites, plus two hotel wings which wrap around the courtyard and swimming pool. Breakfast includes bagels, English muffins, home-baked breads, eggs on request, cereals, fresh fruit, and juice; a complete Southern breakfast is served on weekends. Lunch favorites include chicken with dumplings, fettucini with shrimp, or salmon salad on croissant. Among the dinner entrees are crab cakes with roasted coconut rice, veal with wild mushroom butter and basil mashed potatoes, and beef tenderloin with blue cheese potato gratin.

"Though bordered by busy commercial streets, the hilltop setting surrounded by trees and well-kept flower beds insulates it from traffic noise. Our room in the annex had a king-size bed with a brass headboard, complemented by white wicker furniture—a chaise longue, glass topped table and several chairs." *(Jeanne Smith)* "Best public restaurant in the area, with outstanding soups. Also on the property is a century-old carriage house, restored as a lovely art gallery called the Wren's Nest, emphasizing artwork by well-known local wildlife artist Larry Martin." *(Carol Flaherty)* "Impeccable service, from the valet parking to the attentive waiters in the lovely restaurant, to the pub-style bar with working fireplace." *(Debbie Trueblood)* "Delightful food, service, accommodations. *(Stanley Krawiec)*

Open All year. Restaurant closed Sun.
Rooms 1 cottage, 3 suites in main house, 56 doubles in annex. All with private bath, telephone, TV, air-conditioning.
Facilities Restaurant, bar/lounge, swimming pool, art gallery, valet parking.
Location 60 m E of Birmingham. From I-20, take Exit 185 (Oxford/Anniston); go 4 m N on Quintard (Hwy. 21/431) to inn. Make a U-turn at 17th St. & enter from Quintard.
Credit cards Amex, CB, DC, Discover, MC, Visa.
Rates B&B, $129–299 suite, $79 double, $69 single. Extra person, $10. Children under 12 free. Alc dinner, $25–35.

BIRMINGHAM

Information please: Built in 1914, the **Tutwiler** (Park Place at 21st Street North, 35203; 205–322–2100 or 800–HERITAGE) was restored in elegant and luxurious style, with antique reproduction furnishings created especially for the hotel. The hotel restaurant serves classic American cuisine in an environment meant to simulate that of a private club. Heritage Club rates include use of the Club Lounge, with free breakfast and evening hors d'oeuvres. "Just as wonderful on a return visit. Everything is beautifully maintained by a caring staff; courteous service by all. The restaurant continues to be one of the best in the South. Exceptional duck. Everything we tried from the large menu was excellent."*(HJB)* Double rates for the 148 guest rooms range from $140–180 double, $175–650 suite.

FAIRHOPE

Fairhope makes an ideal base for touring Mobile and the Alabama coast. It's a charming little town, with appealing shops, a lovely park and fishing pier on Mobile Bay, and several enjoyable restaurants. Within an easy drive are the sugar sands of the Gulf beaches, Fort Morgan and the ferry across the bay, and the dozens of factory outlet shops of Riviera Centre. Golf, tennis, and horseback riding are all available as well.

Fairhope is located on the Eastern Shore of southern Alabama, 15 miles southeast of Mobile. Take I-10 E across Mobile Bay to Route 98 south. Follow 98 south for 8 miles, then turn right at sign for Fairhope/Point Clear, and follow road (Section Street) into Fairhope.

Reader tips: "Fairhope is a quiet residential community. The pier and cozy village streets are ideal for an evening stroll. Several sidewalk cafes offer dining under the stars." *(Joe Schmidt)* "A jewel of a town, with unusual shops and restaurants. At night the main streets twinkle with tiny white lights, and by day the flower beds and hanging baskets are equally lovely." *(Nancy McFadden)*

Bay Breeze Guest House/Church Street Inn   ⅁   ¢   *Tel:* 334–928–8976
742 South Mobile Street, 36533   *Fax:* 334–928–0360

As you might expect from its name, the Bay Breeze Guest House sits right on Mobile Bay, offering lovely water views from its common rooms, a beach to explore, and decks for fishing and crabbing. Owners Bill and Becky Jones welcome guests to their stucco home, built in the 1930s, now restored, remodeled, and enlarged. Furnished with family heirlooms and period antiques dating back five generations, the decor includes wicker, stained glass, hooked and Oriental rugs. Under the same ownership is the **Church Street Inn**, listed on the National Register of Historic Places, and offering three guest rooms ($85 double) with turn-of-the-century ambiance just steps from Fairhope's charming shops and galleries. A full breakfast is served at both properties, and includes fresh fruit and juice, plus such entrees as French toast or omelets and Southern-style apples.

About Bay Breeze: "Ideal for peace, quiet, and a charming waterfront location, with friendly hosts, cheerful common areas. The long dock is a focal point for many activities, including breakfast." *(Joe & Shelia Schmidt)* "The flower-filled yard has a winding entrance bordered with hundreds of narcissus. Little touches include miniature pralines at bedside, and fresh flowers in the rooms. Breakfast began with fresh fruit garnished with homemade sorbet, followed by perfect eggs Benedict." *(Nancy McFadden)* "Blooming camellias, azaleas, well-maintained gardens; food available to feed dozens of wild ducks. Plenty of good coffee, served promptly at breakfast." *(Patricia Waters)* "The beautiful Camellia Room had white wicker furnishings with quilted cushions, and a comfortable bed with a lovely old quilt and a ruffled eyelet bedskirt. The bathroom was sparkling and tidy. The Joneses shared some pointers about good local restaurants while we enjoyed wine, toasted pecans, and a view of the bay at sunset." *(Fran Langley)* "Beautifully decorated with antiques, family heirlooms, quilts, and plants, enhanced by fragrant gardens, birdsong, and the bay waters lapping at the shore." *(Kenneth Blad)* "Good jogging route along the beach, pier, and city parks." *(Janet Wright)* "Becky took our hands and greeted us very warmly; she joined eagerly in our conversations at breakfast." *(SC)* "Homey, comfortable rooms, highlighted by family antiques; wonderful food. Nothing does more to relieve stress than strolling through Becky's wonderful gardens to the pier, feeding the ducks and sea gulls, and watching the world go by." *(Lynn Edge)* "Well-maintained inn. Bill and Becky treat guests like family. Comfortable beds." *(Charlotte Reid)* "Fabulous breakfasts, never a repeat. Quiet location." *(Sarah M. Polhemus)*

About Church Street Inn: "Beautiful antiques provided warmth, character, and comfort. Coffee always available. Enjoyed the charming courtyard with a fountain and comfortable seating, and the front porch with wicker furniture. Delightful in-town location." *(Dr. Evelyn Laycock)* "Lovely innkeeper, Alayne; delightful food and conversation at breakfast. Different place settings each day. Best of all was the freezer stocked with Blue Bell Ice Cream, always available." *(Kelly Heath)*

Open All year.

Rooms 1 cottage suite with kitchenette, 4 doubles—all with full private bath and/or shower, clock, TV, air-conditioning, fan. 2 with telephone, radio, desk.

Facilities Dining room; sitting room with fireplace, piano; living room with books; family room with TV/VCR; sun porch; family kitchen. 3 acres with camelia, azalea gardens. On beach with private pier, fishing, crabbing.

Location To Bay Breeze: At 3rd light (Magnolia Ave.), turn right. Go 4 blocks, turn left on S. Mobile St. at Municipal Pier. Go approx. 1 m to inn on right. To Church St.: From U.S. Hwy. 98 exit right onto Scenic/Alt. Hwy. 98 at "Welcome to Fairhope" sign. At 4th light (Fairhope Ave.), go right. go 1 block & turn left on Church St. to inn on next corner.

Restrictions No smoking. Facilities for children very limited.

Credit cards Amex, MC, Visa.

Rates B&B, $105 suite, $95 double. Extra person, $15. Some weekend minimums.

Extras 1 cottage wheelchair accessible. Limited Spanish spoken.

MONTGOMERY

State capital of Alabama, Montgomery also served as the first capital of the Confederacy; today it is equally renowned for its role in the Civil Rights movement. For evening entertainment, call 800–841–4273 for information on the Alabama Shakespeare Festival, which offers high quality repertory theater by the Bard as well as contemporary playwrights. Montgomery is located in central Alabama, 85 miles south of Birmingham, 160 miles north of Mobile.

Also recommended: The **Red Bluff Cottage** (551 Clay Street, P.O. Box 1026, 36101; 334–264–0056 or 888–551–CLAY; www.bbonline.com/

al/redbluff) was built in 1987 in the traditional style of a raised cottage, and is owned by Anne and Mark Waldo; Anne is the cook and gardener, Mark, a retired Episcopal priest, is the handyman and assistant. Breakfasts of peach cobbler, cherry waffles, or maybe eggs and grits are served in the dining room, or on the front porch overlooking the river plain. Four guest rooms are available at the B&B double rate of $65–75. "Convenient location, close to many cultural events. The congenial atmosphere and stimulating breakfast table conversations will ensure our return."(EC)

Lattice Inn ¢ ♿   *Tel:* 334–832–9931
1414 South Hull Street, 36104   800–525–0652
Fax: 334–264–0075
URL: http://members.aol.com/latticeinn

Michael Pierce welcomes guests to the Lattice Inn, built in 1906, and restored as a B&B in 1993; he notes that he "strives to be attentive without intruding on guests' privacy."

"We were made to feel welcome from the first minute. Our wonderful room had a king-size bed with a good reading light on each side. Delicious breakfasts of smoked sausage with apple pancakes one day, turkey and tomato omelets the next. Michael and his nephew Richard were most helpful with tips and advice on restaurants, sights, and the excellent Shakespeare Theater. Our favorite dinner was at the Vintage Year restaurant, just five minutes away." *(Ian & Irene Fisher)* "Michael, the consummate host, accommodates dietary needs without sacrificing taste." *(David Clark)* "The parrot, Rene, and the dogs, Alexandra and Katie, make wonderful, relaxing companions." *(Tina Wyatt)*

"Our favorite place to stay during the Alabama Shakespeare Festival. Exquisite yet comfortable furnishings, highlighted by the host's personal collections." *(MR)* "Delicious homemade cookies; beautiful, tasty fruit basket in our room. Michael willingly shares his recipes." *(Jane & Walter Little)* "A beautiful dining room and two living areas where guests can watch TV, read, or chat. Ideal location, in a historic neighborhood three blocks from the Governor's Mansion, charming for jogging or walking. A large deck and swimming pool offer privacy and comfort in the shade of lovely hardwood trees. Breakfasts are a highlight, with a bowl of fresh-cut fruit (kiwi, raspberries, blackberries, and more), and an array of delicious homemade muffins." *(Joy Satterlee)*

"The neighborhood is quiet and unhurried, yet conveniently located for access to the interstates, downtown, or suburbs. Michael is witty, urbane, erudite, and charming." *(David Clark)* "The rooms have high, beamed ceilings, four-poster beds, antiques, and an elegant country feel." *(Vicki Ford)* "Michael provided a bag of cookies for the ride home. Wonderful breakfast with fresh fruit, great coffee, eggs Benedict, and macadamia French toast." *(Laura Ward)* "Michael's rooms are immaculate, his breakfasts are superb. More than that, though, Michael is gracious host, determined to meet his guests' needs. He has earned the nickname 'The Cookie Man,' and leaves wonderful cookies in each room along with fresh fruit." *(Lynn Edge)* "Genial host, excellent breakfast. The outdoor hot tub and lap pool were a plus." *(Hans & Fran Wriedt)*

Open All year.

Rooms 1 cottage, 4 doubles—all with full private bath, radio, clock, desk, air-conditioning, fan. 2 with telephone (on request), fireplace, deck; 1 with refrigerator, TV. Cottage with living room, kitchen, TV, telephone.

Facilities Dining room, living room with fireplace, library with TV, fireplace, porch, decks. Gazebo, swimming pool, fish pond, patio, hot tub, off-street parking.

Location Historic garden district. Approx 1 m (or less) from downtown, Capitol, I-85, I-65; approx. 6 m from airport, Shakespeare Festival. Exit I-85 at Union St., & go W on service rd. to Hull. Go S on Hull to inn on right, between Maury & Earl.

Restrictions No smoking. Children welcome in cottage.

Credit cards Amex, MC, Visa, Discover.

Rates B&B, $95 cottage, $75–90 double. Extra person, $10. Discount for 3-night stay or longer.

Extras Limited wheelchair access.

We Want to Hear from You!

As you know, this book is effective only with your help. We really need to know about your experiences and discoveries. If you stayed at an inn or hotel listed here, we want to know how it was. Did it live up to our description? Exceed it? Was it what you expected? Did you like it? Were you disappointed? Delighted? Have you discovered new establishments that we should add to the next edition?

Tear out one of the report forms at the back of this book (or use your own stationery if you prefer) and write today. Or email us at afi@inns.com. *Even if you write only "Fully endorse existing entry" you will have been most helpful.*

Thank You!

Alaska

Pearson's Pond Luxury Inn and Garden Spa, Juneau

Alaska is one of our most extraordinary states and a fantastic place to visit. Its size and scope are difficult to imagine: It encompasses an area one-fifth the size of the continental United States and has 3,000 rivers, 3 million lakes, 19 mountains higher than 14,000 feet, and more than 5,000 glaciers—one of which is larger than the state of Rhode Island.

Peak travel season to Alaska is during the summer months, when the weather is warmest and the days are the longest. Travelers are learning that the weather can be nearly as nice in the late spring and early fall, when the need for advance reservations is less pressing.

Alaska is the only state that Americans tend to visit by cruise ship and tour bus—as though it were some exotic foreign country. While it's true that old "Sourdoughs" refer to the U.S. as the "Lower 48" and any-place outside of Alaska as "Outside," the fact remains that the state is easily accessible by air, road, and ferry. The people speak English, willingly accept U.S. dollars, and are extremely friendly and hospitable!

For more information, contact the Alaska Tourism Marketing Council (P.O. Box 110801, Juneau, AK, 99811–0801; 907–465–2010), for a copy of the helpful "Alaska Official Vacation Planner." Both the state of Alaska and the province of British Columbia maintain extensive schedules on their modern, well-equipped ferries; contact them at Alaska Marine Highway, P.O. Box 25535, Juneau, 99811 (907–465–3941 or 800–642–0066); and BC Ferries, 1112 Fort Street, Victoria, BC, V8V 4V2, Canada (604–386–3431). It's also worthwhile getting information on the AlaskaPass (P.O. Box 897, Haines, 99827; 907–766–3145 or

33

800–248–7598) offering unlimited travel within a specified time period on 10 Alaska surface transport companies, including Alaska and BC ferries and rail companies, as well as numerous bus routes. Whatever your route, early reservations are *essential* for peak season travel; cabins on the ferries are often fully booked before February for summer sailings, as are rooms in the most desirable inns and B&Bs in popular destinations.

In planning your Alaska trip, contact Pat Niven at **Alaska Northwest Travel Service** (3303 148th Street Southwest, Suite 2, Lynnwood, WA, 98037; 425–787–9499 or 800–533–7381; Alaskan@aol.com), who has specialized in individually planned itineraries of Alaska for years, and is very knowledgeable about its B&Bs. Pat specializes in individual travel, and can assist with B&B reservations, ferry bookings, airplane flights, wilderness trips, and more; she has personally visited a great many Alaskan properties.

Reader tip: "Many Alaska B&Bs are simple homestays, not elegant inns. Be flexible, open-minded, adventurous, and you'll have a wonderful time. On two-night stays our room and bath were untouched; we were told it was considered an intrusion. The hosts wait until after you leave. Don't forget to bring your rain gear. The Inland Passage is a coastal rain forest; expect changeable weather frequent rain. Yes, the sun does come out and when it does, it is glorious." *(Kip Goldman & Marty Wall)* And: "Although the views were unsurpassed and the price was right, don't expect anything remotely resembling a cruise on the Alaska ferries. The facilities were spartan, sometimes old and frayed around the edges. Cleanliness could have been better, and often the staff was less than available. Omnipresent video games and average cafeteria food were typical. BC Ferries are far better maintained and appointed and the staff was friendlier." *(AP)*

ANCHORAGE

With nearly 250,000 inhabitants, Anchorage is Alaska's largest and most cosmopolitan city. Its modern skyscrapers contrast vividly with the surrounding miles of wilderness—it's not unheard of for a moose to take a wrong turn and come wandering into town. Anchorage is the gateway to South Central Alaska, and is a key stopover for anyone heading north to Denali and Fairbanks, the Arctic Circle, or south to the Kenai Peninsula.

Reader tips: "Anchorage has plenty of traffic, and diesel buses and trucks can endanger your sleep far more than the proverbial midnight sun. If you're a light sleeper, *insist* on an upper-floor room, away from the street, for any of the downtown hotels." *(DK)* "Good seafood at Simon & Seaforts, downtown; reservations necessary." *(Kip Goldman & Marty Wall)*

Also recommended: A log church built in 1946, **Bed & Breakfast On The Park** (602 West 10th Avenue, 99501; 907–277–0878) has been renovated as a B&B by Helen Tucker and Stella Hughton. Each of the guest rooms has a private bath and TV, and the B&B double rates of $70–80 (two-night minimum) include a full breakfast. In the heart of downtown is the **Copper Whale Inn** (440 L Street, 99501; 907–258–7999), overlooking Bootleggers Cove and Cook Inlet. B&B double rates range from $100–125, less in winter, and include a continental breakfast. Located in a residential neighborhood near the airport, the **Fancy Moose** (3331 West 32nd Avenue, 99517; 907–243–7596) is a 7,000 square-foot home built in 1993 as a B&B. Its three guest rooms have private baths, and are decorated with dark green and soft pink floral fabrics. B&B double rates of $100–125 include a home-baked continental breakfast. Additional comments welcome.

A stunning contemporary home designed to resemble a swan in flight, **Swan House B&B** (6840 Crooked Tree Drive, 99516; 907–346–3033 or 800–921–1900; www.alaska.net/~swan1) overlooks the city of Anchorage, framed by Mt. McKinley in the distance. Furnishings include lovely European antiques, and the B&B double rates for the three guest accommodations, including a full breakfast, are $139.

For a taste of the real Alaska, stop at **Yukon Don's** (Yukon Circle, 1830 East Parks Highway #386, 2221 Yukon Circle, Wasilla, 99687; 907–376–7472 or 800–478–7472), a restored barn, now offering ample common areas and seven well-equipped guest rooms. Decor includes antiques and Alaska collectibles. Guests are delighted with the beautiful mountain views, comfortable accommodations, and most of all, the warm hospitality and knowledge of Alaska of host family Don and Kristan Tanner. B&B double rates range from $85–125, and children are welcome. Wasilla is an hour north of Anchorage, and is on the way to Denali, Fairbanks, and Valdez.

Information please: Built in 1916, the **Anchorage Hotel** (330 E Street, 99501; 907–272–4553 or 800–544–0988) was remodeled in 1993 with contemporary furnishings, done in muted shades of dusty green, pink, and taupe. The rates include a light continental breakfast and the morning paper, delivered to your door. B&B double rates for the 26 rooms range from $199–229 in summer, $89 off-season.

Voyager Hotel 🏃‍♀️
501 K Street, 99501

Tel: 907–277–9501
800–247–9070
Fax: 907–274–0333
E-mail: rsvp@alaska.net
URL: http://www.alaska.net/~rsvp

"This sturdy brick and concrete four-story building has a small but pleasant lobby with ample couches for comfortable seating, with coffee, tea, and cocoa available each morning. Most of the spacious guest rooms have two double beds, one set up much like a couch. There's a sturdy table to use for eating or as a desk. Each room has a kitchenette, with plates and cutlery free on request. The decor includes good lighting, firm beds, and sturdy, well-made furnishings. The showers offer strong water pressure, steady hot water (no fluctuations) in ample supply. Owner Stan Williams is often at the front desk, available to answer questions and chat. He bought the hotel in 1979, when it was a rundown boarding house, and each year has worked to upgrade some facet of the hotel. In 1996, he installed central air-conditioning, updated the bathrooms, and replaced the carpeting; in 1997, he replaced the bed-spreads and drapes, and added additional electric outlets and phone jacks for computer use." *(SWS)*

"Stan is personable but not intrusive; the morning hostess is cheer-ful and gracious. The staff care about guests' comfort." *(Maria Rutigliano)* "Spotlessly clean and bright even in the dark of winter." *(D. Titus)* "The hotel's location is a plus—across the street from the well-known Captain Cook Hotel." *(Stephen Holman)* "Our nonsmoking room was impeccably clean, with lots of fluffy towels and plenty of hot water." *(Susan Prizio)* "Helpful, cheerful staff; high standards of clean-liness and comforts for a moderate price." *(Irving Carlisle)* "We used the Voyager as our home base. The attitude and efficiency of the reception desk made each return trip a positive experience; our luggage awaited us in our room and Stan greeted us like old friends." *(Bill & Liz Dingle)* "Friendly atmosphere; great front desk attitude." *(JM)*

Open All year. Closed Christmas.
Rooms 38 doubles—all with full private bath, telephone with dataport, voice mail, air-conditioning, radio, TV, desk, kitchenette, hair dryer, coffee maker (coffee supplied), ironing board (irons at front desk).
Facilities Restaurant, bar/lounge with TV, lobby, parking lot. Valet service. Health club access. Parks, walking trails nearby.
Location City center. Junction K and 5th Sts., near Cook Inlet.
Restrictions No smoking in guest rooms.
Credit cards Amex, DC, Discover, MC, Visa.
Rates Room only (includes morning coffee), $79–159 double, $74–149 single. Extra person, $10. 10% senior discount. Off-season weekend specials.
Extras Crib.

DENALI NATIONAL PARK

Denali National Park covers 5.7 million acres of land and is home to 35 kinds of mammals, from grizzly bears to caribou and moose, plus a va-riety of bird and plant life. Mosquitoes are probably the most populous species in the park; fortunately they diminish by the latter part of the sea-son. Private cars are discouraged in the park; shuttle buses bring guests to campgrounds and transport visitors to places of interest throughout the park. Area activities include hiking, canoeing, natural history and photography trips, rafting, bicycling, fishing, and panning for gold.

The park is 240 miles north of Anchorage, 120 miles southwest of Fairbanks.

Also recommended: A few miles past North Face Lodge (see below) is the **Kantishna Roadhouse** (P.O. Box 130, Denali National Park, 99755 or in winter, P.O. Box 80067, Fairbanks, 99708; 800–942–7420 or 907–479–2436), offering daily guided hikes and horse-drawn wagon trips for sightseeing and gold panning; naturalists and photographers offer evening programs. The 27 cabins have private baths, plus there's a lodge with family-style dining room and saloon, and a sauna along the creek. Rates, including bus transportation for the 90-mile trip from Denali Depot, all meals and activities, are $570 per day for two people; it's open from early June to early September, and families are welcome. "A true wilderness experience; we spotted bear, moose, fox, and eagles. Our cabin had running water, electricity, comfortable bed, and a loft to accommodate two more. Delicious food." *(Kathleen Olson)*

North Face Lodge/Camp Denali

Denali National Park Wilderness Centers, Ltd.   *Tel:* 907–683–2290
P.O. Box 67, Denali National Park, 99755   *Fax:* 907–683–1568
E-mail: dnpwild@alaska.net
URL: http://www.gorp.com/dnpwild

Imagine waking from a good night's sleep, throwing back the covers of your handmade down-filled quilt, and stepping outside to watch the sun transform Mt. McKinley's 20,000 feet of majestic whiteness to a rosy pink. Then add a caribou grazing in the foreground to complete this idyllic picture, and you'll be on your way to understanding what it's like to stay at either the North Face Lodge or Camp Denali.

Longtime owners Wallace and Jerryne Cole have done an exceptional job of creating two havens from which to enjoy the wilderness, and are eager for their guests to appreciate the surrounding wilderness and its inhabitants. Stays emphasize active learning experiences, including guided hikes and wildlife observation; guest lecturers are hosted at special sessions at Camp Denali.

The Cole's first effort, Camp Denali, consists of a central dining room, living room, and restroom/shower buildings along with the cabins, scattered along a high ridge. In 1987, the Coles renovated nearby North Face Lodge. An L-shaped building, the lodge consists of a spacious living/dining area, with a guest-room wing. A covered veranda provides an ideal place to relax and enjoy the view. Electricity to power everything from the reading lights to the pumps that supply hot water for your bath is produced by the inn's own generators. A hearty breakfast is served promptly at 7:30 A.M.; at 8:30 A.M., the lunch fixings are set out; at 6:30 P.M., the single-entree dinner is served.

"A hand-hewn log building with a central stove, large collection of books, telescopes, and audio-visual equipment serves as the main lodge at Camp Denali. Our cabin had bunks for the kids, a hot plate, woodstove, beautiful quilts, a writing table, and a comfortable sofa. The kids were thrilled to ring the big triangle to announce the meals; the atmosphere is casual, with staff and guests mixed randomly at long tables." *(Chuck Darby)* "Our room at North Face had a down comforter and four pillows on the firm queen-size bed, and bedside lamps and tables on each side of bed. The chairs on the porch outside our room were perfect for reading or chatting in the long evenings—sunset in mid-August came around 10:30. We breakfasted on French toast one day and eggs the next. We made lunch from a buffet of cheese, ham, and tuna spreads, homemade bread, sprouts, apples, oranges, cookies, plus plastic bottles to fill with water or lemonade. Dinner included halibut in sour cream sauce, rice, carrots and snow peas, and Waldorf salad, with strawberry rhubarb pie for dessert. The delightful staff mixed easily with guests, creating a warm, friendly, and knowledgeable atmosphere. The living room is handsomely furnished with plenty of comfortable couches, chairs, tables for games, and a stone fireplace." *(SWS)* "Our naturalist/driver made the long trip to the lodge an unforgettable experience." *(Janet & Howard Emery)* "Knowledgeable staff who are pleased to share their expertise with guests. Wonderful food with Alaskan specialties: salmon or halibut, local blueberries or lingonberries." *(Anne Clouser)* "The cabins are snug and attractive with quilted bed covers, photographs of Alaska, wood stoves, and kerosene lamps." *(Catherine Cooper)*

Open Early June–early Sept.
Rooms North Face Lodge: 1 suite, 14 twins—all with full private bath. Camp Denali: 18 cabins—each with wood-burning stove, running water, gas hot plate, propane lights, outhouse. Shared shower facility.
Facilities Both lodge & cabins: Dining rooms, library/living rooms, natural history resource room, darkroom. Naturalist program in evenings. Greenhouse, pond, hiking trails. Daypacks, fishing poles, rain gear, boots provided. Inquire about science, photography, environmental special sessions; academic credit available.
Location In center of park, 90 m W of Denali Station.
Restrictions No smoking. Alcoholic beverages permitted in cabin/room only. No fresh milk served. Children over 7 preferred.
Credit cards None accepted.
Rates Full board: $325 per person, double, $425 single. Family, children's rates. 2–4 night minimum stay.
Extras Narrated safari and picnic from Denali Station included in rates. Crib. French, German spoken.

FAIRBANKS

When you consider the fact that Fairbanks is America's northernmost city, just 150 miles south of the Arctic Circle, it's not surprising that the local baseball team can play a midnight game on June 21 without the benefit of artificial light. Fairbanks was settled in 1901, and was first populated by gold miners. A second wave of growth came in 1968, with the discovery of black gold in Prudhoe Bay and the building of the Alaska Pipeline. Sights of interest include the University of Alaska Museum, depicting the state's natural history; a 36,000-year-old preserved bison, killed by a lion, is the star attraction. Families will enjoy a visit to the pioneer theme park, Alaskaland, offering historic buildings, a sternwheeler, trains, and a salmon bake.

Reader tip: "Pike's Landing was superb for salmon; reservations needed." *(Kip Goldman & Marty Wall)*

Also recommended: The **Forget-Me-Not Lodge–The Aurora Express** (P.O. Box 8001128, 99708; 907–474–0949) overlooks Fairbanks and the Tanana Valley, and offers excellent views of the Aurora Borealis. Three guest rooms are available in the contemporary lodge, while another six guest accommodations await in the restored train cars. B&B double rates of $85–140 include a full breakfast served family-style at 8 A.M. Guests are welcome to relax in the TV lounge, the glassed-in living-dining area, or on the deck. "Susan and Mike Wilson are gracious hosts, helpful with advice on area sights. The lodge was immaculate and beautifully decorated. Breakfast was a fabulous spread in the dining room, with a great view. We stayed in the Golden Nellie Caboose, with gilded ceilings, burgundy velvet drapes, a queen-size bed, and private bath." *(Margaret Choa)*

Seven Gables Inn ¢ ♿
4312 Birch Lane, P.O. Box 80488, 99708

Tel: 907–479–0751
Fax: 907–479–2229
E-mail: gables 7@alaska.net
URL: http://www.alaska.net/~gables7

Despite its name, the Seven Gables doesn't really have seven gables, but fourteen, seven along the front of this 7,000-square-foot Tudor-style house and another seven along the back. Custom-built by Paul and Leicha Welton in 1982, this B&B has many other unusual touches, including a flower-filled two-story atrium greenhouse, a foyer with a seven-foot rock waterfall and stained glass ceiling insets, and a living room with a cathedral ceiling 23 feet high. The Welton's home is simply furnished with contemporary decor. The well-equipped bedrooms are compact, and most have queen- or twin-size beds with cheerful floral bedspreads and curtains.

"Cozy Alaskan lodge, with all the comforts of home. Delicious breakfasts, different each day. Leicha prepared breakfast in plenty of time for us to catch an early train. Guests are asked to leave their shoes by the door, which keeps the inn exceptionally clean and quiet. Appreciated extras include the availability of refreshments, and use of the freezer and washer/dryer." *(Jack Johnstone)* "Friendly, clean, and comfortable. Enjoyed the canoeing." *(Mrs. Tom Livengood)*

"Set in a residential neighborhood, this B&B is private, secure, and homey, with a flower-filled greenhouse." *(Lynn Watson)* "An enormous home, built for B&B, with excellent soundproofing between rooms. A full breakfast is served at 7:15 and 8:15; although a continental breakfast is available for late risers, early birds are well rewarded. The first morning we had a delicious meal of cheese-baked eggs with freshly baked apple muffins; the second we feasted on crepes stuffed with a cream cheese and pecan mixture, topped with peach sauce. The Weltons are friendly, hospitable innkeepers, eager to introduce visitors to Fairbanks." *(Pat Niven)* "Leicha's breakfasts were so wonderful, that I bought a copy of her cookbook." *(TL)*

Open All year.
Rooms 4 suites, 9 doubles—all with full private Jacuzzi bath, TV/VCR, telephone, clock/radio, desk, fan. 4 suites in annex.
Facilities Living room with piano, balcony, books, videos; dining room, garden solarium, multipurpose room with fireplace; freezer, refrigerator, laundry privileges. ½ acres with canoes, kayaks, bicycles, children's play equipment. Off-street parking. Skiing, snowmobiling nearby.

Location From Parks Hwy., turn onto Geist Rd. Go right at Loftus Rd., left at Birch Lane to inn on left. Walking distance to U. of Alaska/Fairbanks.
Restrictions Smoking in 2 suites only. No shoes in house.
Credit cards Amex, DC, Discover, MC, Visa.
Rates B&B, $75–130 suite, $50–120 double, $50–110 single. Extra person, $10. No tipping. Weekly, seasonal discounts.
Extras Crib. Spanish, German spoken.

GUSTAVUS

Gustavus is a small and isolated community on southeast Alaska's famed Inside Passage about 50 miles west of Juneau. Located on a large sandy plain created by receding glaciers, the area contrasts with the typical rocky wooded shoreline of southeast Alaska. There are no roads or ferry service the only way to get here is by plane; the only paved surface in town is the landing strip.

The key attraction here is Glacier Bay National Park, a series of fjords and active tidewater glaciers extending over 65 miles. Activities include hiking in the rain forests of hemlock, spruce, and pine; cruising up the bay to watch for whales, bald eagles, black bear, deer, and 200 varieties of birds; or climbing into a kayak for a close-up look at the seals and porpoises that will accompany you. Fishermen will opt for deep-sea and river fishing for salmon, halibut, cutthroat, and Dolly Varden trout, while winter visitors can add cross-country skiing to the recreation list. Another highlight is a bush plane flight-seeing tour of the park, revealing the bay's deep crevasses, enormous ice fields, jagged peaks, and breathtaking beauty. Berry-picking and picnicking on the beach are a delight for children of all ages.

Although outdoor activities are limitless, one thing the town does not have is a liquor store; if you enjoy a glass of wine with dinner, bring your own. Remember that the weather can be cool and damp even in summer, so bring along warm and waterproof clothing, including hat and gloves.

Reader tip: "Don't come to Glacier Bay for the weather; it's often cold and rainy, with low clouds obscuring the views. Bring warm clothes and foul weather gear."

Also recommended: "A truly rustic lodge with a beautiful setting overlooking Bartlett Cove and the Fairview Mountains is **The Glacier Bay Lodge** (P.O. Box 199, Glacier Bay National Park, 99826; 907–697–2226). Rooms are spacious and comfortable, with high ceilings. Eat on the deck overlooking the cove and 'drink' in the scenery. Breakfast is a full, fixed-price buffet. A courtesy shuttle to and from the Gustavus airport is convenient, as is the express check-in for departures on Alaska Air—an efficient and organized operation." (*Kip Goldman & Marty Wall*) A national park concessionaire, lodge rates for the 56 rooms, all with private bath, include complimentary morning coffee, and a nightly film presentation on Glacier Bay; the restaurant is open from 5:45 A.M. until 10 P.M. and offers a health-conscious menu. Double rates are $156 for the mid-May to mid-September season; also available are dorm beds for $28 per night.

For a country inn experience, a favorite choice is the **Glacier Bay Country Inn/Whalesong Lodge** (P.O. Box 5, 99826; 907–697–2288 or 800–628–0912; www.glacierbayalaska.com), with charming, rustic accommodations at the two properties. Rates including all meals are $240–270 double; a total of 15 guest accommodations are available in the two lodges and several cabins. "Food, facilities, service were outstanding. The owners' logistical skills ensured that all ran smoothly, whether guests need to get to the airport, a whale-watching trip, or a kayaking excursion." *(Nigel Franks)* "I felt welcome from the moment I stepped off the plane. The food is plentiful and delicious. The inn is small enough so that you are treated as an individual, not a number." *(Wayne Reynolds)*

JUNEAU

Set at the northern end of southeast Alaska, Juneau is Alaska's capital city. It is the only state capital unreachable by road, and has the additional distinction of having a glacier (the Mendenhall) just 12 miles from town. The city dates to 1880, when gold was discovered by Joe Juneau and Dick Harris. Mining provided the underpinnings of the local economy for years; these days, government jobs provide most paychecks.

Reader tips: "Be sure to drive up to the site of the AJ Mine, either for the salmon bake or to picnic. You can pan for gold or hike one of the many trails. The setting is beautiful—steep forested hillsides and dozens of waterfalls." *(Lewis Bennett)* Also: "The Second Course restaurant on Front Street serves pan-Asian food, and is open only for lunch. The Monday vegetarian buffet was excellent, with spicy tofu." *(Kip Goldman & Marty Wall)*

Information please: Within walking distance of the historic downtown area, the **Mt. Juneau Inn** (1801 Old Glacier Highway, 99801; 907–463–5855) is surrounded by gardens, wetlands, and native-carved totem poles. Innkeepers Karen and Phil Greeney have named their seven guest rooms after animals in the native Tlingit culture; each room is decorated with Alaskan photographs and native art capturing each animal in its natural environment or depicting its mythical powers. They also offer a furnished one-bedroom cottage with a kitchen. Breakfast includes a hot entree, Karen's wild berry jams and fireweed honey, and possibly some of Phil's homemade sausage. Double B&B rates are $55–95; cottage rate is $115.

Pearson's Pond Luxury Inn and Garden Spa   *Tel:* 907–789–3772
4541 Sawa Circle, 99801–8723   *Fax:* 907–789–6722
E-mail: pearsons.pond@juneau.com
URL: http://www.juneau.com/pearsons.pond

A contemporary home built in 1987, Pearson's Pond was opened as a B&B in 1991 by Diane and Steve Pearson. Highlights include the lovely setting, and the balance of warm hospitality with respect for guests' privacy. Diane can serve a breakfast of cereal, fruit, juice, yogurt, home-baked breads, and jams between 8–10 A.M. in the great room; if you prefer, or would like to eat earlier or later, she keeps each guest's kitchen stocked so guests can fix themselves a light meal at their own convenience, to enjoy in their room or on the deck in the gardens.

"Lovely, spacious, well-equipped room. Beautiful setting, with dramatic views of Mendenhall Glacier. Real Alaskan hospitality; inviting rooms with country decor." *(Linda Maybury, also Michael Young)* "We fixed ourselves a casual breakfast and ate it at the table in our room. Beautiful gardens, inviting hot tub." *(Kathy Halvorson)* "Unusually luxurious and well equipped for an Alaska B&B." *(MW)*

Open All year.
Rooms 3 suites—all with private shower bath, telephone, dataport, clock/radio, TV/VCR, desk, kitchenette, private entrance, deck, CD player, electric fireplace.
Facilities Great room with dining area, fireplace, TV/VCR, books, games, musical instruments; deck with 2 hot tubs. 1 acre with gardens, fountains, barbecue/firepit, berry-picking; pond with dock, rowboat, kayak. Skis, bicycles, ice skates, portable gym, masseuse; health club privileges. River, ocean nearby. Hiking, fishing nearby.
Location SE AK. 10 m from downtown, 3 m from airport/ferry, 1 m from Mendenhall Glacier. Call for directions from ferry, airport, downtown.
Restrictions Absolutely no smoking. Children over 3.
Credit cards Amex, CB, DC, Discover, MC, Visa.
Rates B&B, $179–529 2-3 bedroom suite, $89–199 suite, $89–169 single.
Extras Limited wheelchair access. Car needed; no airport/ferry pickups.

Free copy of INNroads newsletter

Want to stay up-to-date on our latest finds? Send a business-size, self-addressed, stamped envelope with 55 cents postage and we'll send you the latest issue, *free!* While you're at it, why not enclose a report on any inns you've recently visited? Use the forms at the back of the book or your own stationery.

Arizona

The Inn at 410, Flagstaff

Arizona is a land of dazzling extremes. It will shake up your preconceptions about deserts with its varied plant and animal life; even the Grand Canyon won't look like the pictures you've seen (unless you have wide-angle eyeballs). Except for the greater Phoenix area, this is a state with little pollution and many wide open spaces and surprises.

Nature's many gifts to Arizona extend far beyond the Grand Canyon. Visit Organ Pipe Cactus National Monument in the southwest and take the self-guiding Ajo Mountain Drive; see the huge weathered columnar lava cliffs at Chiricahua National Monument in the extreme southeast. Along the New Mexico border, take the scenic high-mountain drive on Route 666 between Clifton and Springerville. And be sure to include Sedona's fairyland Red Rocks on your itinerary—a logical overnight en route from Phoenix to the Grand Canyon.

A trip to Arizona isn't complete without an introduction to prehistoric and contemporary Indians. At Painted Rocks State Park (in the southwest, near Gila Bend) stands an isolated outcropping of petroglyphs that keeps its mysterious meaning to itself. In the Flagstaff area, the 500- to 700-year-old cliff dwellings at Tonto, Montezuma Castle, and Walnut Canyon national monuments seem alive with their former occupants, while the striking tenth- to twelfth-century pueblo ruins at Wupatki give evidence of skilled craftsmanship in the decorative placement of lava. This same grace and craftsmanship can be found today at the Hopi Reservation in northeastern Arizona where the casual visitor will feel he has stepped into another century, a foreign land. Other Arizona diversions include glitzy Phoenix art galleries, houseboat rentals in Lake Havasu City, and the historic Hubbell Trading Post (west of Ganado) established in 1876 and still selling everything from bread to Navajo rugs.

Guest ranch rates typically include all meals and activities in one comprehensive daily rate, sometimes referred to as "Arizona Plan;" a service charge of 15% is added to the total.

Also recommended: If you can't find a room at the inns listed here, or if the rates are too high, we'd suggest calling Ruth Young, the long-time and knowledgeable owner of **Mi Casa–Su Casa/Old Pueblo Homestays B&B Reservation Service** (P.O. Box 950, Tempe, 85280-0950; 800–456–0682 or 602–990–0682; www.mi-casa.org) covering Arizona and Nevada. Readers have been delighted with the B&B homestays that Ruth has booked for them.

FLAGSTAFF

An altitude of nearly 7,000 feet keeps Flagstaff pleasantly cool in summer, and often snowy in winter. Shaded by ponderosa pines, the Museum of Northern Arizona is worth a short visit, especially in July when Navajo and Hopi crafts people exhibit their work. Room rates are reasonable here, making Flagstaff a good base for touring Sedona and Oak Creek Canyon, Montezuma's Castle, Wupatiki and Sunset Crater National Monuments, and of course, the South Rim of the Grand Canyon. There's hiking nearby in the Coconino National Forest, and downhill and cross-country skiing in winter. Flagstaff is located in central northern Arizona, 80 miles southeast of the Grand Canyon, and 142 miles north of Phoenix.

Reader tips: "We had a wonderful natural foods and vegetarian cuisine at Cafe Express on San Francisco Street." *(Gail Davis)* "We had an elegant European-style dinner at the Cottage restaurant." *(Chrys Bolk)* "Tea and Sympathy, at 409 North Humphreys Street, is a first class tea shop, with many varieties of loose tea, plus delicious savories and sweets. The Lowell Observatory and the Arboretum are worth visiting." *(Emily Hoche-Mong)*

Also recommended: The **Birch Tree Inn** (824 West Birch Avenue, Flagstaff, 86001-4420; 520–774–1042 or 888–774–1042; birch@flagstaff. az.us) is a fully renovated 80-year-old Western-style bungalow; its five guest rooms are furnished in Southwestern decor, and rates range from $69–109, including early morning coffee and a full breakfast, often served on the veranda in Flagstaff's cool mountain air; afternoon tea or wine is also offered. "Tasty breakfasts with fresh fruit, just-baked muffins, and a turkey sausage strata with salsa. The innkeepers suggested a great daytrip to Walnut Canyon, with 800-year-old cliff dwellings, and recommended the Beaver Street Cafe, a local microbrewery, for great beer and a fine dinner." *(Eloise Danniel)* "Friendly, delightful innkeepers; we enjoyed the spacious Southwestern suite, with a king-size bed." *(Sharon Bielski)*

The Inn at 410 &.
410 North Leroux Street, 86001

Tel: 520–774–0088
800–774–2008
Fax: 520–774–6354

Built in 1907 by a wealthy banker-rancher, The Inn at 410 was used as a fraternity house in the early 1970s, and was later remodeled into apartments. Restored as a B&B in 1991, the inn was purchased by Sally and Howard Krueger in 1993, and has now made a full return to elegance, with decor ranging from Victorian to contemporary Southwestern. On-going improvements and refurbishing ensure that standards remain high. The parlor and stairs are handsomely trimmed with beautiful oak, original to the house. Breakfast, served from 8 to 9 A.M., might include fresh fruit with cinnamon and honey, scones and jam, and peaches and cream cheese bread pudding with raspberry sauce; or minted fruit, blue corn blueberry muffins, and eggs with black bean, corn, and red pepper relish. Early or late risers may request a continental breakfast in their room. Freshly baked cookies, nuts, and iced tea or hot cider are available in the dining room from 4 to 8 P.M.

"Genuine hospitality, good breakfast, tasty snacks, beautifully decorated rooms. Loved the privacy afforded by the cottage. Neither your writeup nor their brochure does it justice." *(Carol Blodgett)* "We arrived in time for desert flower tea and white chocolate cookies. Immaculate rooms, newly renovated. Careful attention to all the little details that make guests feel welcome and comfortable; their young staff is helpful and pleasant. The Canyon Memories room was spacious, with a mural of the Grand Canyon, a big bathroom with a refrigerator and counter for the coffee maker. Special breakfast of blended juices and corn muffins, baked scrambled eggs with asparagus, sour cream, and salsa; plus kiwi, blueberries, and melon. We had breakfast on the porch, surrounded by flowers. The gazebo and wicker chairs on the porch are great places to relax, as are the large, soft sofas in the sitting room." *(Marilyn Parker)* "Rooms are spacious, modern, spotless, and beautifully decorated; each different, each special. The bathrooms have modern fixtures and luxurious towels and amenities. In the common rooms, classical music plays softly in the background. Breakfasts are robust, delicious, and imaginative. The inn is within walking distance of downtown shops and restaurants, convenient to the highway, yet located in a pleasant, wooded residential area. Howard and Sally are charming, courteous, and helpful, but never intrude upon guests' privacy." *(Mr. & Mrs. L. K. Bret Harte)*

"Delicious chocolate chip cookies. The Sonoran Serenade room is done in bright, Mexican-printed wallpaper with a stunning tile fireplace to warm the cool evening, and a queen-size wrought iron bed draped in Spanish lace. Corner windows looked out to a full moon lighting up the gazebo below. Breakfast was served on the patio, and looked as good as it tasted. Although the area offers much to do, my favorite activity is sitting on the porch rocking chair with a good book." *(Sue Herrmann)* "Howard and Sally are happy to accommodate special dietary needs (with advance notice)." *(Gail Davis)* "The portable phone reserved for guests insures privacy." *(Jerry Shannon)* "The Southwest Room was quiet and relaxing with a comfortable bed and kiva-style fireplace. Terrific advice on hiking." *(Ingrid & Rick Adams)* "The staff made our dinner reservations and pointed us in the right direction. The comfortable Dakota Room has a charming cowboy theme." *(Judith Krone)*

Open All year.

Rooms 5 doubles, 4 suites—all with private bath and/or shower, 2 with double Jacuzzi. All with radio, clock, air conditioning, refrigerator, coffee maker; most with fireplace.

Facilities Dining room, living room with fireplace, books, games, stereo, porch, patio, gazebo. Off-street parking.

Location 4 blocks to historic downtown. From I-40, take Exit 195B N onto Milton. From I-17, continue N onto Milton. Follow Milton under the railroad overpass & curve to right. Turn left at 1st stoplight (Humphreys St.). At Dale turn right. Turn left on Leroux, then go right into inn parking lot, just beyond inn.

Restrictions Absolutely no smoking.

Credit cards MC, Visa.

Rates B&B, $125–165 suite, double. Extra person, $10. 2 night weekend minimum. AAA discount.

Extras Wheelchair access; 1 room specially equipped.

GRAND CANYON—SOUTH RIM

People go to the Grand Canyon to see the Grand Canyon, and the quality of accommodations, beyond the basics, is relatively unimportant. Although obvious, this fact is fortunate, since reports on area accommodations include minor complaints about service and maintenance. However, given the choice of mediocre accommodations at the rim, or better ones 50 miles away, we urge that you choose the former. Two concessionaires control all accommodations and tours—hotels, motels, cabins, lodges, campgrounds, mule trips, and more—in the Grand Canyon. For information on the South Rim, including El Tovar Hotel, Bright Angel Lodge, Kachina and Thunderbird Lodges, Maswik Lodge, Moqui Lodge, Yavapai Lodge, and Phantom Ranch (on the canyon floor), contact: Grand Canyon National Park Lodges, P.O. Box 699, 86023; 520–638–2631 or in advance, contact Amfac Parks & Resorts, 14001 East Illif, Suite 600, Aurora, CO, 80014; 303–29–PARKS. For information on the North Rim, see the entry for the Grand Canyon Lodge below.

Reader tips: "In addition to room reservations, make an advance reservation for dinner at El Tovar. The most popular time to eat is right after sunset, so there's often a wait. The steak house at Bright Angel Lodge doesn't take reservations, so arrive early. Breakfast service at El Tovar begins at 6:30 A.M. We arose early, saw the sunrise, and arrived in time for an early breakfast. Old-fashioned atmosphere, great food, well priced, excellent service. Getting an early start allowed us to hit the trails early and beat the heat. Cancellations for both meals and accommodations are frequent, so if they're full keep calling to check for openings." *(Pam Phillips)* "In most national park lodges, meals are served by college students. While they are generally cheerful and friendly, some are quick and efficient, others slow and careless. Given the 100% occupancy rates much of the year, it's not surprising that housekeeping and maintenance is barely adequate." *(MW)* "Reserve ahead for the trip to Phantom Ranch at the bottom of the canyon. Unforgettable scenery and experience; rustic accommodations; fabulous, filling food." *(Mary Jane Skala)*

Also recommended: Built as a luxury hotel shortly after the Santa Fe Railroad reached the Grand Canyon in 1901, the **El Tovar Hotel** (P.O. Box 699, 86023; 520–638–2631, for advance reservations 303–29–PARKS) has been under the continuous management of the Fred Harvey Company since it opened in 1905. Double rates for the 92 rooms are $119–179; suites to $280; children under 12 stay free. The general consensus on El Tovar is that if you are lucky enough to get a reservation, grab it; that the guest rooms in both the original hotel and the motel wings are uninspired but adequate; and the hotel's public areas are strikingly beautiful, well worth visiting for a drink, a meal, or a look-see. "Built at the most spectacular and colorful section of the South Rim, some of the rooms in the El Tovar and the nearby Kachina Lodge have canyon views, extraordinary at sunrise and sunset. The exterior of the original building, including the grand entrance, is in the 'log cabin' style, constructed of native boulders and Oregon pine. The interior common areas are large with Southwestern Indian motifs." *(Willis Frick)* "Food was good; service was attentive and friendly. Softshell crab salad and cavatelli with wild mushrooms were a pleasant surprise." *(Carolyn Myles)*

We've had relatively good reports on the **Bright Angel Lodge and Cabins** (address above). Lodge rooms are $60 double, historic cabins are $69, and rim cabins are $97–119. "We booked a year ahead for a rim cabin with a fantastic view, simple furnishings, a nice fireplace, and an unnecessary TV. The dining room was excellent, with a wide variety of simple dishes, well prepared. " *(Duane Roller)* Also: "Our historic cabin was comfortable, small, and rustic." *(Daena Kluegel)* "Our 'hiker's special,' was plain but clean and comfortable with knotty pine walls and country furniture. It had a private bath with toilet and sink, and shower down the hall (accessible with the room key). The lodge has a coffee shop, a steak house providing decent food at reasonable prices, gift shop, and a patio area overlooking the canyon with an old-fashioned snack bar." *(Pam Phillips)* "Adequate meals, pleasant serving staff. The location is convenient to everything, with trails and the rim walk from the front door." *(Eloise Danniels)* Less favorably: "Absolutely no soundproofing, so it was rather noisy. We couldn't control the heater and it went on and off mysteriously." And: "Our only difficulty was getting our room made up before late afternoon." Plus: "Our bedspread and carpet were stained and needed a thorough cleaning; lighting was inadequate."

Another possibility is **Yavapai Lodge**, (see El Tovar above) "away from the hordes of tour buses and an easy mile-long walk along the canyon rim to El Tovar. It's also a short trip to the cafeteria for a zero-atmosphere meal. On the other hand, our motel-like room was spacious, clean, and comfortable with TV and telephone, good lights for reading, makeup and shaving, and ample hot water with good pressure. At $100 a night, the price was right." *(Carolyn Myles)*

For additional area entries, see **Flagstaff**.

GRAND CANYON—NORTH RIM

If you're going to visit the Grand Canyon in July or August, and have limited time, give serious thought to bypassing the South Rim altogether, and head directly for the North Rim. Although advance reservations are just as essential, given the extremely limited accommodations, the statistics are telling: of over five million annual visitors, about 10% go to the North Rim. Another advantage is its location 1500 feet higher than the South Rim, keeping temperatures delightfully cool, even in August. Snow keeps the road closed from late October to mid-May.

Reader tip: "Don't assume that there's nothing to do but look at the canyon and leave. There are lots of trails to hike, and it's well worth the cost and effort to book in advance for the full-day mule trip down to Roaring Springs, both for the canyon views and to see the springs, where a great torrent rushes out of the rock, supplying drinking water for the entire canyon. Equally impressive is the ride to Angel's Window, where the view is framed by a natural rock 'window.' " *(SWS, also Amy Siegel)*

Also recommended: Authorized concessionaire AmFac Parks & Resorts operates the **Grand Canyon Lodge** (AmFac Parks & Resorts, 14001 East Iliff, Suite 600, Aurora, CO, 80014; 520–638–2611 or 303–297–2757) at the North Rim, as well as lodges at Zion and Bryce National Parks in Utah. At the North Rim, 201 units are provided in a motel wing, and three different kinds of cabins: most luxurious are the Western Cabins; more rustic (and slightly cheaper) are the Frontier and Pioneer Cabins, with shower baths only. Double rates range from $65–105. Meals in the dining room are adequate and reasonably priced (reservations essential) and a snack bar is also available. The stone and timber main lodge is a classic of park architecture, with a huge high-ceilinged dining room, a "viewing lounge," and wonderful patios where park rangers give lectures—all with spectacular canyon views.

ORACLE

Triangle L Ranch 🐎 ¢   *Tel:* 520–896–2804
Highway 77, P.O. Box 900, 85623   888–782–9572
            URL: http://www.trianglelranch.com

"Birdwatchers, hikers, outdoor enthusiasts, and those who appreciate the plants and animals of the desert find themselves very much at home at the Triangle L Ranch," report Tom and Margot Beeston, who bought the ranch in 1978. Set in the Santa Catalina Mountains, at an altitude of 4500 feet, guests stay in restored cottages dating from the 1890s, furnished with comfortable antiques. The breakfast buffet is set out on the original ten-foot farm table in the ranch kitchen, and includes homemade whole grain breads, pastries and granola, fresh fruit, cereal, and Tom's great coffee/espresso/cappuccino/latte creations. The meal is offered from 8–9:30 A.M., and guests seat themselves either in the sun room, the ranch dining room with two adobe fireplaces, or the screened porch—the birder's choice. Guests also enjoy visiting Tom's shop, where stringed instruments are crafted and restored.

"Located in a secluded spot on the edge of Oracle, near back country wilderness. Our favorite cottage is Hill House, set up on a hill behind the main house with scenic views of the surrounding area. Delightful, healthy breakfasts with just-laid eggs from the ranch chickens. Much of the original furniture is still in place at this century-old ranch, and all is well maintained and comfortable, immaculate and homey. Margot rescues birds of prey, and is a wealth of avian information. If she has 'patients,' you get to see them, up close and personal." *(Red & Dusty Levangie)* "Incredible sunsets, homey atmosphere." *(Sandra Smyre & Mary Pollock)* "Margot and Tom are extremely knowledgeable about wildflowers, birds, and animals." *(Juliana Hazard)* "The Beestons work together to grind the wheat for fresh bread, muffins, or scones. Tom and Margot are loved by all the guests. Each morning one of the friendly, playful ranch dogs walked us to the main house for breakfast." *(Jody Reynolds)*

"The ranch reflects the love that gracious hosts, Margot and Tom, have for this beautiful landscape. The homey Foreman's House had with ample storage space and a wonderful, old-fashioned kitchen. Ample hot water and an excellent shower head for the clawfoot tub. Fluffy towels with extras available in the hallways linen shelf. Placemats, cloth napkins, a big jug of drinking water next to the kitchen sink, fresh flowers on the kitchen table, and cookware ample for a family of four. Flannel sheets for cool April nights. Windows that open easily; screens in place. An efficient gas heater. Interesting books and games for kids and adults. Lovely patio, perfect for relaxing with books, binoculars, and beverage. Margot and Tom never seemed rushed or frazzled by their responsibilities. Both were genuinely interested in learning about their guests' lives and were generous in sharing information about their own. Margot, a wildlife rehabilitator was a wealth of information on local flora, fauna, and hiking trails. Tom told us about his work as a restorer and builder of stringed instruments. Through a telescope, we watched a red-tailed hawk nesting and were amazed to see that the chicks had hatched." *(Marcia Milner-Brage)* "The old live oaks sheltered us from the heat of the day and provided great shade for the swing just outside our door. We stayed in both the Hill House and the Guest House; both were clean and comfortable, furnished with sturdy antiques and intriguing old photographs. Natural plantings complement the wall-maintained adobe buildings. We were totally spoiled sitting in either the formal ranch dining room with its magnificent double fireplace and beamed ceiling or the bright sunny breakfast room overlooking the walled courtyard where birds flock to feed. The ranch is an island of beauty in an area of encroaching development." *(Patty Ryan & David Westphal)* "Another era, from the piled mesquite fences to large old trees. Apple-scented bubble bath was a treat in the old-fashioned clawfoot tub. Electric bedpads and fluffy quilts kept the beds warm and cozy. The blue porch swing in the big tree made a wonderful place to relax." *(Rae Strong)* "Our children love getting up early to gather eggs from the chicken coop. Peaceful setting, no TV or ringing telephones." *(Lucia Gibson)*

Open Oct. through May.
Rooms 4 1-3 bedroom cottages—all with private bath and/or shower, refrigerator, coffee maker, hair dryer, porch/patio. 2 with living room, equipped kitchen, air-conditioning; 1 with fireplace.
Facilities Kitchen; dining room, living room, both with fireplace; porches. 80 acres with garden, greenhouse, picnic area. Hiking, bicycling, birdwatching.
Location SE AZ, 35 m NE of Tucson. Take Rte. 77 N to Oracle. Turn left on Rockcliff Rd., crossing Rte. 77. Turn right on Oracle Ranch Rd., go ¼ mile to Triangle Ranch Rd, turn left to ranch. *Watch carefully for the turn-off from Rte. 77.*
Restrictions No smoking.
Credit cards MC, Discover, Visa.
Rates B&B, $95–125 double, $80–110 single. Extra adult, $15; child, $10.
Extras Spanish spoken.

PHOENIX

Capital of Arizona and a sprawling city of over 850,000 people, Phoenix grew rapidly throughout this century, as it was connected to the East by the railroad, supplied with ample water, and lastly (but far from least) equipped with air-conditioning to temper its 110°F summer highs. Among its outstanding sights is the Heard Museum of anthropology and primitive art, a fine introduction to the Native American culture you'll encounter throughout the state.

Reader tips: "For moderately priced, authentic Mexican food, try Julio G's for dinner. Incredible tortilla soup and tamales in green sauce. Splurge on lunch at Windows on the Green at the Phoenician golf resort; incredible bread and innovative vegetarian sandwiches. Kids of all ages love miniature golf at the Family Golf Center, at the corner of McDonald and Hayden, complete with waterfalls and rushing streams." *(Eloise Danniels)*

Also recommended: For a peaceful desert setting, visit **Gotland's Inn Cave Creek** (Cave Creek Road, P.O. Box 948, Cave Creek, 85327; 602–488–9636; www.arizonaguide.com/gotlands) located 25 miles northeast of Phoenix, adjacent to Carefree. An adobe-style ranch home built in 1994 by owners Jan and Al Gotland, four suites are available at B&B double rates of $110–195; each one has a television, TV, air-conditioning, fireplace, deck, refrigerator, microwave, and more. Breakfast is brought to guests' rooms, and includes homemade granola and baked goodies, fresh fruit and juice, yogurt, and Kona coffee; bottled water and afternoon snacks are also provided. Guests are thrilled with the comfortable accommodations, careful attention to detail, and ideal balance of privacy and hospitality.

For an additional area entry, see **Oracle**, 35 miles northeast of Tucson.

Maricopa Manor   ♦   ♿   *Tel:* 602–274–6302
15 West Pasadena Avenue, 85013-2001   800–292–6403
Fax: 602–266–3904
E-mail: mmanor@getnet.com
URL: http://www.maricopamanor.com

This Spanish-style home was built in 1928 on what was then a quiet country road, miles from downtown Phoenix; today, Maricopa Manor is in the city, close to museums, theaters, restaurants, and shops. After raising 11 children in the house, innkeepers Mary Ellen and Paul Kelley found a way to keep it full of friends in 1990—by opening their home to B&B guests. Breakfast is brought to your room at the time requested; you'll find a picnic hamper filled with lovely crockery, and such goodies as individual cheese souffles, fresh fruit, home-baked breads and muffins.

"A delightful inn in an unexpected setting. Friendly but unobtrusive hosts." *(Bill Hussey)* "Located on a residential street, with well-maintained single family and apartment houses; at either end of the block are major commercial thoroughfares, placing you within easy reach of downtown Phoenix, Scottsdale, and the airport. Guests tend to gather outside on the patios or in the comfortable family room at the back of the house, with ample couches for relaxing, and a table ideal for games or cards. The Library Suite has a small denlike room with good working desk, small pull-out couch, a spacious bathroom, and in a separate room done in blue and white, a beautiful canopied king-size bed. Across the courtyard is a casita with additional suites. One, in chrome, black, and white, has a living room, well-equipped kitchen, and bedroom; there's a prettily flowered room with antique twin beds and enclosed porch, and another with rich tapestry colors and fabrics." *(SWS)*

"An elegant urban B&B. Paul and Mary Ellen were gracious hosts who have obviously thought of everything down to the smallest detail. The canopied king-size bed in the Reflections Past suite was extremely comfortable and cozy with a down comforter. Individually controlled reading lights were cleverly tucked in the overhead canopy. The huge walk-in closet had a microwave, small refrigerator, iron, and ironing board. The grounds are lovely, with a pool, lawn furniture, and tall palms." *(Mark Mendenhall)* "We requested breakfast at 7 A.M.—plenty of orange juice, coffee in a Thermos, fresh fruit, a hot egg dish, and pastries—and made an early start." *(Alex & Beryl Williams)* "We enjoyed a delicious breakfast on our private patio; flowers bloomed everywhere and roses cascaded from the trellis." *(Joanne & David Mahler)* "Lush green landscaping surrounds the private redwood deck of the Library Suite. Oversized fluffy towels were tucked into the cupboards in the bath, along with extra pillows, terry robes, disposable razors, an ironing board, and iron. A coffee pot and a selection of tea, coffee, and hot chocolate were also provided." *(Charlotte Brooks)* "Tasty breakfast, lovely grounds, cordial staff." *(Ruth Hurley)*

Open All year.
Rooms 7 suites—all with private bath and/or shower, telephone, radio, TV, air-conditioning, fan, hair dryer. Some with whirlpool tub, desk, refrigerator, microwave, fireplace, patio.
Facilities Living room with fireplace; family room with fireplace, TV, stereo; music room with organ, harp; laundry facilities. 1 acre with hot tub, gazebo, patios, fountains, pool.
Location N central Phoenix. From I-17, take Camelback Rd. to 3rd Ave. Turn left onto 3rd, go 1 block, turn right onto Pasadena.
Restrictions No smoking.
Credit cards Amex, Discover, MC, Visa.
Rates B&B, $99–229 suite. Extra person, $25. Extended stay discount.
Extras Wheelchair access. Pets permitted by prior arrangement.

SEDONA

Beautiful Sedona was named after Sedona Schnebly, wife of the town's founding father. Today's tourist industry can be thankful that her appealing given name was chosen, or they would be struggling to promote the Red Rocks of Schneblyville today. Most popular with tourists in spring and fall, Sedona's 4,500-foot altitude provides a climate that is relatively mild year-round. Visitors come to see the striking red rock formations and the cool depths of Oak Creek Canyon. Other activities include golf, tennis, horseback riding, hiking, swimming, fishing, hunting, Jeep tours, and visiting the many boutiques and art galleries of this popular resort. Sedona is in central Arizona's Red Rocks Country, 115 miles north of Phoenix, halfway between Phoenix and the Grand Canyon.

Sedona's growth has been recent and fast. Most homes are relatively new; the more attractive ones were built in adobe style, but the majority appear to be 1960s- and 70s-era tract homes of minimal charm. Most of Sedona's B&Bs are in residential neighborhoods, closely bordered by private homes, so don't expect an isolated setting.

Reader tips: "We thought that the famous Jeep tours were well worth the high price. We took Outdoor Expeditions archaeology tour and found it fascinating; everyone we spoke to loved the Pink Jeep tour too. We browsed through Tlaquepaque's elegant but expensive galleries, and enjoyed ourselves completely." *(SWS)* "We stopped at the Heartline Cafe for great espresso and cappuccino—a welcome change from the weak, watery brew we were usually served in Arizona." *(Eloise Danniels)* "We were disappointed with Sedona's many T-shirt and cheap curio shops, a typical blight in many tourist destinations." *(CM)*

Also recommended: The **Briar Patch Inn** (3190 North Highway 89A, 86336; 520–282–2342 or 888–809–3030; briarpatch@sedona.net) is a compound set along the banks of spring-fed Oak Creek in Oak Creek Canyon. The rustic cottages, most built in the 1940s, are furnished with

Native American and Mexican decorations. Double rates of $149–295 for the 17 accommodations include a breakfast of home-baked breads and muffins, granola, yogurt, fresh fruits and juice, and eggs in the shell, to be enjoyed by the fireside lounge, on a tray in your cottage, or at creekside. "Lush greenery and flowers; rustic but comfortable cabins; friendly staff; generous, healthy breakfasts." *(MR)*

Built in 1992, the luxurious **Canyon Villa Inn** (125 Canyon Circle Drive, Oak Creek, 86351; 520–284–1226 or 800–453–1166; www.arizonaguide.com/canyonvilla) offers unrestricted views of Sedona's famous Red Rocks, including Bell, Castle, and Courthouse rocks. Room decor ranges from Santa Fe to Victorian; each of the ten guest rooms have a whirlpool tub. B&B double rates of $135–215 include generous full breakfasts, afternoon snacks, and bedtime cookies or brownies.

One of the best buys in Sedona is the **Cathedral Rock Lodge** (Red Rock Loop Road, Star Rte. 2, P.O. Box 856, 86336; 520–282–7608), with one cabin, one suite, and two doubles, with B&B double rates of $80–150, including breakfasts of homemade breads and jams, plus afternoon snack. This B&B is set on a quiet country road, with breathtaking views of Cathedral Rock. Guest rooms are furnished with family antiques and handmade quilts.

An outstanding choice in the Oak Creek residential section of Sedona is **The Graham Bed & Breakfast Inn** (150 Canyon Circle Drive, 86351; 520–284–1425 or 800–228–1425; www.sedonasfinast.com). Decorated with a contemporary Southwestern look, incorporating the work of local artisans, the inn offers excellent views of the nearby red rock formations. B&B double rates range from $159–249, and include a full breakfast and afternoon refreshments. Four casitas were completed in 1997, each with a bedroom/living room with fireplace, king-size bed, double Jacuzzi tub, and kitchenette. Although expensive ($309–369), guests rave about the beautiful decor, fine construction, and careful attention to every detail. "Incredibly romantic, creative, homey, and comfortable. The double Jacuzzi overlooking the beautiful red rocks, with a potbelly stove and waterfall shower is incredible for romance and hedonism. Fresh bread is baked in your room each day, and the fridge is stocked with butter, jelly, milk, delicious granola, and drinks. They also provide lovely bathrobes to cuddle up in. The owners and staff are friendly, caring, and giving. Delicious snack and breakfast are served each day." *(Laurie Gross)*

The Lodge at Sedona (125 Kallof Place, 86336; 520–204–1942 or 800–619–4467) was built in 1959 of rough-hewn timbers and native red sandstone, and was redone as a B&B in 1993. The thirteen guest rooms vary from spacious country suites with fireplaces, to rooms with private decks. Double rates range from $120–225 a night including private bath, full breakfast, and evening refreshments.

Information please: Listed in many past editions is the well-known **L'Auberge de Sedona Resort** (301 L'Auberge Lane, P.O. Box B, 86339; 520–282–1661 or 800–272–6777) offering a variety of luxury accommodations in the European-style lodge, individual cabins, or motel units; double rates range from $180–425. The motel units, called The Orchards, are at the top of the hill, right in town; the lodge and cabins are down by Oak Creek; a little tram connects them. The inn's two restaurants include the formal L'Auberge, and the Orchards Restaurant, specializing in light American cuisine. Some readers are delighted with the food, service, setting, and accommodations, others less so.

TUCSON

Once a sleepy desert town called Old Pueblo, Tucson now has a population of over 600,000. Spanish, Mexican, Native American, and pioneer influences have combined with a sunny, dry climate to draw increasing numbers of tourists from October to May. Its status as a winter resort has resulted in a wide variety of attractive accommodations, quite unlike the situation 100 years ago. Then, a room in the town's best hotel was typically occupied by a dozen drunk or hungover men and the washing facilities consisted of a ten-foot trough sink that emptied into the street!

Area attractions include the Sonora Desert Museum, an outstanding natural history facility and zoo; the Tucson Museum of Art; the Arizona Heritage Center; the Flandrau Planetarium; the Mission San Xavier del Bac; Saguaro National Park and Colossal Cave; Old Tucson, a combination western movie studio and theme park; the Kitt Peak National Observatory; and Tombstone, an infamous spot in the history of the Wild West. Of course, a full complement of recreational activities await: golf (over 20 courses), tennis, jogging, hiking, skiing, and horseback riding.

Tucson is located in southeastern Arizona, 118 miles southeast of Phoenix and 63 miles north of Nogales, Mexico.

A note for those who like it hot: Tucson room rates drop as precipitously as the summer temperatures skyrocket!

Reader tip: "Two great half-day trips out of Tucson are to the artist colony of Tubac, and to the Amerind Foundation, with a wonderful collectin of artifacts from Native American cultures." *(Kip Goldman & Marty Wall)*

Also recommended: Although the softly pink-stuccoed outside walls of the **Arizona Inn** (2200 East Elm Street, 85719; 520–325–1541 or 800–933–1093) convey its Southwestern character, the interiors have a more traditional look of homey elegance, with comfortable slipcovered couches highlighted by European antiques. "Discreetly hidden by trees and shrubs, our room had windows on three sides and a private patio. Swimming in the pool by moonlight was pleasant, and the poolside ice-cream bar was a treat." *(Duane Roller)* "Beautiful gardens; immaculate rooms; exceptional service." *(Susan Ulanoff)* Double rates range from $115–280.

Car-Mar's Southwest B&B (6766 West Oklahoma Street, 85746; 520–578–1730) is a lovely Southwestern home built in 1980 by Carole Martinez. This four guest room B&B is convenient to the airport and the Sonora Desert Museum, and offers B&B double rates of $65–125. Guest rooms are light and airy, with lovely arched windows and alcoves, decorated with lodgepole and saguaro rib furniture. Handmade comforters top the lodgepole, canopy, and elaborate iron beds. Extras include the luxurious robes in each room, poolside refreshments at sunset, and home-baked goodies at evening turndown.

Located in the West University Historic District, the **Catalina Park Inn** (309 East First Street, 85705; 520–792–4541 or 800–792–4885; www.catalinaparkinn.com) is a renovated 1928 Mediterranean-style home, decorated with eclectic antique flair by owners Mark Hall and Paul Richard. Each of the six guest rooms has a private bath, TV, telephone, bath robes, hair dryer, down comforter, and pillows. The B&B rates of $65–125 include a full breakfast, the morning newspaper, and access to the guest pantry for tea or coffee. Guests can't stop raving about the exceptional hospitality, comfort, dècor, grounds, food, and ongoing improvements at this delightful B&B.

Set in the downtown historic district, **El Presidio B&B Inn** (297 North Main Avenue, 85701; 520–623–6151 or 800–349–6151) combines Victorian detailing with adobe walls nearly two feet thick. The three elegant guest suites are extensively appointed with antiques and collectibles, and a flower-filled courtyard is highlighted by a traditional fountain. The B&B rates of $75–120 include a full breakfast, afternoon tea, and complimentary cheese, wine, juice, and mineral water.

Re-opened after a major renovation is an old favorite, the **Hacienda del Sol Guest Ranch Resort** (5601 North Hacienda del Sol Road, 85718; 520–299–1501 or 800–728–6514; www.haciendadelsol.com), a 34-acre retreat in the foothills of the Santa Catalina Mountains. Adobe casitas house the 31 guest rooms, and rates range from $90–140; two-bedroom suites to $385. Facilities include the swimming pool, tennis court, horseback riding, and hiking, as well as the restaurant, which reopened in 1997. "We had a fabulous two-bedroom casita at a reasonable price, and actually saw a bobcat outside our window." *(Kerck Kelsey)*

Whether you are an artist yourself or like to watch those who are, you will enjoy a peaceful stay at **Rim Rock West** (3450 North Drake Place, 85749; 520–749–8774), converted into an inn in 1985 by Val and Mae Robbins. Mae notes that "our main concern is to provide quiet tranquility amid this beautiful scenery. Birders and hikers enjoy our abundant wildlife. Val is a sculptor and painter, while I do enamel work, and love to garden and cook." B&B double rates are $120 for the three double rooms, $175 for the cottage, including a full breakfast. Each room has a private bath, TV, air-conditioning, and private entrance.

For an additional area inn, see **Oracle.**

Lazy K Bar Guest Ranch ¢ ⋔
8401 North Scenic Drive, 85743

Tel: 520–744–3050
800–321–7018
Fax: 520–744–7628
E-mail: lazyk@theriver.com
URL: www.lazykbar.com

If you want gorgeous views down into the Santa Cruz valley and up into the Saguaro National Park and the Tucson and Catalina mountains, excellent trail rides for all abilities seven days a week, gorgeous hiking trails, plus home-style cooking and comfortable accommodation at reasonable all-inclusive rates, visit the Lazy K Bar Ranch. Set at 2,300 feet, the ranch has been owned since 1975 by William Scott. Longtime manager Carol Moore reports that "the atmosphere here is informal and relaxed—blue jeans, comfortable shirts, and sturdy shoes are the usual dress around here. Most of our guests are active people who enjoy the outdoors; children are welcome and are included in all activities." All meals are included, with hearty breakfasts cooked to order. At lunchtime, there is both a salad buffet and a hot casserole or sandwich, with hot soup during cool weather. Dinner is buffet-style, with baked chicken, mashed potatoes, biscuits, gravy, and carrot cake one evening and sliced steak, Caesar salad, steak fries, and lemon meringue pie the next. At Saturday cookout you can feast on mesquite-grilled steaks, cowboy beans, corn-on-the-cob, salad, and homemade ice cream.

"Totally relaxing, comfortable, and friendly, with a wonderful rapport between the staff and the guests. The wranglers balance humor with safety consciousness. Many activities kept my son busy, and gave me a chance to relax in one of the many hammocks. Other events we could enjoy together. Great food, too." *(Patricia Rodgers)* "The rooms are charming, comfortable, and well-maintained. The meals offered a nice balance between good-to-eat and good-for-you." *(Eileen & Tom Hughes)* "From the moment we were met at the airport by a friendly face and a waiting van, we weren't disappointed; our children were delighted to learn that horses awaited them for the afternoon ride. Although the riding and scenery were splendid, the accommodations and facilities more than satisfactory, the food ample and tasty (especially the Saturday night steak barbecue), best of all was the staff. The Lazy K has a team dedicated to making sure that its guests have a great time—both children and adults." *(Gary Blake)* "The wranglers are real cowboys who entertain with stories and poems about the old west, and who provide many riding tips for beginners. Carol Moore is caring and solicitous. Our spacious room had a comfortable king-size bed, rustic furnishings, and a large bathroom with double sinks." *(Laurie Gianturco)* "Wonderful bird life. Free van rides to the Sonora Desert Museum; long trail rides into Saguaro National Park." *(Lydia Adelfio)*

Open Mid-Sept.–mid-June.
Rooms 4 suites, 19 doubles—all with full private bath, desk, air-conditioning. Located in individual cottages.
Facilities Dining room, living room with fireplace, TV room with wide-screen TV/VCR, bar (bring your own liquor), library with games, Ping-Pong, billiards, patio. Evening progams: country western dance lessons, cookouts, hayrides, etc. 160 acres with heated swimming pool, hot tub, 2 lighted tennis courts, horseback riding, shuffleboard, horseshoes. Golf nearby.
Location 16 m W of Tucson. Exit I-10 at Cortaro Rd.; go W to Silverbell. Turn right (N) on Silverbell Rd.; left (W) on Pima Farm Rd. to ranch at intersection with Scenic Dr.
Credit cards Amex, Discover, MC, Visa.
Rates Full board, $225–300 suite, $185–275 double, $115–175 single. Extra adult, $85; child 6–17, $67.50; child under 6, $25. 15% service. 3-night minimum stay. Weekly rates.
Extras Free airport/station pickup. Crib, baby-sitting.

Arkansas

The Heartstone Inn, Eureka Springs

Rugged mountain individualism is one of the first things that comes to mind when Arkansas is mentioned. Although the Ozarks are a very old mountain chain and not terribly high, the terrain is rugged and transportation was, until quite recently, very difficult. Distinctive crafts, cuisine, and culture developed as a result, much of which has been preserved through the Ozark Folk Center, located in Mountain View (see listing). Many famous springs dot this region of northwestern Arkansas as well, particularly Hot Springs National Park, 55 miles southwest of Little Rock, and Eureka Springs, in the north.

If you want to add sparkle to your Arkansas trip, visit Crater of Diamonds State Park, southeast of Hot Springs—it's America's only public diamond-hunting field. Outdoor enthusiasts generally head to the state's rivers for white-water canoeing or a fight with a largemouth bass, while amateur spelunkers visit what experts call the greatest cave find of the 20th century, Blanchard Springs Caves near Mountain View.

Reader tip: "For Appalachian antiques and crafts, avoid the overpriced shops of Eureka Springs, and stop in Van Buren, near Fort Smith and I-40, at the Antique Warehouse and Mall; the shops in the restored downtown area are also worth a look." *(MA)*

EUREKA SPRINGS

Eureka Springs is the site of natural springs first discovered by the Indians, then lost for decades until rediscovered in the 1850s by a local doctor. The curative powers of the spring waters soon became renowned, and by the 1880s this hillside town boasted dozens of hotels. As the decades passed and medicine advanced, the town was forgotten and its Victorian charms thus preserved. The local Historic District Commission now stands guard to make sure that nothing is changed without its approval.

Local attractions include dozens of art galleries and mountain craft shops, the steam train ride through the Ozarks, the Passion Play, and the Pine Mountain Jamboree. Beaver Lake and the Buffalo and White rivers are nearby for swimming, boating, fishing, and canoeing.

Eureka Springs is located in northwest Arkansas, 50 miles northeast of Fayetteville, 200 miles northwest of Little Rock. From Missouri, it's approximately 100 miles south of Springfield, and 50 miles southwest of Branson. It is best reached via Highways 62 or 23.

Reader tip: "Parking on Eureka Springs' narrow, hilly streets ranges from difficult to impossible. Once you have found a space on the street or at your inn, leave your car and get around on the convenient trolley, which stops in front of many inns." *(GR)*

Also recommended: It's hard to forget a B&B with a name like **Arsenic and Old Lace B&B** (60 Hillside Avenue, 72632; 501–253–5454 or 800–243–5223; www.eureka-usa.com/arsenic). Built as a B&B in 1992, this B&B was constructed in the Queen Anne style, following a set of century-old blueprints. State-of-the art plumbing in spacious bathrooms and up-to-date insulation were combined with period moldings and cornices, tin ceilings, and antique doors, mantels, and stained glass windows. The elegant furnishings include antiques and period reproductions; guest rooms have a queen- or king-size bed, TV/VCR, and Jacuzzi tub. A three-course breakfast is served at 9 A.M., with such entrees as baked eggs with three cheeses or apple pecan pancakes, in addition to a fruit course, and home-baked breads and muffins. B&B double rates for the five guest rooms range from $125–160.

Dairy Hollow House   👤 ♿
515 Spring Street, 72632

Tel: 501–253–7444
800–562–8650
Fax: 501–253–7223
E-mail: frontdesk@dairyhollow.com
URL: http://www.dairyhollow.com

When the doors of Dairy Hollow House opened in 1981, it was one of the first bed & breakfast inns in the state. Since then, innkeepers Crescent Dragonwagon (she adopted the name after moving to Arkansas at age 18) and her husband, Ned Shank, developed a nationwide reputation for their "Nouveau Zarks" cuisine, combining classic French with the Ozarks' best regional ingredients. Guests can savor their specialties at quarterly special occasion feasts, or buy a copy of one of Crescent's wonderful cookbooks.

The Dairy Hollow House encompasses the Farmhouse in the Hollow, a fully renovated 1880s farmhouse, housing three guest rooms, all with fireplaces, handmade quilts, and period antiques; the Main House, with three suites with fireplaces; and the Restaurant at Dairy Hollow, on the garden level of the Main House. The central reception area is here also. Breakfast specialties (delivered to your room) include fresh fruit or juice, perhaps featherbed eggs and chicken-apple sausages, accompanied by homemade jams and jellies, gingerbread muffins, or blueberry coffee cake. Rates also include a check-in beverage and homemade cookies.

"Genuine concern for guests' comfort and scrupulous attention to detail, while maintaining a casual, easygoing atmosphere. It's rustic in style, luxurious in service. The old-fashioned cast-iron bedstead with colorful quilt and a surfeit of pillows covers a top-of-the-line mattress. Wooden floors and calico curtains make the bathroom look homey, but a spanking clean, perfectly functioning Jacuzzi makes one feel pampered." *(Ronni Lundy)* "Delightful town off-season, great for walking and relaxing. The Spring Garden Suite has a lovely sun room, full of wicker furniture, a perfect spot to enjoy the amazing breakfasts. The Summer Meadows suite has a large inviting living room. Rooms in the Farmhouse are smaller, but charming and quiet." *(LI)*

"Every little detail spoke of warmth and hospitality, beginning with the warm spiced cider awaiting us on arrival." *(Tracey Corbin)* "The Rose Room in the 1888 farm house was furnished with authentic Ozark antiques. Our breakfast of German baked pancakes topped with lemon powdered sugar arrived at our door piping hot." *(Jane Maas)* "Convenient kitchenette in our suite; the Jacuzzi tub was great for relaxing soaks before hopping into our featherbed and snuggling into the down comforter. Afternoon cookies—different each day—and fruit juice coolers were a treat after a day of exploring." *(Cheryl L. Gray)* "Our room refrigerator was stocked with milk, fresh-ground coffee, and wonderful ice tea; homemade cookies appeared every day; lavish displays of fresh flowers ornamented the breakfast table and the bathroom. A letter from Ned accompanied the breakfast basket, described the meal, and suggested local excursions of interest. Exceptionally congenial staff; cheery, comfortable rooms with touches of Ned and Crescent's humor, plus copies of Crescent's children's book. Set in the woods, the inn offers ample privacy without sacrificing convenience." *(Megan Isaac)* "The hot tub under starry skies was just the right temperature." *(Greg & Eileen Thomas)* "Ned is a Renaissance man with a vast knowledge of Eureka Springs; Crescent is a wonderful cook, and should you have the good fortune to attend one of their dinners, you may never want to leave." *(Michael & Deann Collins)* "Our windows opened right over our pillows to let in the clean Ozark night air and the morning sound of birds chirping. Tiny details of note: no dust— anywhere (hard to pull off with a wood stove in the room); perfect little soaps molded especially for the inn, fresh-cut flowers, real cinnamon sticks in the cider, a restaurant guide that lets the guests participate, creative and delicious breakfasts delivered to your room hot and fresh, and the blissful quiet." *(William Dale Harrison, and many others)*

Open Feb. through Dec. Restaurant open for 8 special event dinners annually. **Rooms** 3 suites, 3 doubles—all with private bath and/or shower, air-conditioning, fireplace, mini-refrigerator, coffee maker. 4 rooms with desk. 2 rooms with Jacuzzi, kitchenette. 1 with deck. Rooms in 2 buildings.

Facilities Restaurant, lobby. Music entertainment holidays/festivals. 3 acres with flower gardens, woods, hot tub, children's games. 15 min. to water sports.
Location 1 m from downtown.
Restrictions Smoking restricted. BYOB.
Credit cards Amex, DC, Discover, MC, Visa.
Rates B&B, $135–205 suite, double, plus optional $2–5 daily for service. Extra person, $10. 2-3 night minimum weekends/holidays. Off-season discount for longer stays. Mystery, gardener, winter weekend packages. Prix fixe dinner, $49–59 plus service.
Extras Restaurant wheelchair accessible. Crib, baby-sitting. Open for eight special event dinners per year.

The Heartstone Inn and Cottages ¢   *Tel:* 501–253–8916
35 Kingshighway (Highway 62B), 72632   800–494–4921
Fax: 501–253–6821
E-mail: heartinn@ipa.net
URL: http://www.eureka-springs-usa.com/
lodging/heartstone.html

A long-time reader favorite, innkeepers Iris and Bill Simantel have owned The Heartstone since 1985. Guest rooms are decorated with antique and reproduction furniture and decorative Victorian touches—including plenty of hearts; most have queen- or king-size beds.

"Delicious meals, gracious atmosphere, lovely decor, good-natured innkeepers and staff." (*Virginia Ozarzak*) "Iris and her assistant prepared the wonderful breakfasts, which were served by Bill. He was friendly and genuinely concerned that everyone was having a good time and had everything needed. Lovely scent to the room, sheets, and towels." (*Debbie Chilcout*) "Comfortable and clean, lots of antiques, quilts, nicely coordinated wallpaper, plenty of light and hot water." (*Judy Glantz*) "The owners care, and it shows in the impeccable cleanliness and careful attention to detail throughout the inn. Helpful with restaurant recommendations and area hints. A wonderful breakfast room and great deck for relaxing with iced tea or lemonade, watching the birds at the feeders." (*HJB*) "Great location, off the main drag, yet close enough to walk almost everywhere. Delicious breakfasts, not high in fat." (*Regina Donnell*) "Iris is from England and has an extensive collection of Torquay pottery." (*Joanne Ashton*)

"Iris and Bill provided candid restaurant suggestions, gave us accurate directions, and supplied us with blankets for an outside event. In the morning, guests gather for coffee on the deck overlooking the wooded hollow behind the house. Promptly at nine, all are invited to breakfast in the dining room." (*Linda Logsdon*) "Hanging pots of Boston ferns sway lazily above the long front porch, and huge crocks spill over with salmon-colored geraniums. The Bridal Suite has an old lace wedding dress and dried bridal bouquet; a queen-size bed was covered with a red, white, and blue quilt in the double wedding-band pattern." (*Mr. & Mrs. J.D. Rolfe*) "The inn is a beautiful pink Victorian with white trim. We breakfasted on delicious German apple pancakes with bacon, fresh fruit, and chocolate chip muffins." (*Howard & Rebecca Harmon*) "No need for a car with the trolley stop directly in front of the inn."

(Michael Kavanaugh) "The beautifully decorated Victorian cottage was meticulously clean and comfy." *(Mary Corbitt)* "Few places display as much creativity per square foot in the form of antiques, collectibles, art, and tasteful dècor. The deck overlooks a ravine of huge trees, with a variety of birds and squirrels. If not relaxed enough, the on-premises masseuse is a master." *(Wayne Irvine)* "Bill and Iris make their guests feel special and right at home. Iris is an exceptional cook—breakfasts are different each day." *(Linda & Greg Fine)*

Open Late Feb.–late Dec.

Rooms 1 2-bedroom cottage, 1 1-bedroom cottage, 2 suites, 8 doubles, all with full private bath, TV, radio, air-conditioning, ceiling fans. 1 with Jacuzzi. 4 rooms in annex.

Facilities Dining/breakfast rooms, guest lounge with piano, stereo, games, veranda, decks, gazebo; massage therapy; gift/pottery shop. Off-street parking. Live music during May, Sept. festivals. Golf privileges.

Location Historic district, 4 blocks to downtown. Trolley stop near house.

Restrictions No smoking. Limited facilities for older children.

Credit cards Amex, Discover, MC, Visa.

Rates B&B, $97–120 cottage, $89–125 suite, $68–85 double. Extra person, $15. 2-3 night weekend/holiday minimum. Tipping envelopes.

HOT SPRINGS

A visit to Hot Springs will allow you to take your place in a long line of tradition; records indicate that the Indians used this site 10,000 years ago. The springs reached their height of popularity in the 19th century, and the area became a national park in 1921. The bath houses are still well worth a visit; the naturally hot water will soothe your aching muscles after a day of hiking or horseback riding in the surrounding Zig Zag Mountains. And the price is right—call the historic Buckstaff (501–623–2308), where steaming, soaking, and massage costs under $30 (tips extra). Several lakes—Catherine, Hamilton, and Ouachita— are nearby for all water sports. Hot Springs is located in central Arkansas, 55 miles southwest of Little Rock.

Information please: Though too large for a full entry with almost 500 rooms, readers are pleased with **The Arlington Resort Hotel & Spa** (Central Avenue and Fountain Street, P.O. Box 5652, 71902; 501–623–7771 or 800–643–1502; www.arlingtonhotel.com). "The Arlington is an old-fashioned historic hotel with a large staff and excellent service at moderate prices. Fine location overlooking the national park. Large and well appointed room; buffet breakfast included in the reasonable rates." *(Duane Roller)* "This 70-year-old hotel has been updated with bright yellow flowered wall paper, and brightly painted corridors. Our room was large and clean, with a comfortable king-size bed. Breakfast was served with flowers and a smile at a reasonable price." *(Martha Banda)* Rates range from $60–180 for a double and $295 for a suite; children under 18 stay free. Ask about spa, family, and golf packages.

ARKANSAS

Stitt House B&B Tel: 501–623–2704
824 Park Avenue, 71901 Fax: 501–623–2704
URL: http://www.bbonline.com/ar/stitthouse

A 6,000 square-foot Italianate Victorian mansion, the Stitt House was built in 1875 by Samuel Stitt, and is listed on the National Register of Historic Places. Said to be Hot Springs' oldest home, it remained in the Stitt family until 1983, when it was purchased by Linda and Horst Fischer, who lived in the house with their four children, and also ran it as a well-known restaurant from 1983 to 1991. Horst is also the manager of the Arlington and Majestic Hotels, and Linda has operated both restaurants and retail clothing shops.

In 1995, the Fischers restored Stitt House as an elegant B&B, complementing the original crystal chandeliers, hand-carved oak staircase, and imposing mahogany and cherry wood fireplace mantels with period antiques and reproductions. Named for the Fischer's grown children, each of the guest rooms is individually furnished in period, and has a king-size bed and sitting area. Guests can select the time, place, and menu for breakfast. The meal is served between 8–10 A.M., and can be enjoyed at the dining room table, on the veranda, or in bed. Guests can select one of two entrees—perhaps eggs Benedict with French crepes or a quiche with paprika potatoes, accompanied by their preference of fresh-squeezed orange or grapefruit juice, fresh fruit, bacon or sausage, toast or English muffins.

"Horst and Linda were exceptionally helpful in identifying hiking trails and in making restaurant recommendations and reservations. Our lovely room had a high four poster bed with fresh, crisp sheets, and comfortable sitting areas. Lovely swimming pool, perfect temperature. Scrumptious breakfast, served on the veranda." (Kelly Welsh) "Welcoming glass of wine on arrival." (Linda Clinger) "The Fischers came to greet us as we rode up the driveway. Pampering touches included the complimentary beverages, shampoo, toiletries, and soft white terry robes. At breakfast, the dining room was set with beautiful china and silver." (Janis & Ed Tidwell) "This beautiful Victorian home sits atop a hill surrounded by lush greenery; we viewed the lovely scenery from the front porch." (Nancy Bingamon) "Impeccably appointed rooms; ours had a canopied king bed with Battenburg lace linens. Warm, hospitable innkeepers." (Julie R. Salmon) "Early each morning, tea and coffee is set out on a sideboard close to the guest rooms; the upstairs refrigerator is stocked with soft drinks, and fruit, crackers, and cookies are available for munching. At night, beds are turned down with chocolates." (Kim James & Philip Snyder)

"Overlooks a peaceful neighborhood, surrounded by flower gardens and magnolia trees. We were welcomed with cold drinks and assisted with luggage. The inviting common areas include a beautiful formal dining room where the Fischers serve delicious breakfasts on fine china, silver, and crystal. In the upstairs social room, guests can help themselves to hot and cold beverages. Loc's Room is sunny with pleasant views of the grounds, a comfortable queen-size bed, and a large bath with a Jacuzzi. Exceptionally gracious hosts." (Jim & Shirley McCurdy)

"Our room had a king-size wrought iron canopy bed with Battenburg lace. The Fischers offered evening wine and beer with cheese and fruit." *(Curtis & Chris Shoemaker)* "The hospitable innkeepers maintain a quiet atmosphere in which guests can relax and be pampered. Excellent value." *(Margaret & Cliff Brown)* "Innkeepers who really go out of their way for guests. Comfy, homey suite. Impressive home and grounds, perhaps the nicest in town; convenient location; very clean." *(Bruce Bilmes)*

Open All year.

Rooms 1 suite, 3 doubles—all with full private bath, radio, clock, TV, desk, air-conditioning, robes. 3 with ceiling fan; 1 with double whirlpool tub.

Facilities Living room with fireplace, piano, TV/VCR, books; family room, library with fireplace, books; guest refrigerator; porch. 2 acres with off-street parking, heated swimming pool. ¾ m to Natl. Park for hiking.

Location Historic district; 1 m to center of town. N end of town on Scenic Hwy. 7.

Restrictions No smoking or chewing tobacco. Children 12 and over.

Credit cards Amex, Discover, MC, Visa.

Rates B&B, $110 suite, $95 double. Extra person, $15. 10% senior, AAA discount. 2-3 night weekend/holiday minimum.

Extras Airport/station pickups, $20. German spoken.

LITTLE ROCK

Little Rock is the capital of Arkansas and its largest city. Bill Clinton lived here when he was governor of Arkansas, and the city soon adjusted to the unaccustomed glare of media attention after his election as President of the United States. The oldest section of the city is the Quapaw Quarter, which has many fine antebellum and Victorian homes; typical for a historic district, some houses are beautifully restored, others are not.

Reader tip: "Little Rock is like any other city: do not leave valuables visible in the car."

Also recommended: Located in the Governor's Mansion District and listed on the National Register of Historic Places, the **Hotze House** (1619 Louisiana Street, Little Rock, 72216; 501–376–6563) was built in 1900. The double rates range from $90–100 and include a full breakfast served in either the formal dining room or the sunny conservatory. Each guest room has a fireplace, private bath, telephone, TV, air-conditioning, and a king- or queen-size bed.

A Gothic Queen Anne mansion, **The Empress** (2120 South Louisiana, 72206; 501–374–7966) was built in 1888 and is listed on the National Register of Historic Places. Architectural highlights include the fine floors and woodwork, the divided stairway, the lofty corner tower, stained glass skylight, and octagonally shaped rooms. Guests have a choice of an early continental breakfast or a full gourmet brunch. Double rates for the five guest rooms range from $120–150.

A country alternative is the **Pinnacle Vista Lodge** (7510 Highway 300,

72212; 501–868–8905), a historic log cabin with three guest rooms. Situated on 23 wooded acres, the inn is located minutes from the State Park and offers a great view of Pinnacle Vista Mountain from the veranda. Double rates range from $95–125, with a hearty breakfast included.

Information please: Built in 1876, **The Capital Hotel** (111 West Markham, 72201; 501–374–7474 or 800–766–7666; hospitality@capital-hotel-lr.com) is listed in the National Register of Historic Places. The spectacular two-story lobby has a stained glass ceiling panel, a mosaic tiled floor, marble walls, faux marble columns, and a marble grand staircase leading to the mezzanine. Ashley's Restaurant offers regional specialties, fresh seafood, and continental dishes. The 123 guest rooms are furnished with period reproductions, and some have canopy beds; double rates range from $148–168, suites to $385; ask about special weekend packages.

Key to Abbreviations and Symbols

For complete information and explanations, please see the Introduction.

¢ Especially good value for overnight accommodation.

👫 Families welcome. Most (but not all) have cribs, baby-sitting, games, play equipment, and reduced rates for children.

✕ Meals served to public; reservations recommended or required.

🎾 Tennis court and swimming pool and/or lake on grounds. Golf usually on grounds or nearby.

♿ Limited or full wheelchair access; call for details.

Rates: Range from least expensive room in low season to most expensive room in peak season.

Room only: No meals included; European Plan (EP).

B&B: Bed and breakfast; includes breakfast, sometimes afternoon/evening refreshment.

MAP: Modified American Plan; includes breakfast and dinner.

Full board: Three meals daily.

Alc lunch: A la carte lunch; average price of entrée plus nonalcoholic drink, tax, tip.

Alc dinner: Average price of three-course dinner, including half bottle of house wine, tax, tip.

Prix fixe dinner: Three- to five-course set dinner, excluding wine, tax, tip unless otherwise noted.

Extras: Noted if available. Always confirm in advance. Pets are not permitted unless specified; if you are allergic, ask for details; *most innkeepers have pets.*

California

Churchill Manor, Napa

California is the nation's third largest state and the most populous. Its terrain is incredibly diverse, offering virtually every possible land- and seascape, much of it of great interest to tourists. Though the clock puts them three hours behind the East Coast, Californians tend to think of themselves as being ahead of the rest of the country. Many of the country's dominant trends got their start here and spread eastward across the country—not the least of them being the popularity of the small hotels and inns described in this guide. Small wonder then that this is our longest chapter.

There is one category for which we'd really like to request more recommendations: inns that actually *welcome* children! We're all in favor of romantic adult getaways, but there are regions of California—the Wine Country, for example—where there is hardly a place that will tolerate children, let alone welcome them. Perhaps as a reaction to this, a law was passed in California making it illegal for hotels and inns to discriminate on the basis of age. As a result, if we note under Restrictions "No children under 12," this has no legal bearing whatsoever. It is rather an indication given to us by the inns involved that they feel their property is more appropriate for older children.

In general, there's not too much seasonal variation in the rates of California's inns and hotels, although they do tend to be 10% to 20% higher on weekends in most areas. Exceptions are the North Coast region, where midweek rates are lower off-season (November to March), and the desert areas, where brutal summer heat cuts rates in half.

The California Office of Tourism divides the state into 12 distinct regions; we've noted them below, along with a few annotations and subdivisions of our own. At the end of each region, we list the towns with recommended inns and hotels, to help you in using this chapter. When reading the entries, you'll see the 12 regional divisions noted in the "Location" heading for each entry. Check back to these thumbnail sketches if you are liable to get Monterey mixed up with Mendocino.

Finally, please note that most of the greater Los Angeles area (excluding Orange County) is listed under Los Angeles, so you don't need to look through the entire chapter to find out what's available in this most sprawling of cities.

Shasta-Cascade This relatively undiscovered region in north-central and northeast California offers a dramatic introduction to California's wilderness and geologic past. Best known is the Whiskeytown-Shasta-Trinity National Recreation Area, near 14,000-foot Mt. Shasta, where you can backpack or rent a houseboat on Lake Shasta. At Lassen Volcanic National Park, see the strange formations and caves left by wide-ranging volcanic activity. Even more unusual is Lava Beds National Monument, near the Oregon border, where the Modoc Indians made their last stand, using volcanic rubble for protection. This area fronts on Tule Lake, where over one million waterfowl visit each fall and huge populations of bald eagles spend the winter. At the southern edge of this region, take Route 70 through Quincy and the spectacular Feather River Canyon.

North Coast This region has three distinct subregions. The **Wine Country** is located northeast of San Francisco, along Routes 29 and 12. In addition to over 200 wineries with free tours and tastings, there are rolling green hills, mud baths in Calistoga, gliding, and ballooning. Not to be missed is Petaluma Adobe, a restored 1840s headquarters of the Vallejo agricultural empire.

Not surprisingly, food is taken as seriously here as wine, and the area is noted for its many outstanding restaurants. If you'll be visiting on a weekend, ask your host to make dinner reservations when you book your room. Keep in mind that the Napa Valley, in particular, surpasses Disneyland in popularity with tourists; unless heavy traffic is your thing, avoid fall weekends when everyone goes wine-tasting!

The **Coast** area on Highway One north of San Francisco includes world-class scenery, shorelines, and accommodations. Near Jenner the road cuts through steep green slopes that sweep down to the sea. Close by is Fort Ross, an 1812 Russian trading post, complete with an onion-domed Orthodox church. To the north are tiny towns and perfect beach-combing shores near Sea Ranch and Gualala, Elk, Little River, and trendy Mendocino. The area then becomes more remote and wild as it passes through Westport. One recommended side trip for the experienced driver is the back road to Ferndale (from South Fork past Cape Mendocino), which winds up high bluffs with superb ocean views.

The **Redwood Empire** on Highway 101 stretches from Piercy to Crescent City. It's worth putting up with the cutesy tourist offerings to see the real scenery. Especially recommended are Avenue of the Giants near Pepperwood; Big Tree at Prairie City, north of Orick; and the Jedediah Smith area east of Crescent City.

North Coast towns with inns/hotels listed: Wine Country: Calistoga, Geyserville, Healdsburg, Napa, St. Helena. **Coast:** Ferndale, Fort Bragg, Little River, Mendocino. **Redwood Empire:** Eureka.

San Francisco Bay Area   Here and elsewhere along the coast, fog often shrouds the area in spring and early summer. To some this means unwanted cool weather only miles away from a sunny, warm interior. To others this underlines the special romance and mystery of the area. Although few cities can surpass San Francisco for culture, shopping, and sightseeing (see description in listings), there is more to the Bay Area. Across the Golden Gate Bridge are Sausalito and Tiburon, both artists' colonies with unusual homes clinging to the cliffsides. Nearby Muir Woods provides an easy introduction to the giant redwoods. The East Bay includes Berkeley with its hillside residential area, lively university district, and excellent botanical garden. To the south, stroll the seaside boardwalk at Santa Cruz, and visit Ano Nuevo State Reserve to see lolling elephant seals and rocks covered with fossilized seashells.

San Francisco Bay Area towns with inns/hotels listed: San Francisco.

Central Valley   Extremely hot during the summer, this region offers comparatively little of interest to tourists. Extending south from Chico through the central portion of California to Bakersfield, this area has over 11 million acres of rich farmland, and produces an astonishing variety of fruits, nuts, and vegetables. Worth seeing: the Chinese temple in Oroville; Old Sacramento (take the walking tour); and Route 160 from Sacramento to Isleton which winds along dikes, past almond and fruit groves, and through Locke, a bizarre, two-block, two-level town built in 1915 by Chinese workers. In the south, Bakersfield is near California's oil fields and is known as the state's country music center.

Central Valley towns with inns/hotels listed: Sacramento.

Gold Country   Gold mining brought thousands of people to this region in the 1850s, but these days the only thing that is mined are the tourists. Overcrowded with visitors in the summer, this area nevertheless has retained a genuine Old West flavor and should not be missed. Be sure to get off Route 49 to some of the smaller towns like Murphys and Volcano; see nearby Grinding Rocks State Park where the Mi-Wok Indians lived for centuries, and the restored town of Columbia, now a state historical park. Don't avoid the unnumbered back roads that wind up hills and through picturesque farms. To the north, visit Downieville, which is tucked into the northern Sierras, then take passable dirt roads to Malakoff Diggings to see how hydraulic placer mining washed away a mountainside.

Gold Country towns with inns/hotels listed: Nevada City, Sutter Creek.

High Sierras   For 400 miles, the Sierra Nevada mountain range defines eastern California, from north of Lake Tahoe to the northern terminus of the desert region. Yosemite, Kings Canyon, and Sequoia national parks provide unlimited outdoor opportunities for everyone from car window sightseers to rugged backpackers. See 14,495-foot Mt. Whitney, giant sequoias, and torrential waterfalls, or ski at one of 20 areas. Lake Tahoe provides resort offerings, with famous casinos, gambling, and glitzy shows nearby at Stateline Nevada. The crowning jewel here is Emerald Bay. For a bizarre foray into history, visit Donner Memorial Park, two miles west of Truckee, where an 1846 pioneer group, stranded by heavy winter snows, resorted to cannibalism.

High Sierras town with inns/hotels listed: Yosemite.

Central Coast   This photogenic region stretches from the Monterey Peninsula south to Santa Barbara. Inland, Pinnacles National Monument's volcanic spires, bluffs, and crags are worth a visit. On the coast, from Monterey (see description in listings), tour the peninsula via Seventeen-Mile Drive (a toll is charged) past Pebble Beach, wind-sculptured cypresses, cavorting otters, and on to Carmel. Highway One cuts through misty, ragged cliffs that rush into the sea. This is Big Sur—wild, beautiful, with almost no off-road access and too many crowds in the summer. To view the excesses of the rich, visit Hearst's San Simeon Castle (reservations required). To the south, Morro Bay marks the start of the renowned California beaches. Stop to see Solvang, a 1911 Danish settlement, and Santa Barbara, the heart of Spanish Mission country.

Central Coast towns with inns/hotels listed: Big Sur, Cambria, Carmel, Monterey, Pacific Grove, Santa Barbara.

Greater Los Angeles   This city-region includes not only LA itself but the myriad surrounding cities, beaches, and islands. For relaxation, sail or fly to Santa Catalina Island, one of the top resort locations in the country. See listings for more information about the area.

Greater Los Angeles area towns with inns/hotels listed: Los Angeles (also includes Beverly Hills, Malibu, North Hollywood, Santa Monica).

Orange County   Welcome to the California of commercials and legend. Here you can experience the mythic and somewhat crazed California beach life at Newport, Laguna, and Balboa. It's all here: sun, sand, surfers, theme parks (Disneyland, Knott's Berry Farm, Magic Mountain), nouveau everything, Super Hype. Your children will love it, but you may need a week on a desert island to recover.

Inland Empire   From the San Gabriel Mountains in this region you can look down over Los Angeles. Route 2, east of Pasadena, twists through the mountains and past ski areas. East of San Bernardino, Route 18 is called the Rim of the World Drive. Although an overstatement, it is a pretty mountain road that leads to overdeveloped Lake Arrowhead and Big Bear Lake resort area. Southwest is Riverside, California's "citrus

capital" and home of the famous Mission Inn, touted by Will Rogers.
Inland Empire towns with inns/hotels listed: Orland.

San Diego County Although San Diego (see description in listings) is the star of this region, there are several nearby areas in the county worth noting. La Jolla's natural caverns, formed by waves pounding against the sandstone cliffs, and the Mingei International Museum of prehistoric and contemporary crafts make for a special stop. I-8, which becomes Route 79, is a pretty drive to the old mining town of Julian. Farther on is the retirement community of Borrego Springs, with its superb Anza-Borrego Desert State Park. Stop at the headquarters for an excellent introduction to the varied plant and animal life of California's desert country.

San Diego County towns with inns/hotels listed: La Jolla, San Diego.

The Deserts From posh Palm Springs to Nevada, from Mexico to Death Valley, this region is unlike anything else on earth. Since the desert area covers almost one-sixth of the state, it is important to plan your itinerary carefully. Unless you are a dedicated desert aficionado, it can get repetitive. South of Palm Springs, don't miss the enormous date groves near Thermal and Mecca, or the restaurants offering date milkshakes and date pecan pies. Just to the south, senior citizen communities dot the shoreline of Salton Sea, created in 1905 by human error during the construction of the Colorado River aqueduct. To the east are the Chocolate Mountains and the sprawling Sand Hills. North is Joshua Tree National Monument, best in spring when the cacti blossom. Finally there is Death Valley, a bewitching place of startling contrasts in altitude, colors, vegetation, formations, and texture. Close to the Nevada border is the equally fascinating but less well known Mojave National Preserve, established in 1994. Ranging in elevation from 1,000 to 8,000 feet, its 1.4 million acres include mountains, mesas, and more. Also of interest are ancient Indian rock art and abandoned mines. *A few reminders:* Try not to visit this region in the summer, always heed the warning to stay on the highway, and carry extra water in your car.

Desert Country towns with inns/hotels listed: Palm Springs.

BIG SUR

Novelist Henry Miller, Big Sur resident for 20 years, noted that "there being nothing to improve on in the surroundings, the tendency is to set about improving oneself." Unfortunately, news of Big Sur's breathtaking beauty is now well-known, and summer traffic jams often clog the hairpin turns of Highway One. Our advice is to travel off-season, or to leave the crowds behind by hiking the beautiful trails of Pfeiffer–Big Sur State Park, Julia Pfeiffer Burns State Park, and the Ventana Wilderness. May and October are probably the best times for minimal crowds and maximal weather. During the winter storm season, be sure to check ahead on road conditions—during the El Nino winter of 1998, Highway One was closed for months as the result of mud slide damage.

Reader tip: "Dinner at Deetjen's was pricy but delicious; reservations essential. For breakfast, head up the road to Cafe Kevah or Nepenthe, both with a fabulous 20-mile coastal view."

Also recommended: Those interested in a taste of "old California" should try **Deetjen's Big Sur Inn** (Highway One, 93920; 408–667–2377), a 20-room rustic retreat built in the early 1930s by Helmuth and Helen Deetjen, Norwegian immigrants. The simple rooms rent for $75–180, and the restaurant has a good reputation. "A rustic hideaway built of rough-hewn dark wood, situated along the edges of a redwood-lined ravine on an isolated bend of scenic Highway One. The Fireplace Room has a working fireplace, a firm bed with a warm comforter, and windows covered with calico curtains. The bath was across the hall. What it lacks in creature comforts, Deetjen's makes up in charm, romance, and isolation." *(Mark Mendenhall)* "Our favorite room was just as lovely on a return visit; less appealing for this shared-bath room is the year-round rate of $160." *(MM)* "Deetjen's is an acquired taste with its simple furnishings, nonexistent sound-proofing, and 'funky style,' but is very popular because of its pretty setting by a babbling brook, historic appeal, and in-room guest journals. We paid $90, the rate for a small double with shared bath and an electric heater; no meals included." *(LMS)* "Great food. Beautiful, but rustic and somewhat primitive; beautiful stone fireplaces." *(Doug Phillips)* "New innkeepers have done wonders to improve this old place." *(AH)*

If expense is no object, then try the ultra-chic, ultra-expensive **Post Ranch Inn,** (Highway One, P.O. Box 219, 93920; 408–667–2200 or 800–527–2200) just across Highway One from the Ventana. This "environmentally sensitive" luxury retreat will pamper you with magnificent cliffside ocean views, polished wood and natural stone decor, in-room slate-lined Jacuzzi tubs, designer robes, and fold-away massage tables, but you'll have to be "green" financially as well as ecologically: rates range from $365–645 (an increase of approximately $100 per room from 1997 to 1998) for the 30 rooms, either set on stilts or burrowed into the hillside to minimize environmental impact. "On the ocean side of the Coast Highway and beautifully integrated into its bluff-top locale. The rooms have an unobtrusive, original, and contemporary design, and are spacious and comfortable. Take advantage of the complimentary guided hikes." *(Adam Platt)* "Pricy but beautiful; excellent food. Our room had a huge stone bath and lovely teak paneling." *(Doug Phillips)* "We must have hit an off-day at the restaurant. The view was breath-taking, as was the bill, but the food and service were just average." *(PB)*

A long-time reader favorite, the **Ventana Inn** (Highway One, 93920; 408-667-2331 or 800–628–6500) has 60 guest rooms spread over 12 buildings on very ample grounds; 34 have ocean vistas, while the remainder overlook the mountains or forest. B&B double rates range from $260–625, with suites to $725. The restaurant, one-eighth of a mile from the inn, has spectacular views of the Pacific and specializes in California cuisine, with an emphasis on fresh seafood, vegetables, and fruits; advance reservations are essential. Rates include breakfast, with fresh fruits and home-baked breads and pastries, brought to your room or available buffet-style in the lobby, and an afternoon wine and cheese buffet. Careful attention to detail in all areas—service, comfort, cuisine, and atmosphere—produces consistently positive reports from all sources: "Measures up to every super comment we've ever heard about it. Wooded setting with views. Spectacular food. Friendly staff provided help before we realized we needed it." *(Pat Hardy)* "Sheer perfection in every detail.

Information please: A reasonable alternative in a pricy area, the **Big Sur Lodge** (Highway One, P.O. Box 190, 93920; 408–667–3100) or 800–424–4787 is located in the center of Pfeiffer–Big Sur State Park, across from the ocean. The restaurant serves good food at reasonable prices. Depending on the season, rates for its simply furnished 61 units and condo-style cottages range from $80–180. A swimming pool, grocery store, and hiking trails make it a reasonable family choice. Another affordable option is the **Big Sur River Inn** (Highway One at Pheneger Creek, 93920; 408–667–2700 or 800–548–3610, with 20 motel units overlooking the river, restaurant, swimming pool, general store, and gift gallery. Rates range from $70–170, but the best deal is the midweek off-season package, starting at $99 for breakfast, dinner, and accommodations for two; children are welcome. Halfway between Carmel and San Simeon, is **Harlan's Lucia Lodge** (Highway One, 93920; 408–667–2391), overlooking the south coast of Big Sur. Five hundred feet above Lucia Bay, the lodge has ten adjacent cabins—most with ocean views—and a restaurant with waterview dining from the deck. Furnishings are modest and simple, but the view is unparalleled.

CALISTOGA

Set in the North Coast's Wine Country, Calistoga is located at the northern end of the Napa Valley, about 75 miles north-northeast of San Francisco. Nestled in the foothills of Mt. St. Helena, it was founded in 1859 by Sam Brannan, a New Englander who moved west and started California's first newspaper. Brannan was familiar with New York State's Saratoga Springs, and his goal was to make the mineral springs of Calistoga equally well known. People still come for the spas—to sit and soak in tubs filled with volcanic-ash mud and naturally heated mineral water and in mineral-water whirlpools.

Other area attractions include the dozens of area wineries, many first-class restaurants and shops, a petrified forest, a lake for water sports, and a geyser, along with hot-air ballooning and a glider port, tennis, golf, hiking, bicycling, and outdoor summer concerts. The Sharpsteen Museum depicts Calistoga's early days. Summer and fall weekends are very busy; visit during the spring if possible. To reach Calistoga, take Route 29 (St. Helena Highway) north from Napa.

Worth noting: Route 29 is the major north/south route through the Napa Valley, and traffic can be heavy in peak periods. If you're staying at an in on this road, be sure to ask if road noise is an issue. Route 29 is called Lincoln Avenue in Calistoga.

Reader tip: "Excellent dinner at All Seasons on Lincoln Avenue. Memorable duck with sour cherry sauce, and extensive wine list. Enjoyed the mud baths (the thin kind) at Lavender Hill. They have couples tubs and you have a little atrium to yourselves. At the end, the attendant gives you both a foot massage on the twin tables in the room." *(Barbara Ochiogrosso)* "Wonderful dinner at Catahoula, a Louisiana-style restaurant in the Mount View Hotel." *(SH, also SWS)*

Also recommended: The **Foothill House** (3037 Foothill Boulevard, 94515; 707–942–6933 or 800–942–6933) is a luxurious B&B set in a turn-of-the-century farmhouse; the $150–275 rates include excellent breakfasts with fresh fruit, homemade breads and muffins, juice, and an afternoon wine and cheese hour. Guests rave about the food and the innkeepers' hospitality and attention to detail. "Doris is warm, welcoming, mothering but not hovering, and makes a point of staying on top of guests' needs. Guest rooms are private and lovely, with maintenance and upgrading an on-going process. Every room has a special feature, whether a fireplace and double Jacuzzi or a private deck with hot tub. Best of all is the spacious Quail's Nest Cottage, with a cathedral ceiling and a soothing decor of soft florals and shades of mauve, cream and gray, perfect for a romantic splurge." *(SWS)* "Amenities include clean, spacious rooms decorated with Laura Ashley fabrics, private entrances and patios, fireplaces, firm mattresses, reading lights, gourmet breakfast brought to your room, complimentary wine and hors d'oeuvres before dinner, and off-street parking. Sherry, cookies along with other surprises await when you return from dinner." *(Jerralea & Hal Brown)*

For a different experience, *Mark Mendenhall* suggests **Indian Springs** (1712 Lincoln Avenue, 94515; 707–942–4913), California's oldest continuously operating spa facility, with its own 120-by-600-foot steaming spring-fed mineral pool, using 100% volcanic ash in its mud baths. "Meticulously maintained facilities; courteous, efficient front desk service; white adobe cottages all in a row, plus a clay tennis court. The studio and 1-bedroom cottages have wide-board bleached wood floors, built-in cabinets, and big brass beds. New owners have undertaken considerable remodeling to improve the creature comforts without reducing the cottages' charm (though increasing the rates). The pool remains a heavenly experience, especially at midnight. Excellent mudbath treatments." The rates for the cottages, ranging from a studio to a 1-bedroom unit, are $150–180 double occupancy; the midweek off-season rate includes free mud bath treatments; children welcome. "A cool-weather dip in the thermally heated waters of the enormous pool is a serene experience." *(Susan Rather)*

A turn-of-the-century farmhouse, **Scarlett's Country Inn** (3918 Silverado Trail North, 94515; 707–942–6669), is built on the site of a Wappo Indian settlement; obsidian arrowheads are still to be found on the grounds. Guests are accommodated in one of two suites in the cottage or in a room in the nearby main house. Families should note that Scarlett's is one of the very few B&Bs in this area that *welcomes* children. "Highlights are the lovely, peaceful country setting, yet convenient to all area attractions; the lovely grounds, inviting swimming pool, and old-fashioned rope tree swing; and Scarlett herself, a warm and welcoming innkeeper." *(SWS)* B&B rates range from $115–175, including a full breakfast.

CAMBRIA

Cambria is a good base from which to visit Hearst Castle in San Simeon six miles to the north and Morro Bay and San Luis Obispo to the south; it's located on the Central Coast, midway between Los Angeles and San Francisco. Winter visitors should take time to visit the town's seaside parks for a glimpse of sea otters and migrating gray whales. Take time to drive inland 25 miles to the Paso Robles wine country to visit the dozens of area wineries; you'll find enthusiastic vintners, uncrowded tasting rooms, and reasonable prices.

Reader tips: "The view from Moonstone Drive is exquisite. Trails follow the bluffs, and paths lead to the rock outcroppings and tidepools where you can watch the seals sun or frolic in the water. Surfers are a little farther away, and there's plenty of beachcombing to be done." *(Erika Holm)* "Don't miss driving along Route 46; it's what California beauty is all about." *(Diana Chang)* "We ate dinner at Ian's, probably the best place in town." *(Stephanie Roberts)* "Cambria is a good base for exploring Hearst Castle and for starting up a dramatic stretch of coastline. Although we did not care for the shops in town, we enjoyed the ocean views offered by our Moonstone Drive motel." *(SR)* "A few miles north of Hearst Castle, we were able to see many baby elephant seals. Definitely worthwhile." *(Ruth Hurley)*

Also recommended: Moonstone Drive, just across the road from the ocean, is home to a number of motel-cum-inns which some readers adore, while others are left cold. While the architecture is basic motel, most have an appealing common area where breakfast and tea is served, and guest rooms done in French country decor. Typically, these properties are not owner-operated, but do have friendly, accommodating innkeepers and homemade breakfasts. The majority of guest rooms have canopy beds, ocean views, gas fireplaces, whirlpool tubs, refrigerators, telephones, and color cable television with VCRs—perfect for travelers who value privacy and modern conveniences over historic ambience. One excellent choice is the six-room **Blue Whale Inn** (6736 Moonstone Beach Drive, 93428; 805–927–4647). "Decorated in pink and mint green, Room #6 was immaculate. The homemade breakfast and hors d'oeuvres were fabulous, as were the friendly but unobtrusive innkeepers." *(Janet Emery)* B&B double rates range from $160–210.

A family-friendly, affordable choice on Moonstone Beach is the **San Simeon Pines Resort** (Moonstone Beach Drive, P.O. Box 117, San Simeon, 93452; 805–927–4648), with 60 guest rooms, and double rates of $78–110 (ask about special AAA rates). "Across from the beach, on forested acreage, with a playground, inside swimming pool, shuffle board, par-3 golf course, and private beach access. While not fancy, our room was large, clean, and pleasant; deluxe units have a fireplace. One-night stays are allowed on the weekends." *(Ruth Hurley)*

Olallieberry Inn &
2476 Main Street, 93428

Tel: 805–927–3222
888–927–3222
Fax: 805–927–0202
E-mail: olallieinn@thegrid.net
URL: http://www.olallieberry.com

"A darling Greek revival-style house built in 1873, the Olallieberry Inn is filled with Victorian antiques and country charm." *(Gail Davis)* "The marvelous back porch and yard with flower gardens and flowing stream is perfect for relaxing." *(Nancy Wood)* "Breathtaking gardens. The breakfast and late afternoon hors d'oeuvres were exquisitely prepared. Great location, within walking distance to shops and restaurants." *(Bill & Leah Lipps)*

"The friendly owners, Peter and Carol Ann Irsfeld, are available to help with reservations or other information. Just a short walk to restaurants and shops. The sitting room has an antique sofa and chairs, and is a quiet place for reading. The bedrooms are beautifully furnished with queen- and king-size beds, with antique dressers, armoires, and chairs. The Harmony Room was fresh and immaculate with an English carved wooden double bed, rocking chair, armoire, and dresser. The bed had a peach-colored patchwork quilt, plenty of soft pillows, and rose-patterned cotton sheets. Fresh flowers in a vase and chocolates were set on the dresser. The bathroom had a clawfoot tub with shower and a pedestal sink. Breakfast is served family-style from 8–9 A.M., around the long wooden table in the kitchen." *(Wendy Kameda)* "The Creekside Suite has a sitting area, king-size bed in an alcove, dressing area, private bath, and a balcony overlooking the creek. Frogs in the creek provide a restful country atmosphere at bedtime, while morning brings birdsong. Tasty breakfast of fresh-baked bread, granola, cereal, yogurt, juices, plus such entrees as souffle or stuffed French toast." *(Willie & Susan Geoghegan)*

"A warm and tranquil place; soft classical music sets the tone. The cordial, friendly staff provided helpful suggestions about restaurants, sights, and activities. Guests sit and chat during the 5 P.M. cocktail hour, while sampling local wines and such homemade hors d'oeuvres as goat cheese and roasted garlic with foccacia bread or dilled salmon cream cheese, plus black bean and corn salsa, crudites, and terrific cookies. Bowls of M&Ms and candies are always available. Carol Ann prepares a sumptuous breakfast of rich coffee, granola, ollalieberry jam, homemade muffins, and fresh fruit crepes or eggs baked in potato crust. Special dietary needs were graciously met. The Room at the Top is small but comfortable and attractive, with a gas fireplace that lit with the flick of a switch. Robes and bubble bath were provided for our private bath across the hall." *(Diana Chang)* "We stayed in the romantic San Simeon room, overlooking a small garden. Lovely furnishings; clean, modern bath with sunken tub/shower." *(Stephanie Roberts)*

Open All year.
Rooms 1 suite, 8 doubles—all with private bath and/or shower. 6 with gas fireplace. 3 rooms in cottage.
Facilities Dining room with fireplace, parlor, porch, deck. Guest refrigerator. ½ acre with lawn games, gardens, stream.

Location East Village. In Cambria, turn E on Main St. Go 1 m to inn on left (watch for redwood tree in front of inn).
Restrictions No smoking. "Not really suitable for children, over age 10 preferred."
Credit cards MC, Visa.
Rates B&B, $175 suite, $90–150 double. 10% senior discount over 60.
Extras Wheelchair access; 1 room equipped for disabled.

CARMEL

Carmel dates back to the early 1900s when it was an artists' colony and a popular summer resort for well-to-do San Franciscans. Opinion is divided on Carmel—most people think it's a charming seaside town filled with darling shops and beautiful art galleries; others find it a bit much. Whatever your opinion, there's no lack of suitable accommodations. Carmel probably has more attractive inns in its zip code than any other town in the country except Cape May, New Jersey! A number of them were built in the 1950s as motels, with doors opening to a public walkway/balcony, and have since been renovated as inns, making for an interesting hybrid—the mood, decor, and amenities of an inn, added to the convenience and privacy found in a motel; inside common areas are generally limited or nonexistent.

Location is important when booking an inn in Carmel. Parking in town is impossible, so be sure to book a place that's "within walking distance" of the places you want to see.

Other than shops and art galleries, Carmel's attractions include the historic Carmel Mission, golf and tennis, music festivals, and excursions to Big Sur, Monterey, and the Seventeen-Mile Drive. Both Carmel Beach and Point Lobos State Reserve are nice for walking, but the water is generally too cold for swimming, and the undertow is treacherous.

Carmel, also known as Carmel-by-the-Sea, is located just south of the Monterey Peninsula, 120 miles south of San Francisco. Most of Carmel is laid out in a grid pattern, with numbered avenues running east/west, starting at First in the north end of town and ascending as you go south. The exception is Ocean, the town's main east/west thoroughfare. Streets are named and run north/south; Junipero is the main drag. The center of town is Carmel Plaza, where Junipero and Ocean avenues meet. There is no numbering system for buildings.

Word to the wise: Most Carmel inns define a two-night weekend minimum as being either Thursday and Friday nights *or* Saturday and Sunday nights; some charge a premium for a Friday/Saturday combination. Call to double-check. Except for the occasional midweek, off-season bargain, room rates in Carmel range from expensive to astronomical, so plan accordingly. Due to water-use restrictions, most of Carmel's inns have showers, not tubs or Jacuzzis in their guest rooms.

Reader tips: "Carmel has a marvelous climate—cool, clean air encourages the lush growth of beautiful trees and abundant flowers. Rolling surf and clean white beaches where evenings find couples, families, and lone strollers." *(Dianne Evans)* "Recommend the Casanova for a lovely, romantic dinner." *(Stephanie Roberts)* "Although most

Carmel visitors just stop at the beach in town, at the end of Ocean Drive, it's well worth the short drive to Point Lobos State Reserve for beautiful beaches, huge dunes, and marvelous hiking trails; you can watch for whales, seals, and sea lions, plus a wide range of sea birds. When I was there on a Saturday morning in July, the parking lot was almost empty, though the town was jammed full." *(SHW)* "Second your recommendation of Point Lobos—our favorite part of Carmel. Breathtakingly beautiful hikes along the rocky shoreline, with cypress trees and rocks carved by wind and water. Bring a picnic and stay all day." *(RSS)* "The cute fairytale bungalows of Carmel and the little shops of Ocean Avenue made for a pleasant afternoon of strolling mid-week, off-season. Sidewalks are narrow, and can be quite crowded weekends in season. Parking was not a problem on an early April Tuesday morning." *(SWS)*

Also recommended—resorts: Renovated in 1992 by Clint Eastwood is the **Mission Ranch** (26270 Dolores Street, Carmel, 93923; 408–624–6436 or 800–538–8221). The ranch has 31 guest rooms, located in the original 1850s farmhouse, bunkhouse, and in several newer buildings; furnishings combine antiques and custom-designed ranch-style pieces, and some rooms offer sunset views over the pastures to the ocean beyond. Guests have use of the tennis courts and exercise room, and the popular restaurant has an informal piano bar nightly. Double rates range from $85–235. "Cozy and comfortable. Our room had country decor, distant ocean view, Jacuzzi tub with big thick towels and robes, plus a coffee maker. Breakfast was an attractive buffet of fresh fruits, bagels, sweet rolls, cereals, and yogurts." *(Donna Pekkonen)* "Peaceful setting close to the Carmel Mission. Nothing pretentious or ostentatious; inviting and low-key." *(SWS)*

Carmel has two outstanding luxury golf resorts, the **Quail Lodge** (8205 Valley Greens Drive, 93923; 408–624–1581 or 800–538–9516) and the **Carmel Valley Ranch Resort** (1 Old Ranch Road, 93923; 408–625–9500 or 800–422–7635). Each has championship 18-hole golf courses, tennis courts, swimming pools, hot tubs, and fine dining, and each has about 100 guest rooms with rates starting about $250 double, with packages available.

Also recommended—hotels: The **Cypress Inn** (Lincoln and 7th, P.O. Box Y, 93921; 408–624–3871 or 800–443–7443) is a 33-room Spanish Mediterranean-style hotel built in 1929. Rooms are individually furnished, some with patios or ocean views, and gas fireplaces; double rates range from $110–285, and pets are welcome. "In-town location, close to all shops and restaurants, six blocks from the beach. Fresh, clean rooms." *(SWS)* "Delightful architecture, small flower-laden courtyard, spacious guest rooms and common areas. Our favorite rooms are those on the second floor overlooking the courtyard with a balcony offering a distant ocean view." *(Hugh & Marjorie Smith)*

Originally built in 1904 as a private Spanish-style mansion is **La Playa Hotel** (Camino Real and 8th, P.O. Box 900, 93921; 408–624–6476 or 800–582–8900). The 75 guest rooms are done in soft apricot colors, with good lighting and hand-carved Spanish mission-style furniture with the hotel's mermaid motif. Double rates range from $125–230; 5

cottages are also available, at rates of $230–495. "Delightful lunch on the terrace overlooking the beautiful gardens; excellent dinner, too." *(Tom Wilbanks, also Peter Brebach)* "Beautiful gardens, meticulously maintained; comfortable room with Spanish-style decor. Convenient location in a quiet residential area, a few blocks to the beach or shops." *(Susan Lane)* "Though not on the beach (despite its name), this small hotel is beautifully maintained and run, inside and out, with a friendly, delightful atmosphere." *(SWS)*

Also recommended—B&B: Readers are delighted with the friendly staff, tasty food, and comfortable rooms at the **The Cobblestone Inn** (Junipero and 8th, P.O. Box 3185, 93921; 408–625–5222 or 800–833–8836), a former motel, refaced with Tudor-style detailing and beautiful stonework. Each of the 24 guest rooms has a private entrance, opening to the walkway or second-floor balcony. B&B double rates of $95–175 include a generous buffet breakfast, afternoon wine and hors d'oeuvres, evening sherry and fresh-baked cookies, and always available soft drinks and fruit. "We had our choice of having breakfast in our room, in the cozy parlor/lobby by the fireplace, or at one of three tables in the beautiful garden patio." *(Roxanne Mita, also JP)* "Rooms face a charming garden courtyard, where several cars are allowed to park, due to tight in-town parking. Spacious living/dining area for guests to enjoy; delightful, recently redecorated guest rooms with lots of charm and the inn's signature teddy bears. Ask for an upstairs room for more light and privacy. Close to shops and restaurants, a bit further to the beach." *(SWS)*

The **Happy Landing Inn** (Monte Verde between 5th and 6th, P.O. Box 2619, 93921; 408–624–7917) is just a block from Ocean Avenue, next door to an excellent restaurant. Built in 1925 in an early Comstock design, this B&B has seven guest rooms, with B&B double rates of $90–165, including a continental breakfast and afternoon tea or sherry. "A breakfast of coffee cake, quiche, fruit, juice, and a hot beverage is brought to your room any time after 8:30 A.M." *(MK)* "A good value in pricy Carmel. Darling cluster of steep-roof pink cottages encircle beautiful gardens. Snow White could appear in at any moment. The largest cottage is where guests check in, and can enjoy a cup of tea. Charming guest rooms with fireplaces, some with pretty stained glass windows, Victorian antiques, cathedral ceilings. A touch dated and worn, some bathrooms are small, but not a big deal. Ideal location, quiet, convenient, and central." *(SWS)*

The **Sea View Inn** (Camino Real, between 11th and 12th, P.O. Box 4138, 93921; 408–624–8778) offers eight guest rooms decorated with four-poster canopy beds and other antiques, Oriental rugs, fresh flowers, and whimsical toys; B&B double rates are $80–125. "A convenient walk from both the beautiful waterfront and the heart of Carmel, on a quiet residential street. Our cozy little room had a nice-sized bathroom with a clawfoot tub. Healthy continental breakfast served between 9 and 10 A.M.. Cookies and tea in the afternoon, and sherry, wine, and cheese in the evening provided a nice touch." *(Karl Wiegers & Chris Zambito, also SWS)*

Located on the former estate of California Senator and Mrs. Edward

Tickle, the **Tickle Pink Inn at Carmel Highlands** (155 Highland Drive, 93923; 408–624–1244 or 800–635–4774; www.ticklepink.com) was named for Mrs. Tickle's favorite color. Her garden was filled with pink flowers, a tradition that continues at the inn today. The inn has 35 guest rooms, many with balconies and fireplaces, and the rates range from $189–305, including continental breakfast and afternoon wine and cheese. "Overlooks an awesome craggy inlet, complete with seagulls and incredible sunset views." *(GG)* "Wonderful views, well maintained, spacious rooms, good breakfast, pleasant housekeeping staff." *(Steve Holman)*

EUREKA

Visitors come to Eureka, still a major lumbering center and fishing port, to wander through its Old Town—once home to the area's many lumber barons—hike in the area's parks and forests, explore area beaches, and fish in Humboldt Bay. Eureka is located on the North Coast (Redwood Country), 250 miles (5 hours) north of San Francisco. To reach Eureka from the north or south, take Highway 101; from the east, follow Route 299 to 101. The town is laid out in a grid, with the numbered streets running north/south, parallel to the water, and the lettered streets running east/west.

Also recommended: The **Carter House Victorians** (301 L Street, 95501; 707–444–8062; www.carterhouse.com) is comprised of three Victorian buildings: the old Hotel Carter built in 1906; the original Carter House, a reproduction Victorian mansion built in 1982; and The Bell Cottage, a turn-of-the-century home recently restored in 1996. Each is decorated with rich fabrics, antiques, and original local art; some have marble fireplaces and whirlpools with views of the marina; most have queen-size beds. Open daily for dinner, Restaurant 301 in the Hotel Carter showcases herbs, greens, and vegetables from the inn's extensive gardens, as well as local delicacies; its wine list has been recognized for excellence by the *The Wine Spectator*. B&B double rates for the 32 guest rooms range from $131–250 and include a continental breakfast, afternoon wine and hors d'oeuvres, and evening tea and cookies.

Abigail's Elegant Victorian Mansion B&B	*Tel:* 707–444–3144
1406 C Street, 95501	*Fax:* 707–442–5594

URL: http://www. bbonline.com/ca/abigails

This meticulously restored Queen Anne–influenced, Eastlake Victorian inn was built in 1888 for Eureka mayor and county commissioner William S. Clark. A National Historic Landmark, the inn has been owned by Doug and Lily Vieyra since 1989, who have made it into a showcase of authentic High Victorian decor. Doug describes the inn as a "living history house-museum of the Victorian experience." Rates include a "French gourmet" breakfast and a "horseless carriage" ride through town.

"Doug and Lily have made their elegant home into a warm and restful escape from everyday life. Attention to detail includes comfortable queen-size beds, plenty of clean, crisp towels, and fresh bathrobes. Lily's wonderful breakfast included fresh fruit with a light puffed pastry with eggs. They joined us at breakfast and fascinated me with stories about Eureka and the Victorian era." (Paula Adams, also MW) "Welcoming hospitality from the first phone call." (Beth & Roger Emerson) "Doug and Lily greeted us, gave us a tour of the inn, and shared its history. In the morning, we feasted on waffles with real whipped cream and sweet, fresh strawberries, and great coffee." (Robin Christian) "If you've ever wanted to step past the velvet cord in a museum and spend the night, Abigail's is the place for you. The house is filled with Victorian memorabilia which you are encourage to enjoy." (Alicia Oliver) "Authentic yet comfortable atmosphere; attentive but not obtrusive service. Impeccably maintained; convenient parking; safe and secure location." (Mary Kay & Allen Feller) "Every room was a visual delight, filled with Victorian bric-a-brac, furniture, tapestries, floor and ceiling decorations." (Joel & Janice Boyle)

"My immaculate bedroom had an antique bed with a firm queen-size mattress, two bedside reading lights, overstuffed chairs, and a desk. Our afternoon croquet game was followed by tea and delicious scones. Breakfast included fresh-ground coffee, Austrian apple strudel, eggs Benedict, fruit, and freshly baked muffins." (Cindy Jansen) "Freshly squeezed orange juice, mango juice, and a wonderfully light almond cake began our breakfast." (Jesse Ortel) "Belgian chocolate truffles at bedtime." (Troy Sustarson) "We had three bathrooms to choose from down the hall; bathrobes, thirsty towels, soaps and shampoo, hair dryer were all supplied. One bathroom had a sauna and a shower for two; another had an old-fashioned tub." (Nancy Male) "Doug and Lily provided us with a selection of menus from local restaurants and helped us make an excellent choice." (Bernard & Catherine Bishop) "Secure garaged parking protected our bicycles." (Bill & Gail Smithman) "The inn is in a modest residential district, a 10-12 block walk to restaurants." (Heather Allen) "Well-kept Victorian gardens." (Lola & Philip Sherlock) "Extensive collection of classic movies, plus a wide variety of reading material. Ample information on sightseeing and local restaurants." (Virginia Sril)

Open All year.
Rooms 1 suite, 3 doubles—1 with private bath, 3 sharing 3 baths. All with desk, air-conditioning, telephone.
Facilities Dining room, breakfast room with fireplace, living room with fireplace, books, TV/VCR, stereo; parlors, masseuse service, laundry service. Evening movies, chamber music weekly. Gazebo, Victorian flower garden, croquet, sauna, bicycles. Off-street garage parking. Tennis, health club nearby.
Location Historic residential district. From Hwy. 101, go E on C St. to inn at 14th St.
Restrictions Absolutely no smoking. No children under 15.
Credit cards MC, Visa.
Rates B&B, $125–165 suite, $85–135 double, $69–90 single. Midweek, off-season rate. Extra person in suite, $35. 10% AAA discount.
Extras Station pickup; airport pickup, $15. Dutch, French, German spoken.

FERNDALE

Thought by many to be California's best-preserved Victorian village, the entire village of Ferndale is registered as a State Historic Landmark. The town has more than its share of pretty Victorian homes, originally called "butterfat palaces," since their owners made their money in the dairy industry. At the midpoint of Redwood Country, set off the tourist trail, Ferndale is a perfect town for an overnight stay. Although activities are planned year-round, a special effort is made for Christmas, highlighted (literally) by a 125-foot spruce, decorated with over 9,000 lights. Be sure to stop in at any shop for a free walking-tour brochure. Ferndale is located in the North Coast region (Redwood Country), 260 miles north of San Francisco, 15 miles south of Eureka, and five miles from Highway 101.

Reader tips: "During the late spring, Ferndale's rhododendrons are in bloom; each home seems to have huge bushes of gorgeous flowers." *(Erika Holm)* "Bibo's restaurant was superb." *(Margaret Sievers)* "Ferndale is lovely. We were pleased with our dinner at Curley's, with several vegetarian choices." *(Gail de Sciose)* "Be sure to visit Golden Gate Mercantile on Main Street, a fascinating old-time general store complete with every ointment and liniment that our grandparents used. Also unusual is the Museum of Kinetic Sculpture, home to several dozen vehicles, raced once a year. Entertaining for all ages." *(Christopher Hart Johnston, also Julie Phillips)* "A delightful array of Victorian buildings, well worth a detour. We took the long loop off Highway 101 on Highway 211 through Honeydew. Wild views and adventurous road, but fill up the gas tank before leaving 101." *(Carol Moritz)* "A charming and quiet little Victorian town, a good base for area explorations, including the incomparable redwoods." We found the area's best food at the Larrupin Cafè in Trinidad." *(Peter Brebach, also JF)*

The Gingerbread Mansion
400 Berding Street, P.O. Box 40, 95536

Tel: 707–786–4000
800–952–4136
Fax: 707–786–4381
E-mail: Kenn@humboldt1.com
URL: http://www.gingerbread-mansion.com

Within seconds of your first glimpse of the Gingerbread Mansion, you'll know why long-time owner-innkeeper Ken Torbert chose that name and why this is the most photographed Victorian in northern California! Rates include breakfasts of fresh fruit and juice, local cheeses, homemade granola, just-baked coffee bundt cake, nut breads, and muffins, plus a daily entree, perhaps eggs Benedict with Hollandaise and baked polenta, plus afternoon tea and turndown service. Breakfast is served from 8 to 9:30 A.M.; guests are asked to request a seating time the night before.

"The Fountain Suite was spotless and well-equipped; the bathroom had side-by-side clawfoot tubs, a gas fireplace, and was equipped with ample towels and amenities. At 7:00 A.M., the innkeepers set up coffee and tea for early risers. During breakfast, the housekeeping staff makes the beds, replenishes towels, and opens the shutters in the guest rooms.

Afternoon tea included such goodies as rum balls, petit fours, fresh fruit, chocolates, and more. The breakfast entree was stuffed cinnamon raisin French toast one day, a ham and egg souffle the next." *(Julie Phillips, also Peter Brebach)* "Breakfast consisted of fluffy, light pancakes served with real maple syrup; a wonderful apple, cinnamon, and raisin compote; and an assortment of sliced fresh fruit, local cheeses, and warm cranberry muffins." *(Joan Merrill)* "Beautifully decorated in high Victorian style, yet without excess. Common areas and guest rooms were immaculate and carefully thought out. The small garden next to the inn is a masterpiece. We were especially impressed by the helpfulness of Dave, the resident innkeeper." *(John Felton)*

"The Heron Suite was beautifully done in dark wood and various shades of green, with a separate sitting room and a comfortable queen-size bed. Exquisite touches include the antique lamps, old photographs, and such thoughtful amenities as comfortable robes, bathroom nightlights, and magnifying mirrors. Delicious food and coffee at breakfast; the chef modified the menu for our vegetarian diet." *(Gail de Sciose)* "This ornate gingerbread mansion is located off the main street in a quiet, well-lit residential neighborhood close to the well-preserved historic downtown area." *(Patrick & Gloria Smith)* "The Rose Suite has a fantastic mirrored bathroom, complete with an enormous claw-foot tub and shower." *(Jan & Barry Olsen)* "On a stroll through town you may pass a candy shop where you can watch the workers hand-dip chocolates; at night, you'll find these same delicious chocolates by your pillow." *(Erika Holm)* "Tea and bottled water always available in the kitchen." *(Barbara Ruppert)*

Open All year.
Rooms 5 suites, 5 doubles—all with private bath and/or shower. 4 with gas fireplace. Some with desk, twin claw-foot tubs.
Facilities 4 parlors with 2 fireplaces and library, dining room, porches. Guest pantry. Formal English gardens, fountain. Ocean, river, wilderness park nearby.
Location Take Ferndale exit off Hwy. 101, 5 m to Main St. Turn left at Bank of America; 1 block to inn.
Restrictions No smoking. Children over 10 preferred.
Credit cards Amex, MC, Visa.
Rates B&B, $150–350 suite, $140–180 double, $140–160 single. Extra person, $40. 2-night holiday/weekend minimum.

FORT BRAGG

Located on the North Coast, Fort Bragg is eight miles north of Mendocino and approximately 160 miles northwest of San Francisco. The town's best-known tourist attraction is the scenic "Skunk Train" through the redwood forest to Willits; its name came from the smell of its original gas-powered engines. Also of interest in Fort Bragg are the miles of trails in the Mendocino Coast Botanical Gardens, where flowers frame ocean views nearly year-round; and in March, the Whale Festival, celebrating the migration of the California gray whale. Other activities include fishing and whale-watching trips, horseback rides on the beach, and even a repertory theater company. Several of its B&Bs

are on Main Street (Highway One), so expect *significant* traffic noise in front rooms; some B&Bs have rooms with ocean views, but it's a distant one—there's an industrial area between the residential section and the water.

Reader tips: "Fort Bragg is an honest working town, complete with a Georgia Pacific sawmill in its center. Be sure to follow the Noyo River road and explore the harbor, complete with seals, working fishing boats, funky shops, and casual waterside restaurants." *(SWS)* "Fort Bragg has nooks and crannies to explore, including a neighborhood of 1903s shingled arts-and-crafts style homes. Many Mendocino galleries have moved here due to lower rents." *(CB)* "The Wharf restaurant is a great place to view the boats coming in and out of the harbor." *(Carol Moritz)*

The Grey Whale Inn ¢ ♿   *Tel:* 707–964–0640
615 North Main Street, 95437   800–382–7244
Fax: 707–964–4408
E-mail: stay@greywhaleinn.com
URL: http://www.greywhaleinn.com

The Grey Whale Inn, a Mendocino Coast landmark since 1915, has been handsomely restored by long-time owners John and Colette Bailey. Once the town hospital, it now looks as though it has always been an inn, and is furnished with pleasantly eclectic decor, featuring country quilts, antiques, local art, and reproductions. The expansive breakfast buffet changes daily and includes such favorite as Greek frittata, eggs rellenos, or poached eggs and spinach with Hollandaise sauce, plus fresh fruit and juices, hot and cold cereals, home-baked coffee cakes, toasting bread, sliced cheeses, homemade jams, house-blend coffee, teas, and hot chocolate.

"Guest rooms, hallways, and common areas are exceptionally spacious, allowing guests a degree of privacy unknown at many other inns. Built as a hospital, the only remaining clue to the inn's origins are the ramps which lead from floor to floor, making the inn especially welcoming to the disabled. Colette is a warm and caring innkeeper, knowledgeable about Fort Bragg and area activities." *(SWS)* "Large, well-furnished rooms. The Sunset room has a private covered veranda looking out towards the ocean. Large public areas, a strong interest in local history, many reading books, tea available all day, and a first-rate buffet breakfast, with a wide variety of breads, hot dishes, fruit, jams, and more. Walking distance to the train station and several local restaurants. The owners live on site and also have a staff, so everything runs right." *(Duane Roller)* "Even better on a return visit. The Whale Watch room now has a remote-controlled fireplace, ceiling fan, and TV/VCR; my husband felt like a king with three remotes to hold! Well-equipped little kitchenette. Breakfast included fresh fruit salad, vanilla yogurt, cranberry coffee cake, artichoke mushroom frittata, sourdough bread, and more. Impeccably clean and well maintained, friendly owners and staff. Easy walk to shops and the ocean." *(Julie Phillips)* "Quiet and relaxing; rooms to suit all budgets, some with kitchenettes if you're cooking in. Knowledgeable staff helps with directions, reservations, activities. Wonderful mattresses. Guest suggestions are taken seriously and utilized." *(Peggy Lagomarsino)*

"The hallways and entrance are decorated with fine prints, paintings, and old photographs of logging days and of the great whales. Helpful, candid, guest critique book of local restaurants." *(Donald Hook)* "Coffee is ready at 7A.M., and breakfast is served buffet-style from 7:30 to 10 A.M. Four tables await guests, but you can easily take breakfast to your room. After breakfast, we walked along the cliffs and down the walking path. Colette is knowledgeable about area activities and the inn's history. The Sunrise Suite features a king-size bed with hand-embroidered pillows and a matching quilt, comfortable chairs for reading, a table and chairs, an armoire, a space heater for chilly fog-bound evenings, and ample bedside reading lights. The bathroom has a huge whirlpool tub and separate shower. Large windows look out onto a private deck with patio furniture and views of town and the ocean." *(Thomas Layton)*

Open All year.
Rooms 14 doubles—all with private bath and/or shower, telephone, clock radio, TV. Some with VCR or VCP, fireplace, whirlpool tub, balcony or patio, refrigerator and/or kitchenette, ceiling fan.
Facilities Parlor, breakfast room, lounge with fireplace, guest refrigerator, recreation room with pool table, conference room, TV/VCR room, fax/copier. Garden, lawns. 4 blocks to ocean.
Location North Coast. On Hwy. 1.
Restrictions No smoking. "Facilities for children very limited." White noise machine, ear plugs for street noise if needed in a few rooms.
Credit cards Amex, Discover, JCB, MC, Visa.
Rates B&B, $95–190 suite, double, $75–175 single. Extra person, $25. 2–4 night weekend/holiday minimum. Winter midweek rate. Corporate rate.
Extras Wheelchair access; 1 room equipped for disabled. Building has ramps throughout. German, Spanish spoken.

GEYSERVILLE

People go to the Sonoma Valley to explore the area wineries, visit the Russian River resorts, and enjoy the area's inns and restaurants. In general, the pace here is quieter and slower than in the neighboring Napa Valley.

Geyserville is located in the North Coast region, in the center of Sonoma County Wine Country, Alexander, and Dry Creek Valleys. It's 75 miles north of San Francisco and eight miles north of Healdsburg.

Campbell Ranch Inn 🏃
1475 Canyon Road, 95441

Tel: 707–857–3476
800–959–3878
Fax: 707–857–3239
URL: http://www.campbellranchinn.com

Located in the heart of the Sonoma County wine country, the Campbell Ranch Inn is a large, comfortable home, set on a hilltop surrounded by gardens, terrace, and deck. The rooms all have comfortable king-size beds, quality linens, fresh fruit, and flowers.

"Delightfully situated in the middle of rolling vineyards and wonderful gardens. After a sumptuous breakfast of fresh-squeezed orange juice, home-baked breads, and egg puffs, we were off on the inn's bikes to ride to a local winery. Later we enjoyed a game of tennis on their court, and splashed in the pool and hot tub. Skip dessert at dinner, and have coffee and a sweet treat back at the inn with the Campbells and the other guests. We felt like family, especially with Maggie, their family dog who adopts all the guests." *(Toni Adler)* "Especially comfortable beds in the spacious, private guest rooms. Ample common areas, both for quiet reading or watching the huge TV. Easy highway access, yet a completely quiet setting." *(Sue Lippman)* "Highlights include the splendid panoramas, the music of the frogs, the flowers, the comfort, and the delicious food. Pleasant fellow guests. Mary Jane and Jerry are superb innkeepers—organized, hard-working, and capable, with genuine warmth and humor." *(Bob Davis)* "The helpful hosts have a telephone set up to speed dial favorite local restaurants. Soft and luxurious linens." *(Lydia Terrill)* "The fireplace was ready to light; a basket of fresh fruit and assorted beverages were at our fingertips. Our spacious cottage had a spectacular view of the vineyards. After returning from dinner, Mary Jane served peach pie and chocolate cake." *(Betsy Buckwald, also Clint & Pam Guillory)* "Easy to find, convenient parking, spacious guest room with great lighting. Friendly hosts, great food." *(Karen Everhart)*

"Selected the night before, breakfast includes a choice of fruits and cereals, omelets, fried eggs, or an egg puff with chilies or mushrooms, plus homemade jam, muffins, and breads, served at guests' convenience from 8–10 A.M." *(Phyllis & Walt Reichle)* "The second-story bedrooms have balconies, and the tree-shaded terrace is equally inviting." *(Stephen & Judy Gray)* "The good-sized rooms are quiet and well insulated, with good temperature control. Great recommendations for touring, restaurants, and local wineries. The breakfast table is set for ten; guests may eat together or take their food to individual tables on the deck or around the pool. My favorite rooms were #4 for privacy and #2 for the larger bathroom and the views." *(SHW)*

Open All year.

Rooms 1 2-bedroom cottage, 4 doubles—all with private bath and/or shower, air-conditioning. Cottage with cassette player, fireplace, hot tub on deck; 4 with desk, balcony.

Facilities Living room with fireplace, family room with fireplace, games, TV/VCR; dining room, terrace. 35 acres with flower gardens, heated swimming pool, hot tub, tennis court, aviary. Ping-Pong, horseshoes, bicycles, model trains. 3 m to Lake Sonoma for boating, swimming, fishing; 3 m to Russian River for fishing, canoeing.

Location 2 m from town. Take Canyon Rd. exit off Hwy. 101, go 1.6 m W to inn.

Restrictions No smoking. Young children not encouraged.

Credit cards Amex, MC, Visa.

Rates B&B, $225 cottage, $125–165 double, $100–155 single. Extra person, $25. 2–3 night weekend/holiday minimum.

Extras Local airport/station pickup.

HEALDSBURG

Taking a break from the serious business of wine tasting, visitors to Healdsburg enjoy swimming, fishing, boating, and canoeing in the Russian River and Lake Sonoma, plus hot-air ballooning, hiking, bicycling, tennis, and golf. Five wine tasting rooms are right in town, with 50 more within an easy drive.

Located in the Sonoma Valley, along the Russian River Wine Road in California's North Coast region, Healdsburg is 70 miles north of San Francisco, and 13 miles north of Santa Rosa, on Highway 101.

Reader tips: "In the past decade Healdsburg has gone from a sleepy little nothing to a real destination with wonderful wineries and restaurants, yet is still relatively undiscovered. Room rates are relatively reasonable, too." *(Katherine Owen, also SWS)*

Also recommended: An 1869 Italianate Victorian home, the **Camellia Inn** (211 North Street, 95448; 707–433–8182 or 800–727–8182; www.camelliainn.com) combines period decoration—antiques and Oriental rugs—with soft shades of salmon and peach to create a warm and soothing atmosphere. Breakfasts include homemade jams and breads, fresh fruit, yogurt, granola, tea, coffee, juice, and perhaps huevos rancheros. Complimentary beverages, cheese, and crackers are served in the early evening around the inn's swimming pool. B&B rates for the nine guest rooms range from $75–155. "The inn is painted a lovely shade of soft apricot, surrounded by camellia trees—all blooming when I visited. Inside, the double parlors are warm and inviting, a lovely place for guests to relax. Lucy is a delightful innkeeper, warm and friendly, sensitive to guests' needs." *(SWS)*

The **Grape Leaf Inn** (539 Johnson Street, 95448; 707–433–8140; www.grapeleafinn.com) is a Queen Anne Victorian home built in 1900; B&B rates for the seven guest rooms range from $90–150, including a full breakfast and afternoon wine tasting. "At the evening social hour, everyone talked about the great wines they had tasted that day. On Saturday night, the owner of a local winery came to the inn and led us through a tasting of his wines." *(Sue & Tom Nardi)* "Warm, friendly innkeepers. Our favorite rooms are Merlot and Zinfandel on the second floor, with skylights above the double Jacuzzi tubs, so you can see the stars overhead." *(Vicki & Paul Helbig)*

Madrona Manor ✕ ♿	*Tel:* 707–433–4231
1001 Westside Road, P.O. Box 818, 95448	800–258–4003
	Fax: 707–433–0703
	E-mail: madronaman@aol.com
	URL: http://www.madronamanor.com

Originally built in the 1881 by a wealthy San Francisco banker, Madrona Manor sits on a high knoll overlooking the town of Healdsburg and nearby vineyards. In 1983 it was bought by John and Carol Muir, who have turned it into an elegant country inn. Most of the space on the first floor of the main building is devoted to dining rooms, although the front parlor has a five-piece Victorian suite with carved griffin arms.

Guest rooms in the main house are very large, and those on the first and second floors have furnishings original to the house; those in the Carriage House are luxuriously furnished with more modern decor. Most have queen- or king-size beds. The Manor is a busy place in season, and reservations are essential for both the rooms and restaurant, especially on weekends.

Todd Muir is the executive chef, and a recent dinner included sea scallops with artichoke puree, rack of lamb with potato terrine, and cappuccino pots de creme with fresh fruit and cookies. Be sure to save room for the breakfast buffet of juice, fresh fruit, and granola; a selection of European hams and local and imported cheeses; vegetable frittata with salsa; toast, homemade raspberry jam, and bread pudding.

"Lovely hotel. Excellent dinner on the outside patio." *(Pat & Doug Phillips)* "Our dinners were prepared by an outstanding Italian guest chef; excellent service by knowledgeable, intelligent wait staff. Highlights included the lobster quenelles, veal filet with spinach, frozen mascarpone with blueberries." *(SWS)* "We relaxed by the fire, had a wonderful dinner, and woke up to a great breakfast. The reception staff was gracious, helpful, and knowledgeable with good recommendations on wineries and antique shops." *(Edwin Jones)* "The gardens were appropriate to Victorian era, beautifully maintained with a fountain, flowers, herbs, and vegetables." *(Helen Nicholas)* "Through the French doors on either side of the 10-foot-high carved headboard in our bedroom was a terrace from which we could see across the valley to the mountains." *(Virginia Severs)*

Open All year.

Rooms 5 suites, 17 doubles—all with full private bath, telephone, radio, desk, air-conditioning, fan. 20 rooms with fireplace (gas or Duraflame), 7 with balcony, 3 with Jacuzzi tub. 8 rooms in main house, 9 in Carriage House, 5 in 3 cottages. TV/VCR on request.

Facilities 3 dining rooms, bar/lounge, music room, lobby, terrace. 8 acres with gardens, fountains, orchard, walking trails, swimming pool. Golf, tennis, swimming, canoeing, horseback riding nearby.

Location ¾ m from town. From Central Healdsburg exit of Hwy. 101, go left on Mill St., which becomes Westside Rd.

Restrictions Occasional traffic noise midweek. No smoking.

Credit cards All major.

Rates B&B, $225–255 suite, $155–220 double. Extra person, $30. Three-course dinner, $40; four-course dinner, $48.

Extras Wheelchair access. Local airport pickup, $25. Pets by arrangement. Crib, baby-sitting. Spanish spoken.

INVERNESS

Although Point Reyes almost became as developed as the rest of Marin County, it was saved by the environmental movement in the 1970s and was declared a National Seashore. Only an hour northwest of San Francisco, the area offers magnificent beaches, hiking trails in the forests, and Inverness Ridge with abundant wildlife including deer, fox, rabbits, and birds. Other activities include fishing, whale-watching, tennis, golf, kayaking, horseback riding, birdwatching, and attending theater at the Point Reyes Dance Palace.

Inverness is located in the southernmost part of the North Coast area, in west Marin County. Visitors frequently make Inverness their base for explorations of the Point Reyes National Seashore.

Also recommended: The **Holly Tree Inn** (3 Silver Hills Road, Inverness; mailing address: P.O. Box 642, Point Reyes Station, 94956; 415–663–1554; www.hollytreeinn), set amongst the trees, offers hospitality, firm beds, and a relaxing, quiet environment. In addition to the four guest rooms and cottage at the main location, the innkeepers also have a one-bedroom cottage with a fireside living room set on pilings out in Tomales Bay. B&B double rates rooms range from $120–175, with the cottages at $200–230.

Guests can take a swim in Tomales Bay, only steps from the door of **Sandy Cove Inn** (12990 Sir Francis Drake Boulevard, P.O. Box 869, 94937; 415–669–COVE or 800–759–COVE; www.sandycove.com). Each of the three suites offers a skylit ceiling, sitting area, private bath, fireplace, a well-stocked in-room refrigerator, and a private deck. Owners Kathy and Gerry Coles serve a hearty breakfast in their sunny solarium or in guests' rooms. Rates range from $145–225. "Outstanding features include the attention to details—everything you could imagine wanting is supplied—the breakfast, the location, and the gracious hosts, Kathy and Gerry. Gerry was great with directions and helpful hints on exploring Point Reyes. On the grounds are horses, sheep, and even a beach." *(James Whitaker, also Patricia Bell)*

Ten Inverness Way	*Tel:* 415–669–1648
10 Inverness Way, 94937	*Fax:* 415–669–7403
	E-mail: inn@teninvernessway.com
	URL: http://www.teninvernessway.com

"The inn for people who like books, long walks, and cottage gardens," is how Scott and Teri Mowery describe the well-known inn they bought in 1998. Opting out of corporate life, they left Silicon Valley for the natural beauty of Point Reyes National Seashore and Marin County. In their new life as innkeepers, they welcome guests to start the day with Scott's hearty breakfasts of pecan Belgian waffles, blue cheese and portabello mushroom quiche, or perhaps guests' old favorite, banana-buttermilk-buckwheat pancakes. After a day of exploring the nearby trails and beaches, or the sights of San Francisco, Napa, and Sonoma—just an hour away—guests come "home" to enjoy the gardens, soak in the hot tub, and read or chat in the living room. The guest refrigerator is kept stocked with complimentary sodas and water. The inn was built in 1904 and is decorated with comfortable antiques; guest rooms have shiplap siding and quilt-topped queen-size beds. While maintaining its well-loved charms, the Mowerys plan to refurbish the inn with new upholstery, linens, and paint, and establish a botanical garden of indigenous Point Reyes plantings.

"Set on a quiet, green street, the inn is unassuming from the outside.

Inside, all is calm, inviting, and immaculately kept by Teri and Scott. Everything calms the senses: the dècor, the garden, the food, even the hot tub in a lovely garden shed, reserved one-half hour at a time by guests. Breakfasts are a special treat with lots of love lavished on original dishes. The rooms are equally tasteful and comfortable, with well-appointed baths, and no TV in sight. The innkeepers are friendly, interested in their guests, helpful, and happy to assist. Parking is easy. The town invites walking and splendid Point Reyes is just minutes away." *(Max Lowenstein)* "Cozy, restful ambiance. Through the skylights, we could see the softly falling rain and enjoy a gentle breeze. Scott and Teri went to great pains to include the little things that make for a special visit—fresh flowers, incredible breakfasts, and a cracking fire in the evening. The relaxing hot tub overlooks a beautifully terraced English garden filled with fresh herbs and flowers. Within walking distance is Manka's, a wonderful restaurant." *(Elizabeth Ripley)* "We were welcomed warmly with tea and just-baked cookies. After a tasty breakfast of fresh fruit and eggs, we were given a bag of local apples for snacking. Returning that night, we were guided to the house by delightful garden lights which lent an air of enchantment." *(WF Gregson)*

"Though not large, the rooms are extremely comfortable, with excellent mattresses and pillows, luxurious towels, and beautiful quilts. Lovely floral bouquets in the rooms, too." *(Joan Simon)* "On stormy days, a fire is always going in the living room, accompanied by hot tea and cookies. Ample reading lights in common areas and guest rooms. The tasty breakfasts are tailored to the needs of cholesterol-conscious people if desired." *(Rena Ziegler)* "Woodsy seclusion. Our room had a high window running the length of the room with a view of the back gardens." *(Diane Schwemm)* "The living room was exceptionally homey and warm, with a beautiful stone fireplace, bay windows with built-in seating, and plump sofas." *(Linda Goldberg)* "They mapped out excellent paths for us to hike, along ocean shores teeming with wildlife." *(Heide Bredfeldt)*

Open All year.

Rooms 1 suite, 4 doubles—all with private bath and/or shower, clock/radio, fan/heater. Suite with kitchen, private garden patio.

Facilities Sunroom with wood stove, library; living room with fireplace; guest refrigerator. ¼ acre with garden, hot tub.

Location From San Francisco, take Hwy 101 N to San Anselmo-Sir Francis Drake Blvd exit. Follow Drake Blvd. to Olema. Turn right onto Hwy. 1, then left at Bear Valley Rd. Go 3 m to stop sign, go left again, and continue 4 m to Inverness. In village, turn left at 2nd Inverness Way to house on immediate right.

Restrictions No smoking. Small closets in most rooms.

Credit cards MC, Visa.

Rates B&B, $145–180 double, $135–170 single. Extra person, $15, 2-3 night weekend/holiday minimum.

LA JOLLA

La Jolla (pronounced "La Hoya") is a suburb of San Diego, about a 20-minute drive north of downtown. Not just a bedroom community, this sophisticated village on the Pacific Ocean has a number of attractions, including the Museum of Contemporary Art, the Scripps Institute of Oceanography, and U.C. San Diego, along with over 30 restaurants and 120 shops, which range from trendy to traditional. Cove Beach, a marine-life preserve, is a favorite for snorkeling. The Torrey Pines Golf Course and the Del Mar Racetrack are a short drive away to the north.

La Jolla is located 89 miles south of Los Angeles and 12 miles north of San Diego.

For additional area entries, see **San Diego.**

Reader tip: "We were delighted with our stay in La Jolla. It was wonderful walking along the cliffs watching the huge waves, the seals, and the pelicans." *(Alex & Beryl Williams)*

Also recommended: The **Bed & Breakfast Inn at La Jolla** (7753 Draper Avenue, 92037; 619–456–2066) is a beige stucco home built in 1913 and one of the first examples of Irving Gill's "Cubist" architecture. Conveniently located within two blocks of restaurants and shops, it is across a grassy park from the cliffside cove path. The 15 guest rooms (in two buildings) are beautifully decorated in Laura Ashley fabrics, although some are small; many have fireplaces, refrigerators, and/or ocean views, with either queen- or king-size beds. B&B double rates of $110–250 include a home-baked continental breakfast and afternoon wine tasting. "We were warmly welcomed by the innkeeper, Louise, who made us a lovely pot of tea which we enjoyed in the pretty garden. Our rooms, Country Village and Ocean Breeze, were at the lower end of their price range but nevertheless we were delighted to find that they were most attractive with beautiful comforters and drapes. The bathrooms were well equipped with hair dryers, terrycloth robes, and lovely fluffy towels. Additional amenities included a thermos of iced water, fresh fruit, sherry, and flowers. Immaculate housekeeping throughout. Morning coffee is ready at 7:30, with breakfast beginning at 8 A.M.; guests have their choice of small tables or a large one, or the garden. Excellent breakfast on the first morning of our stay, with cereals, fruit, yogurt, juice, muffins, and pancakes with strawberry sauce. Lovely cookies and scones were available all day. Convenient location close to beaches, shops, and restaurants, with easy parking available." *(Alex & Beryl Williams)*

Information please: Built in 1926 of pink stucco and red tile, **La Valencia Hotel** (1132 Prospect Street, 92037; 619–454–0771 or 800–451–0772) overlooks Cove Beach and Scripps Park and is surrounded by some of La Jolla's finest boutiques and art galleries. Rooms are traditionally decorated, and most have ocean views. "In the heart of the village, steps from all attractions." *(Sally Ducot)* "Incredibly romantic, incredibly beautiful. In my next life, I'd like to live here." *(BNS)* "Exceptionally friendly staff; wonderful food. Careful attention to detail, from the Crabtree and Evelyn soaps and lotions, to the thick terry cloth robes and slippers for trips to the hot tub. Our partial ocean view room was picturesque, overlooking the ocean and seaside park." *(Debbie Bergstrom)* Rates for the 90 double rooms range from $205–450; the 10 suites cost $550–850.

Overlooking La Jolla Cove, the **Prospect Park Inn** (1110 Prospect Street, 92037; 619–454–0133 or 800–433–1609), a four-story hotel/motel, was built in 1945. "Great location near the ocean and steps from stores and scores of restaurants. While not large, our second story room (#15) had a balcony, kitchen, plus ample reading lights and storage space; furnishing were standard. You can breakfast in your room or on the sun deck, overlooking the Pacific." *(ABK)* Double rates for the 24 guest rooms are $120–185, ocean-view suites to $325, including a continental breakfast, afternoon beverages, and parking.

An excellent value in a pricy town is the **Scripps Inn** (555 Coast Boulevard South, 92037; 619–454–3391), offering 14 guest rooms at B&B double rates of $105–205, including a continental breakfast and parking; some have fireplaces, ocean views, and/or kitchenettes; most have queen- or king-size beds. "Flower-filled courtyard, ideal location by the art museum and the ocean. Advance reservations essential in summer." *(EG)*

LITTLE RIVER

Little River is located two miles south of the Victorian town of Mendocino. You can easily visit all of Mendocino's boutiques and restaurants during the day and then escape the evening noise and bustle by staying in Little River. Located on the North Coast, it's 155 miles north of San Francisco. The area was originally settled in the 1850s as a major source of redwood lumber for San Francisco. (Redwood, being pitch-free, was found to be more fire-resistant than other woods.) Logs were floated down the river to the coast, then taken by schooner to San Francisco.

Worth noting: If an unobstructed, panoramic ocean view is a priority for you, be sure to ask for details; many inns claim a "water view," but all you get is a glimpse of blue in the distance. If you care about proximity to the ocean, ask if you can *hear* the waves. Many inns are on Highway One, so be sure to ask about traffic noise if you're a light sleeper.

Also recommended: The **Heritage House** (5200 North Highway One, 95456; 707–937–5885 or 800–235–5885) gets our vote for the most beautifully situated inn in northern California. Except for a few units, the inn is located west of Highway One, so all you see from your room is green lawns, beautiful flowers, dramatic cliffs, crashing waves, and endless ocean. The beautiful restaurant and bar offer equally gorgeous views from huge windows. Guest rooms are comfortable, with double rates ranging from $99–305, depending on room, view, and season. "We were pleased with our spacious room, Deerfield #7, with a nice deck and ocean views." *(Tom Wilbanks)* "Beautifully situated on a cliff overlooking the ocean. The whole property is a glorious garden. Our cottage had an enormous bedroom and sitting room, with good light-ing, comfortable reading chairs, fireplace with lots of wood, with one wall entirely of windows. Exceptional food in the restaurant." *(Linda Chisari)*

For unobstructed ocean views and reasonable rates in this expensive area, it's hard to beat the **Little River Inn** (Little River, 95456; 707–937–5942 or 888–INN–LOVE; www.littleriverinn.com). This family-owned facility offers satisfactory motel rooms with spectacular vistas in the moderate $90–130 price range, as well as luxury cottages with fireplaces and whirlpool tubs ($190–275); with the exception of a couple units, rooms are not affected by traffic noise. Facilities include a modest but fun nine-hole golf course, and a tennis court. "Pleasant staff, good restaurant, convenient location. Well-kept grounds with beautiful flowers blooming everywhere; walking distance to Van Damme State Park with a beach and hiking trails into Fern Canyon. The food was quite good, highlighted by the Swedish pancakes at break-fast and the ollalieberry cobbler at dinner." *(SWS)* "Our favorite is the Coombs Cottage across the street on the ocean side. This private little cottage is perfect for romance and privacy, with a Jacuzzi tub and a wonderful stone fireplace, beautiful French doors looking out to spec-tacular ocean views, and a private sundeck." *(Linda Haakenson)*

For additional area entries, see **Mendocino** and **Fort Bragg.**

LOS ANGELES

Larger than Rhode Island and Delaware combined, Los Angeles is both linked and separated by an amazing maze of freeways. In fact, if the people of Detroit could have dreamed up the perfect town, they would have invented Los Angeles, where it is impossible to get anywhere without a car.

Los Angeles is a hodgepodge of different ethnic groups—you can visit different restaurants and shops for a taste of countries from Hun-gary to Thailand, from Polynesia to Ethiopia. Large Mexican, Japanese, Chinese, and Southeast Asian neighborhoods are intrinsic parts of Los Angeles. There's really a lot to see in Los Angeles—not just the TV and movie industry tours but other kinds of cultural and historic sights as well, including a number of outstanding art museums.

To make things a little easier, we've grouped most of our suggestions for the Los Angeles area in this section, so you won't have to check through the whole California chapter to find Beverly Hills or Santa Monica. Before you make reservations, it's a good idea to look at a map and identify the areas where you'll be spending most of your time; then book your room in that area of the city. Los Angeles is so spread out and the traffic so heavy (the afternoon rush hour starts at 3 P.M.) that you could easily spend your entire day in the car (and a car you must have). If you're traveling with the family and will mainly be doing the theme-park circuit, you'll be better off staying in Orange County to the southeast.

LA is a four-area-code town: downtown remains 213; to the north it's 818; and the area south and west of downtown has become 310 and 562. Los Angeles is located in Southern California, about 400 miles south of San Francisco and 125 miles north of San Diego.

To save money on many Los Angeles area hotels, call **Express Hotel Reservations** at 800–356–1123 or 303–440–8481. They offer discounts of 20–50% off rack rates, and since they receive a commission from the hotels, there's no charge to you. Don't feel you have to get stuck with a chain property—the Los Angeles area has many hotels of style and distinction worth checking out.

Reader tip: "The Huntington Library, Museum, and Gardens in Pasadena is well worth a visit; stay for a delicious lunch or a bounteous tea. Tea lovers will also enjoy a visit to the Chado Tea Room (213–655–2056) in Los Angeles, with dozens of teas to sample. Delightful French-Mediterranean dinner at Cafe Pierre in Manhattan Beach." *(Emily Hoche-Mong)*

Also recommended: The Channel Road Inn (219 West Channel Road, Santa Monica, 90402; 310–459–1920) is just a block from the beach in Santa Monica Canyon. A Colonial Revival home built in 1910, it was restored as a B&B in 1988; readers are delighted with the antique decor, continental breakfasts, afternoon wine and cheese, hillside hot tub overlooking Santa Monica Bay, and last but far from least—the warm and welcoming innkeepers. B&B rates range from $125–275. Under the same ownership is the **Inn at Playa Del Rey** (435 Culver Boulevard, Playa Del Rey, 90293; 310–574–1920), close to the airport yet within walking distance of the beach, and located on a 350-acre bird sanctuary. Rates of $85–200 for the 23 guest rooms include a full breakfast, afternoon tea, wine and cheese, and use of the inn's bicycles and hot tub; most rooms have decks, porches, canopy beds, Jacuzzi tubs, and/or fireplaces. Readers rave about the inn's warm hospitality, and beautifully decorated, well-equipped rooms.

Two good choices directly on the beach are the **Malibu Beach Inn** (22878 Pacific Coast Highway, Malibu, 90265; 310–456–6444 or 800–4–MALIBU), a three-story, Mediterranean-style building offering 47 guest rooms, some with gas fireplace and balcony with ocean view (B&B $149–275 double, suites to $325); and **Shutters on the Beach** (1 Pico Boulevard, Santa Monica, 90405; 310–458–0030 or 800–334–9000), highly recommended for "its distinctive style, beautifully designed public areas, well-equipped, handsome guest rooms with huge, comfortable beds, highest quality electronics, luxurious bathrooms, attentive service, lovely swimming pool, and excellent food in two restaurants." *(Mark Tattersall)* Double rates for the 200 guest rooms range from $325–525 (suites from $700).

Glowing superlatives seem to be the operative mode when it comes to describing the **Hotel Bel-Air** (701 Stone Canyon Road, Los Angeles, 90077; 310–472–1211 or 800–648–4097)—it receives top honors in nearly every hotel ranking survey. Rates for the 91 guest rooms are $325–450 for doubles, with suites starting at $525, although promotional rates are sometimes available. "A classic pink stucco building in a spectacular setting—a wooded, secluded canyon close to the Bel-Air Country Club.

Beautifully landscaped grounds, with a fabulous swimming pool. The lobby is cozy and well appointed, with a fireplace. The luxurious rooms are individually done in pastel colors with down comforters. The restaurant is excellent, and the bar is the former haunt of Humphrey Bogart and other movie stars of the 1940s." *(Linda & Paul Duttenhaver)* "We couldn't afford to stay overnight, but came for lunch and relished every moment and every bite." *(MA)*

The Kimco Hotel chain, well-known for its boutique hotels in San Francisco, operates the **Beverly Prescott Hotel** (1224 South Beverwil Drive at Rodeo Drive, P.O. Box 3065, Beverly Hills, 90212; 310–277–2800 or 800–421–3212). Most of the 140 luxurious guest rooms have balconies, plush overstuffed furnishings in florals and stripes, two telephones, terry robes, and more at rack rates of $225–275 double, suites to $850 (ask about promotional rates). There's even a swimming pool for a cooling dip. Ask for a high-floor room facing the hills to avoid traffic noise. "Our room was beautifully furnished; delicious dinner in the hotel restaurant. The rate for our club level room included a continental breakfast and evening cocktails. Good location; pricy valet parking." *(Helen Scheuer)*

MENDOCINO

Originally founded by Maine sea captains, Mendocino still looks a bit like a New England fishing village, and has even been used many times as a set for movies meant to be taking place on the East Coast.

Aside from looking into the many craft shops and art galleries and discovering the area restaurants and vineyards, take the time to explore the shore and the redwood forests, accessible in the area's five state parks. Canoeing, trail rides along the beach, river and ocean fishing, whale watching, tennis, and golf are all favorites. For more information on area attractions, please see the "North Coast" section of the chapter introduction, plus the listings for Fort Bragg and Little River.

Mendocino is located about 150 miles north of San Francisco, in the center of the Mendocino coast. From San Francisco, take Highway 101 through Santa Rosa to Cloverdale. Then take Route 128 to Highway One north to Mendocino. From Eureka, take Highway 101 south to Leggett, and follow Highway One through Fort Bragg to Mendocino.

Rates in the Mendocino area are *high*, with no difference between weekday and weekend rates from July through October; 2-night weekend minimums are the rule. Winter rates are in effect from November through March, with the best values available midweek. Your biggest decision in selecting a room is the question of a view. Some inns have dramatic water views, with the sound of the waves to lull you to sleep, while others offer only a glimpse, through the trees, of a relatively distant bay or shoreline. If there's any question in your mind, be sure to ask for specifics, and *don't* pay a premium for a water view unless you'll really get one. Inns located right in the village or on the east side of Highway One are *least likely* to offer unobstructed ocean views. Of course, if the fog rolls in, all views are obliterated, so factor that in as well. If you're traveling on a budget, our advice would be to book a no-view room on a waterfront property; if the weather is clear, you can enjoy the views from the gardens without breaking the bank.

Reader tips: "Book early if you're planning to visit on the weekend, and make dinner reservations ahead. The Mendocino Botanical Gardens are a must." *(Nancy Cohn)* "The fog may not lift until noon in summer—sometimes it stays all day." *(Ron Kahan)* "Although it's crowded in summer, the village was charming for strolling during our October weekend visit. Delightful hiking in Russian Gulch State Park, up through the redwoods to a lovely waterfall." *(RSS)* "Visit the wonderful store called Out of This World, where you can look through fifteen telescopes pointed at the ocean." *(Christopher Hart Johnson)*

Also recommended: Right next door to the Agate Cove Inn (see below) is the **Sea Rock Inn** (11101 Lansing Street, P.O. Box 906, 95460; 707–937–0926 or 800–906–0926; www.searock.com) with an equally wonderful ocean view. An excellent value for this expensive area, the inn's 18 little cottages and guest rooms have been pleasantly refurbished, and the $85–250 rates include a generous homemade continental breakfast. "Clean, comfortable room; cordial owners; delicious banana bread for breakfast." *(Tina Hom, also SWS)*

When the **Whitegate Inn** (499 Howard Street, P.O. Box 150, 95460; 707–937–4892 or 800–531–7282; www.whitegateinn.com) was built in 1883, a newspaper article described it as "one of the most elegant and best appointed residences in town." Under its current ownership, this description applies equally today. The elegant dining and living rooms have coordinating Oriental carpets, hand-painted wallpaper borders, and beautifully upholstered Victorian furniture. Rates of $119–229 include a full breakfast, afternoon cookies, pre-dinner refreshments, and bedtime chocolates.

For additional area entries, see **Little River**, just 2 miles away, and **Fort Bragg**, 8 miles north.

Agate Cove Inn ♿	*Tel:* 707–937–0551
11201 Lansing Street, P.O. Box 1150	800–527–3111
95460	*Fax:* 707–937–0550
	URL: http://www.agatecove.com

The main structure of this 1860s farmhouse was built by Mathias Brinzing, Mendocino's first brewer. The exterior of the building appears much as it did at the turn of the century; the candlestick fence still graces the entry garden. In 1994, the inn was purchased by Scott and Betsy Buckwald; the inn was handsomely redecorated in 1996 by a noted interior designer, and combines country-style furnishings with lavish use of designer fabrics. The family-style breakfasts, prepared on an antique woodstove, include home-baked bread or scones, fresh fruit and juice, jams and jellies, coffee and tea, plus an entree of omelets, cheese frittata, or French toast, with country sausage or baked ham. Rates also include in-room sherry and the morning newspaper.

"Gets my vote for the best situated inn in Mendocino, on a quiet street, yet an easy walk from town. Breathtaking views of ocean and cliffs; lovely gardens. Appealing guest and common rooms; ample privacy." *(SWS, also Mary Jane Campbell)* "In the afternoon, we relaxed on the front lawn in Adirondack chairs, looking out across the water, enjoying an excellent bottle of Anderson Valley wine, and strolling through the stunning gardens." *(Phill Emmert)* "Our room had a four poster bed, country decor, antiques and a wood-burning Franklin stove. The sherry decanter was replenished daily. The breakfast room has panoramic water views. Our first morning began with baked apples stuffed with cranberries and walnuts topped with vanilla yogurt, followed by hot quiche and home-fries, garnished with an edible flower." *(Merrily Basham)* "Magnificent ocean views from the dining room and some of the guest rooms. The garden is lovely, and the buildings are well-maintained. When we called for reservations, Joan, the resident innkeeper, provided an exceptionally clear description of the guest rooms." *(John Felton)*

Open All year.
Rooms 2 doubles in main house, 8 cottages—all with private bath and/or shower, writing table, TV/VCR, fireplace, deck. 1 with spa tub.
Facilities Dining room, living room with fireplace, games; guest pantry. 1½ acres with gardens, off-street parking.
Location Take Lansing St. exit off Hwy. 1. ½ m N of town center.
Restrictions No smoking. No children under 12.
Credit cards MC, Visa.
Rates B&B, $109–250 double. Extra person, $25. 2-night weekend minimum and 3-4 over holidays.
Extras Airport/station pickup. Wheelchair access; 1 room specially equipped.

Stanford Inn by the Sea	*Tel:* 707–937–5615
Big River Lodge 🛏 ♿ ✕	800–331–8884
44850 Comptche-Ukiah Road	*Fax:* 707–937–0305
and Highway One, P.O. Box 1487, 95460	

The Stanford Inn has been improved and enhanced every year since Joan and Jeff Stanford bought it in 1980. Their latest project—a longtime dream of Jeff's—was to open a vegetarian restaurant, Raven's, now open for breakfast and dinner. Their other endeavors include raising their two children, operating a canoe livery service, breeding llamas, and growing organic produce. Breakfast consists of fresh fruits and juices, oatmeal or granola, yogurt, home-baked pastries, and a choice of such entrees as blue corn waffles, vegetables scrambled with tofu and basil, omelets with goat cheese and butternut squash, or burritos with eggs or tofu and black beans. Rates also include afternoon tea, and evening hors d'oeuvres, served in the spacious common room, furnished with antiques and collectibles.

"Enjoyed the canoe ride and bicycling along the river path. Welcoming staff, excellent housekeeping." *(AJK)* "Beautifully landscaped hillside overlooking the ocean and the town. Plumbing is modern, with good water pressure; quality soaps and toiletries were supplied. The staff assisted us with restaurant advice and reservations." *(Timothy &*

Cynthia Egan) "While not large, my room was amply furnished with a four-poster king-size bed, great reading lamps, remote-control TV, and a sofa. The radio was playing, the fireplace was ready to light, there were chocolates, crackers with herb cheese dip, fresh flowers, and crystal decanter of red wine and two crystal wineglasses ready on the coffee table." *(Linda Goldberg)* "The indoor swimming pool is also a giant conservatory with flowering shrubs and trees, and translucent walls." *(Hugh & Marjorie Smith)* "We took our breakfast tray to our room to eat in privacy. At night, we left our window open and one of the friendly inn cats came to pay a welcome visit." *(MW)* "The inn's terraced grounds have organic vegetable and flower gardens, suppliers to many of Mendocino's best restaurants." *(SWS)* "Wonderful breakfast of poached eggs on portabello mushrooms, black pepper scone, and herbed potatoes." *(HAS)* "Each return visit allow us to renew previous pleasures and experience new ones. The Stanfords are gracious hosts." *(Joy & Howard Bauman)*

Open All year.

Rooms 5 2-bedroom suites, 4 1-bedroom suites, 1 cottage, 22 doubles—all with private bath and/or shower, telephone, radio, TV/VCR, desk, wood-burning fireplace, coffee maker, refrigerator, deck. Some with kitchen.

Facilities Restaurant, common room with fireplace, reception area; deck; videotape library; gift shop; dining room. 10 acres with enclosed heated greenhouse, swimming pool, sauna, hot tub; flower and vegetable gardens, horses, ducks, llamas. Mountain bicycles, fishing; canoe, kayak, outrigger rentals. Beaches, dock nearby.

Location ¼ m S of village, at corner of Hwy. 1 & Comptche-Ukiah Rd.

Restrictions No smoking in common areas.

Credit cards Amex, CB, DC, Discover, Enroute, MC, Optima, Visa.

Rates B&B, $250–625 suite, $215–275 double. Extra person, $35. 2–3 night weekend/holiday minimum. Gardening seminars, March–Oct. Off-season packages.

Extras Wheelchair access; bathroom equipped for disabled. Airport/station pickup. Pets permitted by arrangement, $25 per stay for first pet, $7.50 additional pets. Crib. French, German, Spanish spoken.

MONTEREY

Originally built up around the sardine fishing and canning business (which collapsed about 40 years ago), Monterey was first made famous by John Steinbeck's novel *Cannery Row*. The old cannery buildings have long been renovated and now house art galleries, antique shops, restaurants, and inns. Its newest attraction is the Monterey Bay Aquarium, an imaginatively designed building, that is now home to over 500 species of ocean life. Unfortunately, only a few of the side streets retain any real character; the rest is all for "show."

For more information on the Monterey peninsula, see the Central Coast section of the introduction to this chapter; for additional area entries, see **Pacific Grove**.

On scenic Highway One, Monterey is located about 120 miles south of San Francisco and 320 miles north of Los Angeles, on California's central coast. From Los Angeles, drive up Highway 101 to Salinas, then west on Route 66. If you have more time, take exit 101 at San Luis Obispo and stay on Highway One to Monterey. From San Francisco, take Highway 101 to Route 156 to Highway One, or stay on Highway One the whole way.

Reader tips: "Be warned that Cannery Row is wall-to-wall T-shirt shops and junk food carry-outs, and that there are long lines to get into the aquarium on weekend afternoons in summer; ask your innkeeper about obtaining tickets." *(SHW)* "Rent a bike and follow the rec path from Cannery Row along the water into Pacific Grove, and into Seventeen-Mile Drive, for breathtaking water views." *(RSS)*

Also recommended: Graceful adobe architecture and lush courtyard gardens highlight the **Hotel Pacific** (300 Pacific Street, 93940; 831–373–5700 or 800–554–5542). The 105 guest rooms are furnished with original art, goose-down featherbeds, hardwood floors, and wet bars; the double rates of $189–349 include a continental breakfast, afternoon tea, and nightly turndown. "Walking distance to the historic center of Monterey and Fisherman's Wharf. Our handsome junior suite had a kitchen, bedroom, and sitting areas, plus a fireplace. Generous breakfast buffet of pastries, cereal, fruit, yogurt, fresh orange juice, and more. Some traffic and airplane noise, but nothing significant." *(Duane Roller)*

Old Monterey Inn
500 Martin Street, 93940

Tel: 831–375–8284
800–350–2344
Fax: 831–375–6730
E-mail: omi@oldmontereyinn.com
URL: http://www.oldmontereyinn.com

A consistent reader favorite, the Old Monterey Inn is a half-timbered Tudor-style residence built in 1929, by the town's first mayor. It was bought in the 1960s by Ann and Gene Swett as their private home; as their six children grew up and moved out, their rooms were gradually redone as guest rooms. The inn is decorated with stained glass windows and skylights, period furniture, and family antiques; guests stay cozy with European goose-down comforters and featherbeds.

"Attention to detail is the hallmark of this inn, from the gorgeous gardens to the impeccable interior. Gene, Ann, and their staff welcome you warmly, and strive to make your stay special. Guests can choose to have the delicious breakfast served in the dining room by the roaring fireplace, delivered to their room, or enjoyed in the rose garden." *(Patricia & Charlie Bell)* "The Brightstone room is small but cozy, with charming French country decor. I relaxed on the chaise with a good book and a glass of wine. The armoire had a few nice surprises—old books, a writing desk, and thoughtful amenities. The little bathroom was fully stocked, and the corner window offered a pretty view through the trees to the garden. The first morning we had breakfast outside: their signature orange juice with banana slices, fruit compote, and baked crunchy French toast with orange marmalade sauce. After a day of exploring, it was pleasant to return to the inn and help ourselves to hors d'oeuvres and wine. The second morning was cooler, so we had breakfast in the lovely dining room: baked pear with mandarin oranges, and baked apple pancakes. Another nice touch is the stocked refrigerator on the second floor." *(Lynne Derry)* "Staff attentive to every detail. The wonderful garden enhances the sense of space and privacy. Our room had a luxurious featherbed, plenty of hot water, and a magnifying mirror in the bath. Casement windows, stained glass, and a Dutch door allowed us to enjoy the cool air. Social hour between 5–7 P.M.; hot and cold beverages always available." *(Sherry & Clif Daniel)*

"The fountain edged with carnations was a prelude to the beautiful gardens." *(Tom Wilbanks)* "The lavish breakfasts can be packed in a basket for those leaving before 9 A.M." *(Ellin Spitzer)* "The innkeepers prepare helpful newsletters with tips on picnicking, restaurants, and shopping." *(Jane & Rick Mattoon)* "We felt like we were visiting friends—if we had friends with impeccably decorated mansions with the most cordial of staff, that is. Enjoyed a breakfast of yogurt and granola, bread pudding, and shortbread. While not large, the Rookery is beautifully decorated in green and white florals, with a comfortable white wicker chairs, fireplace, skylight, and a beautifully tiled shower in the bathroom." *(SWS)* "Helpful, friendly staff; convenient parking; quiet location; delicious food." *(John & Jennifer Patterson)* "We treated ourselves to a stay in the newly redone cottage, complete with a double Jacuzzi with a marble surround." *(NJS)*

Open All year. Closed Dec. 25.

Rooms 1 suite, 8 doubles, 1 cottage—all with private bath and/or shower, radio. 9 with fireplace. Guest refrigerator, deck. 3 rooms with private entrance, double whirlpool tub.

Facilities Dining room, living room both with fireplace. 1 acre, flower gardens, sitting areas, hammocks, picnic area. Near Monterey Bay & Aquarium.

Location 4 blocks from center. From Hwy. 1 S, take Soledad-Munras Ave. exit. Cross Munras Ave., then go right on Pacific St. Go ½m to Martin St. on left. From Hwy. 1 N, take Munras Ave. exit. Take immediate left on Soledad Dr., then right on Pacific St. Go ½m to Martin St.

Restrictions No smoking.

Credit cards MC, Visa.

Rates B&B, $350 cottage, $280–300 suites, $200–260 double. Extra person (in suite only), $50. 2–3 night weekend/holiday minimum.

NAPA

Although Napa's founding about 100 years ago was due to the gold rush, today's gold flows from the wine industry and the extensive tourism industry that has developed along with it. The town is a popular base for wine touring—perhaps overly so during fall harvest weekends. Napa is located in the North Coast region, in Napa Valley Wine Country, just one hour north of San Francisco.

Reader tip: "If you have any money left after visiting the local wineries, the Napa Factory Outlet will be happy to slenderize your wallet further." *(MW)*

Also recommended: A twenty guest-room luxury inn, **La Residence** (4066 St. Helena Highway North, 94558; 707–253–0337) is characterized by its 1870 mansion and the French-style barn, decorated with antiques, designer fabrics, lush landscaping, and towering oak trees. Rates of $165–235 include a full breakfast, plus wine and hors d'oeuvres, served by the fire or outdoors by the swimming pool.

Churchill Manor ¢ ⚹   *Tel:* 707–253–7733
485 Brown Street, 94559   *Fax:* 707–253–8836

Churchill Manor is a magnificent three-story mansion built in 1889, now listed on the National Register of Historic Places, and restored as a B&B in 1987 by Joanna Guidotti and Brian Jensen. The manor encompasses 10,000 square feet, with seven fireplaces and 12-foot carved redwood ceilings and columns, and is decorated primarily with European antiques, Oriental rugs, and brass and crystal chandeliers. Breakfast includes omelets or perhaps French toast, afternoon fresh-baked cookies; rates also include afternoon tea and cookies, Napa Valley wines and cheeses from 5:30 to 7:30 each evening, and use of the inn's tandem bicycles.

"Gorgeous mansion, with charming, energetic innkeepers who are constantly working to improve their inn—upgrading bathrooms with oversize clawfoot tubs and double showers, adding fireplaces, and improving wheelchair accessibility. Brian and Joanna are friendly, hospitable, energetic, and gregarious innkeepers. Lots of common space, inside and out, for guests to relax in privacy or with the other guests. Despite the scale of this impressive mansion, the atmosphere is warm and friendly, not stiff and formal. The guest rooms are spacious, attractive, and well equipped. My favorite was Rose's Room (#4), done in soft shades of pink and cream, with exuberant floral wallpaper, a king-size bed, exquisite original tiling. There's an oversize clawfoot tub in the corner of the room, in addition to the private bath and shower. The less expensive rooms are one of the best buys in expensive Wine Country." *(SWS)* "Enjoyable stay; wonderful antiques throughout this beautiful home. Charming Christmas decorations. Cookies are set out during the day, and lovely cheese and wine are served in the afternoon." *(Carolyn Alexander)*

"The huge grounds were lovely, and the common areas were like something out of a different era (which they are)." *(Mark Mendenhall)* "After one early morning walk, we sat down to relax on one of the pretty wicker settees on the veranda overlooking the beautiful gardens." *(Wilfred Sweet)* "Beautiful bouquets of roses had been brought in from the garden. The breakfast room is sunny and cheerful with individual tables. We were served fresh fruit, juice, muffins, croissants, and a choice of French toast or an omelet." *(DG)* "Friendly cats." *(MW)* "A beautiful old house with friendly owners." *(Carol Blodgett)*

Open All year. Closed Dec. 24, 25.
Rooms 10 doubles—all with private bath and/or shower, telephone, radio, desk, air-conditioning. 5 with fireplace.
Facilities 3 living rooms with fireplace, games (1 with TV/VCR); music room with grand piano, fireplace; garden breakfast room, veranda. 1 acre near river.

Off-street parking. Tandem bicycles, croquet. Tennis, golf, health spa, wine train, mud baths, balloon rides nearby.

Location Nat'l. historic district, 4 blocks from center. From Hwy. 29, take Imola Ave. exit; go E to Jefferson; turn left & go ¾m to Oak; turn right & go 7 blocks to Brown. Manor on right corner.

Restrictions No smoking. Children over 12.

Credit cards Amex, Discover, MC, Visa.

Rates B&B, $95–195 double. Extra person, $25. 2-night minimum with Sat. stay.

Extras Wheelchair access; bathroom specially equipped. Spanish spoken.

NEVADA CITY

Founded in the heat of the gold rush, Nevada City remains one of the most picturesque towns along the Mother Lode. Victorian homes, white frame churches, and covered sidewalks still line the hilly streets, in spite of two fires that ravaged the town in the 1800s. Excellent restaurants and charming shops invite strolling and browsing. Nevada City is located in the Sierra foothills, approximately 50 minutes northeast of Sacramento, and 3 hours northeast of San Francisco. Nearby are golf, tennis, swimming, hiking, fishing, downhill and cross-country skiing, river rafting, and horseback riding, as well as a winery and brewery.

Ten miles north of Nevada City are the Malakoff Diggins, the site of the world's largest hydraulic gold mining operation where miners directed high-powered streams of water onto the hillsides. Effective as the practice was, entire mountainsides were washed away before some of the earliest environmental legislation stopped the destruction.

Information please: Built in 1863, **Flume's End B&B** (317 South Pine, 95959; 530–265–9665 or 800–991–8118) overlooks spring-fed Gold Run Creek. Although the furnishings of the inn's common areas are basic, its six bedrooms are appealing with country Victorian floral fabrics and wallcoverings, and modern baths. The cozy Creekside Room is cantilevered over the creek—you look through floor-to-ceiling windows to the rushing waters below. Breakfasts, served on the terrace deck, might include a smoked salmon and dill tart, spicy browned potatoes, and locally made sausage. Homemade fudge, brownies, and cookies are put out each evening to tempt guests. B&B double rates range from $80–140.

The Red Castle Inn   *Tel:* 530–265–5135
109 Prospect Street, 95959   800–761–4766

On a steep hillside overlooking Nevada City sits this dramatic four-story Gothic Revival redbrick mansion, dripping white icicle trim with elaborately carved balconies. Long-time owners Mary Louise and Conley Weaver have furnished this 1860 mansion with period antiques, historic memorabilia, and family heirlooms. Realizing that antique charm can end at the bathroom door, the Weavers redid all the inn's bathrooms in 1998, adding custom tilework, wainscoted walls, tall showers, and ample shelves for guests' toiletries; one bath has a deep soaking clawfoot tub.

A special feature at the Red Castle is the horse-drawn carriage ride through the historic district every Saturday morning; on special occasions, "Mark Twain" or "Lola Montez" will join guests for tea. Breakfast is served between 8–10 A.M. on weekends, and at 9:00 A.M. on other days; coffee is ready at 7:30.

"Mary Louise has a talent for decorating with comfortable and inviting antiques. Scrumptious breakfasts enjoyed on our private balcony, with specially blended coffee, fresh fruit, freshly baked breads, granola, and delicious egg dishes. In the afternoon, tempting sweets and a special ginger ale punch were served. Our well-maintained room was furnished in period, with a four-poster bed, dresser, and marble-top washstand. It's a comfortable walk down the lighted path to the main shopping and historic district, and two fine restaurants are just down a short walk away. The delightful garden has lots of areas to sit and chat with the other guests or to read in a secluded, fragrant corner." (Darlene Harper) "The gardens and walkways enhanced the quiet, beautiful, and restful atmosphere. The 'conversation with Mark Twain' was a highlight." (Anne & George Derfer) "Mary Louise has a wealth of wonderful knowledge about the house, its history, and furnishings. She has created a comfortable but authentic Victorian ambiance with lovely shawls draped over antique chairs and knickknacks. The grounds were lovely, with little ponds, beautiful plants, and Victorian gazing balls." (Sarah & Jan Williams) "Delicious grilled grapefruit with ginger at breakfast. Owners friendly and knowledgeable but not cloying." (David Kobosa)

"Thoughtful details included ice brought to our room, lovely background music, and books on the Gold Country everywhere." (Susan Payne) "Tasty breakfast with breakfast breads, rice pudding, orange compote, and a wonderful quiche." (Lois Revlock) "The Garret West was small but cozy, with a great view of the town. We enjoyed Mary Louise's stories about the Inn and its ghost (we didn't see her)." (Sharon Bielski) "The Rose Room opens onto a large hall where a delicious breakfast buffet was set out at 9:00 A.M., including an unusual cheese-tomato-egg dish, toast, yogurt breakfast cake, and berry cobbler." (Joyce Rinehart) "We were welcomed by Mary Louise, then shown to our room, with a handsome canopied bed and love seat. Across the hall in the living room, guests gathered for tea, a delicious whipped-cream cake, and chocolate nut cookies. In the morning, it was too chilly to eat outside, so we took our breakfast tray into the living room." (SWS)

Open All year.

Rooms 3 suites, 4 doubles—all with private shower and/or bath, ceiling fan. 4 with desk, air-conditioning. 2 with radio. Most with private balcony.

Facilities Parlor with pump organ. 1½ acres with terraced English rose gardens, three fountains, fish pond, footpaths, arbors, trellises, croquet, swing. Off-street parking.

Location Historic district, walking distance to downtown. From Hwy. 49, take Sacramento St. exit and turn right just past Chevron station. Turn left on Prospect St.

Restrictions No smoking. "Children must be carefully supervised." No candles in rooms.

Credit cards MC, Visa.
Rates B&B, $110–150 suite, $75–145 double, $70–140 single. Extra person, $20. 2-night holiday/weekend minimum April–Dec. Corporate rates. Christmas Dinner with entertainment.
Extras Airport/Amtrak connector pickup.

ORLAND

Also recommended: An ideal stopover for those traveling between California and Oregon, **The Inn at Shallow Creek Farm** (4712 County Road DD, P. O. Box 3176, 95963; 530–865–4093 or 800–865–4093) offers "a quiet location, close enough to the freeway so as not to get lost, but far enough away not to hear it." *(Norma & Mike McClintock)* Kurt and Mary Glaeseman have owned the farm since 1982, and in addition to the care and feeding of their guests, tend to citrus orchards and poultry flock. "Peaceful setting; comfortable accommodations and common areas; graciously served breakfast with homemade jams and jellies." *(Barbara Green)* B&B double rates for the four guest accommodations (two with private bath), range from $65–85. The inn is located less than three miles west of I-5, 100 miles north of Sacramento.

PACIFIC GROVE

Set on the Monterey Peninsula, bordering the town of Monterey, Pacific Grove begins at the Monterey Bay Aquarium on Cannery Row and extends along the bay to the beginning of the Seventeen-Mile Drive. Many think this is the peninsula's best town for bicycling and shore-walking. The town was founded by Methodists in 1875 as a "Christian seaside resort"; most of its Victorian inns were built during this period. Its rather stodgy character lingered on—until the late '60s, liquor could be bought in Pacific Grove only with a doctor's prescription. The town is filled with flowers in the spring, but its most famous site is "Butterfly Park" (George Washington Park), where thousands of monarch butterflies winter from October to March.

Pacific Grove is located about 120 miles south of San Francisco. For more information on the Monterey Peninsula, see listings for Monterey and Carmel (three miles away) as well as the Central Coast section of the introduction to this chapter.

Also recommended: Built in 1888, the **Green Gables** (104 Fifth Street, 93950; 408–375–2095 or 800–722–1774) is a half-timbered, many-gabled Queen Anne Victorian mansion with beautiful stained glass and leaded small-paned windows. Most of the eleven guest rooms have private baths, and are decorated with antiques, ruffled curtains, and wall-to-wall carpets. B&B double rates of $110–225 include a full breakfast; afternoon tea, wine, and hors d'oeuvres; a stocked refrigerator; and evening turndown service with chocolates. "Room #7 in the carriage house was spacious and well equipped; we could see the water, and hear the waves all night. Wonderful breakfasts." *(Julie Phillips)* "Helpful concierge service. Guests have the option of eating at tables for two, four, or six. An exceptionally well-run inn." *(Jim & Mary White)*

The Martine Inn   ♿   *Tel:* 408–373–3388
255 Oceanview Boulevard, 93950   800–852–5588
                                      Fax: 408–373–3896
                  URL: http://www.martineinn.com

Although built in 1899 as a Victorian cottage, the Martine Inn was remodeled over the years as a pink-stuccoed Mediterranean mansion. The inn was bought by the Martine family in 1972 and was opened as an inn by Marion and Don Martine in 1984. It has been fully restored and decorated in period, from authentic wall coverings to museum-quality antique furnishings. Breakfast is served from 8:00 to 10:00 A.M.; wine and hors d'oeuvres are offered from 6 to 8:00 P.M..

"Beautiful location overlooking the cliffs and the Pacific. The light, creative breakfast was nicely served, as were the evening refreshments. Lovely antiques throughout the Inn. Comfortable, well-lit rooms with windows that opened to enjoy the sea breeze. Pleasant staff." *(Sandy Truitt)* "Perfect location within walking distance of the aquarium, Cannery Row, and the Wharf. Right on the ocean with a jogging trail that goes along the shore for miles." *(F. T. McQuilkin)* "From the parlor, you get a magnificent view of the rocky coastline, while enjoying wine and hors d'oeuvres. Breakfast included fresh fruit, homemade muffins, a hot entree, and piping hot coffee." *(Mrs. Donald Hamilton)* "Elegant, romantic ambiance. Spectacular oceanfront setting, high above the street below. Incomparable water views. Lace-curtained French doors separated the bedroom and bath. Bedside lights made reading in bed a pleasure. A vase of roses and bowl of fresh fruit was set on our dresser. At night, our bed was turned down, a chocolate placed on each pillow. We fell asleep to the sounds of the gently pounding surf. The large dining room also has picture windows, with binoculars set on the windowsills to enhance viewing." *(Gail Davis)* "The Eastlake room is beautiful and private, with a view of the Pacific." *(Willie & Susan Geoghegan)* "Magnificent views from common areas and guest rooms. Beautiful antiques. Good location." *(SWS)*

Open All year.
Rooms 25 doubles—all with private bath and/or shower, telephone, desk, refrigerator. Many with fireplace. 6 rooms in adjacent house.
Facilities Dining room, parlor with fireplace, piano entertainment nightly; library with fireplace, conference room with TV/VCR, game room with pool table, 2 sitting rooms. Courtyard with fountain, garden, gazebo, hot tub. Fishing, jogging, bicycling, tennis, golf nearby. Limited on-site parking.
Location ¾ m from center, directly on Monterey Bay. 4 blocks to aquarium.
Restrictions Smoking permitted in guest rooms with fireplace only. "Children discouraged."
Credit cards Amex, Discover, MC, Visa.

Rates B&B, $150–295 double. Extra person, $35. 2–3 night weekend/holiday minimum. Picnic lunches on request.
Extras Wheelchair access; 1 room equipped for disabled. Airport/station pickup, $16.

PALM SPRINGS

Located in California's Desert Country, Palm Springs is 115 miles east of Los Angeles, 26 miles east of Joshua Tree National Monument. Palm Springs is famous for its warm and dry winter climate and its championship golf courses. For instant air-conditioning, the tramway to the top of the San Jacinto Mountains is also a favorite; you can even cross-country ski there in winter. Hiking in nearby Palm Canyon, home to trees over a thousand years old, is also popular. Because summer is very definitely off-season here, rates drop considerably during the hottest months. Palm Canyon Drive (Highway 111) is the main street in town, and most directions use it as a point of reference.

Reader tips: "Be aware of the college 'spring break'; Palm Springs gets a bit noisy when overrun with students, motorcycles, and police." Also: "Be aware that the desert can be windy."

Also recommended: Decorated in Santa Fe style, **Casa Cody Country Inn** (175 South Cahuilla Road, 92262; 760–320–9346) is situated at the base of Mount San Jacinto—away from the bustle of downtown but within walking distance of shops and restaurants. Many of the one- and two-bedroom units have kitchens and wood-burning fireplaces. "Our high-ceilinged casita had a king-size bed (twin beds skillfully put together), saltillo tile floors, color TV, a full kitchen, a private shower bath supplied with thick towels, and French doors leading to a totally private fenced yard. The lush landscaping and the inn's location at the base of the mountains were spectacular. Peaceful, relaxing atmosphere; I enjoyed reading and lounging at one of the inn's two pools." *(Gail Davis)* A continental breakfast is served around the pool. "A bargain and just a short block to the main drag. Spacious rooms, simply furnished." *(Ruth Tilsley)* B&B double rates range from $49–199.

Twelve miles north in Desert Hot Springs is the **Travellers Repose** (66920 First Street, P.O. Box 655, Desert Hot Springs, 92240; 760–329–9584). Built in 1986, this neo-Victorian home is complete with gingerbread trim and fish-scale shingles. The interior decor includes iron and brass beds, country-floral wallpapers, and hardwood floors. B&B double rates for the three guest rooms, each with private bath, are $65–99, including a home-baked breakfast and afternoon tea.

Information please: Two adjacent villas—one Mediterranean, the other Moroccan, comprise the **Korakia Pensione** (257 South Patencio Road, 92262; 760–864–6411), with twenty lovely guest rooms surrounding garden courtyards. Most rooms have full kitchens; some have fireplaces. Continental breakfast is served in the garden, where fruit trees surround tiled Moroccan fountains and a swimming pool. B&B double rates range from $99–239.

The Willows Historic Palm Springs Inn
412 West Tahquitz Canyon Way, 92262

Tel: 760–320–0771
E-mail: innkeeper@
thewillowspalmsprings.com
URL: http://www.thewillowspalmsprings.com

Albert Einstein slept here, and so did Carole Lombard and Clark Gable, and while owners Tracy Conrad and Paul Marut can't promise you either brilliance or beauty, they can assure you of comfortable accommodations in a lovely setting, good food, welcoming hospitality, and excellent service. The Willows was built in 1927 as the private winter getaway of New York attorney and human rights activist Sam Untermeyer, and was later owned by Marion Davies, lifelong mistress of newspaper magnate William Randolph Hearst. When Tracy and Paul—both emergency room physicians—first saw the mansion in 1995, it needed immediate emergency attention as well. Abused and neglected, the mansion needed huge transfusions of cash and careful renovation to restore its original elegance. Tracy supervised the work personally, overseeing the restoration of the mahogany beams of the Great Hall, the frescoed ceiling of the dining room, and much more, complementing these fine architectural details with elegant fabrics and antique furnishings.

Breakfast, served 8–10 A.M. at individual tables, varies daily, but might include puffed pancakes, baked eggs with white truffles and Parmesan, pecan praline bacon, and apple sausages. Rates also include evening wine and hors d'oeuvres, served 4–7 P.M. Guests have the option of having lunch or dinner from Le Vallauris—an excellent French restaurant located across the street—served to them at the inn.

"Comfortable and luxurious, yet low-key and unpretentious. Breakfast is served in the beautiful and comfortable dining room with an entire glass wall just a few feet from a dramatic 50-foot waterfall that flows over the rocky hillside." *(John Gartland)* "Delicious wine and hors d'oeuvres served in a lovely homey atmosphere before a fireplace glowing with real logs." *(Raquel Ross)* "In the evening, we followed a path up the hill behind the inn to a sitting area where we enjoyed the cool night air and the city lights below. The inn's lap pool and hot tub are supplied with lots of large fluffy towels." *(Mary Seward)* "Quiet setting, just a block from Palm Springs' main street. Luxurious antique furniture, hardwood floors, armoires, four-poster beds, wood paneling, rich rugs, and French doors in a 1920s and 30s atmosphere. Comfortable beds, luxurious linens. Our bathroom had a spacious shower; the water poured straight down from above, like a warm rainstorm. The house is built with the stone stucco and tile roof of desert architecture, surrounded by palm trees, bougainvillea, desert flowers, and citrus trees. Immaculate throughout, with friendly, efficient staff." *(Lee Hubbard)* "Careful attention to detail; sensitive to guests' needs for privacy; responsive to social interaction." *(Ellen Palo)*

Open All year. "Abbreviated hours July/Aug."
Rooms 8 doubles—all with private bath and/or shower, telephone, clock/radio, TV, desk, air-conditioning. 4 with fireplace, refrigerator; 2 with balcony/deck.

Facilities Dining room with fireplace, living room with fireplace, piano, library; porch, veranda. Pianist in evening. 1 acre with heated pool, hot tub, gazebo, locked off-street parking.
Location From Los Angeles, take I-10 to Hwy. 111 to Palm Springs. Becomes Palm Canyon Dr. in town. Go right on Tahquitz Canyon Way to inn on right. Adjacent to Desert Museum.
Restrictions *Absolutely no smoking whatsoever.* Children over 16.
Credit cards Amex, CB, DC, Discover, MC, Visa.
Rates B&B, $175–550 double. 10% AAA discount. Alc lunch, $15; dinner, $50 (at La Vallauris).
Extras Airport/station pickup. French, Spanish spoken.

SACRAMENTO

Sacramento was founded by John Sutter, who is best known as the man on whose property gold was discovered in 1848, precipitating the great California Gold Rush of 1849. The town grew into a key supply source for the northern Mother Lode country and was named the state capital in 1854. It remains a major transportation hub to this day. It has a few sights of interest—the State Capitol, Sutter's Fort, Old Sacramento, and the California State Railroad Museum—but most Sacramento visitors come for the business of government or the business of business. Those who want to get out of town enjoy swimming, fishing, and rafting in the nearby Sacramento and American rivers.

Sacramento is located in Gold Country, 90 miles northeast of San Francisco and 90 miles southwest of Lake Tahoe. The center city is laid out in a grid pattern of numbered and lettered streets, with the former running east/west and the latter running north/south.

Information please: Abigail's (2120 G Street, 95816; 916–441–5007 or 800–858–1568) is a 1912 Colonial Revival mansion owned by Susanne and Ken Ventura, who describe their inn as being "especially good for the business traveler. Since this is our home, we have all the little things people tend to forget—an iron or hair dryer, aspirin, razors, and so on. They also enjoy the extra touches—beds turned down, evening tea and hot chocolate, and extra-soft towels." All rooms have private baths, and the $115–165 double rates include a full breakfast. Reports appreciated.

Amber House B&B
1315 22nd Street, 95816

Tel: 916–444–8085
800–755–6526
Fax: 916–552–6529
E-mail: innkeeper@amberhouse.com
URL: http://www.amberhouse.com

Amber House, a brown Craftsman-style home from the early 1900s, has been owned by Jane and Michael Richardson since 1987. The inn has the original stained glass windows and distinctive woodwork of the period, and is furnished with Oriental rugs, velvet wingback chairs, antiques, and collectibles. Guest rooms have antique beds and patterned wallpapers; fresh flowers accent the colorful glass in the windows. The renovated 1913 bungalow next door offers marble-tiled bathrooms with Jacuzzi tubs for two. A third building—an 1895 Colonial Revival home—was renovated in 1997, and offers five equally luxurious rooms with marble bathrooms, some with whirlpool tubs, fireplaces, and/or a deck overlooking the delightful garden. Rates include early morning coffee and a full breakfast served in the dining room, on the veranda, or in your room.

"The spacious Renoir Room has a comfortable king-size bed, TV/VCR in an armoire, and the best lighting we've encountered in our B&B travels; the tiled bathroom had a large Jacuzzi. Coffee and newspaper were at our door at 7 A.M., followed by scrumptious breakfasts with freshly baked croissants; bedtime cookies are brought to your room." (Happy Copley) "The library is stocked with books and local restaurant menus, and sherry is always available. At 5 P.M., Michael joined us for wine in the living room and we chatted about area attractions and restaurants." (JoAnn Davis) "Accented by blue stained glass windows, the dining room was a perfect setting for Michael's hearty breakfast of melon with poppy seed dressing, followed by fluffy scrambled eggs with scallions and cream cheese, potatoes sauteed in lemon pepper, and a ham-and-cheese croissant. The inn's residential location is quiet and convenient, a medium walk or an easy drive downtown." (SWS) "The Lord Byron Room had a marvelous marble bath and Jacuzzi. Hospitable, genuinely caring hosts, excellent breakfasts." (MR) "Spotless; careful attention to detail. Friendly staff, excellent service; easy parking." (Carrie Hagerty)

Open All year.
Rooms 14 doubles—all with full private bath, robes, telephone with voice mail, radio/cassette players. TV, desk, air-conditioning. 11 with double Jacuzzi tub, VCR; 3 with fireplace. Guest rooms in 3 adjacent buildings.
Facilities 3 living rooms with fireplace, 2 dining rooms, library, veranda, patio, meeting room. Bicycles. Garden weddings.
Location Midtown. 7 blocks E of Capitol building, between Capitol Ave. and N St. 8 blocks to convention center.
Restrictions No smoking.
Credit cards All major.
Rates B&B, $129–249 double, $119–179 single. Extra person, $20. Corporate rates.

ST. HELENA

St. Helena is located 60 miles north of San Francisco, in the Napa Wine Valley region of the North Coast. Although there are many things to do in the area, the main activity is visiting wineries—there are nine in St. Helena alone. Keep in mind that this area is extremely popular from June through October, especially on weekends. Try November, April, and May for good weather and smaller crowds.

For more information, see the North Coast section of the chapter introduction and the listings for Calistoga.

Also recommended: For an elegant small resort, suitable both for families or romantic escapes, the **Meadowood Resort** (900 Meadowood Lane, 94574; 707–963–3646 or 800–458–8080) may be a good choice. Although reminiscent of an old-style Adirondack lodge or Newport cottage, Meadowood was originally built as a private country club in the 1960s, and was expanded into a full-scale luxury resort in the 1980s. Guest rooms are clustered in gabled cottages scattered around the grounds, while the main lodge is home to an elegant restaurant and a more casual grill. In addition to a heated swimming pool, 7 tennis courts, a 9-hole golf course, hiking trails, a fitness center, and a playground, Meadowood has two championship croquet courts, with a resident teaching pro. Double rates for the 85 guest rooms range from $310–675, one-bedroom suites to $825, with packages available. "Quiet country setting just off the Silverado trail; charming Craftsman-style bungalows scattered in the wooded hillside house the restaurants, meeting rooms, and 100 guest rooms. Guest rooms are spacious and handsome, equipped with all amenities, as you would expect in this price range." *(SWS)*

The well-known **Auberge du Soleil** (180 Rutherford Hill Road, Rutherford, 94573; 707–963–1211 or 800– 348–5406), is located about 5 miles south of St. Helena. Its restaurant is famous for creative California cuisine, and the 48 luxurious guest rooms occupy a series of elegant cottages with stunning views of the Napa Valley, plus such amenities as fridges stocked with champagne and juices, a wet bar with coffee maker, whirlpool baths, lounging robes, and fireplaces. The 33 acres offer a heated swimming pool, hot tub, 3 tennis courts, health spa, bicycles, and hot air ballooning. B&B double and suite rates range from $300–900; private cottages to $2000.

Information please: A sister property to Meadowood, the **Inn at Southbridge** (1020 Main Street, Highway 29, 94574; 707–967–9400 or 800–520–6800) takes its inspiration from the small town squares of Europe, and is located in town. The 21 guest rooms are designed with vaulted ceilings and fireplaces; French doors open onto private balconies with views of the courtyard and the vineyards. A short walk away is the noted restaurant Tra Vigne. Guests may take advantage of all of Meadowood's facilities, a few miles away. B&B double rates range from $235–445, including a continental breakfast.

SAN DIEGO

San Diego is located in southernmost coastal California, 127 miles south of Los Angeles and about 20 miles north of Tijuana, Mexico. For many years a sleepy coastal town, San Diego didn't really start to grow until World War II, when the U.S. Navy moved its headquarters from Honolulu to San Diego. Since then, the city has grown to become California's second largest. San Diego's climate is arguably one of the best in America—very little rain, with an average winter temperature in the mid-60s and summer in the mid-70s. Major sights of interest include

Balboa Park's many museums, the world-famous zoo, Old Town San Diego, Cabrillo National Monument, Sea World, the Maritime Museum, and trips on the Tijuana Trolley to Mexico.

To make sure you're getting the best rate available, it's worth calling **San Diego Hotel Reservations** (619–627–9300 or 800–SAVE–CASH), offering discounted rates at over 250 hotels throughout San Diego County, including several recommended here.

Reader tips: "We enjoyed dinners at Cafe Bacco, close to the U.S. Grant Hotel, at Croce's in the Gaslamp Quarter, and at Poehe's on Coronado Island, about a block from the ferry landing." *(KLH)* "The Gaslamp Quarter is a lively scene. We had a wonderful dinner at an Italian restaurant called Fio's. The district is quite safe and heavily patrolled, but not far away are some rough neighborhoods, so stay within the tourist area." *(JMW)* "We were told that air-conditioning is not necessary here, but during our August visit, they had an atypical heat wave, and the un-conditioned air in our room was uncomfortably warm." *(RW)* "Due to the airport and military bases, airplane noise is fairly common." *(MW)*

Also recommended: The **Balboa Park Inn** (3402 Park Boulevard, 92103; 619–298–0823 or 800–938–8181; www.balboaparkinn.com) is a complex of four pale pink Spanish Colonial-style buildings with a variety of individually furnished rooms, each with queen-, king-, or twin-size beds and a sitting area. The furnishings range from Spanish to Southwestern, Victorian to country, and the rates include continental breakfast and the daily paper. In addition to its pleasant ambience and reasonable rates (rooms range from $85–200), the inn's key advantage is its convenient location across the street from Balboa Park. Balboa Park is the cultural hub of San Diego and offers a full range of sport and cultural activities, including seven museums, the famous San Diego Zoo, and the Old Globe Theater. "Perfect location, pleasant service, adequate accommodations, tasty breakfast brought to the room." *(Joanne Ashton)*

For more information on San Diego area accommodations, see listings under **La Jolla,** 20 minutes north of the city.

Heritage Park Inn ♿	*Tel:* 619–299–6832
2470 Heritage Park Row, 92110	800–995–2470
	Fax: 619–299–9465
	E-mail: innkeeper@heritageparkinn.com
	URL: http://www.heritageparkinn.com

Heritage Park is a seven-acre site, home to seven classic period structures from the 1800s. The buildings, originally located on Third Avenue in San Diego, were saved from the wrecker's ball and moved here in 1978. The B&B is a 1889 Queen Anne mansion, adorned with a variety of chimneys, shingles, a corner tower, and encircling veranda. In 1992, the inn was bought by longtime San Diego residents Nancy and Charles Helsper. Rooms are furnished with 19th-century antiques, and rates include breakfast, afternoon social hour, and a classic film shown in the parlor, evenings at 7 P.M. Breakfast is served by candlelight in the dining room at 8:30 A.M., and a typical menu might include Victorian French toast with apple cider syrup and sour cream-peach coffee cake; plus homemade granola, yogurt, fruit, juice, coffee, and herbal teas. A light continental breakfast is available for those leaving earlier.

"Our room had a plump featherbed and a teddy bear on the bed, with soft lighting. At breakfast we were seated with placecards and could meet the other guests; the food was delicious. Efficient staff, helpful with all requests. Beds were turned down each evening with chocolates and a rose. Quiet setting, yet convenient location, with public transportation nearby; easy parking." *(Sue & Steve Bond)* "The two-bedroom Manor Suite was clean, attractive, with lots of extras: an ironing board and iron, hair dryer, drinks in the fridge. Tasty afternoon tea with finger sandwiches, fruit, and cookies. Tasty breakfast of chicken-filled crepes. Our children were welcomed with chocolate chip cookies. Nancy greeted us on arrival and helped serve breakfast." *(Ruth Hurley)*

"Delightful meeting the other guests and sharing stories over afternoon tea. Conversation continued at breakfast, as we lingered over fresh fruit, orange juice, apple crepes." *(Joanne & Chuck Edmondson)* "Beautifully coordinated wallpapering and stenciling throughout the house." *(Anne Mietzel)* "Loved the crab souffle and raspberry almond scones." *(Jeannie Bell)* "An easy stroll downhill to Old Town, the trolley, sight-seeing, and dining. The innkeepers helped with restaurant and concert reservations. Comfortable wicker furniture on the veranda, perfect for afternoon tea, reading, and enjoying the view." *(Peggy Kontak)* "Nancy and Charles go out of their way to accommodate business travelers. Fax lines have been placed in all the rooms; and desks or tables provide working space for laptops. Attention to detail includes ironed sheets and pillowcases; robes, bath salts, and shampoo; plus fruit, cookies, tea, and coffee always available. The inn feels safe and secure; parking is convenient and well lighted." *(Linda Jones)*

Open All year.

Rooms 1 family suite, 10 doubles—all with private bath and/or shower, radio, clock, telephone, desk. 3 with fan or fireplace. Suite with double Jacuzzi. Suite in adjacent building.

Facilities Parlor with fireplace, TV/VCR, dining room, guest refrigerator, veranda. Meeting room. Croquet. In 7-acre Victorian park. Off-street parking.

Location 1 block to Old Town. 2 m from downtown. Follow I-5 to Old Town Ave. exit. Turn left on San Diego Ave., right on Harney to Heritage Park to inn on right.

Restrictions No smoking.

Credit cards MC, Visa.

Rates B&B, $225 suite, $90–160 double, single. 15% senior, AAA discounts. 2-night weekend minimum. Candlelight dinner, $110 per couple plus 15% service. Special occasion packages.

Extras First floor wheelchair accessible; bathroom specially equipped. Spanish, French, German spoken.

SAN FRANCISCO

Romanticized in song, hyped in commercials, featured in movies and sitcoms, San Francisco is everything promised and more. Compact, ethnically diverse, culturally rich, filled with wonderful stores, cable cars, and restaurants, it's what every city should aspire to be. The weather is best in late summer and early fall, but you don't come here to get a tan, so what does it matter? Bring your walking shoes and a sweater (even summer can be cool), and explore everything. Less well known but worth visiting are the exquisite Japanese Tea Garden and Asian Art Museum in Golden Gate Park and the museums and bookstores at North Beach. Watch the sea lions from Cliff House near Point Lobos Avenue.

For discount rates of 10 to 60% at many San Francisco hotels and B&Bs, including several listed here, call **San Francisco Reservations** (22 Second Street, 4th floor, 94105; 415–227–1500 or 800–677–1500) or **California Reservations** (3 Sumner Street, 94103; 415–252–1107 or 800–576–0003). California Reservations also handles properties in the Wine Country, Carmel area, and other cities.

Reader tips: "San Francisco has excellent public transportation, even by East Coast standards, and it's a very economical and practical alternative. Parking costs $10–20 a day, and in some areas, on-street parking requires you to move your car every two hours 8 A.M. to 9 P.M." *(Adam Platt)* Also: "San Francisco is noisy at all hours. If you're a light sleeper, be sure to let the innkeeper know when making reservations!" *(SHW)* "Even in San Francisco's newly renovated hotels, all rooms are *not* created equal. If you are shown a room that is too small, noisy, musty-smelling, or whatever, politely note that it simply won't do and ask to be shown another." (BI) "North Beach is a great multicultural neighborhood, with busses and cable cars nearby for convenient transportation. Fantastic Italian and Chinese restaurants abound, and there are many bars with music on the weekend." *(KMC)*

Also recommended: The **Monticello Inn** (127 Ellis Street, 94102; 415–392–8800 or 800–669–7777) has patterned its decor after its namesake, with Colonial reproduction furnishings and Williamsburg colors. B&B double rates for the 91 guest rooms range from $115–195. In addition to valet parking, the inn offers a free morning transportation to the financial district. "Room charming and spotless; luxurious bath. Inviting public spaces with two fireplaces. The breakfast buffet nicely set up with juice, coffee, breads, and cold cereals plus an ample supply of morning papers." *(Ruth Tilsley)* "Small, pretty, and quiet yet just a block from tons of activity. *(Randi Rubin)* "Good location, close to Union Square. Lovely, spacious lobby." *(SWS)*

Readers are delighted with the **Washington Square Inn** (1660 Stockton Street, 94133; 415–981–4220 or 800–388–0220), which is located in the Italian District of North Beach, almost midway between Fisherman's Wharf and Union Square. The 16 guest rooms are decorated with English and French antiques, and the B&B double rates of $120–200 include continental breakfast, afternoon tea, wine, and hors d'oeuvres; valet parking is $20 daily. "Just as delightful on a return visit—one of my favorite inns. My second floor room had a window seat with a view of Coit Tower. Inner rooms are quieter, but lack the view; front rooms may be noisy." *(KMC)* "We had breakfast sent up to our room each day (no extra charge), and it always arrived at the time requested. Our quiet, inside room had a small sitting area with a sofa, a king-size bed, an armoire, dresser, small TV with remote, and a telephone. The bath needed a touch of sprucing up, but had an excellent shower. If you are an early riser, you can join those doing Tai Chi in the park." *(WAG, also Michael Crick)*

Also recommended—nearby: Two favorite B&Bs are just 30 minutes south of the city and west of the San Francisco airport, on the ocean side of the San Francisco peninsula, and are ideal spots to begin or end your San Francisco trip, or to use as a base for exploring both the city and the coast. The **Seal Cove Inn** (221 Cypress Avenue, Moss Beach, 94038; 650–728–4114) overlooks a field of wildflowers, with the ocean in the distance. Constructed in 1991, the inn has handsomely decorated guest rooms, in a variety of styles from English country to American Amish. "Careful attention to detail throughout. Our room had a king-size bed, fireplace, high ceilings, large windows, thick carpeting, a VCR, and a double Jacuzzi tub." *(Abigail Humphrey & Karl Sikkenga)* "All the comforts of modern construction, all the warmth and charm of a well-run inn." *(SWS)* B&B double rates for the 10 guest rooms range from $180–260 and include a full breakfast and afternoon snacks.

Equally welcoming is **The Goose & Turrets B&B** (835 George Street, P.O. Box 370937, Montara, 94037-0937; 650–728–5451), a Northern Italian villa-style home built in 1908. B&B double rates for the five guest rooms range from $105–145. "Spotless, quiet, and comfortable. Excellent and unobtrusive service, convenient and abundant parking. Lovely yard, faultless plumbing, plenty of good reading material. Friendly atmosphere; marvelous multi-course breakfasts." *(Frank Mayer, Jr.)* "Charming, original, well-traveled innkeepers. A tea-drinker's mecca." *(SWS)*

Hotel Vintage Court ¢ ♀ ✕ ♿
650 Bush Street, 94108

Tel: 415–392–4666
800–654–1100
Fax: 415–433–4065
URL: http://www.vintagecourt.com

A reader favorite, this appealing little hotel is located a few blocks from Union Square, just off the Powell Street cable-car line. Always available coffee and tea service, plus afternoon wine-tasting are included in the hotel's reasonable rates. For dinner, guests may want to try Masa's, one of the city's top French restaurants, with possibly the largest selection of California wines. Guest rooms are named for Napa and Sonoma vineyards, and feature artwork and an information binder of the wineries.

"Our spacious twin room was decorated in an appealing dark flowered chintz and had good reading lights, a comfortable chair, and ample closet space." *(CM)* "Our room was small but comfortable and charming. Accommodating staff, excellent location. We enjoyed sipping wine by the fire and meeting the other guests." *(Nancy Sinclair)* "Pretty lobby with lighted fireplace and gracious staff; quick and courteous check-in. Our spacious eighth-floor room had a lovely window seat and adequately sized bathroom. We enjoyed hearing the not-too-distant clang of the passing cable cars." *(Gail Davis)* "Safe, convenient, appealing neighborhood. Lovely lobby where wine was served each afternoon. Our recently redecorated room was delightful, done in vibrant pink and green florals." *(Betsy Immergut)* "Friendly and personable employees. This hotel does all the little things without being asked." *(Philip Houser)* "Delightful property. Pleasant staff, cheerful hallways. If you're used to city noises, ask for one of the bright and sunny room on the street side; if not, you'll sleep better with an inside room. " *(SWS)*

Worth noting: We have also had positive reports on other hotels in the Kimpton Group, including the **Bedford**, the **Monticello**, and the **Prescott**.

Open All year. Restaurant closed Sun., Mon., also Dec. 25 through 2nd week of Jan.

Rooms 1 suite, 106 doubles, singles—all with private bath and/or shower, telephone with voice mail, clock/radio, TV, desk, air-conditioning, minibar, cable TV, pay-per-view movies, hairdryer, irons/ironing boards. Suite with fireplace, Jacuzzi.

Facilities Lobby with fireplace; restaurant; meeting room. Room service (through outside service) 11 A.M. to midnight. Valet, laundry services. Health club facilities nearby. Parking garage ½ block away, $16.

Location Nob Hill/Union Square. 1½ blocks N of Union Sq., between Powell & Stockton. 10-min. walk to financial district; 5 min. to Chinatown.

Restrictions Smoking in designated areas only. Double-glazed windows in streetside rooms.

Credit cards All major cards.

Rates Room only, $275 suite, $129–169 double. Extra person, $10. AARP discount. Corporate rates. Prix fixe dinner, $70 & $75. Continental breakfast, $8.

Extras Wheelchair access; some rooms equipped for the disabled. Crib, baby-sitting. Spanish, Tagalog, Chinese spoken. Member, Kimpton Group. Complimentary morning limo service to/from financial district.

SANTA BARBARA

With its crystal-clear skies and steady 65-degree temperatures, Santa Barbara has been a popular winter seaside resort for over 50 years. The rest of the year has always been just as nice, with summer temperatures rarely exceeding the 70s, but people have only recently begun to discover Santa Barbara's year-round appeal. Most activities here are connected with the ocean—the beautiful beaches are ideal for swimming, surfing, diving, sailing, as well as whale and seal watching—but the city is also becoming known as an arts center, with several museums and galleries of interest. In addition to lots of lovely shops, Santa Barbara is the place to go for some of California's best food. Of course, there's no shortage of golf courses or tennis courts either.

The city's appearance is generally Spanish—adobe walls and red-tiled roofs abound. Part of this is because of the city's Spanish heritage—it was ruled by Spain for over 60 years—but a 1925 earthquake, which leveled much of the town, is also responsible. When rebuilding began, the local Architectural Board determined that Spanish, not Victorian, style would prevail.

Santa Barbara is located at the southern end of California's Central Coast, 91 miles north of Los Angeles, via Highway 101, and 335 miles south of San Francisco. Weekend traffic coming up from LA can be heavy.

Worth noting: Santa Barbara is an expensive town; $100–150 per night gets you adequate, not luxurious, accommodations. If you'll be in Santa Barbara during the week on business, don't make a reservation without inquiring about corporate rates; nearly every establishment offers them. Rates also tend to be 10 to 20 percent lower from October to May.

Reader tip: "Fun, excellent lunch at Matte's Tavern in Los Olivos; superior dinner at the Montecito Inn Cafe." *(Ruthie Tilsley)*

Also recommended: Named for characters in *Alice in Wonderland*, **The Cheshire Cat Inn** (36 West Valerio Street, 93101; 805–569–1610; www.cheshirecat.com) occupies two of Santa Barbara's oldest adjoining homes. Most of the 14 guest accommodations have Laura Ashley–style fabrics and sitting areas highlighted with English antiques. Breakfast includes freshly squeezed orange juice, baked apples with yogurt, just-baked breads, pastries, an egg casserole or quiche; locally made chocolates and imported cordials are placed in each guest room as a welcome gift. The inn is located within a pleasant walk of Santa Barbara's shops and restaurants. B&B rates range from $140–300, with a midweek corporate rate of $89.

Travelers who steer clear of B&Bs because of enforced early-morning camaraderie will enjoy the **Glenborough** (1327 Bath Street, 93101; 805–966–0589 or 888–962–0589; www.silcom.com/~glenboro). A delicious full breakfast is delivered to each room between 8:30–9:30 A.M. The inn comprises a 1906 Craftsman-style building with beveled glass windows and cross-cut oak beams, plus two Victorian cottages across the street. Guest rooms are decorated with queen-size brass, iron, or canopy beds, and floral fabrics. Guests enjoy gathering for wine and hors d'oeuvres from 5–6 P.M.; tea and cookies are available after dinner. B&B double rates range from $100–250. "Charming, spotless, private. A gated entrance led to our suite with its own private garden and hot tub." *(Randi Rubin)*

Simpson House Inn ♿
121 East Arrellega Street, 93101

Tel: 805–963–7067
800–676–1280
Fax: 805–564–4811
E-mail: SimpsonHouse@compuserve.com
URL: http://www.simpsonhouseinn.com

Owned by Glyn and Linda Davies since 1976, Simpson House consists of a beautifully restored 1874 Eastlake Victorian home, a renovated 1878 barn, and three garden cottages. This luxurious B&B has earned a five-diamond rating from AAA—the only one in the U.S. as far as we know. Served between 8:30–9:30 A.M., a typical breakfast might include baked pears with whipped cream, eggs with garden herbs, and scones with lemon curd and raspberry preserves. The extensive evening wine and Mediterranean hors d'oeuvres buffet offers such temptations as marinated mushrooms, focaccia with pesto and sun-dried tomatoes, baked Brie, olive tapenade with sourdough toast, and vegetable antipasto. Rates also include a free 90-minute trolley pass, and evening turndown service with chocolate truffles.

"The staff greets us with a smile, and are ready to accommodate any special requests. There is always a warm or cool drink to enjoy and some delicious treat awaiting us. Although our favorite cottage is Abbeywood, we have also enjoyed the beautiful Hayloft with its pitch-beamed ceiling and lovely view of the garden. The rooms and baths are always impeccably clean, the beds piled high with pillows and down comforters. The fire needs only a match to start, wonderful tapes are there for our favorite music, and warm robes wait in the closet. One can walk, bike, or take the State Street trolley to shops and restaurants." *(Geoff & Carole Gillie)* "Each cottage is secluded behind a veil of lush flowers, plants, and assorted hedges; the gurgle of running water mixes with the subtle sounds of classical music. We enjoy the whirlpool bubble bath, and sip complimentary glasses of wine from a local vineyard. Requests to the staff are handled immediately, restaurant reservations made, and directions provided. Breakfasts are fresh and creative, hors d'oeuvres unique and plentiful. The evening often ends sipping a glass of port on the rear veranda. " *(Jeffrey Weber)*

"Huge living and dining room with beautiful Oriental rugs. Guest rooms in the main house are decorated with lovely antiques; the handsome barn suites have king-sized beds and a rustic country look, accented with antique farm equipment." *(SWS)* "A magnificent breakfast of freshly squeezed orange juice and blintzes topped with luscious strawberries was delivered to the private patio of our cottage at the time specified." *(Ron Kahan)* "Attentive staff. A lightbulb over our vanity was changed within minutes. Fresh orchids in every room." *(Jill Hennes)* "A minor plumbing problem was fixed within the hour, and a bottle of wine was sent to us as an apology for the inconvenience. Wonderful thick, fluffy towels changed twice daily." *(Yvonne Stoner)* "The standard by which we measure all other inns." *(Christine Lungren-Maddalone)*

Open All year.

Rooms 3 cottages, 4 suites, 7 doubles—all with private bath and/or shower, desk, telephone, air-conditioning. 4 suites in restored barn—all with telephone, TV/VCR, wet bar, fireplace, deck. Cottages with fireplace, stereo, hair dryer, double Jacuzzi tub, TV/VCR, patio with fountain.

Facilities Dining room, living room with fireplace, library, porch. 1 acre, garden, sitting areas, croquet, picnic area. Bicycles, beach equipment. On-site spa services; gym, pool, health club nearby. Golf, tennis nearby.

Location 5 blocks from center. From Hwy. 101 N take Garden St. exit. Go right 13 blocks then left on Arrellega St. From Hwy. 101 S take Mission St. exit. Go left on State St., left on Arrellaga St.

Restrictions No smoking.

Credit cards Amex, Discover, MC, Visa.
Rates B&B, $330–360 cottage, $315–365 suite, $160–270 double. Extra person, $25. 2-3 night weekend/holiday minimum.
Extras Wheelchair access. French, Danish, Spanish spoken.

SUTTER CREEK

Sutter Creek is located in Gold Country, in Amador County, about 45 minutes west of Stockton and Sacramento and 2½ hours from San Francisco. In addition to gold panning, visitors look for gold of another sort in the liquid found at the many area wineries.

Reader tip: "Stop for afternoon tea at Somewhere in Time, a combined antique and tea shop." (*Julie Phillips*)

Also recommended: With the look and feel of an English manor house, the 19th century **Grey Gables Inn** (161 Hanford Street, 95685; 209–267–1039 or 800–GREY GABLES) brings a touch of the English countryside to Gold Country. There are eight comfortable bedrooms, a formal dining room, and a large parlor with a double alcove; rates range from $90–150, and include a full breakfast, afternoon tea, and evening hors d'oeuvres. "Beautiful both inside and outside with lovely gardens. The rooms have fireplaces, queen-sized beds, private baths, and air-conditioning. Delightful, accommodating owner/innkeepers." (*JP*)

From Highway 49, all you can see of **Hanford House** (61 Hanford Street, Highway 49, P.O. Box 1450, 95685; 209–267–0747 or 800–871–5839; www.isgnet.com/hanford_house) is an old brick building. The majority of the B&B was added much more recently to the back, and includes spacious common and guest rooms, with a cheerful, relaxed, largely contemporary decor. The dining room walls are covered with the owners' "guest book" of signatures and sketches by guests, often with a teddy bear motif. B&B double rates for the eleven guest rooms range from $89–125. "Owner Karen Tierno welcomed us warmly, and told us all about the inn, including the kitchen stocked with snacks for guests, with just-baked cookies. Breakfast is served from 8:30 to 9:30, and guests have a choice of a light or hearty meal. We were invited to relax in the Hanford Room with a huge TV and a large video library. Appealing roof deck for sun-bathing. Room Eight had a queen-size bed and pull-out couch, a beautiful sparkling white fireplace, ceiling fan, reading materials, and a binder with information about the inn and area. Our bed was turned down with rose petals on the pillows; in the morning, we were brought the newspaper and coffee. Tasty breakfast of banana smoothies, homemade granola, and caramel pecan custard French toast and sausage." (*Melissa Phillips*)

YOSEMITE

Yosemite's proximity to California's major cities make it one of the country's most popular national parks. Recent statistics indicate that well over 4 million visitors come to Yosemite annually, *with over 500,000 arriving in July alone.* January visitors number closer to 100,000, most of them day-trippers not competing for scarce beds at prime hotels. So, if you can, go off-season, and bring along snowshoes or cross-country skis, and explore the deserted trails in peace—and remember that Yosemite is far more congested than Yosemite Valley.

Reader tip: "Keep in mind that Yosemite is an extremely large park, and slow-moving traffic makes for sluggish travel. In September, it took us one hour to get from Fish Camp to Yosemite Village, and 2½ hours to reach Tuolumne Meadows at the park's eastern end. Overall, this is a difficult, crowded park to visit in season, with expensive, disappointing accommodations and food." *(Adam Platt)* "Although car travel in this park can be slow and frustrating, the scenery is unmatched. Park your car (come early to find a space), then take shuttles, ride bikes, and hike around the valley." *(JTD)*

Also recommended: Everyone knows the adage: The three most important rules about real estate are location, location, and location. The Ahwahnee proves that these rules apply equally to inns as well. Built in 1927, **The Ahwahnee** (Yosemite National Park, 95389; Yosemite Reservations, 5410 East Home Avenue, Fresno, 93727; 209–252–4848) is a massive seven-story structure with three wings faced with native granite and concrete stained to look like redwood. The 123 guest rooms and common areas are decorated with Yosemite Indian motifs, including original craft and art work. A two-year, $1.5 million renovation of all common areas and guest rooms was completed in 1997; soft goods and furnishings have been replaced or restored. Immensely popular despite rates of $210–240 (no meals), summer and holiday reservations are recommended one year ahead. A regular contributor who visited on a nonholiday winter trip reports that the service was friendly but inexperienced, the housekeeping satisfactory, and the dining room experience such a lengthy ordeal that they resorted to room service as the only way to obtain adequate meals in a timely manner. Although her room in the main hotel was quiet, sound-proofing between the rooms in the cottage buildings was less so. Nevertheless, she noted that "there's so much tradition, and the public rooms are so inspiring that we plan to return anyway." *(SD)* Another reader noted that the hotel was "wonderful as usual. We will continue to return because of the elegance and character of the hotel and the beauty of the location." *(Patricia Bell)* More comments welcome.

Just two miles from Yosemite's South entrance is the **Tenaya Lodge** (1122 Highway 41, P.O. Box 159, Fish Camp, 93623; 209–683–6555 or 800–635–5807; www.tenayalodge.com), a 242-room hotel with a full range of resort activities, including three restaurants, a children's program, fitness center, swimming pools, and more. Double rates range from $69–239, with lowest rates available midweek, off-season; ask about special promotions and AAA rates. "Great location, near the park, but with modern touches some of the park rooms lack. Ask for a room that's been refurnished recently." *(RH)* Another option is **The Narrow Gauge Inn** (48571 Highway 41, Fish Camp, 93623; 209–683–7720), a 26-room motel combining western-style architecture with Victorian decor, most of the latter obtained from the now-defunct Pony Express Museum; double rates from $85–130. "We ate in the restaurant every night, enjoying the well-prepared food, the friendly service, and the views of the moonlight on the mountains through the large windows." *(Carol Dinmore)* "Our room was furnished in 'basic motel' but the view of the Sierra National Forest from our balcony made up for it." *(Glenn Roehrig)*

On Route 120, 23 miles west of Yosemite is **The Groveland Hotel** (18767 Main Street, P.O. Box 481 Groveland, 95321; 209–962–4000), built of adobe in 1849, and restored as an inn and restaurant in 1992. The guest rooms have coordinating floral fabrics and wallpapers, antique beds (most queen-size or twins), down comforters, and robes. Next door is California's oldest saloon, the Iron Door, with great Old West atmosphere. B&B double rates for the 17 guest rooms range from $95–175, including a continental breakfast.

Fifteen miles south of Yosemite's South Entrance is **The Estate by the Elderberries** (48688 Victoria Lane, P.O. Box 577, Oakhurst, 93644; 209–683–6860), constructed to resemble a manor house from the south of France, complete with stucco facade and tile roof, and previously called the Chateau du Sureau. The ten luxuriously appointed rooms are complete with stereo/CD system, imported linens, woodburning fireplace, and marble bathrooms; one is wheelchair accessible. Open for lunch, brunch, and dinner, the restaurant, Erna's Elderberry House, is well regarded for its innovative and elegant cuisine. Double rates of $285–435 (plus 12% service) include a European-style breakfast with cold meats, cheeses, fruit, freshly baked breads, and coffee. "The six-course dinner is an outstanding value. Wonderful hospitality; immaculate, beautifully furnished rooms with all amenities. Delicious breakfast is served on the patio." *(Tina Hom)* "Spectacular dinner, makes any occasion special." *(ACR)*

Can't Find It Here?

Our regional guides include *two to three times* the number of entries contained here. Pick up a copy of our *New England* (plus Eastern Canada), *Middle Atlantic, South, Midwest* (plus Ontario), *Rocky Mountains & Southwest*, or *West Coast* (plus Western Canada) edition for lots more information on great places to stay. If your bookstore doesn't have a current copy in stock, ask them to order it for you or call 800–288–2131. You can also order copies from our Website at http://www.inns.com.

Colorado

Briar Rose, Boulder

Running from east to west, Colorado is divided into four distinct regions, each completely different from the others. The **eastern section** of the state is part of the Great Plains—flat, dusty, and sparsely settled. Next comes the **front range corridor,** where 70% of the population lives snuggled up against the Rocky Mountain foothills, running from Pueblo in the south, through Denver, to Fort Collins in the north. Natural attractions here include the Garden of the Gods and Cave of the Winds, located west of Colorado Springs; Elitch Gardens and Red Rocks State Park near Denver; and the Flatirons of Boulder. The **Rockies** make up the third region, dominating the state with their well-known ski areas, as well as remote ghost towns, invigorating hot springs, and hidden lakes. You can step back to the re-invented 1860s with a visit to Central City or Georgetown (best in spring or fall when the crowds have thinned out), or travel back roads for a rare glimpse of bighorn sheep and elk. Don't miss the incongruous Great Sand Dunes National Monument, located west of the Sangre de Cristo Mountains in south-central Colorado. Standing in the midst of over 36,000 acres of dunes up to 700 feet high, it's easy to imagine Lawrence of Arabia and a host of camels heading over the next ridge. Moving west to the fourth region are pine forests and wide plateaus, cut by deep canyons, that prevail on the **western slope** of the Rockies. Drive the spectacular rim road of the Colorado National Monument, peer into a 12-mile-long gorge at the Gunnison National Monument, or attend film and music festivals in Telluride. In nearby Durango ride a narrow-gauge Victorian passenger train through rugged mountains to Silverton. To visit Colorado's prehistoric past, stop by Mesa Verde Cliff Dwellings or the less crowded Hovenweep National Monument, where you'll find a variety of pueblos, cliff dwellings, and towers over 600 years old.

ASPEN

Aspen has come a long way from its mining-town heritage. Now a famous ski resort and artists' colony, the area offers mountain beauty and outdoor sports all year round. An Aspen summer offers a relaxed pace, an excellent music festival, fine trout fishing, and crisp mountain air, but skiing is still the premier tourist attraction, so winter hotel rates are nearly *double* those of summer. If you want to visit Aspen but haven't made a killing on the stock market, go in October or early November, when prices plummet to affordable levels. Call Central Reservations at 800–262–7736 (or check www.skiaspen.com) for information; call the hotels directly for last-minute off-season specials.

Reader tips: "Aspen is wonderful, but prices have gone crazy. The best deal in town is Gracie's, a resale clothing shop on Main Street, a few doors down from Sardy House. Whatever the Aspen glitterati toss from their closets is fabulous." *(CJ)* "Aspen is a charming town, with a mix of haughty shopkeepers, fickle restaurateurs, and demanding, pretentious customers. We paid over $200 for a tiny hotel room during our July visit, and had to close the windows and turn on a window air-conditioner to block the traffic noise. Ask for details about your room's size and location when making reservations!" *(AP)*

Also recommended: Arguably the most popular hostelry in town is the newly restored **Hotel Jerome** (330 East Main Street, 81611; 970–920–1000 or 800–331–7213). Its 93 rooms are all beautifully decorated with Victorian antiques, period wallpapers, and modern baths and amenities. The Jerome's three restaurants range from casual to elegantly opulent, and its bars are longtime favorites. Double rates range from $160–805, with suites to $2000.

Opened in 1989 and located at the foot of Aspen Mountain is the 92-room **Little Nell Hotel** (675 East Durant Avenue, 81611; 970–920–4600 or 888–843–6355), just steps from the Silver Queen gondola. Rooms are luxuriously furnished with every amenity (including marble baths, gas fireplaces, and VCRs), and service is attentive and friendly. Double rates range from $105–700 depending on size of room, view, and season; suites, which fall into the category of "if you have to ask, you can't afford it," could easily match a mortgage payment for one night's lodging. "One of the best in town. Rooms are spacious and beautiful. An excellent value off-season." *(Tina Kirkpatrick)*

Information please: For the ultimate in luxury, privacy, and elegance, a good choice may be **The Residence Suites** (305 South Galena Street, 81611; 970–920–6532; www.aspenlg.com/residence), offering seven spacious fully equipped suites (from 600 to 1700 square feet in size) at rates of $175–3900, depending on room and season. Built in 1886 in the Aspen Block building, owner Terry Butler has converted this former brothel into posh suites, each equipped with European antiques, museum-quality artwork, designer fabrics, and such amenities as wood-burning fireplace, TV/VCR/CD players, Jacuzzi and soaking tubs, steam showers, and other luxuries. Offering mountain views from its balconies and patios are the 34 affordable units of the **Boomerang Lodge** (500 West Hopkins Avenue, 81611; 970–925–3416 or 800–992–8852) offering comfortable, contemporary dècor and a swimming pool in the double rates of $110–289, including continental breakfast. The location a few blocks from downtown is fairly quiet, and some rooms have a fireplace and/or a kitchenette.

Sardy House ✕
128 East Main Street, 81611

Tel: 970–920–2525
800–321–3457
Fax: 970–920–4478
E-mail: hotlsard@rof.net
URL: www.aspen.com/sardylenado

A turreted Victorian, the Sardy House was built in 1892 by "Three-Fingered Jack" Atkinson and was one of the first houses in Colorado with central heating, indoor plumbing, and electric lights. It was renovated in 1985 by the same group that redid Aspen's Hotel Lenado, in a decor combining period elegance with luxurious contemporary flair. Many of the rooms have hand-rubbed cherry furnishings; some have a view of the ski slopes. The redbrick inn is composed of two buildings, the original mansion and the newly constructed carriage house, connected by an enclosed gallery. Breakfast might include omelets, or a daily special such as oatmeal waffles with bacon, along with home-baked fruit bread, and fresh juices; dinners are pricey but delicious, with Colorado specialties such as rack of lamb and pan-seared red trout.

"My room had a comfortable brass bed with the best of linens, vaulted wooden ceilings with architectural trim, and a bathroom with heated towel racks and a Jacuzzi tub. The restaurant, Jack's, presided over by Charlie Norman, offers grand, charming Aspen cuisine throughout the day. Breakfasts are the best in town and open to the public. I enjoyed beautiful linens and a bright Aspen Victorian dining room full of sunlight and views of the towering evergreens." *(Chris Johnston)* "An elegant, private, small hotel; friendly atmosphere. When shown to our room, we were given a full description of all facilities, including the steam shower. They parked our car and swept off the snow. Exceptional dinner of minted roast lamb, a medley of vegetables cooked with lots of garlic, and fabulous homemade pumpernickel/white rolls. Fine service. At breakfast we enjoyed the freshly squeezed orange juice, blueberry pancakes, and bowl of fresh fruit." *(Jeff Soule)*

Worth mentioning: The Sardy House and Hotel Lenado are under the same management so be specific when making reservations to avoid confusion.

Open Late Nov.–mid-April; June 10–mid-Oct.
Rooms 6 suites, 14 doubles—all with full private bath, telephone, radio, TV, desk. Suites with whirlpool tub, stereo, VCR, bar. 12 doubles with whirlpool bath.

Facilities Dining room, bar, parlor, conference room, porch. Swimming pool, sauna, hot tub. Off-street parking.
Location 3 blocks from center.
Restrictions Smoking in bar only. $45 handling fee on all cancellations.
Credit cards Amex, DC, MC, Visa.
Rates B&B, $275–795 suite, $145–495 double, plus service. Weekend, holiday minimum stay. Alc dinner, $35–50.
Extras Crib, baby-sitting.

BOULDER

Boulder is home to the University of Colorado and to outdoor sports of every kind. It is a friendly but sophisticated place, set against the backdrop of the Flatirons, a massive rock formation that juts 2,000 feet up from the edge of town. Boulder is located in north central Colorado, 35 miles northwest of Denver via Highway 36.

Reader tips: "We enjoyed a free tour of Celestial Seasonings (as well as Coors Brewery, in nearby Golden), and found the small town of Niwot to be a pleasant surprise for antique shops." *(Joyce Wood)* "Real comfort food in the Teddy Roosevelt Grill at the Hotel Boulderado. Meat loaf and mashed potatoes, plus pecan tart with fudge sauce. Wow!" *(Peggy Kontak)*

Also recommended: With flower gardens and a brick Victorian exterior, the **Briar Rose** (2151 Arapahoe Avenue, 80302; 303–442–3007), is reminiscent of an English country house, and offers nine guest rooms. The B&B double rate of $99–159 includes a breakfast of croissants and freshly baked breads with homemade lemon curd, jams, granola, plus yogurt with fruit, fresh juice, coffee, and tea, as well as afternoon tea and sherry. Children are welcome.

The Inn on Mapleton Hill (1001 Spruce Street, 80302; 303–449–6528 or 800–276–6528; maphillinn@aol.com) is an elegant, 100-year-old Edwardian-style bed and breakfast, located in the historic Mapleton Hill neighborhood, just two blocks from festive Pearl Street. The seven guest rooms are individually decorated with many antiques, and the B&B double rates of $80–145 include breakfasts of homemade breads and fresh fruit, plus afternoon refreshments. "Little touches make the difference—help with dinner reservations, brushing an unexpected snowfall off the car, flannel sheets to keep the bed cozy in winter, and sensitivity to guests' privacy." *(Penny Pestle)*

The Boulder Victoria   *Tel:* 303–938–1300
1305 Pine Street, 80302   *Fax:* 303–938–1435
                          E-mail: vicearl@bouldernews.infi.net
                          URL: http://www.bouldervictoria.com

"The handsomest residence exterior in the city," reported the June 19, 1895 issue of the *Boulder County Herald*, describing this showpiece of Colonial Revival style. Purchased in 1990 by Matthew Dyroff and Jeffrey White, a top-to-bottom restoration project produced a beautiful "painted lady," with a color scheme of light tan, accented in shades of cream, rust, and dark green. Furnished entirely in American antiques dating from the late 1800s, light streams in through the Palladian window in the entry hall and sparkles on the leaded glass in the bay window of the dining room. Early-bird coffee is available and breakfast is served from 7 to 9 A.M. weekdays, and 8 to 10 A.M. on the weekends. The breakfast buffet includes juice, fresh fruit, homemade granola with milk and yogurt, croissants with spiced fruit compote, fresh bagels with smoked ham and tomato, plus fruit breads, muffins, and coffee cake. Tea is served from 4 to 6 P.M. daily, featuring scones with lemon curd, homemade toffee, cookies, and Scottish shortbread; Port wine is available in the evening. Meredith Lederer is the innkeeper.

In 1996, Dyroff and White opened a second inn, two blocks away; the **Earl House** (2429 Broadway, 80304; 303–938–1400) is an 1880s Gothic Revival mansion with six luxurious guest rooms and B&B double rates of $109–169, suites to $350, including a full breakfast and evening refreshments.

"Excellent breakfast, friendly staff." *(Michael Crick)* "We were warmly welcomed and were well taken care of by the friendly staff." *(Lois Wysocki)* "A meticulously and tastefully restored Victorian home." *(Barbara Mullin)* "Understated elegance with thoughtful in-room touches: terry robes, sweet-smelling roses, and delicious mocha-chip cookies." *(Jayne Reed)* "The Dwight Room is bright and airy, overlooking Pine Street. Great location for walking to the pedestrian mall downtown." *(Marilyn Boling)* "Ideally situated. Guest rooms are furnished with queen-size brass beds with down comforters. The view of the Flatiron Mountains from the balcony of the Nicholson Room more than makes up for its unattached private bath." *(Raquel Levin)* "Fragrant dried flowers everywhere. Hearty and delicious breakfast, especially the raspberry coffee cake." *(Carolyn Sikes)* "Clean, comfortable rooms; delightful staff; everything we asked for we received with a smile." *(Wallace Perlick)* "Relaxing, friendly atmosphere; wonderful food; our well-equipped room had a great steam shower." *(Mary Dinunno)*

Open All year.

Rooms 1 suite, 6 doubles—all with private bath and/or shower, telephone, radio, clock, TV, desk, air-conditioning. 5 with fan, 3 with deck; some with steam shower.

Facilities Dining room with library; living room; guest refrigerator, guest laundry (for fee); porch. Patios with gardens. 5 off-street parking spaces.

Location In center of town. Hwy 36 turns into 28th St. Turn left on Canyon Blvd. Turn right on 13th St. & go to Pine St. to inn on NE corner.

Restrictions Street noise in some rooms. No smoking. Children 12 and over.

Credit cards Amex, MC, Visa.

Rates B&B, $159–189 suite, $109–169 double. Rollaway bed, $20. Breakfast buffet (outside guests), $7. Corporate rates midweek. 2-night minimum weekends May–Oct.

Extras Limited wheelchair access. Spanish, French spoken.

BRECKENRIDGE

Breckenridge is Colorado's oldest Victorian mountain town, and is located 87 miles west of Denver. Home to a first-rate downhill ski area,

"Breck" also offers a pleasant place for a summer vacation, at exceedingly reasonable rates. Winter activities focus on skiing, skating, and sleigh rides, while warm weather brings opportunities for golf, tennis, hiking, river rafting, fishing, bicycling, and sailing, plus a variety of music festivals.

Also recommended: Built in 1886, the **Evans House B&B** (102 South French Street, P.O. Box 387, 80424; 970–453–5509; colorado-bnb.com/evanshse) features photos and relics from the W.H. Evans Pharmacy, circa 1906. Breakfasts include such treats as crepes with sausage, buttermilk pancakes, baked eggs in bacon rings, or apple-cinnamon French toast; B&B double rates of $65–140 also include afternoon refreshments. After an active day of hiking, riding, golf, or skiing, guests enjoy a relaxing soak in the eight-person hot tub, housed in a historic shed with stained glass windows, Tiffany-style lamps, and mountain views. Each of the six guest rooms has a private bath, and are decorated in Victorian, Southwestern, or Rocky Mountain dècor, and have either queen-size or king/twin-size beds. Well-supervised children are welcome.

Allaire Timbers Inn   ♿   *Tel:* 970–453–7530
9511 Highway 9, South Main Street,   800–624–4904
P.O. Box 4653, 80424   *Fax:* 970–453–8699
         E-mail: allairetimbers@worldnet.att.net
         URL: http://www.allairetimbers.com

Set in the trees at the south end of historic Main Street is the Allaire Timbers Inn, built in 1991 by Kathy and Jack Gumph of Colorado lodge-pole pine. The inn's ample common areas include the spacious great room, the cozy loft for reading or movies, and the relaxing sunroom. Guest rooms are named for Colorado mountain passes, with decor inspired by the name and history of the pass. Especially romantic are the two suites, each with a private hot tub and river rock fireplace. Early-bird coffee is ready by 6:00 A.M. in winter, followed by breakfast served from 7:30 to 9:00 A.M. A typical meal includes fresh fruit and juice, cereal and homemade granola, apple-cheddar quiche, honey wheat bread or perhaps sourdough bread, strawberry-nut cake, homemade raspberry jam and honey-nut butter; 24-hour beverage service with coffee, tea, and cider; and an evening social hour, with wine and hors d'oeuvres, served in winter by a crackling fire.

"Kathy and Jack attend to every detail to ensure guests' comfort and enjoyment. The friendly atmosphere encourages guests to make new friends among the other guests; many even return each year to ski together." *(Louis & Virginia Childers)* "Jack has the ability to help the guests feel connected to one another, and Kathy is an outstanding cook. Each member of their well-trained staff introduced him- or herself to us. Meticulously maintained and cleaned. Typically thoughtful touches are the humidifiers available to guests unused to the dry mountain air, and the headphones provided so one can watch TV without disturbing other guests. The fantastic hot tub on the back deck has an unparalleled view of the Rockies." *(Daniel & Nancy Walsh)* "Kind and friendly owners and staff. Breakfast and happy hour are both wonderful treats." *(Brenda Jones)* "The Bear Creek Room has numerous teddy bears and two wooden carved bears on the headboard. Generous, well-made breakfast." *(Robert Motylenski)*

"Beautiful columbine flowers are hand-painted on the bathroom tiles of the Columbine Room." *(Debbie Cowel)* "Only a ten-minute walk from town." *(Debra Byram)* "Our immaculate room was cozy, with hand-made quilts and stuffed animals to match." *(Jeanette Fitzgerald)* "Special touches included fluffy robes, early morning coffee, afternoon cheese and crackers, and hot-from-the-oven chocolate chip cookies. Breakfast favorites were the Belgian waffles with strawberry Grand Marnier sauce, the blueberry nutmeg coffee cake, and the apple sausage quiche." *(Michele Rickert)* "The oversize windows of the great room overlook the town below and the snow-capped mountain peaks of the Ten Mile Range in the distance." *(Pam Phillips)*

Open All year.
Rooms 2 suites, 8 doubles—all with private bath and/or shower, radio, clock, telephone, TV, deck. 2 with fireplace, hot tub.
Facilities Dining room, great room with fireplace; loft with TV/VCR, library, games; deck with hot tub, ski room. Off-street parking.
Location Take I-70 W from Denver to Exit 203 at Frisco. Go S on Hwy 9 to Main St., Breckenridge. Go through town; inn is just past Boreas Pass Rd. on right.
Restrictions No smoking. Children over 12 preferred.
Credit cards Amex, Discover, MC, Visa.
Rates B&B, $225–325 suite, $135–205 double. 2-night minimum suites; 7-night minimum at Christmas.
Extras 1 room equipped for disabled.

COLORADO SPRINGS

Colorado's second largest city has two key attractions—the U.S. Air Force Academy and Pikes Peak. Other historic sights, both natural and man-made, include the Garden of the Gods, with unusual geologic formations, and a wide variety of museums and ranches, all commemorating various aspects of western history.

Reader tip: "Golfers should definitely try to get on one of the courses at the Broadmoor, up in the foothills, with lovely mountain and city views. The old hotel has been recently renovated and is well worth a walk-through." *(Carol Moritz)*

Also recommended: The **Cheyenne Canon Inn** (230 West Cheyenne Boulevard, 80906; 719–633–0625 or 800–633–0625; www.cheyennecanoninn.com) is a 10,000-square-foot Mission-style mansion near the Broadmoor hotel. Restored as a luxurious B&B in 1994, with a four-diamond rating from AAA, it offers five doubles and three suites, each with private bath, king- or queen-size beds and decor inspired by different regions of the world; oversize windows provide beautiful mountain views. B&B double rates range from $90–190, including a full breakfast. Though only minutes from downtown, it borders 10,000 acres of parkland for hiking.

Built in 1902, the **Holden House** (1102 West Pikes Peak Avenue, 80904; 719–471–3980) is an antique-filled painted lady; its five guest rooms are furnished with heirloom quilts, brass and iron queen-size beds, puffy comforters, and down pillows. The $120–135 rates include creative breakfasts like eggs fiesta, German puff pancakes, or ruffled crepes Isabel. "Located in a quiet residential area, with knowledgeable owners, lovely antiques, and great food." *(JP)*

Built as a B&B in 1997, **The Old Town GuestHouse** (115 South 26th Street, 80904; 719–632–9194 or 888–375–4210) is located in the heart of Old Colorado City, on the site of the 1892 city hall and jail. Its eight guest rooms are individually decorated, some with fireplaces, Jacuzzi tubs, steam showers, and/or porches; all accommodate business travelers with TV/VCRs, coffee makers, refrigerators, working desks, and telephones with voice mail and data ports; one exceeds ADA guidelines for the disabled. The B&B double rate of $80–155 includes a full breakfast, afternoon hors d'oeuvres, access to the stocked butler's pantry, and game room with pool table. "Wonderful location in the historic district; elegant and inviting, with a touch of the Old West; careful attention to detail in every regard, from careful soundproofing to classical music for the CD player. Kaye and David Caster are wonderful hosts, helpful with area information. Enjoyed breakfast and the evening wine and cheese." *(Dixie Kapitula, and many others)*

Just four miles from Colorado Springs, the **Two Sisters Inn** (10 Otoe Place, Manitou Springs, 80829; 719–685–9684 or 800–274–7466), built in 1919, was restored in 1990 and named in honor of the siblings who built it. The five guest rooms are decorated with family collectibles, antiques, and fresh flowers; breakfasts include fresh fruit, home-baked muffins, homemade sausage, maybe an apple puff pancake or stuffed French toast with fruit coulis. B&B double rates are $69–105.

DENVER

The "mile-high" city sits on the high plains, as flat as a pancake, with the Rockies rising majestically in the near distance (when you can see them through the smog). Settled in the middle of the nineteenth century, Denver left behind its origins as a mining town to become the largest city in the Rockies. A major business and convention center, Denver also offers first-rate museums and theaters—the Natural History Museum and Planetarium, Museum of Western Art, the Denver Art Museum, and the Denver Center for the Performing Arts—as well as excellent shopping at Larimer Square and the Sixteenth Street Mall. And after watching all your cash disappear, you can stop by the U.S. Mint (several blocks from the capitol) to see more being made (no free samples).

Most hotels reduce their rates substantially for the weekend; be sure to inquire about special rates.

Note: Several of Denver's B&B inns are in historic neighborhoods, currently in states of upward transition; rough areas may be close by.

As in any major city, there are street people, and not every building has been restored. Night-time walking requires vigilance here as elsewhere; some streets are fine, others inadvisable, so ask your innkeeper for advice. As in any city, when parking on the street, do not leave anything that appears valuable exposed in the car.

Also recommended: For European elegance, fine food and warm hospitality, visit the **Haus Berlin** (1651 Emerson Street, 80218; 303–837–9527 or 800–659–0253; www.hausberlinbandb.com), a century-old Victorian home, decorated with antique and modern furnishings from Europe and South America, complemented by art from Haiti, Brazil, and Mexico. B&B double rates of $95–130 for the four guest rooms include outstanding full breakfasts and pillow chocolates at night. "Immaculate housekeeping, beautiful artwork. Light and airy parlors with comfortable seating, reading lamps strategically placed, and soft music to soothe the day's tensions." *(Janis Williams)*

Castle Marne—A Luxury Urban Inn	*Tel:* 303–331–0621
1572 Race Street, 80206	800–92–MARNE
	Fax: 303–331–0623
	E-mail: themarne@ix.netcom.com
	URL: http://www.castlemarne.com

One of Denver's grandest historic mansions, Castle Marne is a massive stone fortress, built of rusticated rhyolite for a 19th-century silver baron, and listed on the National Register of Historic Places. It was designed in Richardsonian Romanesque style in 1899 by the same architect, William Lang, who planned the Molly Brown House. After years of deterioration, the mansion was restored in 1989 as a B&B by owners Jim and Diane Peiker, their daughter Melissa, and son-in-law Louie. Breakfast menus change daily, and might consist of orange or cranberry juice, Dutch babies with maple syrup, home-baked whole wheat oatmeal toast, and triple chocolate and blueberry buttermilk muffins. Afternoon tea might feature scones with raspberry butter and lemon bars, or apricot bars and chocolate-covered berries. A recent menu for the candlelight dinner noted deviled crab, asparagus soup, salad greens with raspberry vinaigrette, strawberry sorbet, Cornish game hen or beef tenderloin, sugar peas and baby carrots, and chocolate cheesecake with raspberries, coffee, and chocolate truffles.

"Romantic, elegant ambience; pampering service." *(DG)* "Beautiful antiques, warm hospitality, good breakfast. Best of all was our room's private hot tub, enclosed in a trellis on our private balcony." *(William Lloyd)* "The Peikers have a deep and personal relationship with the historic preservations of their neighborhood. We had a lovely self-guided tour with the Peiker's assistance. The inn and all its amenities are a joy, from the tasty breakfast to afternoon tea to a late-night treat." *(Susan Chilcote & Stacey Lamirand)* "I went to plug something in beneath the nightstand, only to find a lovely little card under the bed that said 'Yes, we even clean under the bed!' It was spotless." *(Carla Steele)*

"Innovative, first-quality food. Beautifully restored, attractively decorated and furnished." *(Kurta Lueddeling)* "The Peikers are cordial hosts,

127

knowledgeable about Denver. Tea time is a welcome opportunity to meet and visit with the other guests." *(Bonny McAllister)* "So much to do I didn't even miss having TV—antique puzzles, pool table, darts, chess, and more. Mrs. Peiker was helpful with restaurant advice and reservations." *(Marie Karr)* "I love the peacock stained window, and the tea-time raspberry bars, chocolate truffles, and shortbread." *(Ira May)*

"Jim and Diane have decorated every corner with Victorian charm." *(Debra Day)* "The original hand-rubbed woodwork, ornate fireplaces, and stained glass have all been returned to their original beauty." *(PG)* "Ample space for all our belongings, and modern conveniences to complement the period decor." *(Susanne Stotsky)* "Close to the performing arts complex, the zoo, botanic gardens, and shopping." *(Connie Ondreka)* "Convenient to both the Cherry Creek Mall and downtown." *(WN)* "When Diane found out we were vegetarians, she immediate changed the next day's breakfast to waffles—light, crispy, and delicious." *(LAL)* "The wonderful breakfasts are accompanied by interesting conversation with the other guests. Beds are turned down with chocolates and a wish for sweet dreams. Upon returning home, I found a note of thanks." *(Mary Perrier)*

Open All year.
Rooms 2 suites, 7 doubles—all with private bath and/or shower, telephone, clock/radio, desk, ceiling fan. Some with fireplace, whirlpool tub, hot tub, and/or balcony.
Facilities Dining room, parlor, game room with TV, guest refrigerator; guest office with computer, fax; veranda, porch. Flower and vegetable gardens. Croquet. Off-street parking.
Location 20 blocks E of downtown. 1 block N of Colfax Ave., at East 16th Ave.
Restrictions No smoking. Not suitable for children under 10.
Credit cards All major.
Rates B&B, $180–220 suite, $85–180 double, $70–165 single. 5% senior discount. Candlelight dinners by reservation, $120 per couple.
Extras Hungarian spoken.

Queen Anne Bed & Breakfast Inn
2147–51 Tremont Place, 80205

Tel: 303–296–6666
800–432–INNS
Fax: 303–296–2151
E-mail: queenanne@worldnet.att.net
URL: http://www.bedandbreakfastinns.org/queenanne

Once home to Denver's early leaders, the historic Clements district nearly fell to the wrecker's ball in the mid-1970s. Fortunately, the first owners of the Queen Anne Inn were among the preservationists who helped save the area; in 1992 the inn was bought and expanded by Tom King. This 1879 mansion is decorated with period antiques without abandoning more creative approaches: The Aspen Room, for example, is highlighted by a wraparound hand-painted mural of a golden grove of trees; the Tabor Room has a mural of a garden party, circa 1894; and the Park Room mural depicts the view from the front window as it looked in 1879. The inn's suites are named for Tom's favorite artists: Frederic Remington, Norman Rockwell, John James Audubon, and

Alexander Calder. Guest comfort is a key concern, with good lighting, a working desk, easy chair, and fresh flowers in nearly each room, plus such luxuries as king-size beds and whirlpool tubs in several rooms. The buffet-style breakfast is served from 7:30 to 9:30 A.M., and offers fresh fruit, juice, granola, scones, croissants, and a hot entree; Colorado wine is served in the parlor or garden from 6 to 7:30 P.M.

"The two Victorian homes that comprise the Queen Anne are a treat to the eye. Tom King provided many entertaining stories about Denver's history, and his sons were attentive hosts at breakfast. The innkeepers directed me to the Buckhorn Exchange, a steakhouse where I could sample Rocky Mountain oysters and buffalo meat. Evenings find guests gathered in the sitting room sipping local wine and sharing their experiences." *(Marie Giarniero)* "The third floor Park Room has a wonderful view of Benedict Fountain Park and the city skyline. Cold drinks and juices are always available. A terrific walking tour starts at the nearby park." *(Dianne Crawford)* "The Alexander Calder suite has an energizing primary-color scheme, gas log fireplace, and luxurious Jacuzzi with built-in pillow. Tom is a congenial host who made us feel like pampered, well-regarded guests in a private home." *(Melissa & Bill Schnirring)* "The bath was spotless and sparkling, with plenty of hot water and my favorite glycerin soap. Local papers and a vast collection of menus help guests choose where they'd like to eat." *(Tammy Woodring)* "Breakfasts are varied and ample; I appreciated being able to take a tray to my room." *(Timothy Hartzer)* "The sound system plays classical music, but can be turned off if it's not to your taste. Delightful garden where one can take coffee, tea, or wine." *(Carol Worth)* "The third-floor Rooftop room was charming and homey, with eclectic decor; outside was a private deck with a hot tub, and a spectacular view of the Denver skyline. Breakfast was delicious, with a low-fat Southwest quiche." *(TK)* "The innkeepers went above and beyond the call of duty to make our stay pleasant." *(Carol Barrett)*

Open All year.
Rooms 4 suites, 10 doubles—all with private bath and/or shower, telephone, radio. Most with desk, air-conditioning; 2 with fan, gas log fireplace. 4 suites with soaker or whirlpool tubs; 3 doubles have tubs for two, 2 of them jetted. Rooms in 2 adjacent Victorian homes.
Facilities Parlor with stereo, dining room. Garden, limited off-street parking. Benedict Fountain Park across street.
Location Clements Historic District, 4 blocks from business district. On Tremont, between 20th and 22nd Sts. 1.5 m to I-25 & I-70.
Restrictions No smoking. Children over 12 welcome.
Credit cards Amex, DC, Discover, Eurocard, MC, Visa.
Rates B&B, $145–175 suite, $75–145 double. Extra person, $15.

DURANGO

At the base of the San Juan Mountains, Durango was once a tough and rowdy western town. Today summer visitors make it their base for a ride on the spectacularly scenic Durango & Silverton Narrow Gauge Railroad and for trips to the mysterious cliff dwellings of the Anasazi Indians at Mesa Verde National Park, about two hours away; other activities include hiking, mountain bicycling, golf, rafting, and fishing. Summer is peak season here, when rates are at their highest and advance reservations are needed. Winter travelers head for first-rate skiing at Purgatory, 25 miles north, on Route 550; cross-country skiing is also available.

Durango is located in the southwestern corner of Colorado, at the intersection of Routes 160, running east/west, and 550, running north/south. The town is 174 miles south of Grand Junction and 349 miles southwest of Denver.

Also recommended: Although it looks like a century-old Colorado farmhouse, the **Apple Orchard Inn** (7758 County Road 203, 81301; 970–247–0751 or 800–426–0751; www.appleorchardinn.com) was built as a B&B in 1994. Guests can enjoy the views of the Animas River Valley and mountains, or watch the Durango-Silverton narrow gauge train chug by the orchards. At dusk, deer and elk often come to nibble on fallen fruit. Guests are delighted with the inn's convenient but quiet setting, the beautiful mountain and valley views, the excellent food served at breakfast and (by request) dinner, and the warm and friendly hospitality provided by owners Celeste and John Gardiner. B&B double rates for the four guest rooms and six cottages range from $85–150. "I don't believe John and Celeste have ever met a stranger. They are friendly, warm, and gracious, spending time chatting with each guest. We stayed in the Cortland Cottage, decorated to perfection down to the smallest detail. Immaculate, well-lit, and quiet. The feather beds are so comfortable we slept like babies. Sitting in the rockers on the porch, with the sound of water rushing in the stream, and the mountain views, was heavenly. We enjoyed a breakfast of omelets made to order, fried potatoes, fresh fruit, and cinnamon biscuits right out of the oven. John and Celeste have put a lot of thought and love into creating such a wonderful inn. The eight-mile drive from Durango is pleasant, and is well worth it, to reach such a refreshing, relaxing, quiet place."*(Pat Malone)*

With a convenient, quiet location one block off Main Street, the **Leland House** (721 East Second Avenue, 81301; 970–385–1920 or 800–664–1920) offers ten suites decorated with southwestern art and memorabilia; most have a living room, kitchen, and bedroom with modern bath. Under the same ownership is the **Rochester Hotel** across the street, with 15 spacious rooms with Western motifs, inspired by the many Western movies filmed in the Durango area. B&B rates of $95–185 include breakfasts of cranberry scones and egg veggie scramble with toast and hashbrowns, or blueberry coffee cake and multigrain waffles with cream and berries.

Four miles west of town, **Lightner Creek Inn** (999 C.R. 207, 81301; 970–259–1226 or 800–268–9804; www.lightnercreekinn.com) is an expanded and remodeled 1903 house in a quiet green valley with grazing horses, perennial gardens, meandering creek, trout pond, and surrounding hills. The house is fresh and bright with floral wallpapers and quality linens. Nine guest rooms (three of them suites in a carriage house) are furnished with comfortable Victorian beds, armoires, and rocking chairs. A delicious full breakfast is included in the $75–185 B&B rates.

Built in 1887, the **Strater Hotel** (P.O. Drawer E, 699 Main Avenue, 81301; 970–247–4431 or 800–247–4431) has 93 guest rooms with double rates ranging from $99–225. "All you could ask for in a quaint Victorian hotel. Beautiful antique furniture, convenient and comfortable. Attractive guest rooms and common areas. Good restaurant too." *(Lisa Hering)* "Beautifully decorated and furnished, impeccably maintained rooms. Attentive service at the reception desk, plus help with our luggage. Good restaurant with marvelous honky-tonk piano player in the saloon. Welcoming lobby area." *(Diana Inman)*

ESTES PARK

A popular resort town, especially in summer, Estes Park serves as the gateway to Rocky Mountain National Park. To avoid crowds and traffic on such beautiful highways as the park's Trail Ridge Road, try to avoid visiting in July or August. Estes Park is located in north central Colorado, 65 miles northwest of Denver, at the intersection of routes 34, 36 and 7. Activities include hiking, mountain biking, fishing, and cross-country skiing.

Reader tips: "Route 34 west of Estes Park becomes the Trail Ridge Road through Rocky Mountain National Park, the highest continuous road in the country (closed in winter), with views of spectacular snow-capped peaks. Can be crowded in summer and even the fall when the elk bellow their mating calls. Chances are good of wildlife sightings: moose, elk, deer, marmots, and more. Going east on 34 out of Estes Park towards Loveland along the Big Thompson River is a geologist's dream and is also quite spectacular." *(Carol Moritz)* "I was not impressed with Elkorn Avenue, a long strip of mom-and-pop motels, with a bunch of tourist-trap shops at one end." *(ND)*

Also recommended: Guests are delighted with the friendliness and hospitality of the owners, Harry and Norma Menke, at **The Anniversary Inn** (1060 Mary's Lake Road, Moraine Route, 80517; 970–586–6200), and equally pleased with the delicious food and charming rooms of this 1877 log home. "Wonderful owners. Beautiful breakfast area with large timber ceilings." *(Lisa Hering)* B&B double rates for the four guest rooms, all with private bath, range from $90–150.

Romantic RiverSong ♿   *Tel:* 970–586–4666
1765 Lower Broadview Road,   *E-mail:* riversng@frii.com
P.O. Box 1910, 80517   *URL:* http://www.romanticriversong.com

Set at the end of a winding country lane, RiverSong was the site of lavish Great Gatsby–style parties in the 1930s. In 1986, Sue and Gary Mansfield converted the house into a B&B, perfect for the occasional weddings at which Gary, an incurable romantic and mail-order minister, officiates. Guest rooms are named for Rocky Mountain wildflowers; Indian Paintbrush has a southwestern decor with a swinging bed (suspended from the ceiling), Cowboy's Delight has rustic charm with a jetted tub in front of a woodburning stove, and a queen-size four-poster bed, and Meadow Bright has a Colorado mountain decor, massive log bed, rock fireplace, and waterfall shower. Breakfast, served at a table for eight and at tables for two, is highlighted by such dishes as poached pears with raspberry sauce, boysenberry cobbler, John Wayne casserole, or cranberry bread with apricot cream cheese; afternoon refreshments are offered, and candlelight dinners can be arranged.

"The ultimate romantic getaway. Exceedingly well run, with afternoon tea and cookies, evening turndown service, fires laid, and woodpiles restocked daily. Excellent breakfasts, with no repeats. The living room has a large circular sectional sofa in front of the fireplace, while the well-stocked library is amply supplied with books and local information." *(Duane Roller)* "Beautiful woodland setting, with deer strolling through the yard. The Mountain Rose room has a huge shower built into a dormer, with a skylight as well as full-length windows (with well-placed curtains) so you could be surrounded by stars and sky. The old-fashioned tub is set beneath a bay window; on the sill were gorgeous blooming orchids. The young staff offered helpful information about hiking trails and restaurants." *(Phyllis Salesky)*

"The inn is located in a heavy stand of pines, with a view of the mountains and a gorgeous trout stream running through the front yard." *(Fred & Kathleen Hoster)* "The tree swings provided good spots to relax and enjoy the abundant wildlife." *(Marilyn & Ed Brill)* "Wood Nymph is a beautiful room with reading nook, whirlpool tub in a greenhouse, and a river birch bed with a canopy of branches." *(Rebecca Nangle)* "Pleasant stay, nice rooms, great service, beautifully situated." *(Wade Clement)*

Open All year.
Rooms 6 suites, 3 doubles—all with private shower and/or bath. Most with fireplace, balcony; 5 with whirlpool for two, refrigerator. 5 rooms in carriage house or cottages.
Facilities Breakfast room with fireplace, great room with fireplace, games, library, greenhouse, patio, gazebo with fireplace. 27 acres with tree swings, trout streams, ponds, hiking trails, picnic area. Tennis, golf nearby. 5 m to snowshoeing, cross-country skiing.
Location From Hwy. 36 in Estes Park, turn left at 4th light. Remain on Hwy. 36. At next light, turn left & take 1st right to end of road.
Restrictions No smoking. Children over 12 welcome in carriage house.
Credit cards MC, Visa.
Rates $135–250 cottage, $160–250 suite, $160–190 double. Extra person, $25. 2–3 night minimum. Holiday, honeymoon packages. Prix fixe dinner, $30.
Extras Wheelchair access in 2 cottages, 1 suite in lodge.

OURAY

Named after a famous Ute chief, the town of Ouray (pronounced "you-RAY") experienced a population explosion when both gold and silver were discovered here in 1875. Now a historic district, the town's modern-day attractions include the many waterfalls in deep and narrow Box Canyon, dipping in the natural hot-springs swimming pool, gold mine tours, llama tours, plus horseback riding, hiking, trout fishing, mountain biking, hunting, and cross-country skiing in the surrounding San Juan Mountains. Many inns participate in a program offering half-price rates for skiing at Telluride.

Ouray is located on Route 550, the "Million Dollar Highway" blasted out of solid rock in southwestern Colorado, 98 miles south of Grand Junction, 75 miles north of Durango, and 45 miles east of Telluride.

Reader tip: "We loved Ouray. It is definitely a tourist town, but feels authentic, and is less pretentious than Aspen or Telluride. Wonderful area for hiking. Also worthwhile is the museum, especially for mining history. We had a great meal at The Pinon; try the trout with pine nuts." *(Christine Hines)*

Also recommended: The **Damn Yankee B&B** (100 Sixth Avenue, P.O. Box 410, 81427; 970–325–4219 or 800–845–7512) is a modern wood, stone, and glass home rising three stories above the Ouray Valley floor. The third floor observatory offers panoramic views of mountains and waterfalls; in the afternoon snacks and beverages are served here. The guest rooms have queen- or king-size beds with down comforters, private bath, and outside entrances. B&B double rates for the 10 guest rooms range from $89–189. "Outstanding breakfast, attentive owners, charming town." *(Elisabeth McLaughlin)*

The **St. Elmo Hotel** (426 Main Street, P.O. Box 667, 81427; 970–325–4951; www.colorado-bnb.com/stelmo) was built in 1898, and is furnished with period antiques, stained glass, polished brass, and hand-carved wood detailing. The breakfast buffet includes fresh fruit and juice, granola, cereals, a hot entree, and homemade breads and muffins; advance notice required for special diets. B&B double rates for the nine guest rooms range from $65–105, and also include a wine and cheese social hour. The hotel's restaurant, the Bon Ton, offers a largely Italian menu, with veal and pasta dishes as particular favorites. "Careful attention to detail. Cheerful breakfast room. After a day of cross-country skiing, the hot tub feels wonderful; delightful afternoon wine and cheese." *(Laura Reeves)*

TELLURIDE

A wild mining town when first settled in the 1870s, Telluride came close to being a ghost town when the mines shut down. Originally called Columbia, the town's name was changed to Telluride after the tellurium ore in which gold and silver was found; others say the name is a contraction of "to hell you ride." Discovered by hippies in the '60s, Telluride today has mellowed into a small and isolated town, offering an authentic taste of Western history (the town is a National Historic District), uncrowded yet challenging ski slopes, music festivals all summer long, and outstanding scenery. Telluride's airport, with frequent daily flights from Denver, has made the town accessible to travelers with limited time. Inn rates and minimum stay requirements *double* during festival periods. When booking ski trips, be sure to ask about off-peak "ski free" periods, and remember that strict cancellation penalties generally apply.

Reader tip: "Highway 145 between Cortez and Telluride goes over Lizard Head Pass and is far less crowded than the Durango-Silverton Highway. Following 145 northwest of Telluride, you can take Highway 62 to Ridgway (at Highway 550), with more incredible mountain views." *(Carol Moritz)*

Also recommended: The luxurious **San Sophia** (330 West Pacific Avenue, P.O. Box 1825, 81435; 970–728–3001 or 800–537–4781; www.san-sophia.com) was built in 1988, in a turreted neo-Victorian style with an interior in soft desert colors and whitewashed oak woodwork. The 16 guest rooms, each named for a local mine, have brass beds, handmade quilts, and walls highlighted by original artwork, photography, or wall hangings. Terry robes keep guests warm en route to the hot tub in the gazebo. The breakfast buffet changes daily—egg casserole and poppy seed orange cake one day, pumpkin pancakes and applesauce cake with raisins the next; also included in the rates are afternoon hors d'oeuvres and beverages. Dinners are served nightly, and a recent menu included sweet potato-parsnip-apple soup, trout with grapefruit-butter sauce or venison with coriander, mixed vegetable salad, and pears with hazelnut liqueur and chocolate sauce. B&B double rates range from $115–295. "We were pleased with the Morningstar room on the second floor. Superb breakfast; owners and staff were friendly and helpful." *(Tom Wilbanks)*

On historic Main Street is the **Bear Creek B&B** (221 East Colorado Avenue, P.O. Box 2369, 81435; 970–728–6681 or 800–338–7064), a contemporary brick rowhouse with superb views from its rooftop deck. The nine guest rooms have private baths, telephone, and TV. Rates range from $87–227 and include a full breakfast, afternoon tea, discount lift tickets, and apres ski.

Pennington's Mountain Village Inn (100 Pennington Court, P.O. Box 2428, 81435; 970–728–5337 or 800–543–1437) is a French country-style inn set on a high mountain meadow. Each of the 12 guest rooms have private bath, deck, telephone, TV, and a refrigerator stocked with complimentary snacks. Doubles rates are $140–300. "The service was friendly and the breakfast was good. We enjoyed meeting the other guests over afternoon hors d'oeuvres. Pretty wallpapers and furnishings." *(Lisa Hering)*

Extensively restored is the **New Sheridan Hotel** (231 West Colorado Avenue, P.O. Box 980, 81435; 970–728–4351 or 800–200–1891). Welcoming guests since 1898, the New Sheridan combines genuine Victorian atmosphere with a taste of the Wild West. "Much improved. Restaurant next door serves fine food, a little pricy. Drinks and food are also served on the top floor sundeck during ski season. The wonderful old bar, a favorite gathering place, was held up by Butch Cassidy. Great location, right in the middle of town." *(Jeanne Boutelle)* B&B double rates range from $65–285, and include a full breakfast and afternoon wine and hors d'oeuvres.

Alpine Inn *Tel:* 970–728–6282
440 West Colorado Avenue, P.O. Box 2398, 81435 800–707–3344
Fax: 970–728–3424
E-mail: dhw@alpineinn.com
URL: http://www.alpineinn.com/telluride

You won't need to listen to a radio ski report if you stay at the Alpine Inn—just look out the window! From the inn's lovely glass-walled sun-room, guests can enjoy views of the ski slopes along with breakfasts of juices and cereal, cinnamon-cooked apples with vanilla yogurt and granola, followed by orange French toast; or spiced pears and peaches plus eggs Benedict. Built as a hotel in 1903, this B&B has been owned by Denise and John Weaver since 1992. Floral fabrics, handmade quilts, and soft colors create rooms that are comfortable, with a Victorian flavor and king-, queen-, or twin-size beds.

"We were warmly welcomed by Denise and John, who offered us a tour of the inn and refreshments. Immaculate inn; Victorian decor." *(Diane Kimberling)* "Great breakfast, central location, knowledgeable and helpful staff. Incredible views of the ski slopes from dining room. Cozy, comfortable rooms with great beds. Spectacular apres-ski buffet." *(Pat Hardy)* "Welcoming, professional owners. Convenient in-town location with fabulous views." *(Karen Sands-Levine)* "Delightful, clean, well-maintained inn. The basics are all there, plus the extras: the hot tub with awesome views, exquisite furniture and decorating, environmentally conscious policies, and Grand Marnier French toast. Denise and John took the time to find out what we liked and suggested activities of interest." *(Charlie & Barbara Mead)* "Right on the main street, walking distance to everything. Our lovely room had a king-size bed, antique armoire, two large armchairs, lace curtains, TV, and telephone with an answering machine. John cooks a wonderful breakfast; Denise has a great sense of humor." *(Sunny Piken)*

Open Late Nov.–early April; mid-May–late Oct.
Rooms 1 suite, 7 doubles—6 with private shower and/or bath, 2 with maximum of 4 people sharing bath. All with telephone, clock, fan. 1 with radio, desk, kitchenette, balcony. 6 with TV.
Facilities Breakfast sunroom with TV, stereo, parlor with books, fireplace, deck with hot tub. Off-street parking. 1½ blocks to downhill, 1 block to cross-country skiing.
Location Historic district; 1 block to town center. Enter Telluride on Colorado Ave. & continue for approx. 4 blocks to inn on right. Park at rear of inn.
Restrictions No smoking. Children over 10.
Credit cards MC, Visa.
Rates B&B, $135–230 suite, $85–170 double. Extra person, $15. Tipping encouraged. Senior discount. 3-4 night minimum stay in winter season; peak events. Ask about ski-free packages, off-site cottages.

VAIL

Unlike many of the towns in Colorado whose history dates to either the boom days of the gold and silver rush, or to the early days of cattle ranching, Vail was created after World War II by ski paratroopers who had trained in the area. Expanded substantially in recent years, it offers some of North America's best skiing. The town has built up along both sides of Interstate 70, and a great many of its lodges overlook the highway and the mountains beyond.

Black Bear Inn   ♿
2405 Elliott Road, 81657

Tel: 970–476–1304
Fax: 970–476–0433
URL: http://www.vail.net/blackbear

Unlike much of Colorado, Vail has no handsome turn-of-the-century Victorian mansions, because the town dates back only to the 1960s, when it was developed as a ski area. Combine a lack of housing stock suitable for B&B conversion with soaring land prices, and you'll know why we are delighted with the Black Bear Inn, built in 1991. Both David and Jessie Edeen bring years in the hospitality business to innkeeping. The generous common room has ample couches and chairs for relaxing, plus plenty of tables for enjoying breakfast and afternoon snacks. The spacious guest rooms contrast log walls and ceilings with simple white walls and rich green carpeting; most rooms have a pull-out sofa and Mexican tiled bathroom. The overall effect is relaxing and comfortable, highlighted by the work of local artists.

"Located amid pines and aspens, on babbling Gore Creek. The inn's warmth is due not only to its hand-crafted architecture but also to its wonderful innkeepers. Great basement game room." *(Lexy & Craig Zachrich)* "Our breakfast of orange juice, granola with fresh fruit salad and yogurt, frittata with ham and home fries, homemade cinnamon buns and blueberry muffins was served in the sunny breakfast area." *(SWS)* "Awesome apres-ski with tortilla pizzas, a full spread of cheeses, tarts, soda, beer, and wine. Rooms have down comforters, ample bedside lighting, and a small desk with telephone." *(Jeff Daniel)* "Lovely big screened porch overlooking the stream. After dinner we returned for hot drinks, cookies, and conversation. We were enchanted by the clever use of the black bear motif in many of the furnishings." *(Carol & George Worth)* "Wonderful mountain views; delicious homemade breads; ideal location." *(Scott Matula)* "Jesse and David are warm, friendly, and accommodating hosts." *(Mr. & Mrs. James H. Howren)* "Beautiful grounds with many flowers in bloom. The spacious rooms have comfortable beds with fine linens. Friendly, helpful staff who treat the inn as if it were their own." *(Carol Voss, and others)*

Open Winter, summer, fall seasons.
Rooms 12 doubles—all with full private bath, telephone.
Facilities Living/dining area with antique stove, TV; game room with pool table, pin ball machine, TV; screened porch. Conference room. 1 acre with outdoor hot tub. On bus route for skiers.

Location W Vail. 3 m from town. Take Exit 173 off I-70 to S. Frontage Rd. Turn W & take 1st road on left across bridge to inn.
Restrictions No smoking. Well-supervised children welcome.
Credit cards Discover, MC, Visa.
Rates B&B, $106–245 double. Extra person, $35.
Extras 1 room wheelchair accessible. German spoken.

Key to Abbreviations and Symbols

For complete information and explanations, please see the Introduction.

¢ Especially good value for overnight accommodation.

👪 Families welcome. Most (but not all) have cribs, baby-sitting, games, play equipment, and reduced rates for children.

✗ Meals served to public; reservations recommended or required.

🎾 Tennis court and swimming pool and/or lake on grounds. Golf usually on grounds or nearby.

♿ Limited or full wheelchair access; call for details.

Rates: Range from least expensive room in low season to most expensive room in peak season.

Room only: No meals included; European Plan (EP).

B&B: Bed and breakfast; includes breakfast, sometimes afternoon/evening refreshment.

MAP: Modified American Plan; includes breakfast and dinner.

Full board: Three meals daily.

Alc lunch: A la carte lunch; average price of entrée plus nonalcoholic drink, tax, tip.

Alc dinner: Average price of three-course dinner, including half bottle of house wine, tax, tip.

Prix fixe dinner: Three- to five-course set dinner, excluding wine, tax, tip unless otherwise noted.

Extras: Noted if available. Always confirm in advance. Pets are not permitted unless specified; if you are allergic, ask for details; *most innkeepers have pets.*

Important Note on Area Codes

Telephone area codes are changing faster than a two-year-old's attention span. Although we've tried to incorporate all the new ones in our listings, many numbers were still in the "to be decided" state at press time. *If you dial a number listed here and get an announcement that it's not in service, we urge you to call the information operator and see if that region has been assigned a new area code.* Please forgive the inconvenience!

Connecticut

The Griswold Inn, Essex

As small as Connecticut is, the state has several areas of interest to tourists, which are where the best inns tend to be found. Because the listings for each area are scattered throughout this chapter (listed alphabetically by town), here are a few notes on the different regions. (Check the "Location" heading for each entry.)

Connecticut River Valley Although the Connecticut River extends far past Connecticut all the way to northern Vermont, the area we're describing starts just below Middletown and extends south about 25 miles to the river's mouth at Old Lyme/Old Saybrook. Due to a happy accident of nature—a sandbar at the mouth of the river prevented deep-draft ships from entering—commercial traffic after the 1840s went to deep harbors such as New Haven. Consequently, these unspoiled river towns retain much of their early character.

Area attractions include the Goodspeed Opera House at East Haddam, Gillette Castle at Hadlyme, Florence Griswold Museum in Old Lyme, and the antique shops and train and riverboat rides starting in Essex. It's about a 2½-hour ride from New York and Boston, and only 45 minutes from Hartford.

Fairfield County Although it's better known for high-priced real estate than tourist attractions, this pretty part of New England is closest to New York City and its airports. Its inns are convenient for weekend getaways from the city, and good places for a first or last night's stay if you're touring New England.

Litchfield Hills Litchfield Hills occupies the northwest corner of the state and used to be known as the foothills of the Berkshires. This area was a popular summer retreat 100 years ago; many of the places we list were built either as inns or as private mansions during that period.

Today the area still offers beautiful lakes, mountains, and picturesque villages and is only 2 to 2½ hours from New York City. A full range of recreational pleasures is available, from tennis, golf, hiking, and canoeing to cross-country and downhill skiing, plus a number of art and antique shops, summer theater, and concert programs. Rates are highest in summer and during October fall foliage, when two-night weekend minimums are the rule.

Reader tip "If you're traveling north from coastal Connecticut to the Litchfield Hills area, take Interstate 684 to Route 22 in New York State, or Route 8 from Bridgeport. Route 7 often has heavy traffic and congestion, with tantalizing snippets of superhighway." *(RSS)*

Mystic/Eastern Connecticut Shore From Madison up to the Rhode Island border at Westerly, the Connecticut shore offers many lovely towns and beaches. Areas of major interest are Mystic, with its maritime museum and aquarium; Groton, with the USS *Nautilus* National Submarine Memorial and Connecticut College Arboretum; New London, home to the U.S. Coast Guard Academy, and home port to the tall ship *Eagle*; Ledyard with the immensely popular Foxwoods Casino on the Mashantucket Pequot Indian reservation; and Stonington Borough, one of the prettiest coastal villages in Connecticut. This area is 125 miles northeast of New York City, 100 miles southwest of Boston.

Northeastern Connecticut If it's possible to have an "undiscovered" section of a state as small as Connecticut, then this area wins first place—even its tourist council calls it "The Quiet Corner." Area attractions include wineries, herb farms, and greenhouses of note, as well as such historic sites as the home of Nathan Hale, America's first spy, and a museum devoted to the history of textiles. Those who love antiques will enjoy its many shops. For more information contact the Northeast Connecticut Visitors District, P.O. Box 598, Putnam, CT, 06260; 860–928–1228 or 800–CT–BOUND.

Peak-season rates along the shore generally run from May or June through October. Off-season rates are considerably lower and represent an especially good value during April and May, when the weather is usually just right for sightseeing.

CLINTON

For additional area inns, see Chester, Deep River, East Haddam, Essex, Ivoryton, Madison, Old Lyme, Old Saybrook, and Westbrook.

Captain Dibbell House ¢   *Tel:* 860–669–1646
21 Commerce Street, 06413   *Fax:* 860–669–2300
                    URL: http//www.clintonct.com/dibbell

Just crossing the century-old wisteria-covered footbridge that leads to the Captain Dibbell House will put you in the mood for a relaxing visit at the shore. Built in 1866, this house has been owned by Ellis and Helen Adams since 1986. Furnishings include a comfortable mixture of antiques, family heirlooms, auction finds, and New England artwork and crafts. Breakfast includes fresh fruit and juice, cereal, home-baked muffins, scones or coffee cake, plus such entrees as baked French toast with sausage, or perhaps buttermilk waffles with bacon. Other thoughtful touches include fruit baskets, afternoon treats, fresh flowers (in season), bathrobes, twice-daily housekeeping, and turndown service with chocolate pillow treats.

"Beautiful setting with a large, private, fenced yard, complete with a gazebo where we enjoyed our breakfast. The guest pantry is well-stocked with glasses and a small refrigerator filled with cold drinks. Ellis bakes delicious cookies and scones." (Richard & Holly Benton) "Helen Adams was a wonderful hostess, acquainting me with the house, and making sure I was comfortable. Tucked under the eaves, the delightful Garden Room has lots of plants, unusual ceiling angles, double wedding ring quilt, a wooden bench, a white wicker rocker, sun pouring in the windows with hunter green wooden slatted shutters, and a welcoming atmosphere. I also liked the Morning Room, with a huge bay window, a white iron bed, blue wallpaper, and red accents, for a spacious, nautical feel. The Captain's Room was more traditionally Victorian with a queen-size brass bed, lace curtains, a dried flower arrangement above the bed, and an antique washbasin. Off the comfortable sitting room is the breakfast room, where we enjoyed a baked egg dish with delicious, melt-in-your-mouth buttermilk scones, baked by Ellis." (Abby Humphrey)

"Helen and Ellis know when guests want to chat, and when they want privacy. Breakfast included melon, coffee cake, strata, and sausage. Ellis bakes delicious afternoon cookies—chocolate chip one day, oatmeal raisin the next. A cat motif runs throughout the decor; two beautiful Abyssinian cats have the run of this spotlessly clean house. Our room had a small but modern bathroom and a firm, comfortable bed." (John Corcoran) "Quiet side street, yet close to the main one; first-rate B&B with lots of character." (Elizabeth Dakin)

Open April through Dec.

Rooms 4 doubles—all with private bath, radio, air-conditioning, ceiling fan.

Facilities Living room with fireplace, TV, games; breakfast room. Guest refrigerator, bicycles, beach towels & chairs. ¾ acre with gardens, gazebo. Swimming, sailing nearby.

Location CT shore. 38 m S of Hartford, 25 m E of New Haven. Walk to town & beach. From I-95, take Exit 63 to Rte. 81 S to stoplight at intersection of Rtes. 81 & 1. Go through light (Library Lane), go right onto Commerce St. to inn immediately on right.

Restrictions No smoking. No children under 14.

Credit cards Amex, MC, Visa.

Rates B&B, $85–105 double, $65–85 single. Corporate rates. Discount for 3-night stay.

Extras Airport/station pickups.

ESSEX

A most appealing town, Essex is home to the Connecticut River Museum, the Essex Steam Train and Riverboat ride, and a delightful Main

Street, perfect for strolling, with many intriguing shops. For additional area inns, see Chester, Clinton, Deep River, East Haddam, Ivoryton, Madison, Old Lyme, Old Saybrook, and Westbrook.

The Griswold Inn ¢ ♦ ✕
36 Main Street, 06426

Tel: 860–767–1776
Fax: 860–767–0481

Built as an inn in 1776, the Griswold claims to be America's oldest continually operating inn, and is a longtime reader favorite. In its long history, the Gris has been owned by only six families; in 1995, it was purchased by three brothers, all Essex natives: Gregory, Douglas, and Geoffrey Paul. The decor is eclectic, with an exceptionally fine collection of maritime art and antiques from many periods; some guest room floors have a "port or starboard list," a few are quite small. The Tap Room, where lively music—from sea chanteys to Dixieland—rings out nightly, was originally built as a schoolhouse in 1738, but was pulled to this location by a team of oxen in 1801. The Griswold serves hearty American food; the Sunday Hunt Breakfast is a tradition dating from the War of 1812. The breakfast for overnight guests includes fresh fruit and juice, cereal, English muffins, coffee, and tea, served in the library.

"The rooms are quaint, cozy, and comfortable—some with exposed rough-hewn rafters." *(Betty Norman)* "The inn serves excellent and abundant portions of food in the attractive dining rooms (the Library was our favorite). The tavern is inviting, a gathering place for locals as well as guests. Our room in the annex was tiny but cozy and well decorated, with flowered print wallpaper, simple curtains, and a white bedspread. We especially liked the rustic Garden Suite, with a loft bedroom. Their wonderful-smelling soap is made from a century-old recipe." *(Sally Ducot)* "Lovely, spacious guest room." *(Tina & James Kirkpatrick)* "Packed to the rafters on a Saturday night with banjo players and a great sing-along." *(William Gerhauser)*

"An old favorite that is only improving under new owners. Careful attention to detail. Although we had the last room available, the effective air-conditioner provided ventilation and sound-proofing. Quality mattress, pillows, towels. Freshly wallpapered; new sink and toilet; good bedside lights. Good water pressure in the shower; ample hot water. The restaurant is a New England classic, with a pub-type bar and a variety of interesting dining rooms. Pleasant, intelligent waitress. Complimentary corn relish and herbed cottage cheese spread and crackers. Delicious sausage sampler on sautèed spinach as a first course, followed by salmon with leeks and crabmeat. An excellent value." *(Nancy Barker)*

Open All year. Restaurant closed Christmas Eve & Day.
Rooms 13 suites, 17 doubles—all with private bath, telephone, air-conditioning, clock/radio. 8 suites with fireplace, 1 with wet bar, some with desk. Some rooms in annexes.
Facilities Restaurant, tavern with live entertainment, lounge with TV, library, fireplace in all public rooms.
Location CT River Valley. From I-95, take Exit 69, Rte. 9 N, to Exit 3. Go left at end of ramp, then right at light. Go to stop sign; take Middle Road to bottom of hill. Bear right at rotary onto Main St. to inn ¼ m on right.

Restrictions Restaurant/bar noise in some rooms. No smoking in guest rooms.
Credit cards Amex, MC, Visa.
Rates B&B, $135–185 suite, $90–115. Extra person, $10; no charge for children under 6. Alc lunch, $10–15; alc dinner, $20–35; Sunday brunch, $12.95; children's menu.
Extras Station pickups. Crib; baby-sitting by arrangement. French spoken.

GREENWICH

If Greenwich is the starting point for your New England tour, you'll find a community that is an unusual (and expensive) mix of a New England coastal town, bedroom suburban community, and corporate head-quarters. Greenwich celebrated its 350th anniversary in 1990, and history buffs can find a taste of the town's past at the Bush-Holley House and Putnam Cottage. Among corporate headquarters, Pepsico in neighboring Purchase, New York, is a standout; open to the public, its beautifully landscaped grounds are studded with museum-quality sculptures by Henry Moore, Brancusi, Calder, and many more.

Greenwich is located in Fairfield County, 29 miles northeast of New York City, just off both I-95 and the Merritt Parkway.

Also recommended: The **Stanton House Inn** (76 Maple Avenue, 06830; 203–869–2110) is an imposing Colonial frame house, built around 1840 and enlarged in 1890 under the supervision of noted architect Stanford White. Restored as a B&B in 1985, rooms are bright and cheery, furnished simply with Ashley-style fabrics. Warm weather visitors will enjoy the attractive swimming pool. B&B double rates for the 20 guest rooms range from $89–179. "A charming, spotlessly clean inn with a warm, friendly atmosphere. Tasty breakfast buffet. Ideal for business and vacation travelers; close to charming shops and restaurants. Wonderful grounds and swimming pool." (*Richard Varney*)

The Homestead Inn ✕   *Tel:* 203–869–7500
420 Field Point Road, 06830   *Fax:* 203–869–7502

The Homestead was built in 1799 by Augustus Mead; in 1859 it was sold and converted into an inn. Architecturally, it was transformed from a Colonial farmstead into a Victorian Italianate Gothic house, complete with distinctive belvedere and wraparound porches. In 1978, the Homestead was restored as an elegant hostelry, and was purchased by Theresa Carroll and Thomas Henkelmann in 1997. Guest rooms are found in both the original home, as well as in converted out-buildings. Rooms in the former have a more genuine historic feel, while the newer rooms tend to be more spacious, with modern baths, and better sound-proofing. The inn, set in the beautiful Belle Haven residential area—full of lovely old Victorian homes—is convenient to the interstate and to downtown Greenwich. The Homestead is also well known for its French restaurant, Thomas Henkelmann, which has garnered praise from local and national media. Under the supervision of master chef

Thomas, breakfast choices range from eggs Benedict to brioche French toast. Lunch entrees might include striped bass with mushroom risotto and grilled veal with basil tomato fondue; dinner possibilities are Dover sole with artichoke puree and rack of lamb with herb crust.

"Our room was superior in every sense. Good reading lamps, terry bathrobes, huge towels, bidet, and all the shampoos and bath salts one could use." *(MAA)* "We had an exceptional dinner with two standout entrees of amazingly flavorful lamb and veal. Servings were generous, and both dishes were individually garnished with a variety of perfectly prepared vegetables. Service was attentive and professional, never intrusive or familiar." *(SWS)* "We stayed in the General's Suite, a comfortable room with lovely facilities." *(Mr. & Mrs. K.C. Keller)* "Evening conversation on the veranda is special. A steaming cup of strong black coffee, ready before 7 A.M., sets the stage for early morning contemplation of the dew glistening on the grass of the expansive front lawn. Then breakfast in the enclosed front dining porch. Especially good bran and corn muffins." *(John Blewer)* "A sophisticated country inn; excellent housekeeping, food, service." *(MP, also Pam Phillips)*

Open All year. Restaurant closed Labor Day and New Year's Day.

Rooms 6 suites, 14 doubles, 3 singles—all with private bath and/or shower, telephone with call waiting/voice mail/dataport, radio, TV, desk, air-conditioning. 8 rooms and suites in the "Inn Between," and 3 in the "Cottage."

Facilities Bar, restaurant, common room, meeting room, porch. Three acres with gardens, lawn furniture, and terrace. Large park, tennis, golf nearby.

Location 1 m from town center. From NY, take I-95 to Exit 3. Turn left at bottom of ramp. Go to 2nd light, turn left onto Horseneck Lane. At end of road, go left onto Field Pt. Rd. to inn on right.

Credit cards Amex, DC, MC, Visa.

Rates Room only, $250–300 suite, $150–185 double, $110 single. Alc breakfast $10–16; alc lunch, $35–55; alc dinner, $55–75.

Extras Three working fireplaces in the restaurant. Crib. German, French, Spanish, Arabic, and Portuguese spoken.

HARTFORD

Also recommended: A short walk from the Mark Twain House is **The 1895 House** (97 Girard Avenue, 06105; 860–232–0014 or 860–232–0594), a Colonial Revival home with bay and Palladian windows. Three guest rooms are available at B&B double rates of $70–85, including a full breakfast. Six miles north of Hartford is **The Charles R. Hart House** (1046 Windsor Avenue, Windsor, 06095; 860–688–5555), a century-old Queen Anne mansion, beautifully restored with Victorian antiques and rich Bradbury & Bradbury wallpapers. The double rate of $65–109 for the four guest rooms includes a full breakfast. "Gracious hospitality, lovely decor, excellent breakfast." *(Rose Ciccone)*

IVORYTON

Copper Beech Inn ✕
46 Main Street, 06442

Tel: 860–767–0330
Fax: 860–767–7840
URL: http://www.copperbeechinn.com

The Copper Beech Inn was built about 100 years ago by a wealthy ivory merchant. As the town's name suggests, ivory was once its principal product and source of income. The sprawling mansion derives its current name from the enormous copper beech tree that spreads over the front lawn.

Eldon and Sally Senner bought the inn in 1988 and have worked hard to maintain and improve it. They expanded a side porch to create a Victorian-style conservatory for quiet seating or predinner cocktails, and rejuvenated the gracious terraced English gardens with thousands of spring-flowering bulbs. The inn is well known for its restaurant, offering country French cuisine in an elegant, formal setting. A recent dinner began with country sausage with herbs and apples, followed by lamb with white beans and cumin, and concluded with chocolate cake with raspberry mousse.

"Ivoryton is a peaceful town featuring wonderful old homes and the Ivoryton Playhouse. A perfect base for exploring Connecticut's historic seaport towns, minutes away from Essex on the Connecticut River and close to Goodspeed Opera House and Gillette's Castle." *(Maria Schmidt)* "The breakfast buffet of fresh fruit and juice, cereal, croissants, and assorted pastries was served in the same dining room as dinner. The attentive innkeepers ensured that supplies were ample. We had a spacious room in the carriage house, with a four-poster bed, couch, table, a Jacuzzi in the bathroom, and a deck in back. Pretty grounds, too." *(Lynda Worrell)*

"Our upstairs room in the carriage house had access to a porch overlooking the quiet hillside. The vaulted ceilings were supported by old barn beams." *(June Horn)* "Our spacious room at the back of the main house was quiet and relaxing." *(Mrs. Michael Cromis)* "My spacious room upstairs in the main house had wing chairs, a rocker, plants, a bay window, and plenty of closet space." *(Melissa Robin)* "The public areas and guest rooms are well appointed and carefully maintained, with fresh flowers and live plants. The comfortable guest rooms have good reading lights, lovely sheets and quilts, comfortable mattresses, and current magazines. Dinner is expertly prepared, and most entrees have wonderful sauces. The vegetarian entrees are complex and delicious—perhaps glazed root vegetables with grilled polenta and black bean puree. The service is professional, friendly, and personable; desserts are extraordinary." *(Holiday Collins)*

Open Closed 1st week of Jan., Dec. 24–25. Restaurant closed Mon., also Tues. Jan.–Mar.
Rooms 13 doubles—all with private bath and/or shower, air-conditioning, fan, telephone/fax link, clock/radio. 9 with Jacuzzi, TV, balcony or deck. 2 with desk. 9 rooms in carriage house.

Facilities Restaurant, lounge, parlor with books, conservatory, antique shop with collection of Chinese porcelain. 7 acres with gardens. Tennis, swimming, boating, fishing nearby.

Location Lower CT River valley. 30 m E of New Haven. 30 m W of Mystic, CT. 3 blocks from center of town. From I-95 take Exit 69 to Rte 9. At Exit 3, turn left and go 1¾ m to inn.

Restrictions Light sleepers should request rooms away from street and restaurant. No smoking. "Facilities not well suited for children under 10. " Room #1 has a small tub, no shower.

Credit cards Amex, DC, MC, Visa.

Rates B&B, $125–180 double. Extra person, $30. 2-night weekend/holiday minimum. Alc dinner, $50–60.

Extras Restaurant wheelchair accessible with lavatory equipped for disabled. Some Portuguese, Spanish spoken.

MYSTIC AREA

There's a lot to see and do in the Mystic/New London/Stonington area, but no one inn we want to single out as a special favorite. Described below are a number of fine choices of varying style, size, and price.

Also recommended: Three miles from downtown Mystic is the **House of 1833** (72 North Stonington Road, Mystic, 06355; 860–536–6325 or 800–FOR–1883; www.visitmystic.com). This Greek Revival mansion offers five guest rooms, each beautifully decorated with antiques. Some have a canopy bed, whirlpool tub, and/or a fireplace. B&B double rates of $95–225 include a full breakfast, and use of the inn's swimming pool, tennis court, and bicycles. "Blissful setting for a romantic getaway." *(LP)*

Nearby is the **Old Mystic Inn** (58 Main Street, P.O. Box 634, Old Mystic, 06372; 860–572–9422) built in 1794. The original chestnut and pine flooring and woodwork were all retained in the restoration, complemented by modern baths, four-poster canopy beds, and wicker furniture. Breakfast may include Belgian waffles with pecans or ham-and-cheese strata along with fresh fruit, juice, and homemade muffins. Eight rooms are available, four located in the carriage house (children welcome), and the $115–150 B&B rates include Saturday night wine and cheese. "Delightful rooms, wonderful breakfasts, delicious chocolate chip cookies, charming innkeepers." *(Leigh Robinson)*

Composed of the Haley Tavern, circa 1740, and the Crary Homestead, circa 1770, the **Red Brook Inn** (Gold Star Highway, Route 184, P.O. Box 237, 06372; 860–572–0349) gives guests an authentic taste of Connecticut's Colonial past. The guest rooms are decorated with period furnishings, stenciled wide plank floors, and canopy beds with hand-embroidered linens. Seven of the ten guest rooms have fireplaces; two have whirlpool tubs; B&B double rates range from $95–189. Full breakfasts are served family style before the cooking hearth in the keeping room. "Our spotless, spacious room had a queen-size canopy bed plus a twin-size bed; linens were crisp. The knowledgeable innkeeper explained the fascinating utensils used in the open hearth cooking." (*Pat Borysiewicz*)

A Georgian Colonial home built in 1807, **Stonecroft** (515 Pumpkin Hill Road, Ledyard, 06339; 860–572–0771 or 800–772–0774; www.stone croft.com) is surrounded by meadows, woodland, and stone walls, and is only a ten-minute drive from Mystic. Public rooms include the Great Room with its nine-foot wide fireplace, and for quiet pursuits, the Snuggery, once the birthing room and now a small library. In cool weather, breakfast is served by the dining room fireplace; in summer, guests dine on the terrace. Favorite entrees include omelets with smoked salmon and herbs, and buttermilk waffles with blueberries and whipped cream; special diets are accommodated with advance notice. B&B rates for the ten guest rooms range from $99–250.

NEW PRESTON

Set in the Berkshire Hills, New Preston's key attraction is Lake Waramaug, an inviting spot for swimming, fishing, and boating in summer, and skating in winter. Other area activities include hiking to the top of Pinnacle Mountain for views reaching to Massachusetts and New York, canoeing, bicycling, golf, and horseback riding; in winter, there's sledding, plus cross-country and downhill skiing. Many plays and concerts are offered in the summer, along with craft fairs, and the supply of antique shops is plentiful year-round.

New Preston is located in northwestern Connecticut, 45 miles west of Hartford and 85 miles north of New York City. From NYC, take Hutchinson River Pkwy. to I-684 N, then I-84 E to Exit 7 onto Rte. 7. In New Milford take Rte. 202 (formerly Rte. 25) to New Preston. From Hartford, take I-84 W to Farmington to Rte. 4 to Rte. 118 to Litchfield. Take Rte. 202 to New Preston, then left on Rte. 45 to Lake Waramaug.

Rates are highest here in summer, and on weekends year-round, and are considerably lower midweek from November through May.

Also recommended: An affordable alternative eight miles to the south is **The Homestead Inn** (Elm Street, New Milford, 06776; 860–354–4080), close to the village green. The inn itself dates back 140 years; there is also a small adjacent motel and many small shops and restaurants are within walking distance. A self-service breakfast buffet of fresh fruit and juice, cereal, English muffins, bagels, and breads, with coffee and tea, is included in the B&B double rates of $80–105; children welcome.

For a special occasion splurge, consider the **Mayflower Inn** (118 Woodbury Road, Washington, 06793; 860–868–9466), a luxurious country hotel. Imported linens, down comforters, and custom-blended toiletries are the appropriate complement to the king-size four-poster canopy beds and antiques found in the 25 guest rooms. Baths are fitted with marble, mahogany wainscoting, Limoges sinks, and deep tubs. The inn's restaurant utilizes local New England produce, from both land and sea. Double rates are $250–415, suites to $620, exclusive of meals.

Boulders Inn ✕ 🕭 ৬.
Route 45, 06777

Tel: 860–868–0541
800–55–BOULD
Fax: 860–868–1925
E-mail: boulders@bouldersinn.com
URL: http://www.bouldersinn.com

Set in the hills overlooking Lake Waramaug, the Boulders was built in 1895 as a private residence. Converted to an inn 45 years ago, the inn was purchased by Kees and Ulla Adema in 1988, assisted by their son, Eric, the inn's talented chef. Rooms in the inn are handsomely appointed in country decor with antiques and handmade quilts, while the rebuilt carriage house has a pleasing mix of antiques and contemporary furnishings. The cottages were recently renovated, adding new bathrooms, some with whirlpool tubs, and decks with lovely views of the lake. Breakfast includes a buffet of freshly squeezed orange juice, both fresh and dried fruit, yogurt, and lemon poppy seed muffins, orange walnut scones, or other pastries from the inn's bakery. Daily entrees might be a choice of ham and Swiss cheese omelets or cinnamon French toast; eggs any style are always available. Elegant, leisurely dining is a highlight at the Boulders; a recent dinner included an appetizer of jumbo scallops in a crispy potato puree with a sweet and sour blood orange sauce; sesame-seared yellowfin tuna with wasabi whipped potatoes, Oriental vegetables, and ginger cream sauce; and fresh fruit tart with apricot glaze. The wine list includes about 400 wines, with two dozen available by the glass.

"Appealing location, set back from the road with attractive landscaping and good lighting from the parking lot to the main entrance. Our carriage house room had a cathedral ceiling, Shaker-style four-poster bed, fireplace, comfortable seating areas, an antique bureau, quality bath amenities, and a good supply of fluffy towels. The living room in the main house is inviting, with lots of polished woodwork, a lively mix of floral fabrics, antique lamps, overstuffed sofas, and beautiful vistas of the lake through large windows. The renovated, circular porch offers an equally good view.

"Breakfast is hearty, starting off with a buffet of fruit, juices, granola, yogurt, and freshly made muffins and breads, followed by a cooked-to-order hot entree—I especially liked the omelets with fresh herbs and the waffles with fresh berries. For a magnificent view of the Litchfield Hills, follow Kees' directions up the small mountain behind the inn; it's an energetic 45-minute climb, but it's worth it." *(NB)* "We walked the entire seven miles around the lake, as a soft snow fell. Later, couples gathered in the living room, reading, listening to the softly playing classical music, or talking quietly." *(Mary Beth O'Reilly)* "Our lovely cottage room had a deck with a lake view, charming country-style furnishings, and a delicious plate of home-baked cookies." *(SWS, also MC)*

Open All year. Restaurant open Thurs.–Sun, Jan.–April, except holiday weekends; Memorial Day weekend through Oct. 31, restaurant open Wed.–Mon.
Rooms 8 cottages, 2 suites, 7 doubles—all with private bath and/or shower, telephone, air-conditioning. Some with desk, double whirlpool tub. Cottages

with deck, refrigerator, fireplace. Carriage House rooms with fireplace, refrigerator.

Facilities Restaurant, living room with fireplace, library/TV den with fireplace, terrace, game room with pool table, darts, piano, antique pinball machine. 27 acres with swimming, canoeing, sailing, paddleboats, tennis court, bicycling, hiking.

Location On Lake Waramaug, 7 m N of New Milford.

Restrictions No smoking in guest rooms, cottages, dining room. Children under 12 by arrangement.

Credit cards Amex, MC, Visa.

Rates B&B, $150–275 double. Extra person, $25. MAP, $225–325 double, $200–350 single. Extra person, $50. 15% service. 2–3 night weekend minimum. Alc dinner, $35–40.

Extras Wheelchair access to restaurant, 1 guest house. Dutch, German, French, Spanish spoken.

OLD LYME

Old Lyme has a reputation as an art colony and is the home of the Florence Griswold Historical Museum, with an excellent collection of American Impressionist paintings, the Lyme Art Association Gallery, and many fine antique shops.

Bee and Thistle Inn ✕
100 Lyme Street, 06371

Tel: 860–434–1667
800–622–4946
Fax: 860–434–3402
URL: http://www.beeandthistle.com

Longtime innkeepers Bob and Penny Nelson, assisted by their son, Jeff, and daughter, Lori, describe their inn as "a relaxing getaway, in a gracious warm setting, appealing to sophisticated adults." The Bee and Thistle serves breakfast, lunch, and dinner daily, and brunch on weekends, and menus change with the seasons. The breakfast menu includes raspberry crepes, beef and bacon hash, artichoke-dill omelets, and popovers filled with scrambled eggs, bacon, and cheese. Lunch favorites range from crab cakes to smoked chicken salad, and dinner entrees might include grilled shrimp with garlic couscous and tomato pesto, rack of lamb with potato flan, duck with mushroom risotto, and veal with lemon sage. From November through May, a proper English tea is served three days a week in the parlor or garden porch, including finger sandwiches, scones, and desert.

"Wonderful location, next door to the Florence Griswold Museum, and an easy drive to the Goodspeed Opera House. Lovely rooms with canopy beds. Relaxing grounds with flower gardens and river views." *(Marilyn Parker)* Exceptional dinner; creative menu, fine service, lovely atmosphere. Be sure to make reservations." *(SWS)* "One of the least expensive, our room was quite small but lovely; we had a chance to see many of the others, and especially liked rooms 1, 2, 5, and 11 in this well-maintained inn. We had a drink in the inviting bar, then a superb dinner which included homemade scones with honey, delicious salad with raspberry vinaigrette, wonderful clam chowder, trout, and an apple tart with ginger ice cream. The accommodating innkeepers offered us iced tea to take down to the river, where we relaxed and read." *(Trudy Selib)* "The bathroom was small but well supplied with lotions and soaps, and large, fluffy towels. The dinner menu was inventive, the atmosphere incredibly romantic with a harpist." *(Pamela Carafello)*

"Built in 1756, the building was moved several hundred feet away from the road about 65 years ago; various wings and porches were also added over the years." *(EL)* "The immaculate cottage has a sitting room with a fireplace and sofa bed, a bedroom with a dressing room, kitchen stocked with coffee and tea, a TV room with a brick floor and floor-to-ceiling windows opening onto a large deck, a private garden, and a path down to a private dock on the river. Private and quiet." *(William Gerhauser)*

Open Closed 1st 2 weeks in Jan.
Rooms 1 cottage, 11 doubles—all with private bath and/or shower, desk, air-conditioning, fan. Cottage with TV, kitchen, fireplace.
Facilities Restaurant with guitarist and harpist on weekends. 2 parlors with fireplace, bar; porches, library with books. 5½ acres with gardens. Swimming, boating, tennis, golf nearby.
Location E CT shore. Midway between NYC and Boston. 30 m E of New Haven. In historic district. From I-95 N, take Exit 70. Go left off ramp to 2nd traffic light, turn right (Rte. 1 E). Go to "T" in road & turn left to inn on left. From I-95 S, take Exit 70, turn right off ramp, third bldg. on left.
Restrictions Smoking in parlor only. No children under 12. Restaurant noise possible in two rooms until 11 P.M. on weekends.
Credit cards Amex, DC, MC, Visa.
Rates Room only, $215 cottage, $75–210 double. Extra person, $15. Alc breakfast, $5–7 (extra charge for breakfast in bed). Alc lunch, $20; alc dinner, $40–50; afternoon tea, $13; Sunday brunch, $15. Tips welcome.

SALISBURY

Salisbury is located in northwestern Connecticut, at the junction of Routes 41 and 44. Explore the stores and antique shops of this village, or use it as a base to explore the area's many lakes and mountains; activities include hiking, canoeing and kayaking, fishing, swimming, golf, and tennis, with downhill and cross-country skiing in winter. Car racing is a few miles south at Lime Rock, open from July through October. A number of summer music programs are within an easy drive, and Tanglewood, in Lenox, Massachusetts, is just 24 miles north.

In neighboring Lakeville (originally part of Salisbury) is Lake Wononskopomuc, one of the state's loveliest, deepest, and hardest to pronounce (try Wuh-NON-skuh-PUH-mic). This area has almost as many prep schools as antique shops, so reservations during parents' weekends and graduation can be tough to find.

Under Mountain Inn ✕

482 Undermountain Road (Route 41), 06068

Tel: 860–435–0242
Fax: 860–435–2379

"This inn is under Bear Mountain, one of Connecticut's 'loftiest' peaks at 2,300 feet; after one of Peter and Marged Higginson's full English breakfasts, guests will want to follow the nearby Under Mountain Trail to its peak, to ensure that they'll have room for afternoon tea and short-bread, served from 4 to 5 P.M., plus the American and English dinners prepared nightly by chef Peter. The oldest parts of the inn date back to the early 1700s, with the wide boards and uneven floors you'd expect. The common rooms and the bedrooms are highlighted with antiques; five guest rooms have canopy beds (most queen-size). My two favorite rooms are the corner rooms at the front of the inn, one with a king-size canopy bed. Most appealing is the cozy pub with its 250-year-old paneling, found hidden in the attic when the inn was restored. Just across the road is a pretty lake and a country road that invites strollers and joggers. The Higginsons have owned the inn since 1985 and are friendly and relaxed innkeepers." *(SWS)*

"Relaxing and rejuvenating. A beautiful area of Connecticut, close enough for a perfect weekend getaway. The rooms are bright, quiet, well-maintained, and attractively furnished. Marged is a charming hostess, most attentive to her guests, while Peter is the quiet man-behind-the scenes, serving up delicious English meals, with generous portions." *(Richard Boas)* "The English atmosphere, the excellent food, and fine service brought back memories of our cruise on the *QEII*." *(Marcela Dios)* "Nicely prepared and presented meals, even steak and kidney pie prepared for American palates. We used the inn as a base for day trips, antiquing in the treasure trove of area shops." *(John Blewer)* "Peter's English heritage permeates the inn with the many books on England and afternoon tea at four." *(Phyllis Fredericks)* "Exudes warmth and country inn hospitality from the minute you walk through the door." *(Jedd Savel)*

Open All year.

Rooms 7 doubles—all with private bath and/or shower, air-conditioning.

Facilities Living room with games; 3 dining rooms with fireplaces; pub; library with British books, books-on-tape, videos. 3 acres with croquet; lake nearby for swimming, canoeing; horseback riding. 15–20 min. to downhill and cross-country skiing. 40 min. to Tanglewood.

Location 4 m N of village center on Rte. 41.

Restrictions No smoking. Not suitable for children under 6.

Credit cards MC, Visa.

Rates MAP, $170–200 double, $115–150 single, plus 7% service. Extra person, $50. Senior discount midweek. 2–3 night weekend/holiday minimum. Mid-week/weekend, theme packages. Christmas, New Year's 3-night packages, MAP, $595–725 double.

Extras Restaurant wheelchair accessible.

TOLLAND

Set halfway between Hartford and Sturbridge, Tolland remains a traditional New England town, with many buildings clustered around the central town green. Founded in 1715, Tolland has long served as a resting point for travelers on the old post road from New York and Boston.

Area activities include bicycling, golf, swimming, fishing, and boating, plus cross-country skiing and ice-skating. Also of interest is Caprilands Herb Farm, and many antique shops and auctions.

Tolland is located in northeastern Connecticut, just a half-mile from Interstate 84, 25 minutes southwest of Sturbridge Village, 25 minutes northeast of Hartford, and 15 minutes northeast of the University of Connecticut at Storrs.

Also recommended: For a truly Colonial experience, visit the **Old Babcock Tavern B&B** (484 Mile Hill Road, 06084; 860–875–1239), dating back to 1720. Rooms are decorated with early-American antiques, and the double rate of $70–85 includes a full breakfast, plus a welcoming tray of tea and cookies. "Warm and attentive owners, excellent service, beautifully furnished rooms with private baths. Breakfast was exactly what we wanted after a relaxing night's sleep." *(William Lukas)*

The Tolland Inn (63 Tolland Green [Route 195], P.O. Box 717, 06084; 860–872–0800) combines careful craftsmanship, history, and a convenient location. The eight guest rooms are comfortably furnished with attractive wallpapers, comfortable beds, and antiques, and the B&B double rates of $70–130 include afternoon tea and cookies and a full breakfast.

Delaware

Lord and Hamilton Seaside Inn, Rehoboth Beach

Delaware is a small but historic state. The Brandywine Valley, over-lapping both Delaware and Pennsylvania, is particularly rich in sites of cultural interest such as Winterthur, the Hagley Museum, and the Nemours Mansion. Wilmington, Delaware's major city, has restored many of its historic areas in recent years. History buffs will also enjoy the 18th- and 19th-century houses of Odessa (including a Muskrat Skinning Shack), and the Victorian architecture of Dover's Historic District. If you're traveling through on I-95, be sure to stop in lovely, historic New Castle for at least an hour or preferably overnight.

The beaches of Rehoboth and Lewes are favorite escapes from the heat and humidity of summertime Washington. They are 120 miles (approximately 3 hours) from Washington, Baltimore, and Philadelphia. If you're coming from New York or New Jersey, take the New Jersey Turnpike over the Delaware Memorial Bridge, then take Route 13 to Route 1 to Lewes and Rehoboth. An alternate route (suggested for the trip home) is to take the 70-minute ferry ride from Lewes to Cape May to the Garden State Parkway (call 800–64–FERRY for details); it's about a 5-hour drive to New York City. A recommended short detour is the Bombay Hook National Refuge (northeast of Dover) where migrating ducks and geese stop by in spring and fall, and herons, egrets, and other wading birds spend the summer.

Peak rates generally run from June 15 to September 15; off-season rates are considerably less. Rehoboth is a favorite family resort, combining all the boardwalk stuff kids love with chic shops and gourmet restaurants; Lewes is a bit more sedate.

Worth noting: Delaware has no sales tax, so outlet malls have sprung up in tourist areas faster than mushrooms after rain.

NEW CASTLE

Delightful New Castle is an ideal spot to stop if you're traveling along I-95 between Washington and New York. In the few minutes it takes to drive from the highway to the historic section, you can travel back 250 years to a living Colonial village.

Founded in 1651 by Peter Stuyvesant, New Castle was claimed alternately by both the Dutch and the Swedish governments, until the Duke of York took it for the British in 1664 and renamed it New Castle. The town was Delaware's capital until the early eighteenth century, when it was shifted to Wilmington. Development stopped, and a lovely piece of history was preserved. The town is built right along the Delaware River, nearly under the Delaware Memorial Bridge.

Reader tips: "Within easy walking distance are a magnificent 1732 Court House, Delaware's Colonial capitol, the home of George Read II, and a lovely and inspiring Presbyterian church built in 1707. Be sure to see how the Dutch settlers lived by visiting the Amstel House and the Old Dutch House museums." *(Nancy Harrison & Nelson Ormsby)* "Old town New Castle is a historic delight with cobblestoned streets, a lovely waterfront park, and charming small shops. The David Finney Inn had not yet reopened when we visited, so we had dinner at the Old Arsenal—pleasant ambiance, satisfactory food." *(PB)*

Also recommended: Built in 1732 and renovated as a B&B in 1995, **The Armitage Inn** (2 The Strand, 19720; 302–328–6618) overlooks the Delaware River. The four guest rooms have queen- or king-size beds, private baths, central air-conditioning, telephones with dataports, and cable TV. The B&B double rates range from $105–150. "The spacious White Rose Room has a high king-size four-poster canopy bed, draped in white fabric, with a floral rose comforter, and lace curtains. The bathroom was large with whirlpool tub, ample counter space, and soft fluffy bath towels on brass racks. The other guest rooms were equally lovely. The parlor, dining room, and library on the first floor contain many mementos, collections, and family treasures. The delicious breakfast included juice, freshly ground coffee, fresh fruit, yogurt, cereals, homemade zucchini bread, and baked French toast." *(Rose Ciccone)*

REHOBOTH BEACH

Rehoboth is located on Delaware's Atlantic shore, 125 miles east of Washington, D.C., and has been a mecca for Washingtonians escaping the oppressive summer heat and humidity ever since the Chesapeake Bay Bridge was completed in 1952. Rehoboth's beautiful white sands are bordered in most areas by shady pine forests, offering a welcome respite from the summer sun. Children love the mile-long boardwalk, complete with snack bars alternating with miniature golf courses and video games and capped with the rides at Funland. Those in search of more sedate entertainment will prefer the weekend evening concerts at the bandstand nearby on Rehoboth Avenue. Area activities center on the water, and include swimming, surf-casting, sailing, windsurfing, clamming, and fishing, plus the favored indoor sport of the 1990s: the designer outlet mall.

As is the case in most beach towns, parking is a pain in season, when Rehoboth's population zooms from 3,000 to 90,000. Once you've found an unmetered parking space, just leave your car where it is, and walk or bicycle to in-town destinations. To avoid congestion, visit midweek.

Reader tips: "In Lewes, don't miss dinner at Rosa Negra and a sandwich from Taste of Heaven." *(Donna Bocks)*

Also recommended: The **Lord and Hamilton Seaside Inn** (20 Brooklyn Avenue, 19971; 302–227–6960 or 800–637–2862) offers a cozy sitting room and a sunny, sprawling veranda for convivial breakfasts or lazy afternoon conversations. The rooms are decorated with family antiques, canopy beds, quilts, overstuffed chairs and lounges. The location is quiet, just a half-block from the beach, and two from the town center, so you can forget about your car. All rooms have private baths and air-conditioning, and the B&B double rates range from $85–105, including a continental breakfast.

A little farther away is the historic Dutch seaport town of **Lewes**, with its canal which carries fishing and pleasure boats to sea. The gingerbread Victorian **Wild Swan Inn** (525 Kings Highway, Lewes, 19958; 302–645–8550), offers lovely gardens, a swimming pool, bicycles, a homemade breakfast, and quiet guest rooms decorated in period. B&B double rates range from $85–120. Guests rave about the delightful innkeepers, delicious breakfasts, and charming Victorian decor.

A good choice for families is the **Blue Water House** (407 East Market Street, Lewes 19958; 302–645–7832 or 800–493–2080; bluewater-house@lewes-beach.com) at Lewes Beach, just a short walk from the bay beach and a quick drive to the ocean at Cape Henlopen. Built in 1993, the six guest rooms open onto a wraparound veranda, each with a private bath and air-conditioning. The upper level offers spectacular views, board games, and TV. Breakfast includes home-baked breads with fresh fruit and cereal. Guests are welcome to borrow the inn's beach balls, boogie boards, and bicycles. Furnishings are casual, and the B&B double rates are $80–140 double.

Information please: The **Royal Rose Inn** (41 Baltimore Avenue, 19971; 302–226–2535) is a 1920s beach cottage, restored as a B&B in 1989, and purchased by Andy Dorosky in 1998. The breakfast menu changes daily: perhaps fresh fruit cup, juice, praline French toast, Canadian bacon, blueberry muffins, and granola one day; and grapefruit, orange juice, sausage quiche, banana muffins, poppy seed bread, and baked apple oatmeal the next. "The inn is an easy walk to the beach, boardwalk, shops, and restaurants; its off-street parking is a real plus in a town where parking is metered and spaces are not easy to find. Our favorite spot was the screened front porch where breakfast is served; we relaxed there in the early morning, watching the town wake up, and in the evening enjoying the breeze." *(Robert & Judith Nulton)* B&B double rates for the seven guest rooms range from $95–115. Reports appreciated.

WILMINGTON

Reader tip: "Compared to New York, Wilmington seems more like a town than a city, but despite its many charms, it also has urban problems, including crime. Use your street smarts and ask your innkeeper for advice. As is true in any city, never leave valuables visible in a locked car." *(DGW)*

Also recommended: Beautifully renovated in 1993, the famous **Hotel Dupont** (11th & Market Street, 19801; 302–594–3100 or 800–441–9019) has classic charm in its restaurants and common areas, and lovely guest rooms showcasing the latest Dupont products in baths, on walls, floors, and beds. Double rates for the 216 rooms run from $149–385; weekend packages are an especially good deal.

Ten minutes north of Wilmington is the 18th-century Dutch Colonial that was home to Felix Darley, a popular illustrator of books by Edgar Allan Poe and James Fenimore Cooper. **Darley Manor** (3701 Philadelphia Pike, Claymont, 19703; 302–792–2127 or 800–824–4703; http://www.dca.net/darley) was renovated in 1991 and is extensively decorated with antiques, reproductions, and collectibles. Ideal for the business traveler, the inn has a convenient location, just off the interstate, efficient phone service, good working space, modern amenities, and flexible full breakfasts. B&B double rates range from $79–99.

Four miles northwest of Wilmington is the village of Montchanin, a compound of modest Greek- and Gothic-Revival buildings, dating to 1870, that once housed workers from the Dupont powder mills. Five generations and millions of dollars later, Dupont descendants Missy and Daniel Lickle have restored the eleven buildings to form the **Inn at Montchanin Village** (Route 100 at Kirk Road, Montchanin, 19710; 302–888–2133 or 800–COWBIRD; www.montchanin.com) with 26 luxury suites and doubles, all with marble baths and state of the art amenities; a 55-seat restaurant, Krazy Kat's, is housed in a renovated barn, and features seasonal American cuisine. Double rates of $150–325 include a continental breakfast.

The Boulevard B&B ¢
1909 Baynard Boulevard, 19802

Tel: 302–656–9700
Fax: 302–656–9701
E-mail: blvdbb@wserv.com

The Boulevard is an imposing redbrick house built in 1913, with neoclassical and Federal elements; Chuck and Judy Powell opened it as a B&B in 1986. Served from 8–9 A.M., breakfast includes fruit and juice, cereal, muffins or coffee cake, eggs to order or the daily special—perhaps lemon pancakes with raspberry syrup, pecan waffles, or cinnamon French toast—and sausage or bacon. Depending on the season, afternoon snacks are accompanied by iced or hot tea, lemonade or hot mulled cider.

"Spacious home, eclectically furnished with traditional pieces and antique accents. Warm, inviting living room; the little library has an unusual tiled fireplace. Especially pretty is the second floor landing, with a comfy window seat. Our favorite room, tucked under the eaves on the third floor, is done in shades of rose and pink, with a queen-size bed, sitting area, and a Jacuzzi. Guest rooms are bright and sunny, comfortable but modest." *(SWS)*

"Delicious breakfast, beautifully served in the spacious and bright dining room, or on the porch in warmer weather." *(Elaine Bermas)* "We appreciated the comfortable chairs in our room, ideal for reading and conversation." *(Debra Hood)* "Spacious bathrooms with soaps, shampoo, and fluffy towels. Quiet residential neighborhood with a park and zoo just down the road." *(Fenella Thornton)* "Our spacious room had a loveseat, desk, large closet, big thirsty towels, fresh flowers, and chocolate mints. Loved having a choice at breakfast; conversation was so relaxed and pleasurable that it was hard to leave the table." *(Ron & Jean Alexander)* "We were treated like family, with high chair and toys for the kids, plus a playground nearby." *(Pat Bradle)* "Comfortable atmosphere, immaculate rooms, wonderful food. Gracious hosts, well informed about local attractions and restaurants." *(Steve & Ann Hunt)* "The hospitable Powells gave us great advice on what to see and do in Wilmington. The breakfast of home-baked muffins, fluffy pancakes, and grapefruit with raspberries was delicious." *(Debra Hood)*

Open All year.

Rooms 6 doubles—4 with private bath and/or shower, 2 with maximum of 3 sharing bath. All with radio, TV, desk, air-conditioning. 4 with telephone, 3 with ceiling fan. 1 with whirlpool tub.

Facilities Dining room, living room with fireplace, stereo, organ; library with fireplace, TV/VCR; sun porch. Meeting room.

Location Historic district. 10 blocks from center. Take Exit 8 off I-95 onto Concord Pike (Rte. 202 S). Go right at 2nd light onto Baynard Blvd. B&B on right after 20th St.

Restrictions No smoking.

Credit cards Amex, MC, Visa.

Rates B&B, $70–85 double, $60–75 single. Extra person, $10–15.

Can't Find It Here?

Our regional guides include *two to three times* the number of entries contained here. Pick up a copy of our *New England* (plus Eastern Canada), *Middle Atlantic, South, Midwest* (plus Ontario), *Rocky Mountains & Southwest*, or *West Coast* (plus Western Canada) edition for lots more information on great places to stay. If your bookstore doesn't have a current copy in stock, ask them to order it for you or call 800–288–2131. You can also order copies from our Website at http://www.inns.com.

District of Columbia

Swann House

Everyone needs to visit "DC" at least once in their lives. Early spring is the prettiest time, with cherry blossoms adding color and softness to a city that can seem rather cold and impersonal. In addition to the obligatory monuments, museums, and other famous tourist spots, add some less-visited stops to your itinerary: See hundreds of water plants at the Kenilworth Aquatic Gardens, wander through sprawling Rock Creek Park, stroll along the B&O Canal just west of Georgetown, or drive up MacArthur Parkway to Great Falls—a spectacular setting for picnics. If Congress is in session when you're in town, be sure to watch your lawmakers in action (night sessions are particularly intriguing). From late June to early July, join the throngs at the Festival of American Folklife. For a more sedate cultural experience, attend a performance at the Folger Shakespeare Theater (September to June).

Spring and fall are peak periods in Washington, when rates are high and space is tight. You can get the best deals on weekends year-round, and from December through February and during the summer, when Congress adjourns and many Washingtonians escape the city's infamous heat and humidity. When making reservations always ask if any special rates are in effect. To save money on hotel reservations, call **Capitol Reservations** (1730 Rhode Island Avenue N.W., Suite 506, 20036; 202–452–1270 or 800–VISIT–DC), which can book you into 75 local hotels (including Loew's L'Enfant Plaza described below) at a lower price than you could get by calling the hotel directly.

Another option is a B&B reservation service called **The Bed & Breakfast League, Ltd./Sweet Dreams & Toast, Inc.** (P.O. Box 9490, 20016–9490; 202–363–7767). The accommodations have been inspected; the criteria for membership includes safe neighborhoods, comfortable bedrooms, immaculate baths, hearty continental breakfasts, and location within an easy walk of the public transportation system.

Reader tips: "Washington is a busy, noisy city. In popular areas like Georgetown, street noise can continue into the wee hours, especially in summer. If you are a light sleeper, you might need to sacrifice a view for a quieter courtyard room." Also: "Staying in Georgetown is great if you have a car or can take taxis. There's no Metro stop, a definite problem for sightseers." *(Robin Clarke)* "Some areas are pretty rough—definitely unsafe for night-time strolls. Ask for advice and pay attention." *(MW)*

Also recommended—moderate: The **Dupont Plaza** (1500 New Hampshire Avenue, N.W., 20036; 202–483–6000 or 800–841–0003) has 314 guest rooms with private baths, two-line phones with voice mail and dataports, refrigerators, and coffee makers. Double rates range from $95–205, and children under 17 stay free. "Pleasant staff who know me by name. The neighborhood is safe (for D.C.), and full of ethnic restaurants and great bookstores. The outer rooms have wonderful big bathtubs, but are noisier than the inner rooms. The Metro is only a block away. My favorite room overlooks Starbuck's outdoor cafe—great coffee aroma." *(CMK)*

Based in two grand townhouses dating to 1864 plus a contemporary addition, the **Morrison-Clark Inn** (Massachusetts Avenue at 11th Street, N.W., 20001; 202–898–1200 or 800–332–7898) enjoys a top reputation for the creative international cuisine served in its charming dining rooms. Reports on the rooms vary, although the Victorian rooms in the original mansions seem to be the first choice. The location is convenient to the convention center, although some nearby streets are not appealing. Rates range from $165–260, with lower rates on weekends. In an appealing neighborhood, ten minutes by Metro to the White House, Capitol, and the Mall is the **Kalorama** (1854 Mintwood Place, N.W., 20009; 202–667–6369), comprising four townhouses with 30 guest rooms, in a location convenient to the Kalorama Park and Adams Morgan neighborhoods. B&B double rates range from $55–125. "Our room was comfortable, not fancy; the bathroom was small. Ample breakfast/sitting area. Great neighborhood, with lovely streets of private houses and plenty of good restaurants nearby." *(Bill Hussey)* "Comfortable bed, spotless bathroom. Ample breakfast with fruit juice, nice baked goods from a local bakery, yogurt, cereal; afternoon cookies and lemonade also served. Cordial staff; convenient location. Be sure to inquire if you have trouble with steps." *(Carol Dinmore)*

Across the Potomac in Virginia, about 10 miles from Washington, is the elegant Federal-style **Morrison House** (16 South Alfred Street, Alexandria, 22314; 703–838–8000 or 800–367–0800), built in 1985. A European-style luxury hotel, it is furnished with high-quality period reproduction furnishings, brass and crystal lighting, and elaborately swagged curtains. The inn's dining room offers an intimate setting with an 18th-century decor, while the clubby grill room has leather chairs and a mahogany bar. Double rates are $150–205, suites to $295. "Convenient location, charming area, wonderful hotel. Tasteful decor, pleasant and helpful staff, a delicious continental breakfast. Our lovely room was at the front corner, top floor. Three-day package an excellent value." *(Stephanie Roberts)* "Although the management has changed, the service has not. Every need is anticipated with a smile." *(Lorraine Cromis)*

For lots of character, try the **Tabard Inn** (1739 N Street, N.W., 20036; 202–785–1277), located on a quiet side street close to Dupont Circle and its Metro stop. Composed of three linked Victorian townhouses, the inn is furnished with well-used period furnishings, and offers idiosyncratic charm that will delight some, but not all, readers. B&B double rates range from $90–110 for the shared-bath rooms; $115–175 for rooms with a private bath. "Tasty breakfasts, central location, reasonably priced. Chaucer theme gives it a bit of a British feel, with a pub-type bar, panelled lounge, and well-spaced tables for breakfast. Service mostly good." *(Caroline Raphael)* "Great location in a residential area near Dupont Circle. Guest rooms are a bit on the shabby side, with furnishings that are equal parts 'attique' and antique, but are a fair value. The best part of the Tabard are the intimately arranged parlor, great room, and dining room. It's a great place to settle down for an evening of conversation, by the fireplace and fine food." *(KMC)*

Also recommended—luxury: The **Hay-Adams Hotel** (16th & H Streets, N.W., 1 Lafayette Square, 20006; 202–638–6600 or 800–424–5054). Known for its luxurious atmosphere and excellent service, the hotel has handsome rooms, excellent service, and delightful food and ambiance in its restaurant. Located directly opposite the White House facing Lafayette Square Park, its 137 rooms rent for $255–395. Children under 16 stay free and weekend rates are available. "Quiet location, yet ideally located within walking distance of most major attractions. Staff friendly, and extremely helpful. Old-fashioned charm with beautiful wainscotting throughout the lobby and dining rooms. Our room had a beautiful modern marble and brass bathroom, several telephones, and more than ample closets. Romantic, cozy pub in the lower level." *(Betsy Sandberg)*

On Capital Hill, near Union Station is the newly renovated **Hotel George** (15 E Street, N.W., 20001; 202–347–4200 or 800–576–8331), with luxurious contemporary décor in its 140 guest rooms. "Sleek marble and glass modern design. Friendly staff." *(KLH)*

Built as a luxury apartment building in 1923, **The Jefferson** (16th & M Streets, N.W. 20036; 202–347–2200 or 800–368–5966) offers 100 elegant guest rooms, individually decorated with rich fabrics, canopy beds, original paintings, and antiques. Located just four blocks north of the White House, its restaurant has long been a place to see and be seen. Double rates range from $265–305, suites from $350. "Extremely spacious room; 'old money' elegance to the décor. Pleasant, if pricy breakfast. A lovely experience." *(EA)*

Swann House　　　　　　　　　　　*Tel:* 202–265–7677
1808 New Hampshire Avenue, N.W., 20009　　*Fax:* 202–265–6755
E-mail: swannhouse@aol.com

Architect Walter Paris designed and built the Swann House, one of the area's oldest free-standing mansions, for his personal use in 1883, in the grand Richardsonian Romanesque style. In 1996, Richard and Mary

Ross restored the building to its original elegance, complete with 12-foot ceilings with 18-inch crown moldings, fluted woodwork, inlaid wood floors, crystal chandeliers, and elaborately carved wood mantels. Dozens of shops, restaurants, and art galleries are close by; major sights and government buildings are easily reached by car, Metro, or on foot. David Story is the manager.

"A tray of cookies sat on the dining room table and tea was offered on arrival. Later, we sipped wine while perusing restaurant menus. Mary made recommendations and then our dinner reservations. The common areas are spacious, attractive, uncluttered, and comfortable, with ample seating and lots of fresh flowers and live plants. The sun room, which opens to a balcony overlooking the swimming pool, is used for breakfast in the warmer weather; it has a wet bar and refrigerator stocked with soft drinks and bottled water. The Jennifer Green Room has a balcony overlooking the garden, a fireplace, a comfortable queen-size bed, bedside tables with reading lamps, and a leather armchair with ottoman. The yellow-, green-, and rose-colored bedding matched the quilt and drapes. The sectioned bathroom had a vanity and sink area separate from the over-sized shower; a basket contained shampoos, conditioners, and lotions in large bottles. Large bath towels were nice and fluffy. The Regent Room is done in blue, with handsome woodwork, a king-size bed, plus a double marble shower, and a Jacuzzi in the bath. Breakfast was served in the dining room between 8 and 10 A.M., and included granola and cereals, juice, muffins and scones, and a wonderful assortment of fresh fruit. Coffee was plentiful and good." (Rose Ciccone)

"David and Mary provide first-class service and hospitality. Rooms are extremely clean and well maintained. The inn itself is a magnificent historic home in downtown Washington's most livable and civilized neighborhood. A small city park is directly across the street, and abundant excellent restaurants are within a short walk. The Il Duomo room has skylights, Gothic windows, clawfoot tub in the turret, as well as a hand-painted ceiling mural. Great scones, too." (Paula Chiarmote) "Delicious, hot-from-the-oven apple muffins. Friendly, hospitable atmosphere." (Karen Mannes) "Our room was beautifully decorated and clean. The owners were friendly and helpful with area history and information." (Sandy Pare) "We played the grand piano, sat in the living room and read, and enjoyed wine and cheese in the evening." (Barry Pollara) "Outstanding features include large rooms, fireplace with lots of wood, quiet atmosphere, and the welcoming atmosphere of this beautiful mansion." (Mary E. Malcuit) "Spacious, yet cozy, public areas—good for reading, conversation—even parties."(Joan Ewald) "The deck, garden, and pool was a wonderful treat after a day in the summer heat." (Jane Arthur, and others)

Open All year.

Rooms 3 suites, 6 doubles—all with private bath and/or shower, telephone with voice mail/dataport, TV, radio, clock, air-conditioning. Some with fireplace, refrigerator, deck, whirlpool tub.

Facilities Dining room, living room with fireplace, piano, parlor with fireplace, sun room with guest refrigerator, guest laundry, porch, deck, patio. Garden, swimming pool, 3 off-street parking spaces (reserve ahead).

Location Dupont Circle neighborhood, 1 m from White House. 3 blocks to Metro. On NH Ave., between S & T Sts., 17th & 18th Sts. From I-95 S, take I-495 W to Exit 30B, Colesville Rd. S, toward Silver Spring. Go 2 m to 16th St. & go left. Go 5 m past V St. At next corner, turn right onto NH Ave., through 1 light to house on right.

Restrictions No smoking. Children over 12.

Credit cards Amex, DC, MC, Visa.

Rates B&B, $125–200 suite, double; $110–200 single. Corporate, government, long-term rates. Extra person, $20.

Key to Abbreviations and Symbols

For complete information and explanations, please see the Introduction.

¢ Especially good value for overnight accommodation.

♦ Families welcome. Most (but not all) have cribs, baby-sitting, games, play equipment, and reduced rates for children.

✗ Meals served to public; reservations recommended or required.

⚂ Tennis court and swimming pool and/or lake on grounds. Golf usually on grounds or nearby.

& Limited or full wheelchair access; call for details.

Rates: Range from least expensive room in low season to most expensive room in peak season.

Room only: No meals included; European Plan (EP).

B&B: Bed and breakfast; includes breakfast, sometimes afternoon/evening refreshment.

MAP: Modified American Plan; includes breakfast and dinner.

Full board: Three meals daily.

Alc lunch: A la carte lunch; average price of entrée plus nonalcoholic drink, tax, tip.

Alc dinner: Average price of three-course dinner, including half bottle of house wine, tax, tip.

Prix fixe dinner: Three- to five-course set dinner, excluding wine, tax, tip unless otherwise noted.

Extras: Noted if available. Always confirm in advance. Pets are not permitted unless specified; if you are allergic, ask for details; *most innkeepers have pets.*

Florida

Thurston House, Orlando (Maitland)

There *is* a real Florida apart from giant theme parks, condo developments, and endless chains of cloned hotels and motels. Although theme parks, beaches, and retired relatives are three popular reasons for visiting Florida, we'd like to suggest some less-well-known Florida highlights. In the southeast, visit the tranquil Japanese flower gardens at the Morikami Cultural Complex west of Delray Beach, or drop by a professional polo match. On the Gulf Coast, travel back roads to find isolated coastal inlets, drop by the Salvador Dali Museum in St. Petersberg, or visit unspoiled Honeymoon and Caladesi islands that are maintained as state parks.

Although best known for its theme parks, Central Florida also boasts miles of grassy prairies, flowering fruit groves, horse farms, 1400 lakes and the world's largest sandy pine forest. In Northeast Florida don't miss the Spanish flavor of St. Augustine, the oldest city in the United States. The Florida Panhandle, in the northwest, offers miles of sugarwhite sand, rolling hill country near Tallahassee, the Alaqua Vineyards (one of only four wineries in the state), and an unusual mixture of Creole, Victorian, and other architecture in Pensacola's Seville Historic District.

Peak season rates in most of Florida generally extend from December 1–15 through May 1–15; off-season rates are considerably lower. Do remember that August and September are the height of the tropical storm/hurricane season, so keep this in mind when planning a trip.

AMELIA ISLAND

Amelia Island's only town is Fernandina Beach, at its north end, but since the two addresses are used interchangeably, and the island name is better known, we've listed our entries here. Amelia Island is located in the northeast corner of Florida, just south of the Georgia border, and 35 miles north of Jacksonville. Area activities focus on the area's wide sandy beaches, with ample opportunities for swimming, boating, and fishing, but golf and tennis are available as well. The scent of the sea is sometimes mixed with the less appealing odor of the island's paper mills, but this doesn't seem to bother the island's many enthusiasts.

Reader tips: "The historic district of Fernandina Beach feels the way Key West did 25 years ago. Friendly people, interesting shops, and good places to eat." *(Joe & Sheila Schmidt)* "The Kingsley Plantation south of Amelia Island is worth visiting, as are the state parks at Little Talbot Island and Fort Clinch, where there are reenactments of military drills of the 1860s." *(April Burwell)* "The historic district is compact, making walking delightful." *(SWS)*

Also recommended: Constructed in an 1890s Nantucket shingle style, with a maritime theme, the **Elizabeth Pointe Lodge** (82 South Fletcher Avenue, P.O. Drawer 1210, 32034; 904–277–4851 or 800–772–3359;) has 25 guest rooms with B&B rates ranging from $130–210, most with ocean views, and some with Jacuzzi tubs (the sand dunes are just steps away). Rates include a full breakfast, the morning newspaper, afternoon lemonade, and wine at 6 P.M. "Hotel-style convenience with inn-style caring; the staff was friendly, helpful, and professional. Lovely water views from most common areas, guest rooms, and porches. The cool ocean breezes allowed me to open the windows wide and sleep like a baby to the sound of the waves lapping the shore. You can enjoy your breakfast in the dining room or on the porch, chatting with the other guests or in privacy, as you prefer. The evening social hour was set up in the library, with fresh fruit and sliced cheese, spinach dip and crackers; we took our glasses and snacks out to the porch to enjoy the ocean air." *(SWS)*

Built in 1856, **The Amelia Island Williams House** (103 South 9th Street, 32034; 904–277–2328 or 800–414–9258; www.williamshouse.com) was completely restored by owners Dick Flitz and Chris Carter, who refinished over 6500 square feet of woodwork and hung over 350 rolls of wallpaper. Opulent and elegant, the inn is furnished with antiques. A sweeping cherry and mahogany staircase leads to the four guestrooms; each has access to the wraparound veranda. B&B double rates range from $145–190. "Outstanding accommodations, impeccable service." *(Tom Wilson & Cynthia Hermes)*

Florida House Inn ✕ ♿   *Tel:* 904–261–3300
20 & 22 South 3rd Street, P.O. Box 688, 32034   800–258–3301
                              E-mail: innkeepers@floridahouseinn.com
                              URL: http://www.floridahouse.com

One-time Florida resident Thomas Alva Edison is said to have remarked that: "Invention is 1% inspiration, 99% perspiration." When you see the "before" and "after" pictures of the Florida House, you may decide that restoring an old inn follows a similar ratio. In 1991, Karen and Bob Warner completed a total renovation of the Florida's oldest sur-

FLORIDA

viving (but just barely) hotel. During the 19th century, its many famous guests included General Ulysses S. Grant, Jose Marti, plus assorted Rockefellers and Carnegies; in those days, the inn had 25 guest rooms and no indoor plumbing—now all have private baths, many with luxurious double Jacuzzi tubs! Rates include a full Southern breakfast, served from 8 to 9:30 A.M.; also available is a restaurant offering "boarding house" dining—fried chicken and catfish with fresh Southern-style vegetables, served family-style at tables for twelve.

"Karen, Bob, and their staff will cater to your every whim, making your stay exactly as you want it. After a wonderful breakfast of French toast and other treats, served on beautiful china, I love to finish my coffee on the patio, enjoying the breeze, with a fuzzy kitten curled into my lap." *(Lisa Kittrell)* "Southern hospitality; down-home cooking." *(Eleanor Smith)* "Good lighting and strong showers. An excellent breakfast is served on the back porch or in the sunny breakfast room. Sipping afternoon lemonade on the wooden rockers of the second floor porch was equally pleasant." *(Shirley Hall)* "The shade of time-twisted oaks makes the porch an inviting place to gather over evening wine." *(Michael & Jeanne Green)* "The annual May seafood festival is conveniently located right at the inn's front door." *(Mr. & Mrs. John Cheetham)* "Extensive insulation added during the renovations kept our room extremely quiet." *(Robert & Donna Jacobson)* "Crisp cotton sheets; clean, spacious bathroom; warm hospitality." *(SW & AB)*

"Karen and Bob have done a wonderful job of preserving the inn's historic charm, while adding all modern conveniences. Lunch and dinner are very reasonably priced; along with gallons of iced tea, I sampled delicious sweet and sour cabbage, collard greens, chicken and dumplings, candied yams, and cornbread, and even found room for a bite of apple crisp. The fun, low-key, cozy pub has an incredible collection of bottled brews that are well worth a detour for beer lovers. Antique quilts line the hallway walls, and accent the simple but pleasing furnishings of the guest rooms. Color schemes are soothing and uncomplicated, rooms uncluttered. The two least expensive rooms are small, but a super value." *(SWS)*

Open All year.
Rooms 1 suite, 14 doubles—all with private bath and/or shower, telephone, radio, TV, air-conditioning, ceiling fan. Most with desk; 10 with fireplace, double Jacuzzi tub. 12 rooms in North Bldg; 3 rooms in South Bldg.
Facilities Breakfast room, restaurant, pub with fireplace, TV; parlor with fireplace, games. Gazebo, garden courtyard with fountain. Fax, copier, laundry facilities. Off-street parking. Tennis, golf nearby. 5 min. from Atlantic Ocean for boating, fishing, swimming; 2 blocks from marina.
Location Historic District. From I-95, take Exit 129 and follow Rte. A1A to Amelia Island, Fernandina Beach. Rte. A1A turns into 8th St. on island. Follow 8th St. to the intersection of 8th St. & Atlantic/Centre St. (Shell gas station on left). Turn left on Atlantic/Centre St. Go 5 blocks to S 3rd St. & turn left. Florida House Inn is ½ block from Centre on left.
Restrictions Smoking only in pub, on porches, patio.
Credit cards All major.

Rates B&B, $145 suite, $75–140 double. Extra person, $15. 2-night weekend minimum.
Extras Limited wheelchair access. Some pets by arrangement. Local airport/marina pickups. Limited Spanish spoken.

APALACHICOLA

Although once a major Gulf port, Apalachicola (known locally as Apalach) is now a sleepy town in the Florida Panhandle, with shrimp and oysters being the primary cash crops.

Information please: A magnificently renovated 1905 Victorian home, the **Coombs House Inn** (80 Sixth Street, 32320; 850–653–9199; www.coombshouseinn.com) is located in the historic district, minutes from the bay. The ten guest rooms in the main house are beautifully done with elegant antiques and fine reproductions, English chintz fabrics, and Oriental carpet atop gleaming hardwood floors. More casual in decor are the eight rooms in the restored 1907 Coombs Cottage annex. B&B double rates of $79–139 include a continental breakfast served from 8 to 11 A.M. and use of the inn's bicycles.

A plantation home built in 1838, **Magnolia Hall** (177 5th Street, 32320; 850–653–2431) has a swimming pool and rose garden for guests' relaxation. The two guest rooms occupy the entire second floor; each has a gas log fireplace and private bath. The B&B double rates of $150 for the first night, $100 the second, including wake-up coffee, a full breakfast, and afternoon wine and cheese.

The **Gibson Inn** (51 Avenue C, 32320; 850–653–2191) is a large blue building surrounded by two-story white verandas and topped by a cupola. The 31 guest rooms are furnished in period, with four-poster beds, ceiling fans, antique armoires, brass and porcelain bathroom fixtures, and clawfoot tubs. Its popular restaurant serves three meals a day, from a full range of standard breakfast favorites, to a lunch of fried oysters, to a dinner of seafood gumbo; shrimp and scallop Dijon; and chocolate bourbon pecan pie. Double rates range from $70–115. Reports welcome.

JACKSONVILLE

Located in northeastern Florida, Jacksonville is a major port and business center. The St. John's River loops through the city, and the Riverwalk area on the south bank has been attractively preserved.

Also recommended: A prairie-style home in the Riverside district, the **Cleary-Dickert House** (1804 Copeland Street, Jacksonville, 32204; 904–387–4762) offers comfortable suites in a 1914 Prairie-style home in charming garden setting, just 50 yards from the river. B&B double rates of $85–99 include a full breakfast, afternoon tea, and evening wine and cheese. "Delightful owners; Joe's English, Betty's Southern. Rooms are

FLORIDA

quiet, comfortable, and immaculate; the hospitality is unbeatable." *(Bill MacGowan)*

House on Cherry Street ¢   *Tel:* 904–384–1999
1844 Cherry Street, 32205   *Fax:* 904–384–5013
                        E-mail: houseoncherry@compuserve.com

Those who have stereotypical ideas of Floridian decor will be amazed when they see the House on Cherry Street, a Colonial-style home built in 1909, overlooking the St. John's River, and owned by Carol and Merrill Anderson since 1984. Its guest rooms are handsomely decorated in rich, deep colors, with period antiques, canopy beds, handwoven coverlets, and Oriental rugs. The historic mood is further enhanced by the owners' collections of tall-case clocks, duck decoys, baskets, and pewter. No less inviting is the screened porch, equipped with an ample supply of old wooden rocking chairs. "Beautiful house with wonderful river views; a dock, just steps from the back door, is surrounded by azaleas. Our favorite is the Rose Room with a canopy bed, and a day bed in the sitting area." *(Kathryn Stuart)*

"Lovely historic neighborhood. Our room had a four-poster bed with a 150-year-old woven coverlet, antique clock, freshly cut flowers, an ice bucket, glasses, and a thirst-quenching drink." *(Alice Schalk)* "The Duck Room is decorated with duck paintings, decoys, and wallpaper. It is small but comfortable with its own sitting room across the hall, looking out to the river." *(William Novak)* "Exceptional cherry muffins. Evening wine and hors d'oeuvres give guests the opportunity to meet the Andersons and each other, share stories and recommendations." *(Linda Hardy)* "Great location with easy access to restaurants, shopping, and the Gator Bowl." *(Sheila Herndon)* "Carol is personable and friendly, concerned with her guests' comfort. The delicious breakfast of fresh fruit, cereal, and homemade biscuits was graciously served in the dining room, at the time requested." *(Lynda Hinshaw)* "A wonderful experience from its beautiful riverside location to the delicious evening hors d'oeuvres and wine to the delightful, well-mannered yellow lab Chardonnay." *(Cec Nieminen)*

Open All year.
Rooms 4 doubles—all with private bath or shower, telephone, radio, TV, desk, air-conditioning, ceiling fan. Some with balcony/deck.
Facilities Dining room, living room, family room, screened porch. 1 acre with lawn games, off-street parking. Fishing, canoeing, kayaking, dockage, tennis, golf nearby.
Location NE FL. Riverside; 10 min. from downtown; 5 min. from I-95; 25 min. from airport. 1 block from St. John's Ave. From I-95, take Exit 113, Stockton St. Go S 12 blocks & turn right on Riverside, go 4 blocks, & go left on Cherry to inn, last building on right at river. On bus rte.
Restrictions No smoking in guest rooms. No children under 10.
Credit cards MC, Visa.
Rates B&B, $80–105 double, $75–90 single. Extra person, $10. 2-night minimum special events.

KEY WEST

Key West is the southernmost city in the continental United States, located 161 miles south of Miami. The completion of the Overseas Highway in 1938 brought major changes to Key West. No longer a sleepy fishing village, the town is often filled with tourists and hustlers. International travelers discovered its allures, and are providing a foreign accent to the goings-on. Its gay population is estimated at 25 percent.

If the sun and water overwhelm, some other Key West sights of interest include Ernest Hemingway's Home, Key West Lighthouse Museum, Wrecker's Museum, and Mel Fisher's exhibit of sunken treasure. Those who feel their stay will be incomplete without a taste (or two or three) of key lime pie may want to sample the offerings at the Deli Restaurant, the Buttery, Pier House, or Sloppy Joes; remember the real thing is *never* green or thickened with gelatin—it's yellow, creamy, and sweet.

A word of advice about navigating in the Keys—the Florida Keys' Overseas Highway (U.S. 1) is studded with 126 mile markers starting at the corner of Fleming and Whitehead streets in Key West and ending near Florida City. Watch for the small green signs with white writing, found on the right shoulder of the road, since they're often used as reference points when directions are given.

Budget travelers should note that hotel rates are substantially lower from June through November, with the exception of holiday weekends.

Reader tips: "On your way to or from Key West, stop at Montes at MM 25 in Summerland Key for excellent seafood, inexpensively served in a casual setting. Don't miss Mangrove Mama's (MM 20) for Key lime pie. Camille's on Duval offers delicious breakfasts and lunch at very reasonable prices." *(Sheila & Joe Schmidt)* "The streets of Key West are narrow and congested, making car travel a problem. Park your car and walk!" *(Howard Addis)* "The tour of the Hemingway House is interesting but overpriced." *(Hilary Soule)*"Tour the Audubon House using the recorded tape; actors portray the actual lives of the family. Beautiful old Florida mansion filled with wonderful James Audubon prints." *(Christopher Johnston)* "We gotten bitten up by no-see-ums during our early June visit; bring insect repellent! Not all inns supply beach towels, so bring your own, along with a hat and suntan lotion. We rented bicycles and rode to the beach at Ft. Zachary Taylor Park. Lots of wonderful restaurants in town, though the really imaginative ones have entrees priced at $25–30." *(Carolyn Myles)* "Key West is great for shoppers and bar and restaurant lovers who enjoy the beautiful weather and stars, but I don't think it's great for kids." *(MP)* "Water pressure is not great anywhere in Key West, and can be a minor annoyance at some inns." *(MW)* "In addition to the beach at Zachary Taylor Park, be sure to tour the fort itself; the ranger-led tour at noontime is interesting and free. If you have time, it's worth taking the trip out to the Dry Tortugas as well. Parts of Duval are so tacky that we were reminded of Bourbon Street in New Orleans." *(Steve Soule)*

Also recommended: Formerly a private residence, the **Gardens Hotel** (526 Angela Street, 33040; 305–294–2661 or 800–526–2664) was refurbished as a luxury hotel in 1993. The 17 guest rooms overlook a half-acre garden of fragrant flowering plants. Double B&B rates range from $270–625; less in summer. "Ample places to sit in shade or sun, with as much privacy as you desire. Everything is immaculate and totally first class, including the splendid continental breakfast buffet. Our attractive room in the main house facing Angela Street had a porch and comfy chairs. The staff is extraordinarily friendly and helpful." *(Judith Brannen)* "Once the island's largest estate, now a luxurious retreat from nearby Duval Street." *(Joe Schmidt)* "Lovely staff, beautiful property, quiet but central location in the historic district. Well-furnished, gracious common areas; private, well-tended gardens and swimming pool. Even the least expensive room is well-furnished and appealing." *(SWS)*

The **Center Court Historic Inn & Cottages** (916 Center Street, 33040; 305–296–9292 or 800–797–8787, www.centercourtkw.com) is a cluster of cottages surrounding a central garden courtyard with an inviting swimming pool. B&B double rates for the 14 units range from $88–298. "Convenient but quiet location on a modest residential street just a block from Duval. The availability of inside common areas a big plus, since most inns in Key West don't have any. Handsome, well-equipped guest rooms are mercifully clutter free. An excellent value." *(SWS)*

The **Duval House** (815 Duval Street, 33040; 305–294–1666 or 800–22–DUVAL) is formed by a cluster of Victorian homes, furnished with a simple mix of wicker and antique furnishings. B&B double rates for the 29 guest rooms range from $90–195 double, suites $200–285. Guests especially enjoy the secluded backyard, with ample sun and shade. "Inviting grounds, relaxing setting, excellent service; adequate room and breakfast." *(GC)* "In the heart of Key West. Ask for a room overlooking the lush tropical gardens which surround the swimming pool. Continental breakfast is served in the breakfast house overlooking the pool and parklike grounds." *(SWS)*

Marquesa Hotel ✕ ♿
600 Fleming Street, 33040

Tel: 305–292–1919
800–869–4631
Fax: 305–294–2121

Listed on the National Register of Historic Places, the Marquesa is comprised of two 1880s boarding houses rescued from near destruction by hard work, good taste, and over $3,000,000 in renovation costs, plus the vision of owner/manager Carol Wightman. A waterfall, two swimming pools, and a variety of flowering plants enhance this intimate outdoor retreat. A concierge tends to your every whim, and your senses will be soothed by bedtime Godiva chocolates, fresh flowers, and Caswell Massey toiletries. The hotel restaurant, the Cafe Marquesa, offers a creative menu, with such entrees as mahi mahi with garlic mashed potatoes, beef tenderloin with red pepper aioli, and lamb shanks with white beans.

"Fully endorse all the accolades awarded this hotel. Ideal balance of respect for privacy with attentive service; furnishings in the best of taste, carefully maintained and immaculate. Conveniently located, within walking distance of most places of interest. Prompt help with luggage. Wonderful continental breakfast with ample choice; breakfast orders are left at the reception desk the night before, designating the time and selections. Each morning our meal was delivered exactly on time; excellent croissants and banana bread, outstanding granola. Most people choose to eat at tables on their porches, overlooking the wonderfully peaceful gardens with orchids and other flowers." *(HJB)* "Most rooms face the courtyard, with lush tropical plantings, swimming pools, and waterfall. The elegant restaurant is located in a corner of the building, with a separate entrance, so overnight guests are undisturbed. Highlights of our dinner included roast duck and grilled shrimp, with tempting desserts of key lime Napoleon and profiteroles." *(SWS)*

"The decor, porch, furnishings, amenities, and overall comfort of our new junior suite were exceptional." *(Sheila & Joe Schmidt)* "Each morning the *New York Times* was delivered to our door and when we went out to dinner, the bed was turned down, the towels changed, and waste baskets emptied." *(JS)* "Perfect location, on a quiet street off Duval, just a short walk to Mallory Square. Beautiful antiques and marble baths. Wonderful breakfast, served in the room or by the pool and fountain." *(Bill & Kim Barnes)* "The excellent restaurant has an imaginative menu and style that is reminiscent of San Francisco–style dining." *(Stephen & Ellise Holman)* "Great food. Quality abounds, with tasteful colors and fine furnishings." *(Christopher Johnston)*

Open All year.
Rooms 27 suites, doubles—all with full private bath, telephone, TV, air-conditioning, stocked minibar. 17 with deck. Rooms in two buildings.
Facilities Lobby, parlor, restaurant, terraces, decks, 2 heated swimming pools. Full concierge service. Off-street parking.
Location Historic district, corner Fleming and Simonton Sts. 5 blocks from Gulf, 10 blocks from Atlantic, 1 block to center.
Credit cards Amex, DC, MC, Visa.
Rates Room only, $205–325 suite, $135–260 double. Extra person, $15. 2–3 night weekend, holiday minimum. Off-season packages.
Extras Wheelchair access. Baby-sitting.

MIAMI/MIAMI BEACH

Most small hotels are found in the section of Miami Beach known as South Beach or SoBe. This mile-square Art Deco district encompasses 800 buildings dating from the 1930s and 1940s, and has grown immensely popular in recent years. Wander Ocean Drive and Collins Avenue between 5th and 15th streets to see the best of them. Many have been restored as hotels, as noted below. In general, rooms in the Art Deco hotels are considerably smaller than most modern hotel rooms are today, and remember that water view rooms on Ocean Drive in SoBe are *noisy*—day and night.

Don't forget that Miami is a big city, where the twin scourges of crime and drugs can quickly sour the vacation of any traveler who isn't citywise. Consult your hotel staff about which neighborhoods are safe, and which routes to walk.

Reader tips: "Miami, once known for Jackie Gleason on Saturday night, bathing beauties on the beach, and a new showplace hotel each year (in 1955, a night at the Fontainebleau Hotel cost an astronomical $55), has become a sophisticated subtropical city. Leading attractions are the beach and lighthouse at Bill Baggs State Park, the dolphin show at the Seaquarium, and the tropical Fairchild Garden. In the winter there is opera, in summer a film festival. For strolling and sidewalk cafes, try the Art Deco area of Miami Beach, Coconut Grove, or Bayside. The elegant Grand Bay Hotel, a short walk from downtown Coconut Grove, serves high tea in the lobby and has one of Miami's best restaurants. The Biltmore Hotel, restored to its 1920s glory, is a reminder of old Miami; a special treat is the Sunday brunch. Your visit will not be complete without a dinner at Joe's Stone Crab Restaurant in Miami Beach. Close to 400,000 diners annually enjoy terrific seafood year-round; stone crabs are in season from mid-October to mid-May. Sport enthusiasts will find the Dolphins, the Heat, the Marlins, Grand Prix, Lipton Tennis, and the Doral Open. Hialeah Racetrack is one of the country's most beautiful. You don't have to bet; have lunch and enjoy the scenery. The best buy is a half-hour ride around downtown on the rubber wheeled people-mover, which stops conveniently near the Bayside shops. On Saturday afternoon, park on the MacArthur Causeway and watch the parade of departing cruise ships. South Miami Beach and Coral Gables have many outstanding ethnic restaurants; check the 'Weekend' section of the Friday *Miami Herald* for a good list." (*Joe Schmidt*)

"In South Beach, shoppers should not miss the boutiques, galleries, restaurants, and cafes on Collins, between 7th and 9th; the recently renovated Lincoln Mall, parallel to Collins and Ocean near 17th Street; and Espagnola Way, just west of Washington Avenue between 14th and 15th Streets. Also worth seeing is the Wolfsonian Museum of Decorative Arts. Best of all is people watching and Rollerblading on the east side of Ocean Drive." (*GC*) "Renovation and reconstruction is going full-blast in SoBe, with renovated hotels opening frequently. Overall it's a lively, international scene, with lots of appealing shops, restaurants, and bars." (*SWS*)

Worth noting: Come to South Beach for tropical excitement—not peace and quiet. Traffic and people noise at all hours will disturb light sleepers in the rooms of many hotels, although some have invested in surprisingly effective soundproofing. Ask for a quiet room when making reservations, and bring ear plugs. Rooms at most of the Art Deco hotels are small, and rates vary with the view or lack thereof. Among SoBe's many Art Deco hotels, here are some intriguing choices (in alphabetical order):

Also recommended: At the heart of the action is the **Cardozo Hotel** (1300 Ocean Drive, 33139; 305–535–6500 or 800–782–6500), a 44-room hotel built in 1939, and refurbished in vibrant Art Deco colors. "Owned by Gloria Estefan, it's a favorite with musicians, models, photographers, and foreign tourists. Although street noise forced us to keep our windows closed and the air-conditioning on, this was also part of the hotel's appeal. The excellent restaurant has a large outdoor cafe, a perfect spot for watching Rollerbladers of all sizes, ages, shapes, sexes, and passing media types. Informal, helpful, and friendly staff. The guest rooms were well maintained but small." *(Steve Holman)* Rates range from $150–460, including continental breakfast.

One of SoBe's hottest hotels is the icy cool 238-room **Delano Hotel**, (1685 Collins Avenue, Miami Beach, 33139; 305–672–2000 or 800–555–5001) opened in 1995 by hotelier Ian Schrager. "Imagine a hotel done all in white. Now add a balmy Miami evening with that famous moon floating over the ocean. Four-story floor-to-ceiling draperies in the lobby billow in the breeze. Plus a wonderful restaurant, done in African wicker with huge white pillows, overlooking the swimming pool. Flickering white candles line the garden paths." *(Chris Johnston)* Fantasy has its price; rates range from $300–800, and some may not think it's worth it.

Effective soundproofing is a big plus at the **Ocean Front Hotel** (1230-38 Ocean Drive, 33139; 305–672–2579), with 27 guest rooms individually furnished in a 1930s Mediterranean theme. Double rates range from $180–250, with suites to $515; some rooms have whirlpool tubs, balconies, and/or ocean views. "The hotel's restaurant, Les Deux Fontaines, offers a breakfast buffet, served on the terrace in front of the hotel, a great value with good service; in addition to adequate French toast, eggs, potatoes, and sausage, they served wonderful fresh-squeezed orange juice, strong coffee, and genuine French rolls and croissants. We also enjoyed a delicious lunch of French-style mussels with more great bread. Cozy inviting bar, with lots of couches for a relaxing atmosphere. Great French service. Guest room décor includes both French country and Art Dèco touches, and some of those on the upper floors have water views." *(SWS, also EE)*

Information please: Built in 1929 and renovated in 1996 is the **Hotel Leon** (341 Collins Avenue, 33139; 305–673–3767; www.hotelleon.com). Conveniently located in the heart of the Art Deco district, the hotel is just just one block from Ocean Drive. Double rates for the 18 guest rooms range from $100–215, plus $315–375 for the penthouse suite. The décor includes Mexican tiles, wood floors, original fireplaces, and oversized bathrooms with sunken bathtubs, and pets are welcome. Comments?

ORLANDO

Reader tip: "For a fun evening, visit Church Street, a historic railroad depot converted into an entertainment center, with a wild-west saloon and 'opera house,' a ballroom and dessert cafe, a seafood bar, and a wine cellar." *(PB)*

Also recommended: The **Courtyard at Lake Lucerne** (211 North Lucerne Circle East, 32801; 407–648–5188 or 800–444–5289) is comprised of three buildings sharing a common garden courtyard. The 1885 Norment-Parry Inn is Orlando's oldest house, and is furnished with American and English antiques, accented with floral wallcoverings and fabrics. The Wellborn, one of the finest surviving Art Deco buildings in town, has been furnished with the eclectic styles popular in the Twenties. The I.W. Phillips House, a 1916 antebellum-style manor house, has wooden verandas wrapping around three sides and a Tiffany stained glass window. A fourth building—an eclectic Queen Anne/Colonial Revival mansion—was restored in 1998, and houses a fine dining restaurant and additional guest rooms. Rates for the 14 suites and 6 doubles range from $85–165 and include a breakfast buffet, plus a welcoming bottle of wine. "Breakfast, served buffet-style in the ballroom of the Phillips House, was abundant—fresh strawberries, orange juice, fruit compote, English muffins, blueberry muffins, bagels and cream cheese, and a selection of cold cereals. Sitting on the veranda, by the gently splashing fountain, smelling the fragrances of the courtyard, it's hard to believe you are right in downtown Orlando." *(NB)*

Designed as an eight guest-room B&B, **Perri House** (10417 Centurion Court, P.O. Box 22005, Lake Buena Vista, 32830; 407–876–4830 or 800–780–4830; www.perrihouse.com) was built by Angi and Nick Perretti and their family in 1990; this one-story, pale brick building is located literally at the back door to Disney World, yet the inn's landscaped acres include a bird sanctuary and swimming pool. The Perrettis have skillfully planned their home to provide space and privacy for their guests (all rooms have queen- or king-size beds and outside entrances). Angi notes that "because of our location, we heartily welcome children of all ages." B&B double rates of $99–129 include a self-serve breakfast of fruit, muffins, pastries, toast, and cold cereal. Opening in 1999 are four deluxe cottages with a birdhouse theme, and such luxuries as king-size canopy beds, see-through fireplaces, media center, wet bar, and double whirlpool tub.

Just five miles north of Orlando is the **Thurston House** (851 Lake Avenue, Maitland, 32751; 407–539–1911 or 800–843–2721; www.thurston-house.com), a 1885 Queen Anne Victorian home with an idyllic lakeside country setting. Architectural features include the cross gable roof and corbeled brick chimneys, while the inside is highlighted by the beautifully restored pine and curly cypress woodwork and floors. The rooms are spacious and airy, furnished with an attractive balance of Victorian antiques, Colonial reproductions, and traditional pieces. A typical breakfast might include honey peaches, granola, French toast casserole with maple syrup, raisin scones, and zucchini bread. "Just minutes from the charming village of Winter Park, yet tucked away on a quiet country lane. In addition to the idyllic screened porch, there's an inviting, comfortable back parlor, a slightly more formal front parlor, and a dining room with three or four small tables where guests enjoy breakfast." *(SWS)* B&B double rates for the four guest rooms ranges from $110–120.

ST. AUGUSTINE

St. Augustine, founded in 1565, is the oldest city in North America. With a few interruptions, it was under Spanish rule until 1821; many of its restored Spanish colonial homes were built in the 1700s. The city's architecture also has a strong Victorian component, dating back to the 1880s, when Henry Flagler did much to popularize St. Augustine as a fashionable resort. St. Augustine is on the northeast Florida coast, 30 miles north of Daytona and south of Jacksonville, and 100 miles northeast of Orlando.

As you would expect, parking in this historic city is extremely tight. Ask your innkeeper for specific advice and information. Once you have parked your car, you may not need it again until you leave. The city is compact and delightful for walking, and many restaurants provide free shuttle service in the evening. Given its considerable charms, St. Augustine is a popular destination, and the better inns are often booked well in advance, so make resevations early.

Reader tips: "Many inns include free passes to the Oldest House in their rates." And: "We had a delightful meal at Le Pavillon, including a lovely salad of Bibb lettuce, delicious cheese bread, and Florida-style bouillabaisse." *(SWS)* "Recommend a visit to the Lightner Museum, built by Flagler at the Alcazar Hotel, with displays of decorative objects, from Tiffany stained glass to early photographs. Had lunch at the museum, then spent the afternoon visiting Flagler College, just across the street."

Also recommended: Just a few blocks away from the Oldest House, is the **Kenwood Inn** (38 Marine Street, 32084; 904–824–2116). Rooms are decorated in a wide variety of New England styles, from Shaker to country Victorian. The self-service continental breakfast includes fresh orange juice, pastries, and coffee. You can eat at the large dining room table, in front of the living room fireplace, in the light and airy wicker-furnished sunroom, or outside in the courtyard. The B&B double rates of $85–175 include use of the inn's small swimming pool.

The **St. Francis Inn** (279 St. George Street, 32084; 904–824–6068 or 800–824–6062; www.stfrancisinn.com) was built in 1791, became a boardinghouse in 1846, and was extensively renovated in 1996. Although its historic charms were undisturbed, all the plumbing and wiring were replaced, along with the carpeting and wood flooring. In-room telephones and TVs make it a fine choice of the business traveler; fireplaces and double Jacuzzi tubs are appealing for weekend getaways. Rates include a full breakfast buffet, coffee and iced tea at any time, and wine and cheese before dinner. Guests can relax on one of the balconies, in the charming garden courtyard, or by the swimming pool. B&B double rates for the 15 guest rooms range from $85–175.

Casa de la Paz	*Tel:* 904–829–2915
22 Avenida Menendez, 32084	800–929–2915
	Fax: 904–824–6269
	E-mail: delapaz@aug.com
	URL: http://www.oldcity.com/delapaz

Location, location, location are the first three rules of real estate, and they make a great starting point for a B&B as well. The Casa de la Paz complements its superb location overlooking Matanzas Bay and the

Bridge of Lions with lovely rooms, charming innkeepers, and delicious food. Built in 1915, the "House of Peace" is a Mediterranean Revival-style home, with white stucco walls and a hipped roof, purchased by experience innkeepers Bob and Donna Marriott in 1996. Inside, the original nine-foot ceilings, polished heart of pine and oak floors, and leaded glass windows and doors are enhanced by period decor.

"Owners Donna and Bob Marriott are experienced, knowledgeable, involved, active, personable, and friendly innkeepers. The inn overlooks the bay, with beautiful views from the parlor and front guest rooms. Common areas include the spacious parlor with ample comfortable seating, and Donna's music box collection; early morning coffee is available here at 8:00 A.M.. The breakfast buffet is set out from 9:00 to 9:45 A.M., and can be enjoyed at the dining room table, for those who enjoy a communal meal, or at a tables for two in the delightful solarium. You can be done in minutes, or linger for an hour, chatting with the other guests, as you wish. The generous array of dishes included fresh fruit, yogurt, granola, cottage cheese, toasted bagels, delicious turkey crepes, and coffee cake. The staff was attentive with refills of caf and decaf coffee. At the back of the inn is a little garden patio, where guests can sit out and enjoy the shade and cool ocean breezes. My room at the back of the inn was delightful and comfortable, with pale lilac walls, soft green colors, lots of white trim, and a white iron Victorian-reproduction queen-size bed. Good lighting at bedside and in the bathroom. Even a small private balcony." *(SWS)* "Thoughtful touches included the availability of cold wine and soda, coffee cake in the living room, and sherry in our room. Beautiful antiques throughout the inn; lovely chandelier in the formal dining room." *(Ginette Brainard)* "Wonderful bayside location within walking distance of major sites; flower-filled courtyard. Our suite was clean, quiet, and nicely appointed." *(Charlotte Steiner)* "Bob and Donna are totally dedicated innkeepers, available when you need them with any assistance you require. Our room overlooked the Ponce de Leon bridge and bay. The sun porch is inviting both for breakfast and for afternoon relaxing, with refreshing drinks available. Wonderful breakfasts with Italian quiche, chocolate chip banana muffins, grits, fresh fruit and juice, and more; the second morning brought banana almond pancakes with sausage links." *(HJB)*

Open All year.
Rooms 2 suites, 4 doubles—all with full private bath, clock/radio, TV, air-conditioning, ceiling fan, hair dryer.
Facilities Living room with fireplace, dining room, sunroom. Garden courtyard, off-street parking.
Location Historic district. On Ave. Menendez, just N of Bridge of Lions, S of fort.
Restrictions No smoking. Children over 15.
Credit cards Amex, Discover, MC, Visa.
Rates B&B, $119–174 suite, $89–189 double.

SANIBEL

For a change of pace from shell collecting and lazing on the wonderful beaches, spend time hiking, canoeing, or bicycling in the "Ding" Darling National Wildlife Preserve, or cross the causeway back to Fort Myers to visit the winter home of Thomas Edison. You can see his home, research labs, and 14-acre botanical gardens.

Reader tip: "Kayaked through the beautiful Ding Darling Wildlife Refuge. The only drag was the no-see-ums which come out in the morning and before dusk, and eat you alive. Wear plenty of insect repellent!" *(Andrew Arntfield)*

Information please: The **Song of the Sea** (863 East Gulf Drive, Sanibel Island, 33957; 941–472–2220 or 800–231–1045) is a 30-room European-style seaside inn, made up of a cluster of pink buildings framed by tropical foliage, right on the beach. Each unit has a kitchen, dining area, bathroom, screened porch, ceiling fan, air-conditioning, TV, VCR, and telephone; the decor includes French country furniture, Mediterranean tile floors, and down-filled comforters. The $160–350 rates include wine and flowers, free bicycles, swimming pool and hot tub, laundry facilities, and a breakfast of pastries, bagels, coffee, tea, and juice; golf and tennis privileges are offered at a nearby club. "Excellent breakfast, convenient location, free videos, friendly innkeepers." *(Robert Mandell & Deborah Brown)* The inn is managed by South Seas Resorts, which also manages several other small places of interest, including the Seaside Inn and the Sanibel Inn.

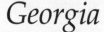
Georgia

The Veranda, Atlanta

There's more to Georgia than peaches and peanuts, Jimmy Carter and Scarlett O'Hara. For urban delights, visit Atlanta, one of the country's most sophisticated cities combining contemporary culture and "Old South" charm; tour graceful historic homes in Savannah; or time-travel to Macon's antebellum mansions. In northwestern Georgia, visit New Echota (outside of Calhoun), the former Cherokee capital where Sequoyah developed a written language for his people; then stop by nearby Chatsworth to see the Vann House, a mansion built by a Cherokee chief and noted for its unusually colored interior paint. In northeastern Georgia, tour the mountains, then stop by 1000-foot Tallulah Falls. Want more water? Get your fill canoeing through the Okefenokee Swamp or visiting posh St. Simons Island.

ATLANTA

Virtually leveled by General Sherman during the Civil War, Atlanta recovered fairly quickly, becoming a major rail hub by the end of the century. Today, Atlanta is a modern city whose population has exploded in the past three decades; its airport is one of the busiest in the country, and its traffic jams rival those of Los Angeles.

Also recommended: Thirty miles south of the Atlanta airport is **The Veranda** (252 Seavy Street, P.O. Box 177, Senoia, 30276; 770–599–3905) built in 1907. The original tin-covered ceilings and stained-glass windows are complimented by antiques, memorabilia, and Oriental rugs. Breakfast includes fresh fruit with strawberry sorbet, granola, and a hot entree; outstanding dinners are available by advance reservation. B&B

double rates for the nine guest rooms range from $99–150. "Delicious meals, exceptional hospitality, comfortable accommodation." *(MR)*

Gaslight Inn
1001 Saint Charles Avenue, 30306

Tel: 404–875–1001
Fax: 404–876–1001
E-mail: innkeeper@gaslightinn.com
URL: http://www.gaslightinn.com

Taking its name from the flickering gas lanterns outside the inn, as well as the original gas lighting inside, the Gaslight Inn is a Craftsman-style home, built in 1913, and restored as a B&B in 1994 by Jim Moss. Breakfast, served 8:30–10 A.M., consists of fresh baked breads, muffins, croissants, bagels, potato rolls, Danish, fresh fruit and juice, cereals, yogurts, and coffee. Guests are delighted with the warm yet professional hospitality, the first-rate location, and most of all the exceptionally lovely decor of this B&B.

"Unparalleled elegance, genuine comfort, impressive guest rooms and common areas; an ideal balance of comfort and elegance. The guest rooms are furnished with lovely antiques, queen- or king-sized beds, thick terry robes, and thoughtful amenities. The English Suite has a four-poster mahogany bed with a draped canopy, and a separate sitting room which opens to a private veranda overlooking the formal gardens. The bathroom has double sinks and a double Jacuzzi for two, a tiled steam shower, and a wet bar. The other guest rooms and common areas are equally impressive. All was furnished under the supervision of Jim's partner, an architect and interior designer. You can relax on the front porch rockers, on in the screened porch overlooking the garden. Terrific neighborhood, with wonderful shops and restaurants literally around the corner. Host Jim Moss is warm, hospitable, and a knowledgeable Atlanta native." *(Susan Poole)* "The private Ivy Cottage has a light, bright, informal Nantucket look." *(MW)* "Exquisitely decorated. Close to trendy North Highland Avenue." *(Millie Ball)* "Fully endorse entry. The delicious breakfast was served in a well-decorated dining room. Comfortable places to sit and read on the front porch, in the backyard, and in the back parlor. The staff was pleasant and helpful with suggestions on places to go and things to see. Great old neighborhood with interesting walks nearby." *(Leigh Robinson)*

Open All year.

Rooms 3 suites, 3 doubles, 1 cottage—all with full private bath, telephone, clock, TV, desk, air-conditioning, ceiling fan, refrigerator. Some with double whirlpool tub, fireplace, radio, wet bar, veranda. Cottage with kitchen, washer/dryer.

Facilities Dining room, living room, both with fireplace. Sunroom/den with piano, TV/VCR, stereo, books. Veranda, screened porch. Courtyard garden with fountain, off-street parking.

Location 2 m NE of downtown Atlanta, in Virginia Highlands historic district. From I-75/85, take Freedom Pkwy (Hwy 10 E) to Ponce de Leon Ave. Go left on Fredrica (between bank & library). Go left on St. Charles to inn on right. Walking distance to Emory, Piedmont Park, Callanwolde Fine Arts Center; public transportation nearby.

Restrictions No smoking. Children over 12 years old.
Credit cards Amex, Discover, MC, Visa.
Rates B&B. $149–195 suite, $95–125 double, $85–125 single.
Extras Wheelchair accessible; 1 suite specially equipped.

Shellmont Bed & Breakfast Lodge
821 Piedmont Avenue N.E., 30308

Tel: 404–872–9290
Fax: 404–872–5379

Built in 1891, and listed on the National Register of Historic Places, Shellmont is an excellent example of Victorian design. Stained, leaded, and beveled glass abound, as do intricately carved interior and exterior woodwork, elaborate mantels, mosaic-tiled fireplaces, documented Bradbury and Bradbury wall coverings, and accurately reproduced original stenciling. The inn is furnished throughout with Victorian antiques. Ed and Debbie McCord, owners since 1984, work hard to improve the inn each year, both in terms of the lovely decor and, equally important, to ensure guest comfort and convenience; although the beds are antiques, all have new, top-rated queen-size mattresses. The Shellmont is located in midtown; restaurants, live theaters, art cinemas, museums, and shopping are within walking distance. Breakfast is served at 7:30 or 8:30 A.M. on weekdays (an hour later on weekends) and includes cereal, granola, yogurt, fresh fruit, homemade breads, and such entrees as Belgian waffles with whipped cream and fresh strawberries, frittatas, and specialty egg dishes.

"A smooth and efficiently run inn. Well decorated rooms with nice touches and amenities, spotlessly clean." *(Shirley Dittloff)* "This lovely Queen Anne home is painted pale green with cream trim; the carved shell woodwork above the bay window is gorgeous. The parlor sitting room has window seats in the lovely curved windows. At night, the lovely Tiffany window is back lit from inside the house." *(SHW)* "Debbie intuitively knew when solitude was preferred." *(Barbara Cordaro)* "My room had a comfortable antique bed with a matching dresser, a modern tiled shower with tons of hot water, and plush towels. The high ceilings were painted a beautiful shade of dark green with a stenciled border. Scrumptious chocolates were put on the pillow at night; fresh fruit and an assortment of soft drinks were set on the dresser." *(Nina Piccirilli)* "Debbie is a jewel—sweet, funny, and helpful." *(Dianne Crawford, also Stephanie Roberts)* "Well-maintained inn. Debbie was always available to chat about Atlanta and suggest touring ideas. Delicious breakfast." *(Happy Copley)*

Open All year.
Rooms 1 carriage house suite, 4 doubles—all with private bath and/or shower, telephone with dataport, TV, air-conditioning, radio, ceiling fan. Suite with kitchen, steam shower.
Facilities 3 parlors, library, all with books, magazines, games, fireplaces, guest refrigerator/pantry, veranda. Shady garden with fish ponds; off-street parking. ¼ m to Piedmont Park.
Location Midtown; 1¼ m from city center. From I-75 & I-85 N, take Peachtree exit to Piedmont; southbound, exit at North Ave. to Piedmont. MARTA stop nearby.

Restrictions No smoking. Traffic noise in some rooms. Children under 12 in carriage house only. Limited off-street parking.
Credit cards Amex, DC, Discover, MC, Visa.
Rates B&B, $120–150 suite, $110–125 double, $90–125 single. Extra person, $25. 2-night minimum weekend stay.
Extras Crib in carriage house.

CLARKSVILLE

Clarksville is about 75 miles northeast of Atlanta, in a rural yet historic area known for its waterfalls, Chattahoochie National Forest, and the Blue Ridge mountains. Area activities include golf, horseback riding, fishing, canoeing, whitewater rafting, kayaking, hiking, and bicycling. Several national forests and state parks are nearby, including the spectacular Tallulah Gorge State Park.

Also recommended: In Clarkesville's historic district, and listed on the National Register of Historic places is the **Burns-Sutton House** (855 Washington Street, 30523; 706–754–5565). Built in 1901, the house has wraparound porches, stained glass windows, and ornate woodwork. The seven guest rooms are furnished in period antiques (some with four poster canopy beds and gas-log fireplaces), and the $65–125 rates include a full breakfast. Dinners are served at the inn's restaurant, Jeffrey's Fine Dining. "Jaime Huffman is a cheerful, friendly innkeeper; she keeps the house spotless, prepares a delicious breakfast." (*Pat Borysiewiez*)

Glen-Ella Springs Inn ✕ ♿   *Tel:* 706–754–7295
1789 Bear Gap Road, 30523   *Fax:* 706–754–1560
                                     E-mail: info@glenella.com
                         URL: http://www.glenella.com

In the early 1900s, Atlanta tourists came to "take the waters" at the Glen-Ella Springs Inn. When Barrie and Bobby Aycock purchased the inn in 1986, it had essentially been unaltered since its construction, so the Aycocks' restoration started with the addition of indoor plumbing and electricity. Well off the highway on a quiet gravel road, the inn is surrounded by pine forests and meadows of wildflowers. The gardens supply the herbs and vegetables for summertime dining. Breakfasts include fresh fruit compote, homemade granola, cereal, home-baked breads, and battered French toast with orange sauce or perhaps blueberry granola pancakes—plus coffee, tea, and juice. Favorite dinner entrees might include grilled swordfish with lemon herb butter, duck with roast vegetables and fettucini, and honey peach-cured pork chops.

"Charming country setting, yet convenient to lots of activities. Although we had the smallest room, it was cozy and comfortable." (*David & Linda Ackerson*) "The whole Aycock family works at the inn, and all are kind and cheerful." (*Marian Anderson*) "Atmosphere and charm to match the inn's history: heart pine floors, ceilings, and walls; stacked rock fireplaces; primitive antique furnishings." (*Don Depew*) "The porch overlooks a lovely meadow; you can hear a swift running creek nearby." *(Francine Hollowell)* "A restorative place, with its wraparound porches and white rocking chairs. The lobby has a variety of chintz-covered sofas, chairs, and loveseats." *(Nancy & John Schultz)* "Our suite was furnished with antiques, handmade quilts, and rugs, with a modern bathroom." *(Anna Culligan)* "Our rustic room had plenty of reading material and a checker board." *(Beth Webster)*

"The innkeepers make everyone feel welcome, comfortable, and at home. Although they were busy with a full house, they still graciously took care of our needs. While not large, the rooms are clean, comfortable, and nicely decorated. The swimming pool is clean, with a nice size and depth. Plenty of big towels for pool and bath. Delightful herb lotion, soap, and shampoo for the bathroom." *(Bill & Becky Yeatman)* "Delicious breakfast of spinach frittata, country sausage, fresh fruit, oat bran scones, and cinnamon rolls; equally wonderful dinners of trout cakes with horseradish cream sauce, prime rib with rosemary blue cheese butter, peach cured pork chops, and sinful chocolate molten lava cake for desert. Plus lovely mountain views and cool breezes." *(Kim Cornish)* "Wonderful location, near both sights and hikes. Barrie and Bobby were delightful hosts and the breakfast of blueberry pancakes was delicious. The porch rockers were great place for relaxing." *(Anne Jackson)*

Open All year. Restaurant open for dinner by reservation. Hours vary in winter, early spring.

Rooms 2 suites with fireplace, Jacuzzi; 14 doubles—all with full private bath, telephone, radio, air-conditioning, porch with rocking chairs.

Facilities Restaurant, gift shop, living room with fireplace, TV/VCR, games, books, terrace. 17 acres with swimming pool, gardens, nature trails.

Location NE GA. 85 m NE of Atlanta. From Atlanta, take I-85 N to I-985, Exit 45. Becomes GA 365, then US 441 N of Cornelia. Follow US 441 N for 15 m. Go left on G. Hardeman Rd. at Turnerville, then right on Historic Old 441 for ¼ m. Left on The Orchard Rd. Follow signs 2 ½ m to the inn.

Restrictions No smoking in dining room or guest rooms. Limited interior sound-proofing. "Well-behaved children welcome." BYOB.

Credit cards Amex, MC, Visa.

Rates B&B, $190 suite, $120–150 double. Extra person, $10. 2-night weekend minimum May–Nov. Alc dinner $30.

Extras Wheelchair access.

MACON

A trading center since its founding, Macon remains a manufacturing center to this day. Much of the downtown business area and the College Hill residential neighborhood has been designated as a historic district. The city is located in central Georgia, 82 miles southeast of Atlanta.

Reader tip: "Of the three restaurants we've tried in Macon, the best is Natalia's on Riverside Drive, a five-minute drive away, located in the shopping plaza behind Wendy's. Excellent continental/Italian food and fine service." *(HJB, also B. Crawford Hitt)*

1842 Inn   ♿
353 College Street, 31201

Tel: 912–741–1842
800–336–1842
Fax: 912–741–1842

The 1842 Inn consists of an imposing antebellum Greek Revival mansion, restored in 1984, and an adjacent Victorian cottage. The luxurious rooms are furnished handsomely with Oriental rugs, antiques, and quality reproductions; Phil Jenkins is the managing partner. Rates include a light breakfast, brought to your room with the morning paper; shoeshine; afternoon coffee or iced tea; predinner hors d'oeuvres; and evening turndown service.

"Exceptionally lovely garden, parlors, front porch, and guest rooms. Appreciated extras included fresh flowers in our room, a pleasant cocktail hour with plentiful hors d'oeuvres, nightly turndown service with pillow chocolates, and the friendly, helpful staff. An added plus is its proximity to the Hay House and the surrounding historic district with self-guided, illuminated, walking tour." *(Sona Nast)* "The facility is beautifully decorated with a mixture of antiques and reproductions; our room had cut flowers in the bathroom and a live orchid on the desk. Service is solid with a well-trained staff." *(B. Crawford Hitt)* "As pleased with our stay in the cottage as we were with our room in the main house. The breakfast of juice, muffin or croissant, and tea or coffee was brought to our room at the time requested; we could have had it brought to a table in the garden. Immaculate rooms, excellent condition, gracious and helpful staff; warm greeting by Phil Jenkins." *(HJB, also Donna Jacobson)*

"This beautiful Southern mansion sits on a street of beautiful houses, in a city of beautiful streets. Double-floor columns extend across the front, with splendidly proportioned rooms inside." *(Robert Freidus)* "Within walking distance of many fine antebellum homes and the fabulous Hay House home museum." *(Celia McCullough & Gary Kaplan)* "A beautiful inn, lovely town. Delicious breakfast; helpful, caring staff." *(Doris Easton)*

Open All year.
Rooms 21 doubles—all with full private bath, telephone with voice mail, radio, TV, desk, air-conditioning. 9 rooms in annex. Some with whirlpool tubs, gas fireplaces.
Facilities 2 parlors with piano; occasional pianist. 1 acre with garden. Secure off-street parking. Private club golf, tennis, dining privileges.
Location 1 m from center. Exit 52 off I-75; go left on Forsyth St.; from N, go left on College to inn; from S, go right on Forsyth.
Restrictions Children over 12. Light sleepers should request a second floor room away from lobby, or in adjacent cottage. When booking, inquire if a group will be in residence.
Credit cards Amex, MC, Visa.
Rates B&B, $125–185 double, $115–145 single. Extra person, $20.
Extras Wheelchair access.

ST. SIMONS ISLAND

Also recommended: For a truly exceptional experience, visit **Little St. Simons Island** (P.O. Box 21078, 31522; 912–638–7472 or 888–733–5774; www.pactel.com.au/lssi), about as close as most of us will ever come to having our own unspoiled waterfront paradise. Since only 30 people can be accommodated on this 10,000-acre private island, you'll find as much solitude as you desire. With the variety of habitats on the island, and its location in the path of a number of migratory patterns, the opportunities for bird-watching are outstanding. Resident naturalists are available to answer questions, and readers report that their presence really enhances the experience. Debbie and Kevin McIntyre are the long-time managers of both the inn and island's resources. All-inclusive double rates of $300–540 daily include three meals a day, evening hors d'oeuvres, wine with dinner, snacks and hot and cold beverages on request, picnic lunches, use of all facilities and equipment, and access to all experts. Long-time reader *Pat Malone* represents the opinion of LSSI guests when she reports: "Indescribably beautiful; friendly, supportive staff; delicious food; relaxed atmosphere."

SAVANNAH

Savannah was founded in the eighteenth century by the English general James Oglethorpe and has been a major port ever since. Today, elegant yachts have replaced the pirate ships and China clippers of the early days, but a surprising number of Savannah's original buildings have survived. In fact, Savannah now claims to have the largest urban National Landmark District in the U.S., with over 1,000 restored homes in an area 2½ miles square. Some are now museums; many more are inns and restaurants. In fact, it seems to us that Savannah has more B&Bs these days than you can shake a croissant at!

Savannah is located 255 miles southeast of Atlanta, 136 miles north of Jacksonville, Florida, and 106 miles south of Charleston, South Carolina. It's a 16-mile drive to the Atlantic Ocean beaches. Start your exploration of the town at the Visitors Center on West Broad Street. There's an audiovisual program to introduce you to the city, lots of brochures, and a well-informed staff to answer questions.

Worth noting: Walking at night in some parts of Savannah is inadvisable; ask your innkeeper for advice. Parking in Savannah's historic district can also be a problem. Some inns have a limited number of on-site spaces, while others do not. If you're traveling by car, be sure to get details; ask about city parking passes, which eliminate the constant need to feed meters. The front doors of most historic inns in Savannah are reached by a flight of steps; guest rooms at the ground level look out onto sidewalk at the front of the house and the garden to the back, and usually have exposed brick walls and more rustic furnishings than upstairs guest rooms; these "garden-level" rooms may be dark and sometimes lack privacy.

Reader tips: If you don't mind waiting on line, head for Mrs. Wilkes Boarding House (107 West Jones Street), where enormous Southern-style breakfasts are served at penny-pinching prices. There's no menu, but your table will be covered with a dozen dishes. "I loved the old-fashioned farm-style Southern cooking; you'll have to wait but don't let them rush you once you're seated." *(PP)* And: "Well worth a splurge was dinner at Elizabeth's on 37th. Not a neighborhood for strolling, though." *(SWS)* "Wonderful meal at The Olde Pink House (an 18th century mansion) on Abercorn Street at Reynolds' Square; some say it's better than Elizabeth's. Excellent duck with berry sauce; reservations essential. The 1790 Restaurant also a good choice. Hueys on River Street is a popular casual spot serving New Orleans fare; great beignets at breakfast." *(Rose Ciccone, also HJB)* "Enjoyed the fine beer, tasty sandwiches, and delightful pub decor at the Six Pence Pub." *(Susan Woods)* "Exceptional dinner at The Crab Shack Restaurant on Tybee Island with mounds of crawfish, crab, shrimp, and veggies, all steamed to perfection. Casual outdoor setting with Jimmy Buffet music wafting though the area and lanterns hanging from the trees." *(Scott & Stephanie Williams)*

"Read John Berendt's *Midnight in the Garden of Good and Evil* (known locally as 'The Book,') before your trip for a different picture of Savannah; the statue on the book's cover has been removed from Bonaventure Cemetery, so don't bother looking for it. Loved the tour of the Green-Mildrem House and the Andrew Low House, but recommend skipping the Hamilton-Turner House. Enjoyed the Art & Craft Center on Bull Street, and the E. Shaver Bookstore in Madison Square. Took a day trip out to Tybee Island for some sunning. Recommend a visit to Fort Pulaski; take time to watch the introductory movie. You can still see shells in the masonry of the fort where it was attacked." *(Penny Poirier)*

Also recommended: Overlooking lovely Chippewa Square, **The Foley House** (14 West Hull Street, 31401; 912–232–6622 or 800–647–3708) was built in 1896 and is decorated in typical Savannah colors of dark reds, and soft greens. The 19 guest rooms are beautifully furnished with four-poster Charleston rice beds, antiques and period reproductions, and Oriental rugs; most have either king- or queen-size beds, although a few have two doubles. Guests can enjoy breakfast in their room, the lounge, or the courtyard, selecting serving times between 7:30 and 10:00 A.M.; choices include orange juice or a grapefruit, granola with milk or yogurt, and a basket of just-baked breads. The B&B double rates of $120–235 also include afternoon tea, evening hors d'oeuvres with a cash bar, and nightly turndown service.

The Gastonian ♿
220 East Gaston Street, 31401

Tel: 912–232–2869
800–322–6603
Fax: 912–232–0710
URL: http://www.gastonian.com

Savannah's best known luxury inn was purchased in 1996 by Anne Landers, who is working hard to make a lovely inn even more so. The Gastonian is comprised of two connecting Savannah mansions, built in

GEORGIA

1868 in the Regency Italianate style. The interiors are highlighted with
fine woods and heart pine floors, decorative moldings and brass, and
wallpapers in the original Scalamandre Savannah pattern. Depending
on the room, the luxurious decor ranges from French, Italianate, English, Victorian, or Colonial, but both common areas and guest rooms
are stunning with authentic antiques, Persian rugs, and rice poster or
Charleston canopied beds. Recent improvements include a complete re-
painting of the inn's interior; replacement of all mattresses and most
draperies and upholstery; resurfacing of all sinks and bathtubs, the in-
stallation of an up-to-date telephone system; replanting the gardens and
sprucing up the hot tub area. Several king-bedded rooms were added
at street level, ideal for those who have difficulty with stairs; breakfast
and afternoon tea can be delivered to these rooms on request.

Anne notes that "it is our pleasure to make dinner reservations,
arrange tours, and answer questions about this lovely city. A bellman
is available to assist with luggage at check-in. Using fine china, crystal,
and silver, we serve a beautiful sit-down breakfast between 8 and 10
each morning with home-baked breads and such dishes as German
apple pancakes; in the afternoon complimentary wines are available in
the parlor; each evening guests may come relax in the candlelit parlor
over a glass of port or sherry. Iced tea and lemonade are always available in warm weather, along with chocolate chip cookies. Bottled water
is delivered daily to each guest room, and a Savannah praline accompanies evening turndown service."

"Elegant decor, immaculate housekeeping, delicious breakfast, welcoming tea service. Attention to detail includes the fresh flowers in the
room, the fire crackling in your room on a chilly evening, and the attentive staff's guidance with restaurant reservations and shopping options. Anne is a delightful innkeeper." (Pat Conner) "Located in a quiet
residential area near Forsyth Park, the inn is within walking distance
of Savannah's attractions." (Susan Rasmussen) "Our room was high up
in the connecting house, next door, with a four-poster bed and a separate sitting room." (Lee Todd) "We stayed one night in one of the most
expensive rooms, and the next in one of the least costly; both were
wonderful, creatively and comfortably furnished, with every amenity
one could wish." (Sally Schenk) "Anne Landers is the perfect hostess.
An absolutely first-class experience. Perfect service. Total concern for
each guest's needs" (Richard & Jaclin Farrell)

Open All year.
Rooms 2 suites, 15 doubles—all with private bath and/or shower, telephone
with dataport, radio, TV, air-conditioning, fireplace. 9 with whirlpool tub. Some
with desk, ceiling fan.
Facilities Kitchen/breakfast room, parlor, dining room, gift shop. Garden
courtyard with hot tub. Limited off-street parking.
Location Historic district.
Restrictions No smoking. No children under 12.
Credit cards Amex, MC, Visa.
Rates B&B, $195–350 suite, double. Extra person, $25. Midweek corporate rate
off-season. 2-night weekend minimum.
Extras Limited wheelchair access.

THOMASVILLE

Thomasville is centrally located in south Georgia, 28 miles north of Tallahassee, Florida. Once the train lines were repaired after the Civil War, wealthy Northerners traveled here to hunt quail, breathe the pine-scented highland air, and escape the harsh winters; many built lavish "cottages" and "shooting plantations" for the winter season. The mild winter climate hasn't changed over the last century; now travelers detour off I-10 or I-75 to enjoy Thomasville's leisurely pleasures—visits to historic homes and plantations, two challenging golf courses, tennis, and sporting clays. The town's biggest event is the Rose Festival, held the fourth week of April, when reservations are essential.

Reader tip: "Well worth visiting are the Lapham-Patterson House and Pebble Hill Plantation." *(Imogene Tillis)*

Also recommended: An eclectic Victorian mansion built in 1893, **The Grand Victoria Inn** (817 South Hansell, 31792; 912–226–7460) was restored as a B&B in 1991; guest rooms are handsomely decorated with period antiques. The four guest rooms have private baths, and the B&B double rates range from $70–90. Listed on the National Register of Historic Places and overlooking Paradise Park, **Our Cottage on the Park** (801 South Hansell Street, 31792; 912–227–0404), is a Queen Anne Victorian home built in 1893 and opened as a B&B by Connie Clineman in 1992. B&B double rates for the two guest suites are $60 double; children are welcome. The **Serendipity Cottage** (339 East Jefferson Street, 31792; 912–226–8111 800–383–7377) is a four-square house built in 1906 by a lumber baron; the interior has handsome oak trim and stained glass windows. Each of the four guest rooms has a private bath, telephone, and TV, and the $85 double rate includes such delicious breakfasts as apple Calvados French toast with sourdough bread.

Evans House B&B ¢
725 South Hansell Street, 31792

Tel: 912–226–1343
800–344–4717
Fax: 912–226–0653

Built in 1898, the Evans House is located in an area of late Victorian houses built across from 27-acre Paradise Park, in what was then suburban Thomasville. Its transitional style bridges the asymmetry of the Victorian era and the formality of the emerging Neo-classical style. Lee and John Puskar, who have owned Evans House since 1989, have furnished it with quality Victorian antiques; guest rooms have either queen- or king-size beds. Breakfasts vary daily, but might include fresh-squeezed orange juice, baked grapefruit, almond-poppy seed muffins, strawberry crepes with orange sauce, and bacon; or apple cinnamon muffins, bananas and strawberries in cream, eggs Dijon, and sausages. Rates also include evening turndown service with after-dinner liqueurs, sweets, and fresh towels.

"Hospitable, ready-to-please hosts; they made our dinner reservations, and the chef came out to greet us personally. Immaculate and well maintained; carefully manicured grounds." *(Terry Taylor)* "John and

Lee are a charming couple; hospitality and comfort come first here. We especially like the Regency Room with a wonderful king-size bed." *(Donna Jacobson)* "With their security system I felt extremely safe." *(Rita Gable)* "Our room, with twin beds, two comfortable chairs, and good lighting, was clean and quiet. The old-fashioned bathroom was well supplied with towels. Superb breakfast with fresh peach crepes and excellent coffee."*(ELC)* "Lee brought me a plate of homemade brownies and iced tea, and provided helpful information about the area's historic homes." *(Bill Novak)* "The bed was so comfortable I wanted to take it home with me. Delicious, beautifully presented breakfasts. At night, I found my bed turned down, towels replenished, plus homemade cookies, a pillow sweet, and even a little nightcap." *(Nancy Smith)*

Open All year.

Rooms 1 suite, 3 doubles—all with private bath and/or shower, radio, desk, air-conditioning, fan, queen- or king-size beds. Telephone on request (jacks in rooms).

Facilities Dining room, living room with TV, entrance hall & library with fireplaces, guest kitchen with refrigerator and refreshments. Off-street parking, bicycles. Paradise Park across street.

Location Park Front Historic District. ¼ m from downtown.

Restrictions No smoking.

Credit cards None accepted.

Rates B&B, $135 suite, $75–90 double, $70–85 single. Extra person, $20. Corporate rates.

Extras Airport/station pickups. Wheelchair access; 1 room specially equipped. Pets by arrangement.

We Want to Hear from You!

As you know, this book is effective only with your help. We really need to know about your experiences and discoveries. If you stayed at an inn or hotel listed here, we want to know how it was. Did it live up to our description? Exceed it? Was it what you expected? Did you like it? Were you disappointed? Delighted? Have you discovered new establishments that we should add to the next edition?

Tear out one of the report forms at the back of this book (or use your own stationery if you prefer) and write today. Or email us at afi@inns.com. *Even if you write only "Fully endorse existing entry" you will have been most helpful.*

Thank You!

Hawaii

Kilauea Lodge, Volcano Village

In planning your Hawaii vacation, you may want to consider the "Seven Wonders of Hawaii," as compiled by readers of the *Honolulu Star-Bulletin:* Kilauea in Hawaii Volcanoes National Park and 420-foot Akaka Falls on the Hamakua Coast on the Big Island of Hawaii; the cliffs of the Na Pali Coast and Waimea Canyon on Kauai; the 10,000-foot-high Haleakala Crater on Maui; and Hanauma Bay, a marine preserve, and Diamond Head on Oahu. And remember, to leave crowds and stress behind, hike the trails and walk the beaches whenever you can.

Remember that each island has two weather zones: the leeward side, to the south and west, where the weather is sunny and dry; and the windward side, to the east and north, which is rainier but has the lush vegetation one associates with Hawaii. On the Big Island, for example, monthly precipitation is typically two inches on the leeward side, ten on the windward. Check the map and plan in accordance with your preferences.

Note: With the exception of the island of Hawaii, a restaurant license is required for B&Bs to serve a hot (or full) breakfast, so most serve expanded continental.

Homestay B&Bs have become quite popular throughout the islands, and are typically booked through a reservation service; rates are often very reasonable. **Hawaii's Best Bed & Breakfasts** (P.O. Box 563, Kamuela, 96743; 808–885–4550; or in continental U.S., 800–262–9912; www.bestbnb.com) is the brainchild of Barbara Campbell. After years with one of the big resorts, Barbara has not only her own B&B cottage in Waimea near the Parker Ranch, but also represents many others throughout the islands.

Hawaiian tips: "As far as we can tell, a *lanai* (la-NIE) is used interchangeably in Hawaii to mean a balcony, porch, or deck." And: "Speaking of Hawaiian words, although there are only twelve letters in the Hawaiian alphabet, it seems like thirteen of them are vowels. When trying to say a Hawaiian word, pronounce every vowel separately. Thus *Pu'upehe*, Sweetheart Rock, is said poo'-oo-peh'-heh. Got it?"

Entries are listed alphabetically, first by island, then by town.

HAWAII—THE BIG ISLAND

Twice the size of any other Hawaiian island, the Big Island offers the greatest variety of scenery, with the drama of active volcanoes, stark lava flows, black sand beaches, and great hiking.

HILO, HAWAII

Hilo (pronounced Hee'-low) was the headquarters of King Kamehameha I, who used it as a base to conquer all the islands by 1810. It later became a center for Christian missionaries, sugar plantations, and a thriving port. Devastated by tsunamis in 1946 and 1960, the town slowly decayed until a restoration program began in 1985. Since then there's been a turnaround, with many of its historic buildings handsomely restored. Don't forget an umbrella—Hilo has 120 inches of warm rain annually, making for lush vegetation and lots of rainbows.

Also recommended: Built in 1900, **The Shipman House Bed & Breakfast** (131 Ka'iulani Street, 96720; 808–934–8002 or 800–627–8447; www.hilo-hawaii.com) once hosted Jack London, author of *Call of the Wild*, as well as Hawaii's last queen, Lili'uokalani, who enjoyed playing the grand piano in the parlor and enjoying a cigar with her friend, Mary Shipman. Known locally as "The Castle," the 9,000-square-foot structure is one of the few remaining Victorian mansions in the state of Hawaii. This Queen Anne–style house features a striking three-story rounded tower with a conical roof, accented by a circular veranda, and four curved bay windows on both the first and second floors. Restored as a B&B in 1994, it offers five guest rooms at B&B double rates of $140–160. Rates include a generous breakfast buffet, afternoon lemonade, iced tea, and cookies.

KAILUA-KONA, HAWAII

Also recommended: About 15 miles north of Kailua-Kona via Highway 19 is the well-known **Kona Village Resort** (P.O. Box 1299, Kaupulehu-Kona, 96745; 808–325–5555 or 800–367–5290) built on the site of the ancient Hawaiian village of Kaupulehu. In 1801, when Mt. Hualalai erupted, this cove was the only one spared the massive lava flows that devastated the area. The village's 125 thatched *hales* (Polynesian-style bungalows) have been built among the actual stone platforms of the ancient Hawaiians, and are located around the lagoon, along the beach, and in a lava field along the ocean. Many have been recently renovated, and some have a private hot tub. Although its not for everyone (no TV, no AC), many feel that Kona Village Resort is still the best Polynesian resort on the island, and one of the finest tropical resorts in the world. Popular with both couples (excepting school vacations) and families alike, activities include pool and ocean swimming, tennis, snorkeling, sunfish sailing, canoeing, boat excursions, children's program, and a new fitness center. All this does not come cheap; all-inclusive double rates range from $425–735, plus 15% service. "I was warmly greeted, given a flower lei, rum punch or pineapple juice, and then driven on a golf cart to my thatched-roof Lava Tahitian hale, set on stilts overlooking a black pebble and rock lava beach. Open-air laundry rooms with complimentary washers, dryers, and laundry soap were greatly appreciated. The food was outstanding, chosen from a menu at breakfast and dinner, with a buffet set out at lunch—creative, imaginative, and delicious. I also toured a renovated hale, and would highly recommend requesting one." *(Linda Goldberg)*

Information please: The **Kailua Plantation House** (75–5948 Alii Drive, 96740; 808–329–3727; www.tales.com/KPH), offers superb ocean views and relaxing accommodations. Built as a B&B, it faces the Pacific from atop a promontory of black rocks formed by ancient lava flows. Most rooms have tiled floors and sliding glass doors that lead out to balconies; furnishings are spare but elegant, mostly bamboo with soft Hawaiian print fabrics. Double rates for the five guest rooms range from $160–235, including a breakfast of breads, muffins, Hawaiian fruits, Kona coffee, tea, and juice, plus a hot entrée such as Belgian waffles, French toast, or quiche, served from 7:30–9:30 A.M. "Beautiful setting, delicious breakfast. We watched dolphins playing in the surf, a 100 yards from the lanai. Our comfortable room had a great bed and was well equipped with such extras as beach towels, a thermos, and coolers." *(Mike & Cindy Wilkinson)*

VOLCANO, HAWAII

Try to spend a couple of days exploring Hawaii Volcanoes National Park, one of only two national parks devoted to active volcanoes; the park is bigger than the island of Oahu, so allow ample time. The summit areas are in a subalpine tropical rain forest zone, with about 125 inches of rain annually, making for lush green forests. At an elevation over 3,500 feet, the weather is typically cool and rainy, so come prepared with warm, comfortable clothes, sturdy hiking shoes (an extra pair is good when the first pair gets wet), and rain gear; binoculars are recommended for bird-watching. Stop at the visitors' center for details on the drives around the Kilauea caldera or down the Chain of Craters road, and maps for the many exciting hiking trails; heli-tours are also a thrilling option. Area restaurants options are extremely limited, so ask your innkeeper about advance reservations. The park is about 25 miles southwest of Hilo on the "Big Island" of Hawaii.

Reader tip: "Cold, wet, and rainy throughout our visit. The wood and paper were too wet to light for a fire; our towels never dried. Bring warm clothes and ask if your room is heated!" *(MW)* "Kilauea is a very active volcano; ask a park ranger for safety advice and follow it!" *(WT)*

Also recommended: The **Chalet Kilauea, The Inn at Volcano** (Wright Road, P.O. Box 998, 96785; 808–967–7786 or 800–937–7786) has elegantly decorated guest accommodations with marble Jacuzzi baths. B&B rates of $125–395 include a full breakfast and afternoon tea; six vacation homes have kitchens and go for $125–395 including afternoon tea. "A wonderful escape: romantic room, gorgeous greenery, elegant bathroom, delicious candlelight breakfast, and the fascinating park itself." *(Linda Goldberg)*

Kilauea Lodge ♀ ✕ &

P.O. Box 116, 96785

Tel: 808–967–7366
Fax: 808–967–7367
Email: staff@kilauea-lodge.com
URL: http://www.kilauea-lodge.com

Hawaii may not be the first place that comes to mind when "mountain country inns" are mentioned, but that's just what Kilauea Lodge is. Built in 1938 as a YMCA lodge, it was converted into an inn in 1987 by Albert and Lorna Jeyte. Lorna notes that "I was raised on the Big Island, and have decorated our inn with original Hawaiian art and furnishings made from local woods. Our menu combines local specialties with dishes reflecting Albert's European background." The inviting guest rooms are country comfortable with colorful comforters, and breakfast is a hearty meal of bacon and eggs to order, pancakes, or Hawaiian-style French toast with fresh fruit.

"Our serene room featured a king-sized bed, a wood-beamed cathedral ceiling, and garden views. The inviting dining room is decorated with eye-catching local artwork and an imposing stone fireplace. Chef Albert accommodated our strict vegetarian diet with a special entrée, and the staff served us breakfast before our early morning flight." *(Gail Davis)* "Blissfully quiet location, with wonderfully starry skies at night. Friendly dogs, cats, and birds." *(Jennifer Baker)* "Charming setting among tree ferns and cypress. Rooms are immaculate, with flowers and Hawaiian prints." *(Carol Lied)*

"The common room has books and video tapes about Hawaii, comfortable seating, and a fireplace to take off the chill. Birds sang outside our window; a couch was placed in front of the fireplace, which needed only a match to light. Our room also had a comfortable king-sized bed, and a double-headed shower." *(Pam Thatcher)* "Convenient parking. Insider books and area information; pottery and pictures enhanced the decor of our spacious room. The fireplace was replenished daily, and the bathroom towels were heated by a warmer." *(George Vorhauer)* "Comfortable, spacious guest rooms; one of the best restaurants on the island." *(Joseph Lacey)* "Clean, cozy, well-run lodge at the park entrance, set in a tree fern forest. Guest rooms are cheerful, individually decorated, and comfortable." *(Silvey Carmen)* "Superb staff—attentive, eager to help, and very friendly." *(Randall Schmitt)* "Impeccably maintained. Every member of the staff treats you as an old friend." *(Linda Eggerking)* "Delicious meals with ample choices featuring locally grown produce. My dinner favorites include the potato leek soup and duck l'orange; at breakfast, I love the French toast with coconut syrup." *(Teri Childers)*

Open All year.
Rooms 3 cottages, 11 doubles—all with private bath and/or shower, clock. Some with fireplace, desk, balcony. Rooms in several buildings.
Facilities Restaurant with bar, books, fireplace; common area with games, books, fireplace. 10 acres with off-street parking, croquet, hiking trails.
Location From Hwy 11 S, exit at Wright Road & bear left on Old Volcano Hwy. to lodge on right. From Hwy 11 N, bear left after Visitors' Center to village. Approx. 1 m from park entrance.
Restrictions No smoking.
Credit cards Amex, MC, Visa.
Rates B&B, $135–145 cottage, $95–135 double. Extra person, $15. No charge for children under 2. Tips welcome. Alc dinner $35.
Extras Wheelchair access. Cribs, baby-sitting. German, Spanish spoken.

KAUAI

Although hardly undiscovered (it's third among total visitors), Kauai has maintained its relaxed island pace despite increased traffic. Visitors will especially enjoy its challenging golf courses and spectacular scenery. Tropical vegetation doesn't last long without ample rain, so try the Poipu area for the best chances for sun.

Reader tips: "A drive to the north shore is a must, as it is the most picturesque and peaceful part of the island, with many beautiful white-sand beaches, high cliffs, lush foliage, and natural, rugged beauty. This side is the least crowded, with less traffic and many tiny villages. There are many interesting things to do on Kauai, other than lounge on the beach. Try a drive to Waimea Canyon, where you can also hike, or a helicopter tour, or an exciting boat trip to view the humpback whales and the impressive Na Pali cliffs." *(Linda Goldberg)* And: "Kauai's red earth stains shoes, clothes, carpets, and more. Many B&Bs ask that you leave your shoes outside, and provide slippers." *(JR)*

KOLOA/POIPU

Gloria's Spouting Horn B&B   *Tel:* 808–742–6995
4464 Lawai Beach Road, 96756   *Fax:* 808–742–6995
                              E-mail: glorbb@hotmail.com

Extensive renovation is a normal part of innkeeping, but at Gloria's Spouting Horn B&B, Mother Nature took charge of the job; in 1992, Hurricane Iniki swept Bob and Gloria Merkle's home out to sea. Plans to rebuild better than ever were drawn up, and sixteen months later, this custom-built cedar home was completed, securely anchored by deep pilings. Balconies stretch along the first and second floors of the house, overlooking the beach below and the ocean beyond. The three ocean-view rooms have queen-size beds; one has a dramatic curved willow branch canopy queen bed. Each room has a wet bar with a refrigerator stocked with cold drinks, lots of shuttered windows, and a balcony with spectacular coastal views. Bathrooms have deep soaking tubs, separate shower and dressing areas, and ample closet space. Breakfast, served 7–9 A.M., might include fresh tropical fruits, orange-guava juice, macadamia nut or raspberry-chocolate Kona coffee, and such entrees as peach French toast with warm peach syrup, seafood frittata with salsa and bran muffins, spinach souffle with coffee cake, and perhaps home-baked crusty Cuban or Irish soda bread. Rates also include evening liqueurs and snacks

"Superb physical facilities, with large, private bedrooms which front directly on the Pacific. I'd bet there are cruise ship cabins further from the water than our room. Friendly gracious hospitality; fabulous breakfasts." *(Allan & Judy Rachap, also Connie Howard)* "We appreciated the option of having breakfast either in the living room or in our beautiful bedroom." *(Jerry & Judy McGrath)* "Married on the beach by Bob, Gloria's was the perfect honeymoon retreat. Convenient minikitchen in each room." *(R.J. Thiessen)* "Bob welcomed us to breakfast playing beautiful Hawaiian music on the guitar. We watched whales while feasting on walnut French toast with maple syrup and whipped cream. Helpful, charming innkeepers." *(Nancy & Mark Donatelli)* "An elegant and intimate seaside retreat combining Gloria's mouthwatering breakfasts with Bob's classical guitar serenades." *(Barbara & Jim Oilar)* "We woke to the sound of the surf crashing on the rocks below, and the sun streaming into our room. From our balcony we watched sea turtles graze. Rich Kauai coffee." *(Craig Swanson)* "Wonderful location—beautiful views, quiet and serene. Superb snorkeling and great restaurants nearby." *(Nancy Fengold)* "Our refrigerator was stocked with juice and chocolate macadamia nuts. Thoughtful extras included beach chairs and a cooler for day trips. An extensive collection of books, videos, and local guide books as well as snacks and liqueurs were readily available." *(Theresa Brink)*

Open All year.

Rooms 2 suites, 1 double—all with full private bath, telephone, ceiling fan, clock/radio, TV/VCR, desk, fan, wet bar with refrigerator, microwave, coffee maker; balcony.

Facilities Dining room, living room, library with books, lounge, guest kitchen, balcony. Occasional classical guitar music. ¼ acre on ocean; off-street parking, koi ponds.

Location Poipu Beach, 3 m from Koloa. From Lihue Airport, follow Hwy. 50 W to Koloa-Poipu turnoff at Hwy. 520 (Tree Tunnel) Go left (S) & continue to Koloa. Turn right at Kolua Rd. Go left at Poipu Rd. At "Welcome to Poipu" sign, take right fork on Lawai Rd. and proceed 1.5 miles to inn.

Restrictions No smoking. Children over 14.

Credit cards None accepted.

Rates B&B, $200–225 suite, $170–195 double. Extra person, $25; three-night minimum. Ask about vacation rental homes nearby.

PRINCEVILLE, KAUAI

Also recommended: Noted for its extraordinary setting and lushly landscaped grounds and cascading waterfalls is the **Hanalei Bay Resort and Suites** (5380 Honoiki Road, 96722; 808–826–6522 or 800–367–5004). Extensively renovated in 1995 after Hurricane Iniki, the hotel has 280 well-equipped guest rooms and suites spread over 16 separate buildings; facilities include eight tennis courts and two swimming pools. Guest rooms and studios range from $160–240, with 1-3 bedroom suites from $290–750 suite, with many package rates available. "An exceptional setting, beautifully landscaped, amazing views, wonderful swimming lagoon, comfortably furnished rooms." *(Linda Goldberg)* "Although our room was one of the less expensive ones, it was large, well equipped, and clean. We made our own breakfast (utensils provided) and ate on our own lanai, with views of the mountains, pool, and gardens. Although popular with tour groups, we didn't see them or feel their presence." *(Michael & Dina Miller)*

Hale 'Aha B&B   *Tel:* 808–826–6733
3875 Kamehameha Road, P.O. Box 3370, 96722   800–826–6733
                                      Fax: 808–826–9052
                             E-mail: kauai@pixi.com
                    URL: http://www.pixi.com/~kauai

"Princeville is a planned recreational community on the north coast of Kauai, consisting of championship golf courses, many beautiful condominium projects, exclusive homes, and the Hanalei Bay Resort. A 20-minute scenic drive will take you to the start of the Na Pali hiking trails, and some of the most beautiful beaches on the island are just a short car ride away. Hale 'Aha (pronounced hah-ley-ah'-ha), meaning 'house of gathering,' was built as a B&B in 1990 and is lovingly maintained by owners Herb and Ruth Bockelman. The house overlooks the golf course, with distant sea and mountain views. The decor is soothing, in shades of peach, blue, and beige, with houseplants and flowers. The 1,000-square-foot penthouse suite has open-beamed ceilings, and a deck with panoramic views of Bali Hai and the Kilauea lighthouse." *(Linda Goldberg)*

"I felt comfortable enough to stretch out on the couch with one of their delightful books on Kauai. We stayed in the least expensive room with a mountain view; it was sizable with a large closet and bathroom, and separate entrance. We enjoyed talking with Herb and Ruth each morning after breakfast. They are knowledgeable about the island's many attractions and helped us plan our activities." *(John Dearborn)*

"Spectacular drive to the inn, past the Hanalei Valley lookout, famed Lumahai Beach where South Pacific was filmed, the one-way bridges, the quaint green church in the town of Hanalei, the dry and wet caves, the state park, streams, and craggy mountain peaks. The beautifully decorated honeymoon suite is comfortable, peaceful, and homey, with a well-equipped kitchenette, and a private entry leading to a deck over-looking the golf course. The bedroom has a king-size bed; the bathroom is done in pale peach tiles and has a large Jacuzzi tub and separate shower. The penthouse suite is even more special, but all the rooms are lovely. Breakfast was served at the dining room table, and included poppy seed muffins with guava butter, blueberry coffee cake, and steamed brown rice and raisins, topped with fresh pineapple, straw-berries, brown sugar. Fruit smoothies were blended from guava, pas-sion fruit, banana, orange juice, and strawberries." *(LG)*

Open All year.
Rooms 2 suites, 2 doubles—all with full private bath, private entrance, radio, TV, desk/table, deck, ceiling fan, refrigerator. Some with air-conditioning. Suites with whirlpool tub, kitchenettes. Penthouse suite with laundry, deck, gas grill.
Facilities Dining room, living room with fireplace, balconies. 1½ acres on golf course. Trail to secluded beach. Tennis, fitness center, horseback riding nearby.
Location N coast. From Lihue airport take main road N past Kapaa to Princeville. Turn right on Ka Haku at main entrance to Hanalei. Go past golf course, turn right on Kamehameha Rd. to inn on right.
Restrictions No smoking. No children. Sunday check-ins discouraged; by spe-cial arrangement only.
Credit cards MC, Visa.
Rates B&B, $220 suite, $88–150 double. Weekly discount. Extra person in suite, $15–20. 3-night minimum.

LANA'I

Once known for its pineapple—not its tourist—crop, Lana'i offers a minimum of crowds and beautiful beaches. Plan to rent a car to get around on Lana'i; it may be worth it to pay the extra for four-wheel drive, since there are only 30 miles of paved road on the island.

Reader tips: "To get to Lana'i, try the ferry. It's cheaper than the plane, more reliable in poor weather, fun, and a pretty ride, and you will likely see humpback whales." *(Carol Blodgett)* "Although once known as the 'Pineapple Island,' the only pineapples I saw were in a small field near the airport. The weather on Lana'i is much wetter at higher elevations; when I was at the Lodge at Koele for tea it rained buckets; Manele Bay stayed completely dry." *(LG)* "Lana'i City offered interesting morning walks. The island of Lana'i is peaceful, unlike the bustle of the other islands. Excellent food at Koele, Manele Bay, and the Hotel Lanai." *(Leigh Robinson)*

Also recommended: Originally built in 1923 as a guest house for the Hawaiian Pineapple Company, you can still find a taste of old Hawaii (along with your fresh pineapple juice) on the **Hotel Lanai's** (P.O. Box 520, Lana'i, 96763; 808–565–7211 or 800–795–7211) verandas, shaded by towering pines. Each of the 11 guest rooms are similarly furnished with natural wood floors, bleached pine furniture, and patchwork quilts. Guests can enjoy cocktails and appetizers at the knotty pine bar or on the front lanai, and enjoy dinner in the hotel restaurant, Henry Clay's

Rotisserie, specializing in spit-roasted meats and fish, Cajun and Creole-style dishes, pizza, and salad. B&B double rates are a reasonable $95–105, including continental breakfast; a cottage is available at $135. Children under 8 stay free.

Opened in 1991, the 250-room **Manele Bay Hotel** (P.O. Box 310, Lanai City, 96763; 808–565–7700 or 800–321–4666) was designed to take full advantage of its spectacular location overlooking the beach on Hulopoe Bay, rugged coastline, and the blue Pacific Ocean beyond. "An elegant Mediterranean villa–style hotel, with an ornate lobby with high ceilings and walls decorated with massive Oriental murals. My exquisite ocean-view suite had Oriental decorative accents, beautiful floral fabrics, and a bathroom with all possible amenities. Sliding glass doors opened to a patio overlooking the gardens and ocean. Inviting swimming pool and spa were especially private at night, as was sitting in the moonlight on the sugar-fine white sand beach. Dining options range from several reasonably priced, casual options to the acclaimed (and expensive) Ihilani Restaurant." *(LG)* Double rates range from $275–525, suites from $525–$2,000; meal plans available.

Lodge at Koele 🏃 ✕ 🎿   *Tel:* 808–565–7300
P.O. Box 310, Lana'i City, 96763   800–321–4666
                                       Fax: 808–565–4561

The don't-blink-or-you'll-miss-it town of Lana'i City will leave you totally unprepared for the luxurious experience offered by the Lodge at Koele. The Lodge sits on a 59,000-acre up-country estate, and both its architecture and decor evoke turn-of-the-century English manor elegance, from the Great Hall with two stone fireplaces to the Library and Trophy rooms, and outside to the croquet lawns and Orchid House. The decor is lightened with a mix of country antiques, folk art by local Lana'i artists, and Asian accent pieces. Guest rooms have dark bamboo furnishings and four-poster beds with pineapple finials, and luxuriously equipped bathrooms. The Lodge's restaurant offers an imaginative menu featuring such entrées as skillet chicken on field greens with chive onion rings, lamb shanks with polenta, and grilled fish with fennel citrus vinaigrette.

"Because of its 1,700-foot hillside elevation, the Lodge is sometimes shrouded in mist from nearby Lana'i Hale, the highest point on the island, but that only adds to its appeal. Upscale atmosphere, yet low-key and livable." *(BN)* "Beautiful grounds, outstanding decor. Service is professional and helpful. You can use all the beach facilities at the sister resort, Manele Bay, where sometimes you can see spinner dolphins playing in Hulopoe Bay; there's free shuttle service for the 20-minute drive. Lana'i is fascinating in a stark way. You really feel the old Hawaii on this island, with long stretches of uninhabited beaches." *(Carol Blodgett)* "The lodge is surrounded by acres of manicured lawns and pine trees, and there is a magnificent pond surrounded by flowering bushes; its golf course is among the world's most scenic and challenging. Rustic but elegant common rooms, with cozy fireplaces; spacious, well-appointed guest rooms, with oversized furniture and spacious ornate bathrooms with wonderful magnifying mirrors for makeup. Delight-ful 4:00 afternoon tea with a variety of teas, pastries, miniature cran-berry scones, clotted cream, and lemon cream." *(Linda Goldberg)* "Fully endorse entry. Both the hotel and Lana'i itself were an outstanding va-cation choice. Our package rate included many activities. Both our guest room and the common areas were spacious and beautifully dec-orated. Extensive landscaping around the hotel with a lake and a white conservatory building full of orchids. Excellent food; friendly, kind staff." *(Leigh Robinson)*

Open All year.
Rooms 14 suites, 88 doubles—all with private bath and/or shower.
Facilities Restaurants, lounge, lobby, gift shops. Orchid house, sporting clays course, golf, fitness center, swimming pool, Jacuzzi, tennis, croquet, lawn bowl-ing, horseback riding, mountain biking. At Manele Bay: spa, beach, snorkeling, children's program. Scuba diving, sailing, fishing nearby.
Location Lana'i City.
Credit cards Amex, CB, DC, JCB, MC, Visa.
Rates Room only, $600–1,500 suite, $325–485 double. Extra person, $40; no charge for child under 15 in parents' room. MAP, add $100 per person. FAP, add $125 per person. Minimum stay Dec. 18–Jan. 2. Package rates. Picnic lunches by arrangement.
Extras Airport pickups by arrangement. Shuttle van between Koele, Manele Bay, Lana'i City.

MAUI

Years ago, we saw a corny bumper sticker which proclaimed: "Here today, gone to Maui." Unfortunately, millions of others have been so inspired, making Maui second only to Oahu in popularity. Don't expect isolation here, although you will find the full spectrum of accommo-dations, shopping, night life, water sports, beautiful beaches, and dra-matic scenery.

KAHULUI/WAILUKU, MAUI

Information please: What better way to start your visit to Maui than with a stay at a beautiful 1920s island home, owned by born-and-raised Hawaiians Janice and Tom Fairbanks, and dedicated to Hawaii's poet laureate of the 1920s, Don Blanding. From your arrival at Kahului Air-port, it's less than a ten-minute drive to **The Old Wailuku Inn at Ulupono** (2199 Kaho'okele Street, Wailuku, 96793; 808–244–5897 or 800–305–4899; www.aitv.com/ulupono). B&B double rates for the seven charming guest rooms, all with air-conditioning, TV/VCR, telephone, private bath, and heritage Hawaiian quilts (some have a king-size bed, private lanai and/or whirlpool tub) range from $120–180, including a full breakfast and afternoon refreshments.

LAHAINA, MAUI

Old Lahaina Town plays a distinguished part in the history of Hawaii; as the first capital of the Hawaiian Kingdom, it was the center of Maui's cultural and social life. Later it became the whaling capital of the Pacific in the 1860s, with all the diverse personalities of that era.

Reader tips: "Although touristy, we enjoyed Lahaina and used it as a base for touring Maui. The Banyan Tree Park leads to charming renovated 1800s buildings. The Court House and two art galleries in the old prison have crafts not found elsewhere; admission is free." *(Michael & Dina Miller)* "Lahaina serves as headquarters for whale-watching cruises, snorkeling tours, shopping, and nightlife." *(SHW)* "It's not hard to find surviving landmarks from the days of whalers and missionaries." *(PG)*

Also recommended: Located in a residential area convenient to the town of Lahaina and the beach resort of Kaanapali, **The Guesthouse** (1620 Ainakea Road, 96761; 808–661–8085 or 800–621–8942; guest-house@compuserve.com) offers clean, comfortable rooms and hospitable owners, Tanna Swanson and Raphael and Tammy Djoa, who really enjoy having guests. Four guest rooms, each with private Jacuzzi bath or hot tub, have contemporary decor, and the $95 double rate includes a casual family-style breakfast, use of swimming pool, kitchen, and laundry.

Imagine waking up to breathtaking views of the Pacific, with Lana'i and Moloka'i in the distance. The **House of Fountains** (1579 Lokia Street, 96761; 808–667–2121 or 800–789–6865; private@maui.net) enhances this view with an inviting swimming pool, hot tub, and barbecue area. This recently remodeled home has five guest rooms, furnished with island-style white rattan, floral fabrics, private baths, and all modern conveniences. Laundry facilities and beach towels are also available. The B&B double rates range from $85–125, and include a full buffet breakfast, with fresh fruit and juice, cheese and salami, home-baked bread, rolls, and croissants. "German-born Daniela and Thomas Clement are gracious, charming innkeepers. Their elegant home has high ceilings in the living room, lots of windows, and white marble floors; the spacious, immaculate guest rooms are well equipped but uncluttered." *(Linda Goldberg)* Comments welcome.

Recommended for its "fabulous location in the heart of town" is **The Lahaina Inn** (127 Lahainaluna Road, 96761; 808–661–0577 or 800–669–3444; www.hawaiionsale.com/lahainainn), a re-creation of a Hawaiian Victorian hotel, with walnut banisters, cast-iron chandeliers, and period antiques. The guest room furnishings include antique brass, iron, and carved walnut beds, Laura Ashley and Ralph Lauren fabrics, and lace curtains. B&B double rates for the 12 guest rooms range from $89–169.

Located on ten secluded acres on Napili Bay is the **Napili Kai Beach Club** (5900 Honoapiilani Road, 96761; 808–669–6271 or 800–367–5030; www.napilikai.com), eight miles north of Lahaina. Magnificent ocean views abound from the private lanais of the 162 well-equipped studios and suites, with double rates of $170–275, suites $265–580; many have kitchenettes, and package rates are available. The resort claims to have the largest hot tub in Maui, plus four swimming pools and two 18-hole putting greens. Championship golf and tennis is nearby. "My newly renovated deluxe sea-view studio unit had a kitchen and a large bedroom with a king-size bed, cable TV, air-conditioning, ceiling fan, Japanese screens, a large covered terrace, and a spacious bathroom. Gorgeous view of one of the swimming pools and the white sand beach, excellent for swimming and snorkeling." *(Linda Goldberg)* "A great place for families, with a kids' vacation program; a far better choice than the area's tacky condos, and a much better value than the fancy big-name resorts." *(HAS)*

Information please: Built in 1987, **The Plantation Inn** (174 Lahainaluna Road, 96761; 808–667–9225 or 800–433–6815; www.maui.net/~inn/) is an elegant gray and white wood-frame building. Its 19 guest rooms are decorated with stained glass windows, brass and four-poster beds, flowered fabrics and wallpapers, and oak flooring; the baths have Victorian pedestal sinks and chain-pull toilets. The inn's restaurant, Gerard's, is well established and reputed to be one of Maui's best, specializing in French cuisine. B&B double rates range from $135–215, and include early morning coffee and a breakfast of fresh fruit, French toast, Kona coffee, and hot chocolate. The inn came under new ownership in 1997, and a refurbishing program as well as a 14-room expansion to an adjacent home are planned. Reports welcome.

OAHU

Hawaii's most crowded island, Oahu is still a must-see for first-time visitors. Explore Waikiki and climb up Diamond Head for a fabulous view, then visit Honolulu's downtown, with its fine museums and Chinatown markets. Get a car and discover Oahu's magnificent beaches, many ideal for mile-long walks, unspoiled by development.

HONOLULU, OAHU

Overcrowded, overbuilt, overwhelming, Honolulu is both a big city and a major resort area—an unusual combination. It is perhaps the one place in Hawaii where man-made attractions outnumber those of nature. Go to spiffed-up Waikiki to do your souvenir shopping, then to Diamond Head and Ala Moana Beach Park to clear your head. Visit Iolani Palace to understand a bit about Hawaii's monarchy, and the Bishop Museum for a look at the island's Polynesian heritage. Chinatown will give you a taste of the East, and Pearl Harbor's Arizona Memorial pays homage to America's entry into World War II.

Also recommended: In one of Waikiki's best neighborhoods, a 12-minute walk from Sans Souci Beach and Kapiloani Park is the **Diamond**

Head B&B (book through Hawaii's Best B&Bs, P.O. Box 563, Kamuela, HI, 96743; 808–885–4550 or 800–262–9912; www.bestbnb.com), located on the west slope of Diamond Head. B&B double rates for the three guest rooms, each with private bath and lanai range from $100–125. "A lovely 50-year-old island home handsomely decorated with heirloom Hawaiian furniture, including a huge four-poster koa wood bed which belonged to Hawaiian Princess Ruth. Breakfast one morning was a complete luau; the next we had bagels and cream cheese with smoked salmon caught and smoked by our hostess. Beach mats, towels, and coolers were supplied for a picnic. Beautiful grounds with tropical flowers and huge trees." *(Barbara-Ann Andersen, also LG)*

New Otani Kaimana Beach Hotel   🏃 ✕   *Tel:* 808–923–1555
2863 Kalakaua Avenue, 96815   In U.S./Canada: 800–35–OTANI
Fax: 808–922–9404
E-mail: kaimana@pixi.com
URL: http://www.kaimana.com

The Kaimana was built in 1964, and is ideally located in the center of Kapiolani Park, adjacent to Waikiki's central hotel and shopping area. It overlooks Sans Souci beach, one of the best swimming beaches on Oahu, according to long-time general manager Stephen Boyle.

"A favorite haunt of Robert Louis Stevenson. Today the area includes the hotel, the beach and ocean, 500-acre Kapiolani Park, and Diamond Head. The hotel has one of the few outdoor restaurants in Waikiki, the Hau Tree Lanai, plus an excellent Japanese restaurant, Miyako. A short walk away are the Honolulu Zoo, Waikiki Aquarium, the Waikiki Shell, and bus stops." *(Michael Virgintino)*

"We stayed in Room 8, a park-view studio facing Kapiolani Park. From our small but private lanai we could sit and watch the sunset and enjoy the island breezes. Diamond Head overshadows the hotel and makes for a very picturesque setting. We joined the New Otani Club (it's free), and were given a $6.50 breakfast credit." *(Michael Miller)* "The Kaimana has a wonderful open-air tiled lobby with flowers, ferns, and mosaic paintings. Excellent dinner at the Hau Tree Lanai of papaya mint soup, shrimp curry, and Midori cheesecake. Standard guest rooms are not large, but all are pleasantly decorated in pastel shades of lavender, aqua, and beige; most popular are the ocean-view studios." *(SHW)* "Clean room and friendly atmosphere." *(Juan C. De Tata MD)* "Wonderful and friendly staff." *(Geary B. Southard)* "Quiet and convenient location. Happy and helpful staff. Very clean." *(J. Shukla)*

Open All year.
Rooms 30 suites, 94 doubles—all with full private bath, TV, telephone, radio, desk, air-conditioning, balcony, minibar. Some with kitchenette, hair dryer, coffee maker, microwave, large-screen TV.
Facilities 2 restaurants, room service, beach. Concierge service. Swimming, windsurfing, golf, tennis, kayaking, hiking, jogging, bicycling nearby.
Location 1 m S of Waikiki, at Diamond Head. 10-min. walk to main Waikiki strip.

Restrictions Rooms on the corner next to the Sans Souci condominium are quite close.
Credit cards Amex, CB, DC, Discover, JCB, MC, Visa.
Rates Room only, $180–620 suite, $115–260 double. Extra person, $15; no charge for children under 12. 10% AARP, NARFE discount. "Room & Car," 5-night minimum stay, Dec. 20–Jan. 5.
Extras Crib, baby-sitting. Japanese, Korean, Spanish, German, Tagalog, Ilokano spoken.

Key to Abbreviations and Symbols

For complete information and explanations, please see the Introduction.

¢ Especially good value for overnight accommodation.
♗ Families welcome. Most (but not all) have cribs, baby-sitting, games, play equipment, and reduced rates for children.
✕ Meals served to public; reservations recommended or required.
♟ Tennis court and swimming pool and/or lake on grounds. Golf usually on grounds or nearby.
♿ Limited or full wheelchair access; call for details.
Rates: Range from least expensive room in low season to most expensive room in peak season.
Room only: No meals included; European Plan (EP).
B&B: Bed and breakfast; includes breakfast, sometimes afternoon/evening refreshment.
MAP: Modified American Plan; includes breakfast and dinner.
Full board: Three meals daily.
Alc lunch: A la carte lunch; average price of entrée plus nonalcoholic drink, tax, tip.
Alc dinner: Average price of three-course dinner, including half bottle of house wine, tax, tip.
Prix fixe dinner: Three- to five-course set dinner, excluding wine, tax, tip unless otherwise noted.
Extras: Noted if available. Always confirm in advance. Pets are not permitted unless specified; if you are allergic, ask for details; *most innkeepers have pets.*

Idaho

Idaho Rocky Mountain Ranch, Stanley

Idaho was the only western state settled by an eastward flow of settlers—waves of prospectors swarmed here from California and other western regions when gold was discovered in 1860. Now prospectors have largely been replaced by tourists (and disenchanted Californians), but Idaho's rugged terrain still provides the allure. With 200 mountain peaks over 8,000 feet in height, Idaho also boasts North America's largest gorge (Hell's Canyon), rivers turbulent with white-water rapids, remote forests, numerous large lakes, and Craters of the Moon National Monument—83 acres of twisted globules, rivers, and cones of lava.

Idaho is ideal for the outdoor enthusiast: rafting, fishing, hunting, hiking, mountain climbing, cross-country and downhill skiing. The list is endless. The less energetic can take comfort in the fact that many tempting spots can be seen along the state's two north-south highways. North of Twin Falls, State Route 75 winds through farmland, past Hailey (where Ezra Pound was born), then climbs to Ketchum/Sun Valley (a ski resort since 1936) and on to the magnificent Sawtooth Mountains. From here north to Salmon (route number changes to State Route 93), every bend in the road looks like a picture postcard. In June, the road is bordered by a profusion of delicate wildflowers. For a different view, take State Route 95 north from Weiser to the Canadian border. Broad valleys, steep mountains, and rolling fields of alfalfa lead to the forests and famous lake country of northern Idaho.

Cutting across Idaho? Take U.S. 12, which follows Lewis and Clark's 1805 trail from Lolo Pass on the Montana border (west of Missoula) through lush forest along the Lochsa River, one of Idaho's prettiest. Staying in Boise? You'll find it one of the friendliest capital cities in the country. While here, don't miss the capitol rotunda, where huge, beautiful faux marble columns blend in spectacularly with the real thing from Vermont and Italy. One warning: Southern Idaho (including Boise) can be very hot in summer; when you reserve a room, make sure it is air conditioned.

BOISE

Notwithstanding the fact that it is the capital and largest city in Idaho, Boise is a pleasant small city in southwest Idaho and serves as a gateway for those en route to Sun Valley.

Also recommended: Listed on the National Register of Historic Places, the **Idaho Heritage Inn** (109 West Idaho, 83702; 208–342–8066) was built in 1904 by Henry Falk, and remained in the Falk family until 1943, when it was purchased by Governor Chase Clark. The governor passed along the house to his daughter Bethine and son-in-law, Senator Frank Church, who owned it until Tom and Phyllis Lupher restored the home as a bed & breakfast inn in 1987. The inn is within walking distance of several good restaurants, the city zoo, art museum, historical museum, Boise State, and the Greenbelt, a paved path following the Boise River. B&B double rates for the six guest rooms range from $60–95 and include a full breakfast and evening refreshments; guest rooms have private baths, queen-size beds, and telephones. Comments welcome.

COEUR D'ALENE

Coeur d'Alene is a lovely resort town set on the banks of the lake of the same name. Located in Idaho's northern panhandle, it's only 30 miles east of Spokane, Washington, and is a very popular getaway with the inhabitants of that city. Activities include lake cruises, canoeing, paddleboating, plus hiking, picnicking, and, in winter, cross-country skiing and snowmobiling. About 30 minutes away is downhill skiing.

Also recommended: The turn-of-the-century **Gregory's McFarland House** (601 Foster Avenue, 83814; 208–667–1232 or 800–335–1232; www.bbhost.com/mcfarlandhouse) is a beautifully restored home with birds-eye maple flooring, leaded glass windows, and period decor. Ample common areas for guests include a living room with piano, a family room with TV and pool table, a wraparound porch with swing, and a redwood deck overlooking the garden. B&B rates for the five guest rooms range from $105–135. "Comfortable room with excellent lighting. Delicious breakfast with fresh fruit and apple-filled crepes with huckleberry sauce." (*Chris Zambito & Karl Wiegers*) Comments appreciated.

Ten miles north of Coeur d'Alene is **The Clark House** (East 4550 South Hayden Lake Road, Hayden Lake, 83835; 208–772–3470 or 800–765–4593; www.clarkhouse.com), a beautiful Colonial Revival home built in 1910 and extensively restored by Monty Danner and Rod Palmer. B&B double rates for the four guest suites, each with queen- or king-size beds, fireplaces, and private baths, range from $85–$225, including a full breakfast. Six-course dinners are served by reservation only. "Peaceful atmosphere and setting, overlooking Hayden Lake.

Warm welcome from the innkeepers. Beautifully decorated rooms, immaculately clean. Wonderful meals. A fireplace gave our room a romantic glow, and the bathroom had a two-headed shower. Soft robes and plenty of towels." *(Shelley Worsham)*

PRIEST LAKE

Hill's Resort ¢ ♄ ✕ ⽊ ♿
4777 West Lakeshore Drive, 83856

Tel: 208–443–2551
Fax: 208–443–2363
URL: http://www.hillsresort.com

Owned by the Hill family for over 50 years, this family resort offers cottage and townhouse-type accommodation in a relaxed and casual setting. A relatively undeveloped wilderness, Priest Lake is likely to retain its pristine beauty—nearly 80% of the shoreline is controlled by state and federal governments. As Teri Hill says: "Hill's is a family resort where friends and family can rediscover each other in a homey setting, without the many interruptions of daily life."

"Fully endorse entry. Picture windows in the dining room offer incredible views of the lake, islands, and mountains. The delicious dinners include local trout and morels; reservations a must on summer weekends. Our knotty pine cottage had a full kitchen, bathroom, pleasant living and dining rooms, small bedrooms with good bedside lighting, window screens, and a front porch for relaxing." *(Mark Mendenhall)* "Returning after two years, I'm delighted to report that Hill's has retained its charm, excellent service, and wonderful feeling of being a special getaway. Our cottage deep in the woods gives one a sense of roughing it without really doing so; the food and service in the lodge were easily up to city folks' standards. The real draw, as always, is the lake with its mountain backdrop. Truly a family resort in a spectacular setting. And Priest Lake offers some of the best lake swimming—crystal clear cool waters—you'll find anywhere." *(MM)*

"We return year after year to the private cabins in the woods, to white sand beaches, and to the friends we've made here." *(Steve & Darcy Wells)* "A member of the friendly Hill family is always around to solve the need of every guest." *(Mr. & Mrs. Byron Stephan)* "Accommodations range from rustic cabins to luxury chalets with picture windows, plush carpets, and king-size beds." *(Janice Adams)* "Favorite dinner entrees include baby back ribs, and Margarita shrimp sauced with cream, tequila, and lime juice." *(KG)* "Ample parking, even for trailers and boats." *(Suzanne Close)*

Open All year. Restaurant open daily May through Oct., Dec. 26–Jan. 1; open weekends rest of year.

Rooms 53 1- to 3-bedroom housekeeping units with kitchen. All with telephone, radio, desk, fireplace, dishwasher, balcony. TV on request.

Facilities Restaurant, living room with fireplace; lounge with dance floor, live music during summer; game room with stereo, TV; gift/sport shop, grocery store, guest laundry May 15–Sept 15. 12 acres on lake with beach for swimming, fishing, water-skiing, sailing, canoeing, wind-surfing. 2 tennis courts, pickleball court, golf, cross-country skiing, snowmobiling, hiking, mushroom & berry picking, bicycling. Children's games, play equipment.

Location N ID, Bonner County, 85 m N of Spokane, WA. In Luby Bay, at SW end of Priest Lake.

Restrictions No smoking in dining room.

Credit cards Discover, MC, Visa.

Rates Room only, $100–350 cabin/chalet/suite (sleep 6–10). Extra person, $10. 7-night minimum July, Aug. Weekend packages. Alc breakfast, $3–7; alc lunch, $6–12; alc dinner, $22–30.

Extras Limited wheelchair access. Pets permitted in some units, $10 daily; must be leashed. Crib.

STANLEY

Reader tips: "Stanley is basically a one-block-long village, with funky little log-cabin shops and restaurants lining both sides of a narrow dirt road. Good place to buy gear and clothing for fishing, river rafting, and hiking. Decent newish supermarket/gas station as well." *(Nancy Debevoise)* "Unbelievable alpine hiking in the Sawtooth National Forest. Plan to stay several days, or even better, for a week." *(NED)*

Also recommended: About a mile down river from town is **Jerry's Motel** (Highway 75, HC 67, P.O. Box 300, Lower Stanley, 83278; 208–774–3566 or 800–972–4627). Double rates range from $45–65, and each room has two queen-sized beds, private bath, TV, and fully equipped kitchenette. "Although unassuming from the road, we were delighted to find that our room was unusually spacious, welcoming and cozy, with woodsy rustic charm. It was immaculate, with good lighting, and quite inviting. The back door of the room opened onto a redwood porch (with chairs for lounging) about six feet above the Salmon River. The view was breathtaking, with the Sawtooth Mountains as a backdrop. Even the adjacent country store had high quality meats and veggies, and a cooler jammed with microbrewed beer. I even found a bottle of my favorite, Alaska Amber Ale. Overall, a great value in a sensational setting." *(Steve Holman)*

Idaho Rocky Mountain Ranch 🏃
HC64, P.O. Box 9934, 83278

Tel: 208–774–3544
Fax: 208–774–3477
E-mail: idrocky@cyberhighway.net

It's worth a trip to the Idaho Rocky Mountain Ranch just to grab a seat on the front porch to see the Sawtooth Mountains silhouetted against a brilliant sunset. Established as the Idaho Rocky Mountain Club in 1930, it's now listed on the National Register of Historic Places. Accommodations are available in cabins and a main lodge handcrafted of lodgepole pine with rough rock fireplaces; the furniture is handmade, from the bent willow pulls on the dressers to the rush-plaited backs of the porch rockers.

Under the longtime ownership of Rozalys Bogert Smith, the ranch was reopened to guests in 1975 as the Idaho Rocky Mountain Ranch, and is managed by Bill Leavell and Sandra Beckwith. Guests enjoy hiking and horseback riding in the Sawtooth Wilderness and exploring the hundreds of high mountain lakes linked by miles of trail. The Salmon River and Redfish Lake are close by for all water sports, but even more convenient is the ranch's own natural hot springs swimming pool, kept at 103° by a hot mineral spring nearby.

Dinners include delicious appetizers, home-baked bread, salad, homemade soup, Idaho potatoes or rice pilaf, and tempting desserts; a choice of three entrees is offered nightly—perhaps chicken with pasta in avocado cream, salmon with rum-butter sauce, or steak with mustard-pepper sauce. Popular weekly events are the Western barbecue, and horse-drawn wagon ride to a Dutch oven cookout, both accompanied by music from local cowboys. A breakfast buffet starts each day at 7 A.M., and from 7:30–10 A.M. a hot entree is also served; a typical menu includes egg quesadillas, sliced ham, bread pudding with berries, and muffins; or pancakes with fruit, sausages, strudel, and coffee cake.

Winter operations are limited; the main lodge is closed, but one log cabin and a three-bedroom house are available, both with fully equipped kitchens, at B&B double rates of $85–140. The setting by the hot springs pool is quiet and peaceful, ideal for cross-country skiing and snowshoeing. "The friendly welcoming staff provides great information on local hiking, bicycling, and fishing spots. The accommodations are sparse and rustic; each unit has its own beautiful rock fireplace and some have unusual rock showers." *(Rebecca Obletz)* "Unstructured ranch environment, with plenty of outdoor activities; you can also just sit on the front porch and read, paint, and enjoy the views. A nice selection of appetizers accompany the predinner socializing on the front porch. Memorable evening events—barbecues, wagon rides, and country western singers." *(Kenneth Murray)* "A good place to get a sense of Idaho's colorful history. Numerous spectacular hiking trails in the Sawtooths nearby." *(Richard Stephan)* "Peaceful, relaxed, casual atmosphere. Friendly staff who take the time to visit. Clean, well-maintained cabins. Excellent food; the chuckwagon dinner was especially enjoyable with spectacular mountain views and cowboy music." *(Burt Young)* "Each cabin has a fireplace with ample kindling, an easy chair, a desk/night stand, a large dresser, and either a queen-size or two twin beds. All the windows open and there are room darkening shades. The large walk-in closet space had a dressing table and a mirror. Our rustic but immaculate bathroom had a clawfoot tub with a shower ring; water pressure was strong and hot water was ample. Very good food at both the evening barbecue dinner and generous breakfast buffet. The young staff was efficient and cheerful , and the manager made it a point to come around and introduce herself to the guests. " *(Susan Ulanoff)*

Open Dec. 20–April 1; June 1–Sept. 20.
Rooms 21 doubles—all with private bath and/or shower, desk, fireplace, electric heating. 4 rooms in main lodge, 17 rooms in duplex log cabins.

Facilities Dining room, lobby with fireplace, porch. Music 3-4 times per week during summer; guest laundry. 1,000 acres with natural hot springs swimming pool (approx. ½ m from main lodge), private stocked fishing pond, horseback riding, hiking, mountain bike rentals. Fishing, white water rafting, water sports, river float trips nearby.

Location Central ID. 125 m E of Boise, 50 m N of Sun Valley, 9 m S of Stanley. From Stanley take Hwy. 75 S to ranch.

Restrictions No smoking. Limited soundproofing between some lodge rooms.

Credit cards Discover, MC, Visa.

Rates MAP, $138–230 double, $100–192 single. Extra person, $30–69. 15% service. Picnic lunches available. Riding program, $55 half day; $95 full day. 3-night, weekly rates.

SUN VALLEY/KETCHUM

Also recommended: An elegant, European-style hostelry, the **Knob Hill Inn** (960 North Main Street, P.O. Box 800, 83340; 208–726–8010 or 800–526–8010; knobhillinn@sunvalley.net) is a Tyrolean chalet-style building. The decor is light and elegant, with Southwestern touches in some rooms, European country in others. Most rooms have king-size beds, and each has a marble bathroom with separate shower and tub. Glass doors open from each room to the balconies that run the length of the hotel, offering sweeping mountain vistas. Breakfast includes fresh fruit, granola, and yogurt, with waffles, pancakes, or frittatas, plus home-baked goods. The menu at the inn's restaurant includes such entrees as veal with morel sauce, wine-braised lamb shanks, and spice-crusted salmon with lime-orange salsa. B&B double rates for the 24 guest rooms range from $160–350. "Beautiful inn, excellent service, delightful ambiance." *(BJ Hensley)*

Built in 1985, the **River Street Inn** (100 River Street, Ketchum, 83340; mailing address, P.O. Box 182, Sun Valley, 83353; 208–726–3611; home.sprynet.com/sprynet/riverst) was constructed in a neo-Victorian style with Palladian windows, offering beautiful views of Mt. Baldy. The living room is done in shades of dusty rose, sage green, and ivory, while the guest room decor is softer, with pastels and subtle prints. Double rates of $140–195 include a full breakfast. "The Japanese soaking tubs were much appreciated after a day of skiing, as were the laundry facilities. We walked to restaurants and shops in Ketchum every afternoon; and returned to apres-ski snacks." *(Linda Smalley)*

Information please: A massive stone, log, and frame lodge, the **Idaho Country Inn** (134 Latigo Lane, Ketchum, 83340; mailing address, P.O. Box 659, Sun Valley, 83353; 208–726–1019 or 800–250–8341) offers beautiful mountain views from almost every window. The ten beautifully furnished, spacious guest rooms each have private bath, telephone, TV, and refrigerator. The B&B double rates of $132–205 include a full breakfast and afternoon hors d'oeuvres. Although a reader favorite in past years, more comments are now needed.

TETONIA

Teton Ridge Ranch   *Tel:* 208–456–2650
200 Valley View Road, 83452   *Fax:* 208–456–2218
E-mail: atilt@aol.com

Longtime managers Albert (Skip) and Chris Tilt describes the Teton Ridge Ranch as "an upscale, small, luxurious guest (but not *dude*) ranch located on the western border of the Yellowstone ecosystem—the quiet side of the Tetons. We offer a wilderness program with lots of personal attention, in an unstructured environment." The lodge was built in 1984 of pine and other local materials. Unlike most ranches, where riding is a regimented affair, Teton Ridge "provides riding at no extra charge with an experienced wrangler any time the guests desire."

Hearty breakfasts and lunches are prepared to suit guests' tastes. At dinner, innovative American fare is served in the candle-lit dining room where guests dine before two fireplaces with close-up views of the Teton mountain range. Accompanied by good wine, dinner might include mixed greens with creamy vinaigrette, cumin-roasted rack of lamb, grilled vegetable Napoleons, with chocolate crème brulee for dessert. Freshly baked bread accompanies each meal; in the summer months, dinner includes home-grown vegetables, herbs, and greens.

"What really sets this ranch apart is its friendly and helpful personal service. Exceptional dinners served by candlelight; the chef considerately prepared a vegetarian entree for our teenage daughter. Skip, Chris, and the staff are friendly and helpful; we assisted with a cross-country ski tour and snowmobiling in Yellowstone. Equally enjoyable was the evening social hour, with delicious wine and hors d'oeuvres, served in the spacious lodge living room. Guests mingle and compare notes about past activities and future plans." *(Robert Boas)* "Heaven. Our room had a king-size bed, Jacuzzi for two, and a steam shower. Dinner is served at a large table if only a few guests are there, or several tables if the group is larger. Excellent service; wide variety of activities. Chris and Skip are gracious hosts." *(Norma Simon)*

"A special experience from the moment we turned in at the entrance gate, nearly two miles from this majestic lodge. Where else can one eat breakfast while watching moose and a variety of birds less than 50 feet away? Rooms are spacious and immaculate; every window offers views of the Tetons. Decor is simple Southwestern with an elegant twist." *(Amy Hammel)* "Delicious meals were individually prepared to our personal taste by the chef." *(David Marcus)* "The large stone fireplaces, over-stuffed chairs, and ample reading materials create a homey atmosphere." *(Ellen Dwinell)* "Treated us like family and attended to every need or desire. Great food, beautiful setting, wonderful staff. Doesn't get any better than this." *(Lisa Ottinger)*

Open Dec.15–March, June–Oct.
Rooms 6 suites—all with private bath with Jacuzzi, steam shower, wood-burning stove, balcony, desk.
Facilities Living room with bar, fireplace, stereo, TV; dining room with fire-

place, library with fireplace; game room with billiards, TV; western entertainment weekly. 4,000 acres with horseback riding, mountain bikes, hiking, fly fishing, white water rafting, sporting clays, 25 km groomed cross-country trails, snowmobiling, dog sled rides. Gliding nearby. Guided fishing, pack trips.

Location E ID. 38 m NW of Jackson, WY; 70 m NE of Idaho Falls.

Restrictions Sound of coyotes could disturb light sleepers. No smoking in dining room. Wine served; BYOB. No children under 12.

Credit cards None accepted.

Rates Full board, $358–475 per day suite, $250–350 single. 7-night minimum, July 1–Aug. 1. Child on rollaway, $100.

Extras Airport pickups, $50–60. Some pets permitted by prior arrangement.

We Want to Hear from You!

As you know, this book is effective only with your help. We really need to know about your experiences and discoveries. If you stayed at an inn or hotel listed here, we want to know how it was. Did it live up to our description? Exceed it? Was it what you expected? Did you like it? Were you disappointed? Delighted? Have you discovered new establishments that we should add to the next edition?

Tear out one of the report forms at the back of this book (or use your own stationery if you prefer) and write today. Or email us at afi@inns.com. *Even if you write only "Fully endorse existing entry" you will have been most helpful.*

Thank You!

Can't Find It Here?

Our regional guides include *two to three times* the number of entries contained here. Pick up a copy of our *New England* (plus Eastern Canada), *Middle Atlantic, South, Midwest* (plus Ontario), *Rocky Mountains & Southwest*, or *West Coast* (plus Western Canada) edition for lots more information on great places to stay. If your bookstore doesn't have a current copy in stock, ask them to order it for you or call 800–288–2131. You can also order copies from our Website at http://www.inns.com.

Illinois

Hellman Guest House, Galena

Chicago, with its dynamic business and convention activities, outstanding museums, and cultural offerings, is the key attraction of Illinois. Ten miles west is Oak Park, which has the world's largest collection of Frank Lloyd Wright architecture. Southern Illinois is rural and agricultural, home to Springfield, the state capital and hometown of Abraham Lincoln. Other areas of interest lie along the Mississippi, from Galena in the north, to St. Louis, on the Missouri side, in the south. Drive along the river on Rte. 96, the National Great River Road, stopping by Historic Nauvoo, a restored 19th-century town. Or visit Bishop Hill, north of Galesburg, formerly a 19th-century Swedish religious communal society known for its fine crafts.

CHICAGO

Set along the banks of Lake Michigan, Chicago has much to offer the business traveler and tourist alike. The list of must-see attractions is a long one, but the following rank high on any list: the Art Institute, the Field Museum of Natural History, the Shedd Aquarium, and the Museum of Science and Industry. And a trip to the top of the Sears Tower or the John Hancock Center for wide-ranging views is a must. Those with more time to spare will enjoy the city's many ethnic and special-interest attractions, ranging from institutions devoted to Lithuanian culture to free tours of the world's largest post office facility.

As is the case in most major cities, weekend rates at Chicago's hotels offer substantial savings over midweek rates. Always inquire if any promotional rates are in effect when making reservations. To get a hotel room for less, contact **Hot Rooms** (One East Erie Street, Suite 225, 60611; 773–468–7666 or 800–468–3500; www.hotrooms.com), a free reservation service offering discounted rates at participating hotels, including some recommended here. Budget travelers, particularly those visiting midweek, may want to contact **Bed & Breakfast Chicago** (West Deming Place, Chicago, 60614; 773–248–0005 or 800–375–7084), a reservation service offering accommodation in B&Bs and unhosted apartments from high rises on the Gold Coast to Victorian brownstones on the Near North Side and Lincoln Park. Rates range from $75–195 for B&Bs, and $125–350 for apartments.

Also recommended—in Chicago: Business travelers will appreciate the historic Printer's Row location of the **Hyatt on Printer's Row** (500 South Dearborn, 60605; 312–986–1234 or 800–233–1234), just south of the city's financial district. It's also home to Prairie, acclaimed for its regional cooking. *Adam Platt* notes that "it's a great area for architecture buffs; take a walking tour led by the nearby ArchiCenter." Its small size (161 rooms) combined with an attentive staff results in a reputation for good service. Rooms are equipped with two phones, TVs, and VCR; double rates range from $100–210. "Shops and restaurants nearby; short, wonderful walk to Harold Washington Library, Art Institute, and the western Loop. Taxis readily available. Pleasant staff. Our room was large, high-ceilinged, with simple furniture, nice green/gray/black color scheme. Big hotel services, with the feel of a small hotel." *(MM)*

Just off Michigan Avenue in the heart of the Magnificent Mile, **The Tremont** (100 East Chestnut Street, 60611; 312–751–1900 or 800–621–8133) is an appealing 129-room hotel. Guest rooms are equipped with traditional furnishings, plus armoires housing mini-bars, CD players, and VCRs, and 2-line telephones with fax/modem hookups. Double rates range from $220–299, with corporate/weekend rates at $175. "Beautifully furnished hotel on a pretty tree-lined street. Excellent restaurant, Cafe Gordon. Friendly, helpful staff; efficient service." *(Annabel Royden)*

Fully renovated in 1995 was the elegant, European-style 221-room **Whitehall Hotel** (105 East Delaware Place, 60611; 312–944–6300 or 800–948–4255). The 18th century English decor with Oriental accents is complemented by such amenities as terry robes, hair dryers, makeup mirrors, and Crabtree & Evelyn toiletries. The hotel's restaurant features a blend of Continental and American cuisine with daily fresh-baked breads, pastries, and desserts from the Whitehall's bakery. Double rates of $179–349 include afternoon tea served in the lobby.

Information please: Originally built in 1894 and rebuilt in 1926, the **Hotel Allegro** (171 West Randolph Street, 60601; 312–236–0123 or

800–643–1500)was renovated in 1997 by the Kimpton Group (well-known for its West Coast "boutique" hotels). A block from City Hall, and just three blocks from the theater district, the 18-story Allegro has 483 guest rooms boldly decorated in warm, vibrant colors, plus all the amenities: including two-line speaker-phones, in-room fax machines, and CD/tape stereos. Double rates of $145–215 (suites $185–395) include evening wine service.

Recently refurbished and offering "high ceilings rather than high tech," is **The Seneca** (200 East Chestnut, 60611; 312–787–8900 or 800–800–6261), located on the Magnificent Mile, just east of Michigan Avenue and two blocks from the beach, and just across from Water Tower Place. Most of its 95 suites have kitchenettes, and all have TV and air-conditioning; each floor has laundry facilities, plus there's a rooftop sundeck and fitness center. Double room rates of $135–189 include in-room coffee service.

Located on a quiet, residential street close to the Lincoln Park Zoo, and a ten-minute cab ride from downtown is the **Surf Hotel** (555 West Surf Street, 60657; 773–528–8400 or 800–SURF–108), a renovated 1920s hotel. While the 40 guest rooms are on the small side, so are the double rates of $95–119, which include a continental breakfast and daily newspaper. "Charming lobby, adequate rooms, small but immaculate bathrooms, outstanding value." *(EE)*

Also recommended—nearby towns: Bordering Chicago to the north, along Lake Michigan, is the college town of Evanston, home of Northwestern University. **The Margarita Inn** (1566 Oak Avenue, Evanston 60201; 847–869–2273) is a Georgian-style inn in the heart of town. A parlor, library, and den provide ample common areas, and a Northern Italian restaurant is open for lunch and dinner. The 48 guest rooms have period furnishings, high ceilings, and leaded windows; B&B double rates range from $70 (for shared baths) to $90–155 for a private bath. "Pleasant rooms, gracious staff, excellent restaurant." *(CEC)*

A bit further north, just two blocks from the Chicago train, is **The Deer Path Inn** (255 East Illinois Road, Lake Forest, 60045; 847–234–2280 or 800–788–9480), a Tudor-style mansion constructed in 1929. The decorating theme is English, from the reproduction antique furniture to the artwork and accessories. The inn has three separate eating areas, popular with locals as well as guests. Double rates from $140–300, with weekend rates available. "Our suite included a kitchenette and overlooked the courtyard, complete with fountains." *(Susan Woods)* "Excellent food; pleasant, helpful staff." *(Duane Roller)*

Sutton Place Hotel ✕ ♿
21 East Bellevue Place, 60611

Tel: 312–266–2100
800–606–8188
Fax: 312–266–2141
E-mail: sales@chi.suttonplace.com
URL: http://www.chi.suttonplace.com

Built in 1988, Sutton Place's exterior is smoked glass and brown marble, as is the lobby, with its four-story mirrored atrium. Theme colors of mushroom, plum, peach, and turquoise, and a piano key motif are used throughout the Art Deco interior design. The Brasserie Bellevue, a glassed-in cafe, is located in the atrium area.

The Art Deco motif is reflected in the cleanly designed wooden furniture with black glass tops, white globe lights, and black and white covers for the down duvets. Turndown service includes a weather forecast and treats. Guests have a choice of four newspapers and an overnight complimentary shoe shine. The marvelous, high-tech bathrooms have black and white tiles, black marble sinks, a deep soaking tub, plus separate clear glass-walled shower stalls with thermostatic controls to adjust the temperature before you enter the shower. "My minisuite had a corner wall of curved glass overlooking the lights of Rush Street—pretty at night and spectacular in a snowstorm. The comfortable king-size bed was triple-sheeted. The hotel feels safe, and is quiet; I heard no noise from the hall or other rooms. The custom omelet bar at breakfast was out of this world, with numerous choices." (Susan W. Schwemm)

"Excellent location, a block from Michigan Avenue shopping and within walking distance of restaurants and pubs on Rush and Division Streets. Courteous, efficient, friendly staff. A great touch was the car service to take me to work. Complimentary midweek breakfast buffet for Sutton Club members from 6:30 to 9:30 A.M." (John Dillon) "Located in a vibrant section of Chicago. Spacious rooms, exceptional service. Excellent early morning coffee and newspapers." (Jim Findley)

Open All year.
Rooms 40 suites, 206 doubles, all with soaking tub, shower; telephones with voice mail, fax, dataport; clock/radio, TV/VCR, CD player, air-conditioning, minibar. Suites with 2-line phones, in-room safe, iron/ironing board.
Facilities Restaurant, lobby, bar/lounge, fitness room, video rentals, valet parking.
Location 2 blocks W of the N end of Michigan Ave., at junction of Rush St.
Credit cards All major cards accepted.
Rates Room only, $350–775 suite, $280–325 double, $255–300 single. Weekend rate, $189. Alc breakfast, $8–11; alc lunch, $10–15; alc dinner, $25–35.

GALENA

A handsome river town, Galena boasts such sights as Grant's Home, Grant Park, and the Belvedere Mansion, plus many craft and antique shops. The town's original fortune (and even its name) came from the local lead mines and later from the steamboat business on the river. When the mines were depleted and the railroads came through in the 1850s, prosperity ended and construction stopped. As a result, nearly 85 percent of the town's buildings are listed in the National Register of Historic Places.

In addition to seeing the sights and shops of the town, area activities include canoeing, fishing, boating, and steamboat rides on the Mississippi and Galena rivers, along with swimming, tennis, golf, horseback riding, and downhill and cross-country skiing in season.

Galena is located in the northwest corner of Illinois, 150 miles west of Chicago and 15 miles south of Dubuque, Iowa.

Reader tips: "Galena is understandably popular as a weekend getaway for Chicago folks. If you're on a tight budget, try to visit midweek, when rates are about a third less." Also: "The trolley tour is recommended; I also stopped by the historical society, public library, and drove to Dubuque, Iowa to see the maritime museum. Parking is a problem in Galena. If you don't mind a hike back uphill, consider staying in an inn within walking distance of town." *(Bill Novack)* And: "Being a serious foodie from the West Coast, I feared severe food deprivation syndrome would be my lot in the land of massive hog farms. The Kingston Inn was an oasis; I set up camp in their café-style dining room, or would lounge in the pub, playing dominos and drinking ales brewed on the premises. The chef, Toni, brings touches of her native Iberia to the eclectic preparations of beef, veal, pork, chicken, and fish. And the wine list is substantial, too." *(Ray Sundstrom)* "Recommend the El Dorado for unusual dishes, excellent food quality, nice selection of reasonably priced wines, and good, informed service—a true find." *(Peter Brebach)*

Also recommended: A Southern-style 1855 home with floor-to-ceiling walk-through windows and a two-story porch, the **Captain Gear Guest House** (1000 South Bench Street, P.O. Box 1040, 61036; 815–777–0222 or 800–794–5656) has three guest rooms with private baths (one with whirlpool tub). B&B double rates range from $155–175. "Immaculate, beautifully decorated home. Superb breakfast, elegantly served." *(Pat Malone)*

A Second-Empire Victorian mansion, **The Felt Manor** (125 South Prospect Street, 61036; 815–777–9093 or 800–383–2830), sits high on Prospect Street overlooking the town and surrounding countryside. The five guest rooms are furnished with antiques or reproductions and have the original marble sinks which date to the 1870s. B&B double rates range from $80–150 and include a full breakfast and afternoon tea. "Lovely rooms, delicious food, charming owners. Convenient location overlooking the town, a short (but steep) walk to Main Street." *(Bill Novack)*

About a 15 minute-drive from Galena, the **Wild Turkey B&B** (1048 North Clark Lane, 61036; 815–858–3649) is a new farmhouse set on 25 peaceful acres complete with deer and wild turkeys. Decorated with antiques and memorabilia, each of the three guest rooms has a private bath. Double rates are $75–90 and include a generous continental breakfast. "The Stoneburners are cordial, welcoming innkeepers. Cozy, homey, two-story living room with a fireplace; large, pleasant guest rooms." *(Vince & Carol Rauner)* "Delightful rural setting, ideal for bird-watching. Exceptionally nice innkeepers." *(Peter Brebach)*

Hellman Guest House   *Tel:* 815–777–3638
318 Hill Street, 61036   *Fax:* 815–777–3658
                    E-mail: hellman@galenalink.com
                    URL: http://www.galena.com/hellman

A Queen Anne brick mansion built in 1895, the Hellman House is a testament to the rewards of Victorian entrepreneurship. Originally constructed for John Hellman, a wealthy merchant, and his wife, Wenona, daughter of a shipping magnate, the house still reflects Victorian splendor—complete with turret, stained glass windows, and fine oak paneling. Restored by Merilyn Tommaro in 1987, it is decorated with a mixture of period and contemporary furnishings, with comfortable overstuffed couches in the parlor; the large windows throughout give it a light, airy look. Guest rooms have country Victorian appeal, with queen-size antique-painted iron bedsteads, wicker furniture, and light floral fabrics and wallcoverings. Breakfast menus change daily; in addition to fresh fruit and juice, Merilyn might offer blueberry buttermilk pancakes with sausage and pumpkin bread or possibly French toast, bacon, and cranberry muffins.

"Superb breakfasts; marvelous conversation among the guests." (*Joe Jarosz*) "Merilyn's breakfasts included sliced fruit, quiche, home fries with vegetables and cheese, enhanced by soft music and candlelight. The parlor has an antique brass telescope for the view across Galena to the river. The updated bathrooms have glass-enclosed showers." (*Kristi Kuhnau*) "Merilyn is always willing to assist without being intrusive." (*Bill Novack*) "The magnificent old woodwork in all the upstairs bedrooms is complemented by an inspired selection of wallpaper patterns and fabrics." (*Jim & Krisha Pennino, also RSS*) "Friendly, well-informed innkeeper; incredible views of the town and countryside. Charming library in which to read and relax." (*Lourdes Rivadeneira*)

Open All year.
Rooms 4 doubles—each with private bath and/or shower, air-conditioning. 1 with fireplace.
Facilities Parlor with fireplace, library with fireplace, dining room, porch, patio. Off-street parking.
Location Quality Hill district. If approaching on Rte. 20 from E, go 2 blocks past bridge. Turn right onto High St. (up steep hill) & continue to corner of High & Hill Sts. to inn. Short (but steep) walk to Main St.
Restrictions No smoking. Children over 11.
Credit cards Discover, MC, Visa.
Rates B&B, $99–169 double, $94–165 single. 2-night weekend, holiday minimum.

Indiana

The Book Inn, South Bend

While few travelers plan a trip just to see Indiana, many come on business, or to visit friends, relatives, or kids at college; plenty of others pass through on cross-country trips. Those who like to explore will discover that the state has much more to offer than most people realize. From the Lake Michigan beaches in the north to the wooded hill country along the Ohio River at the Kentucky border, there are a surprising number of places worth visiting.

CHESTERTON

Chesterton is a gateway to the Indiana Dunes National Lakeshore, a sizable memento of the last ice age. Stop by the visitor center for information on this geological phenomenon, hike the many trails that follow Lake Michigan, then cool off with a swim.

Also recommended: About a minute from I-94, hidden behind a Pizza Hut (!), is the delightful **Gray Goose Inn** (350 Indian Boundary Road, 46304; 219–926–5781 or 800–521–5127; graygoose@nii.net). You will be amazed by the juxtaposition of its shady, peaceful, lakeside setting with its incredibly peaceful location. The eight guest rooms are beautifully furnished with English and French country antiques, with queen- and king-size beds. Tasty full breakfasts are served at private tables on a flexible schedule; rates also include afternoon tea and cookies. B&B double rates range from $80–160. Guests are delighted with the warm hospitality, attention to detail, and delicious breakfasts they consistently find at the Gray Goose.

FORT WAYNE

Fort Wayne is located in north-central Indiana, two hours north of Indianapolis and 3 hours southeast of Chicago.

Reader tip: "A nice dinner spot is Henry's on Main Street, an old-fashioned tavern with lots of wood paneling. It's also close to the Allen County Public Library, one of the top genealogical research centers in the U.S." *(Jennifer Harrison)*

Information please: The childhood home of actress/comedienne Carole Lombard, the eponymous **Carole Lombard House** (704 Rockhill Street, Fort Wayne, 46802; 219–426–9896 or 888–426–9896) is a turn-of-the-century Victorian home located in the historic West Central neighborhood. Nearby is the library, and adjacent is the River Greenway with its miles of trails for biking, jogging, and walking. The four guest rooms, each with private bath, TV, telephone, and air-conditioning, have double rates of $60–85. A breakfast of fresh fruit, a hot dish such as blueberry pancakes and Canadian bacon, juice, and gourmet coffees and teas is served at the dining room table. "Warmly decorated, in a historic district of old homes; yummy breakfast and lovely perennial garden." *(JH)*

GOSHEN

The Checkerberry Inn ✕ 🕭 ⅋   *Tel:* 219–642–4445
62644 County Route 37, 46526   *Fax:* 219–642–4445
                      E-mail: inns@npcc.net
        URL: http://www.checkerberryinn.com

If you'd like to combine a visit to Indiana's Amish Country with elegant accommodations reminiscent of a European country hotel, try the Checkerberry Inn. John and Susan Graff, who built the inn in 1987, offer comfortable contemporary decor amid acres of rolling farmland. The inn is equally renowned for its restaurant. Dinner includes soup, salad, and dessert, and a choice of such entrees as grilled veal medallions with roasted red pepper and blue cheese polenta; roasted salmon with a shallot, spinach, and red potato ragout; or Amish chicken stuffed with pistachios and brie.

"Elegant, attractive, and restful, neither cutesy nor cluttered. The guest rooms are done in shades of beige and white, with bright color accents and a signature row of three Amish-style hats on the wall over the bed. Beautiful location in the remote countryside, surrounded by Amish farms, with horse-pulled buggies clip-clopping by. The spacious great room is warm and inviting, with several seating groups. The restaurant is at the opposite end of the inn, and includes the original dining room and even lovelier solarium which was added on." *(SWS)* "Peaceful and relaxing, light and airy. Excellent dinners; save room for dessert. Enjoyed walking on the quiet country roads near the inn." *(Donna Bocks)*

"An oasis of tranquility, with pastoral views of cornfields and trees. Welcoming hosts; spacious, inviting, well-lit guest room. Excellent dinners of tandoori pork and beef tenderloin." *(Detlef Herbst)* "We enjoyed touring the nearby craft shops." *(Janet Diederichs)* "While not ostentatious, luxury abounds—eye-catching artwork, fresh flower bouquets, down comforters and pillows." *(Susan Dutmers)* "An amazing find in the midst of a heavily touristed countryside. Tasty breakfast buffet of homemade granola, fruit, hot muffins, and fruit breads, with juices and coffee." *(John Blewer)*

Open Tues.–Sat., Feb.–Dec.; also open for lunch Wed. in summer.

Rooms 2 suites with whirlpool tub, 11 doubles—all with private shower and/or bath, telephone, clock-radio, TV, desk, air-conditioning, coffee maker.

Facilities Dining room, library with fireplace, TV/VCR, porch. 100 acres with swimming pool, tennis, croquet green, hiking. Golf, bicycling nearby.

Location N central IN. Amish country. 120 m E of Chicago, 150 m N of Indianapolis, 30 m E of South Bend. 6 m from Goshen, 16 m S of I-80/90. From I-80/90, take Exit 107 (Middlebury); go S (right) on S.R. 13, W (right) on Rte. 4, S (left) on C.R. 37 to inn on right.

Restrictions No smoking.

Credit cards Amex, MC, Visa.

Rates B&B, $350 suite, $120–200 double, $80–100 single. Extra person, $30–50. Prix fixe lunch, $12; dinner, $45. 2-night minimum on Notre Dame football weekends.

Extras Wheelchair access.

INDIANAPOLIS

Indianapolis dates back to 1820, when it was selected as the site for the state's capital because of its location at the geographical center of the state. Streets were laid out in a wheel pattern similar to Washington, D.C.'s.

Sights of interest include, of course, the Indianapolis Speedway and Hall of Fame. Hotel rates skyrocket on Memorial Day weekend, when the famous "Indy 500" is held. Cultural attractions include the Museum of Art, with collections of Medieval, Renaissance, and 19th-century arts; the Children's Museum, with carousel, Egyptian mummies, and limestone cave; and the Eiteljorg Museum of American Indians and Western Art.

Also recommended: Six miles north of Indianapolis are the two deep-green farmhouses that comprise the **Frederick-Talbott Inn** (13805 Allisonville Road, Fishers, 46038; 317–578–3600 or 800–566–BEDS; www.fredtal.com). Just across the street is the Conner Prairie Museum, a living history museum depicting the lives of early Indiana settlers. The inn includes an 1870s Gothic-style farm house and the North House, a 1906 cottage. The ten guest rooms are furnished in antiques and reproductions, each with a different rich-toned color scheme accented by white-painted woodwork with white lace curtains. A breakfast buffet of fresh fruit, apple French toast strata, raspberry breakfast cake, and butterscotch pecan rolls, plus access to the guest pantry is included in the double rates of $94–180.

The Canterbury Hotel (123 South Illinois Street, 46225; 317–634–3000 or 800–538–8186) a 99-room luxury hotel located downtown, close to the Hoosier Dome and Union Station. The well-equipped guest rooms are furnished with Chippendale four-poster beds and Queen Anne furniture and a full complement of amenities. Its fine-dining restaurant has an excellent reputation. B&B double rates range from $220–245 double; regular suites to $550; weekend rates start at $145 and include lots of extras, an excellent value. Reports please.

In a convenient historic neighborhood, the **Old Northside B&B** (1340 North Alabama Street, 46202; 317–635–9123 or 800–635–9127; www.hofmeister.com/bbb/bbb.htm) is a brick Romanesque Revival mansion built in 1885. The original wood floors and carved cherry woodwork are complemented by hand-painted murals and turn-of-the-century furnishings. Each of the six guest rooms are decorated with a different theme from the Theatre Room with posters and playbills, to the Literary Room with memorabilia from Indiana authors, to the 500 Room with Indy maps and mementos. All have private baths, telephone, TV, Jacuzzi tubs, and fireplaces. A full breakfast is included in the B&B double rates of $95–165.

Built in 1929, the recently renovated **Renaissance Tower Inn** (230 East 9th Street, 46204; 317–261–1652 or 800–676–7786) offers 80 suites with fully equipped kitchens, furnished with Queen Anne cherry reproduction furnishings, including four-poster beds. The hotel is a project of Robert Borns, who restored Union Station; the hotel has a three-diamond rating from AAA, and costs $75 daily; advance reservations strongly advised.

MADISON

Set on the Ohio River in southern Indiana, Madison reached its zenith in the 1850s with the rapid growth of river traffic. Much of its downtown area, now listed on the National Register of Historic Places, dates from this period. Architecture buffs will enjoy the variety of styles of its restored buildings, including Gothic Revival, Classic Revival, Federal, and Italianate.

Madison is located in southeast Indiana, near the Kentucky and Ohio borders, about a 1½-hour drive from Louisville, Cincinnati, and Indianapolis.

Reader tip: "Historic Madison also offers good restaurants and a winery." *(Lawrence Schwartz)*

Also recommended: Restored in 1993 by Judy and Bill Gilbert, **Schussler House** (514 Jefferson Street, 47250; 812–273–2068 or 800–392–1931) is a beautifully restored 1849 Federal-Greek Revival home built by Civil War surgeon Dr. Charles Schussler. Decorated with antiques and reproduction furniture, the decor is highlighted by Judy's handmade quilts and needlework. B&B rates for the three guest rooms, each with private bath, are $99, including a full breakfast and afternoon refreshments. Guests are especially delighted with the handsome decor and careful attention to detail. "Inviting common areas, ample privacy, beautifully restored rooms. All amenities from early morning coffee to nightly turndown service. Lovely breakfast with bread pudding with raspberry sauce, ham, and fresh fruit. Madison is full of antique stores; it's lovely for strolling, and everyone seems to be a gardener." *(Thomas Wittenberg)*

Main Street B&B ¢
739 West Main Street, 47250

Tel: 812–265–3539
800–362–6246
Fax: 812–265–3153
E-mail: mbalph@seidata.com

Located in Madison's historic district, the Main Street B&B is a Classic Revival-style home built in 1843. Long-time owners Mark and Mary Balph have decorated elegantly with antique and period reproductions. Guest rooms have king-, queen-, and double-size beds to assure that all can be accommodated in comfort. Guests get a key to the front door, so they can come and go privately and independently; the innkeepers' quarters are in the rear of the house.

"The Balphs are witty, intelligent hosts with a flair for knowing exactly how to pamper each guest in their beautiful, comfortable, immaculate house. Delicious, imaginative breakfasts." *(CR Scott-Seville)* "Wake-up coffee and juice delivered to our room each morning at the time requested; while there were other guests, we still enjoyed our privacy." *(Jerry & Nola Rairdon)* "Impeccably clean, with every effort expended to ensure guest comfort." *(Bessie Klein)* "Stimulating breakfast conversation among guests and hosts. Spacious rooms with antiques and firm mattresses. Clean, modern bath with abundant towels." *(Tom Ryther)* "We heard no traffic noise, even though our room faced the street. Many interesting books and magazines." *(BL)* "Walking distance to shops and historic sites, with convenient on-street parking. The big front bedroom has a large dressing-shower area with great lighting." *(MY)* "Breakfast was served in the dining room between 8 and 9:30 A.M., and consisted of an egg casserole, fabulous blueberry oatmeal muffins, baked French toast, fresh fruit, and fresh-squeezed orange juice or a fruit smoothie. Helpful collection of lunch and dinner menus from local cafes and restaurants." *(Shari & Greg Burrows)* "Mary and Mark kindly arranged for us to play golf at a local club." *(Marsha Linnemann)*

Open All year.
Rooms 1 suite, 2 doubles—all with private bath and/or shower, radio, desk, air-conditioning, fan.
Facilities Dining room with fireplace, parlor with fireplace, piano, stereo, books, sunroom. Golf, swimming nearby.
Location Historic district. On Hwy. 56 (Main St.)
Restrictions No smoking. No off-street parking. Children over 12.
Credit cards MC, Visa.
Rates B&B, $150 suite (for 4), $89 double. Extra person, $25.
Extras Some French, German.

MICHIGAN CITY

Located at the southern end of Lake Michigan, Michigan City is best known for the beautiful sand dunes of Indiana Dunes State Park and National Lakeshore. Area activities include the lake for water sports, hiking and cross-country skiing in the park, plus golf, tennis, and horseback riding. On rainy days, the Lighthouse Place Outlet Mall awaits with dozens of shops. Michigan City is 30 miles west of South Bend, and 60 miles southeast of Chicago.

Also recommended: Built in 1880 as a parsonage, **The Brickstone** (215 West 6th Street, 46360; 219–878–1819) offers four guest rooms, each with a whirlpool tub, at B&B double rates of $80–140 including a full breakfast and afternoon refreshments. Serious shoppers will especially enjoy the location, two blocks from Lighthouse Place Outlet Center.

If you'd prefer the atmosphere of a country hotel, just minutes from the interstate, we recommend the **Creekwood Inn** (Route 20 35 at I-94, 46360; 219–872–8357). "Built in the 1930s as an English cottage-style manor house, its 13 well-equipped hotel-style guest rooms are in a wing added in 1984. The spacious accommodations are decorated with coordinated fabrics, quality reproduction furniture, and queen- or king-size beds. Guests can relax in the two-level solarium with a fireplace and windows overlooking the woods; doors open to an equally inviting deck with a hot tub; wooded setting, with trails for walking. Pleasantly served breakfast of cereal, fresh fruit, store-bought croissants and blueberry muffins; attractive dining rooms." *(SWS)* B&B double rates range from $113–148.

An imposing 1875 Queen Anne brick mansion, the **Hutchinson Mansion Inn** (220 West 10th Street, 46360; 219–879–1700) has beautiful stained glass windows, ornamented ceilings, and is decorated with family antiques and reproductions. Guests are encouraged to wander about the house, exploring its nooks, crannies, and alcoves—there's even a secret door in the dining room paneling. B&B rates for the 10 suites and doubles range from $85–140 including a full breakfast and afternoon refreshments.

MIDDLEBURY

Northern Indiana's Crystal Valley, just south of the Indiana Toll Road, is best known for its large Amish population, and for the famous Shipshewana Auction and flea market, open Tuesday and Wednesdays, May 1 through October 31. Middlebury is located in northeastern Indiana, 15 miles east of Elkhart, 30 miles east of South Bend, and 10 miles west of Shipshewana. It's approximately three hours driving from both Detroit and Indianapolis.

Reader tips: "We thought the Menno-Hof's visitor center across the street from the Shipshewana auction house was excellent, with informative exhibits and displays to tell the story of the Anabaptist Mennonite movement." *(John Blewer)* "The flea market is irresistible for most women, a nightmare for most men; wear comfortable shoes, and prepare for endless lines for the bathrooms. Stock up on delicious cheese at the Amish cheese factory en route from Middlebury to Shipshewana. And don't miss downtown Shipshewana. Most shopping is in individual houses with great crafts and interesting tidbits." *(B.J. Schwartzkopf)* Also: "Popular area restaurants are mobbed on weekends and in summer." *(MW)*

Also recommended: For a quiet, uncommercial adult atmosphere, contact the **Empty Nest B&B** (13347 County Route 12, 46540; 219–825–1042), a large contemporary home with three guest rooms, offering a hillside view of the fish pond, gardens, and lawns. The B&B double rates of $70–80 include a full breakfast. Guests are delighted with the inn's peaceful country setting, its friendly, knowledgeable owners, the delicious breakfasts, and the comfortable, private accommodations.

The **Essenhaus Country Inn** (240 U.S. Route 20, P.O. Box 2608, 46540; 219–825–9447 or 800–455–9471) is part of a busy complex including shops and the well-known restaurant, Das Dutchman Essenhaus, famous for huge portions of hearty food at reasonable prices. The 35 guest rooms are furnished with hand-crafted Amish furniture, quilts, country prints, and decorative touches, and open to a spacious atrium lobby area. Rates range from $73–120. The **Patchwork Quilt B&B** (11748 County Road 2, 46540; 219–825–2417) is known for its delicious all-you-can-eat Amish dinners. Fifteen guest rooms offer private baths and beds topped with handmade quilts, at B&B double rates of $75–100.

NEW HARMONY

The town of New Harmony was founded in 1814 by a group of Harmonists, who were persecuted in their native Germany and came to the fertile Wabash valley to start anew. After eleven years of hard work they moved to Pennsylvania, leaving many sturdy and ingeniously constructed buildings behind. They sold the town to the British social reformer Robert Owen, who arrived in 1825 with many distinguished scholars to start an experiment in communal living. Although the experiment failed, much of its intellectual heritage lives on. Many of the historic buildings have been restored, contrasting modern ones have been built, and a variety of music, art, and drama programs are offered.

Also recommended: The New Harmony Inn (North Street, P.O. Box 581, 47631; 812–682–4491 or 800–782–8605) is a simply designed contemporary structure, blending well with the clear lines of the town's original Harmonist structures. The Shaker-style furnishings are complemented by original artwork and antiques found throughout the inn and restaurants. Two restaurants are connected with the inn, the Red Geranium and the Bayou Grill. "Peaceful, lovely, and uncluttered. Paul Tillich is buried next to the inn." *(Betty Sadler)* "Nothing has changed at our old favorite. Excellent meal at the Red Geranium, and the Bayou Grill is a wonderful value." *(Duane Roller)* "The bedsteads are maple, the simple window drapes were of early 19th-century design." *(Bill MacGowan)* "Gorgeous flower gardens. Our kids were delighted with the greenhouse-enclosed swimming pool." *(James & Janice Utt)* Rates for the 90 guest rooms are $85 double; off-season rates of $125 include breakfast and dinner for two. Facilities also include conference rooms, tennis courts, indoor swimming pool, exercise room with sauna and hot tub.

Built in 1899, the **Raintree Inn** (503 West Street, P.O. Box 566, 47631; 812–682–5625 or 888–656–0123; www.raintree-inn.com) is a Classic Revival home with quarter-sawn golden oak woodwork, antique decor, and period wallpaper. Each of the four guest rooms has a private bath, and the B&B double rate of $95–115 includes a full breakfast, and afternoon tea on weekends. "A beautifully restored home in the heart of New Harmony with inviting guest rooms. Innkeepers Scott and Nancy McDonald were very approachable and seemed to thoroughly enjoy hosting guests at their inn." *(Greg & Grace Munson)*

SOUTH BEND

Best known as the home of the University of Notre Dame, South Bend was an early industrial center for the manufacture of steel and of Studebaker automobiles.

Reader tip: "Small college towns like South Bend are great places to stay. They combine the advantage of small cities (safety, accessibility, spaciousness, warmth, slow pace) with galleries, museums, good restaurants, entertainment, and appealing parks. Excellent dinner at the bistro-style LaSalle Grill; unforgettable onion rings." *(Eric Friesen)*

Book Inn ¢
508 West Washington Street, 46601

Tel: 219–288–1990
Fax: 219–234–2338
E-mail: BookINN@aol.com
URL: http://www.members.aol.com/bookinn

An outstanding example of Second Empire architecture, the Book Inn was built in 1872; its elaborate entry doors reportedly won first place for design at the 1893 Columbian Exposition. The house returned to public attention in 1991, when it was restored as a decorator's showcase. The inn has 12-foot ceilings and original butternut woodwork, highlighted with antiques, marvelous faux paintings and murals, and fresh flowers; most guest rooms have king- or queen-size beds. The inn has a quality used book store on the downstairs level, and guest rooms named for famous authors. Owners Peggy and John Livingston note that "innkeeping is like travelling without having to pack. We meet new people, and guests become like family and friends." Served at the dining room table, breakfast includes fresh-squeezed orange juice, a hot entree, five-fruit compote, and tea and coffee. A butler's pantry is available for the guests to help themselves to water, soft drinks, beer, and wine.

"The Cushing Suite is spacious and gracious, with handsome antique furnishings, appealing colors, and good bedside lighting. Charming hand-painted 'wallpaper' and radiator covers painted as humorous bookshelves. The small private bathroom is across a narrow hall; robes are provided. A lovely hand-painted floral mural transforms the narrow circular back stairs to the kitchen into a 'secret garden.' More than ample common areas include the inviting living room, cozy library, sun porch. The Livingstons are warm and accommodating hosts. Next door is Tippicanoe Place, a handsome old stone mansion, now an atmospheric restaurant. Breakfast included fresh fruit salad followed by stuffed blueberry French toast the first day, and baked apples with sausage strata and English muffins the next." *(SWS)* "The comfortable Charlotte Bronte room is done in burgundy and gold; the queen-size bed was made up with linens in a cabbage-rose pattern, and had wall-mounted glass lamps on either side of the bed. The bathroom had a shower, good lighting, and an assortment of soaps, shampoos, lotions, and more in the oversized wall cabinet. Breakfast included waffles with bacon; Peggy and John joined the guests for coffee once they finished serving." *(Rose Ciccone)*

"High ceilings, large comfortable beds with beautiful linens, lovely antique furnishings, picture books, novels, cozy reading chairs, fresh flowers, lush terry robes, private bath—everything I could possible want. The entire house, from the well-stocked library and kitchen to the dining room table set with crystal, linen, great coffee, and tasty breakfast fare, is a weary traveler's dream. Peggy and John made me feel welcome, relaxed, and pampered." *(Suzanne Peck)* "Elegant designer decor; loved the Alcott room." *(PBN)* "Good location near downtown; you can walk to Tippecanoe Place and the LaSalle Grill to eat." *(Robin Clarke)* "Gracious atmosphere, with delicious evening glass of wine." *(KB)* "The Livingstons are excellent hosts, friendly but not intrusive. The house is magnificently restored and refurbished, within walking distance of almost everything. Loving books as we do, it's fun after breakfast to go down into Peggy's basement shop and browse. You always find something you're looking for, and so did we." *(Eric Friesen)*

Open All year.

Rooms 2 suites, 3 doubles—all with private bath and/or shower, telephone, radio, clock, desk, air-conditioning.

Facilities Dining room, living room with fireplace, TV/VCR, stereo, family room, library, book store, guest refrigerator, porch. Off-street parking.

Location 5 blocks to town center. Take Exit 77 of I-80/90 Toll Rd., & take Rte. 31/33 S to Main St. Go W on Washington to inn on left. Next door to Tippecanoe Place.

Restrictions No smoking. "Limited children."

Credit cards Amex, MC, Visa.

Rates B&B, $80–120 suite, double. Corporate rates. 2-night minimum during Notre Dame functions.

Iowa

The Mandolin Inn, Dubuque

Since you've turned to this chapter, we assume you know better than to think of Iowa as an endless cornfield. There's a lot to do here. Many of the historic towns along the Mississippi and Missouri rivers sponsor summertime events and river excursions, while other towns proudly display their ethnic heritage—Dutch, German, Czech, and Native American. The Amana Colonies, in eastern Iowa, offer a fascinating glimpse into a religious communal society dating back to the mid-1800s. Several historic reconstructions will appeal to visitors, from the Living History Farms and the Boone & Scenic Valley Railroad near Des Moines, to the Fort Museum at Fort Dodge. Iowans love fairs, and you'll find them sponsored by towns around the state from April through October. Highlights include the Iowa State Fair in Des Moines and the National Hot Air Balloon Championships at Indianola.

DAVENPORT (QUAD CITIES)

Davenport is the largest of the four towns which make up the Quad Cities: Davenport and Bettendorf, Iowa; and Rock Island and Moline, Illinois. The area first prospered because of its riverside location, then continued to grow when the railroad bridged the river between Illinois and Iowa in 1856. Shipping by river and rail continues to support the economy today. For entertainment, visitors can choose from riverboat gambling cruises, harness racing, a Civil War muster, and blues and jazz festivals. The Quad Cities are located midway between Chicago and Des Moines, 160 miles to the east or west, and 79 miles southeast of Cedar Rapids.

Also recommended: Built in 1871, **Fulton's Landing Guest House** (1206 East River Drive, 52803; 319–322–4069) offers rooms overlooking the Mississippi. After a hearty breakfast, all can enjoy the river views from the walking/jogging/bicycling path which runs directly in front of the house. B&B double rates for the five guest rooms—each with private bath, TV, air-conditioning, and balcony—range from $60–125. "This brick and stone Greek Revival mansion has stained glass windows, carved oak woodwork, and handsomely curved ceilings. Wonderful breakfasts of oven-baked pancakes or apple cinnamon baked French toast." *(Phyllis Seidler)*

Just west of Davenport is the **Abbey Hotel** (1401 Central Avenue, Bettendorf, 52722; 319–355–0291 or 800–438–7535), a four-diamond AAA-rated hotel and restaurant set on a bluff overlooking the Mississippi River. A Romanesque-style building originally constructed as a Carmelite monastery and now listed on the National Register of Historic Places, the Abbey has 19 luxuriously appointed guest rooms, with queen- or king-sized beds, marble bathrooms, cable TV, and direct dial phones with dataports; most have river views. Double rates of $75–149 include a complimentary breakfast, and smoking is allowed only in the bar. "Our river-view room was spacious and elegant, the immaculate bathroom outfitted with marble. On a return trip, we stayed in Room 207, with a sitting area with sofa and chairs, plus a door to the balcony which opens to the garden and swimming pool. The staff is very hospitable, and we were directly to wonderful restaurants on the river. An honor bar with hors d'oeuvres and snacks are available in the early evening, and dinner may be ordered in advance and served to one's room." *(Doris & Bud Longfellow)*

DUBUQUE

Iowa's oldest city, Dubuque grew prosperous in the 19th century, first from lead mining, later from lumber, meat packing, and other industries. The city's many handsome Victorian buildings are a legacy of this prosperity, and many have been restored as art galleries, B&Bs, and theaters. If you have just a short time for sightseeing, take a ride up the Fenelon Place Elevator, billed as the country's "shortest, steepest railway," for a three-state view of the Mississippi and beyond. If you've a little more time, we'd suggest a visit to the Woodward Riverboat Museum and a ride on a Mississippi River sternwheeler. Exercise enthusiasts will enjoy the 26-mile-long Heritage Trail, a railroad track now converted for hiking and bicycling. Riverboat gambling cruises, with Las Vegas–style entertainment and food, are very popular.

Dubuque is located on the Mississippi River, 185 miles northwest of Chicago and 150 miles northeast of Des Moines.

Reader tip: "I was surprised to find the area surrounding Dubuque to be so hilly, and learned that this area is the 'un-glaciated' region of the Midwest, and so was spared nature's bulldozer that shaped (or unshaped) the rest of the surrounding country." *(Ray Sundstrom)*

Also recommended: Set high on the bluffs of Dubuque with a grand view of the river and three states is **The Hancock House** (1105 Grove Terrace, 52001-4644; 319–557–8989). A large Queen Anne Victorian home built in 1891, its nine guest rooms have private baths, queen-size featherbeds, and air-conditioning; some have whirlpool tubs. The B&B double rates of $75–150 include breakfast and complimentary beverages. "The house is comfortable, and elaborately decorated with original antiques. The innkeepers were warm and hospitable and breakfast was delicious. We stayed in Florence's Room which had a white iron bed set inside a turret and had views looking over the river." *(Mary Ellen Cassman)*

Just over the hill from the Sundown Ski Area (eight miles from town) is the **Juniper Hill Farm** (15325 Budd Road, 52002; 319–582–4405 or 800–572–1449). B&B rates for the three guest suites range from $80–140, and include a full breakfast and use of the hot tub on the deck. Forty acres of woods and walking trails provide ample opportunity for appreciating Iowa's natural beauty.

The **Mandolin Inn** (199 Loras Boulevard, 52001; 319–556–0069 or 800–524–7996; www.mandolininn.com) is an Edwardian mansion built in 1908, with original wall murals, floors of inlaid oak and mahogany, ornate plaster moldings, and Italian tiled fireplaces. The eight guest rooms are furnished with period antiques, queen-size beds, and down comforters. The $75–135 double rates include afternoon beverages and a full breakfast.

The **Redstone Inn** (504 Bluff Street, 52001; 319–582–1894) was built in 1894 by A.A. Cooper as a wedding present for his daughter. In 1984 the Redstone was converted into an elegant small hotel. Now listed on the National Register of Historic Places, it combines Victorian furnishings with such modern amenities as whirlpool tubs and in-room telephones with dataports. B&B rates for the 15 guest rooms range from $60–175, including a continental breakfast and the morning paper.

Richards House ¢   *Tel:* 319–557–1492
1492 Locust Street, 52001   *URL:* www.the-richards-house.com

The Richards House is a magnificent Stick-style Victorian mansion built in 1883. Over 80 dazzling stained glass windows shed light on the ash, butternut, oak, maple, and cherry woodwork. Two rooms boast fireplace tiles painted by children's illustrator Kate Greenaway, and all have Victorian antique lighting, wallcoverings, and furnishings. Owners David Stuart and Michelle Delaney have been working on the home for many years, and have done an incredible job of restoration. David alerts guests that while the interior renovation is complete, restoration of the exterior is an on-going project, designed to save as much as possible of the original. Eventually the house will be repainted in its original "painted lady" color scheme of chocolate brown, rust, pumpkin, and moss green.

Breakfast is served in the elegant dining room around an antique table. A typical menu includes sour cream–cinnamon breakfast cake, baked apples, waffles, and eggs with cheese and chives.

"Arriving in the dark, my first thought was of the Addams family house, but once inside, we fell in love with this beautiful mansion. The buffet and refrigerator in the hall was supplied with fresh-baked cookies and soda. Off the kitchen was a microwave with popcorn plus the makings for coffee and tea. Breakfast was served at our convenience: pumpkin bread, apple cake, sliced fruit, five-cheese scrambled eggs and bacon, and homemade raisin-bread French toast." *(Chris Dabrowski)* "We stayed in the library suite, surrounded by bookshelves, with a walnut bed, fireplace, and a spectacular stained glass window. In the second room, an antique clawfoot tub sat before another fireplace, and floor-to-ceiling windows let in the morning sunlight." *(Sharon TeRonde)*

"Our spacious room had a concealed TV, and the queen-size bed had a beautiful comforter with matching pillows and sheets; lamps on either side of the bed provided adequate reading light. Several restaurants are within walking distance, including a beautiful old mansion called the Ryan House. Parking is ample on the street in front and on the side. Though it's only about five minutes from Cable Car Square, the location is fairly quiet." *(Chrys Bolk)* "Beautiful lace window treatments and antique chandeliers." *(Pamela Stremick)* "Michelle had a booster seat and toys ready for our toddler." *(Daniel Witte)* "Michelle gave us an informative tour of the antique-filled rooms. Our room's old-fashioned bath had a tall water closet, marble sink, and clawfoot tub, enhanced by a hand-held shower, ample soft, fluffy towels, and toiletries. Magnificent stained and cut glass accents in the dining room." *(MR)* "Breakfast included cheese omelets, waffles, baked peaches, banana nut bread, bacon, and wonderful coffee. " *(Pamela Stewart)* "Tasty evening treats." *(Richard Jackson)* "Beautiful vaulted ceilings, ornate wall coverings, period furnishings, and authentic knickknacks take one back to the 19th century." *(Deborah LaBeau)* "Michelle is knowledgeable and makes you feel like a member of the family, plus being a great cook." *(Sherry, Steve, & Stephanie Byriel)*

Open All year.
Rooms 1 suite, 4 doubles—4 with private bath and/or shower, 1 with a maximum of 4 sharing bath. All with telephone, radio, TV/VCR, air-conditioning. Some with desk, fireplace, balcony, whirlpool tub.
Facilities Dining room, living room, both with fireplace, library, music room with fireplace, pianos, TV/VCR, guest pantry, laundry, porch. Off-street parking. Riverboat cruises nearby. 10 m to downhill skiing.
Location Jackson Park National Historic District.
Restrictions Smoking restricted to kitchen.
Credit cards Amex, DC, Discover, MC, Visa.
Rates B&B, $50–95 suite, $45–85 double. Extra person, $10. Midweek rate.
Extras Airport/station pickup. Pets permitted by prior arrangement. Crib.

NEWTON

LaCorsette Maison Inn ¢ ✕
629 First Avenue East, 50208

Tel: 515–792–6833
Fax: 515–792–6833

Cognoscenti in the laundry business may know Newton as the home of the Maytag Company, but few would think of this town as the place to go for a leisurely gourmet dinner, served by tuxedoed waiters to the accompaniment of a pianist playing a baby grand. Kay Owen has always enjoyed cooking, and in 1984 she opened LaCorsette as a restaurant and inn. There's no choice of menu at dinner; the entree of the evening is determined by the first caller to make reservations. The rest of the six-course meal is decided by Kay and what's fresh in her garden. A recent menu included cheese ramekins, onion soup, greens with Maytag blue cheese and orange vinaigrette, salmon filet, mushroom potatoes, asparagus and baby carrots, French bread, and pecan meringue torte. Dinner is preceded by a tour of the inn, a Mission-style mansion built in 1909 and listed on the National Register of Historic Places. The original Mission oak woodwork, Art Nouveau stained and beveled glass windows, and brass light fixtures highlight the decor; guest rooms are eclectically furnished with French country motifs, with down comforters and pillows. In 1995, Kay restored the adjacent century-old Federal-style house, and has created two luxurious suites for special-occasion romance.

"A wonderful house, clean and well decorated. Delicious breakfast." *(Pat Malone)* "We stayed in the penthouse suite, and awoke to a dazzling display of rainbows emanating from the cut glass windows." *(Mark Sherman)* "Breakfast is served in a spacious dining room on an oak table with Kay as hostess; exceptional dinners are served at separate tables." *(Patricia Olsen)* "Kaye's wonderful hospitality enhances her clean, charming, and welcoming inn." *(Douglas Bahr)* "Fully endorse existing entry. Excellent dinner. Exceptionally pleasant innkeeper; friendly, unstuffy atmosphere." *(MM)*

Open All year. Restaurant open "several nights a week by reservation only."
Rooms 3 suites, 5 doubles—all with private bath and/or shower, telephone, air-conditioning. TV available. 3 with double whirlpool or soaking tub, 2 with fireplace, CD player. 2 suites in adjacent Sister Inn.
Facilities Restaurant with pianist, living room with fireplace, den with fireplace, atrium. 15 miles to lake for swimming, fishing, boating.
Location 23 m E of Des Moines. 7 blocks from center of town. From Des Moines, go E on I-80 and exit at Newton. Go E on Hwy. 6 (First Ave.) to inn.
Restrictions No smoking. No facilities for infants.
Credit cards Amex, MC, Visa.
Rates B&B, $75–185 suite, $60–85 double. Extra person, $20. Prix fixe dinner, $35–38 plus 18% service, 5% tax.
Extras Some pets permitted by prior arrangement. Airport/station pickups, $10.

Kansas

Circle S Guest Ranch & Country Inn, Lawrence

Set right at the center of the continental U.S., Kansas has a history far more complex than most people realize. From 1492 to 1845 six nations claimed all or part of what is now Kansas. Although included as part of the U.S. with the Louisiana Purchase, it became part of the Republic of Texas until that state was admitted to the Union in 1845. Kansas's own admission to the Union was delayed until 1861 by intense and bloody feuding between the territory's pro- and anti-slavery factions.

Although Kansas is known as one of the country's leading wheat producers, its farmers have never had it easy, from the hardships faced by the first settlers of the early 1800s, through the "dust bowl" period of the 1930s, to the present day. Industry now plays an important role in the state's economy, with meat packing and aviation among the leading fields.

While it is by no means a tourist mecca, Kansas does have many towns of interest, including Wichita, center of the state's aircraft industry; Lawrence, home of the University of Kansas; and Dodge City, once known as the Wickedest City in America, with a saloon for every 50 citizens. Many towns sponsor fairs and festivals during the warmer months; ask the tourist office for a calendar of events.

COUNCIL GROVE

Also recommended: The Cottage House Hotel (25 North Neosho, Council Grove, 66846; 316–767–6828 or 800–727–7903) dates back to 1867, and offers 28 rooms decorated with Victorian antiques, including lace curtains and stained glass windows. Guests enjoy relaxing on the hotel's gazebo-style verandas after a hearty made-from-scratch meal at the Hays House, just around the corner. Council Grove was the last out-fitting point on the Santa Fe trail, and is about 50 miles southwest of Topeka. B&B double rates range from $60–130 (less for the motel rooms). "Wonderful old Victorian hotel, lavishly decorated, with excellent lighting. Just a block from the historic Hays House restaurant. Nice lounging areas with newspapers, books, etc. The generous breakfast is available from 6:30 A.M. and includes cereal, all kinds of breads, juices, fruit. Highly recommended." *(Duane Roller)*

LAWRENCE

Located halfway between Kansas City and Topeka, and bisected by the Oregon Trail, Lawrence is the home of the University of Kansas, founded in 1866, and the country's only intertribal American Indian educational institution, the Haskell Indian Nations University, founded in 1884. On the 1,000-acre KU campus is the Kenneth Spencer Research Library, with a major rare book collection; the Museum of Anthropology; the Natural History Museum; and the Spencer Museum of Art. Local history is the focus of the Watkins Community Museum of History, housed in a restored 1888 bank at the edge of the Old West Lawrence Historic District. Two outlet malls provide relief in cases of cultural overdose.

Also recommended: Situated on a working ranch, about 15 minutes from downtown Lawrence, and 40 minutes from both Kansas City and Topeka is the **Circle S Guest Ranch & Country Inn** (3325 Circle S Lane, Lawrence, 66044; 785–843–4124 or 800–625–2839; www.CircleSRanch. com). Fifth generation ranchers Mary Beth and Mitchell Stevenson built a barn-style guest house on their 1,200 acre property in 1997. Each of the 12 guest rooms has a private bath, telephone, TV, and air-conditioning, and many have whirlpool tubs and fireplaces as well; the silo houses a large hot tub. A full breakfast and four-course dinner is included in the double rates of $149–250. "Mary Beth and Mitchell are gracious hosts, ready to do anything for their guests' comfort. Each of the guest rooms has a different theme, but all offer country elegance—like Martha Stewart teamed up with a wealthy rancher. We walked the rolling hills, followed by two friendly dogs, explored the barn with its cats and kittens, and greeted the handsome strolling peacocks. Lawrence is an easy drive for lunch, shopping, and museums." *(Marilyn Brown)*

LINDSBORG

Located 70 miles north of Wichita, the Smoky River Valley was homesteaded in the 1860s by Swedish immigrants, and its Swedish heritage has been well preserved. Lindsborg, known as Little Sweden, is the area's hub and offers a number of Swedish-style restaurants and shops selling Scandinavian imports.

Also recommended: A Dutch colonial home built in a Swedish community in Kansas sounds like an all-American B&B, and the **Morning Mist B&B** (618 North Chestnut, Lindsborg, 67456; 785–227–3801 or 888–566–MIST; www.morningmistB-B.com) fills the bill. Gary and JoAnn Mattison renovated their 1907 home in 1997, adding private baths to each of the five guest rooms; some have a whirlpool tub and fireplace. Breakfast is served at the large dining room table at 9 A.M. or earlier, if guests prefer, and includes fresh fruit, juice, coffee, a breakfast meat (such as link sausage) and a hot entree, perhaps peach-stuffed French toast. B&B double rates are $50–85. "Gary and Jo Ann have done a superb job of restoration; our Grand Room had a fireplace operated by a push button, a wonderful, deep whirlpool tub, and the most comfortable bed and linens we've ever had. Best of all are Gary and JoAnn, who have vivacious and nurturing personalities, yet are sensitive to guests' needs for privacy. They gave us excellent dining recommendations and good shopping tips. The delicious breakfasts were reason enough to return." *(April & Ove Johansson)*

WAKEENEY

Thistle Hill B&B ¢ ♦♦
Route 1, P.O. Box 93, 67672

Tel: 785–743–2644
URL: http://www.bbonline.
com/ks/thistlehill

"Our guests enjoy the quiet vastness of the western Kansas prairie in this secluded rural area; ours is a simple lifestyle close to nature. We have a variety of farm animals, including cows, draft horses, and chickens. Floral arrangements, both fresh and dried, decorate our contemporary cedar farmhouse, and are available for sale in the remodeled barn," report longtime owners Dave and Mary Hendricks. "We've also built a solarium hot tub for our guests to enjoy." Freshly ground coffee, herbal teas, and juice are always on the breakfast menu, along with homemade muffins and pastries, home-grown fruit, and such entrees as whole wheat pancakes made from Thistle Hill's own wheat, topped with homemade syrups.

"We had always heard that driving across Kansas was the ultimate drudgery, but we found the landscape beautiful in its vast loneliness. Out in the middle of the plains is this warm and cozy B&B. The Oak Room has a bed Dave and Mary built themselves from fence posts. We sat down to breakfast with the Hendricks, and Dave said grace. Our meal included eggs from their chicken house, seasoned with rosemary from their greenhouse." *(Park Burroughs)* "We stayed in the largest room, with an elegant shower stall and a separate enclosure for the sink and toilet. We breakfasted on wonderful harvest bread, fruit, juice, and eggs." *(Carol Worth)* "Wonderful restored prairie setting; quiet and peaceful, though in sight of I-70. The buildings are within a three-sided evergreen windbreak. The first floor has a huge kitchen-dining area, with a big table looking out to the garden, where we could watch a variety of birds at the feeders. The breakfast schedule was set by mutual agreement; the meal was tasty, but the conversation was even better." *(Fred Markham)* "The Hendricks are delightful people of varied interests, much enthusiasm, and considerable knowledge of the environment and local history. A convenient stopover between Kansas City and the Colorado ski slopes." *(Linda & Kirk Dodge)* "We were fascinated by the owners' returning some of their farm acreage to grassland prairie. Mary shared seeds and cuttings from the herb garden with us. Both she and her husband were gracious hosts."*(Sara Moore)* "Fully endorse entry. A lovely experience and one of the delights of our trip." *(BJ Hensley)* "Hosts were friendly and helpful as to places to see; food was delicious." *(Phyllis Bales)*

Open All year.

Rooms 1 suite, 3 doubles—3 with private bath and/or shower, 1 with a maximum of 4 people sharing bath. All with clock, air-conditioning. 2 with desk, 1 with telephone, fan.

Facilities Dining room with fireplace, living room with fireplace, piano, TV/VCR, stereo, library, family room, solarium with hot tub, guest refrigerator, guest laundry, 2 porches, gift shop in barn. 7 acres with herb, flower gardens; 60-acre prairie-wildflower restoration project; 600-acre farm with farm animals. 30 m to Cedar Bluff Reservoir for fishing, hunting, swimming, boating. Castle Rock, Sternberg Museum, Cottonwood Ranch nearby.

Location NW KS. Halfway between Kansas City & Denver, CO (325 m from each). 125 m W of Salina. 7 m from town. 1 ½ m from I-70 interchange. Call for directions.

Restrictions No smoking.

Credit cards MC, Visa.

Rates B&B, $75 suite, $59–69 double, $45 single. Extra person, $10.

Extras Local airport/station pickups, $5.

WICHITA

A bustling and prosperous city, Wichita was for years a wide-open "cow town"; later grain and oil became key sources of income, and today Wichita is also known as a center for the manufacture of small aircraft. Sights of note include the Old Cow Town Museum, the zoo and botanical gardens, and the outdoor sculptures at Wichita State University.

Also recommended: One of Wichita's newest inns is the **Castle Inn Riverside** (1155 North River Boulevard, 67203; 316–263–9300 or 800–580–1131; castle@gte.net) overlooking the Arkansas River. A limestone mansion built in 1888, and modeled after a Scottish castle, it was extensively (and expensively) renovated in 1995. B&B double rates for the 14 guest rooms range from $125–250, and include a full breakfast, wine and hors d'oeuvres, and evening coffee and dessert. All guest rooms have private baths, TV/VCRs, and telephones with dataports; several have a Jacuzzi tub, fireplace, and/or balcony. "Meticulously restored castle with a rich local history. " *(Tina Kirkpatrick)* "The Lowry clan has done a spectacular job of restoring this mansion and renovating the interior. Beautiful rooms, modern baths, good lighting. Saturday's breakfast was served at the time of one's choice and consisted of juices, wonderful granola, and breakfast burritos with apple-based salsa, plus strong coffee." *(Carol Worth)*

The **Inn at the Park** (3751 East Douglas Avenue, 67218; 316–652–0500 or 800–258–1951), built in 1909, is a brick Colonial Revival mansion restored as a B&B in 1989.

The decor ranges from English Victorian to French country to Oriental, from Neoclassic to Art Nouveau. B&B double rates of $114–164 include a continental breakfast and afternoon coffee and tea. "A designer showcase home, each guest room has a different theme. We stayed in Room #7 with a lovely sitting room, large bathroom, a king-size canopy bed with a lace canopy, and a fireplace with a Duraflame log. Professional, unobtrusive staff. Delicious breakfast buffet with quiche, chocolate muffins, fresh fruit, and more." *(Tina Kirkpatrick)*

Key to Abbreviations and Symbols

For complete information and explanations, please see the Introduction.

¢ Especially good value for overnight accommodation.

☖ Families welcome. Most (but not all) have cribs, baby-sitting, games, play equipment, and reduced rates for children.

✕ Meals served to public; reservations recommended or required.

🎾 Tennis court and swimming pool and/or lake on grounds. Golf usually on grounds or nearby.

♿ Limited or full wheelchair access; call for details.

Rates: Range from least expensive room in low season to most expensive room in peak season.

Room only: No meals included; European Plan (EP).

B&B: Bed and breakfast; includes breakfast, sometimes afternoon/evening refreshment.

MAP: Modified American Plan; includes breakfast and dinner.

Full board: Three meals daily.

Alc lunch: A la carte lunch; average price of entrée plus nonalcoholic drink, tax, tip.

Alc dinner: Average price of three-course dinner, including half bottle of house wine, tax, tip.

Prix fixe dinner: Three- to five-course set dinner, excluding wine, tax, tip unless otherwise noted.

Extras: Noted if available. Always confirm in advance. Pets are not permitted unless specified; if you are allergic, ask for details; *most innkeepers have pets.*

Kentucky

Inn at the Park, Louisville

Kentucky's history is a rich and complex one—Daniel Boone explored and hunted here, Abraham Lincoln was born here, and Stephen Foster and Harriet Beecher Stowe wrote about Kentucky. In the development of the U.S., Kentucky has served as a bridge state: Linking the north and south, it was a slave state but fought for the Union in the Civil War; from Virginia to Missouri, settlers passed through on their way west.

And there is far more to present-day Kentucky than Churchill Downs, the Derby, and horses. A key common denominator is the dominant limestone strata responsible for the state's bourbon (the water), bluegrass (the color), and dramatic scenery (cliffs, canyons, and caves). At Cumberland Falls State Park visitors can walk out on flat limestone slabs to watch a 125-foot-wide, 68-foot-high swathe of water plunge dramatically to the boulders below. During a full moon, the resulting pervasive mist forms a rare "moonbow" visible only here and at Victoria Falls in Zimbabwe, Africa. If you're not claustrophobic, explore some of the 300 miles of charted limestone passages in Mammoth Cave, including some areas used for human habitation over 4,000 years ago.

Other spots to explore: Shaker Village at Pleasant Hill, with its architecturally distinctive buildings where superb design emphasizes stately simplicity; nearby Harrodsburg's Old Fort Harrod—site of the first permanent English settlement west of the Alleghenies; Hodgenville, where visitors can see Abe Lincoln's birthplace and an enormous sinkhole; and the many TVA lakes scattered throughout the state, which offer limitless recreational opportunities.

234

BARDSTOWN

Bardstown is one of Kentucky's oldest towns, with many historic buildings, and is a center for the growing of tobacco and the distilling of bourbon. Sights of interest include the local historical museum, the Getz Museum of Whiskey History—from colonial days to Prohibition—and My Old Kentucky Home State Park. This park is home to Federal Hill, a mansion that probably inspired Stephen Foster to write "My Old Kentucky Home." From June to early September the "Stephen Foster Story," a musical pageant featuring the composer's melodies, is sung in the park's amphitheater. Bourbon aficionados will want to take the tours of the nearby Jim Beam and Maker's Mark distilleries. Here also is a Trappist abbey that sells a very distinctive (and strong) cheese.

Bardstown is in central Kentucky's Nelson County, 35 miles south of Louisville.

Jailer's Inn ¢   *Tel:* 502–348–5551
111 West Stephen Foster Avenue, 40004   800–948–5551
                                                     Fax: 502–348–1852
                                     E-mail: jailersinn@bardstown.com
                                     URL: http://www.jailersinn.com

After two centuries as a jail, Fran, Challen, and their son Paul McCoy bought the old jail and jailer's residence at public auction in 1988, and have converted it into an unusual B&B. Five guest rooms have been decorated with antiques and Oriental rugs; the sixth, the former women's cell, is done in prison black-and-white, with framed reproductions of cell-wall graffiti hung on the walls. Public tours are given from 10 A.M. to 5 P.M.; guests may check in after 2 P.M.

"Helpful suggestions for dining and sightseeing; we had an outstanding dinner at the Bardstonian Restaurant." *(Edward Warner)* "The sitting area has an Oriental theme, with a large couch; the breakfast table was set with beautiful china. Our room, #3—The Library—had green walls, a wallpaper ceiling border, red accent curtains, pretty pictures, a king-size bed with a brass headboard, two brocade sitting chairs, and a modern bath." *(Lynne Derry)* "Breakfast was served in the flower-filled fortress courtyard." *(Gail Greco)* "A special breakfast dish was prepared to meet my dietary needs. Interesting collection of jail memorabilia." *(Patricia Davis)*

"Charming and peaceful, relaxed and friendly. We were welcomed warmly, shown to a lovely guest room, and were given the recipe for our breakfast favorite, peach French toast. It's a short walk to the inn's parking area, but we had no problems. Bardstown is an inviting town for evening strolling." *(Richard Miller)* "Paul was an excellent host, both witty and informative. Delightful breakfast." *(JFH)* "We enjoyed the Dungeon Room, the jail tour, and pleasant conversation with Paul, who is doing an excellent job."*(Mark & Terrie Bryant)*

Open Feb. 1–Dec. 31.
Rooms 6 doubles—all with private bath, desk, air-conditioning, fan. 2 with double Jacuzzi.
Facilities Breakfast room, TV/VCR room, gift shop, courtyard garden, gazebo, picnic area. Off-street parking. Golf nearby.
Location 35 m S of Louisville. 65 m SW of Lexington. Center of town. Adjacent to Court Square.
Restrictions No smoking in guest rooms. House tours held 10 A.M.–5 P.M.
Credit cards Amex, Discover, MC, Visa.
Rates B&B, $65–95 double. Extra person, $10.
Extras Limited wheelchair access. Crib.

HARRODSBURG

The Harrodsburg area is home to two of Kentucky's finest inns. If your time in Kentucky is limited, this town, oldest in the state, is probably the one to visit. Sights of interest include Old Fort Harrod State Park, with its historic buildings and amphitheater, featuring dramatizations of the stories of Daniel Boone and Abraham Lincoln; Morgan Row; and Shakertown at Pleasant Hill.

Harrodsburg is located in central Kentucky's Bluegrass Region, 32 miles southwest of Lexington.

Reader tip: "Mercer County is dry, so come prepared. If you'd like to enjoy a glass of wine with dinner, phone the restaurant in advance to see if it's OK to bring a bottle."

Also recommended: Dating back to 1845, the **Beaumont Inn** (638 Beaumont Drive, P.O. Box 158, 40330; 606–734–3381 or 800–352–3992; www.beaumontinn.com) has been owned by the Dedman family for four generations. Formerly a school for girls, the inn's rooms are spread out over a number of buildings and cottages, including the original main building of the school, a brick building with Greek Revival–style Doric columns. Restaurant specialties include the inn's own Kentucky-cured ham, fried chicken, corn pudding, bread pudding with bourbon sauce, and orange-lemon cake. B&B double rates range from $77–112; three meals are served daily, and are reasonably priced. "Warm hospitality, delicious food, excellent housekeeping, comfortably furnished with many Victorian antiques." *(SHW)* "We were fascinated by the sense of history evoked by the inn. A gracious staff served hearty regional food served in ample quantities."*(Ruthie Tilsley)*

Shaker Village of Pleasant Hill ¢ 🚸 ✕ ♿
3501 Lexington Road, 40330
Tel: 606–734–5411
800–734–5611
Fax: 606–734–5411
URL: http://www.Shakervillageky.org

A longtime reader favorite, Shaker Village preserves 33 original 19th-century buildings, accurately restored and adapted. Visitors take self-guided tours of the buildings where interpreters and craftsmen explain the Shaker approach to life and religion. Shaker music programs are also offered on many weekends. Shakertown at Pleasant Hill is a non-profit educational corporation, listed on the National Register of Historic Places; it is the only historic village offering overnight accommodation in original buildings.

"Well worth a visit; you can really get into the spirit of these extraordinary people. Wonderful musical presentation of the Shaker religious ceremony." *(Robert Freidus)* "The reservationist described the accommodations in detail, helping us to select the East Family Washhouse suite as a good choice. It was airy and light, with seven windows in the bedroom, just a short pleasant walk to the dining hall. Fantastic breakfast buffet; the staff constantly replenished the food." *(Mr. & Mrs. Conrad Schilke)*

"Rolling Kentucky bluegrass, with peaceful vistas in all directions. Tasty down-home cooking with fried fish, fried chicken, and steaks. Family-style vegetables—perhaps green beans with bacon and corn pudding. Furnishings are authentically plain—reproduction Shaker furniture, rag rugs, white walls, dark woodwork. To reach the idyllic Tanyard Brick Shop cottage, you wind through cow pastures down to a small farm pond, surrounded by weeping willows." *(SHW)* "The trundle beds enable a family to share one large room, each with a comfortable bed. Meals are served in the Trustees' House, with spectacular twin spiral staircases." *(Ann Delugach)*

"Our two-room suite in the East Family Wash House was large and private." *(Joyce Ward)* "We enjoyed our stay in the Old Ministry's workshop, with a fireplace and comfortable bed. At night we saw a spectacular sunset over the rolling fence-lined hills." *(Deanna Yen)* "Exceptionally comfortable mattress; excellent home-style cooking at breakfast and dinner." *(Peggy Kontak, also Duane Roller)* "Rooms in the smaller buildings are especially quiet and peaceful. Wonderful evening serenity; cattle low in the distance as you stroll along the dirt road down to the old cemetery." *(CK)*

Open All year. Closed Christmas Eve and Day.

Rooms 1 cottage, 2 conference centers, 78 doubles with full private bath, telephone, TV, desk, air-conditioning. Accommodations in 15 restored buildings.

Facilities Sitting rooms, restaurant. 2,700 acres. Riverboat rides on Kentucky River. Craft shops, demonstrations.

Location Central KY, Bluegrass Region. 80 m SE of Louisville, 25 m SW of Lexington, 7 m NE of Harrodsburg, on US Rte. 68. Use caution on winding, hilly road after dark.

Restrictions No alcoholic beverages in dining room. Traffic noise in North Lot dwelling. Minimal soundproofing; TV noise can sometimes be heard in neighboring rooms.

Credit cards MC, Visa.

Rates Room only, $140–180 cottage, $105–115 suite, $60–80 double, $50–70 single. No charge for children under 17 in parents' room. Extra adults, $10. Country buffet breakfast, $7.50; alc lunch, $6.50–9.50; alc dinner, $13.25–17.75. Children's menu. Seasonal, special event packages.

Extras Crib. Dining room, public restrooms wheelchair accessible.

LEXINGTON

A city wealthy from the tobacco industry, Lexington is home to the University of Kentucky, Transylvania University, and many beautiful antebellum and Victorian buildings, a number of which are now open to the public as museums. But the real attraction here is thoroughbred horses. Head for the Kentucky Horse Park, for 1,000 acres of bluegrass, where you can learn everything you ever wanted to know (and more) about equines, then sign up for a tour of the area's best horse farms. Lexington is located in central Kentucky, 101 miles south of Cincinnati, Ohio, and 78 miles east of Louisville.

Also recommended: A Federal-style mansion built in 1812, **The Brand House at Rose Hill** (461 North Limestone Street, 40508; 606–226–9464 or 800–366–4942; www.brandhouselex.com) offers five guest rooms, each with double whirlpool tubs, at B&B double rates of $89–189, including a hearty yet creative full breakfast. This 4,000-square-foot mansion has a Greek Revival facade, while the interior combines historically accurate colors and fabrics with exceptional charm and the comfort of queen- and king-size beds. "Eclectically decorated with exceptional flair and handsome design. Owners Logan and Pam Leet were extremely accommodating to my husband's conference schedule, and provided an early breakfast. We especially enjoyed the billiard room. If visiting on a spring or summer Saturday morning, don't miss the farmer's market down the street for a colorful, fascinating experience." *(Gary & Sarah Beatty)*

In 1995, lifetime Lexington residents Beverly and Bobby True realized a 20-year dream and opened **A True Inn** (467 West Second Street, 40507; 606–252–6166 or 800–374–6151), Lexington's first small B&B. Built in the Greek Revival style in 1843, their house was remodeled as a Richardsonian Romanesque mansion in 1890. Each of the six guest rooms is named for a famous Lexingtonian, including the infamous Lexington madam, Belle Brezing. Rooms are furnished with antiques, handmade quilts and afghans. The double rates of $85–125 include a full breakfast and afternoon refreshments. "The owners are warm, passionate about their city and their beautifully restored B&B, and are a prime example of the excellence of owner-operated B&Bs." *(Kip Goldman & Marty Wall)*

Just 15 minutes west of Lexington in historic Versailles are two B&Bs of interest. The **Rose Hill Inn** (233 Rose Hill, Versailles, 40383; 606–873–5957 or 800–307–0460; www.rosehillinn.com) is an 1800s home, a block from downtown. The five guest rooms have private baths, and range from a romantic choice with a double Jacuzzi tub, to a quaint brick cottage where children and pets are welcome. B&B double rates of $75–125 include a full breakfast, evening hors d'oeuvres, and bedtime cookies and tea. The **Tyrone Pike B&B** (3820 Tyrone Pike, Versailles, 40383; 606–873–2408 or 800–736–7722; www.bbonline.com/ky/tyrone) is set back from the road on five acres of land. Owner and registered nurse Jean Foreman has created a warm, welcoming atmosphere. "One set of rooms is specifically set up for families, while another is ideal for business travel or a romantic getaway." *(SHW)* B&B double rates range from $95–125, including a full breakfast.

Information please: What is now the **Camberley Club Hotel at Gratz Park** (120 West Second Street, 40507; 606–231–1777 or 800–555–8000; www.camberleyhotels.com), was originally built as an office building in 1916. This 44-room hotel is housed in a Georgian Revival–style building, with a lovely lobby, pleasant guest rooms with English antique reproduction furniture, and king- or queen-size pencil post or rice four-poster beds. The restaurant has gathered excellent reviews for its fine cuisine and elegant atmosphere. B&B double rates range from $130–260, including a continental breakfast and evening turndown service with sherry.

LOUISVILLE

Louisville is known best for the Kentucky Derby (the most famous two minutes in sports), and as the state's cultural center year-round, with great jazz clubs, superb live theater, and several truly gracious residential areas where homes date from the 1870s. Louisville is located in the north central part of the state, on the Ohio River, across from Indiana.

Also recommended: Visitors to Louisville are fortunate to have their choice of two lovely, well-maintained, historic luxury hotels, **The Brown** (4th & Broadway, 40202; 502–583–1234 or 800–555–8000), and **The Seelbach** (500 4th Avenue, 40202; 502–585–3200 or 800–333–3399), each with approximately 300 guest rooms. Although regular double rates at both are in the $180–225 range, it pays to ask about weekend packages and AAA promotional rates. Comments welcome.

Louisville's first B&B inn, the **Old Louisville Inn** (1359 South Third Street, 40208; 502–635–1574; www.digifax.com/oli.html) was built in 1901 in the Second Empire Beaux Arts style; Marianne Lesher has been the innkeeper since the inn opened in 1990. B&B double rates for the seven double rooms range from $75–110; children are welcome. The three romantic suites, each with a double whirlpool tub, cost $135–195. "Our spacious third-floor suite was prettily furnished with period pieces and a king-size bed. Coffee and tea are set out in the afternoon with freshly baked cookies. Breakfast included waffles one day, French toast another, with breakfast breads, juice, yogurt and fruit, and vanilla-flavored coffee. Marianne was helpful, recommended good restaurants, called for reservations, talked when it was clear we were ready for a chat, but didn't intrude when we wanted to be alone. Her terrific cat took a shine to us, and visited through an open window; a real plus." *(Robert Freidus)*

Inn at the Park ⊄
1332 South Fourth Street, 40208

Tel: 502–637–6930
800–700–PARK
Fax: 502–637–2796
E-mail: InnatPark@aol.com
URL: http://www.bbonline.com/ky/innatpark/

In 1886, Russell Houston, president of the L & N Railroad, built a 7,400-square-foot mansion in the massive Richardsonian Romanesque style, with blocks of roughly squared stonework, rounded arches, stone balconies, and more. The interior is equally lavish, with a striking mahogany staircase, rich hardwood floors, 12-foot ceilings, marble fireplaces, and crown moldings. The inn was bought by Sandy and John Mullins in 1995.

The rooms are furnished in period with antiques and reproductions. Breakfast is served between 7:30–9:30 weekdays, 8:00–10:00 weekends, and includes freshly baked muffins, croissants and breads, fresh fruit and juice, coffee and tea, and a such entrees as banana-walnut pancakes with maple syrup and bacon, omelets with grilled ham and whole wheat toast, or vanilla yogurt with granola and honey.

"Appealing neighborhood, including the beautiful park with its summer Shakespeare festival and walking tour of Old Louisville, plus convenient access to downtown. The atmosphere is comfortable, casual, and inviting. Delicious coffee is ready for early risers, and Sandy offers a choice of entrees, usually an egg-based dish and waffles or pancakes; plates are garnished with fresh flowers and herbs from her garden. Each room has its own personality and charm, all are very clean, well lit, beautifully decorated, and private. Sandy and John are friendly, outgoing people who truly enjoy being innkeepers. They respect your privacy, but love to share their stories and hear yours." *(Mary Kasik)* "A gorgeous home in a charming historic neighborhood with an elegant grand staircase, working fireplaces in almost every room, and warm, gracious hospitality." *(Marianna Adams)* "The romantic Parkview Room has a king-size four-poster bed, fireplace, private balcony, and whirlpool tub with a view of the park." *(Pamela Goff)* "Beautifully decorated for Christmas. Delicious omelet with Crimini mushrooms and smoked cheddar cheese; innkeepers accommodating about breakfast times and menus." *(Susan Schwemm)* "Elegant, yet comfortable accommodations; well-prepared food, beautifully presented; but best of all is the hospitality and warmth of innkeeper Sandy Mullins." *(Wanda Tate)* "From the passion fruit bubble bath, delicious breakfast, and guest pantry stocked with drinks and snacks, this is an exceptionally traveler-friendly and romantic spot." *(Timothy Mallon)* "Easy to find and centrally located. The innkeepers offer ample information on area restaurants, events, and attractions." *(BDS)* "Charming garden with fountain; the best Belgian waffles with hazelnut liqueur flavored whipped cream." *(TM)*

Open All year.

Rooms 3 suites, 4 doubles—all with private bath and/or shower, telephone, radio, clock, TV, air-conditioning. Some with ceiling fan, fireplace, desk, double whirlpool tub, balcony. 2 suites in adjacent carriage house with double whirlpool tub, dining room, living room with wet bar, kitchen.

Facilities Dining room, living room, meeting rooms, guest pantry, porch, fax, copy service. Off- & on-street parking. Park adjacent for tennis.

Location Historic district, 5–10 min. of downtown, U. of Louisville, Churchill Downs. From I-65, take Exit 135 A & go W (right) on W. St. Catherine St. 4 blocks. Turn S (left) on 4th St. & go 3 blocks to inn at corner of Park & 4th.

Restrictions No smoking. No children.

Credit cards Amex, MC, Visa.

Rates B&B, $79–149.

Extras German spoken.

Free copy of INNroads newsletter

Want to stay up-to-date on our latest finds? Send a business-size, self-addressed, stamped envelope with 55 cents postage and we'll send you the latest issue, *free!* While you're at it, why not enclose a report on any inns you've recently visited? Use the forms at the back of the book or your own stationery.

We Want to Hear from You!

As you know, this book is effective only with your help. We really need to know about your experiences and discoveries. If you stayed at an inn or hotel listed here, we want to know how it was. Did it live up to our description? Exceed it? Was it what you expected? Did you like it? Were you disappointed? Delighted? Have you discovered new establishments that we should add to the next edition?

Tear out one of the report forms at the back of this book (or use your own stationery if you prefer) and write today. Or email us at afi@inns.com. *Even if you write only "Fully endorse existing entry" you will have been most helpful.*

Thank You!

Important Note on Area Codes

Telephone area codes are changing faster than a two-year-old's attention span. Although we've tried to incorporate all the new ones in our listings, many numbers were still in the "to be decided" state at press time. *If you dial a number listed here and get an announcement that it's not in service, we urge you to call the information operator and see if that region has been assigned a new area code.* Please forgive the inconvenience!

Louisiana

Madewood, Napoleonville

Everybody goes to New Orleans sooner or later, and although it's a big city, you can get a good taste of its delicious food, distinctive architecture, and famous jazz in just a few days' visit. Beyond New Orleans, the state offers a potpourri of cultures and landscapes. North of the city, across Lake Pontchartrain Causeway, horse farms and dense pine forests provide a peaceful contrast to New Orleans' famous excesses. To the south, scenic Route 90 leads to Houma, the heart of Cajun country. Rent a boat here to explore and fish in Louisiana's legendary bayous, swamps, and marshes. Continue west on Route 90, then detour to Avery Island, the home of McIlhenny Tabasco sauce. Up the road, visit the restored antebellum plantation homes in New Iberia.

Note: You'll frequently hear the words *Cajun* and *Creole* used in Louisiana. The former refers to the French settlers of Acadia (present-day Nova Scotia), who were expelled from Canada by the British in the 1750s and settled in Louisiana, which was then French territory. (The word *Cajun* is derived from the word *Acadian*.) The word *Creole,* on the other hand, describes the descendants of the early French and Spanish settlers of this region. Although time has produced some overlapping, their heritage and traditions are quite different.

LAFAYETTE

Located in south central Louisiana, Lafayette is the capital of Cajun country. Of particular interest is Vermillionville, a recreation of the original 18th-century Cajun and Creole village; the Live Oak Gardens, especially beautiful when both azaleas and tulips are in bloom; the Acadian village, a folk museum celebrating 19th-century Acadian life; nearby plantations; and a variety of celebrations and festivals year-round. Ask your innkeeper for advice on the best places for Cajun food, music, and dancing.

Reader tips: "Great food at Prejean's Restaurant and Enola Prud-homme's Cajun Cafe; enjoyed the food and zydeco music and dancing at Mulate's in Breaux Bridge." *(MW, also Emily Hoche-Mong)*

Also recommended: Seven miles north of Lafayette is **La Maison de Compagne** (825 Kidder Road, Carencro, 70520; 318–896–6529 or 800–895–0235), a Victorian plantation home, set among pecan trees and live oaks. B&B double rates for the four guest rooms (each with private bath) range from $100–125, including a full breakfast and use of the swimming pool. "Magnificent Victorian antiques. Fresh baked breads, elegant seafood dishes, superb egg dishes, and wonderful fruit frappes kept us fueled all day." *(Michael Ledger)* "Personable owners, relaxing rural setting, inspired breakfasts, attractive and comfortable rooms." *(Catherine Lyons)*

Bois des Chenes ♦ ♿   *Tel:* 318–233–7816
338 North Sterling Street, 70501   *Fax:* 318–233–7816
E-mail: boisdchene@aol.com
URL: http://members.aol.com/boisdchene/bois.htm

Listed on the National Register of Historic Places, this Acadian-style plantation home has been restored to its original 1820 configuration, and is furnished with Louisiana French period antiques, highlighted by Coerte and Marjorie Voorhies' collections of pottery, antiques, and textiles. Part of the Charles Mouton Plantation, the B&B is housed in an 1890 carriage house at the rear of the plantation house. Each guest room has a different antique decor: country Acadian, Louisiana Empire, and Victorian. Rates include breakfast, a welcome bottle of wine, and a plantation house tour. Readers highly recommend signing up for Coerte's boat tour of the Atchafalaya Swamp.

"Our Carriage House room had convenient parking, and was large, exceptionally clean, and attractively furnished, with lovely fresh towels in the bathroom. Marjorie's delicious breakfasts included pain perdu (French toast) with pecans, maple syrup, and boudin sausage the first day, and eggs, sausages, fruit, and biscuits cooked in a skillet with preserves, the next. Coerte joined the guests at the long table, and talked about the local history." *(Beryl & Alex Williams)* "From entertainment and restaurant recommendations, to lessons on the history and culture of the area, Marjorie and Coerte looked after us well." *(Glenn Roehrig)* "We stayed in the Louisiana Suite, with a high, firm bed. We loved the two family dogs." *(Deborah Ross & Russ Hogan)* "Best of all was the Voorhies' kindness. They provided our toddler with a splendid antique brass child's bed, complete with teddy bear. After breakfast, we got a history and tour of the plantation house, and a slide show of the 'before' pictures." *(Barbara Mast James)* "Huge bathroom, fabulous bed, good bedside lighting, fluffy towels. The Voorhies' son, Kim, led our wonderful swamp tour and gave us a once-in-a-lifetime view of this incredible area. The owners also have an interesting antique business." *(Dianne Crawford)* "Just as wonderful on a return visit. Enjoyable breakfast with hosts and guests. After delicious French toast or pecan waffles we shared experiences; one morning we were treated to a tour of their historic home. Our suite, upstairs in the carriage house, was comfortable, quiet, and very clean, with a good shower and ample counter space in the bathroom. Coerte's boat trip into the Atchafalaya was informative and entertaining; the scenic cypress swamp is in Coerte's words 'Louisiana's answer to the Grand Canyon.'" *(GR)*

Open All year. Closed Christmas Eve.
Rooms 3 suites, 3 doubles—all with private bath, radio, TV, air-conditioning, fan, refrigerator. 1 with fireplace. 1 in carriage house.
Facilities Breakfast room, solarium, porch. 2 acres with patio, aviary. Atchafalaya Swamp expeditions.
Location Historic district. From I-10 take exit 103A S to Evangeline Thruway. Go 3 lights to Mudd Ave. Turn left and go 3 blocks to intersection with N Sterling. Inn is on SE corner. Continue on Mudd past inn and enter circular driveway on right at 35 MPH sign.
Restrictions Smoking in designated areas.
Credit cards Amex, MC, Visa.
Rates B&B, $115–165 suite, $95 double, $85 single. Extra person, $30. Children under 5 free in parents' room. Crib, $10. 10% senior, AAA discount.
Extras Wheelchair access. Airport/station pickups. Pets by prior arrangement. Crib, babysitting. French spoken.

NAPOLEONVILLE

Madewood Plantation House   *Tel:* 504–369–7151
4250 Highway 308, 70390   800–375–7151
                                     Fax: 504–369–9848

A 21-room Greek Revival mansion, Madewood was designed in 1846 and is a National Historic Landmark. The white-painted mansion has six imposing Ionic columns and was built from bricks produced in the plantation's kiln and from cypress grown on its lands. Madewood was purchased in 1964 by Mr. and Mrs. Harold Marshall and is now owned by their son Keith and his wife, Millie. Keith and Millie work in New Orleans during the week, spending many long weekends at Madewood; they are assisted by managers Janet Ledet Michael Hawkins. Rooms are furnished with an extensive collection of antiques, including canopy or half-tester beds, marble fireplace mantels, hand-carved woodwork, and fanned windows. Millie notes that "Madewood is not sophisticated or luxurious, but is a large country mansion. Our food is country cooking, not gourmet; some northerners don't realize that smothered green beans are supposed to be cooked to death."

Guest rooms are located in the mansion, a 1820s Greek Revival cottage, and a three-room cabin with more casual country furnishings. Rates include wine and cheese, family-style dinner, coffee and brandy in the parlor, and full breakfast in the dining room.

"Probably the most authentic plantation that we have visited; we felt that the experience of staying there was very realistic. Impressive home, with towering Greek Revival columns. The atmosphere of grandeur is echoed by the vast public rooms with their large doorways, high ceilings, and fine Waterford crystal chandeliers. Our second floor room opened onto the large front balcony, and was pleasantly furnished with antiques. Enjoyable breakfast of eggs, sausage, grits, biscuits, apple sauce, preserves, orange juice, and coffee." *(Beryl & Alex Williams)*

"Beautiful, yet comfortable mansion. The friendly staff cheerfully provided the recipes for my favorite dishes. I loved hearing about my own room during the informative guided tour." *(Rosemary Combs)* "We liked having the run of the house during the hours it was closed to tours." *(Glenn Roehrig)* "The Girls' Room in the main house has two comfortable four-poster beds, while the big bedroom on the main floor has very impressive furniture. Taking the tour helped us to understand the plantation lifestyle. Keith Marshall joined us and the other guests for wine, Brie, and crackers; we were delighted to hear his stories about Madewood. We had a family-style dinner with the other guests, and were served turkey gumbo, salad, chicken or shrimp pot pie, and bread pudding. Wonderful atmosphere in the dining room, with silver, china, and candlelight. After our meal, the staff opened the huge doors to the drawing room to where we retired for coffee, brandy, or tea. A 17-foot-tall Christmas tree accented the marvelous antiques. Breakfast included a tasty sausage casserole. Overall, we felt as though we'd been transported to an earlier era." *(Lynne Derry)*

Open All year. Closed Thanksgiving, Dec. 24, 25, 31, Jan. 1.
Rooms 1 cottage, 2 suites, 6 doubles with private bath and/or shower, air-conditioning. 3 rooms in annex; 1 2-bedroom cottage. Some with desk, radio, fireplace, refrigerator, balcony.
Facilities Double parlors, dining room, library, music room, verandas. 20 acres with patio, live oaks, bayou. Swamp tours nearby.
Location SE LA. Sugarcane country. 75 m W of New Orleans, 45 m S of Baton Rouge. On Bayou Lafourche, facing LA Hwy. 308. 4 m from town.
Restrictions No smoking. Because of tours, a 5 P.M. check-in and a 10 A.M. check-out is sometimes requested for rooms in the main house.
Credit cards Amex, Discover, MC, Visa.
Rates MAP, $215 double, $185 single. Extra person, $50–60. Reduced rate for small children.
Extras Playpen.

NEW ORLEANS

Cognoscenti inform us that the city under discussion here is called *Nu-Aw'luns*, never *New Or-leens'*.

The French Quarter is roughly rectangular in shape, bordered by Canal Street to the west, Rampart Street to the north, Esplanade to the east, and the river to the south. Canal Street forms a border between the French Quarter and the financial district; the big chain hotels—the Sheraton, Marriott, Westin, etc.—are all in the area around Canal. Bourbon and Royal Streets run east/west, and can be very noisy in the central section of the quarter; the quietest section is the beautiful residential area to the east, just north of the French Market.

Rates may double and triple during Mardi Gras, Sugar Bowl, Super Bowl, Jazz Festival, and other peak festival times; be prepared to pay *in advance*. Bargain summer rates are generally available from June through September, so ask for details when phoning. Parking can be a problem; if traveling by car, be sure to ask for specifics when reserving your room. A few hotels provide on-site parking; most have arrangements with nearby garages.

Many hotel rooms in the French Quarter tend to be small, with a bed and not much in the way of easy chairs or usable desk space. Although most inns have attractive balconies and courtyards, few offer parlors or dining rooms for guests to gather inside. People come to New Orleans for many reasons, but peace and quiet are not usually among them. It is a noisy city, and light sleepers should stay away from rooms in the commercial sector of the French quarter. Visitors should also be alert to the problem of street crime, a real problem in some areas; ask your innkeeper for advice.

Reader tips: "Be sure to allow plenty of time for just hanging out in front of the Cathedral in Jackson Square, where music is always playing and there's always something going on." *(RSS)* "We enjoyed a delightful afternoon tea at the Windsor Court Hotel, complete with delicious sandwiches, scones, preserves, petits fours, and fine tea, delightfully accompanied by harp music." *(Alex & Beryl Williams)* "Wonderful dinner at the Commander's Palace included a divine bread pudding souffle." *(Lynne Derry)* "Once a questionable area with many abandoned homes, the historic Lower Garden District is in transition, with some—but not all—homes beautifully restored. Request secure parking, and expect to encounter street people; caution is especially advisable at night." *(MW)* "We booked a literary walking tour of the French Quarter with Heritage Tours (504–949–9805), led by a knowledgeable New Orleans native, who shared many fascinating anecdotes and stories. Also worth a visit is the Hermann-Grima Historic House, a museum which shows how life was lived before the Civil War." *(Pam Phillips)*

Also recommended: The elegant **Windsor Court Hotel** (300 Gravier Street, 70130; 504–523–6000 or 800–262–2662; www.orient-express hotels.com/) is a big hotel with 324 suites and doubles (rates of $250–675 double). As the city's first and only 5-diamond hotel, *Alex & Beryl Williams* describe it as "a civilized haven of peace and quiet, with high standards of service and comfort. It boasts a fine collection of original oil paintings; it is worth staying there just to see them. We had a beautifully furnished junior suite with a small balcony. The restaurant is most attractive and the food is excellent." *(Alex & Beryl Williams)* "Although on the list for refurbishing, our room was spacious, comfortable, and quiet amidst Sugar Bowl frenzy." *(SDB)* "Nice staff and very personal service. Perfect in every way except for the water pressure in the shower." *(DC)*

Information please—French Quarter: We'd like more feedback on two of New Orleans best-known inns, the **Hotel Maison de Ville** (727

Rue Toulouse, 70130; 504–561–5858 or 800–634–1600) and the **Soniat House** (1133 Chartres Street, 70116; 504–522–0570 or 800–544–8808). The Maison de Ville consists of eight buildings, including its well-known restaurant, The Bistro, and the Audubon Cottages, about a block and a half away. Rates, ranging from $195–250 double, $245–545 for the cottages, include a continental breakfast and afternoon cocktails. "In a quiet part of the Quarter is this European-style inn, with lots of old world charm, and an exceptionally lovely courtyard. The Bistro is also very Parisian. The antiques are beautiful, and the marble bathrooms are nice. I'd love to stay here if I could afford it." *(PP)*

The Soniat House is probably New Orleans' best-known B&B inn, and offers 25 lovely guest rooms, a peaceful setting, and a charming courtyard. B&B double rates range from $160–250, suites $275–565; a light continental breakfast is $7 per person, and valet parking, $14 daily; local telephone calls are extra. "Loved it! Our room had twin beds, two wing chairs, and a lovely bathroom. The people at the front desk were so helpful." *(BJ Hensley))* "Beautiful flower-filled courtyard 'oasis,' firm beds with top-quality linens, great water pressure, and friendly staff, but would rather save my travel dollars for the great New Orleans restaurants." *(DC)*

The Chimes Cottages   🏃 ¢   *Tel:* 504–899–2621
1146 Constantinople Street, 70115   800–729–4640
Fax: 504–488–4639
E-mail: bedbreak@gnofn.org
URL: http://www.gnofn.org./~bedbreak

A consistent reader favorite, the Chimes Cottages encircle the brick courtyard belonging to the 1876 Uptown home of innkeepers Jill and Charles Abbyad. In 1985, the Abbyads bought and restored two attached Victorian cottages, with gingerbread detailing and stained and leaded glass windows. Breakfast is served family-style in the dining room, and includes freshly squeezed orange juice, fresh fruit, muffins, rolls, and coffee; guests may opt to take a breakfast tray to their room.

"I would be amazed if anyone, anywhere, does more to make guests special than Charles and Jill. Breakfast conversation is a highlight; great fellow guests. Jill is a gifted decorator, and has created rooms which are beautiful and fun." *(David Evans)* "My room was large, well lit, and comfortable, with a large clawfoot tub in the bathroom. Convenient and quiet." *(Pam Cook)* "Run with skill by Jill and Charles Abbyad, their children, Alexander and Yasmin, and their resident cats. The small courtyard serves as a gathering place for guests who help themselves to refreshments from the 'honor system' refrigerator. The Abbyads know everything about New Orleans." *(Penny Poirier)*

"Breakfast is hosted by Jill and/or Charles. They introduced the guests and encouraged the exchange of information and suggestions. Their insights made our plans easier, faster, better; they made objective suggestions for dining, tours, and activities without imposing." *(Ri Regina)* "Unbeatable restaurant advice. Fresh gardenias from their bushes were placed by the bedside." *(Beth de Anda)* "Our appealing fireplace room had a comfortable queen-size bed and was accessed by a walk-through window in the courtyard. We appreciated the convenience of an in-room phone, and my husband loved having a cable TV with remote control. Jill was helpful and charming, and suggested we walk a few blocks to Copelands for some great crab cakes. Breakfast included just-baked croissants from a local bakery, with fresh fruit, breads, and cheeses." *(Lynne Derry)* "Romantic, quiet, private, and secluded. The courtyard was shaded by crepe myrtles and palms, and the breeze tickled the chimes. Two cats kept us company, sunning on the doorstep of our little cottage, and coming in to say hello." *(Stephanie Williams)*

Open All year.
Rooms 2 cottages, 3 doubles—all with private bath and/or shower, telephone with dataport, radio, TV, desk, air-conditioning, ceiling fan, refrigerator, coffeemaker. 2 with fireplace. Iron, hair dryer on request.
Facilities Dining room, courtyard with garden trellis, limited off-street parking.
Location Upper Garden district. 2 m from French Quarter; 3 blocks to St. Charles Streetcar. Take I-10 E to Business District which changes to Hwy. 90. Exit at St. Charles Ave. (last exit before Crescent City Connection bridge). Constantinople St. is located between Louisiana & Napoleon on river side of St. Charles.
Restrictions No smoking inside.
Credit cards None accepted.
Rates B&B, $65–125 suite, $50–90 double, $50–75 single. Extra person, $10. 2-3 night weekend minimum Oct.–May.
Extras Pets with approval. Playpen. French spoken.

Le Richelieu in the French Quarter 🛏 ✕ ♿ *Tel:* 504–529–2492
1234 Chartres Street, 70116   800–535–9653
Fax: 504–524–8179
E-mail: nawlinssk@aol.com
URL: http://www.neworleansonline.com/richelieu.htm

Several restored 19th-century buildings make up Le Richelieu. Long-time owner Frank Rochefort and manager Joanne Kirkpatrick make sure their staff "do their best for guests," which is probably why the hotel has such a high rate of both occupancy and returning guests. Another plus is its "self-service" parking lot, avoiding the inevitable inconvenience of valet parking. Refurbishing is a never-ending job at well-run hotels, and Joanne reports that "18 rooms were just redone with new drapes, coverlets, dust ruffles, and carpeting. Ceiling borders have been added to all rooms, and crown moldings to the suites that didn't have them."

"The front desk staff couldn't have been nicer, taking plenty of time to give directions, marking a handy map for us. Our top-floor room was under the eaves, with a great view of the city skyline. It was clean and tastefully decorated, with dark green walls and coordinating floral bedspreads and drapes. Silent ceiling fans enabled us to leave the windows open on a balmy spring night." *(NB)* "Enjoyed breakfast on the glassed-in porch." *(BJ Hensley)* "Convenient but quiet location, excellent parking situation. Enjoyed breakfasting outside in the courtyard." *(Betty Sadler)*

"Our spacious room overlooked the courtyard and swimming pool. It had ample room for a king-size bed, armoire for both the TV and drawers for clothing, easy chairs, and a workable desk. The furnishings are quality reproductions, with coordinating drapes, coverlets, and dust ruffles. The bed was firm and comfortable, the sheets soft. The bathroom was functional, with ample storage space and towels. We loved the quiet location, just a block or two from the French Market." *(SWS)* "Being able to drive right into their parking lot is a big plus at night." *(Mary & Sidney Flynn)* "Charming decor, excellent housekeeping, helpful staff." *(GR)*

Open All year.
Rooms 17 suites, 70 doubles—all with full private bath, telephone, radio, TV, desk, air-conditioning, ceiling fan, refrigerator, hair dryer, ironing board/iron. Some with balcony. Dataport on request.
Facilities Lobby cafe, bar/lounge. Courtyard, swimming pool, free private self-park-and-lock lot. Room service. Tour tickets.
Location French Quarter. On Chartres St. in between Gov. Nicholls and Barracks Sts.
Credit cards Amex, DC, Discover, Enroute, Eurocard, JCB, MC, Visa.
Rates Room only, $160–475 suite, $95–150 double, $85–140 single. Extra person, $15. Packages available. Alc breakfast, $5–6; alc lunch or supper, $7–10.
Extras Limited wheelchair access. Elevator. Crib, baby-sitting. French, Spanish spoken.

ST. FRANCISVILLE

Settled by the English, St. Francisville is in the heart of Plantation Country, an area much favored by Audubon when he worked in this area during the 1820s, living at Oakley Plantation. "St. Francisville is a truly lovely little town, with quiet streets set off the main highway. Listed on the National Register of Historic Places, the handsome restored historic buildings, lovely gardens, and antique shops make Royal Street well worth exploring. Make it your base to visit the area plantations (less commercial than those closer to New Orleans, two hours away); particular favorites are Rosedown (the showiest), Greenwood, Oakley, and Catalpa, the homiest. Also worth a visit are the lovely gardens at Afton Villa." *(SWS)*

St. Francisville is set on the Mississippi River, 25 miles north of Baton Rouge and 60 miles south of Natchez, MS, via Highway 61.

Reader tips: "We had several Po-Boy lunches at Glory B's, and enjoyed dinner at The Cottage." *(Beryl Williams)* "We enjoyed dinner at Maggie's Restaurant at the Cottage Plantation." *(Ian & Irene Fisher)* "Especially recommend a tour of the Catalpa Plantation." *(GLR)*

Also recommended: A working plantation, **Butler-Greenwood** (8345 U.S. Highway 61, 70775; 504–635–6312; www.butlergreenwood.com) was established in 1796, and offers accommodations in six restored dependencies. B&B double rates range from $100–110, and include a tour of the plantation house. "Beautiful setting among moss-draped live oaks. Owner Anne Butler is a local author and the eighth generation of her family to live here. We stayed in the Old Kitchen, which was comfortable and well-equipped, with a double Jacuzzi tub, and a continental breakfast waiting in the refrigerator." *(Ian & Irene Fisher)* "Our favorite cottages are the Gazebo and the Treehouse." *(Jerome Chauvin)* "The Treehouse overlooks a wooded ravine; we enjoyed having breakfast on the secluded deck."*(Glenn & Lynette Roehrig)*

Barrow House ¢
9779 Royal Street, P.O. Box 700, 70775-0700

Tel: 504–635–4791
Fax: 504–635–4769
E-mail: staff@topteninn.com
URL: http://www.topteninn.com

Built in the saltbox style in 1809 with a Greek Revival wing added in the 1850s, Barrow House is listed on the National Register of Historic Places. Owned by Shirley Dittloff since 1985, it is furnished in 1860s antiques. Across the street is the equally historic Printer's Cottage, dating from the late 1700s; its gazebo has a view of the Mississippi. Other cottage highlights include the 21 original 1840s Audubon bird prints in the sun room, and a growing collection of teddy bears. Dinners are served at 7 P.M. by advance reservation, and include an appetizer (chef's choice), shrimp salad with two sauces, and a choice of chicken stuffed with crawfish and vegetables, shrimp with mustard cream, filet mignon, or rack of lamb with Creole mustard glaze, plus dessert and coffee.

"Our charming room was furnished with antiques; the bathroom was spotless. The common areas are also decorated with lovely antiques. Shirley is delightful, personable, and knowledgeable about the area, including historic spots and wonderful restaurants. Her breakfasts are extraordinary, and she even arranged a special plantation tour for us." *(J. Scott Grisby)* "Our energetic hostess served a variety of breakfasts during our stay: quiche, muffins, and bread pudding with maple syrup, plus eggs with Hollandaise, cheese grits, and sweet potatoes; our rooms were made up while we were at breakfast. Shirley is an imaginative cook, and we enjoyed a dinner of crawfish in phyllo, salad, chicken with crawfish and tarragon, and ice cream with praline sauce. The Printer's Cottage is exquisitely furnished and private; breakfast is served at the cottage rather than in the main house. We enjoyed strolling past the well-preserved buildings in the historic district." *(Alex, Beryl & Jonathan Williams)*

"We relaxed with a glass of wine on the screened porch to the sound of the splashing fountain. Take a long walk before breakfast the next morning if you're planning to feast on Shirley's full breakfast—poached eggs with beans and rice or grits, accompanied by spicy sausage." *(SWS)* "Everything is provided, from sherry on an antique table, snacks in the refrigerator, and toiletries in the bathroom. Located on a lovely, safe, quiet street of beautiful historic homes." *(Jerome Klinkowitz)* "You can see where a Union cannonball entered and exited the roof of the

Printer's Cottage." *(Cindy & Bob Cameron)* "Close to numerous local attractions and an easy, scenic drive north to historic Natchez." *(Ellis Locher)* "Our lovely suite in the Printer's Cottage had a great bathroom with a full range of toiletries from shampoo to bubble bath. Delicious breakfast. Shirley was very informative, and helped us plan our visit and choose restaurants."*(Dianne Crawford)*

Open All year. Closed Dec. 22–25.

Rooms 3 suites, 5 doubles—all with private bath and/or shower, TV, air-conditioning. 4 with desk, 2 with kitchen. 2 suites, 2 doubles at Printer's Cottage.

Facilities Dining room, living room, screened porch, sunroom. 1 acre with gazebo, camellia collection. Golf nearby.

Location In town, behind the courthouse.

Restrictions "Well-behaved children welcome." Porch conversation can be heard in downstairs guest room.

Credit cards MC, Visa.

Rates B&B, $130–150 suite, $85–105 double, $80 single. Extra person, $25. Full breakfast, $5 extra. Prix fixe dinner, $25–30, with 24 hrs. advance notice.

Extras Port-a-crib.

Can't Find It Here?

Our regional guides include *two to three times* the number of entries contained here. Pick up a copy of our *New England* (plus Eastern Canada), *Middle Atlantic, South, Midwest* (plus Ontario), *Rocky Mountains & Southwest*, or *West Coast* (plus Western Canada) edition for lots more information on great places to stay. If your bookstore doesn't have a current copy in stock, ask them to order it for you or call 800–288–2131. You can also order copies from our Website at http://www.inns.com.

Maine

Captain Swift Inn, Camden

Coastal Maine has long been one of the foremost tourist areas in the Northeast, with its striking rock cliffs and innumerable coves and sheltered inlets. The coastline is so curving, in fact, that it supposedly twists through 3,000 miles to cover a distance of 240 miles as the crow flies. Inland Maine brings other, quieter pleasures of wooded mountains and peaceful lakes. The Lakes Region, about 100 miles northwest of Portland in the White Mountains along the New Hampshire border, combines relatively easy accessibility with inviting small towns and villages. North of Route 2, the (human) population density diminishes rapidly, with the exception of winter visitors tackling the challenging ski slopes at Sugarloaf, or those making the pilgrimage to the northern terminus of the Appalachian Trail. If getting away from the crowds is your preference, amble up Route 1 north of Ellsworth to discover relatively undeveloped, untouristy Maine. Here you can explore roads leading south from Machias to Roque Bluff State Park, and take Route 191 through sleepy Cutler and on to the fishing village of Lubec. From here cross over to Campobello Island (Canada) to visit picture-postcard villages and FDR's famous "summer cottage." For the more adventurous, head north to explore remote Aroostook County's virgin lakes as well as Baxter State Park's imposing Mt. Katahdin, then try out your college French in border towns such as Fort Kent and Van Buren.

By the way, if you've ever wondered why the natives refer to going "Down East" when the rest of the world thinks of it as "up north," we're glad to report that it dates to sailing days, when the prevailing coastal winds out of the southwest made the trip from Boston to Bar Harbor an easy trip *east*, going *down* wind.

Peak season in Maine runs from mid-June to mid-October, and rates are significantly higher during these months. Two-night to three-night minimum stays on weekends and holidays are the rule. Many coastal inns are open only from May through October, although a few stay in operation year-round. If you can get away in September, the chances are you'll have great weather and fewer crowds. Rates at most coastal inns are lower in May, June, September, and October, and are lowest during the winter months.

Reader tips: "I toured the coast from Camden to Blue Hill to Deer Isle in early November. Although the foliage season was over, Maine's beauty was still breathtaking, with views of tall green evergreens silhouetted against the deep blue sky, and the sun sparkling on the water. The complete lack of crowds and traffic more than compensated for the fact that some inns, shops, and restaurants were closed." *(SWS)* "The black flies can attack with a vengeance in June; if possible, visit during another month, but bring bug repellent for any warm weather visit."

BAR HARBOR

Bar Harbor is Mt. Desert Island's main town. It's where you'll find most of the island's shops and restaurants; in season (mid-May to mid-October), it's the center for a wide variety of shows, lectures, festivals, and theater. From the center of town, it's a short drive to the Bluenose Ferry to Nova Scotia, and to Acadia National Park. The Bangor Airport is 45 miles to the northwest, and Boston is about a 5-hour drive.

Bar Harbor's popularity dates to the turn of the last century, when millionaires from John D Rockefeller to J. P. Morgan built "cottages" for the brief summer season. Unfortunately, many of these mansions were destroyed in a devastating fire in 1947. Most of the island is occupied by Acadia National Park, a Rockefeller legacy of breathtaking beauty. From the top of Cadillac Mountain, to the road along the shore, you'll find extraordinary vistas at every turn. The park is honeycombed with innumerable trails for hiking and wide carriage paths for jogging, strolling, horseback riding, bicycling, and cross-country skiing. Unfortunately, it's hardly a secret: Acadia is the second-most-visited national park, after the Smokies. August is the busiest month; if you can visit the area in June, or better yet, in September, you'll avoid most of the crowds and still have good weather. Aside from the park, area activities include golf, tennis, swimming, as well as whale-watching and kayaking.

Reader tips: "Especially recommended is eating at one of the lobster pounds on the island. You pick out a lobster and it is cooked right in front of you. You then proceed with your plate out to picnic tables on the pier, piled high with lobster traps, and surrounded by lobster boats. A real New England experience. We also suggest getting up very early to see the sunrise at the top of Cadillac Mountain—they say it's the first place in the U.S. from which to view the dawn—and returning at night with a bottle of wine and a hunk of cheese to enjoy the sunset." *(SP)* "Parking is a problem in season; we were glad our inn was within walking distance of shops and restaurants." *(EHM)*

Rates are highest from mid-June to mid-October; off-season rates are typically $50–100 less (reflected in the lower number in our range of rates). Many of Bar Harbor's inns have a two-night minimum stay throughout the summer and early fall; a one- or two-night deposit is typically required to confirm your reservation. Some inns also require full payment for the *entire* stay at check-in.

Also recommended: A good resort alternative is the **Bar Harbor Inn** (Newport Drive, P.O. Box 7, 04609; 207–288–3351 or 800–248–3351; www.blackfriar.com), "a sprawling seven-acre complex on a scenic point just east of town. Rooms are found in the original building, the oceanfront lodge, and the motel. Best of all is the harbor view of ships and boats coming and going." *(Duane Roller)* "Good food and service; generous continental breakfast buffet. Superb views from our ocean lodge room. Great location, close to shops and restaurants." *(Carol & Gil Abernathy)* A total of 130 units are available, with rates ranging from $69–265, depending on view, room size, and season.

The **Black Friar Inn** (10 Summer Street, 04609; 207–288–5091; www.blackfriar.com) is a three-story house built in 1910, set back a short block from one of Bar Harbor's main streets. Restored with all new plumbing and wiring, the inn combines the best of old and new, and is owned by Perry and Sharon Risley. Rates for the seven cozy guest rooms (all with queen- or king-size bed and private bath) are $95–150 double, and include a full breakfast, late afternoon refreshments, and rainy day teas. Guests are uniformly delighted with the food, hospitality, attention to detail, and location.

An excellent choice for both budget travelers and families with school-age children is the **Coach Stop Inn** (Route 3, Bar Harbor Road, P.O. Box 266, 04609; 207–288–9886; www.maineguide.com/bar harbor/coachstop), built in 1804 as a stagecoach stop and tavern. Hand-hewn ceiling beams and wide-board pine floors are complemented by antique and country furnishings, antique coach prints, and Waverly and Schumacher fabrics and wallpapers. The very reasonable rates of $49–99 ($129 for the suite) include a full breakfast and afternoon refreshments; each of the five guest rooms has a private bath.

Breakfast is served from 8 to 9:00 A.M. at individual tables, and includes fresh fruit and juice, cereal, home-baked goods, breakfast meat, plus such daily specials as Colonial bread pudding with warm maple syrup, vegetable frittata, blueberry corn pancakes, or stuffed French toast with sauteed apples. Rates also include afternoon iced tea or apple cider, and wine and a tempting snack.

"Kathy Combs welcomed us warmly and showed us around the inn, explaining about breakfast, afternoon refreshments, local restaurants, special activities, and what to do in Acadia National Park. She did this all with such charm that we felt right at home. Kathy's breakfasts were as delightful as the company. While enjoying the delicious meal, we shared travel stories with the other guests. After a day of exploring, we always made sure to be back around 5:00 P.M. to enjoy the wine and hors d'oeuvres, served in an inviting room with a fire crackling in the fireplace. After browsing through the binder with the menus of local restaurants, we sometimes ended up going out for dinner with other guests. Our room was beautifully decorated—comfortable, clean, and quiet. The inn is perfectly located for exploring Acadia." (*Maaike van Es-Oosting*)

Open Mid-May–late Oct.
Rooms 2 suites, 3 doubles—all with full private bath and/or shower, clock, fan; 1 with TV, desk, fireplace. Some with private entrance, porch/patio.
Facilities Common room with fireplace, TV, stereo, books, guest refrigerator. 3 acres with apple trees, gardens, arbors, outdoor seating. 2 m to Acadia National Park.
Location 5 m from downtown Bar Harbor. From Ellsworth, take Rte. 3 to Bar harbor. At Thompson Island Drive bear left. Inn is on left, 4 m from bridge. From Nova Scotia ferry, make right onto Rte. 3. Inn is on right approx. 5 m from ferry.
Restrictions No smoking. Children 6 and over.
Credit cards Amex, Discover, MC, Visa.
Rates B&B, $75–129 suite, $49–99 double, $44–94 single. Children free in parents' room.

For additional area listings, see **Southwest Harbor**.

The Inn at Canoe Point　　　　　　　　　*Tel:* 207–288–9511
P.O. Box 216, 04609　　　　　　　　　　　　*Fax:* 207–288–2870
　　　　　　　　　　　　E-mail: canoe.point@juno.com
　　　　　　　　　URL: http://www.innatcanoepoint.com

Nancy and Tom Cervelli, who bought the Inn at Canoe Point in 1996, previously owned the Kingsleigh in Southwest Harbor (see listing) for six years. The Cervellis note that "you will never realize that busy Bar Harbor is just two miles away. Lounge on the decks, read in the Ocean Room, walk among the trees, or sit on the rocks and watch the boats sail by." Breakfast is served from 8–9 A.M., and includes fruit juices, muffins or coffee cake, fresh fruit or maybe apple crisp, and a daily special—perhaps eggs Benedict and home fries, blueberry pancakes, or spinach-mushroom quiche. Afternoon refreshments include cheese and crackers, cookies and brownies, and perhaps iced tea and lemonade, or hot cider and cocoa.

"To have a good time, a guest need do no more than sit in the living room or on the deck and stare at the ocean. But Nancy and Tom aren't content to let it go at that. They have made, and are continuing to make, improvements to the inn's facilities. And their style of personal service makes this special location even more so. The Garden Room is a lovely small room with a great water view; everything was in excellent condition and beautifully maintained. Breakfasts are imaginative and delicious. As long as the Cervellis own this inn, we can't imagine staying anywhere else in Bar Harbor." (JF)

"At first, all you see of the inn is a tasteful sign on a road and the beginning of an inviting little lane. Turning in, you come to the inn at the end of the road, a 1889 Tudor cottage set in the pines and rocks just above the water." *(Mrs. James Todd)* "Perfect location—five minutes from Bar Harbor and seconds from the national park." *(Yvonne Stoner)* "All the rooms are comfortable and beautifully appointed. The Master Suite has a fireplace and a private deck; the Garrett Suite has the wonderful sunrise view. Little touches include coffee on the upstairs landing at 7 A.M.; Nancy's lemon French toast at breakfast; tea on the deck in the afternoon or in front of a roaring fire in winter. It's so pristine and quiet, we felt like we were miles from civilization." *(Denise Dixon)*

"Tom and Nancy love sharing their favorite restaurants, hiking trails, and bicycling routes. Humor is always abundant, and guests love to socialize." *(Doug & Marylou Benzel Jr.)* "We walked along the beach, and read books on the deck." *(Edward Rogers)* "Our room's lighting was excellent, with a small Tiffany-style lamp to keep on as a nightlight. Breakfast and snacks are served in the Ocean Room, which has a large fireplace, a spectacular view, and pleasant background music. We enjoyed countless cups of hot cider in front of a blazing fire as the rain came down outside. Tom mapped out a perfect tour of Acadia for us." *(Stephanie Roberts)* "While located just off the main highway leading into Bar Harbor, the inn is secluded from the road by its lower elevation and setting among tall trees. The property is situated on the water and is within easy walking distance of the main entrance to Acadia National Park. Excellent and creative breakfasts are served on the outdoor deck, weather permitting." *(Ellis Locher)*

Worth noting: This inn is deservedly popular. Book well ahead in season to avoid disappointment.

Open All year.

Rooms 2 suites, 3 doubles—all with private shower and/or bath, radio/clock, fan. 3 with desk. 2 with fireplace, deck, private entrance.

Facilities Breakfast room with fireplace, living room with fireplace, piano, ocean room with fireplace, library, deck. Guest refrigerator. 2 acres on waterfront.

Location 2 m from Bar Harbor, 1 m from Nova Scotia Ferry. From Ellsworth, take Rte. 3 approx. 15 m toward Bar Harbor. Just beyond the village of Hulls Cove, watch for entrance to Acadia National Park on right. ¼ m past entrance, watch for inn driveway on left.

Restrictions No smoking. Children 16 and over.

Credit cards Discover, MC, Visa.

Rates B&B, $120–245 suite, $80–175 double.

Extras Airport pickup.

BLUE HILL

Blue Hill is an old shipping town on the east coast of the Penobscot peninsula, bordering magnificent Blue Hill Bay, on the other side of which is Acadia National Park. It's 40 miles south of Bangor and an easy drive to Bar Harbor, Camden, and Rockport. Blue Hill is popular with hikers, bikers, and sailors in warm weather, and cross-country skiers and ice skaters in cold. Summertime brings first-rate concerts to Kneisel

Hall. For those interested in seeing classic old boats and newly constructed ones, the Wooden Boat Museum is 10 miles to the south in Brooklin. Blue Hill is located 40 miles south of Bangor, and 150 miles north of Portland; it's 40 minutes from Acadia National Park.

Also recommended: The **Eggemoggin Reach B&B** (Herrick Road, RR1, P.O. Box 33A, Brooksville, 04617; 207–359–5073 or 888–625–8866; www.eggreachbb.com) is located right on Penobscot Bay, about 10 minutes south of Blue Hill. A post and beam home recently built in the old Maine farmhouse tradition, this B&B is comfortably furnished with antiques and pine-paneled walls. B&B double rates for the ten studio guest rooms (all facing the bay) range from $150–175. "Unparalleled scenery, delicious breakfast served on the porch with unbelievable water views." *(Anne Marie Clark, also SWS)* Offering lovely water views, the **Inn at Ferry Landing** (108 Old Ferry Road, RR 1, P.O. Box 163, Deer Isle, 04627; 207–348–7760) was purchased in 1996 by Jean and Gerald Wheeler. Before the suspension bridge to the mainland was built, this 1840s farmhouse served as the general store and docking facility for the ferry. B&B double rates for the four guest rooms (each with private bath) range from $85–140, including such breakfasts as buttermilk currant scones with calico eggs or Belgian waffles with fresh berries; also available is a charming two-bedroom attached cottage.

For convivial country inn atmosphere and a waterside location, visit the 200-year-old **Pilgrim's Inn** (Deer Isle, 04627; 207–348–6615; www.pilgrimsinn.com). Readers are delighted with its longtime owners, Jean and Dud Hendrick, its rooms, and especially the food. All rave about the delicious hors d'oeuvres, fresh fruits and vegetables, original recipes, attractive presentation, and good service (dinner nightly at seven). Breakfasts (served from 8 to 9 A.M.) come in for similar plaudits, especially the homemade granola and fresh Maine blueberries. Also mentioned by many are the guests themselves: "The inn attracts well-spoken and well-read visitors from all over the U.S. and Canada." *(Langevin Cote)*

The Blue Hill Inn ✕ ♿   *Tel:* 207–374–2844
Union Street, Route 177, P.O. Box 403, 04614   800–826–7415
                                         Fax: 207–374–2829
                  E-mail: bluhilin@downeast.net
                URL: http://www.bluehillinn.com

A brick and clapboard building, the Blue Hill Inn has operated as a village inn since 1840, and has been owned by Don and Mary Hartley since 1987. A consistent reader favorite, guests are delighted with the inn's welcoming atmosphere, warm hospitality, and delicious food. The five-course dinner menu features local meats, fish, and produce. Recent entrees included striped bass with zucchini and porcini mushrooms; pork tenderloin with rosemary and Calvados; or lobster with tomatoes, garlic, and white wine. Breakfasts are no less tasty, with fresh fruit and juice, breads and scones, and a choice of such entrees as feta cheese and tomato omelets, homemade granola with yogurt, waffles with strawberries, almond raisin French toast, and blueberry pancakes. Equal attention is paid to the guest rooms. Beds are turned down nightly, with clean towels provided. Linens are changed daily, with flannel sheets in winter, and cotton ones in summer. Fresh-brewed coffee, tea, and soda are available throughout the day. Completed in 1997 is the wheelchair-accessible Cape House suite, with cathedral ceiling, king-size bed, living area, kitchen, brick fireplace, deck, and private entrance.

"Impeccable service; it seemed that every time we returned to our room, the towels and bedding had been refreshed, and fireplace logs replaced as needed. Superb cuisine at both breakfast and dinner." *(Ron & Andrea Winson)* "Genuinely caring and hospitable innkeepers, who are always working to improve their inn. My spacious, well-equipped, easy-to-access room was right by the front door, with wood laid in the fireplace, ready to light, ample storage space in the closet and dresser, good-sized bathroom, comfortable queen-size bed, desk with a lamp, and two comfortable reading chairs with another lamp. Ample space in the parlors for relaxing and visiting with the other guests." *(SWS)* "We rarely return to an inn, preferring to try new ones, but we always come back to the Blue Hill Inn. The towels are so soft, the rooms immaculate, and the Hartleys so accommodating. My special dietary meals were met with delicious results. Beautiful area for walking." *(Terry Gray)* "The aromas of sumptuous dinners and tasty breakfasts, the soft sounds of classical music, and the comfort of a well-appointed room made the Blue Hill Inn the highlight of our trip. Elegance, class, warmth, and service." *(Donna Bradley)* "An excellent inn, professionally run. We especially enjoyed the cocktail hour and socializing with our fellow guests. Mary mapped out a lovely after-dinner stroll. One night was not enough." *(Ruthie & Derek Tilsley)*

"Competent and friendly staff who make guests feel welcome from the moment they arrive until the day they reluctantly depart." *(Ann Westbrook)* "Blue Hill is small, but lively in a relaxed way, with a number of good restaurants." *(MM)* "Lovely garden, ample and convenient parking. Information and assistance on area sights, shops, and events was readily available." *(Mary Wagner)* "At 6 P.M. guests gather in the sitting room to have cocktails in front of the fire (or in the garden in summer). The warm and friendly atmosphere soon makes it seem like a country house party of old friends. Though there are tables for two and four, the most fun is dining at the table for eight." *(JB)* "All galleries and shops are within an easy walk." *(Arthur Avent)*

Open Mid-May–Nov. 30.
Rooms 3 suites, 9 doubles—all with private bath and/or shower, desk, fan. 4 with fireplace, 2 with air-conditioning, 1 with kitchen, TV, telephone.
Facilities Restaurant, parlor with fireplace, games, library. Chamber music in July. 1 acre with perennial gardens. Concert tickets, day sails, kayaking arranged. Bike rentals by advance notice.
Location Historic district, 1 block from center. Near village intersection of Rte. 15 and Rte. 177.
Restrictions No smoking. Not recommended for children under 13.
Credit cards MC, Visa.
Rates B&B, $90–200 suite or double, $80–160 single. MAP, $140–240 suite, double; $110–180 single. Extra person, $20–50. 15% service. 2-night minimum July

1–Oct. 15. Holiday, wine tasting, sailing packages. Corporate rates off-season. Prix fixe dinner $30. Box lunch by arrangement.

Extras Airport/station pickups. Limited wheelchair access.

BOOTHBAY HARBOR

Like many Maine coastal towns, Boothbay's original reputation as a shipping port made the transition to one as a tourist center at the turn of the century. Visitors endure the inevitable T-shirt and fudge shops, and enjoy boating excursions to nearby islands, deep-sea fishing, and the Marine Aquarium on McKown's Point.

Boothbay Harbor is located in midcoastal Maine, 30 miles north of Brunswick, and 60 miles north of Portland. Also noted here are inns in **East Boothbay** and **Capitol Island**, both on the water.

Also recommended: For a taste of old Maine, adventurous readers will seek out the **Albonegan Inn** (Capitol Island, 04538; 207–633–2521), set on a private island four miles south of Boothbay Harbor. Described as "determinedly old-fashioned," 11 of the inn's 15 guest rooms have shared baths (with a sink in each room), and double rates of $75–125 include a continental breakfast served in the dining room, with ocean views on three sides. "The location is incredible—sounds of the surf and a distant fog horn, the smell of salt water and delicious homebaked breads and muffins, the pleasures of rocking chairs on the porch combine in a sensual delight. Rooms are small but adequate, with either double or twin-size beds and limited storage space." *(Ilene Wolfman)*

Another fine choice is the **Hodgdon Island Inn** (Barter's Island Road, P.O. Box 492, 04571; 207–633–7474), set on a quiet cove just 3½ miles from Boothbay Harbor. A sea captain's home dating back to the late 1700s, the inn offers six guest rooms, each with a new private bath and water views, and a heated swimming pool. B&B rates range from $65–105. "Our lovely, spacious room had a king-size bed and bay windows looking out on the water." *(Bill Hussey)*

Six miles south of Boothbay Harbor is the **Newagen Seaside Inn** (Route 27 South, Southport Island, Cape Newagen, 04552; 207–633–5242 or 800–654–5242), bordered on three sides by the ocean. "A wonderful, old-fashioned resort located at the tip of a peninsula, offering both salt- and freshwater swimming pools, and tennis courts. You can walk around the rocky shore, watch ospreys fly in and out of their nests, or (our favorite occupation) sit on the large deck, read a book, look out at the water, and daydream." *(Suzanne Carmichael)* B&B double rates are $100–175.

Twenty minutes north of Boothbay is the **Newcastle Inn** (River Road, RR2, P.O. Box 24, Newcastle, 04553; 207–563–5685 or 800–832–8669; www.newcastleinn.com). The inn's large deck overlooks the Damariscotta River, and serves as an outdoor dining area for breakfast, evening hors d'oeuvres, and beverages. B&B double rates range from $95–200, including a full breakfast and afternoon hors d'oeuvres. Three- and five-course dinners are served Tuesday–Sunday in season (weekends off-season), and might include mussels in saffron cream, salad, peppered beef filet with mushrooms, and an apricot almond tart ($30–45). Many guest rooms have canopy or four-poster beds; the suites have a king-size double Jacuzzi, and fireplace.

Substantially renovated under the supervision of managing partner Angelo DiGiulian is the **Spruce Point Inn** (P.O. Box 237, 04538; 207–633–4152 or 800–553–0289; www.sprucepointinn.com), located on the water, about two miles from town. Open from late May to mid-October, this famous old coastal resort has been updated and spruced up in recent years, and readers have checked in with glowing reports. Summer rates include breakfast and dinner, as well as use of the tennis courts, heated swimming pools, boat cruises, town shuttle, lawn games, and more, and range from $265–535 for two, plus 15% service. Spring and fall rates do not include meals, and range from $110–$395. Renovations to be completed in 1998 include additional deluxe ocean-front rooms in the Balsam and Sea Breeze Lodges, renovated family cottages, an outdoor dining pavilion, plus a heated freshwater outdoor swimming pool, spa, fitness center, and children's playground. "Our immaculate, peaceful suite in Evergreen Lodge—built in 1997—had a king-size bed, air-conditioning, a spacious well-lit bathroom with a whirlpool soaking tub and oversized shower, and a sitting area with woodstove and big-screen TV. We thoroughly enjoyed the rockers on our deck, overlooking the grounds and the bay. Dinners were delicious, and the breakfast buffet was more than ample, with a delicious egg souffle each day. Despite its size, the inn felt small and personal." *(Pat Malone, also MW)* "Beautiful grounds, full of flowers in summer, with comfortable chairs to enjoy the spectacular harbor views. Wood was supplied daily for the huge rock fireplace in our rustic cabin, with two bedrooms, a living room, a tiny kitchen, and a porch. Quiet, uncrowded location." *(Betty Sadler)*

For an additional area entry, see listing for **The Squire Tarbox Inn** in **Wiscasset**.

Five Gables Inn
Murray Hill Road, P.O. Box 335,
East Boothbay, 04544

Tel: 207–633–4551
800–451–5048

Built circa 1890, the Five Gables sits on a hillside overlooking Linekin Bay. Originally a 22-room (three toilets!) summer hotel, it was extensively renovated in 1987. The fifteen guest rooms all face the bay, and are attractively furnished with reproductions, wicker, some antiques, and country touches. Most rooms have queen-size beds; one has a king-size bed, and one has twin beds that can also be made up as a king.

De and Mike Kennedy purchased the inn in 1995; the Kennedys are world travelers, and have worked everywhere from Europe to Montana to Tahiti. Mike is a graduate of the Culinary Institute of America and also spent ten years renovating Victorian homes in Atlanta. Early morning coffee is available, and breakfast is enjoyed at individual tables between 8–9:30 A.M. A typical morning meal might include puffed apple cinnamon baked pancakes with cider syrup, grilled tomatoes with herbed cornmeal, grilled ham, English breakfast scones, fresh baked whole wheat bread, fresh minted fruit, homemade granola, Birchermuesli, cereal, yogurt, and orange juice.

"The Kennedys are working hard to make a lovely inn even more so." *(SWS)* "De and Mike are friendly and knowledgeable about local activities. Spotlessly clean, beautifully decorated, relaxed, and unrushed. Fantastic food at breakfast, afternoon tea, and evening refreshments." *(Nancy Cowell)* "Peaceful and relaxing atmosphere; wonderful bay views." *(Anne Kollian)* "Afternoon tea and cookies were served in the comfortable common room before a roaring fire or on the porch." *(Mrs. Arthur Wahlstedt)* "Friendly atmosphere, excellent variety at each delicious breakfast. Tempting aromas of freshly baked bread and cookies." *(Ruth Birch)* "Relaxed atmosphere, well-managed inn. Our hosts provided us with excellent area information." *(S.E. Chantler)* "Baskets of fresh flowers everywhere. Our days began with breakfast in the common room by a crackling fireplace, friendly conversation, and a view of Linekin Bay." *(Linda Morin)* "Heirloom patchwork quilts, towels scented with fresh lavender, and natural soaps in the bath. Delicious fresh fruit and yogurt with muesli for breakfast." *(Sonia & Stan Nowak, also Barbara Walsh)*

"The shaded porch and the hammock overlooking the quiet cove were wonderful places to relax with a book and afternoon lemonade while hummingbirds hovered around the fuchsia, and osprey soared overhead."*(John Price)* "Picturesque, quiet location, convenient to Boothbay." *(Mark & Linda Gale)* "Guest rooms on the upper floors offer more privacy than the first floor ones opening onto the porch, and vary in size from small to spacious." *(Pam Phillips)* "Usually the only sounds we heard were seagulls, an occasional boat, and the plaintive tolling of the bell buoys." *(Marsha & Bob McOsker)*

Open Mid-May through Oct.
Rooms 15 doubles—all with private bath and/or shower, telephone, clock/radio, fan. 5 with fireplace, 1 with desk.
Facilities Living/dining room with games, fireplace, stereo; library; wrap-around veranda. ½ acre. Boating, swimming, fishing across street. 1 acre with off-street parking. Overlooking Linekin Bay for swimming, boating, fishing; two boat moorings.
Location Take Rte. 1 to Rte. 27 S to Rte. 96 through East Boothbay. Turn right on Murray Hill Rd. The inn is ½ mile on right. 3.3 m to Boothbay Harbor.
Restrictions No smoking. Children over 8.
Credit cards MC, Visa.
Rates B&B, $95–165 double. Extra person, $30.
Extras Boat moorings by reservation.

CAMDEN

Camden is one of Maine's most popular summer coastal resorts. It's about halfway up the coast, between Portland and Bar Harbor—40 miles east of Augusta, 185 miles northeast of Boston, and 414 miles northeast of New York City; take I-95 to Route 1, and follow it into the town.

A large village by Maine standards, Camden offers lots of shops and restaurants to explore (don't expect to explore them alone in season). Summer activities include tennis, hiking, swimming, sailing, water-skiing, and picnicking. There are chamber music concerts and a resident theater. The Farnsworth Collection in nearby Rockport has a fine Andrew Wyeth collection. The harbor is filled with yachts and with the two-masted schooners of the windjammer fleet. In winter, there's ice-skating and cross-country and downhill skiing within five miles. The tops of the two mountains that rise over the town, Mt. Battie and Mt. Megunticook, offer beautiful views of Penobscot Bay.

Worth noting: Most of Camden's B&Bs are on Route 1, called Elm or High Street as it passes through town. *Traffic is often heavy, so ask for a room facing away from the street if you're a light sleeper.* Most innkeepers have taken steps to minimize noise by plantings, installing double-glazed windows, air-conditioners, and white noise machines; ask for details.

Also recommended: A Federal-style home built in 1810, the **Captain Swift Inn** (72 Elm Street, 04843; 207–236–8113 or 800–251–0865; www.midcoast.com/~swiftinn) has four guest rooms (all with private bath), at B&B double rates of $75–115. "Fully endorse entry. We stayed in a comfortable and spacious downstairs room. As in all our favorite inns, it is the innkeepers who make your stay. Tom and Kathy made us feel right at home, and joined us and the other guests at breakfast and for after-dinner chocolate cake." *(Cecile Desroches)*

A stately Queen Anne Victorian home built in 1894, the **Hawthorn Inn** (9 High Street, 04843; 207–236–8842; www.midcoast.com/~hawthorn) offers lovely views of the harbor and the Camden Hills from many of its ten guest rooms. A breakfast of fresh fruit, an egg dish, and freshly baked breads is included in the double rates of $95–195. "Warm, friendly hospitality; comfortable, homey atmosphere; immaculate accommodations; helpful owners." *(Pamela Johnson & Ed Hirst, also SWS)*

A Little Dream B&B (66 High Street, 04843; 207–236–8742) is a late 1800s house, decorated in "romantic country English Victorian style, combining antique furnishings and a light-hearted whimsical approach." Five lovely guest rooms are available, each with private bath; rates are $95–159 double.

The Inn at Sunrise Point (Fire Road #9, Lincolnville, P.O. Box 1344, Camden, 04843; 207–236–7716 or 800–43–LOBSTER; www.midcoast. com/~oceaninn) is a restored oceanfront estate, offering luxurious accommodations with unrestricted ocean views. There are three rooms in the main house and four cottages (all with fireplaces); double rates of $150–350 include a breakfast buffet and afternoon hors d'oeuvres.

Information please: If you love lighthouses, then make **The Elms** (84 Elm Street, 04843; 207–236–6250 or 800–755–3567; www.midcoast.com/~theelms/) your beacon. Built in 1806, this handsome Colonial home was purchased by Ted and Jo Panayotoff in 1994, who have named the six guest rooms (each with private bath and telephone) for New England lighthouses. B&B double rates of $75–105 include a full breakfast and afternoon refreshments. The Panayotoffs know all about the area lighthouses, and even offer delightful lunch cruises to many which can only be seen from the water.

Blue Harbor House ¢
67 Elm Street, Route 1, 04843

Tel: 207–236–3196
800–248–3196
Fax: 207–236–6523
E-mail; balidog@midcoast.com
URL: http://www.blueharborhouse.com

Warm and gracious hospitality is the cornerstone of the best B&Bs, and that's just what you'll find at the Blue Harbor House, owned by Jody Schmoll and Dennis Hayden since 1989. They extensively restored and renovated their inn, a traditional Cape home built in the early 1800s and added to many times over the years; the decor is highlighted by hand-stenciled walls and colorful handmade quilts, the comfortable king-, queen-, and twin-size beds have good reading lights and bedside tables. Dennis' popular dinners include a lobster feast with lobsters and steamers, garden tomatoes, corn on the cob, and chocolate chip cookies; other days the menu might be Vidalia onion soup, spinach salad with tarragon mustard vinaigrette, poached Maine salmon, and chocolate brownie souffle; or spicy tomato rice soup, salad with blueberry vinegar and goat cheese, grilled filet mignon, and blueberry pie. Breakfasts menus change daily, and are no less tempting: perhaps baked apples with vanilla ice cream and blueberry pancakes with blueberry butter; lobster quiche with Irish soda bread; or breakfast burritos and chocolate tacos.

"Three inviting common rooms for guests to enjoy. Stenciling, plants, fresh flowers, and pretty craft items round out the decor throughout the inn, along with plenty of reading material, menus, and other tourist information. When we returned to our rooms after our lobster dinner, besides Godiva chocolates, we found a split of port with a personal note from Jody and Dennis. Dennis provides each guest with an atlas, marked for great day trips. We started at the top of Mt. Battie for a breathtaking view of Camden harbor and the coast, then followed Dennis' directions to several lighthouses, fishing villages, and a small local place with great chowder." *(Rose Ciccone, also SWS)* "Gracious hospitality, relaxing atmosphere, walking distance to harbor and shops. Our four-poster canopy king-size bed had an excellent mattress and pillows; the whirlpool tub was a real treat." *(Henrietta Sparano)*

"Our tempting breakfast consisted of morning glory muffins and pancakes topped with blueberries, slivered almonds, warm fruit, powdered sugar, and maple syrup. Large, succulent lobster was the highlight of a delicious dinner." *(Ann Tigue)* "Jody and Dennis have scouted out interesting and out-of-the-way spots for guests to visit—whether by foot, bike, boat, or car. Impeccably clean." *(Mary W. Davis)* "Dennis' warmth made us feel like long-lost friends." *(Cheryl Feinberg)* "We were missing our own pets, and were happy to meet their well-behaved Labrador retriever, Bali, and Boots, the inn cat." *(MW)* "Immaculately clean, outstanding food, relaxing atmosphere, and personable innkeepers." *(Linda and Richard Wark)* "So delightful to be welcomed with home-made brownies and lemonade." *(Irene Jacobs)* "A wonderful treat for the business traveler." *(Kathleen Power)* "Relaxing, homey atmosphere; privacy respected." *(Diane Johnson)*

Open All year.
Rooms 2 suites, 8 doubles—all with private bath and/or shower, radio, telephone, hair dryer, robes, air-conditioning, fan. 7 with TV, 2 with refrigerator, kitchenette. 3 rooms in carriage house; 2 with whirlpool tub.
Facilities Dining room, living room, books, games, enclosed sun porch. Patio garden, lawn.
Location On Rte. 1, S of town.
Restrictions No smoking. Traffic noise masked by soundproofing.
Credit cards Amex, Discover, MC, Visa.
Rates B&B, $145 suite, $85–125 double. Extra person, $30. 2-night minimum holiday weekends. Prix fixe dinner (by reservation only), $35; beer, wine for purchase. 2-night package includes 1 dinner for two, $295–340.

The Maine Stay
22 High Street, 04843

Tel: 207–236–9636
Fax: 207–236–0621
E-mail: mainstay@midcoast.com
URL: http://www.mainestay.com

Peter Smith retired from a career in the navy to steer a ship of a different—but no less demanding—kind. In 1989, along with his wife, Donny, and her identical twin sister, Diana Robson, he purchased the Maine Stay, built in 1802. Peter notes that "from the bubble bath beside the clawfoot tubs to the thick terry cloth bathrobes, we have tried to anticipate guests' needs." An innkeeper's work is never done; Peter's most recent project involves creating an attic suite, building a breakfast conservatory, and restoring the barn to create an innkeepers' apartment.

Coffee is out at 6:30 A.M. for early risers, and breakfasts include egg dishes, waffles, French toast, or whole wheat pancakes with Maine blueberry syrup. In good weather, it's served on the deck overlooking the woods with Mt. Battie beyond. Most guest rooms have wide-board floors and are decorated with a mix of antiques and Oriental pieces.

"The Captain and the twins run the inn with great style and enthusiasm. They obviously care about their guests and have invested much time in suggesting walks, drives, and boat rides. The Captain's mapped itineraries include sights, events, routes, and suggested eateries. When we mentioned a hankering for a short sail, they knew the perfect small boat run by a happy and interesting couple, and arranged it all for us. We were pampered in so many ways. Never have I had such an excellent breakfast, with seconds sincerely offered. They give the word *host* added luster. Shops and restaurants are just an easy walk away." *(Ruthie Tilsley)*

"Wonderful antiques and quilts; friendly and comfortable. We love eating around the big dining room table, meeting new people, and sharing travel advice. After breakfast, Peter brings out his folders of information sheets on coastal Maine, filled with tourist information, maps, tips on out-of-the-way places, and driving distances. He takes time with his guests, showing them around the inn, giving a little his-

tory of the house." *(Pam Phillips)* "Occasional comments would remind this dynamic trio of a song and they would spontaneously break into a barber shop rendition." *(Joan & Arnold Kerzner)* "Peter drove us to the start of a trail in Camden State Park, which ends back at the inn where homemade lemonade and cookies awaited." *(Karin & Tom Frood)*

"The spacious sitting rooms provide ample room to accommodate all guests and their varying interests. Peter Smith is genuinely friendly and sincere; guests are drawn to him like a close friend; his wife and sister-in-law are equally pleasant." *(Julie Irmischer)* "Extremely handsome building, impeccably maintained. The kitchen is the heart of the house. Guest rooms have been done with great care for guest comfort, and are mercifully free of clutter. Lovely location, combining in town-convenience with woods and nature trails right behind the inn." *(SWS)* "Wonderful breakfast of granola with yogurt, fresh fruit, quiche, and homemade muffins made with raspberries fresh from the garden." *(Susan Goldblatt)* "Our comfortable room had a large, modern bathroom and was well lit and beautifully decorated. We enjoyed watching TV downstairs in the den. Delicious, plentiful breakfast of baked apples, waffles, and sausage. Diana thoughtfully provided a computer printout with a detailed route to our next destination." *(Stephanie Roberts)*

Note: Though both are highly recommended, this Maine Stay is not affiliated with the Maine Stay listed under Kennebunkport (see entry).

Open All year.
Rooms 1 suite, 10 doubles—all with private shower and/or bath, fan. 3 with fireplace/stove. 1 with patio.
Facilities 2 parlors with fireplace, dining room, conservatory, family room with TV/VCR, videotape library, deck. 2 acres with garden, benches. Walk to state park; drop-offs at state park trail heads.
Location 85 m N of Portland. 3 blocks from harbor/center.
Restrictions Traffic noise in front rooms. No smoking. Children 8 and over.
Credit cards Amex, MC, Visa.
Rates B&B, $125–160 suite, $95–125 double. Off-season rates.
Extras Free station/airport pickups.

FREEPORT

Once a depressed little Maine town, known only as the home of L.L. Bean, Freeport now feels like an outdoor mall, with a variety of newly built, "New England-style" gray clapboard shops housing every brand name known to American consumers (or so it seems), interspersed with little snack bars and restaurants to refuel weary shoppers. Don't expect great bargains during the peak shopping seasons of June to December, although the January sales might justify a detour. Bean's enormous store is still well worth a visit, although for bargains, go across the street and down a bit to their outlet store.

Freeport is close to Wolf's Neck State Park for fishing, boating, and swimming; in winter, cross-country skiing is nearby as well. The town is in midcoastal Maine, 16 miles north of Portland, 125 miles northeast of Boston, and 3 hours southwest of Bar Harbor.

Worth noting: Many of Freeport's B&Bs are located on Main Street. *Expect significant daytime traffic noise in any rooms at the front of a house, and be sure to inquire for details if you're a light sleeper.*

Reader tips: "Tear yourself away from the shops and visit Wolf's Neck State Park, a real jewel." *(SB)* "Although there's a fantastic range of shops to visit, there were few bargains, with the exception of the L.L. Bean Factory Outlet, which offered irregulars, overstocks, and off-season merchandise at sale prices. We also enjoyed Bean's Outdoor Discovery Program; we took a two-hour class in fly fishing, held at a farm they own." *(Susan Harper)* "For a pleasant change of pace, drive down to South Freeport and eat at the lobster pound overlooking the harbor." *(MW)*

Also recommended: A peaceful alternative 20 miles northeast of Freeport is the **Fairhaven Inn** (Route 2, P.O. Box 85, North Bath Road, Bath, 04530; 207–443–4391 or 888–443–4391; www.mainecoast.com/fairhaveninn) a few miles from the historic shipbuilding town of Bath, home of the Maine Maritime Museum. Built in 1790, the Fairhaven is a weathered shingled Colonial home with seven guest rooms in a quiet country setting; B&B double rates range from $80–120. Prior to purchasing the inn, owners Susie and Dave Reed owned a pastry shop in Washington, D.C., so the three-course breakfast is a special treat.

The Bagley House ¢ 👫 ♿   *Tel:* 207–865–6566
1290 Royalsborough Road   800–765–1772
Route 136, Durham, 04222   *Fax:* 207–353–5878
          URL: http://members.aol.com/bedandbrk/bagley

Dating back to 1772, The Bagley House is the oldest home in the hamlet of Durham, and has served as an inn, a schoolhouse, and a dairy farm; today its rooms are furnished with antiques, reproductions, and handmade quilts, highlighted with antique linens and china and glass collections. Purchased in 1993 by Susan Backhouse and Suzanne O'Connor, the "two Sues" describe their B&B as being ideal "for those who love peace and quiet and old homes." The kitchen, probably the oldest room in the house, is the guests' favorite. The huge free-standing fireplace has two cauldrons built into it, and a beehive bread oven. The floor has exceptionally wide pine boards, some of them "illegal," since it was against the law in Colonial days to have any board in your home wider than 23 inches; such trees automatically belonged to His Majesty, King George III, for his ships' masts. Those who like their history tempered by modern construction will enjoy a room in the adjacent carriage house, completed in 1998.

Early morning coffee is left in the upstairs hallway, and guests gather in the kitchen for a family-style breakfast at a time scheduled the night before. The meal starts with fresh fruit, juice, homemade granola and yogurt, and fresh-baked muffins. The entree might be an egg casserole, sourdough waffles with local blueberries, maple syrup, and bacon or sausage.

"Welcoming innkeepers, comfortable room, fascinating history to the house, quiet location. Fun breakfast in the wonderful kitchen, with the innkeepers right there, cooking and chatting. A nice change from

more formal inns—warm, friendly, and casual. I took a long walk on one of the country roads by there—the foliage was glorious " *(Pam Phillips)* "The two Sues know the area well and suggested great places to eat. Lots of repeat guests. The guest refrigerator is filled with fruit drinks and the bottomless cookie jar is always available." *(Mary Bauer)* "We were in a bright, cheery upstairs room, decorated in blue, with a wonderful flower-garden quilt on the bed, and some of Sue's penguin collection decorating the walls. Good bedside lighting, and individual heat controls. My favorite touch was the hot water bottle, tucked in a soft cover trimmed in lace, tucked in our bed while we were at dinner. Coffee was set out at 7:30 A.M., followed by breakfast in the kitchen. We had baked apples with granola and yogurt, an egg dish with homemade rhubarb chutney, English muffins, and scones." *(Suzanne Carmichael)*

"Ten minutes and two hundred years from the bustle of downtown Freeport—the perfect antidote to shoppers' stress. The two Sues have delightful senses of humor, and are doing a wonderful job at this historic home. Rooms are reasonably sized, old-fashioned, simple but comfortable; some love the rustic 'unfinished' barnlike room under the eaves, others will prefer the more traditional look of the other guest rooms. Delicious chocolate chip cookies and tea." *(SWS)* "Conversation with the two Sues was genuine and not forced." *(Tina Hom)* "I'm an animal lover, so Shasta Daisy, a shepherd/lab mix, made me a happy woman." *(Barbara Walsh)* "Sue and Sue make us feel like we were old friends . . . no small feat since we were traveling with a 15-month-old." *(Brooke Perin)* "Perfect location for visiting Bowdoin and Bates." *(MOR)* "Enjoyed the downstairs bedrooms with extra-large bathroom, spotlessly clean, great towels." *(Peggy Kontak)*

Open All year.

Rooms 1 suite, 7 doubles—all with private bath and/or shower, gas or wood-burning fireplace, fan. 3 rooms in carriage house.

Facilities Country kitchen with fireplace, living room with fireplace, library, conference room with wood-burning stove. 6 acres with woods, gardens, berry-picking, cross-country skiing.

Location 22 m N of Portland. 6 m N of Freeport. From I-95, take Exit 20 and go N on Rt. 136 6 m to inn.

Restrictions No smoking. "Children with well-behaved parents welcome." Early morning traffic noise in some rooms.

Credit cards Amex, Discover, MC, Visa.

Rates B&B, $135 suite, $80–125 double, $65–85 single. Extra person, $15.

Extras Wheelchair access; bathroom specially equipped.

White Cedar Inn ¢   *Tel:* 207–865–9099
178 Main Street, 04032   800–853–1269
                E-mail: CapandPhil@aol.com
     URL: http://www/members.aol.com/bedandbrk/cedar.

Arctic explorer Donald MacMillan left his 1880's Victorian home in 1909 to accompany Robert E. Peary as second in command on Peary's epic trip to the North Pole. (Maine winters must have seemed balmy by comparison.) Philip and Carla Kerber, who bought and restored the White Cedar Inn in 1987, report that "our unpretentious inn is uncluttered and clean, with a relaxing atmosphere; rooms are sunny and large."

"Ideally located on the main street, within easy walking distance of Freeport shopping. The Kerbers are charming and helpful, always available but never obtrusive; there is ample quiet and privacy." *(Dr. & Mrs. Arthur A. Mintz)* "I enjoyed sitting in a rocking chair by the potbellied stove, browsing through the albums showing the restoration of the inn. Books, newspapers, games, tourist literature, and restaurant menus are also provided. The guest rooms are color coordinated; if you stay in the blue room, you will have blue wallpaper, blue towels, and blue linens. All are bright, immaculate, and decorated in a modern country motif with a few antiques. Towels are big and thick and bed linens neat and crisp. Delectable breakfasts are served in a breakfast room with three tables seating four people each. Each is set with fresh flowers, place mats, and cloth napkins. There's a choice of juice and plenty of cinnamon-scented coffee. First a fresh muffin arrives on the blueberry stoneware dishes, followed by scrambled eggs with cheese, French toast, or perhaps blueberry pancakes, garnished with Canadian bacon, sausage, or bacon, fresh fruit, and an English muffin or bagel." *(Judith Singer)* "Phil served us juice, Carla's delicious home-baked coffee cake, pancakes, and fruit." *(Marilyn Parker)*

"Early American wallpapers, dried flower decorations, and live plants highlighted the decor. Phil is knowledgeable about the area, and suggested a wonderful trip along the coast for us." *(Jean & Craig Haley)* "The guest rooms have good lighting and comfortable beds with down comforters." *(Dianne Crawford)* "Cordial owners; rooms are well equipped, spotless, simply but comfortably furnished. Phil was most accommodating about preparing an early breakfast when we had to leave early for camp visiting day." *(Helen Stark, also SWS)*

Open All year.
Rooms 6 doubles—all with private shower and/or bath, desk, air-conditioning.
Facilities Dining room, sun porch, living room with games, TV, books, woodstove. ¾ acres with picnic table.
Location 2 blocks N of L.L.Bean.
Restrictions No smoking. No children under 10. Traffic noise possible in front rooms.
Credit cards Amex, Discover, MC, Visa.
Rates B&B, $70–130 double. Extra person, $15.

KENNEBUNK BEACH

The Ocean View *Tel: 207–967–2750*
171 Beach Avenue, 04043 *Fax: 207–967–5418*
E-mail: arena@theoceanview.com
URL: http://www.theoceanview.com

Carole and Bob Arena describe their inn as being "the closest you'll find to a bed on the beach in the Kennebunks. Our inn is casual but elegant, whimsical and colorful, light and airy—befitting its oceanfront setting." All of the bedrooms have hand-painted furniture, some have hand-painted bedspreads and bathroom tiles. The day begins in the sunny breakfast room, with a wall of windows looking out to the water, a charming floral decorating motif, and colorful Fiesta Ware–style china. Guests sit at individual tables, and a typical meal might include baked pears dressed with yogurt, honey, and slivered almonds, followed by yogurt-based Belgian waffles, garnished with seasonal fruits and crème fraiche, and baked honey ham. If staying in one of the suites, you can opt for breakfast in bed, or on your private balcony overlooking the ocean. Rates also include afternoon refreshments, in-room robes, and beach towels.

"Sparkling clean, inside and out; beautiful, bright flowers, too. The front porch is a delightful place to relax, enjoy a cup of coffee, and take in the view. Attention to detail is evident from the individual bottles of water in each guest room refrigerator, the custom-tailored bathrobes, and the wonderfully firm yet comfortable mattresses." (Patricia & James Cadira) "Our oceanfront room was light and airy, decorated in pastel greens, pink, and blue. The location is convenient for shopping, nature walks, biking, and water sports." (Susan Soviero, also Tom Wilbanks) "We slept to the sound of the ocean every night." (Donna Ciezki) "Carole and Bob make guests feel truly welcome yet are never intrusive. The immaculate rooms are furnished in a contemporary and breezy style, with nice touches—two pinpoint reading lights over the bed (a must for avid readers), plenty of closet space, towels for the beach." (Margot Anne Kelley) "We particularly appreciated Carole's helpful recommendations and reservations for theater and dinner." (Suzanne Scutt)

"Cool ocean breezes on the hottest night. An early-morning walk along the beach tunes you up for breakfast." (Roy & Ruth Baltozer) "Only a local two-lane road and a sea wall separates this B&B from the ocean, and a sandy beach is within a short walk. This residential area is about a mile from Kennebunkport's shopping district, giving you easy access to all the sights without the crowds and traffic." (Mary Welch) "The breakfast room is a gem—soft ocean breezes waft through as you eat her marvelous breakfast served on beautifully coordinated china in soft pastel colors." (Susan Tevens) "Room #1, on the third floor, has a Palladian window giving a wonderful view of the ocean, which is echoed in the blues of the decor. You can lie in bed and pretend that you're on a cruise ship. For breakfast we had a huge goblet of fresh-squeezed orange juice and wonderful waffles—crisp yet moist—with fresh strawberries." (SWS)

Open April through Dec.

Rooms 5 suites, 4 doubles—all with private bath, telephone, CD player, ceiling fan, minirefrigerator. Some with TV, wet bar, porch/deck.

Facilities Breakfast room, living room with fireplace, TV room with books, front porch, gift shop, off-street parking. Concierge services. Ocean frontage, short walk to beach. Beach towels. Golf nearby.

Location SE ME, 85 m NE of Boston, 30 m SW of Portland. 1 m from Kennebunkport village. Off exit 3 of ME Turnpike onto Rte. 35. Straight to Beach Ave. #171.

Restrictions No smoking. Children 12 and over.
Credit cards Amex, Discover, MC, Visa
Rates B&B, $120–250 suite, $100–180 double. Extra person, $25.
Extras Airport/station pickups. French spoken.

KENNEBUNKPORT

Kennebunkport is one of Maine's most popular resort towns, located along the coast in the southwest corner of the state. It has many sea captains' homes from the seventeenth and eighteenth centuries, as well as "cottages" built later by wealthy summer visitors. In addition to many fine gift and antique shops, art galleries, and restaurants, sights of interest include the Seashore Trolley Museum, the Brick Store Museum, and the Rachel Carson Wildlife Refuge. Visitors head to the beach for swimming, fishing, and boating; there are plenty of tennis courts in the area, and golf at the Cape Arundel course (also available for cross-country skiing in winter). Bicyclists can bring bikes along or rent them on arrival. Other activities include antiquing, golf, and whale-watching.

Kennebunkport is 264 miles northeast of New York City, 75 miles northeast of Boston, and 30 miles south of Portland. From I-95 (Maine Turnpike), take Exit 3 to Kennebunk, and turn south (left) on Route 35 into Kennebunkport.

Reader tips: "Beach passes are a necessity; most inns provide them, but ask just to be sure when booking." *(LR)* "Kennebunkport was charming and not at all as crowded or commercial as we'd expected." *(RB)* "We visited during a heat wave, and our inn, like most in town, had no air-conditioning."

Also recommended: Readers can't stop raving about the blissful waterside location of **Bufflehead Cove** (Gornitz Lane, P.O. Box 499, 04046; 207–967–3879; www.buffleheadcove.com) and the gracious hospitality of longtime owners Harriet and Jim Gott. The guest room decor includes brass beds, wicker love seats, hand-painted and stenciled walls, and folk art; the Balcony Room and the River Room have the best water views, but even the smallest room is comfortable and appealing. "Most rooms have views of the picturesque Kennebunk River and its abundant wildlife. Breakfast includes fresh-squeezed juices, fruit, home-baked breads with homemade jam, a satisfying hot dish—perhaps puff pastry filled with scrambled eggs and cheese—and delicious coffee." *(Miriam Shark & Frank Harris, also SWS)* B&B double rates for the six rooms range from $115–290.

For an intimate, luxurious, romantic getaway, you can't make a better choice than the **Captain's Hideaway** (12 Pleasant Street, P.O. Box 2746, 04046; 207–967–5711; www.gndesigns.com/hideaway), a Federal-style home built in 1808. The two exquisitely decorated guest rooms have all possible luxuries and amenities—from double whirlpool tubs to fireplaces to TV/VCR/CD players—and owners Judith Hughes-Boulet and Susan Jackson leave no pillow unfluffed to ensure their guests' satisfaction. B&B double rates range from $179–279, and include a full breakfast, plus always available hot and cold beverages, fresh fruit, and sweets.

The 1802 House (15 Locke Street, P.O. Box 646-A, 04046; 207–967–5632 or 800–932–5632; URL, www.1802inn.com) offers six gracious guest rooms, each with a fireplace and/or whirlpool tub, plus CD players and TV/VCR, decorated with period decor. B&B double rates range from $119–299. "Gracious innkeepers, charming decor, peaceful yet convenient location." *(Kathy Banak)* "Enjoyed the luxuriously romantic Sebago Suite, and watching the many birds at their feeders. Tasty breakfast of served baked apples, lemon ricotta pancakes, bacon, cranberry muffins. Genuine hospitality." *(Carol Dinmore)* A rambling shingled home, **The Inn at Harbor Head** (41 Pier Road, Cape Porpoise, 04046; 207–967–5564) overlooks Cape Porpoise harbor. The charming decor of antiques, fine art, and old Oriental carpets are complemented by hand-painted murals and stenciling. A typical breakfast includes apple brown betty, and eggs scrambled with spinach, feta cheese, and tomatoes. "Lovely house, extensively decorated; outstanding location in a quiet neighborhood; beautiful grounds, magnificent views."*(Rose Ciccone)* B&B rates range from $135–275.

An excellent value in a pricy town, **The Welby Inn** (Ocean Avenue, P.O. Box 774, 04046; 207–967–4655) is just a short walk to the beach and to the shops, galleries, and restaurants of Dock Square. This spacious gambrel-roofed home was built in 1900. "Merrianne and Allison, a mother-and-daughter team, were warm, gracious, and funny innkeepers. My room was decorated with bright, cheery pink, blue, and white floral wallpaper, lace curtains, and a beautiful blue-and-white bedding set on the four-poster bed. For breakfast, Allison made light and airy pancakes, sausages, and muffins." *(Kathy Banak)* Double rates for the seven guest rooms range from $70–115, including a full breakfast.

For Kennebunkport's most elegant food and accommodations, your best choice is **The White Barn** (Beach Street, P.O. Box 560C, 04046; 207–967–2321; www.whitebarninn.com), owned since 1988 by experienced hotelier Laurence Bongiorno. Guest rooms in the Main House are decorated with colorful fabrics, floral wallcoverings, and period antiques, while the Carriage House offers luxurious suites with four-poster king-size beds and marble baths with whirlpool tubs. The inn's exceptional restaurant is set in a restored three-story barn; menus are changed weekly to offer the freshest of native ingredients, and service is as outstanding as the food. B&B double rates range from $160–250; suite rates $350–395. "The atmosphere and service have always been excellent at the White Barn, but under chef Jonathan Cartwright, the cuisine has reached new levels of excellence." *(CA)*

Captain Lord Mansion	*Tel:* 207–967–3141
Corner of Pleasant and Green Streets	*Fax:* 207–967–3172
P.O. Box 800, 04046–0800	*E-mail:* captain@biddeford.com
	URL: http://www.captainlord.com

Bev Davis and her husband, Rick Litchfield, escaped to Kennebunkport from the advertising world in 1978. They've devoted incredible amounts of time and energy to bringing the Captain Lord Mansion back to its nineteenth-century elegance, while adding the modern conveniences expected by today's travelers. This Federal mansion, which dates back to 1812 and is listed on the National Register of Historic Places, is truly spectacular both inside and out. Many of the house's original architectural features have been preserved; guest rooms are spacious, immaculately clean, and individually decorated with antiques and quality reproductions. Completed in 1997 is the Captain's Suite, a first-floor river-view room, which now has a king-size carved wood canopy bed, oversize tiled shower with massage jets, as well as a whirlpool tub for two, stereo system, comfortable wing chairs in front of the gas fireplace, a Nordic Track Health Rider, and more (the Captain never had it so good!).

Breakfast is served family style in the country kitchen, and includes fresh fruit, muesli cereal, French vanilla yogurt, home-baked muffins, and such entrees as buckwheat apple pancakes, cinnamon French toast, Belgian waffles, or vegetable quiche, plus a choice of coffees and teas.

"Rick is a most gracious host; his staff is both professional and friendly. Beautiful location, with the lawn stretching down toward the river." *(Priscilla Mason, also KB)* "The staff goes out of their way to help with dining and sightseeing information." *(James Beninath)* "We honeymooned at the inn years ago and returned to restore our beautiful memories. Fantastic lodging; impeccable service." *(Mark O'Brien)* "The focus on the customer, consistency, and attention to detail keep bringing us back." *(Michael Ostergard)* "Excellent breakfasts; useful book of local restaurant menus. Beautiful four-poster bed in the Lois room." *(Judith & Nigel Broderick)* "Quiet, friendly, relaxed atmosphere; staff attentive but not hovering." *(Russ Lawson)* "Rick made everyone feel welcome, and facilitated conversation between guests most effectively." *(Linda Sullivan)*

"Location is excellent—walking distance to town, near the water and famed Ocean Drive." *(Pam Phillips)* "The decor tends toward the formal, with lavish linens and rugs pulling everything together. We sat in front of the sitting room fireplace sipping the inn's special Swedish glog and munching on scrumptious chocolate chip cookies. Large formal portraits of members of the Lord family stared down at us, providing great food for the imagination." *(Freda Eisenberg)* "The many antiques are complemented by good reading lights, night tables, and comfortable chairs." *(SWS)* "Eating breakfast at long tables in the big kitchen is a great way to meet people." *(Judith Brannon)* "Fully endorse entry; our favorite is the Lincoln room." *(Ann Marie Mason, Carol Dinmore)*

Open All year.
Rooms 16 doubles—all with private bath and/or showers (3 baths are very small), hair dryer, makeup mirror, air-conditioning, desk, fan. 14 with gas fireplace, 8 with small refrigerator, 3 with double whirlpool tub.
Facilities Gathering room with fireplace, books, games, country kitchen, gift shop, conference room with fireplace, AV capability. 1 acre with gardens, outdoor seating. Walking distance to ocean, short drive to beach. Off-street parking.
Location Walking distance to village shops and restaurants. In Kennebunkport,

go left at light at Sunoco station, over drawbridge. Take 1st right onto Ocean Ave., 5th left off Ocean Ave. to inn on left.
Restrictions No smoking. Children 6 and over.
Credit cards Discover, MC, Visa.
Rates B&B, $159–399 double. Extra person, $25. Midweek discounts off-season. Special packages. 2–3 night weekend/holiday minimum.
Extras Airport/station pickups, $25 round trip.

Maine Stay Inn & Cottages   *Tel:* 207–967–2117
34 Maine Street, P.O. Box 500A, 04046   800–950–2117
Fax: 207–967–8757
E-mail: innkeeper@mainestayinn.com
URL: http://www.mainestayinn.com

They say "you can't please all the people all the time," but long-time innkeepers Lindsay and Carol Copeland sure come close. If your fantasy of the perfect inn involves climbing the steps of a suspended flying staircase in a historic Italianate mansion built in 1860 and listed on the National Register of Historic Places, then choose one of the antique-filled rooms in the Maine Stay's original building. If you prefer the romantic privacy of your own cottage, complete with a double whirlpool tub, queen-size bed, and remote-control gas fireplace, select one of the remodeled units. And if you're traveling as a family, reserve one of the larger cottages with a fully equipped kitchen.

Breakfast is served in the dining room, although guests in the cottages can have a breakfast basket delivered to their door; at 4 P.M., tea is offered in the parlor. Menus change daily, but a typical morning brings fresh fruit cup, apple spice pancakes with Maine maple syrup, pumpkin ginger muffins, and English muffins with blueberry jam. The inn is on a quiet residential street, and the wicker rockers on its front porch invite guests to relax and watch the passing scene.

"Gracious, personable innkeepers who never stop remodeling and improving their inn, keeping it fresh and inviting." *(Carol Dinmore)* "We love the gorgeous rooms, the afternoon tea and pastries, the neighborhood's history rich architecture, assigned off-street parking, and the proximity to water, shopping, and restaurants. Appealing weekend packages, too." *(Paul Grzywinski)* "Great location, within walking distance of everything. Recent renovations to the cottage rooms are lovely, with fine reproduction furnishings, beautiful wall coverings and window treatments." *(Norma LeBlanc)* "Carol and Lindsey are wonderful, welcoming hosts, always available to recommend activities and restaurants; the inn is immaculate, the breakfasts exceptional." *(Brenda & Howard Leafe)* "Although families with small children are happily accommodated in the cottages, a relaxing and elegant atmosphere is always maintained for adults." *(Jean Foy)* "The furnishings are beautiful, from the quilts to the matching curtains. A highlight of our weekend was a specially arranged maple sugaring tour at one of the local farms." *(Mr. & Mrs. Robert Taft)*

"Service is prompt but unobtrusive. Excellent breakfast served at shared tables so guests have opportunities to meet and converse."

(Roland & Rose Sarti) "Loved the option of a private breakfast. Our basket was always delivered promptly, and included a hot dish, fresh milk for coffee, fresh fruit, raisin bread or English muffins, and juice." *(Fritz Shantz & Tara Neal)* "Our cottage fireplace was cleaned and set up each day; plumbing and electrical systems were in excellent condition." *(Ann Steeves)* "The inn's common rooms were beautifully decorated with antiques; guidebooks, tourist information, and morning papers were available." *(Nora Corrigan)* "Our cottage was comfortable, quiet, and private." *(Cecile Desroches)* "We climbed the curving steps of the suspended flying staircase to our suite, with a lovely sitting area furnished with antiques and a bedroom with a queen-size canopy bed. Thick, thirsty towels, lemon- and wildflower-scented soaps were welcome touches." *(Timothy & Kerry Kenney)*

Note: Though both are highly recommended, this inn is not connected with the Maine Stay in Camden, Maine (see entry).

Open All year.

Rooms 11 1-2 bedroom cottages, 2 suites, 4 doubles—all with private bath and/or shower, radio, TV, air-conditioning. Some cottages with kitchen, 9 with wood-burning or remote control gas fireplace, some with whirlpool tubs.

Facilities Breakfast room, living room with fireplace, books, stereo, porch. 1.2 acres with children's play equipment, picnic area. Cross-country skiing, golf, whale-watching, fishing nearby.

Location Historic district, walking distance to town. Take Rte. 95 to Rte. 35 and go 2½ m to traffic light. Turn left & at next set of lights go right on Rte. 35. Continue 3½ m to Rte. 9 & turn left. Follow Rte. 9 over a small bridge & through Dock Square to top of small hill. Turn right on Maine Street & go ²⁄₁₀ m to inn on left.

Restrictions No smoking.

Credit cards Amex, MC, Visa.

Rates B&B, $85–185 cottage, $110–225 suite, $85–185 double. Extra person, $15–25; children 5–11, $10, age 4 and under free in parents' room. Crib, $10. Weekly discount. Rates higher New Year's and Prelude weekends. 2-night weekend minimum. 2-3 night summer minimum in cottages. Off-season packages.

Extras Crib, baby-sitting.

OGUNQUIT

Ogunquit has one of Maine's best beaches—three miles long, with fine light sand, and water that actually gets warm enough for (some) people to swim in! Walkers will enjoy the Marginal Way, a footpath that follows the tops of the rugged cliffs of this rocky coastline from Perkins Cove to the beach. Ogunquit has been popular with artists for many years, and has over twenty art galleries as well as craft and antique shops, restaurants, and a summer stock theater. Other activities include fishing, surf-boarding, tennis, golf, and cross-country skiing.

Ogunquit is 15 miles north of Portsmouth, New Hampshire, and 70 miles north of Boston.

Also recommended: Readers rave about the warm hospitality, inviting setting, delicious breakfasts, and attractive rooms at the **Trellis House** (2 Beachmere Place, P.O. Box 2229, 03907; 207–646–7909 or 800–681–7609; www.trellishouse.com). Built in 1907 this charming B&B has eight guest rooms with private baths, and a quiet location close to the Marginal Way, the beach, and town. Breakfast, including a hot entree, fresh fruits, muffins, and breads, is served on the wraparound screened porch by owners Pat and Jerry Houlihan. Guest rooms are done in an inviting, uncluttered country cottage style. Double rates range from $75–120. "Plentiful breakfast with tasty ginger pancakes. Loved having wine with the hosts and sitting by the fire; inviting screened porch." *(Ed & Cecile Desroches)*

Rockmere Lodge (40 Stearns Road, P.O. Box 278, 03907; 207–646–2985) enjoys a private but spectacular location just above the Marginal Way, with awesome water views from the porch that wraps around the front of the house; with lots of flowers and comfortable seating, it's the perfect spot for the continental breakfast (served here in good weather) and preprandial wine (byo). Many of the guest rooms have ocean views, and all can enjoy the panoramic view from the third floor solarium. Double rates of $60–145 include a continental breakfast.

PORTLAND

Maine's largest city was virtually destroyed by Indian massacres in the 17th century, British bombardment in the 18th, and fire in the 19th, but has always arisen phoenixlike from the ashes. More recently, it has come back from late 19th-century urban decay to take new pride in its seaport heritage and as Maine's cultural center, with several fine art museums and a performing arts center. Portland is located in south coastal Maine, about 45 miles north of the New Hampshire border.

Reader tips: "Summer or winter, Portland is a walker's city. The Old Port district of the city has galleries, shops, coffee houses, and is within a few blocks of the Museum of Art." *(Jeremiah Reilly)* "In the Old Port area, Street & Co. is an excellent restaurant for fresh fish and homemade pasta. A favorite with locals." *(Lynne Glaser, also NB)* "An excellent restaurant (with lots of vegetarian dishes) in the Old Port is The Pepperclub." *(Dianne Crawford)* "Portland is a lively and interesting small city. We explored an affordable antiques fair, enjoyed lively evening entertainment, and relaxed on a restful walk through a district of historic homes." *(Gail DeSciose)*

Also recommended: For traditional charm and contemporary convenience, in a charming waterside location, visit the appealing **Inn by the Sea** (40 Bowery Beach Road, Route 77, Cape Elizabeth, 04107; 207–799–3134 or 800–888–4287; http://www.innbythesea.com). Built in 1986, the hotel has beautiful views of the Atlantic. Guest rooms in the Main House are furnished with Chippendale reproductions and floral chintz fabrics, while rooms in the Cottages, ideal for families, are furnished informally with such Maine classics as wicker and simple pine pieces. The Audubon Room restaurant serves three meals a day, featuring Maine and international specialities, from lobster and cheese omelets to blueberry pancakes with maple syrup. Facilities include the beach, plus tennis courts and swimming pools.

Pomegranate Inn   ♿
49 Neal Street, 04102

Tel: 207–772–1006
800–356–0408
Fax: 207–773–4426

A consistent reader favorite, the Pomegranate Inn probably has the most unusual decor of any inn in New England. A stately Victorian home, it was restored as an inn in 1988 by Isabel Smiles, and is furnished with her collection of fine antiques; more surprising is its striking and sometimes humorous display of 20th-century art—a wooden cut-out butler proffers a handsome bromeliad; a Picasso-esque wooden pull-toy depicts Lady Godiva on horseback. Mrs. Smiles' daughter painted faux-finishes on columns, mantels, and moldings throughout the house, and Portland artist Heidi Gerquist Harbert created decorative murals in almost every guest room; some take their inspiration from Matisse, others from Japanese designs. Tall French doors open from the common area to an inviting city garden. Breakfasts start with fresh fruit; the menu varies daily, and might include poached eggs on homemade bread with capers, smoked salmon, and tomato; or French toast topped with rhubarb and fresh raspberries, with blueberry syrup and rashers of bacon.

"Creatively decorated by Isabel Smiles, who has an amazing sense of style. From the entertaining folk art to the unusual color combinations, nothing is overdone. We were welcomed with glasses of wine, and given excellent dinner recommendations. Our comfortable, spacious second-floor had a king-size bed with luxurious linens, down pillows, and good reading lights, two large upholstered chairs in the sitting area. The bathroom had a clawfoot tub with hand-held shower and thick towels. The delicious, light, creative breakfast was served at the dining room table, and included raspberry French toast, sliced fruit, peach-orange juice, and coffee." *(Al & Lauren Kenney)* "Superb decor, great food, and wonderful hospitality." *(Rebecca Bernie)* "In an attractive and architecturally interesting part of Portland, a short drive from downtown." *(MM, also Eloise Balasco)* "Delicious breakfast of crepes with apples, currants, nuts, and spices." *(Susan LaCaille)*

"When the Smiles moved to Portland they brought along an incredible wealth of good taste, sensitivity, and creativity, along with a cache of beautiful, witty, and unusual antiques and artwork. Even the table settings in the elegant dining room are gorgeous, with different antique silver at every place. Wonderful breakfast of just-squeezed fruit juice, fruit salad with yogurt, sauteed tomatoes and mushrooms on toast, and exceptional bacon." *(Lucy Price)* "Located in the beautiful residential Western Promenade area. The on-street parking was no problem." *(Nicki Brown)* "Our huge room had high ceilings and beautifully hand-painted walls, ample closet and storage space, and comfortable twin beds, fitted with the finest linens. The bathroom was spacious with a large old-fashioned sink and tub, luxurious white towels, and a night light. Even the hallways had interesting art and glossy tangerine sponge-painting on the walls." *(Lynne Glaser)*

Open All year.
Rooms 1 carriage house suite, 7 doubles—all with private bath and/or shower, telephone, radio, TV, air-conditioning. 4 with gas fireplace.
Facilities Living/dining room; 3rd floor sitting room/library. Garden, patio, off-street parking.
Location West End. From I-295, take Exit 4 and go N on Danforth St. and continue to Vaughn St. and turn left. At Carroll St. turn right, go 1 block and turn left on Neal to inn.
Restrictions No smoking in guest rooms. No guests under 16.
Credit cards All major cards accepted.
Rates B&B, $95–175 double. 2-night holiday/summer weekend minimum.
Extras 1 room with wheelchair access.

SOUTHWEST HARBOR

Southwest Harbor is located on Somes Sound, almost on the opposite side of Mt. Desert Island from Bar Harbor (about a 15-minute drive). It's reached by taking Route 3 onto the island, then bearing right onto Route 102, then right again when 102 and 198 split.

Reader tips: "Southwest Harbor prides itself in being on the 'quiet side' of Mt. Desert Island; it's much more of a working fishing village than Bar Harbor or a Northeast Harbor. The location is perfect if you dislike crowds but still wish to have ready access to Acadia National Park." *(Pamela Vollmer)* "In addition to appealing restaurants and shops, an absolute don't-miss in Southwest is the Oceanarium (207–244–7330), found in an unprepossessing old house on the docks that's been converted into a marine museum. Although we went there 'just for the kids,' the whole family was fascinated. The kids got to touch the sea cucumbers and the adults were riveted by a fascinating lecture on our favorite crustacean—the lobster." *(SS)*

Also recommended: Originally built as an inn, **The Inn at Southwest** (371 Main Street (Route 102), P.O. Box 593, 04679; 207–244–3835; www.acadia.net/innatsw) has nine guest rooms, each named after a historic Maine lighthouse. Breakfast is served from 8:00 to 9:00 A.M. in the dining room or on the wicker- and flower-filled porch. Although menus change daily, a typical breakfast consists of juice, blueberry-apple crisp, lemon poppyseed bread, eggs Florentine, bacon, coffee, and tea. B&B double rates range from $60–135.

The **Kingsleigh Inn** (373 Main Street, P.O. Box 1426, 04679; 207–244–5302; www.kingsleighinn.com) is a turn-of-the-century turreted Victorian inn. Its eight guest rooms are furnished with lace curtains, flowered wallpapers, and antiques; many have harbor views. B&B double rates range from $60–175. The full breakfast might include eggs Florentine, fruit pancakes, blueberry French toast, or waffles. On warm days, iced tea can be enjoyed from a wicker rocker on the flower-filled wraparound veranda overlooking the harbor.

Named for the stately linden trees on its property, the **Lindenwood Inn** (118 Clark Point Road, P.O. Box 1328, 04679; 207–244–5335 or 800–307–5335), built in 1902, enjoys a quiet location on a side street by the harbor, with easy access to the municipal dock. Owner Jim King offers 17 guest rooms in two buildings and three cottages; the large sitting rooms open onto a shady front porch. The decor is contemporary, with ivory fabrics contrasting with brightly colored walls; many guest rooms have water views. B&B rates range from $75 to 225, including a full breakfast, and guests are welcome to enjoy the inn's heated swimming pool, hot tub, and popular restaurant.

WISCASSET

The Squire Tarbox Inn ✕
Route 144, 1181 Westport Island, 04578

Tel: 207–882–7693
Fax: 207–882–7107
E-mail: squire@wiscasset.net

Caring, hands-on innkeepers; comfort without ostentation; good food prepared with love; a peaceful country setting; and a location convenient to all the Maine coast has to offer, is what you'll find at The Squire Tarbox, a longtime reader favorite. Listed on the National Register of Historic Places, this rambling clapboard Colonial farmhouse was built by Squire Samuel Tarbox; part of the building dates back to 1763. Bill and Karen Mitman have owned the inn since 1983. The inn makes a good base from which to explore coastal Maine, and a wonderful place to relax after the day's activities—pleasantly removed from the commotion of Boothbay Harbor. The Squire Tarbox is also home to a herd of friendly Nubian dairy goats—source of the inn's famed goat cheeses (served each evening as hors d'oeuvres) and of considerable guest entertainment.

The food is excellent and freshly prepared, starting with a generous breakfast of homemade bread, muffins, granola, quiche, and fresh fruit, and ending with a five-course set dinner. A typical summer meal might include a chilled carrot soup with dill, garden greens with balsamic vinaigrette, chicken stuffed with herbed goat cheese and baked in puff pastry, vegetable stir-fry, homemade pasta, and lemon mousse. Special diets are accommodated with prior notice.

"Perfectly simple and simply perfect is the best way to describe the dècor of the Squire Tarbox. Our charming, airy room had good lighting and storage space, an amply sized bathroom well stocked with towels, and a private porch with Adirondack chairs and a forest view. Before dinner, we sampled the superb goat cheese and crackers in the homey barn-turned-library, attempted a puzzle, and browsed through the books. The delicious dinner included spinach crepes, Caesar salad, chicken with fresh vegetables, and a slice of chocolate sin pie—the name says it all. After the meal, we enjoyed an introduction to goat milking, complete with kid hugging. In the morning, we walked to the salt marsh, then returned to try the two swings in the barn. Karen and Bill were delightful, helpful innkeepers." *(Hilary Soule & Dave Shea)*

"Well-maintained inn with genuine Colonial charm; beautiful rural setting. Excellent dinner, welcoming ambiance. Our room was large and comfortable, and we enjoyed learning about their goats and cheese-making business." *(Walt & Elinor Hermansen)* "The tiny vases of fresh flowers are typical of the Mitman's careful attention to detail. Every year improvements in safety and convenience are made, yet the atmosphere is unchanged. Good food with occasional flashes of greatness; the whey buns are a celestial experience. Opportunity for solitude along with unforced camaraderie at mealtimes. Wonderful location—isolated from the tourist scene, but close to harbors, beaches, antique shops, museums, lobster pounds, and discount outlet shopping. Observing a working farm and dairy." *(Nancy Keim)* "Loved watching the birds at the feeders, especially the orioles and the hummingbirds. And the goats stole our hearts." *(Karen Hoeb)* "Whether a guest chooses to read in front of the fire or down by the pond, watch birds from the inviting screened porch, work puzzles near the potbellied stove, visit the farm animals, or just watch Karen milk the goats, there is a sense of timelessness." *(Lana Alber)* "The Mitmans treat their animals with love and respect, and it shows. Our dinner favorites included the salmon in pastry crust, the melon with poppyseed dressing, the goat cheese strudel, and the chocolate pound cake with raspberry sauce. Outstanding staff." *(GF)* "Special moments during our stay included playing the player piano, enjoying an excellent fireside breakfast, rowing on a nearby river, bicycling around the inlet on the inn's two fine mountain bikes, relaxing, and dining on healthy and tasteful meals." *(Michelle & Tom Wilson)* "Rooms vary in size but all are furnished with a simple, cozy country charm." *(Pam Phillips)*

Open Mid-May–late Oct.

Rooms 11 doubles—all with private shower.

Facilities 2 dining rooms, library with puzzles, games, and books, music room with player piano, 3 parlors; all with fireplaces. 12-acre grounds include nature walk, barn animals, pond with rowboat, bicycles. Short drive to ocean beaches.

Location Mid-coastal ME. 50 m NE of Portland. On Rte. 144 between Bath & Wiscasset; 8½ m S of Rte. 1, on Westport Island.

Restrictions Smoking on weather-protected deck. Children 14 and over.

Credit cards Amex, Discover, MC, Visa.

Rates B&B, $85–167 double, $75–95 single. MAP, $143–235 double, $104–124 single. Extra person B&B, $30; MAP, $50. 12% service. Prix fixe dinner, $29 for overnight guests, $33 for dinner guests.

Free copy of INNroads newsletter

Want to stay up-to-date on our latest finds? Send a business-size, self-addressed, stamped envelope with 55 cents postage and we'll send you the latest issue, *free!* While you're at it, why not enclose a report on any inns you've recently visited? Use the forms at the back of the book or your own stationery.

Maryland

Chesapeake Wood Duck Inn, St. Michaels, (Tilghman Island)

In addition to Baltimore, historic Annapolis, and the gracious countryside of western Maryland, the Eastern Shore is the state's main area
for attractive inns and hotels. This region is actually part of a large
peninsula, extending south from Pennsylvania and Delaware like a fist
with one long pointing finger. It's often called the Delmarva peninsula,
taking its name from the three states covered: Delaware is on the western side of this peninsula; Maryland is on the east; the "finger" itself is
part of Virginia. The entire area is flat, ideal for bicycling, and, of course,
fishing and other water sports are always options. It's also rich in history, with many well-preserved eighteenth- and early nineteenth-
century houses to be found in Chestertown, Easton, St. Michaels,
Oxford, and Cambridge. For a change of pace, stop in Crisfield, self-
proclaimed "Crab Capital of the World," and a departure point for ferries to Smith and Tangier Islands, both pleasant afternoon excursions.
If you visit the Delmarva Peninsula in late fall you may see hundreds
of snow geese during their annual migration. In learning about the
Chesapeake Bay area, you'll frequently encounter the term "water-
man." This old English word for a commercial fisherman is still in use
today, although the numbers of watermen have declined precipitously
in recent years.

ANNAPOLIS

Annapolis is a historic city with restored buildings spanning three
centuries—a large section has been named a National Historic District.

It's full of interesting shops and galleries; there's the Maryland State House and several eighteenth-century mansions, along with the harbor to tour, and, of course, the U.S. Naval Academy. Streets in the historic district are narrow, and on-street parking is limited to two hours during the week. Unload your luggage at your inn (many do not have parking areas), then park at the Navy Stadium and ride a trolley shuttle back. Forget your car—it's a compact area and everything's in easy walking distance.

Also recommended: Three adjacent 18th- and 19th-century homes, furnished with antiques and highlighted by stained-glass windows, make up **Gibson's Lodgings** (110 Prince George Street, 21401; 410–268–5555; http://avmcyber.com/gibson/). Adjacent to the U.S. Naval Academy, Gibson's is within walking distance of the Capitol and historic sites. B&B double rates for the 20 guest rooms are $68–125. "Attractive room in the Lauer House; pleasant breakfast buffet available from 7:30–10:30 A.M. in the Patterson House. Great location, convenient courtyard parking." *(Jack & Billie Schloerb)*

One block from the city dock, in the historic district, is the **Georgian House** (170 Duke of Gloucester Street, 21401; 410–263–5618 or 800–557–2068; georgian@erols.com). This cozy, elegant home, built in 1747, has three guest rooms, each with private bath. The B&B double rates of $90–135 include a full breakfast, served in the dining room or on the brick patio. We've heard from many of this B&B's guests, all delighted with the hospitality offered by owners Dan and Michele Brown, the careful attention to detail, and the comfortable accommodations. "Delightful and quiet; safety items such as night lights and flashlights are provided." *(Claudia Klahre)* "Tasty and original breakfasts with low-fat options available." *(Kenyon Petura)* "Excellent sitting and leisure rooms, and even a small private guest kitchen for snacks." *(Campbell McCarthy)*

William Page Inn ¢	*Tel:* 410–626–1506, ext. 10
8 Martin Street, 21401–1716	800–364–4160, ext. 10
	Fax: 410–263–4841
	E-mail: WmPageInn@aol.com
	URL: http://www.WmPageInn.com

Robert Zuchelli renovated the William Page Inn and opened it as a B&B late in 1988. He has decorated this turn-of-the-century shingled home with period antiques and collectibles. Rates include a full buffet breakfast, to be enjoyed either in the common room or on the wraparound porch. "Ideal location; easy walking distance to harborfront, shops, restaurants, and Naval Academy. Immaculate, elegant, and comfortable. Most of the guest rooms are named after characters from Charlotte's Web, with the exception of Marilyn, the third-floor suite. This open, airy, spacious room has angled high ceilings, dormered windows with window seats, a queen-size sleigh bed, a sitting area with a pull-out sofa, and a huge, new bath with a whirlpool tub, and separate stall shower. Breakfast is served buffet-style in the common room, and included cereals, fresh fruit, muffins, juice, and out-of-this-world French toast." *(BNS)* "Fully endorse entry. Delicious breakfast of eggs Benedict and fresh fruit, on plates attractively arranged. Rob was helpful, gracious, and an interesting source of information on local history. Excellent lighting; attractive, soothing decor; lovely antiques." *(Helene Doyle)*

"Small amenities added to the ambiance: aperitifs and chocolates at night; fresh flowers in the rooms." *(Michelle Montgomery)* "When leaving and returning at night a porch light automatically goes on, making you feel very safe." *(Lura & Bill Reddington)* "Plenty of extras like a magnified shaving mirror, lots of fluffy towels, and a hamper for the wet towels." *(Ellen Sherling)* "Fully endorse entry. The beautiful Marilyn Suite has soft linens, plush carpets, and careful attention to detail throughout." *(Rebecca Hankin)*

Open All year.

Rooms 1 suite, 4 doubles—3 with private shower and/or bath, 2 rooms with a maximum of 4 people sharing a bath. All with clock/radio, desk, air-conditioning. Suite with TV, hair dryer. 2 with whirlpool.

Facilities Common room with guest pantry, wraparound porch. Off-street parking.

Location Historic district, near East Street. Take Rte. 50 to Annapolis. Take Exit 24 or 24A onto Rowe Blvd. Follow Rowe to end; turn left onto College Ave. Go to traffic light. Turn right onto King George St. Go 3 blocks to Gate #1 of US Naval Academy. Make *sharp* right turn onto East St. Go to 1st stop sign. Turn right onto Martin St. Inn is 1st house on right; 1st driveway on right for guest parking.

Restrictions No smoking. No children under 12.

Credit cards MC, Visa.

Rates B&B, $200 suite, $105–165 double.

BALTIMORE

Baltimore has changed considerably in the past decade. Once a city tourists deliberately bypassed on their way to Washington, it is now a tourist attraction, thanks in part to the stunning National Aquarium (with its new marine mammal pavilion) and the shop-filled Harborplace, along with the renovation of many of its historic areas. Other attractions include the baseball at Camden Yards, Revolutionary War frigate U.S.S. *Constellation,* the Maryland Science Center, the Power Plant indoor amusement park, the Baltimore Museum of Art, the Walters Art Gallery, and the Edgar Allan Poe House. Of no less importance is Baltimore's remarkably varied cuisine, with seafood houses and the restaurants of Little Italy among the leading contenders. The town of Fell's Point was Baltimore's original seaport on the Chesapeake Bay, and dates back to the 1730s. Some of the earliest wharves, taverns, and shops are still in operation, and the area remains a working seaport today.

Baltimore is located 37 miles northeast of Washington, D.C., 67 miles southwest of Wilmington, Delaware, and 96 miles southwest of Philadelphia, Pennsylvania.

Reader tips: Baltimore enjoys an active night life, and from time to time, readers visiting the Fell's Point area on the weekend have reported being kept awake until after 2 A.M. If you're a light sleeper, be sure to request a room away from the street. "The water taxi makes it very easy to stay in Fell's Point and leave the car behind. Stops include the Inner Harbor and the Science Center. We paid a modest amount for one day's unlimited rides. The art museum has a great Matisse collection and a lovely cafe in the sculpture garden." *(Diane Wolf)*

Information please: Although the name has changed from the Peabody Court, to the Latham, and now the **Clarion Hotel** (612 Cathedral Street, 21201; 410–727–7101 or 800–292–5500), this remains an elegant 104-room hotel, with both a casual and fine dining restaurant. Furnishings are traditional, with well-equipped marble bathrooms (some with Jacuzzis), and nightly turndown service includes imported chocolates. Double rates are $150–170, with weekend packages available. The new management spent $1.2 million in floor-by-floor renovations; ask for details when booking. "Beautiful location on Mt. Vernon Place, next to Walter Art Museum and one block from famous Charles Street." *(Gloria King)*

Perhaps the Inner Harbor's most elegant hotel is the luxurious, beautifully furnished 203-room **Harbor Court Hotel** (550 Light Street, 21202; 410–234–0550 or 800–824–0076; www.harborcourt.com), with excellent harbor views from the fifth and sixth floors. Doubles range from $215–300, suites are $435–725, and children under 18 stay free. Weekend packages are an excellent value starting at $170.

For a Fell's Point location, there's the **Inn at Henderson Wharf** (1000 Fell Street, 21231; 410–522–7777 or 800–522–2088; www.hendersonswharf.com), a converted 19th-century tobacco warehouse, now home to 38 guest rooms (no smoking permitted). Continental breakfast is served in the lobby and can be taken to the attractive courtyard; spacious brick-walled guest rooms overlook the harbor or the courtyard. B&B double rates are $130–170, with weekend and package rates available; children under 18 stay free in parents' room.

Ann Street B&B ¢   *Tel:* 410–342–5883
804 South Ann Street, 21231

The town of Fell's Point was Baltimore's original seaport on the Chesapeake Bay, and dates back to the 1730s. Some of the earliest wharves, taverns, and shops are still in operation, and the area remains a working seaport today. The Ann Street B&B, two adjacent 18th-century houses in this historic waterfront district, has been Joanne and Andrew Mazurek's home since 1978; they opened it to overnight guests in 1988. Joanne notes that the inn "offers travelers the opportunity to enjoy the atmosphere of an authentic Colonial home. Our inn has 12 working fireplaces, including three in our guest rooms. Hardwood floors and antiques highlight the decor."

"Wonderful location just a half-block from the wharf, where one can take the water taxi to the Inner Harbor attractions. Impeccably maintained; authentically furnished; warm, welcoming innkeeper. Our suite had two fireplaces, beautifully maintained wood floors, and Oriental rugs. The bedroom was done in blue and white with a canopy bed, while the sitting room had wing chairs, and Windsor chairs flanking a skirted table. Simple Colonial elegance, with folk art, quilts, candle sconces and chandeliers, and dried floral wreaths. Breakfast was served at a communal table overlooking the walled patio/garden, where Max, the cat, posed among the daffodils. We enjoyed fresh fruit, juice, chocolate chip muffins, Belgian waffles, and sausages." *(Betsy Sandberg)* "Like stepping back into the late 1700s. Our room at the back of the house was quiet, overlooking the garden, and had a comfortable canopy bed. Joanne's German pancakes and freshly squeezed orange juice were delicious. Two excellent seafood restaurants are less than a block away." *(Robert & Donna Johnson)* "A pleasure to stay with pleasant innkeepers like Joanne and Andrew in such charming, comfortable, convenient accommodations. Delicious breakfasts, too." *(Jackie Schmigel)*

Open All year.
Rooms 2 suites, 2 doubles—all with private shower and/or bath, radio, air-conditioning. 3 with fireplace.
Facilities Kitchen/dining area, garden. Boat dockage nearby. Innkeeper provides permit for on-street parking.
Location Historic waterfront area. From I-95 N take I-395 downtown to Pratt St. Go E on Pratt St. past Harborplace. Go right on President St. (I-83), left on Fleet St. Continue on Fleet St. one block past Broadway. Go right on S Ann St. From I-95 S, bear right to Baltimore/Washington (Fort McHenry Tunnel). Take Exit 57, O'Donnell St. (2 exits before tunnel). Go right from O'Donnell St. Exit to dead end at Boston St. (1.4 m) & turn right. Go left on Aliceanna St., left on South Ann St.
Restrictions No smoking. Children over 10 preferred.
Credit cards None accepted.
Rates B&B, $110 suite, $95 double, $75–85 single (midweek). Extra person in suite, $15.

Mr. Mole B&B
1601 Bolton Street, 21217

Tel: 410–728–1179
Fax: 410–728–3379

As you've probably guessed, Mr. Mole B&B is named for the character in Kenneth Grahame's *Wind in the Willows* who is always spring cleaning. As Paul Bragaw and Collin Clarke found out when they renovated this 1870 row house in 1991, an innkeeper's life involves constant "spring cleaning," too.

Located in Bolton Hill, Mr. Mole B&B is set in a quiet, tree-lined neighborhood of spacious brick row houses, constructed by wealthy merchants of mid-19th century Baltimore to escape downtown congestion (some things never change). The house is decorated with great style and elegance with many 18th- and 19th-century antiques. The first floor rooms have 14-foot ceilings, bay windows, and nonworking marble fireplaces. A Dutch-style buffet breakfast is served at 8 and 9 A.M., consisting of fresh fruit, sliced meats and cheeses, such home-baked breads as buttermilk-cheese or honey-oatmeal, and dessert, perhaps apricot-pecan cake or brown sugar-cream cheese pie, plus juice, coffee and tea.

"Careful attention has been paid to every decorating detail, with each guest room furnished with a different theme. The Garden Suite has a separate sunroom, perfect for a spring or summer visit. The hosts were warm and friendly and offered excellent dining recommendations in Little Italy. A big plus is the garage parking, complete with your own remote control door opener for the length of your stay. A welcome convenience in this regentrified historic neighborhood." *(LuAnn & Steve Weiner)* "Creative, original decor, great charm and comfort, imaginative food, and marvelously interesting hosts." *(GR, also Susan Berry)*

Open All year.
Rooms 2 suites, 3 doubles—all with private bath and shower, telephone, clock/radio, desk, air-conditioning. 1 with sunroom.
Facilities Dining room, living room with fireplace, parlor, garage.
Location Bolton Hill. 1.5 m to center. 8 blocks to symphony hall, opera house. From I-95 N take Exit 53 to I-395. Go 0.8 m & bear right on Martin Luther King Jr. Blvd. After 2 m, go left on Eutaw St. At 4th stop light, go right on McMechen St. Cross Bolton St. intersection to inn on left. Call for directions from other areas.
Restrictions No smoking. No children under 10.
Credit cards Amex, DC, Discover, MC, Visa.
Rates B&B, $165 suite (for 3), $105–155 double, $105–135 single. 2-night weekend/holiday minimum.
Extras French, German, Dutch spoken.

CHESTERTOWN

A quiet colonial town on the Eastern Shore, Chestertown's area attractions include walking tours of its historic homes, the Eastern Neck Island Wildlife Refuge and the Chesapeake Bay Maritime Museum, while boating, fishing, crabbing, bicycling, hiking, birding, hunting, golf, tennis, and swimming are among the favorite activities. Chestertown is located 90 miles east of Washington, D.C.; take the Chesapeake Bay Bridge to Route 301 north to Route 213 north.

Reader tip: "The Chestertown area is quiet and peaceful, but not isolated. Lots of historic buildings in town, and a wildlife refuge full of migrating waterfowl (in season), deer, and other creatures. Stay to watch the magnificent sunset from the little one-lane wooden bridge leading into the refuge." *(Brad Freden)*

Also recommended: Listed on the National Register of Historic Places, **Brampton** (25227 Chestertown Road, Route 20, RR 2, P.O. Box 107, 21620; 410–778–1860; brampton@friend.ly.net) is a handsome red brick Italianate–Greek Revival home decorated with antiques, period reproductions, and well-chosen contemporary pieces. B&B double rates of $105–155 include a full breakfast and afternoon tea.

A gracious country manor house built in 1938, **Great Oak Manor** (10568 Cliff Road, 21620; 410–778–5943 or 800–504–3098; www.great oak.com) was constructed of bricks from the ballast of W.R. Grace sailing ships. Restored as a B&B in 1993, it offers eleven well-equipped guest rooms, each with private bath, at B&B double rates of $95–145, including breakfast of cereal, fresh fruit, yogurt, home-baked muffins, and on weekends, French toast or perhaps pancakes. "Excellent location on the bay, well-maintained grounds, and gorgeous views from many of the rooms. Beautifully furnished rooms with many antiques and beautiful Oriental rugs. Best of all are owners Don and Diane Cantor, who do everything possible to accommodate their guests." (*Debbie King*)

FREDERICK

Frederick is a historic town, located just 46 miles west of Baltimore. A prosperous agricultural center, it boasts a number of restored eighteenth-century buildings, many now open as museums. It was also a center of fighting during the Civil War and changed hands between the Union and Confederate forces several times. According to local legend, it was here that Barbara Fritchie dared the forces of Stonewall Jackson to shoot her "old gray head" before she would take down her Union flag. Plan ahead if you want to visit the third weekend in May, when the craft fair is in full swing, or in late September, during the county fair. Stop at the Visitor Center (19 East Church Street, 21701; 301–663–8703) for information on walking tours and other activities. The town of New Market, billed as the antiques capital of Maryland, is nearby.

Also recommended: An Edwardian mansion with Georgian Colonial features, the **Turning Point** (3406 Urbana Pike, 21704; 301–874–2421 or 301–831–8232; www.bbonline.com/md/turningpoint) was built in 1910. Food is just as important as handsome decor here, and from 8:00–9:30 A.M., guests enjoy breakfasts with a choice of eggs Creole, blueberry buttermilk pancakes, or perhaps frittata. The four-course dinners offer such entrees as lamb with rosemary, maple-glazed pork with dumplings, or swordfish with sun-dried tomatoes. Charlie Seymour is the long-time innkeeper. "Attractive inn, excellent service, charming decor; my favorite accommodation is the Green Room. First-rate food, with a few exceptions." (*LR*) B&B double rates for the two cottages and 5 double rooms range from $75–150.

Two excellent B&Bs are six miles east in New Market, known as the "Antiques Capital of Maryland." The area's first B&B, the **Strawberry Inn** (17 West Main Street, P.O. Box 237, New Market, 21774; 301–865–3318; www.newmarketmd.com) has five doubles with private baths; B&B double rates of $95–125 include breakfasts of eggs Benedict, ham and eggs, or sausage apple pancakes. "Attractive rooms, pleasant innkeepers, Jane and Ed Rossig. Bountiful breakfasts, artfully presented. The strawberry motif is found on the antique china, on the linens, and even in the candy bowls." (*Allen & Karis Borger*) Dating back to 1796, the **National Pike Inn** (9 West Main Street, P.O. Box 299, New Market, 21774; 301–865–5055) is beautifully decorated with Colonial and Victorian antiques. B&B double rates of $85–125 include a hearty

SHARPSBURG

For additional area inns, see **Shepherdstown, West Virginia.**

Inn at Antietam   *Tel:* 301–432–6601
220 East Main Street, P.O. Box 119, 21782   *Fax:* 301–432–5981

This turn-of-the-century Victorian home has been owned and run by Cal and Betty Fairbourn since 1984. "This large restored home with a wraparound porch borders Antietam Cemetery and the historic Antietam Battlefield, site of the bloodiest day of the Civil War. The tiny town of Sharpsburg is just a short walk down the road. The inn is beautiful with wide-plank hardwood floors and antiques. There's a sunroom at the side of the house supplied with coffee, homemade cookies, and a fruit bowl. The sitting room had a decanter of brandy and glasses set out for guests to help themselves. We stayed in the Master Suite with attractive floral wallpaper, coordinated fabrics, and a beautiful high four-poster antique cherry wood bed. Chocolates were placed by the bed. A delicious breakfast of citrus-melon compote, bacon, homemade waffles topped with fresh peaches, whipped cream, and powdered sugar, plus orange juice and coffee was served in the dining room on antique china and silverware." *(Lori Sampson)*

"Relaxing and peaceful. Breakfast favorites are melon with crepes and bacon, the pan-baked apples, and the strawberry pancakes." *(Sandra Cobden)* "Beautiful flowers; comfortable rocking chairs on the inviting porch. The sunporch has an assortment of cold drinks; in the evening, coffee and cookies await. Beautiful lamps provide plenty of light for reading in bed; excellent plumbing; luxurious, comfortable rooms. Many books on Civil War topics to read." *(Dorothy F. Mullen)* "The porch, brick patio, and backyard garden are quiet, peaceful spots to relax, providing views of the countryside and Blue Ridge Mountains beyond. We stayed in the Bluebird Suite, named for the charming bluebird wallpaper and down comforter on a four-poster bed piled with big fluffy pillows on a comfortable, firm mattress." *(Alissa Lash)* "Friendly, helpful, unobtrusive innkeepers. Spotless throughout; our modern bathroom was ample in size, with plush towels and fresh flowers. The area offers great antiquing and many state parks to explore." *(Carolyn Wesoky)* "Fully endorse entry. Pleasant and lovely, with a wonderful setting overlooking the softly rolling hills. I toured Antietam—an awe-inspiring experience." *(Pam Phillips)*

Open All year. Closed Dec. 15–Feb. 1.
Rooms 4 suites—all with private bath, 1 with tub only. All with air-conditioning, 1 with TV, 3 with desk.
Facilities Sitting room, sunroom, dining room, porches. 8½ acres with patio, gardens. Fishing, swimming, hiking, bicycling, cross-country skiing nearby.
Location W MD. 4 m E of Shepherdstown, WV. 13 m from intersection of I-70 and I-81. From Washington or Baltimore, take I-70 to Braddock Heights, Exit 49 & turn left to Alt Rte. 40 W. Go W through Middletown & Boonsboro to Rte. 34.

Turn left onto Rte. 34, 6 m to Sharpsburg. Approaching Sharpsburg, the Antietam Battlefield Cemetery is on left; inn just past it.
Restrictions No smoking. "Well-mannered children over age 6 are welcome." No pets.
Credit cards Amex.
Rates B&B, $95–115 suite. Extra person, $25. 2-night weekend, holiday minimum.
Extras Airport/station pickup, $25.

Key to Abbreviations and Symbols

For complete information and explanations, please see the Introduction.

¢ Especially good value for overnight accommodation.
♦ Families welcome. Most (but not all) have cribs, baby-sitting, games, play equipment, and reduced rates for children.
✗ Meals served to public; reservations recommended or required.
✵ Tennis court and swimming pool and/or lake on grounds. Golf usually on grounds or nearby.
♿ Limited or full wheelchair access; call for details.
Rates: Range from least expensive room in low season to most expensive room in peak season.
Room only: No meals included; European Plan (EP).
B&B: Bed and breakfast; includes breakfast, sometimes afternoon/evening refreshment.
MAP: Modified American Plan; includes breakfast and dinner.
Full board: Three meals daily.
Alc lunch: A la carte lunch; average price of entrée plus nonalcoholic drink, tax, tip.
Alc dinner: Average price of three-course dinner, including half bottle of house wine, tax, tip.
Prix fixe dinner: Three- to five-course set dinner, excluding wine, tax, tip unless otherwise noted.
Extras: Noted if available. Always confirm in advance. Pets are not permitted unless specified; if you are allergic, ask for details; *most innkeepers have pets.*

Massachusetts

Amadeus House, Lenox

Although there's plenty of beautiful country in between, most of our listings cluster around the East Coast—Cape Cod, Cape Ann, Martha's Vineyard, and Nantucket—and the Berkshires in western Massachusetts.

The Berkshires About a 2½-hour drive from New York and slightly less than that from Boston, this region of gentle mountains is known for Tanglewood—the summer home of the Boston Symphony Orchestra—Jacob's Pillow Modern Dance Theater, the Berkshire Theater Festival, the Norman Rockwell Museum, Chesterwood, the Hancock Shaker Village, and many recreational facilities. The area also features trails for hiking and lakes for fishing and swimming in summer, plenty of golf courses and tennis courts, foliage in October, and downhill and cross-country skiing in winter.

Peak season rates in the Berkshires generally apply in July, August, and October; rates are usually lower the rest of the year. Expect two- and three-night minimum-stay requirements on weekends and holidays in peak season, and book well in advance.

Worth noting: A visit to the Berkshires in season is *expensive,* so make sure you find the inn that suits your needs. Properties right in Lenox offer convenience to Tanglewood, those farther afield generally offer spacious grounds, swimming pools, and tennis courts. Prices off-season vary dramatically. Some inns drop their rates only slightly from November through April, others reduce prices by 50–75%, especially midweek, so shop around if you're on a tight budget, and don't be afraid to ask for "off-season specials."

Here's a list of towns with recommended inns in **The Berkshires:** Great Barrington, Lee, Lenox, Stockbridge.

Cape Cod The Cape officially starts at the Cape Cod Canal, about 50 miles south of Boston, and extends out into the Atlantic like an arm, bent at the elbow at a 90° angle. Buzzards Bay is formed by the shoulder, to the south, and Cape Cod Bay by the bend of the arm, to the north. A highlight of a visit to the Cape is the Cape Cod National Seashore, with 40 miles of beach and dunes to explore; park headquarters, with guided walks and lifeguards in summer, are in South Wellfleet. Equally appealing is the Cape Cod Bike Trail, which follows the route of the old Penn Central Railway tracks for thirty miles, from Dennis to Wellfleet, past forests, ponds, marshes, and beaches.

Peak season rates on the Cape generally extend from mid-June through Labor Day, and on weekends through October. Two- and three-night minimum stays are the rule in peak season. Off-season rates vary significantly; some upscale inns keep their rates quite high all year, others discount significantly in the off-season, so bargain hunters will do well to shop around.

Reader tip: "I particularly enjoy the solitude of winter with its magnificent sunrises and sunsets. Be sure to watch the sunset on the bay side from any beach. My particular favorite though, is Corn Hill in the winter—now that is raw beauty." *(Pamela Conrad)*

Here's a list of towns with recommended inns on **Cape Cod:** Barnstable, Brewster, Chatham, East Orleans, Falmouth, Sandwich, Wellfleet.

BARNSTABLE

Dating back to 1637, Barnstable is a quiet and attractive village, with none of the honky-tonk found in some Cape towns. It is located on Cape Cod's north shore, 75 miles southwest of Boston, and 4 miles from Hyannis. In addition to the town beach on Cape Cod Bay, seven ocean, bay, and lake beaches are within a five-mile drive, and opportunities for golf, tennis and hiking are easily available, as are numerous antique shops.

Also recommended: Dating back to 1699, **Ashley Manor** (3660 Old King's Highway, P.O. Box 856, 02630; 508–362–8044 or 888–535–2246; www.capecod.net/ashleymn) offers evidence of its age in its wide-board flooring, open-hearth fireplaces with beehive ovens, and a secret passageway connecting the upstairs and downstairs suites. The inviting living room has antique side pieces, richly colored Oriental rugs, and dark blue velvet couches, perfect for curling up with a book. A multicourse breakfast is served on the backyard patio in good weather; in cooler months, guests are seated on the Chippendale chairs in the formal dining room, complete with candlelight, fine china, and linens, before a blazing fire. Breakfasts typically include freshly squeezed orange juice, baked apples, granola, home-baked popovers, and crepes with strawberry sauce. Candy, sherry, port, plus afternoon tea, are also included in the B&B double rates of $120–180. Six guest rooms are available, each with private bath; some have a fireplace and whirlpool tub. "Fully endorse existing entry. Donald is sweet and welcoming.

Guest rooms are light and airy, beautifully decorated and well lit. The grounds are carefully maintained, and tennis court was surrounded by flowers." *(RC)*

Built circa 1810, **Honeysuckle Hill Bed & Breakfast** (591 Old King's Highway, 02668; 508–362–8418 or 800–441–8418) is listed on the National Historic Register. Mary and Bill Kilburn, owners since 1997, came to the Cape with years of inn experience, having run Trail's End in Vermont. B&B double rates for the three guest rooms are $115; the two-room suite runs $175. "Mary and Bill are charming, fun, and exuberant innkeepers, and we enjoyed chatting with them on the inviting screened porch. Our lovely room, Morning Glory, was done in white wicker, with a queen-size bed made up with red-and-white gingham-check sheets, bed tables with Tiffany-style reading lamps, a loveseat, and coffee table, antique trunk, and chest. Delicious breakfast of coffee cake, shirred eggs with Brie, bacon, and toast. Fresh flowers everywhere." *(FC)*

The Acworth Inn ¢   *Tel:* 508–362–3330
4352 Old Kings Highway,   800–362–6363
P.O. Box 256, Cummaquid, 02637   *Fax:* 508–375–0304
                    URL: http://www.acworthinn.com

When you picture a classic Cape Cod inn, your first thought may be of a spacious old home with naturally weathered shingles, crisp white trim, and green shutters. Add mature evergreen plantings, overflowing flower boxes, and colorful beds of flowers, and you've just pictured the Acworth Inn, built in 1860 and bought by Cheryl and Jack Ferrell in 1994. Prior to becoming innkeepers, they had spent 30 years in corporate and military environments: Cheryl as a food service manager with Marriott, and Jack as a professor at the Air Force Academy in Colorado. Breakfasts are served from 8:00–9:30 A.M., and might include fresh fruit, cranberry granola, cinnamon rolls, muffins, and sour cream waffles.

"A warm welcome included refreshing glasses of cranberry spritzers. Our first-floor room in the attached carriage house had a queen-size white iron bed with Laura Ashley ivy pattern quilt and shams. The thick towels were changed twice daily. Spotless and meticulous housekeeping. The breakfast room has a fireplace to keep guests cozy on winter mornings, and sliding glass doors to the deck where tables are set on summer days. Guests sit at tables for two or four, but are close enough to chat between the tables if desired. A choice of juices is served at the table along with specially blended coffee. Entrees included an herb omelet with homemade toasted orange cinnamon bread, and heart-shaped miniature waffles with homemade syrups." *(Rose Ciccone)* "First-rate inn. Cinnamon rolls to die for." *(Susan Doucet)* "Just as special on a return visit. The elegant Cummaquid room on the first floor has a fireplace, triple-sheeted queen-size bed, and a soothing ivory color scheme. Cheryl's turndown service included chocolate-cranberry treats and a miniature rose. Rooms also have vases with fresh flowers from the Ferrells' garden. Bathroom amenities included a variety of soaps, shampoo, conditioner, body lotion, shoe mitt, cotton swabs and balls, bath gel, makeup remover pads, and a shower cap. Guests at the Acworth are made to feel like family guests and you can be as social as you wish. Cheryl and Jack offer afternoon refreshments and join guests on the deck to offer restaurant recommendations or help plan outings. Our delicious breakfast included a beautiful platter of fresh fruit, homemade granola, yogurt, just-baked almond rolls and blueberry muffins, followed by multigrain pancakes with some homemade jam and maple syrup." *(RC)*

"Undoubtedly a labor of love; the Ferrells' hospitality is awesome." *(Jeanne King)* "Always fresh flowers and chocolates in our room. Relaxing music throughout the inn." *(Lynnette Ryan)* "Careful attention to detail, from the evening pastries to the fact that our room was cleaned while we were at breakfast." *(Nicole Fortier)* "Gracious owners who exude energy and warmth." *(Peter von Eschen & many others)* "Beautifully landscaped with flowering plants, a garden, and bird feeders outside the kitchen window." *(Ronda Hoag)* "Every conceivable comfort: both soft and hard pillows, fluffy thick towels, thirsty robes. The innkeepers welcome you on arrival and send a thank-you note for staying." *(Abby Green)* "Cheryl and Jack made reservations for us in excellent restaurants and mapped out a tour of the prettiest spots on the Cape. The inn is located on a quiet street where you can walk for miles enjoying the scenery along the water." *(Jeanne & Thomas Russo)* "Cheryl went out of her way to accommodate my dietary restrictions." *(Holly Shaker)* "The innkeepers have decorated the house with light, airy pastel colors and hand-painted furniture." *(Carola Staiano)*

Open All year.

Rooms 1 suite, 4 doubles—all with private bath and/or shower, clock/radio, fan. 1 with TV, desk, wood-burning fireplace, refrigerator, air-conditioning.

Facilities Breakfast room with fireplace, living room, family room with TV, books, porch. Off-street parking, bicycles. Tennis, golf, swimming, fishing, boating nearby.

Location Cape Cod; north side, mid-Cape. 1½ m E of Barnstable, 4 m N of Hyannis. Center of business district. Follow Rte. 6 to Exit 6 at the Rte. 132 exit. Turn left onto Rte. 132 continuing to Rte. 6A. Turn right on 6A. Follow for exactly 4.6 m to inn on left.

Restrictions No smoking. Children 12 and over. Traffic noise possible in some rooms.

Credit cards Amex, Discover, MC, Visa.

Rates B&B, $185 suite, $85–125 double. Extra person, $20. 2-night weekend/holiday minimum. Extended stay rates.

Extras German spoken.

BOSTON

Founded in 1630, Boston is one of America's oldest cities, yet its historic area is compact and easy to explore on foot. This is fortunate, considering that it is nearly impossible for the uninitiated to navigate the center city by car; the town plan was "laid out by the cows," according to legend. Boston is rich in sights and museums of all periods, from the historic Freedom Trail to the John Hancock Observatory, from the

Boston Tea Party Museum to the Computer Museum. Be sure to write or call the Greater Boston Convention and Visitors Bureau, Prudential Plaza, P.O. Box 490, 02199 (617–536–4100) for details.

Reader tip: "If you want vibrant, chic, and trendy, stay on Newbury Street; if you want a quiet, residential area, walk one block north to Commonwealth Avenue, with its broad park down the center; if you want a more busy and bustling city atmosphere, walk one block south of Newbury to Boylston Street." *(Fritz Shantz & Tara Neal)*

Also recommended—luxury: Readers continue to report that all standards—comfort, decor, food, and most important, staffing—have remained at the highest levels at both the **Ritz-Carlton** (800–241–3333) and the **Four Seasons** (800–332–3442). Both typically offer reasonably priced weekend packages, so call for details if you want luxury at an affordable rate.

Another fine luxury choice is the **Fairmont Copley Plaza Hotel** (138 St. James Avenue, 02116; 617–267–5300 or 800–527–4727), in the Back Bay area. Built in 1912, this French Renaissance style hotel building was refurbished in 1992 and 1996 at a cost of millions. It offers grand and elegant common areas, plus 379 guest rooms with antique reproductions and marble baths; double rates range from $160 to $325. "Ask for a recently renovated room facing Copley Plaza with a view of Trinity Church." *(DLG)*

Also recommended—moderate: A traditional turn-of-the-century hotel, the **Lenox Hotel** (710 Boylston Street at Copley Place, 02116; 617–536–5300 or 800–225–7676; www.lenoxhotel.com) underwent a $20 million renovation in 1997. The 214 guest rooms are appointed in either Colonial or French provincial decor; most have walk-in closets. The suites are large, with an elegant mix of designer fabrics, wallpaper, and furniture; some have wood-burning fireplaces. Double rates range from $170 to $295. Although readers continue to be delighted with the hotel's convenient location, excellent soundproofing, and efficient staff, one reader was overwhelmed by a tour group occupying the lobby.

Also recommended—budget: One of Boston's best-kept secrets is the affordable **Eliot and Pickett Houses** (6 Mount Vernon Place, 25 Beacon Street, 02108–2800; 617–248–8707; www.uua.org/ep), with a wonderful location at the top of Beacon Hill. These two 1830s brick townhouses have 20 guest rooms pleasantly furnished in period reproductions, most with a private bath and clock/radio. Guests can relax on the roof deck, watch TV in the den, and play the piano in the living room; you'll prepare your own breakfast in the inn's kitchens; all the fixings are supplied. B&B double rates range from $85–145.

Another good choice is the affordable **John Jeffries House** (14 Embankment Road, 02114; 617–367–1866), offering 46 singles, doubles, and suites, at rates ranging from $85–145, and a fine location at the foot of Beacon Hill at the corner of Charles and Cambridge Streets. Rooms are furnished with private bath, telephone, TV, air-conditioning, and kitchenette; coffee and doughnuts are offered each morning in the double parlor. Reduced rate parking is available at the garage next door. "Great location; quiet despite its facing the highway because of the well-made double-paned windows. My small single room was immaculate. The subway is at the front door, as is all of Beacon Hill." *(Harriet Krivit)*

"Excellent location; serviceable, quiet rooms. Our room had some noise from adjacent elevator and heating system. Friendly, efficient staff; agreeable lounge." *(Caroline Raphael)* Comprised of two adjoining four-story brick and brownstone 1880s townhouses, the **Newbury Guest House** (261 Newbury Street, 02116; 617–437–7666 or 800–437–7668; www.hagopianhotels.com) is located in the heart of Boston's fashionable Back Bay neighborhood. Each of the 32 guest rooms has a private shower bath, and the $100–145 double rate includes a continental breakfast; a limited number of parking spaces are available at $15 daily, by advance reservation. "Vibrant, chic, and trendy Newbury Street location—the hotel's chief asset. Pleasant staff, tasty breakfast of fruit, juice, cereal, muffins, pastries, and bagels, available in a breakfast room with the newspapers and CNN on the TV from 7:30–10:30 A.M. Coffee, tea, and ice were always available. Adequate but uninspired decor." *(FS)* "Excellent location. Friendly staff. Do-it-yourself breakfast." *(Caroline Raphael)*

Also recommended—Cambridge: The four-story red brick **Inn at Harvard** (1201 Massachusetts Avenue, 02138; 617–491–2222 or 800–222–8733) is a 113-room university-owned hotel with rooms facing Harvard Square and Harvard Street. A skylight fills the four-story atrium lobby and balconied hallways with light. Rates range from $189–239. A delightful B&B is **The Mary Prentiss Inn** (6 Prentiss Street, 02140; 617–661–2929), an 18-room historic inn, located a half-mile from Harvard Square. Built in 1843 in the neoclassic Greek Revival style, the inn was purchased in 1992 by Charlotte Forsythe. A generous breakfast, served in either the dining room or on the flower-filled deck, is included in the double rates of $99–229.

Also recommended—North Shore: Just ten miles northeast of Logan Airport (no tunnels or bridges, either), is the **Diamond District Bed and Breakfast** (142 Ocean Street, Lynn, 01902; 781–599–4470 or 800–666–3076; www.bbhost.com/diamonddistrict), a Georgian mansion built in 1911. Common areas include a spacious living room, with ocean views from the veranda, and a swimming beach just 300 feet away. The 11 guest rooms and suites are furnished with antiques and have private baths, telephone, radio, TV, and air-conditioning; some have fireplaces, whirlpool tubs, decks, and ocean views. The B&B rate of $90–225 includes a full, home-cooked breakfast.

Worth noting: Demand for accommodations in Boston is currently very high, while the supply is relatively low—not the best combination for the traveler. Just because you're paying a lot, don't expect to get a lot. Shop around for the best deals, and consider staying outside the city if approriate.

The Eliot 🛏 ✕ ♿
370 Commonwealth Avenue, 02215

Tel: 617–267–1607
800–44–ELIOT
Fax: 617–536–9114
E-mail: hoteleliot@aol.com
URL: http://www.BostBest.com

Recognized as one of Boston's most elegant small hotels, the Eliot was built in 1925 by the family of Harvard College president Charles Eliot, and is located adjacent to the Harvard Club. Owned since 1937 by the

Ullian family, the hotel was renovated extensively in 1991, and received a four-star rating from Mobil in recognition of their efforts. "We strive to provide an intimate European-style atmosphere," reports owner Dora Ullian, "and are most proud of the compliments we receive about our staff." Restaurant Clio features contemporary French-American cuisine and has received rave reviews from the local media. Entrees include glazed short ribs with corn and truffles, rack of lamb with eggplant tagine, and swordfish with lentils and shallots. The hotel's suites are furnished in traditional English-style chintz fabrics, authentic botanical prints, and antiques. French doors separate the living room from the bedrooms; all rooms have imported marble baths and plush terry cloth robes.

"A European-style hotel with a friendly, professional staff. Big, fluffy bath towels and comfy robes. Our suite was clean and comfortable, and included a small bath with Italian marble. If city noise bothers you, request an inside room." *(Pat Malone)* "Excellent Back Bay location, with all the benefits of being close to shopping on fashionable Newbury Street and to the MTA (subway). You can step outside and stroll down the charming streets of the Back Bay, complete with flowering trees in spring. Request a room on the 'Comm Ave' side for lovely views." *(NB)* "The hotel is beautiful, small, European, and intimate; I was upgraded to a spacious suite. Best of all was the staff, who were kind enough to type out directions to my appointments the next day." *(Meg Daly)* "Our suite of two attractive small rooms had a small entryway, kitchenette, plenty of lights, window seats, large botanical and hunting prints, full-length mirror, and ample seating. The bathroom had a nightlight and lots of towels." *(Jennifer Ball)* "After a long flight and a late arrival it was nice to be greeted by a welcoming, helpful staff." *(Margaret Horn)* "Intelligent, friendly front desk staff." *(Lisa Weiner)* "The helpful staff quickly met our request to change our room from one that faced Commonwealth Avenue to a quieter one. The bathroom was small, but had excellent lighting." *(Susan Ulanoff)*

Open All year.
Rooms 95 1-2 bedroom suites—all with private bath and/or shower, 2 dual-line telephones, personal fax machine, radio, 2 TVs, desk, air-conditioning, minibar refrigerator. Most with microwave in minipantry.
Facilities Restaurant, bar/lounge, function rooms. Valet parking.
Location Back Bay district. At the corner of Commonwealth & Mass. Aves.
Restrictions 71 nonsmoking rooms.
Credit cards Amex, DC, MC, Visa.
Rates Room only, $225–395 one-bedroom suite; $460–550 two-bedroom suite. Extra person, $20. Children under 12 free in parents' room. Breakfast $13. Alc dinner, $40. AAA discount.
Extras Wheelchair access. Complimentary shoe shine and newspaper. Crib, baby-sitting. Multilingual staff.

BREWSTER

Brewster is located on the bay side of Cape Cod, north of the "elbow." It's about a 20-minute drive northeast of Hyannis and is 90 miles southeast of Boston. In addition to the usual activities—swimming at nine public beaches, fishing, golf, tennis, hiking, bicycling, horseback riding, and antiquing—nearby attractions include the Brewster Historical Society Museum, the Drummer Boy Museum, and the Cape Cod Museum of Natural History.

Also recommended: The **Captain Freeman Inn** (15 Breakwater Road, 02631; 508–896–7481 or 800–843–4664) was named after a wealthy ship master who acquired his fortune in the clipper ship trade. No expense was spared when he built his home in 1860, complete with ornate plaster moldings, inlaid floors, marble fireplaces, and nine-over-nine windows. The breakfast menu features Cape Cod's famous cranberries: from cranberry granola to cranberry pineapple bread, cranberry applesauce to cranberry scones. The hot entree might be corn and cinnamon pancakes with Canadian bacon, or shrimp and prosciutto omelets. Rates for the twelve rooms are $105–325 double; the three suites have whirlpool tubs and fireplaces.

The **Old Sea Pines Inn** (2553 Main Street, P.O. Box 1070, 02631; 508–896–6114) was founded in 1907 as the Sea Pines School of Charm and Personality for Young Women, but it now welcomes people of *all* ages and sexes to partake of its charms. Michele and Steve Rowan bought the abandoned school in 1977 and opened it as an inn in 1981, after doing virtually all the renovation work themselves. A typical breakfast might include orange juice, honeydew melon, and eggs Benedict; or cranberry juice, grapefruit, omelets to order, and home-baked blueberry muffins. Seafood dominates the menu at night, and a typical dinner might be New England clam chowder; scallop, shrimp, and cod medley; salad with poppy seed dressing; and homemade strawberry shortcake. B&B double rates for the 21 guest rooms range from $55–155, depending on size of room and season. Guests especially enjoy the peaceful grounds, and relaxing on the veranda with an early morning cup of coffee.

CHATHAM

Chatham is located at Cape Cod's "elbow," on the south shore, with Nantucket Sound on one side and the Atlantic Ocean on the other. In addition to the beaches for swimming and other water sports, there is fine salt-water fishing, both amateur and commercial, tennis, golf, a railroad museum, and a 1797 wind-powered grist mill; the Cape Cod National Seashore is nearby. Chatham is approximately 90 miles southeast of Boston. To reach Chatham, take Route 6 to Route 137 South, then follow Route 28 east into town.

Reader tip: "The Impudent Oyster offers fine dining in a casual atmosphere. Excellent menu." *(Rose Ciccone)*

Also recommended: If you prefer the atmosphere of an old-time beach resort, the **Chatham Bars Inn** (Shore Road, 02633; 508–945–0096 or 800–527–4884; www.chathambarsinn.com) combines old-fashioned elegance with a comfortable family atmosphere, attractive rooms, and good food. There's a free activity program for kids in summer (including a new program for teens), and enticing theme weekends for adults in the cooler months. Economic imperatives require this resort to book a great many business groups off-season, so ask for details when booking. "Attractive location, gracious staff. The veranda, sitting rooms, lobby area, restaurant, and tavern were all well attended and comfortable." *(Rose Ciccone)* Double rates for the 150 rooms range from $100 to $380, depending on room and season; suites higher.

The Captain's House Inn of Chatham   ⛿

371 Old Harbor Road, 02633

Tel: 508–945–0127
800–315–0728
Fax: 508–945–0866
E-mail: capthous@capecod.net
URL: http://www.captainshouseinn.com

The Captain's House was built in the Greek Revival style by Captain Hiram Harding in 1839. The original random-width pumpkin-pine floors, fireplaces, and antiques are complemented by four-poster and fishnet-canopied beds. In 1993, this luxurious inn was purchased by Dave and Jan McMaster. Recent improvements include the expansion of the dining room, with French doors leading to a brick patio with a small pond, as well as the addition of the Stables, with several luxury rooms with whirlpool tubs, fireplaces, and more.

Breakfast is served from 8–10 A.M. at individual tables, with a hot entree (maybe lemon yogurt pancakes with cranberry syrup or crustless ham quiche), plus homemade breads and muffins, English muffins, raisin toast, granola, orange juice, and fresh fruit. English tea, with cream scones and jam, cakes, and cookies, all baked fresh daily, is served from 4–5 P.M.; hot chocolate, tea, coffee, and a filled cookie jar are set out each evening; and turndown service is available on request.

"Jan and Dave have a staff of young energetic students from both local schools and a hotel management school in England. Breakfast and afternoon tea are served in a lovely room with floor-to-ceiling windows on three sides, overlooking the gardens. Hanging plant baskets and the slate floor add to the feeling of dining outdoors. The fruit course was poached pears, followed by ginger pancakes with ham. An assortment of teas were available. At teatime, English scones with raspberry jam and whipped cream were accompanied by such treats as orange spice cookies and jelly roll cake. The kitchen is open to the guests, and spring water, ice, as well as tea and coffee, is always available. The grounds are lovely, with formal, semiwalled gardens and a fountain.

"Our spacious room, the Wild Pigeon, was in the carriage house on the second floor, and had a cathedral ceiling. The queen-size lace canopy bed had reading lamps on both sides of the bed. A phone and answering machine were tucked away in a drawer to be connected if desired. The bathroom contained an assortment of shampoo, conditioners, lotions, and a hair dryer."*(Rose Ciccone)*

Open All year.
Rooms 4 suites, 15 doubles—all with private bath and/or shower, air-conditioning, telephone, hair dryer, iron, clock/radio. 13 with fireplace, 3 with

oversize whirlpool tubs, robes, TV/VCR, refrigerator, coffee maker, patio/deck. Rooms in 4 buildings.

Facilities Living room with fireplace, dining room. 2¼ acres with patio, pond, gardens, fountain, croquet, bicycles. ¼ m to ocean.

Location ½ m from town. At rotary at top of Main Street, turn left on Old Harbor Road (Rte. 28) toward Orleans. Inn on left ½ m ahead.

Restrictions No smoking. No children under twelve.

Credit cards Amex, MC, Visa.

Rates B&B, $250–325 suite, $120–275 double. Off-season rates, packages.

DEERFIELD

Old Deerfield consists of a mile-long street of buildings dating back to the early 19th century that, since 1952, have been restored by the Historic Deerfield Foundation. Most of the buildings are lived in by staff members of the foundation, and by faculty members at Deerfield Academy. Fourteen of the buildings are open to the public as museums.

Deerfield Inn ✕ ♿
81 Old Main Street, 01342

Tel: 413–774–5587
800–926–3865
Fax: 413–773–8712
E-mail: frontdesk@deerfieldinn.com
URL: http://www.deerfieldinn.com

The Deerfield Inn was built in 1884 but was seriously damaged by fire in 1979. Fortunately, students, staff, and townspeople arrived with the firefighters and saved virtually all the inn's valuable antiques. The rebuilt inn opened in 1981, with most of its 19th-century atmosphere intact, and with modern heating, cooling, and fire safety systems. Now under the hands-on management of innkeepers Karl and Jane Sabo, the inn is in fine shape, improving each year. Dinners at the inn might include such entrees as sesame-crusted salmon with black beans, osso buco of venison with risotto, and grilled chicken over pasta with a tomato Zinfandel sauce. Formal lunches are served in the restaurant in September and October, although the coffee shop is open for lunch year-round.

The parlors and dining rooms are filled with 18th- and 19th-century antiques, while guest rooms are decorated with antiques and reproduction furnishings, accented with coordinating fabrics and wallpapers. Breakfast features a buffet with homemade granola, yogurt, cereals, sweet breads, muffins, donuts, and fruit, starting at 7:30 A.M.; from 8 to 9 A.M. (until 10 A.M. on weekends) a hot breakfast is served with a choice of entrees. Rates also include afternoon tea.

"The dining room is great, bordering on superb." *(Peter Overing)* "Our room was spotless, our dinner excellent." *(Mrs. Floyd Calley)* "Relaxing afternoon tea in the comfortable living room. Later, I dined by candlelight, with Vivaldi playing softly in the background." *(Marjorie Felser)* "The rooms are well decorated with period reproduction furniture, handsome wallcoverings, and coordinated window treatments.

Wonderful breakfasts: excellent cheddar cheese and tomato omelet with whole-grain toast, French toast with great bread too." *(SWS)* "Lived up to its reputation for comfort, lovely decor, and good food. Very professional staff. It was nice to walk out of the hotel into a living museum." *(Bill Hussey)*

Open All year. Closed Dec. 24, 25, 26.

Rooms 23 doubles—all with private bath, telephone, TV, air-conditioning. 12 rooms in annex.

Facilities Restaurant, coffee shop, tavern, lobby with fireplace, 2 parlors with TV; 3 conference rooms. Fax machine. Downhill, cross-country skiing 10–20 m.

Location Central MA; 100 m W of Boston, 40 m N of Springfield. Historic Old Deerfield. From I-91 N, take Exit 24; from I-91 S, take Exit 25. Old Deerfield just off Rtes. 5 & 10 N.

Restrictions No smoking. "Children are always welcome, as long as they are kept under control. Parents are responsible for all damages."

Credit cards Amex, DC, MC, Visa.

Rates B&B, $140–206 double. Crib, $10; cot, $25. 2-night weekend minimum during peak periods. Alc dinner, $25–40.

Extras Wheelchair access; 2 rooms equipped for disabled.

DENNIS

Dennis, located in almost the geographic center of Cape Cod, has stately homes built by sea captains and summer residents, artists' studios, and the Cape Playhouse, where numerous, notable acting careers have been launched since 1927. The Cape Museum of Fine Arts, located on the grounds of the playhouse, displays the work of 20th century Cape Cod artists.

Dennis is on Cape Cod's North Shore, on Route 6A, 90 miles southeast of Boston and 8 miles northeast of Hyannis. From Mid-Cape Highway (Route 6), take Exit 8 (Union Street) and go north 1.2 miles to Route 6A.

Reader tip: "The beaches of Dennis are two of the most beautiful on the Cape, and may even rival the pristine beaches of the National Seashore, not far away." *(Lon Bailey)*

Also recommended: If you are looking for an old-time family resort, **The Lighthouse Inn** (Lighthouse Inn Road, P.O. Box 128, West Dennis, 02670; 508–398–2244; www.lighthouseinn.com), run by the Stone family since it opened in 1938, may well be the place. This oceanfront country inn complex has accommodations in cottages with fireplaces, Cape-style houses with guest rooms, individual suites, and rooms in the main house, and offers a children's program in summer. *Paula Devereaux* writes that "the inn was just as appealing on a return visit. The grounds are well maintained with an outdoor pool, tennis courts, beach area, and playground. Fine family getaway." And from *Ron Kahan*: "For a family reunion, we stayed in a five-bedroom house next to the tennis court, and were delighted with the accommodating staff and wonderful breakfast buffets. Excellent value." The center section of the main house is officially recognized by the U.S. Coast Guard as the West Dennis Lighthouse. Per person rates range from $111–153, including breakfast, dinner, and service; children pay $40–65 each, depending on age. B&B rates are available off-season.

Isaiah Hall B&B Inn 👣
152 Whig Street, P.O. Box 1007, 02638

Tel: 508–385–9928
800–736–0160
Fax: 508–385–5879
E-mail: isaiah@capecod.net
URL: http://www.virtualcapecod.com/market/isaiahhall

Cranberries are synonymous with Cape Cod, and it may surprise you to find out the Cape's cranberry industry started right here. Built in 1857, this farmhouse was originally home to Isaiah B. Hall, builder and barrel maker. Isaiah's brother Henry cultivated the first cranberry bogs in America behind the inn. With Yankee ingenuity, Isaiah then proceeded to patent the original cranberry barrel to transport the berries. Marie and Richard Brophy restored the home as an inn in 1984 and have furnished it with antiques, quilts, and Oriental rugs.

"Everything you could want in a relaxed country B&B—a comfortable place for families, with rooms that are both casual and inviting. The light and airy common room is filled with white wicker furniture, attractive for games and casual conversation, plus there's a cozy parlor with a fireplace for chilly fall and winter evenings." *(SWS)* "Impeccably maintained, comfortable inn. Lovely grounds. Ideal location on a quiet residential street, yet a short walk to the beach, shops, Cape Theater, and restaurants." *(Joan Farquhar)* "Marie is both extremely welcoming and well informed about local activities, attractions, and more. The rooms were delightful, the breakfast delicious, the atmosphere friendly. We sat at a large table with the other guests and shared experiences of Cape Cod." *(Rosanna Nissen)*

"The delicious breakfast always includes fresh fruit, homemade breads, granola, cereals, and juices. The beautiful garden is a delightful place for relaxing or a game of badminton or croquet." *(Beverly Carpenter)* "Marie provided helpful directions and wonderful advice about area activities. The coffee, tea, hot chocolate, and cookies available from early morning to late evening were a thoughtful touch." *(Elsie Rest)* "Fluffy towels, good bedroom lighting, an efficient breakfast setup with tasty choices, and friendly but unobtrusive hosts." *(Bill Hussey)* "The nearby beach has a gradual slope, making it ideal for children. Coffee is ready for early risers." *(Terry Stapleton)*

Open Mid-April–mid-Oct.
Rooms 1 suite, 10 doubles with private bath and/or shower. All with radio, fan, air-conditioning, most with TV/VCR, some with desk, deck/balcony, 1 with fireplace. 4 rooms in carriage house.
Facilities Dining room, parlor with TV, games, library, great room, porch. 1 acre with gardens, lawn games. ½ m from ocean beach, ¾ m from lake. Bicycle trails, golf, tennis nearby.
Location ⅓ m from village. From Union St. intersection with Rte. 6A, turn E (right) & go 3.4 m to Hope Lane (opposite cemetery & church). Turn left on Hope, to end; go right on Whig St. to inn on left.

Restrictions No smoking. Children over 7.
Credit cards Amex, MC, Visa.
Rates B&B, $156 suite, $93–128 double, $83–117 single. Extra person, $17. 10% weekly discount. 2-3 night weekend/holiday minimum June 15–Sept. 5. Midweek rates, April–June 15.

EAST ORLEANS

East Orleans is home to Nauset Beach, one of the Cape's loveliest. Come off-season to walk for miles in blissful solitude. Its located on the north shore of Cape Cod, at the "bend of the elbow," 28 miles northwest of Hyannis, 100 miles southwest of Boston.

Also recommended: An authentic Cape Cod–style house dating back to 1770, with wide pine floors and low ceilings, **The Parsonage Inn** (202 Main Street, P.O. Box 1501, 02643; 508–255–8217 or 888–422–8217; www.parsonageinn.com) was purchased by Ian and Elizabeth Browne in 1991. Breakfast includes muffins, scones, waffles, French toast, or quiche. "Beautiful, freshly decorated rooms. But the outstanding charm of this place is its owners, Ian and Liz, who seem to truly enjoy their roles as host and hostess. At the end of the day, they invite guests for wine and delicious snacks on the patio. Stories and laughs shared among the guests added to our enjoyment." *(Diana Inman, & others)* Each of the eight guest rooms have a private bath; some have a TV and refrigerator, and B&B double rates range from $80–125.

Nauset House Inn ¢   *Tel:* 508–255–2195
143 Beach Road, P.O. Box 774, 02643   *E-mail:* jvessell@capecod.net
                          URL: http://www.nausethouseinn.com

Diane and Albert Johnson, along with their daughter Cindy and son-in-law John Vessella, have owned Nauset House since 1982. They describe their 1800s farmhouse as a "quiet, old-fashioned country inn. Fresh flowers in each room, edible flowers garnishing breakfast plates, patchwork cats sitting on the beds, and whimsical painted furniture make Nauset House special. We also have a one-of-a-kind conservatory, with Cape Cod flowers and greenery and wicker furniture, attached to our brick-floored pub/dining room." Breakfasts feature home-baked muffins, as well as fresh fruit or juice, plus such specialties such as Portuguese omelets or blueberry pancakes; afternoon refreshments at 5:30 P.M. include wine or cranberry juice and hors d'oeuvres.

"A simple but excellent inn. Always a log fire in the living room and a family member ready to help with plans and reservations. A lovely garden area, game tables, newspapers, and a happy ambience, especially during the wine and treats. Lots of tempting choices at their excellent breakfast. Residential area, yet close to the beach and superior restaurants." *(Ruthie Tilsley)* "The cocktail hour featured tasty dips and crackers. Guests mingled, discussed dinner plans, and chatted about the next day's activities. They also have a little diary with restaurant reviews from past guests; we were encouraged to add our input. The delicious breakfast was served in a beautiful dining room with two large harvest tables, and included homemade granola and ginger pancakes with lemon sauce. Our room was beautifully decorated and provided ample closet and drawer space." *(Lynda Worrell)*

"Quiet, serene atmosphere; helpful innkeepers, who provided valuable hints on exploring the Cape. My room had a lovely homemade quilt on the bed, and walls bordered with a stencil design hand-painted by Diane and Cindy." *(Susan Tirone)* "Our room had a comfortable king-sized bed and a small bath." *(AF)* "Guest rooms are small but charming, with beautiful hand-painted wall borders, furnishings, and mirrors. The conservatory is delightful, with Diane's stained glass windows, white wrought-iron furniture, and lots of plants." *(SWS)* "Even better than we remembered it on our first visit, four years earlier, due to its wonderful innkeepers. Al went beyond the usual restaurant advice, and got us a reservation at a popular place that doesn't normally take them." *(Glenn Roehrig)*

Open April 1–Oct. 31.
Rooms 12 doubles, 1 single, 1 cottage—8 with private shower and/or bath, 6 with maximum of 6 people sharing bath; 5 rooms in carriage house and cottage.
Facilities Living room with fireplace, dining room with fireplace, conservatory, terrace. 2½ acres with picnic tables, gardens. ½ m to Nauset Beach, 3 m to bay, 2 m to lake.
Location 3 m from Orleans. Take Rte. 6 to Exit 12. Go right to 1st light; go right on Eldredge Parkway and straight to light. Straight across Rte. 28 (Tonset Rd.) to next light. Right on Main St. to fork in road at Barley Neck Inn. Bear left on Beach Rd. to inn ⁸⁄₁₀ m on right.
Restrictions No smoking. Children over 12.
Credit cards Discover, MC, Visa.
Rates B&B, $75–135 double, $65 single. 2-night weekend minimum.

FALMOUTH

Falmouth is 72 miles south of Boston and east of Providence, on the south shore of Cape Cod's "shoulder." It's three miles north of Woods Hole, departure point for the Martha's Vineyard ferries. Its Village Green district is listed on the National Register of Historic Places. One delightful way to travel between Falmouth and Woods Hole is via the Shining Sea bike path; some inns have free bikes available to their guests, and rentals are easily available.

Reader tip: "Highly recommended the Chapoquoit Grill in West Falmouth for casual dining. No reservations taken but it's worth the wait. Small menu, with many daily specials; reasonable prices and generous portions." *(Rose Ciccone)*

Also recommended: If you like to be right on the beach, the nearby **Grafton Inn** (261 Grand Avenue South, Falmouth Heights, 02540; 508–540–8688 or 800–642–4069; www.sunsol.com/graftoninn/) is enthusiastically recommended by *Rose Ciccone*. "Unobstructed views of Martha's Vineyard from the breakfast room enhanced the marvelous breakfasts of fresh fruit, juices, muffins, homemade preserves, and choices of such entrees as eggs Benedict, blueberry pancakes, and French toast. After a day on the beach, we returned to the inn for wine, cheese, and crackers. Guest rooms in this Queen Anne Victorian are well-equipped with comfortable queen-size beds, air-conditioning, good lighting, ample towels, English toiletries, and private baths; most appealing are the turret rooms facing the ocean." B&B double rates for the 11 guest rooms range from $75–170.

Mostly Hall B&B (27 Main Street, 02540; 508–548–3786 or 800–682–0565; www.sunsol.com/mostlyhall/)was built in 1849, and listed on the National Register of Historic Places. Set well back from the road, this plantation-style home is located on the historic village green. The inn has 13-foot ceilings; grand, shuttered windows; an enclosed widow's walk; a spacious wraparound porch; and hallways that dominate three floors—the source of the inn's name. Breakfast, served at 9 A.M. on the veranda in warm weather, features low-fat stuffed French toast, eggs Benedict souffle, or cheese blintzes with blueberry sauce, accompanied by fresh fruit and juice, breads and muffins; refreshments are served in the afternoon. B&B double rates for the six guest rooms range from $95–140.

Built in 1910, and restored as a B&B in 1995, **The Wildflower Inn** (167 Palmer Avenue, Route 28, 02540; 508–548–9524 or 800–294–LILY; www.wildflower-inn.com) is located in Falmouth's historic district. Owner Donna Stone offers six individually decorated air-conditioned guest rooms, plus a suite with a living room, kitchen, and loft bedroom. Double rates range from $90–160, including a full buffet breakfast.

Village Green Inn	*Tel:* 508–548–5621
40 Main Street, 02540	800–237–1119
	Fax: 508–457–5051
	E-mail: village.green@cape.com
	URL: http://www.vsc.cape.com/~villageg

Built in 1804, the Village Green Inn was "modernized" later in the century with porches and turrets, inlaid floors, and stained glass windows. The inn is listed on the National Register of Historic Places and has been owned by Diane and Don Crosby since 1995. Early-bird coffee is ready at 7:00 A.M., and breakfast is served at 8:30 A.M. A typical meal might include juice, a fruit and yogurt parfait, glazed lemon knots, and chili-cheese egg puffs. Rates also include afternoon snacks and beverages, plus in-room fresh flowers and chocolates.

"Great location, across from the green, within walking distance of shops and restaurants. Guest comfort is obviously a priority to the friendly innkeepers. Breakfast is served around the dining room table, where everyone is made to feel at home." *(Kathie Farlow)* "Exceptionally warm and caring atmosphere; wonderful innkeepers." *(Kendall Sanderson)* "Don came out to meet us and help with our bags. After checking in, we were offered refreshments and were offered the choice of enjoying them in our room, or with the other guests in the living room. Guest rooms are named for historic Cape Cod figures; ours overlooked the town square, and had a queen-size sleigh bed, reading lights on both sides, two side chairs, and a dresser with area information, a tray with glasses and corkscrew, plus a dish of chocolates and a vase of fresh flowers. The wallpaper had a Wedgewood blue background with a delicate pink and white floral pattern, and was complemented by the pink comforter and white ruffled curtains. The bathroom had adequate counter space for personal items and good lighting for makeup or shaving. The Lord & Mayfair amenities included shampoo, conditioner, and lotion. In the morning, blueberry coffee cake was set along with pitchers of orange and cranberry juice. A grapefruit and strawberry fruit cup was followed by wonderful baked French toast with sautéed apples and cinnamon. Don and Diane joined the conversation after breakfast, and helped to arrange a day trip to the Vineyard for one couple, sailboat reservations for another, plus general shopping tips and restaurant recommendations. We relaxed on the front porch and read the morning papers." *(Rose Ciccone)*

"The Dr. Tripp Room is conveniently located on the first floor, with no stairs. Tempting breakfast specialties include Cape Cod bananas, breakfast ambrosia, lemon-nut bread, and cranberry crescents. Excellent location—convenient, yet quiet and peaceful." *(Suzanne Scutt)* "An immaculate and impressive three-story Victorian surrounded by a white picket fence, on a beautifully landscaped corner lot. The wrap-around porch with hanging geranium baskets and wicker furniture made it even more inviting. Located directly across from the village green, the inn is surrounded by other beautiful period mansions. The Bates Suite is named for the Falmouth native who wrote *America, the Beautiful*; it's inviting and immaculate, with a cozy sitting area." *(Toni Stone)* "Rooms are immaculate, complete with teddy bears—one of Diane's passions. Afternoon sherry and home-baked cookies are available in the parlor along with a books documenting America's history (Don is a retired history/geography teacher). We borrowed bicycles and explored the Shining Sea Bikeway." *(Mark Coyle)*

Open All year.

Rooms 1 suite, 4 doubles—all with private shower and/or bath, radio/clock, TV, fan. 2 with working fireplace, 1 with desk.

Facilities Dining room with fireplace, parlor with books, games, fireplace, porches. ⅓ acre with garden, off-street parking. Bicycles, beach chairs, & towels. Off-street parking. Tennis, golf nearby.

Location Historic district; on village green. In Falmouth, turn left at Queen's Byway. Go right on Hewins St. & right on Main St. to the inn.

Restrictions No smoking. Children 12 and older.

Credit cards Amex, MC, Visa.

Rates B&B, $115–150 suite, $85–130 double, $80–145 single. Extra person, $25. 2-3 night weekend/holiday minimum in season.

Extras Bus station pickup.

GREAT BARRINGTON

Great Barrington is located in the Berkshires of northwestern Massachusetts, at the intersections of Routes 7, 23, and 41. It's 2½ hours north of New York City, and 3 hours west of Boston, and about 30 minutes south of Lenox. Downhill skiing at Butternut and Catamount is just a few minutes away, and the town itself has many appealing shops and inviting restaurants.

Windflower Inn 🚶
684 South Egremont Road, 01230

Tel: 413–528–2720
800–992–1993
Fax: 413–528–5147
E-mail: wndflowr@windflowerinn.com
URL: http://www.windflowerinn.com

The Liebert and Ryan families have owned the Windflower since 1980, and Gerry Liebert reports that "our inn is a family-run endeavor; we are raising the third generation of innkeepers with Jessica and Michael Ryan." Barbara Liebert is the part-time kitchen helper to her daughter, Claudia, the resident chef, and all baking is done on the premises. The large gardens are John Ryan's special interest, supplying organic berries, herbs, and other vegetables for the dining room. Breakfast includes fresh fruit, juice, cereals, homemade muffins, breads, and such entrees such as wild blueberry pancakes, bacon and eggs, or a vegetable quiche in a potato leek crust.

"We arrived Friday afternoon to find tea and delicious homemade cookies. Our cozy room was furnished with antiques and comfortable country furniture; it had a wood-burning fireplace and a private porch overlooking a charming country setting. The breakfasts were delicious, especially the homemade bread and muffins." *(Linda & David Kahn)* "Wonderful hospitality, good food, spacious rooms. Quiet country setting, yet close to restaurants and shops." *(L.A. Colton, also Anita & Marty Elias)* "Our room had a huge stone fireplace, stocked with wood and ready to light, and a comfortable four-poster bed with Laura Ashley linens." *(Maria & Joseph Tufo)*

"Defines the concept of 'country comfortable;' there's nothing stuffy or pretentious about this warm, hospitable inn. Spacious common rooms, one with tables and board games, the other with couches before the large stone fireplace. Guest rooms are comfortable and ample in size, with adequate seating and good lighting; most have antique, queen-size beds, some with canopies. Breakfast consisted of eggs to order, bacon, homemade bread, and raisin bran muffins." *(SWS)* "We had French toast with thick sliced bread for breakfast one day, and waffles the next, accompanied by juice, coffee, muffins, bacon, and cantaloupe with strawberries." *(Christine Zambito & Karl Wiegers)*

Open All year. Dinner served Thanksgiving, Christmas, and New Years Eve.
Rooms 13 doubles—all with private bath and/or shower, TV, air-conditioning. 6 with fireplace.
Facilities Dining room with fireplace, living room with fireplace, sitting room with piano, library, games, screened porch. 10 acres with vegetable & flower gardens, swimming pool. Tennis, golf across street, cross-country, downhill skiing nearby.
Location SW MA, Berkshires. 3 m W of Great Barrington/Rte. 7 on Rte. 23.
Restrictions Traffic noise in front rooms. No smoking in dining room or guest rooms; cigarettes only in living room. "Well-behaved children welcome."

Credit cards Amex.
Rates B&B, $100–200 double. Extra person, $25. 3-night holiday/weekend (July, Aug.) minimum.
Extras Crib.

LEE

Also recommended: Built in 1928, guests are delighted with the warm hospitality, comfortable accommodations, and excellent facilities at **Devonfield** (85 Stockbridge Road, 01238; 413–243–3298 or 800–664–0880; www.devonfield.com), owned by Sally and Ben Schenck since 1994. B&B double rates for the eleven guest rooms range from $75–260, including a full breakfast and use of the inn's swimming pool and tennis court. "Caring, gracious innkeepers; immaculate house and grounds. Ample common areas, tasty breakfasts." (*Michael & Dina Miller*)

Applegate
279 West Park Street, RR1, P.O. Box 576, 01238

Tel: 413–243–4451
800–691–9012
Fax: 413–243–4451
E-mail: applegate@taconic.net
URL: http://www.applegateinn.com

Years ago Rick Cannata and Nancy Begbie-Cannata fell in love with the Berkshires, and spent many vacations here, exploring its B&Bs. In 1990 they found this large Colonial Revival home with dramatic two-story pillars and decided to create their own inn, using their experiences as a guide. Taking its name from the old apple orchard which surrounds the inn, the Applegate is furnished with quality Colonial reproductions and Oriental rugs; teddy bears and dolls add a whimsical touch. Rates include a breakfast of freshly squeezed orange juice, cereal, yogurt, fruit, breads and muffins, coffee, and tea with silver candelabras; afternoon wine and cheese; and bedside chocolates and brandy.

"Warm atmosphere, exceptional hospitality and attention to detail. We became engaged over the weekend and returned to our room to find champagne awaiting us." (*Kim Griffinger*) "Loved both the steam shower for two, the king-size bed, and fireplace in spacious Room #1." (*Ann & Bill Thibaud*) "Delightful little touches include wine and cheese at 5:00, plus bedtime brandy and chocolates." (*Marthe & Steven Hemsen*) "A wealth of entertainment options at the inn. Nancy and Rick offered wonderful dinner recommendations." (*Gwen Goltzman & Ron Zaczepinski*) "Generous little touches included a makeup removal towel, cotton balls, and Q-Tips; down pillows and comforters; large, soft towels." (*Jennifer Laterra*) "The French room was beautifully decorated with a great fireplace. Wonderful guest comment book on local restaurants." (*Mike & Julia Dubisz*)

"Nancy provided menus from at least 25 local restaurants." (*Kimberly Adams*) "I stopped by to visit during the off-season. Everything looked perfect, yet the innkeepers were busy scraping and painting, ensuring that this lovely inn stayed in tiptop shape. The rooms are handsome and well decorated in dramatic colors, from the deep green and rose of the suite, to the lovely Lavender room, to the rich jewel tones of Room #6, the smallest room, done in deep green florals (an excellent value). The dining room has several tables, allowing seating for both couples and groups of guests. Convenient location, yet away from traffic noise." *(SWS)* "The large, well-maintained grounds give the inn a quiet, secluded environment." *(Bonnie & James Surma)* "Extra touches include fresh flowers, classical music, a carafe of brandy in each room, and coffee served in lovely antique cups." *(Mary Jean & David Nelson)*

Open All year.

Rooms 6 doubles—all with private bath and/or shower, radio, air-conditioning. 1 with steam shower. 2 with fireplace. Carriage house apartment with living room, kitchen, 2 bedrooms, bath with Jacuzzi, deck.

Facilities Dining room with fireplace, living room with fireplace, stereo, piano, library, TV/game room, screened porch. 6 acres with swimming pool, bicycles. 5 m to cross-country skiing, 14–20 m to 5 downhill ski areas. Golf and tennis directly across street at country club.

Location W MA, Berkshires. 130 m W of Boston, 130 m N of NYC, 55 m SE of Albany. 3.5 m from Stockbridge, ½ m from center of town. From I-90, take Exit 2, bear right on Rte. 20 into town. Go ½ m past 1st stop sign to inn on left, across from golf course.

Restrictions No smoking. Children over 12 welcome.

Credit cards MC, Visa.

Rates B&B, $1000 apt. (weekly), $95–230 double. Extra person, $30. Tipping encouraged. 2-3 night weekend/holiday minimum. 10% weekly discount. Off-season rates. New Year's, wine-tasting, special event weekends; midwinter packages.

Extras French spoken.

LENOX

Lenox is most famous for Tanglewood, the summer home of the Boston Symphony, in residence from mid-June through August. Call 617–266–1492 for schedules and ticket information. Also in Lenox is The Mount, a restoration of Edith Wharton's house; Shakespeare is presented at The Mount's outdoor amphitheater from July to October.

Rates are highest from late May through October, and 2-3 night weekend minimum stays are the rule; during Tanglewood season, weekend rates generally apply Thursday through Sunday nights. When reading through the rates noted in the following pages, be aware that the off-season rates are *half* the peak season rate—an excellent value. On the other hand, a peak season visit will cost you about $185 per night with service and tax (for two) for a charming—but not at all luxurious—room with a continental breakfast. If you must pay these prices, make sure that you're getting a decent breakfast and afternoon tea, too!

When you need a culture break, you'll find that there are lakes nearby for fishing, swimming, and boating, along with tennis courts and golf courses. In winter, there's plenty of cross-country and downhill skiing nearby. Lenox is in the Berkshires, 7 miles south of Pittsfield, approximately 10 miles west of the New York border, 40 miles east of Albany, and 150 miles north of New York City.

Reader tip: "I'd suggest visiting Lenox during the second or third week of September, when the midweek rates are quite low, but the weather is lovely." *(MW)*

Also recommended: Named to capture the feeling of Lenox as a music haven **Amadeus House** (15 Cliffwood Street, 01240; 413–637–4770 or 800–205–4770; www.amadeushouse.com) includes good music as a major part of one's stay—from the extensive library of recordings and books to the naming of each guest room after a famous composer. Built in 1820 and "Victorianized" in the late 1800s, the Amadeus House has been extensively restored by John Felton and Martha Gottron since they bought it in 1993. "Painted in handsome cream with tan and green accents, with a wonderful wraparound porch, grand old rockers, and bright geraniums." *(Ellen Schecter)* "The well-equipped rooms are light and airy. Great location on a quiet side street." *(SWS)* "Delicious breakfasts of baked French toast, lemon ricotta pancakes, or mushroom, egg and cheese frittata—with fresh fruit and juice, poppy seed muffins or cranberry bread, and great coffee." *(Susan Levy)* "Welcoming innkeepers with excellent suggestions for restaurants, hiking trails, and more. Convenient in-town location, an easy walk to restaurants and shops. Delicious breakfasts and afternoon tea." *(Helen Stark)* Double B&B rates for the eight guest rooms range from $65–195.

A grand Scottish-style manor built at the turn-of-the-century, **Blantyre** (16 Blantyre Road, P.O. Box 995, 01240; May–Oct.: 413–637–3556; or Nov.–April: 413–298–1661; www.blantyre.com) has been lavishly restored and is open from mid-May to early November. Rates for the 20 suites and doubles range from $265 to $700, and include a continental breakfast; prix fixe dinners in the acclaimed restaurant cost $70. "Perfectly manicured grounds (with two competition croquet lawns, tennis courts, and swimming pool), a museum-like collection of antiques, and sheer luxury in everything. Our room had a crocheted spread on the queen-sized bed, a huge bath with everything you could ask for, from towel warmers to the strongest shower I've ever had. Dinners were superlative, from canapes in the Main Hall where we ordered before entering the dining room, to the dessert." *(Mark Traub)*

A century-old Victorian home, **Brook Farm Inn** (15 Hawthorne Street, 01240; 413–637–3013 or 800–285–POET; www.brookfarm.com) has a library of 1,500 books, containing 750 volumes of poetry, with another 70 poets recorded on tape. B&B double rates for the 12 guest rooms range from $80–200. "Welcoming atmosphere with books and music, delicious food, enchanting rooms, and pleasant guests; Bob the cat is a true treasure." *(Kristina Brown & Dale Brunelle)* "Off the main street, with easy access to town. The well-stocked guest pantry enables guests to make themselves at home." *(Lisa Taylor)* "Breakfasts served promptly at 8:30 A.M., with piping hot coffee, fresh fruit, tasty breads, cereal, and a hot entree." *(Cathy Reitz)* "Joe hosts an informal poetry reading during afternoon tea and scones; the atmosphere is casual, with guests feeling free to stay or just enjoy their tea and depart." *(Maria Posella)*

Originally the summer home of Harley Procter of Procter and Gamble fame, **Gateways Inn and Restaurant** (51 Walker Street, 01240; 413–637–2532 or 888–GWAY-INN; gateways@berkshire.net) offers twelve guest rooms and a dining room (open to the public) specializing in Italian cuisine. "The grand staircase designed by Stanford White is magnificent; beautifully decorated rooms with large baths and all the amenities. European flair; excellent dinners." *(Rose Ciccone)* Rates range from $85–380, including a continental breakfast.

Built in 1885 and named for an eclectic kind of Victorian pottery, the **Rookwood Inn** (11 Old Stockbridge Road, P.O. Box 1717, 01240; 413–637–9750 or 800–223–9750; www.rookwoodinn.com) is a "painted lady" covered in shades of cream, salmon, and blue-gray on the outside. Inside visitors discover English and American antiques, Oriental rugs, and period wallpapers. B&B rates of $75–300 include a full buffet breakfast and afternoon tea. "Owners Steve and Amy Lesser provide warmth, hospitality, and charm, along with lovely rooms, delicious breakfasts, and a serene getaway." *(Heather Angstreich)*

MARTHA'S VINEYARD

Martha's Vineyard is a 20-mile-long island, located 5 miles south of Woods Hole in Cape Cod, and 80 miles south of Boston. It is easily reached by air from LaGuardia Airport or White Plains, NY; Bridgeport, CT; New Bedford and Boston, MA; or by a 45-minute ferry ride from Woods Hole or a longer one from Hyannis. Its beautiful beaches—many of them free—offer full surf on the south side of the island, and gentle waves along the state beach between Edgartown and Oak Bluffs. Swimming, fishing, and sailing are always popular, as are horseback riding and bicycling. A 15-mile bicycle path leads along the water and through the woods.

The Vineyard is a popular and crowded place in the summer, so make car reservations for the ferry three to six months in advance. You can also rent a car after you arrive, but again, advance reservations are essential. If you're staying at an inn in Edgartown or Vineyard Haven, you can manage quite well without a car at all; in the up-island towns, such as Menemsha or West Tisbury, it's essential. Rates are highest in July and August, and two- and three-day minimum stays are the rule; a number of inns charge peak season rates from early June through mid-October. We urge you to visit in September or October for sunny weather minus the crowds.

All the towns on the island, except for Edgartown and Oak Bluffs, are dry; when you're going out to dinner, bring your own wine, and the staff will be happy to chill and serve it for you.

Also recommended: A gambrel-roofed cottage built in 1920s, the **Hanover House** (10 Edgartown Road, P.O. Box 2107, Vineyard Haven, 02568; 508–693–1066 or 800–339–1066), has been an inn since 1934. The 15 guest rooms and suites are furnished with vintage or reproduction beds, quilts, antique bureaus, and good bedside lighting; B&B rates range from $75–225, including a continental breakfast. "Our quiet suite had a spacious, cathedral-ceilinged living room; a bedroom with a comfortable four-poster, queen-size wrought-iron bed; a well-equipped bathroom with fluffy towels; and a private patio. Friendly, thoughtful caring owners." *(Amy Silverman)*

Named after the estate that once belonged to its owner's grandparents, **Hob Knob Inn** (128 Main Street, P.O. Box 239, 02539; 800–696–2723 or e-mail: hobknob@vineyard.net) offers 16 beautifullly refurbished guest rooms, most with king-size beds; all are appointed with luxurious down and cotton bedding, select antiques, and fresh flowers. A buffet breakfast, with a choice of hot entree and afternoon tea are included in the double rates of $125–375.

Thorncroft (460 Main Street, Vineyard Haven, 02568; 508–693–3333 or 800–332–1236; www.thorncroft.com) is a secluded, luxurious, couples-oriented country inn. Rates for the fifteen guest accommodations range from $160–450, and include a full breakfast in the dining room, or a continental breakfast in bed. "Beautiful inn with traditional furnishings, plush carpets, immaculate bathroom. Amenities include bathrobes, coffee and the newspaper delivered to the room, stamped postcards, and headphones for the television. Private, romantic escape." *(Louisa Yue-Chan)*

The Charlotte Inn ✕

27 South Summer Street
Edgartown, 02539

Tel: 508–627–4751
Fax: 508–627–4652

The Charlotte has a well-deserved reputation as the most elegant inn on Martha's Vineyard. Each guest room is decorated differently, but all have beautiful European antiques, original paintings and engravings, and brass lamps. Rich, dark-colored wallpapers contrast handsomely with the light-colored carpets and window trim in the main inn.

Gery and Paula Conover bought The Charlotte Inn in 1970, and have gradually expanded it from the original Captain's House, built in 1860, adding suites in the Carriage House and guest rooms in the 200-year-old Garden House, the Summer House, and the Coach House; Carol Read is the general manager. Rates include a breakfast of coffee, juice, and homemade muffins. The inn's restaurant, L'Etoile, serves excellent French cuisine in a beautiful setting. Although the menu changes frequently, a recent choice of entrees included lobster with parsnip and chive custard, pheasant on broccoli rabe, and rack of lamb with spring greens.

"Fully endorse entry. The rooms are wonderful, the grounds are absolutely beautiful, the common rooms are elegant, and the excellent staff can constantly be seen delivering drinks, freshening flowers, and more. Our second floor room in the Summer House was done in green and white, with lovely woodwork, antique furnishings, and silky green wallcovering. Fabric patterned in white dogwood on an ecru background was used for padded headboard, bed tables, and draperies. Linens, pillows, and the down comforter were all top quality. The opulent bath was large as our bedroom. A marble-topped table held a vase of fresh flowers, silver brushes, and a book; other amenities included generous men's and womens' toiletries, terry robes, and a heated towel rack. Towels were changed in the morning and again at night when the bed was turned down. A small alcove held a cabinet with a variety of books, a Bose Wave radio, a selection of CDs, and a silver tray with a bottle of port and glasses. The semiprivate porch was perfect for relaxing. Dinner at L'Etoile was outstanding, with appetizers of veal terrine and lobster and scallop bisque; entrees of rack of lamb and lobster; and desserts of pumpkin creme brulee and a fruit tart. Coffee was accompanied by a liqueur and a plate of shortbread cookies, truffles and chocolate-covered pecans. Breakfast is brought to your room or served in the terraced dining room. Served to our table were coffee, juice, and a tray with toast, croissant, bagel, coffee cake, and muffins. More than ample and all freshly made." *(Rose & Frank Ciccone)*

"Excellent location on a quiet lane, just off one of Edgartown's main shopping streets. The grounds are a lovely expanse of well-tended greenery, and the antique-filled rooms are exceptionally handsome. The restaurant feels much like a greenhouse—it's light and airy with lots of glass, plants, and even a little waterfall." *(SWS)* "Our room had a private terrace that opened to the English garden. The staff attended to every need but were almost invisible." *(Margaret Horn)* "Quite possibly the most relaxing 48 hours we've ever spent. Quiet room, impeccable taste." *(GR)*

Open All year. Restaurant closed Jan. 2 to Feb. 14.
Rooms 2 suites, 23 doubles—all with full private bath, radio, fan, air-conditioning. 16 with TV. Most with telephone, desk. 5 with fireplace. Guest rooms in 5 buildings.
Facilities Restaurant, art gallery. Living room in Garden House with fireplace, TV; sitting room in Main House. Outside sitting areas, decks, porches, gardens. Walking distance to tennis, beaches, charter fishing. Public parking diagonally across the street.
Location 15-minute ride from the ferry. ½ block to Main Street. Follow signs to Edgartown. Turn right onto S. Summer St. (after Town Hall). Inn ½ block down on left.
Restrictions No cigars, pipes or heavy cigarette smoking. Children over 14.
Credit cards Amex, MC, Visa.
Rates B&B, $395–650 suite, $175–450 double. 2-night weekend/high-season minimum. Full breakfast, $9. Prix fixe dinner, $56.

NANTUCKET

Nantucket, a relatively small island, about 7 by 15 miles, located 25 to 30 miles south of Cape Cod in the Atlantic Ocean, was settled in the late 17th century by theological nonconformists who were not welcome in the Puritan Massachusetts Colony. The island thrived as a port for fishing and whaling ships and the profits earned were often invested in stately saltbox or Federal-style houses which still stand clustered cheek-to-jowl in the town of Nantucket. With the decline of the whaling industry, modern development bypassed the community; when it was once again "discovered" by sailors and summer vacationers, the unspoiled Colonial architecture became part of its allure. Strict preservation laws now restrict development, and all new houses must have unpainted clapboard which weathers to that unique shade known as "Nantucket grey." Lovely beaches encircle the island and between the communities of Siasconset (pronounced "Sconset") to the east and Madaket to the west you'll find 7,700 noncontiguous acres of open land, including a nature sanctuary, windswept moors, and cranberry bogs. Of particular interest on rainy days is the Nantucket Whaling Museum and the Peter Foulger Museum covering Nantucket history.

Peak season (when the population can swell from 4,000 to 40,000) runs from Memorial Day through Labor Day weekend although spring, fall, and Christmas are becoming increasingly popular. During July and August, expect crowds, high rates, and minimum-stay requirements at all inns. If you're making last-minute plans and aren't having any luck at the inns recommended here, call the Nantucket Information Bureau (25 Federal Street, 508–228–0925); they can tell you where rooms are available.

You can fly to Nantucket from New York, Providence, Boston, New Bedford, or Hyannis, or take the ferry from Hyannis, or Oak Bluffs (Martha's Vineyard). Reservations are essential in peak season, and should be made several months in advance for cars, but almost all innkeepers recommend leaving your car on the mainland, if possible. Most inns listed below are within a short distance of the ferry dock, in the town of Nantucket itself. *In-season parking is a problem in Nantucket town.* New visitors to the island should familiarize themselves with a map before they start out cross-island on a bicycle (rental shops abound) as distances can be deceiving.

Nantucket is expensive. Prices for everything on the island are higher; fuel for heating and electricity must be brought in on barges, and most food and other commodities make the trip on the ferry, adding to their cost.

When calling for reservations, take the time to shop around, and make sure you're getting the best value for your money. Understand what the total cost will be, and what is included in the price, i.e., light or hearty continental breakfast, afternoon tea or evening refreshments. And let us know what you discover!

Reader tips: "Highly recommend a visit to Nantucket midweek in late October, or even early November. The weather was lovely, the crowds were small, and the room rates were exceedingly reasonable. If you don't mind a bit of uncertainty, you can save even more if you wait until your arrival to look for a room—most inns have irresistible "walk-in" rates—but don't ever try this on a weekend." *(SWS)* "The Brotherhood of Thieves is a fun pub with evening entertainment and appealing dècor. The Atlantic Cafè is also a good choice for late-night fare." *(Sally Ducot)* "Something Natural was our favorite for lunch. We enjoyed the slide film *Nantucket Seasons on the Island* to see what it is like the rest of the year." *(Glenn Roehrig)*

Also recommended: Long-time Nantucket vacationers Sheila and Fred Heap decided to make the island their year-round home when they bought the **Centre Street Inn** (78 Centre Street, P.O. Box 262,

02554; 508–228–0199 or 800–298–0199; www.centrestreetinn.com) in 1994. The 13 guest rooms (most with private bath) are decorated with a light and airy look, with Waverly, Ralph Lauren, and Laura Ashley fabrics, and antique, English pine, and white wicker furnishings. Double rates of $95–205 ($65–125 off-season) include fresh fruit and juice, with yogurt-and-granola fruit parfaits, home-baked breads and muffins, plus afternoon refreshments. The inn is located on a quiet street in the historic district, a short walk from the ferry and Main Street, and is open from mid-April to mid-December. "Excellent location. Rooms fresh with charming dècor and constant upgrading. Though small, even the least expensive rooms are darling, and an excellent value in pricy Nantucket. Caring, hands-on innkeepers." *(SWS)*

The "grand dame" of Nantucket inns, the **Jared Coffin House** (29 Broad Street, 02554; 508–228–2400 or 800–248–2405; www.nantucket.net/lodging/jchouse) is comprised of the Jared Coffin House (1845), two attached wings built in the 1700s and in 1857, two 19th-century buildings (the Henry Coffin and the Harrison Gray) less than 50 feet away, and the Daniel Webster House, built in 1968. Two restaurants, the Tap Room and Jared's, offer casual and more formal dining. Some rooms have been renovated more recently than others, others can be noisy in season, so get details when booking. A full breakfast is included in the $100–225 double rates; there are 60 guest rooms (30 with a queen-size canopy bed). "Enjoyed the food, service, ambiance, and excellent value at the midweek off-season seafood buffet." *(SWS)* "Our favorite rooms are in the Harrison Gray House, offering antique dècor, lots of common space for guests, and quiet atmosphere." *(DLG)*

The **Martin House Inn** (61 Centre Street, P.O. Box 743, 02554; 508–228–0678; www.nantucket.net/lodging/martinn) was built in 1803 and offers four-poster and canopy beds, fireplaces, and period antiques in its 13 guest rooms. Guests can enjoy a breakfast of fruit, granola, and muffins at the elegant dining table, curl up with a book in the window seat or before the living room fireplace, or take a snooze in the hammock on the inviting veranda. Double rates range from $65–165, with both private and shared baths; those with shared bath are a good value in pricey Nantucket.

Named for the Colonial symbol of hospitality, **The Pineapple Inn** (10 Hussey Street, 02554; 508–228–9992; www.nantucket.net/lodging/pineappleinn) was built in 1838 by a whaling ship captain's house. Extensively renovated and redecorated, the inn is furnished with handmade four-poster queen- and king-size canopy beds, Ralph Lauren linens, goose-down comforters, handmade Oriental carpets, white marble baths, and a blend of reproduction furniture and 19th century antiques. B&B double rates for the 12 guest rooms range from $75–250 and include breakfasts of cappuccino, freshly squeezed orange juice, a fresh fruit, and home-baked pastries, served in the dining room or on the garden patio.

Built as a silk factory in 1835, the **Sherburne Inn** (10 Gay Street, 02554; 508–228–4425) has been elegantly restored as a handsome B&B, with a quiet location in the historic district. Rates for the eight guest rooms include a continental breakfast and range from $75–210. "Delightful hands-on innkeepers, Dale Hamilton and Susan Gasparich, always improving their inn, from the addition of central air-conditioning to enhancements of the decor." *(SWS)*

The **Stumble Inn** (109 Orange Street, 02554; 508–228–4482 or 800–649–4482; www.nantucket.net/lodging/stumbleinne) was built in 1704. The building was a private home for most of its history, and was purchased by Mary Kay and Mal Condon in 1985. Although the rooms and breakfasts are delightful, guests especially enjoy the inn's friendly owners. There are nine guest rooms, three in the nearby String Cottage; the double rates vary from $90–250 according to room and season, and include a hearty continental breakfast.

Built in the mid-19th century, **The Wauwinet** (120 Wauwinet Road, P.O. Box 2580, 02584; 508–228–0145 or 800–426–8718) is one of Nantucket's few waterfront inns; after a multi-million dollar restoration, it is now also the island's most expensive. The decor of the 35 guest rooms and cottages includes antique pine armoires, iron or wicker headboards, sisal carpeting, and fresh flowers. The inn's lawns sweep down from the porch to the harbor on one side; to the other, it's a 50-yard walk to the dunes and the Atlantic beyond. B&B double rates $195–$725 (suites to $1,400) include a full breakfast, twice daily maid service, use of the mountain bicycles, tennis courts, and boats, plus jitney service to Nantucket Town, eight miles away. Topper's, the inn's restaurant, combines American cooking with regional specialties. "Magnificent setting with beautifully landscaped grounds and water views. Both the common areas and the guest rooms are lush and stunning." *(SWS)* "Although we had booked the least expensive room for our midweek off-season visit, we were thrilled to be upgraded to one of their best!" *(MW)*

ROCKPORT

Rockport is on Massachusetts's "other" cape—Cape Ann, with a coastline more like that of Maine than Massachusetts, yet only 40 miles northeast of Boston. To get there, take Route 128 north until it ends at a set of traffic lights, then pick up Route 127 to the center of Rockport. Rockport has one of the country's oldest artist colonies, along with dozens of craft and antique shops. Other activities include golf, hiking and bicycling, and of course swimming, fishing, schooner and lobstering trips, boating, and whale-watching in season—from April through October.

Rockport is a "dry" town, so bring your wine from Gloucester; restaurants will gladly chill and serve it for you, charging a modest corkage fee.

Also recommended: A charming in-town choice is the **Addison Choate Inn** (49 Broadway, 01966; 978–546–7543 or 800–245–7543; www.cape-ann.com/addison-choate), a Greek Revival home, built in 1851. Knox and Shirley Johnson, who bought the inn in 1992, have decorated with antiques, reproductions, and original art. B&B double rates for the eight guest rooms and apartment suites range from $85–135, and include home-baked continental breakfast and afternoon tea. Guests are delighted with the Johnson's gracious hospitality, the attractive decor, the convenient location, the lovely gardens, and the inviting backyard swimming pool.

Built as a seaside summer home in 1905, **Rocky Shores Inn & Cottages** (65 Eden Road, 01966; 978–546–2823 or 800–348–4003; www.rockportusa.com/rockyshores) offers eleven guest rooms in the main house, plus eleven rustic, shingled cottages built in the 1940s. B&B double rates of $84–120 include a continental breakfast; the cottages have kitchens, and the weekly rate ranges from $825–1025.

A 1911 manor house, the **Seacrest Manor** (99 Marmion Way, 01966; 978–546–2211; www.rockportusa.com/seacrestmanor) offers lovely water views, handsome rooms, and a convenient location in a quiet residential area. A full breakfast is served on Wedgwood china in the lovely breakfast room. Other amenities include nightly turndown, shoe shine service, and the morning newspaper delivered to your door. Double rates for the eight guest rooms range from $86–135.

The **George Fuller House** (148 Main Street, Rte. 133, Essex, 01929; 978–768–7766 or 800–477–0148; www.cape-ann.com/fuller-house) is conveniently located just ten miles east of Rockport. Built in 1830, the George Fuller House has retained such Federal architectural details as Indian shutters, fireplaces, original paneling and woodwork. Guest rooms are beautifully decorated with antiques and country pieces; the penthouse suite overlooks the Essex River and saltwater marsh. Breakfasts typically include cereals and juice, fruit, coffee, tea, and hot chocolate, home-baked breads, cranberry coffee cake or apricot twists, and Belgian waffles with orange sauce or crêpes with ham and ricotta cheese. Double rates range from $90–145.

SANDWICH

Founded in 1639, Sandwich is the oldest town on Cape Cod, and offers plenty to interest both children and adults. In addition to a walking tour of the village and its historic buildings (several are open to the public), visitors will enjoy the Sandwich Glass Museum, displaying the work which made the town famous in the 19th century, and the nature center and separate museum dedicated to the famous children's writer Thornton Burgess, author of the Peter Cottontail stories. Also worthwhile is Heritage Plantation, a 76-acre open-air museum devoted to different aspects of American life; for collectors of all ages, Yesteryears Doll and Miniature Museum is a don't-miss.

Sandwich is located on Cape Cod, approximately 3 miles west of the Cape Cod Canal and 20 miles northeast of Hyannis. From Bourne Bridge, continue on Rte. 6A into town.

Worth noting: Most of the B&Bs in Sandwich are on its appealing main street, and are buildings of similar size and style. In most, both common and guest rooms are fairly small, typical of the period. For safety reasons, most innkeepers use Duraflame-type logs in guest rooms with working fireplaces.

Also recommended: Captain Ezra Nye House (152 Main Street, 02563; 508–888–6142 or 800–388–2278) was built in 1829 by a packet ship captain, and has been restored with a pleasing mixture of period antiques, Oriental art, and Chinese porcelain. The seven guest rooms are painted in soft pastels with hand stenciling, each with an individual appeal—a queen-size canopy or sleigh bed, or a white wicker king-size bed; double rates are $85–110.

Built in 1835 in the Greek Revival style, **The Summer House** (158 Main Street, 02563; 508–888–4991 or 800–241–3609; www.capecod.net/summerhouse) has five guest rooms, each with private bath, antique furniture, hand-stitched quilts, heirloom linens, and painted hardwood floors. The double rate of $65–95 includes a full breakfast and afternoon tea. "New owners Kevin and Marjorie Huelsman are hospitable and gracious. Convenient in-town location, yet quiet at night. Inviting backyard with flowers, sitting area, and enticing hammock." *(Diana Inman)*

The Dan'l Webster Inn 🛏 ✕ ♿
149 Main Street, 02563

Tel: 508–888–3622
800–444–3566
Fax: 508–888–5156
E-mail: dwi@capecod.net
URL: http://www.danlwebsterinn.com

The Dan'l Webster dates back to 1692, and was operated as a tavern and inn through much of its history. In 1915, it was named for one of its most famous regular guests. The historic building was destroyed by fire in 1971 and rebuilt in Colonial style. The Catania family, owners of the inn since 1980, have renovated and expanded it to an adjacent property, the Fessenden House, built in 1826. The Dan'l Webster is a good choice for travelers who want the mood of a historic inn with the conveniences of a small hotel.

"Exceptional service from every member of the staff, who feel like part of an extended family. Excellent dining and an extensive wine list. Ample parking and a strategic location for those wishing to visit nearby historic sites." *(Patricia & James Donovan)* "Lovely landscaping, with flowers everywhere. Our favorite room is #31, but all are spacious, comfortable, and in excellent condition, with chairs just right for sitting and reading, and extra pillows and blankets. Bathrooms are shiny clean with plenty of big fluffy towels. Ice is delivered to your room in the evening, and coffee awaits early risers in the gathering room." *(Roger Dennis, Jr.)* "Meals are elegant, the food is always good (great sandwiches served in the pub), the staff cordial, the innkeepers warm and friendly, and the guest rooms comfortable." *(Hopie Welliver)* "The owner was helpful with information about restaurants, antiques, and auctions. Our room, with a working fireplace, was furnished with numerous antiques including a canopy bed, trunk, and antique chest." *(Gail Owings)* "Endorse existing entry. A pleasant small hotel, with clean, comfortable rooms and good food." *(Pat Borysiewicz)* "Delightful dinner in the plant-filled Conservatory, with wonderful salad and striped bass from the Catanias' Aquafarm. The apple cranberry bread pudding is a special dessert treat." *(DLG)*

Open All year. Closed Christmas Day.

Rooms 9 suites, 37 doubles—all with full private bath, telephone, radio, TV, desk, air-conditioning. Some with fireplace or whirlpool tub. Guest rooms in several buildings.

Facilities Restaurant, tavern, gift shop. 5 acres with flower gardens, swimming pool, gazebo. Health club, golf privileges.

Location Historic district. Take Rte. 6A to 3rd light, turn right on Jarves St. At end, turn right onto Main St. to inn.

Restrictions No smoking in some guest rooms. No pets.

Credit cards Amex, DC, Discover, MC, Visa.

Rates Room only, $89–199 suite, double. Extra person, $10. MAP, $170–280 suite, double. No charge for children under 12. 2-night weekend/holiday minimum. Alc breakfast, $7; alc lunch, $7–15; alc dinner, $22–45.

Extras Wheelchair access; some guest rooms equipped for disabled. Spanish, French, Portuguese, Italian, spoken. Crib.

STOCKBRIDGE

Reader tip: "The lovely village of Stockbridge is where Norman Rockwell lived and worked; don't miss the display of his famous magazine covers at the Norman Rockwell Museum. In addition to Tanglewood, another Stockbridge attraction is the Berkshire Theater Festival." *(Irving Litvag)*

Stockbridge is located in the Berkshires, just seven miles south of Tanglewood, summer home of the Boston Symphony, and five miles southwest of Exit 2 of the Mass. Pike.

The Red Lion Inn 🛏 ✕ ♿   *Tel:* 413–298–5545
Main Street, 01262   *Fax:* 413–298–5130
                      E-mail: innkeeper@redlioninn.com
                      URL: http://www.redlioninn.com

The Berkshires may now have more inns than antique shops (imagine!), but there is only one Red Lion, a wonderful old hotel of great charm and character. It's a tribute to its long-time owners, the Fitzpatricks, and its management, headed by Brooks Bradbury, that reader reports are consistently so positive. Founded in 1773, the Red Lion burned to the ground in 1896; soon rebuilt, it has since been enlarged and renovated many times, and is furnished with antiques and period reproductions. If you're traveling with friends or family, ask about the inn's annex houses, with a quiet location on the streets behind the inn; if you'd like a romantic escape, reserve the Firehouse, with an enormous common area on the ground floor, and luxurious bathroom and bedroom on the second.

The Red Lion is also a delightful place to eat. Although menus change frequently, a recent dinner included such entrees as roast halibut with parsley risotto; beef tenderloin with mushrooms and leeks; and braised artichokes with red lentils.

"Long-time owners, the Fitzpatrick family continually maintains and upgrades the inn. Our room had furnishings original to the hotel, but had been redone with new fabrics, wallpaper, and paint; feather pillows were on the firm beds, with extra foam ones in the closet. Equal attention to detail can be seen in the flowers which bedeck the inn during the summer; we were told that keeping them blooming is a full-time job. Standouts at dinner were the freshly steamed corn-on-the-cob and the apple pie. Fun Victorian ambience: the original birdcage elevator, assorted antique paintings, sideboards and sofas lining the long halls—even a glass case filled with century-old hats and shoes (the original lost and found, perhaps)." *(SWS)*

"The main dining room offers casual elegance, the tavern is cozy and romantic, and the Lion's Den is a great place for a light meal in an intimate atmosphere; excellent cappuccino, too." *(Sally Ducot, also MW)* "The staff was unfailingly cheerful and helpful." *(NB)* "Our room had twin beds with crisp white linens and lovely old spreads. Two rocking chairs with a reading lamp were by the window and an old pine desk held writing materials and information about Stockbridge. Plenty of electrical outlets and good lighting. Breakfast of fresh squeezed grapefruit juice, fresh muffins, and bagels was delivered punctually to our room. Most impressive is the constant care and updating." *(Wendy Van Exan)* "On a beautiful summer afternoon, there is no nicer place to be than rocking on the front porch of the Red Lion." *(William Gerhauser)*

Open All year.

Rooms 27 suites, 93 doubles—most with private bath and/or shower, 18 with shared bath. All with air-conditioning, telephone, TV, and desk. 18 rooms in adjacent buildings.

Facilities Restaurant, bars, tavern, TV rooms, living rooms, meeting rooms, automatic elevator. Live music in bars, restaurant. Courtyard, gardens, swimming pool, tennis court, exercise room.

Location SW MA, Berkshires. Center of town.

Restrictions Traffic noise in some rooms; light sleepers should ask for a courtyard room. Minimal interior soundproofing. Parking can be tight when inn is full. No smoking in dining rooms, most guest rooms. Most rooms accessible by elevator.

Credit cards Amex, CB, DC, MC, Visa.

Rates Room only, $167–350 suite, $97–165 double, $65–155 single, plus $2 daily housekeeping charge. Extra person, $20. B&B rates. Full breakfast, $5–10. Alc lunch, $9–20; alc dinner, $25–40. Children's menu. Off-season midweek packages Nov.–mid-May. Holiday menus, programs.

Extras Limited wheelchair access; 1 room specially equipped. Japanese, Spanish, German spoken. Crib, baby-sitting.

STURBRIDGE

For additional area entries, see **Tolland, Connecticut.**

Information please: A pleasant B&B choice is the **Bethany B&B** (5 McGregory Road, 01566; 508–347–5993), a Colonial-style home built in 1970 with four guest rooms, two with private baths and air-conditioning. B&B double rates of $85–95 include a breakfast of fresh fruit and juice, bacon and eggs or quiche, and home-baked breads and muffins, served from 7 to 9 A.M. Guests are invited to relax in the extensive gardens. "Colleen and Dennis are gracious hosts; she fixed us a hearty English breakfast, and he's very knowledgeable about area history." *(Susan Doucet)*

Publick House Historic Inn ✕ &.   *Tel:* 508–347–3313
P.O. Box 187, Route 131, On the Common, 01566   800–PUBLICK
                                       Fax: 508–347–5073
                       URL: http://www.publickhouse.com

Founded in 1771 by Colonel Ebenezer Crafts, the Publick House is now a large complex, including the original inn with 16 guest rooms furnished in Federalist Colonial style, plus several restaurants and shops. The 225-year-old slanted floors and exposed beams of the Publick House give a feeling of history to guest rooms furnished with four-poster acorn beds, fluffy pillows, firm mattresses, and period reproductions. The inn's restaurants share the same kitchen; extensive buffet breakfasts are served weekends in the main dining room, originally the stables and carriage house. Next door is Chamberlain House, with four suites and similar reproduction Colonial decor. In the same compound is the 94-room motor lodge, decorated in country decor. Finally there's the Colonel Ebenezer Crafts Inn, dating back to 1786 and located about 1½ miles away; its eight rooms are furnished with antiques and reproductions. Albert Cournoyer is the innkeeper.

"Our room at the Publick House was spotlessly clean, with a high-quality reproduction canopy bed, and fine linens. Excellent value." *(Paul Steinmetz, also BJ Hensley)* "Friendly and helpful staff made our stay delightful. The sticky buns are a highlight of the breakfast buffet." *(JFI)* "The lobster pie is scrumptious. Try the 'Joe Froggers' for dessert—large molasses cookies which arrive with an explanation of their name." *(Mary & Jim Rafferty)* "Every day is Thanksgiving at the Publick House, and the traditional turkey dinner with stuffing was a traditional treat." *(MW)*

Open All year.
Rooms 11 suites, 114 doubles—all with full private bath, desk, air-conditioning, fan. Rooms in 9 buildings.
Facilities 3 restaurants, gift shop, bake shop. 60 acres with swimming pool, tennis court, playground. Boating, fishing nearby.
Location Central MA. From Mass. Pike, take Exit 9, through tolls. Take Exit 3B to lights, turn left on Rte. 131. From I-84, take Exit 2 to Rte. 131.
Restrictions No smoking in some guest rooms. Traffic, restaurant noise in some rooms.
Credit cards Amex, CB, DC, MC, Visa.
Rates Room only, $114–155 suite, $90–135 double. Extra adult, $15; children under 17 free in parents' room. 10% AARP discount. B&B, MAP packages. Alc breakfast, $5–10; alc lunch, $12; alc dinner, $22–30. Theme weekend packages.
Extras Crib, baby-sitting. Wheelchair access to restaurant, lodge.

WELLFLEET

The Inn at Duck Creeke ¢ 👫 ✕ ♿   *Tel:* 508–349–9333
Main Street, P.O. Box 364, 02667   *Fax:* 508–349–0234 (summer)
Fax: 508–349–9333 (winter)
Email: duckinn@capecod.net
URL: http://www.capecod.net/duckinn

Owned by Bob Morrill and Judy Pihl since 1980, the Inn at Duck Creeke is set on a knoll overlooking Duck Pond, a tidal creek, and a salt marsh. The four buildings which make up the inn complex include the Captain's House, built in the early 1800s, and the equally venerable building housing the inn's two restaurants, Sweet Seasons and the Tavern Room. The innkeepers travel each winter to Europe or the Caribbean so that Chef Judy can add new dishes to her culinary repertoire—the Tavern's steak-and-ale puff pie was learned on a recent trip to England and Ireland. Favorite entrees at Sweet Seasons include shrimp with tomatoes, feta, garlic, and ouzo; pork with citrus, cilantro, and pine nuts; and chicken with garlic, sage, and vermouth cream. Choices at the Tavern are no less appealing, ranging from veggie and sirloin burgers to a New England boil: cod with shrimp, kale, and Portuguese sausage in vegetable broth; plus wonderful cod and salmon fishcakes. Although the inn is not a fancy place, upgrading is an on-going process; most recently, Judy notes that they've remodeled bathrooms, added carpeting and ceiling fans, and in 1999, will have new suites in the remodeled Salt-works building.

"The delectable little town of Wellfleet, with its many art galleries and craft shops, is as charming as nearby Provincetown is gaudy and honky-tonk. The simple but comfortable guest rooms are furnished with period pieces—Boston rockers, spool beds, and the like. Breakfasts are basic—served on paper plates with plastic cutlery—with excellent coffee in real mugs." *(Hilary Rubinstein)* "A wonderful creaky old house. We were delighted with the breakfast of fresh muffins and pastries served from 8–10 A.M., along with cereal and juice. We visited during a heat wave but our un-air-conditioned room was comfortable." *(Duane Roller)* "The helpful staff arranged for wonderful babysitters. Rooms are simple and small, yet comfortable; bathrooms basic but functional." *(BF)* "Charming airy rooms. Beautiful, peaceful in the fall. The Tavern offers good food, great fun. Bob and Judy are helpful, willing to accommodate guests' requests." *(Elizabeth McGinty)* "Pleasant atmosphere; peaceful, quiet ambiance. Owners sincerely interested in our comfort and enjoyment during our stay." *(Joseph Laput)*

Open Early May–mid-Oct.
Rooms 25 doubles—17 with private bath and/or shower, 8 with a maximum of 4 people sharing a bath. Some with air-conditioning, all with ceiling fan. 7 rooms in annex.
Facilities Restaurant, tavern with live music, breakfast room, common room, screened porches, veranda. Swimming, boating, fishing, hiking, bicycling nearby.
Location Cape Cod, 17 m S of Provincetown, 100 m SE of Boston. Take Rte. 6

to Wellfleet; turn left at Wellfleet Center sign at traffic lights. Go 500 yds. to inn on right. Historic district; ½ m to village.

Restrictions Traffic, restaurant noise in some rooms. No refunds late June through Labor Day; transferable credit given toward a future stay.

Credit cards Amex, MC, Visa.

Rates B&B, $65–100 double. Extra person, $15; children under 5 in parents' room, $5. 2–3 night weekend minimum in season. Alc dinner $12–20. $10 one-time charge for crib, cot.

Extras Limited handicap access. Crib, baby-sitting.

Key to Abbreviations and Symbols

For complete information and explanations, please see the Introduction.

¢ Especially good value for overnight accommodation.

♠ Families welcome. Most (but not all) have cribs, baby-sitting, games, play equipment, and reduced rates for children.

✕ Meals served to public; reservations recommended or required.

⚲ Tennis court and swimming pool and/or lake on grounds. Golf usually on grounds or nearby.

⚿ Limited or full wheelchair access; call for details.

Rates: Range from least expensive room in low season to most expensive room in peak season.

Room only: No meals included; European Plan (EP).

B&B: Bed and breakfast; includes breakfast, sometimes afternoon/evening refreshment.

MAP: Modified American Plan; includes breakfast and dinner.

Full board: Three meals daily.

Alc lunch: A la carte lunch; average price of entrée plus nonalcoholic drink, tax, tip.

Alc dinner: Average price of three-course dinner, including half bottle of house wine, tax, tip.

Prix fixe dinner: Three- to five-course set dinner, excluding wine, tax, tip unless otherwise noted.

Extras: Noted if available. Always confirm in advance. Pets are not permitted unless specified; if you are allergic, ask for details; *most innkeepers have pets.*

Michigan

Kingsley House, Saugatuck (Fennville)

Taking its name from the Indian words for "the great water" *(Michi gami)*, Michigan is made up of the mitten-shaped Lower Peninsula, and the rugged terrain of the isolated Upper Peninsula; they meet at the Straits of Mackinac. A recommended drive follows Routes 31 and 22, south from the Mackinac Bridge along Lake Michigan through Petoskey (scour the beach here for fossilized coral), Charlevoix (balanced on a narrow strip of land between Lakes Michigan and Charlevoix), around Grand Traverse Bay, and through the Sleeping Bear Dunes National Lakeshore (scenic detritus left by the last glaciers).

The state's economy is diverse, with heavy industry—most notably cars and cereals—based in the south, substantial agriculture, and a prosperous tourist business throughout. Bordered by four of the Great Lakes, and with 11,000 inland lakes, water sports are of course a key attraction on both peninsulas, along with hunting and skiing.

Note to families: State antidiscrimination legislation has caused Michigan's B&Bs to become nervous about prohibiting young children as guests, and a number have asked us to drop the line in their write-up which read "No children under 12" or words to that effect. But, if you're looking for a place where your family will be welcomed—not just tolerated—look for entries with our family symbol:

ANN ARBOR

Named both for a grape arbor and after the given names of the town's founding pioneers—Ann Allen and Ann Rumsey—Ann Arbor is best known as the home of the University of Michigan. Key sights include the Gothic buildings of the Law Quadrangle, the Performing Arts Center, and the sports stadium, seating over 100,000 fans.

Also recommended: With a name like **The Artful Lodger** (1547 Washtenaw, Ann Arbor, 48104; 734–769–0653; www.annarbor.org/artlodger) you could assume that the innkeepers have an interest in literature, theater, a good sense of humor, or all of the above. Edith Bookstein (she's a costume designer) and her husband, Fred, are the owners of this 1859 stone house, built for Professor Henry Simmons Frieze (later president of the University of Michigan. "The Artful Lodger is airy and fanciful with quiet public rooms. The service, hospitality, housekeeping, cleanliness, lighting, parking, and location are the finest. The four guest rooms are off to themselves in various Victorian ways—round little halls, up different stairwells—so you enjoy privacy but are just a stroll away from the grand living/music room for company. The breakfast was lavish and full of choices for nongreasers and anti-egg types. The company of the innkeepers was amusing and kindly." *(Diana Van Fossen)* Double rates are $60–105 (higher on University and sports weekends), and include a continental breakfast midweek, and a full meal on weekends, with vegetarian, kosher, and heart-healthy options available.

DETROIT/DEARBORN

The Motor City is also a major port and industrial center. Of interest to visitors are the shops and restaurants of Greektown, and the Detroit Institute of Arts, one of America's finest art museums. In nearby Dearborn, the Henry Ford Museum and Greenfield Village are home to outstanding collections highlighting the history of transportation and technology in the U.S.

Reader tip: "Be sure to eat at least one meal in Greektown. The Greek food is especially good, and the prices are reasonable. You can get there easily on foot or take the People Mover from downtown."

Information please—hotels: In the heart of Greektown is **The Atheneum** (1000 Brush Avenue, Greektown, 48226; 313–962–2323 or 800–772–2323), a 175-room all suite hotel. Suites are equipped with two-line phones and two TVs; corner suites have whirlpool baths. Rates for most suites range from $125 –250, with special weekend packages available.

Now run by Marriott, **The Dearborn Inn** (20301 Oakwood Boulevard, Dearborn, 48124; 313–271–2700 or 800–228–9290) was Henry Ford's vision of the ideal inn. "Lovingly renovated and enlarged. Beautiful antique reproduction furniture in our room in the newer section of the main inn building. Lovely grounds for strolling—lots of flowers. Directly across from Greenfield Village and Henry Ford Museums." *(HB)* The hotel is set on 23 acres with 234 rooms in the Georgian-style inn, the Colonial-reproduction homes, and a motor lodge; double rates range from $109–159.

Another good choice is the 308-room **Ritz-Carlton, Dearborn** (300 Town Center Drive, Dearborn, 48126; 313–441–2000 or 800–241–3333; www.ritzcarlton.com). Although a new building, the Ritz creates the impression of an older luxury hotel with Oriental rugs, Spanish chandeliers, English porcelain, and original 18th- and 19th-century artwork. Guest rooms come with mahogany antique reproduction furniture, plus all the modern amenities and lots of little extras. Double rates range from $119–195; weekend packages start at $155.

Information please—B&Bs: A half-block from the Detroit River and the mayor's residence is **The Blanche House Inn** (506 Parkview, Detroit, 48214; 313–822–7090; www.millynnium.com/castle-blanche), a 1905 Greek Revival mansion with twenty-foot Corinthian porch pillars and ten-foot entrance doors of etched glass; guest rooms are also available in its sister mansion, The Castle, built in 1898. Interior features include ornate plaster moldings and medallions, beautiful oak woodwork, and Pewabic tiling. Each of the eight guest rooms have antique furnishings, private baths, TV, and telephone. Those at the back of the inn have views of the Stanton Canal, Waterworks Park, the Detroit River, and a working boathouse. B&B double rates include breakfasts of fresh fruit and home-baked goods, and range from $75–125.

In Detroit's historic downtown Corktown neighborhood is the **Corktown Inn** (1705 Sixth Street, Detroit, 48226; 313–963–6688), an American Federal-style row house built in 1850. Completely restored and renovated as a B&B in 1994 by Richard Kokochak and Chet Allen, it is furnished with period antiques and original artwork by local artists. B&B double rates for the four suites are $115–135 and include wake-up coffee, morning paper, breakfast, and a never-empty cookie jar and fruit bowl; each room has a private bath, TV/VCR, air-conditioning, and telephone, and two have whirlpool tubs. Breakfast favorites reflect the area's ethnic diversity with Greek toast souffle or huevos Corktowneros. In good weather, guests enjoy relaxing in the courtyard garden with fountain and pergola.

Built in 1927 by a lumber baron, the **Dearborn B&B** (22331 Morley, Dearborn, 48124; 313–563–2200 or 888–959–0900; www.dearbornbb.com) is a short walk from area shops, museums, and restaurants. The original detailed hand-crafted woodwork is complemented by antique furnishings, Original rugs, goosedown comforters, lace, and fine linens; each of the four guest rooms has a private bath, telephone, and TV. The B&B double rates of $95 ($165 for the suite) include wine and cheese on arrival, and a continental breakfast buffet.

LAWRENCE

Oak Cove Resort ¢ ♀ ✕
58881 46th Street, 49064

Tel: 616–674–8228
In winter: 630–983–8025
Fax: 616–674–3895
E-mail: oakcove@aol.com
URL: http://www.oakcove.com

One of Michigan's oldest and smallest resorts, Oak Cove dates back to the turn of the century, and has been owned by Susan and Bob Wojcik since 1973. Recent improvements include a new, more efficient kitchen, recarpeting of the lodge and dining rooms, redecorating of the lodge guest rooms, new playground equipment, and additional landscaping.

"Susan and Bob are like family after 17 years of vacationing at Oak Cove. They suggest places to see, unique shops, and activities for children if the weather is cool or rainy. Our grown children now come with spouses and friends. The food continues to be a big draw, with a variety of fresh fruits and vegetables. Susan packs a lunch if needed. Every year we return to find improvements have been made." *(Joan Butler)* "The Lake House was a perfect fit for our family, with plenty of room, great views of the lake, and air-conditioning. Excellent food with plenty of variety and seconds always available. Ample paddleboats, canoes, rowboats, and more for our use. The vouchers enabled us to play golf for free each day. Pleasant owners and staff made our stay relaxing and fun." *(PR)* "The kids enjoy going back and forth between the pool and lake, and a selection of bikes are available for riding. If there are any special needs, you know Susan and Bob will do all they can to see that they are met. Not having to worry about cooking or clean-up makes the vacation especially relaxing for me, and the whole family loves Susan's cooking." *(Deborah Janiasz)*

"Susan and Bob are always ready to answer questions, recommend local points of interest, and lend a hand. Our lodge room was kept cool with fans; the shared baths are kept clean, and plumbing problems quickly repaired. Children can enjoy the 'Fun House' without disturbing adults." *(Joan Butler)* "The lodge rooms are decorated with antiques; the air is fresh; and meals are served on a glassed/screened-in porch overlooking the lake. Susan and Bob have retained the ambience of a 1910 summer resort, with some judicious updating." *(Betsy Ray)* "The accommodations range from the quaint and charming lodge rooms, to the rustic older cabins, to the modern and comfortable houses at the edge of the property." *(Jean Karres)* "Beautifully clean, clear lake. The sandy beach has plenty of tree-shaded spots, with delightful wooden swings for lazy reading, and several swing sets for the little ones. Susan and her helpers prepare delicious meat-and-potato meals, with wonderful vegetable side dishes and a big salad bar." *(Cathy Miller)* "The young staff work hard and provide efficient service." *(Charles Wheeler)*

Open Early June–mid-Sept.
Rooms 7 doubles in main lodge share 4 baths. 11 1- to 4-bedroom cottages with shower, porch. 7 with air-conditioning, 4 with fireplace.

327

Facilities Living room with TV/VCR, video library; "Fun House" with pinball, jukebox, pool table, books, games, bar. 16 acres with heated swimming pool, fitness trail, lake with 500 ft. sand beach, boats, canoes, fishing, children's play equipment, bicycling, hiking. Free golf; 18 holes per day per adult.

Location SW MI. 3 hrs. W of Detroit, 2 hrs. E of Chicago, 5 m from Paw Paw. Take Exit 56 off I-94. Go N ½m on Rte. 51 to Red Arrow Hwy. Go W 1 m to fork; bear left and follow signs.

Restrictions No smoking in lodge guest rooms. No daily maid service.

Credit cards None accepted.

Rates Weekly, full board, $720 lodge double, $790 cottage double. Daily, full board, $145–160 double, $65–105 single. Children, $105–275 weekly; $20–60 daily, depending on age. Extra adult, $65. 15% service. Prix fixe lunch, $6.50; prix fixe dinner, $13.50. Golfing weekends.

Extras Airport/station pickups. Crib, baby-sitting.

MACKINAC ISLAND

The Upper and Lower Peninsulas are connected at the Straits of Mackinac by the Mackinac Bridge, at five miles one of the longest suspension bridges in the world—a twentieth-century achievement that forms a pleasant contrast with the nineteenth-century charms of Mackinac Island.

A trip to Mackinac (pronounced *Mackinaw*) Island is a trip back to another era. Cars were banned from the island in the thirties; you drive to either Mackinaw City (Lower Peninsula) or St. Ignace (Upper Peninsula) and park at the ferry. The dock porters meet all boats as they arrive at Mackinac, and help transfer luggage to the hotels. You can get around the island on foot, hire a horse-drawn carriage, or rent a bike from one of the many rental shops.

Reader tips: "It's not difficult to see why Mackinac Island has become such a popular summer resort. As you approach by ferry or hydroplane, you see high cliffs rising from the shoreline change to wooded bluffs dotted with some remarkable houses. Then, rounding a bend, you see a charming village nestled around the harbor. The sheer number of tourists milling about the village, along with the inevitable fudge and T-shirt 'shoppes,' may cause you momentary panic, but don't let it deter you from exploring the island's natural beauty. About 3 miles long and 2 miles wide (four-fifths of the island is a state park), Mackinac is basically a limestone outcropping with ravines, natural bridges, caves, and interesting rock formations. Rent a bicycle and explore the beach road and the cliffs—it doesn't take long to get away from the crowd." *(MS)* "The individual carriage rides are far more enjoyable than the group ones, and are well worth the extra cost." *(Peg Bedini, also RRS)* "Outstanding food at the **Yankel Rebel Tavern**; convenient location just off the main street." *(Pat Malone)*

Also recommended: Although with 275 rooms and plenty of convention business, the **Grand Hotel** (49757; 906–847–3331 or 800–334–7263; www.grandhotel.com) is not right for this guide, it is a splendid century-old establishment, and well worth seeing. You can pay about $5 to tour the grounds, or dress up in your finest and come for dinner. Rates for two range from $310–1020, including breakfast and dinner.

The **Hotel Iroquois** (298 Main Street, P.O. Box 456, 49757; 906–847–3321) is a rambling Victorian structure with plenty of turrets and gables, overlooking the beautiful Straits of Mackinac. Rates for the 47 guest rooms vary with room size, location, season, and view, from $98–365. Continental breakfast is served in the rooms, and breakfast, lunch, dinner, and drinks are available in the hotel's Carriage House restaurant. "An outstanding facility located at the edge of town, in a quiet area, overlooking the water. The lapping of waves and the clip-clopping of horses' hooves will lull you to sleep." *(Robert Johnson)*

Haan's 1830 Inn 🕯

Huron Street, P.O. Box 123, 49757

Winter address: 3418 Oakwood, Island Lake, IL 60042

Tel: 906–847–6244
Winter: 847–526–2662

One of Mackinac's oldest buildings, Haan's 1830 Inn sits on the foundations of a log cabin built in the late 1700s. The present structure, a pillared Greek Revival cottage, dates back to 1830. In the early 1900s, the house served as the residence of Colonel William Preston, an officer at Fort Mackinac and the mayor of the island. The Haan family bought the inn in 1976, and restored it as a bed and breakfast, furnishing it with period antiques. Breakfast includes fruit, juice, and fresh-baked breads, muffins, and coffee cakes.

"Relaxing on one of the three porches, watching the horse-drawn carriages pass by, takes one back to an earlier time. Everything about the inn is top quality, from the linens, to the warm, fresh breakfast muffins, to the beautiful antique furnishings. The Haans' hospitality makes you feel like family." *(Marcia Robbins)* "We enjoyed a tasty breakfast while talking with the other guests at one big table." *(Pat & Glen Lush)* "Away from the downtown crush, the inn has a beautiful setting next to St. Ann's Church. The front yard is highlighted by huge ferns, which give the setting a woodsy look." *(John Blewer)* "Quiet, but close to all activities." *(Hugo & Kathy Ritzenthaler)*

Open Mid-May–mid-Oct.

Rooms 2 suites, 5 doubles—5 with private bath and/or shower, 2 sharing 1 bathroom. All with fan, desk. 1 suite with kitchen.

Facilities Dining room with fireplace, living room with books, games. 2 open porches, 1 screened porch. Large yard adjacent to garden of church. 3 blocks to fort, village. Near ferry dock and charter fishing. Bike, horse, carriage rentals, golf, tennis nearby.

Location 4 blocks E of ferry docks on Huron Street. From MI Lower Peninsula, go N on I-75 to Mackinaw City, then 7½ m ferry trip. From WI and MI Upper Peninsula, take Rte. 2 to St. Ignace, then 3½ m ferry trip.

Restrictions No smoking.

Credit cards None accepted.

Rates B&B, $140–150 suite, $80–130 double. Extra person, $10. No tipping. 20–25% discount midweek off-season.

Extras Cribs, cots.

SAUGATUCK

A well-known art colony close to the shores of Lake Michigan, Saugatuck is an attractive resort town. It's most popular in the summer months for swimming and windsurfing on Lake Michigan, plus hiking in the dunes and canoeing on the Kalamazoo River; cross-country skiing has become popular as well. Visitors also enjoy browsing through the town's lovely shops and art galleries.

The town is located in southeastern Michigan, 35 miles southwest of Grand Rapids and 10 miles south of Holland. Rates are generally highest on weekends, May through October, and a two-night minimum stay on weekends is usually required for advance reservations. Many shops and restaurants are closed midweek off-season, so call ahead if your heart is set on one in particular.

Reader tips: "Parking is a problem in Saugatuck in the summer. Look for an inn close to town, so you can park the car and walk everywhere. The Saugatuck area is appealing in season, with lots to see and do." *(Pam Phillips)* "Although it's impossible to get a table in summer, we needed no reservations for our off-season dinner at Chequers, a British-style pub, with Watney's Ale on tap, and tasty food at reasonable prices. Under the same ownership is Toulouse, a good fine-dining restaurant nearby." *(SWS)*

Also recommended: Built in 1874, **Beechwood Manor** (736 Pleasant Street, P.O. Box 876, 49453; 616–857–1587) enjoys a quiet residential location, yet is just an easy walk to town. B&B double rates for the five guest rooms, each with queen-size bed, private bath, and fireplace, are $105–185, including a full breakfast and use of the inn's tandem bike. "A lovely wraparound porch with rocking chairs overlooks the beautifully landscaped yard. Our room are decorated in cozy fabrics and warm colors with a hardwood floor; the bathroom was pristine and lovely as well. Breakfast was a highlight, from French toast with fresh fruit, to egg souffle, to blueberry waffles to German apple pancakes. Owners Jim and Sharron were kind and great to talk with over breakfast. Wonderful herb garden, too." *(Kim Fitzgerald)*

Built at the turn of the last century as a lumbermen's boarding house is the **Twin Oaks Inn** (227 Griffith Street, P.O. Box 867, 49453; 616–857–1600 or 800–788–6188), just one block from the docks. Each of the ten guest rooms have a private bath, air-conditioning, and a TV/VCR; B&B double rates range from $65–125. Guests can relax with a movie from the extensive library, with refreshments by the common room fireplace, in the garden or hot tub. "Clean, well-maintained, caring staff. Excellent breakfast of fresh fruits and homemade breads. Quiet location, with off-street parking, yet convenient to shops and restaurants." *(HJB)*

Two miles south, across the Kalamazoo River, is the **Sherwood Forest B&B** (938 Center Street, 49453; 616–857–1246 or 800–838–1246; sherwoodforest@hayburn.com), a century-old home opened as a B&B in 1992. Former Chicagoans Keith and Susan Charak have decorated it cheerfully with both period antiques and more contemporary furnishings and artwork; the dark original woodwork contrasts with walls of deep colors and floral wallpapers. Breakfast includes fresh fruit salad, orange juice, cereals, and possibly blueberry bran muffins, lemon yogurt bread, or banana bread. The five guest rooms all have private baths, and there's a separate two-bedroom cottage, with kitchen and laundry facilities, on the spacious grounds; double rates range from $85–165.

Minutes from Saugatuck is the **Kingsley House** (626 Main Street, Fennville, 49408; 616–561–6425), a turreted Queen Anne Victorian built in 1886. The original Kingsleys introduced apples to this part of Michigan over a century ago; guest rooms are appropriately named after locally grown apples: Dutchess, Jonathan, Golden Delicious, McIntosh, and Granny Smith. Double rates of $80–165 include a continental breakfast on weekdays, full breakfast on weekends. "Welcoming owners, beautiful Victorian decor, delicious breakfasts, immaculate housekeeping." *(CP)*

For a convenient in-town location, beautiful dècor, wonderful food, and pleasant staff, a fine choice is the well-known **Wickwood Inn** (510 Butler Street, P.O. Box 1019, 49453–1019; 616–857–1465) owned by Julee Rosso (of *Silver Palate* cookbook fame), and her husband, Bill Miller. Fresh-brewed coffee is set out every morning at seven, and a breakfast of fresh fruit, granola, muffins, and coffee cake is served from 8:00–10:00 A.M. weekdays, with a 9:30 A.M. buffet brunch on weekends. The cocktail hour starts at 6:00 P.M. in the library, with the innkeepers providing hors d'oeuvres and mixers; guests are welcome to supply their favorite beverage. The decor features wonderful fabric combinations, from tartan plaids and cabbage roses in the stunning Carrie Wicks Suite, to the blue and white checked patterns of the appropriately named Wee Bridgadoon room. All are equipped with robes, snacks, and reading materials. B&B double rates for the 11 guest rooms range from $165–215.

SOUTH HAVEN

South Haven is located on Lake Michigan, in the southwestern part of the state, about 2 hours northeast of Chicago, and 3½ hours west of Detroit. Area activities include all the water sports Lake Michigan makes possible (including great beaches), plus golf, cross-country skiing, winery tours, and fruit-picking in season. Summer is the area's busiest season, although the many sugar maples make the fall colors glorious. Winter is the quietest time, although many city visitors savor a pre-Christmas weekend in the country, enjoying the courteous service and free gift wrapping offered in local shops, and bringing home a freshly cut, reasonably priced Christmas tree.

Also recommended: You'll have a choice of two locations if you stay at the **Carriage House** (233 Dyckman Avenue and 118 Woodman, 49090; 616–639–1776); one nine guest-room property is across from Stanley Johnson Park, the other, with 11 rooms, is at the harbor, overlooking the Black River marina. Both recently restored properties are decorated with antiques and Amish furniture; all guest rooms have a private bath, air-conditioning, and TV/VCR, at B&B double rates of $95 to $175; most have a fireplace or whirlpool tub. "Warm, welcoming innkeepers; ample common areas; immaculate rooms. We were welcomed with chocolate chip cookies and cocoa; wonderful hors d'oeuvres and cold drinks were offered before dinner; breakfast was a feast of poppy seed muffins, sausage casserole, potatoes, and coffee cake." *(L. & B.J. Schwartzkopf)*

Yelton Manor B&B   *Tel:* 616–637–5220
140 North Shore Drive, 49090   *Fax:* 616–637–4957
           E-mail: elaine@yeltonmanor.com
           URL: http://www.yeltonmanor.com

A rambling Victorian home, Yelton Manor was built in 1873 for Lulu and Dee Delamere of Chicago. They ran it as a rooming house; in 1947 it was remodeled as a small hotel. Fully restored in 1988, it is now owned by Elaine Herbert and Rob Kripaitis. The outside of this painted lady has soft gray clapboards, contrasting with pale pink fishscale shingles, highlighted by white trim and rose detailing. Rates for guest rooms in the manor include a full breakfast and afternoon refreshments; guests looking for a greater degree of privacy may request a room in the adjacent guest house; rates here include continental breakfast. A typical full breakfast consists of egg strata with fresh salsa, home-fried potatoes, English muffins, orange coffee cake, fresh fruit and juices.

"Terrific inn with great owners who work hard to keep it in top-notch condition, fresh as a pin and clean as a whistle. Guest rooms are beautifully decorated with top quality traditional furnishings, but are mercifully free of cutesy country clutter. The extensive common areas offer ample spaces for both seclusion or sociability." *(SWS)* "Immaculate; beautiful decor; hospitable hosts; delicious homemade food with recipes offered." *(H. Kayayan)* "Wonderful flower gardens. Soda, popcorn, cookies, and candy are always available in the common areas. Elaine and Rob work hard to make you comfortable, and are delightful conversationalists. Wonderful evening appetizers served at 5:30 P.M.; delicious breakfasts. Across the street from Lake Michigan beaches, and a short walk to excellent restaurant and interesting shops. We parked the car on Friday, and never moved it until we left." *(Judith Barnett)* "Great homemade cookies." *(LuAnn & Steve Weiner)* "The Iris Suite has a Jacuzzi tub, king-size bed with canopy, and sitting area." *(Deborah Cortopassi)* "The hearty, delicious breakfast is served in several locations, for your choice of privacy or mingling with other guests." *(Glennyce Moerman)*

Open All year.
Rooms 8 suites, 9 doubles—all with private shower and/or bath, central air-conditioning, TV/VCR. Some with Jacuzzi tub, fireplace. 6 suites in guest house.
Facilities Dining room; 2 parlors with TV/VCR, fireplaces; guest refrigerator; den with TV, books, 1,000-tape video library; porches. Conference facilities with support staff. Perennial, rose gardens. Across street from beach.
Location Take Rte. 196 to Phoenix Street (196 Business). Turn right on Broad-

way. At drawbridge Broadway turns into Dyckman. Take Dyckman to stop sign. Inn is at left corner of Dyckman and N. Shore Dr.

Restrictions No smoking. "Adults only B&B."

Credit cards Amex, MC, Visa.

Rates B&B, $155–230 suite, $90–175 double.

UNION PIER/NEW BUFFALO

Long a getaway resort for Chicagoans (it's just a 90-minute drive), Harbor Country includes the town of New Buffalo, and the adjacent residential resort areas of Union Pier, Lakeside, and Grand Beach. It's located on Lake Michigan in the southwest corner of the state, about five miles north of the Indiana border. Favorite activities include swimming, fishing, golfing, bicycling, and skiing. Roaming local country roads, looking for antique shops, wineries, orchards, and dunes to explore is no less appealing.

Reader tips: "Our favorite pastime is riding our bikes to visit the nearby wineries—it's ten miles to Tabor Hill Winery. The dunes in Warren Dunes State Park make scenic and relaxing hiking terrain; the beaches there are wide and sandy." *(Dave Marzke)* "When my hearty inn breakfast wore off around 3 P.M., I recharged my batteries with an ice cream cone at Oink's in New Buffalo. Good choices for dinner are Brewsters and Millers." *(SWS)*

Also recommended: The **Pine Garth Inn** (15790 Lake Shore Road, P.O. Box 347, Union Pier, 49129; 616–469–1642) is a restored summer estate right on the lake, complete with a 200-foot sugar-sand beach. Nearly all rooms have dramatic lake views, and are decorated eclectically with country florals, brass beds, and some antiques. B&B double rates for the seven guest rooms range from $115–170, and include a full breakfast and afternoon refreshments. Across the street, five adjacent cottages provide housekeeping accommodations ideal for families. "The best lake views of any B&B I saw in Harbor Country." *(SWS)*

Garden Grove (9549 Union Pier Road, Union Pier, 49129; 616–469–6346 or 800–613–2872; www.laketolake.com/gardengrove) is a recently renovated B&B, with bright and fresh common areas, an inviting deck and hot tub, and two friendly, cheerful, young owners, Mary Ellen and Ric Postlewaite. "The comfortable guest rooms are well lit with ample storage; two have double Jacuzzi tubs and gas-log fireplaces. My room was done in rose; another lovely one had a violet color scheme, accented by a white picket fence serving as the bed's headboard. I was welcomed with hot tea and home-baked brownies. Breakfast included fresh fruit salad, apple muffins, pancakes with blueberry sauce, and a chocolate-dipped strawberry for dessert." *(SWS)* B&B double rates range from $80–160.

For a change of pace, try the **Bauhaus on Barton** (33 North Barton Street, New Buffalo, 49117; 616–469–6419), a 1948 International Moderne–style home. Rates for the three guest rooms, each with private bath, range from $95–130; the two-bedroom suite is $200. "Combines modern amenities with 1950s-era furnishings, a nice change from the usual Victorian and Colonial-style B&Bs. Well done with a sense of humor. Next door is Brewster's restaurant, and a block away are the charming shops of New Buffalo's main street. Unusually good full breakfast." *(MM)*

Appealing for both families and private getaways is **Sans Souci** 19265 South Lakeside Road, New Buffalo, 49117; 616–756–3141; www.sans-souci.com), a few miles east of Lake Michigan. The inn is made up of four homes and cottages spread over the ample grounds, with rates ranging from $110–220. "Beautiful area, slightly hilly, with a lovely private spring-fed pond, ideal for swimming; nice walking trails too. Furnishings throughout are clean, bright, simple, uncluttered, inviting. An ideal choice for those traveling with children and/or dogs, since both are welcome. Delightful owner, Angie Siewert." *(SWS)*

The Inn at Union Pier   ♿   *Tel:* 616–469–4700
9708 Berrien Road, P.O. Box 222, 49129   *Fax:* 616–469–4720
                        URL: http://www.innatunionpier.com

Chicagoans are thrilled to have found a relaxing retreat less than two hours' drive around the lake—The Inn at Union Pier. Opened in 1985, it was purchased in 1993 by Mark and Joyce Erickson Pitts. The inn features an open and sunny great room, inviting decks for summer breakfasts or a soak in the hot tub, and elegantly decorated guest rooms. Lake Michigan's beaches are "just two hundred steps from the front door." Breakfast menus change daily, and might include baked apples, blueberry streusel muffins, walnut pancakes with raspberry sauce, and sausages; or fresh berries with vanilla cream sauce, lemon walnut muffins, tomato-basil-mozzarella frittata, and roast potatoes.

"The inn's three white-trimmed blue buildings surround a beautifully landscaped flagstone courtyard. The inn's 19th-century Swedish cottage style blends antiques with clean-lined, unfussy comfort. The huge rose-colored great room with three seating areas, five game tables, and a floor-to-ceiling fireplace is a wonderful place to read, chat, and relax. " *(Susan Woods, also SWS)* "Guests are greeted with fresh baked cookies and lemonade in summer, hot chocolate in winter." *(Kathryn Havlish)* "The antique Swedish kakelugn fireplaces are great in winter. Each room has an assortment of books and magazines. Plenty of hot water, thick towels, and comfy beds. Superb location far from the sounds of traffic." *(Ann Scher)* "The rooms are meticulously clean, furnished with a mix of antiques, new furniture, and great mattresses. Extra touches include a bedside flashlight, an umbrella in the armoire, a sewing basket, homemade cookies and lemonade in the afternoon, as well as wine and popcorn in the afternoon. The delightful breakfast is served over a generous two-hour time span." *(Jane Renkes)* "Spacious Captain's Quarters, with an inviting whirlpool tub. The breakfast room is inviting and sunny; service was friendly and seconds on pancakes were gladly provided. Many thoughtful extras for guests." *(Pat Malone)*

Open All year. Closed Christmas week.
Rooms 2 suites, 14 doubles—all with full private bath, radio, clock, air-

conditioning, fan. 7 with balcony, 12 with fireplace. 1 suite with whirlpool tub, wet bar; 1 suite with Jacuzzi tub, TV, wood-burning fireplace, stocked kitchen, covered balcony. 10 rooms in 2 adjoining buildings.

Facilities Dining room with fireplace, TV/VCR, stereo; living room with fireplace, piano; library; decks. 1 acre with hot tub, sauna, hammock, lawn games, bicycles. Off-street parking. ½ block to Lake Michigan.

Location 4 m from town. Take Exit 6 off I-94 N, go W on Townline Rd. 1 m to flashing light. Turn right on Red Arrow Highway. Go ½ m, turn left on Berrien. Go 1½ blocks to inn on left.

Restrictions No smoking. Children over 12 preferred. Occasional trains.

Credit cards Discover, MC, Visa.

Rates B&B, $175–195 suite; $125–155 double. Extra person, $20. 2-3 night weekend, holiday weekend. Off-season midweek packages.

Extras Station pickups.

Key to Abbreviations and Symbols

For complete information and explanations, please see the Introduction.

¢ Especially good value for overnight accommodation.

♠ Families welcome. Most (but not all) have cribs, baby-sitting, games, play equipment, and reduced rates for children.

✕ Meals served to public; reservations recommended or required.

𝕂 Tennis court and swimming pool and/or lake on grounds. Golf usually on grounds or nearby.

♿ Limited or full wheelchair access; call for details.

Rates: Range from least expensive room in low season to most expensive room in peak season.

Room only: No meals included; European Plan (EP).

B&B: Bed and breakfast; includes breakfast, sometimes afternoon/evening refreshment.

MAP: Modified American Plan; includes breakfast and dinner.

Full board: Three meals daily.

Alc lunch: A la carte lunch; average price of entrée plus nonalcoholic drink, tax, tip.

Alc dinner: Average price of three-course dinner, including half bottle of house wine, tax, tip.

Prix fixe dinner: Three- to five-course set dinner, excluding wine, tax, tip unless otherwise noted.

Extras: Noted if available. Always confirm in advance. Pets are not permitted unless specified; if you are allergic, ask for details; *most innkeepers have pets.*

Minnesota

St. James Hotel, Red Wing

Minnesota is best known for being a nice place to live—but that doesn't mean you wouldn't want to visit there. The Twin Cities, Minneapolis/St. Paul, have outstanding theaters, museums, and cultural attractions; the countryside has more lakes than you can count, as well as numerous historic river valleys to explore by boat, foot, or bicycle. Travelers driving up Route 61 to Minneapolis would do well to stop and explore the historic Mississippi River bluff towns of Hastings, Red Wing, Frontenac, Lake City, Winona, and Wabasha. Duluth and Lake Superior's North Shore are also very popular; see our listings in the Grand Marais area. Other recommendations: Pipestone National Monument, a sacred Indian stone quarry in the state's southwestern corner; Jeffers Petroglyphs (north of I-90, off Route 71); and, in far northeastern Minnesota, Grand Portage National Monument, dedicated to the voyagers who used this 8½-mile portage during the area's fur trade.

COOK

Ludlow's Island Lodge 🏃 🎣
P.O. Box 1146, Lake Vermilion, 55723

Tel: 218–666–5407
877–LUDLOWS
Fax: 218–666–2488
E-mail: info@ludlowsresort.com
URL: http://www.ludlowsresort.com

The Ludlow family has owned and run this rustic family resort for over 50 years. Mark and Sally Ludlow, the second-generation owners, welcome back a fair share of second-generation guests each year. They note that "our staff caters to families with such activities as pontoon rides, hot dog roasts, marshmallow campfires, nature hikes, and fishing contests. Adults are pampered with full-length terry robes and daily newspaper delivery, and all feel safe knowing that only registered guests are allowed on the property. We offer guided trips to nearby lakes for canoeing and fishing; pontoon rides to identify waterfowl, eagles, beaver lodges, and turtles; and picnics at a nearby waterfall with plant and tree identification along the way."

The cabins are spaced out over their small private island, with several more on the nearby south and north shore of the lake, each within 60 feet of the water's edge. To facilitate your travels between your cabin, the main lodge, and the recreation center, rates include shuttle service and free use of their many canoes, kayaks, and sailboats. Lake Vermilion is 40 miles long, with 365 islands and 1,200 miles of shoreline, and offers fishing for walleye, northern pike, large and smallmouth bass, plus crappies and panfish.

"The Northshore cabin is perfect for two, with a kitchen, small living/dining area with fireplace, a bedroom with king-size bed, a bathroom with whirlpool tub, shower, and double sinks, plus a screened porch for afternoon siestas and reading." *(Gail & Myles Brostrom)* "Ideal for families. All the joys (and none of the discomforts) of camping." *(Therese Tulloch)* "The 'gourmet pantry' demonstrates Ludlow's philosophy of hospitality and service; unusual items are stocked in addition to basics like bread and milk. Spices and small appliances are loaned to guests. The pantry is open 24 hours daily, on an honor system, so if you have a taste for an ice cream sandwich at midnight, it's just a short walk away." *(Wanda & Terrence Joy)* "Each cabin's screened-in porch is out of view of neighboring cabins, for privacy. Dock hands will clean your catch, launch boats, and offer guidance." *(Frank Obermeier)* "Meticulously maintained cabins, continually being updated. The staff is well trained and attentive, without intruding on your privacy." *(Barbara Wilson & others)*

"Children can explore the island paths (lighted at night) connecting the cabins, lodge, and beach areas; they can play basketball, football, tennis, racquetball, or watch a movie on a rainy day." *(Al & Joanne Hinderaker)* "Sunsets, loons, and cozy cabins; no TV or telephone." *(Terri & Craig Innes)* "It's an easy drive to town to shop for groceries or essentials." *(Melissa Van Hee)*

Open Early May–early Oct.

Rooms 19 1–5 bedroom cabins—all with full bath, kitchen with microwave, dishwasher, fireplace, deck or screened porch, barbecue grill. Some with whirlpool tub.

Facilities Lodge with fireplace, TV/VCR, library, game room, grocery store, laundry, fax machine. Recreation center with 2 tennis courts, racquetball. Children's program, playground, water slide, camping island. 4 acres with lake for swimming, fishing, boating, hiking trails. Power boat rentals (15–100hp). 5 m to golf.

Location NE MN. 8 m from Cook, 80 m N of Duluth, 225 m N of Minneapolis. From Minneapolis, take Rte. 35 W to Cloquet. Then take Rte. 33 to 53 N to Cook. From Cook, take River St. to Vermillion Dr. Go 3 m to Beatty Rd., at the 1st Ludlow's sign. Go 5 m & turn left at 2nd sign, to 2nd driveway on left.

Restrictions No smoking in lodge.

Credit cards MC, Amex, Visa.

Rates Room only, $165–195 double, daily; $1440–1950 weekly. Extra person, $30 daily, $150 weekly. Weekly maid service $100 for two. 2-night minimum stay. Fishing, honeymoon package. Children under 10 free off-season.
Extras Airport pickup, $20–60; station pickup, free. Baby-sitting.

GRAND MARAIS

Located on Lake Superior in the far northeast corner of Minnesota, Grand Marais is a popular resort for those enjoying water sports in summer, and skiing in winter. It's also the beginning of the Gunflint Trail, leading north into the wilderness of Superior National Forest and Boundary Waters Canoe area.

Reader tip: "Judge Magney State Park offers great hiking in summer, wonderful cross-country skiing in winter." *(Robin Derscherd)*

Also recommended: The **Cascade Lodge** (3719 West Highway 61, 55604; 218–387–1112 or 800–322–9543; www.cascadelodgemn.com) is set in the Cascade River State Park on the shore of Lake Superior. The resort includes about 18 guest rooms in the main lodge, plus log cabins with fireplaces. "Our suite in the main lodge was attractively furnished; with the windows open, we were lulled to sleep by the crashing waves of Lake Superior, just across the road. Several trails take you to the beautiful cascades and waterfalls nearby." *(Celia McCullough & Gary Kaplan)* Double rates range from $67–180; children are welcome, and meals are reasonably priced.

Gunflint Lodge 🏃 ✕
143 South Gunflint Lake, 55604

Tel: 218–388–2294
800–328–3325
Fax: 218–388–9429
E-mail: gunflint@gunflint.com
URL: http://www.gunflint.com

Owned by the Kerfoot family for over 60 years, the Gunflint Lodge consists of the main lodge building and trading post, original cabins built in the 1930s, and newer ones added by current owner/operators Bruce and Sue Kerfoot. The coffee pot is always on (plus hot chocolate and tea), along with a jar of homemade cookies. Breakfast is served from 7–10:00 A.M. each morning, and includes such choices as cheese omelets or blueberry pancakes with fresh-baked pastries. Lunch can be enjoyed in the dining room or as a take-along picnic lunch. Dinner menus change daily, and include homemade soup, salad, breads, fresh vegetables, and dessert, with such entrees as salmon with tarragon peppercorn sauce, steak with tomato thyme salsa, beer-batter fried walleye with horseradish tartar sauce, or venison with wild blueberry demiglaze.

"The Grand Marais area offers a range of outdoor summer activities for families, long weekend getaways, or special romantic times. Gunflint is reminiscent of the fishing camps and lodges from the turn of the century. A big stone fireplace in the main common area offers a cozy feeling in this casual, friendly lodge. The rustic, knotty pine decor is balanced with all modern comforts. The staff is always available to help you plan activities. The setting alone is worth a stay—the beauty of Lake Superior plus the availability of many activities." *(Pam Phillips)* "Superior lakeside location with lots of activities. Good, fresh food in a charming dining room." *(Ruthie & Derek Tilsley)* "Cabins range from older, smaller ones right on the shore of Gunflint Lake, to newer, larger ones with hot tubs and saunas. One can canoe or motorboat across the lake to hike in Canada. Old communal ovens are still visible near the remains of the iron mine railroad beds. Magnetic Rock, a three-story-high magnetite stone on a nearby trail is fascinating. Pontoon boat tours take your to trailheads and sights around the lake. Wildlife included ducks, moose, beaver, river otters, bald eagles, hummingbirds, and more. Helpful hosts and naturalists. Reading Justine Kerfoot's two books on the area really enhanced the experience. Many beautiful waterfalls and cascades. Excellent dinners and breakfasts—no room for lunch." *(Celia McCullough)*

Open All year.

Rooms 4 units in original Trading Post building, 20 1-4 bedroom cabins/chalets with private bath, living room with fireplace. Some with kitchen, sauna, hot tub or whirlpool tub, VCR/CD player, washer/dryer, porch/deck.

Facilities Main lodge with fireplace, games, library, dining room. Canoeing, kayaks, fishing (guides available), boating, swimming beach, hiking, nature activities. Horseback riding, cross-country skiing, dog sledding, snowshoeing, children's activities. Boat rentals.

Location Take I-35 to Duluth, Hwy. 61 to Grand Marais. Go inland on Gunflint Trail (Cty. Rd. 12) to entrance sign.

Restrictions "No coats and ties, please."

Credit cards Amex, Discover, MC, Visa.

Rates Room only, $139–256 double; extra person, $16–54. MAP, $181–299 double; extra person, $38–75. Full board, $213–331 double; extra person, $54–91. Weekly rates. 8% service. Children under 4 stay free. Family, package rates.

Extras Pets permitted, $10; dogs must be leashed.

MINNEAPOLIS

Minneapolis is an inviting modern city, as is its slightly more old-fashioned sister city across the Mississippi, St. Paul. Known for its exceptional cultural and educational facilities, it offers outstanding restaurants, theaters, and museums, and the largest single college campus in the U.S., the University of Minnesota, with about 65,000 students. Modern art fans should head over to the Walker Art Center and Sculpture Garden, and perhaps stay for an evening performance by the renowned Guthrie Theater. Children of all ages will enjoy the city's fine zoo, as well as its extensive network of lakes and parks for bicycling, jogging, swimming, boating, and cross-country skiing.

Also recommended: Built in 1893, the **Nicollet Island Inn** (95 Merriam Street, 55401; 612–331–1800) is a limestone building, originally a built as a factory making wooden window sashes and doors. Restored as a popular inn and restaurant, it offers 24 guest rooms, all with private bath, telephone, TV/VCR, and air-conditioning, and many with river views. Double rates range from $115–150. "Nicollet Island sits in the middle of the Mississippi River in downtown Minneapolis, and is a wonderful place to explore. To the south is a well-kept park with lots of cottonwood trees and grass; just across the bridge to the west is Riverplace and Mississippi Live, with shops, restaurants, and clubs in refurbished warehouses." *(SC)* "Simply furnished, unfussy, comfortable corner room, #209, with river views; central location; parking in front of hotel; morning newspaper and afternoon cookies provided. Beautiful views of Mississippi from the restaurant, and would especially recommend it for breakfast or a predinner drink." *(MM, also Sally Heytens)*

Ten minutes north of Minneapolis is the **Inn on the Farm** (6150 Summit Drive North, Brooklyn Center, 55430; 612–569–6330 or 800–428–8382). Four extensively remodeled farm buildings are the setting for this B&B on the grounds of a former Victorian horse farm, now a state-of-the art commercial convention center and high-rise office park. Guest rooms are individually decorated with period reproductions. Afternoon tea is served daily in the parlor, and a typical breakfast might include fresh fruit, wild rice quiche, sausage, French toast, and muffins. B&B rates range from $110–130.

Information please: Managed by Hyatt Hotels as of August 1997 is the **Hyatt Whitney Hotel** (150 Portland Avenue South, 55401; 612–339–9300 or 800–233–1234; www.hyatt.com), a 96-room luxury hotel located in a retrofitted 19th century flour mill. Double rates range from $155–250. "The hotel has a wonderful location near the Mississippi River near St. Anthony Falls. A lot has been done to enhance the riverfront and make it appealing to locals and tourists alike with walking and biking trails, historical information, and so on." *(GW)* A recent report noted that "our room was adequate, perhaps a bit tired; food and service in the restaurant was good; daytime lobby staffing was OK, but the evening front desk staff did not seem to care about the guests, and were not knowledgeable about local restaurants." *(LF)* We still hope that Hyatt will return the hotel to its earlier levels of fine service and careful attention to detail, complementing its lovely and elegant guest rooms. More reports please.

RED WING

A historic river town, Red Wing was named for a famous Dakota Indian chief. Although known particularly for its pottery, the town is still home to many prosperous industries as well as several beautiful riverfront parks, ideal for hiking and swimming. Climb to the top of Barn Bluff and Sovin's Bluff for dramatic river views and stop by the colorful harbor, Boathouse Village. In winter, both downhill and cross-country skiing are close by.

Located in southeastern Minnesota, Red Wing is set among the limestone bluffs lining the Mississippi River Valley, 55 miles southeast of Minneapolis/St. Paul via Route 61, and about the same distance from Rochester, via Route 58Y.

Information please: Owned for 72 years by the Lillyblad family, the **St. James Hotel** (406 Main Street [U.S. 61], 55066; 612–388–2846 or 800–252–1875) first became famous for fine food. In 1975 the Red Wing Shoe Company bought the hotel, restoring it completely and combining it with a shopping, parking, and office complex. Each of the sixty guest rooms are named for a Mississippi riverboat, and half have views of the river and the bluffs. Still known for good food, the hotel is home to two restaurants: the Port of Red Wing Restaurant, serving American food, and the Veranda Cafe, for breakfast and lunch, overlooking the Mississippi. Double rates range from $92–165. Reports welcome.

ST. PAUL

Just across the river from its flashier twin, Minneapolis, St. Paul offers beautifully restored mansions and historic sights, and a diverse ethnic population. Of particular interest is its impressive turn-of-the-century State Capitol, and the Science Museum of Minnesota, with domed Omnitheater.

Information please: The **Chatsworth B&B** (984 Ashland Avenue, 55104; 612–227–4288) is a 1902 Victorian home with guest rooms eclectically decorated in Victorian, Oriental, African, and antique Scandinavian decor. The $70–125 double rates include a healthy continental breakfast; it's conveniently located two blocks from the Governor's Mansion and three blocks from Grand Avenue restaurants and shops. "The lovely Summit Hills district is a turn-of-the-century neighborhood with many Victorian homes. Interesting shops line nearby Grand Avenue, with many good restaurants." *(Bill Novack)*

In the luxury hotel category, a good choice is the classic **The Saint Paul Hotel** (350 Market Street, 55102; 612–292–9292 or 800–292–9292), with an elegant setting overlooking Rice Park in the heart of St. Paul. Its architects were Reed and Stem, who had just completed New York City's Grand Central Terminal, and the hotel opened to great fanfare in 1910. A complete remodeling was completed in 1992 with designer decorated guest rooms, many with king-size beds. Double rates for the 258 rooms range from $155–179, suites to $675, and include evening turndown service with mineral water, plus the morning newspaper. Meals are available in the St.Paul Grill and The Cafè.

Free copy of INNroads newsletter

Want to stay up-to-date on our latest finds? Send a business-size, self-addressed, stamped envelope with 55 cents postage and we'll send you the latest issue, *free!* While you're at it, why not enclose a report on any inns you've recently visited? Use the forms at the back of the book or your own stationery.

Mississippi

Fairview, Jackson

Andrew Jackson was one of Mississippi's first heroes. After he defeated the Creek Indian nation and won the Battle of New Orleans, the state's capital was named for him. The Civil War played a major role in Mississippi's history; in addition to the famous siege of Vicksburg, innumerable battles took place across the state, leaving tremendous destruction in their wake.

Today history buffs visit Natchez and Vicksburg in search of antebellum ambience, while beach lovers head south to the Gulf Coast. Plan to spend some time (spring and fall are best) exploring the Natchez Trace Parkway, a 400-mile parkway administered by the National Parks Service. Extending from Natchez nearly to Nashville, Tennessee, it follows the historic trail (or trace) that was one of the region's most frequented roads at the beginning of the 1800s.

For additional accommodations in historic private homes and inns, call **Lincoln, Ltd. B&B** (P.O. Box 3479, 2303 23rd Avenue, Meridian, 39303; 601–482–5483), a reservation service operated by Barbara Lincoln Hall since 1983. If you're planning to spend some time exploring along the Gulf, pick up a copy of *Ramblin' and Gamblin' on the Mississippi Coast*, an informative guide written by longtime contributors Lynn Edge and Lynn Fullman ($10.50 including postage and handling; Seacoast Publishing, 110 Twelfth Street North, Birmingham, AL, 35203, 205–250–8016).

Important note: If you're booking a room in an antebellum mansion that can also be visited by the public, remember that rooms on a tour will rarely be available for occupancy before 5 P.M., and must typically be vacated by 9 A.M. Rooms in adjacent buildings may not be quite as fancy, but have more liberal check-out policies. In addition, public rooms on the tour are usually kept locked.

JACKSON

Located in central Mississippi, Jackson is the state capital and its largest city.

Reader tip: "Be sure to call the MetroJackson Convention & Visitors Bureau to find out what's going on in town (800–354–7695 or www.visitjackson.com). When we visited, outstanding exhibits included the Treasures of Versailles (its only U.S. stop), an American art show featuring Winslow Homer and Edward Hopper, a ballet performance, and more." *(Pam Phillips)*

Also recommended: Listed on the National Register of Historic Places, the **Millsaps Buie House** (628 North State Street, 39202; 601–352–0221 or 800–784–0221) was restored as a B&B in 1987, and is beautifully decorated with period antiques. Double rates for the eleven guest rooms, each with king- or queen-size beds, are $100–160. The buffet breakfast includes freshly squeezed orange juice, fresh fruit, homemade blueberry banana bread, biscuits and bagels, cheese grits, eggs, and ham, bacon, or sausage. "We particularly enjoyed the comfortable screened porches." *(Joe & Sheila Schmidt)* " Wonderfully comfortable beds. Tasty pralines were placed on our pillows at night." *(HJB)* "Our first-floor room had a king-size bed, good lighting, and excellent shower." *(John Blewer)* "Professionally managed with all the amenities a business traveler needs. Wine was served in the parlor in the late afternoon." *(KM)*

Fairview ✕	*Tel:* 601–948–3429
734 Fairview Street, 39202	888–948–1908
	Fax: 601–948–1203
	E-mail: fairview@teclink.net
	URL: http://www.fairviewinn.com

Despite its antebellum appearance, Fairview is a Greek Revival–style home built in 1908, and owned by the Simmons family since 1972. This replica of Mount Vernon is listed on the National Register of Historic Places, and was restored as a B&B in 1993 by Carol and William Simmons. The inn is gracious and elegant, with many antiques, while still comfortable and uncluttered. Guest rooms have either queen- or king-size beds. Midweek, business travelers appreciate its convenient location and many amenities; on weekends, Fairview hosts many weddings. The Southern breakfast of bacon, eggs or French toast, grits, and biscuits is cooked to order and is served at guests' convenience. Dinners are served by reservation, and a typical menu might include grilled quail with angel hair pasta; green salad with balsamic vinaigrette; beef tenderloin with morels, asparagus, and roasted potatoes; and lemon glory dessert with coffee.

"This beautiful home is framed by fragrant magnolia and brilliant crepe myrtle. We stayed in the honeymoon suite located on the top floor of the renovated carriage house, with a king-size bed and decorated in ivory and beige. Carol is a well-known caterer and William is rooted deeply in Mississippi history. Wonderful Sunday brunch, complete with flowers and a pianist." *(MR)* "We were personally greeted by the hospitable owners; great breakfast." *(Tersa Lawson)* "Bill and Carol Simmons have meticulously maintained Fairview's original charm and comfort; they know everything about Jackson. In the library, virtually unchanged since 1908, Bill has an excellent collection of Civil War books. Exceptionally maintained; every surface glows from cleaning and polishing." *(Joe & Sheila Schmidt)* "Outstanding breakfast and dinner; wonderful service. Guest rooms are spotless, beautifully decorated, with nice bathrooms well supplied with amenities. Enjoyed meeting a bicycle group that was staying at the inn, as well as a TV producer doing a story on why the memory of Civil War is kept so alive in the South. Also loved sitting out on the deck, listening to the birds." *(Pam Phillips)*

Open All year.

Rooms 5 suites, 3 doubles—all with private bath and/or shower, telephone with dataport, clock, working desk, air-conditioning, TV, robes, hair dryer. 2 with fan, 1 with fireplace, 2 with Jacuzzi tub. 1 suite in carriage house.

Facilities Dining room, living room, library, foyer with fireplaces, garden room with piano, porch, deck with hot tub. 2 acres with gardens, off-street parking.

Location Old Jackson; near state Capitol Building, medical complexes. From I-55 S, take Exit 98A. Go W on Woodrow Wilson Dr. & turn S (left) on N. State St. Go E (left) at Medical Plaza bldg. on Fairview to inn on left. From I-55 N, take Exit 96C & go W on Fortification St. to N. State & turn right. Turn right on Fairview as above.

Restrictions No smoking. Children over 12. No pets.

Credit cards Amex, MC, Visa.

Rates B&B, $150 suite, $100–150 double. Extra person, $15. Prix fixe dinner by reservations only; menus at $35 & $50 plus 20% service; BYOB.

Extras Wheelchair access; 1 room specially equipped. French spoken.

NATCHEZ

Natchez was founded in 1716. Since then the flags of six nations have flown over the city—France, England, Spain, the sovereign state of Mississippi, the Confederacy, and the U.S. Natchez's greatest wealth and prosperity came in the early 1800s with the introduction of cotton and the coming of the steamboat. Extraordinary mansions were built during this period, which ended with the Civil War. Unlike Vicksburg to the north, Natchez was not of military importance, so although little property was destroyed during the war, further development ceased. As a result, over 500 antebellum mansions survive.

Over half the mansions in Natchez are open to visitors year-round. The others are open during festivals, called Pilgrimages, which are held for four weeks in October, two weeks at Christmas, and five weeks in March and April. The Natchez Opera Festival runs throughout the month of May. If you plan to visit during one of these times, make your reservations six weeks to three months in advance. Alternative bed &

breakfast lodging, as well as tickets for the house tours, can be arranged by calling Pilgrimage Tours at 800–647–6742.

Natchez is in southwest Mississippi, on the Mississippi River, 114 miles southwest of Jackson. Try to travel here via the Natchez Trace, once an Indian footpath, now a two-lane parkway run by the National Park Service between Natchez and Nashville, passing centuries of American history en route. Call the Natchez Trace Parkway Visitors Center for more information (601–680–4027).

Reader tips: "Natchez is definitely the jewel in Mississippi's crown, with lovely homes and plantations, and a beautiful setting on the river. Lots to do for history lovers, some shopping too, and riverboat gambling for those who like that sort of thing. We rented bikes to tour historic area, then retired to the lawn to read with our mint juleps." *(Pam Phillips)* "For over 100 years, the Natchez Trace was an important wilderness road. Deep wagon cuts still mark the path followed by settlers. Stretching over 400 miles from Nashville, Tennessee to Natchez Mississippi, the superbly landscaped and maintained parkway provides an opportunity to explore the history of the period while enjoying the quiet beauty of the countryside." *(Joe & Sheila Schmidt)* "Explore Natchez-Under-the-Hill, an area wedged in beneath the Mississippi River bluffs that was once home to gamblers, riverboat hustlers and other ne'er-do-wells." *(SC)* "If you're looking for catfish, go across the bridge to Vidalia, Louisiana (right by the Briars and the Ramada), and just over the bridge, turn right to the Sandbar restaurant. Down-home atmosphere; clean, inexpensive, friendly, and good fish." *(Frances White)* "Three favorite restaurants on the Mississippi are the Wharfmaster, the Landing, and the Magnolia Bar and Grill; wonderful barbecue and gumbo." *(LR)*

Worth noting: In many plantation homes, the common areas are kept locked, except during tours, because of the value of the antique furnishings. Guests are welcome to relax on the galleries and grounds, but rarely have "free run" of the house itself.

Also recommended: Set on a hill overlooking the Mississippi River is **The Briars Inn** (31 Irving Lane, P.O. Box 1245, 39120; 601–446–9654 or 800–634–1818). This plantation-style mansion was built in the early 1800s and was the site of Jefferson Davis' marriage to Varina Howell in 1845. The 13 guest rooms are elegantly decorated, and the $135–360 B&B double rates include a full breakfast. "Beautiful mansion. We were welcomed graciously and shown the first floor. Our large room opened onto the gallery; it was comfortable and well equipped, with terry cloth robes and hair dryer in the bathroom, and a gas fireplace. Breakfast was very good, served with Southern hospitality." *(Frances White)*

Dating back to 1792, **Linden** (1 Linden Place, 39120; 601–445–5472 or 800–2–LINDEN) has been owned by ancestors of the current owner, Jeanette Feltus, since the early 1800s. Nearly all furnishings are original to the house, and Linden is especially noted for its outstanding collection of Federal furniture. Rate for the seven guest rooms, each with private bath and air-conditioning, range from $90–150.

Monmouth Plantation ✕ &.
36 Melrose Avenue at the
John A. Quitman Parkway, 39120
P.O. Box 1736, 39121

Tel: 601–442–5852
800–828–4531
Fax: 601–446–7762

Monmouth, a Greek Revival mansion listed on the National Register of Historic Places, was built in 1818 and was purchased in 1826 by John Quitman, who later became governor of Mississippi and a U.S. congressman. Monmouth stayed in the Quitman family until 1905; its restoration began in 1978, when it was purchased by Lani and Ron Riches. Period antiques, including many of the plantation's original furnishings, decorate the rooms, which are also equipped with thick terry robes, English toiletries, and a welcome basket of pralines and cold drinks. In the evening, guests can order freshly mixed mint juleps to accompany the complimentary hors d'oeuvres. Rates also include a full Southern breakfast, house tour, and evening turndown service with chocolates. Five-course candle-lit dinners are served (by reservation) in the elegant dining room or gas-lit parlors.

"Friendly, professional, efficient staff—exceptionally well trained. Our room was lavishly done plantation-style, with grand antiques, four-poster bed, and fabulous fabrics; well-equipped bathroom. The Carriage House rooms are delightful, have their own porches with rockers, and are a bit more private and quiet than those in the big house. Fine dinner; our waiter, Roosevelt, made it a great experience, with gracious Southern charm. The table was set with china, silver, and elaborate flower arrangements. Well-presented, tasty breakfast buffet. Marguerite, a treasure of Monmouth, gave us a house tour; it was great fun, and she has good stories. Museum-quality furniture and artifacts; it's great learning about the era. The brick patio in the back of the house has beautiful wrought-iron furniture, where drinks are served in the afternoon. Lovely grounds with walking paths, pond, and lots of flowers." *(Pam Phillips)*

"We were warmly welcomed and shown to our Carriage House suite, with a convenient parking space just outside our room. Our request for extra towels was responded to immediately. Though recently built, the architecture of the Carriage House matches the original buildings. Our suite, one of four, had a bedroom with a four-poster bed and armoire, a sitting room with a sofa in front of the fireplace, a private patio, and a well-appointed bathroom. Tasty breakfast of eggs, grits, biscuits, and preserves. At dinner time, we were seated at the long table in the beautifully furnished dining room, with wonderful period atmosphere. The food was very good, the surroundings lovely, and conversation with our fellow guests delightful." *(Alex & Beryl Williams)*

Open All year. Dinner served Tues.–Sat.
Rooms 13 suites, 12 doubles—all with private bath and/or shower, telephone, radio, TV, desk, air-conditioning, hair dryer, robes. Some with fireplace, Jacuzzi. 6 rooms in mansion, 4 in original kitchen building, 4 in former slave quarters, 4 rooms in Carriage House.
Facilities Parlors, study, courtyard patio, gift shop, conference facility (100). 26 acres with gardens, gazebo, fish pond, croquet, walking trails. Golf, tennis nearby.

Location 1 m from downtown. E on State St., at corner of Quitman Pkwy. and Melrose.
Restrictions No smoking. Children over 14.
Credit cards Amex, Diners, Discover, MC, Optima, Visa.
Rates B&B, $175–255 suite, $125–155 double. Extra person, $35. Prix fixe dinner, $38; reservations required. Cocktails, wine not included in rates.
Extras Wheelchair access; some rooms specially equipped.

VICKSBURG

When folks talk about "The War" in Vicksburg, it's the Civil War they're referring to, not any of more recent vintage. Because of the town's controlling position, high on the Mississippi River bluffs, Union forces felt Vicksburg's surrender was essential to victory. Repulsed in repeated attempts both from land and water, the town surrendered to General U.S. Grant only after a 47-day siege of continuous mortar and cannon bombardment.

Must-see sights in Vicksburg include the National Military Park and Cemetery and the nearby Cairo Museum, with numerous exhibits and audiovisual programs that bring the history of the battle and the period to life. Amazingly enough, many of Vicksburg's antebellum mansions survived the siege and can be visited today. Check with the Vicksburg Tourist Commission for pilgrimage dates: 800–221–3536. For a lighter taste of history, stop at the Biedenharn Candy Company Museum to see where Coca-Cola was first bottled in 1894.

Vicksburg is located in southwest Mississippi, 44 miles east of Jackson, via I-20.

Reader tips: "Be sure to visit Vicksburg National Military Park. The battle of Vicksburg was pivotal in the career of General Ulysses S. Grant. It propelled him to command of the Union armies and later to the presidency of the United States. The 15-mile drive through the park travels back and forth between Union and Confederate lines, often only yards apart. The weathered trenches are a reminder of the agony and fury of the battle. During the siege the Union ironside *Cairo* was sunk by a mine. She has been raised from the mud and is the centerpiece of the unique gunboat museum. Nearby, neat rows of white stone monuments mark the National and Confederate Cemeteries. *(Joe & Sheila Schmidt)* "I recommend touring the park with a guide; fascinating history, beautiful setting." *(Pam Phillips)* "Most riverboat casinos offer excellent, well-priced dinner buffets." *(JS)*

Also recommended: An Victorian Italianate home built in 1868, plus an adjacent 1881 cottage, **Annabelle** (501 Speed Street, 39180; 601–638–2000 or 800–791–2000; Annabelle@Vicksburg.com) is located in the historic River View Garden District, just east of the Mississippi River, with the river valley below. B&B double rates of $90–125 include a full breakfast. Each of the eight guest rooms has a queen- or king-size bed, antique furnishings, private bath, telephone, and TV; some have a gas log fireplace and/or whirlpool tub. "New Orleans native Carolyn Mayer and her Czech-born husband, George, offer a historic atmosphere, service, luxury, delicious breakfast, a showcase of antiques, a relaxing swimming pool, and a common room filled with antiques and classical music. The Rose room has an invitingly plump king-size bed, a garden view, and a modern bath well supplied with toiletries. Homemade cookies, delivered as we arrived, set the tone for the gracious hospitality that highlighted our stay." *(Lynn Fullman)*

The **Belle of the Bends** (508 Klein Street, 39180; 601–634–0737 or 800–844–2308) is set high on a bluff overlooking the Mississippi. This 1876 brick Italianate-style home is furnished with period antiques and steamboating memorabilia. Double rates for the four guest rooms are $85–150, and include a plantation breakfast and afternoon tea. "Beautiful architecture, attractively furnished. The solicitous owner/ innkeeper breakfasts with guests; the meal is first class, as is everything about this B&B. Rooms are large and spacious; ours had a river view." *(David Adamson)*

An antebellum mansion built in 1840, **Cedar Grove** (2300 Washington Street, 39180; 601–636–1000 or 800–862–1300) is listed on the National Register of Historic Places. Despite the Union cannonball still lodged in the parlor wall, it survived the Civil War with most of its antiques and architecture intact. The 24 guest rooms are available in the mansion and in the poolside guest cottage; the carriage house has eight suites. Rates of $90–165 include a full Southern breakfast, and a tour of the mansion. Dinners are served in the Garden Room restaurant; grilled chicken, catfish, and filet mignon are among the entrees. "The Grant Room has a high but comfortable king-size four-poster canopy bed, antique furnishings, with a Jacuzzi tub in the bathroom. Tasty country breakfast." *(Sharon Bielski)* "Very good dinner with fine traditional service. Loved the European atmosphere of the bar." *(Pam Phillips)*

The Mission-style **Stained Glass Manor–Oak Hall** (2430 Drummond Street, 39180; 601–638–8893 or 888–VICK–BNB; www.vickbnb.com) was built in 1902 and is highlighted by 38 original stained glass windows. Rooms are furnished with antiques and period reproductions, and are exceptionally spacious. Owners Bill and Shirley Smollen report that "we offer a family-oriented home-away-from home. Guests love Bill's breakfasts, learned after years of cooking with the best New Orleans chefs." B&B double rates for the six guest rooms range from $70–185, and children are welcome. "Our host was both amusing and informative; he even arranged a special breakfast for me when I had to leave early; great homemade bread." *(Phala Patton-Reed)* "Bill welcomed us to his home and treated us like family. He told us which sights to see, where to shop, where to eat, and filled us with Civil War history. The Washington Room has a king-size rice canopy bed, antique furnishings, stained glass windows, working fireplace, and a bath with the original clawfoot tub. Our delicious breakfast consisted of homemade sourdough bread, mimosas, quiche, chocolate fondue, and rich black coffee."*(John & Maryann Merritt)*

Missouri

Boone's Lick Trail Inn, St. Louis (St. Charles)

Missouri's two major cities, Kansas City and St. Louis, developed on the state's two major rivers—the Missouri and the Mississippi—which form its eastern and part of its western borders. Children will enjoy Kansas City's Toy & Miniature Museum, while adults will appreciate St. Louis' sophisticated shops and the Cupples House, an enormous pink granite mansion erected in 1890. Northwest Missouri is Mark Twain country, while the central part of the state is more rural, with the Lake of the Ozarks and the Ozark Mountains regions as major tourist attractions. Don't miss the annual Arrow Rock Invitational Craft Festival in October or the National Ragtime Festival in June.

Reader tip: "Scenic Highway 19 through the Ozark Heritage Section of southeastern Missouri (beginning at I-44) surpasses a lot of the better-known Arkansas back roads—less traffic, less windy, more interesting, heavily tree-lined, with lots of rivers to explore (canoe rentals readily available). Gorgeous and remote; can't wait to return for fall foliage." *(Carol Moritz)*

BRANSON

It's not hard to predict that Orlando is the most popular auto vacation destination, according to the AAA. If asked to name the other top choices, you might guess Yosemite and Williamsburg without difficulty. But how many would know that Branson is in second place? Country music fans, that's who. This tiny (population 4,000) southwest Missouri town now hosts over 5 million people annually who come to enjoy the music and family entertainment in some three dozen theaters. Nearly everything is on Route 76, so expect *major* traffic jams in season, and allow plenty of extra time. Alternative side roads are available, so ask your innkeeper for a map.

Bradford Inn   *Tel:* 417–338–5555
HCR 9, P.O. Box 1276-10, Highway 265, 65616   800–357–1466
Fax: 417–338–4354
E-mail: bobw@dialnet.net
URL: http://www.bransonnow.com/lodging/bradford

Capturing the classic feel of a New England inn amid the serene beauty of the Ozarks is the Bradford Inn, built in 1993 by Bob and Lucyanna Westfall. Taking twenty years' experience building custom homes, the Westfalls designed and built the inn to evoke both Lucyanna's native Connecticut background as well as Bob's Missouri-born down-home country charm. Assisting in the inn's management are their son, Bob III, and daughters Rebecca and Cherie. Guest rooms vary in size and dècor, many with hand-painted scenes that identify the theme, complemented by the room's furnishings and fabrics. The Mountain View room has a faux window above the bed's headboard that gives a "view" of the surrounding hills, while the Secret Garden room has a faux stone wall and iron gates at its entrance. The top-of-the-line beds have pillow-top mattresses, down comforters, and 250-thread count linens. A breakfast buffet is served from 7:30 to 9:30 A.M., and features fruits, orange juice, pastries, cereals, assorted breads, bagels, hot biscuits, sausage, ham, homemade muffins, cooked-to-order Belgian waffles, and eggs.

"Great location, near Branson nightlife but far enough away to be quiet." *(Todd Morriss)* "Serene and restful retreat. The entire family and staff go out of their way to make us feel welcome and pampered." *(Darla Carr)* "Guest rooms are spotless, warm, and inviting, each different." *(Bob & Vi Pilkington)* "Soaking in the whirlpool tub, set in a bay window, with a fireplace burning, was a luxurious experience on a winter evening." *(Peggy Owens)* "The inn sits on top of a hill overlooking Branson and the Ozarks; sunset and sunrise are breathtaking; beautiful view of the city lights." *(James Danley)* "The Lilac room has plenty of space, while the Mountain View is on the cozy side. The Retreat has a comfy king-size bed and plenty of room for luggage, and all are exceptionally clean. Both owners and the staff are pleased to answer any and all questions." *(Marlene St. John)* "Great deck for enjoying the view; no-mess gas-log fireplaces; privacy; great homemade muffins." *(Deborah Duncan)* "Bob and Lucyanna are generous, hospitable folks. Gracious, helpful staff. Made-to-order delicious breakfasts." *(Barbara Hodges)* "Informal breakfast atmosphere makes it easy to meet your fellow guests." *(Kendra Nay & others)* "The Harbor Room had an aquarium next to the whirlpool tub; we toured other rooms and all were decorated beautifully. Plenty of soft towels, good plumbing, fluffy comforters, lots of natural light, ample parking, right in front of our room. Tasty breakfasts of fresh cooked eggs, sausage, waffles, and peach-almond muffins." *(David & Laura Gomez)* "Our room had two queen-size beds, and a huge bathroom." *(Joanne Fogarty)* "Each room has a guest diary, which makes for interesting reading. The stenciled walls, lace curtains, antiques, and accessories create a homey but unfussy atmosphere." *(Linda Doyle)* "Despite the inn's size, the innkeepers made us feel as if we were the only guests. Our private deck had a lovely view of the Ozark foothills." *(Judy Daugherty)* "Bright, colorful, and cozy room; the towels and sheets were scented with potpourri." *(Adrianna & Larry Gilpin)*

Open All year.
Rooms 1 3-bedroom, 2-bath Guest House; 31 doubles—all with full private bath and/or shower, telephone, radio, clock, TV, air-conditioning, fireplace, refrigerator, balcony/deck, private entrance. 22 with whirlpool tub. Most with refrigerator, desk, balcony, or patio. 14 with fireplace, 2 with fan. Rooms in 3 buildings.
Facilities Breakfast room with fireplace, loft, deck, living room, conference room. 4 acres with off-street parking. Near lake for boating. Hiking nearby.
Location SW MO. 5 m NE of town. From Rte. 76, go S 2 m on Rte. 265 to inn on left.
Restrictions No smoking in buildings.
Credit cards Amex, Discover, MC, Visa.
Rates B&B, $59–99 double. Extra person over age 12, $5; under twelve, free. 5% senior, AAA discount. 3 night minimum in Guest House.
Extras 2 rooms with wheelchair access; bathrooms specially equipped. Cribs.

HANNIBAL

Mark Twain lived in Hannibal as a boy and as a young man, when the prosperity of the river and of steamboating were at their height. Scenes from both *Tom Sawyer* and *Huckleberry Finn* were inspired by his days here. Twain remains Hannibal's main claim to fame to this day, and there are many worthwhile historic and entertaining sights to see, including Mark Twain's Boyhood Home; a summer outdoor drama based on his life and characters; narrated riverboat rides; and the Mark Twain Cave, in which Tom Sawyer and Becky Thatcher were lost. Also of interest is the Autumn Folk Life Festival, where traditional crafts are demonstrated; and the high bluffs overlooking the river, the southern migration point for many bald eagles.

Garth Woodside Mansion ¢   Tel: 573–221–2789
New London Gravel Road   E-mail: Feinberg@nemonet.com
R.R.#3, 63401   URL: http://www.hanmo.com/garth

In 1871 John W. Garth built Woodside, an imposing Victorian mansion in the Second Empire style—complete with mansard roof and cupola—as a summer retreat. A longtime friend of Mr. Garth's, Mark Twain stayed in the mansion in 1882 and again in 1902. In addition to breakfast, rates include the use of a Victorian-style nightshirt, and afternoon refreshments served from 4:00–6:00 P.M. The mansion was restored as a B&B in 1987 by Diane and Irv Feinberg.

"We were warmly welcomed with a smile, to a house rich in history and period furnishings, scented with the faint fragrance of roses."

(Sheryl Riley) "Well maintained, with fine attention to detail in accessories and colors. Beautifully presented breakfasts, different each day."
(Marilyn Kollmorgen) "Enjoyed the balance of ample privacy with Irv's witty and interesting conversation. The quiet wooded grounds and flowering garden were wonderful for an early morning walk. The mansion is clean and fresh, decorated with an incredible number of handsome antiques. The spacious Garth Room was beautifully decorated, with a view of the garden and sunrise. The parlor and sitting rooms were inviting for visiting with friends in a comfortable sitting." *(Robert & Raydell Wahlert)* "The Feinbergs are knowledgeable about the mansion's history, and entertained us with stories about the original owners." *(Erik Long)* "Listed on the National Register of Historic Places, the mansion has almost all the original furniture, with 12-foot-high headboards, tables, even knickknacks." *(Cristina Goodman)* "The magnificent flying staircase floats to the third floor with no visible means of support." *(Duane & Clare Baylor)* "Lovely views of the parklike hillside shaded by stately oak and maple trees from our third-floor room." *(Doris & R. B. Thomas)* "Our delicious breakfast included peach French toast, lemon sponge cake, and fresh fruit with sour cream sauce." *(Kimberly Holzerland)* "A thrill to sleep in the same room as Mark Twain." *(Robert Slotta)* "The hallways have museum cases loaded with 19th-century household items and personal accessories; the walls are draped with old hats and garments." *(Jean Rees)*

"Bathrooms are small, but rooms are spacious. Ours had a front view with lace curtains and a gorgeous bed with a crocheted canopy and spread, which was turned down for us at night. Third floor rooms are smaller and the ceilings lower, but are still beautiful. Though not in the country, it feels like no one is around for miles. Diane serves breakfast at a table for sixteen; she quickly started a stimulating conversation among the guests. " *(Elaine Bounds)*

Open All year.
Rooms 8 doubles—all with private bath and/or shower, air-conditioning, some with desk, telephone on request.
Facilities Dining room, living room, parlor, library, verandas, porches. Parking on site. 39 acres with gardens, fish pond. Swimming, boating nearby.
Location NE MO. 2 m S of town. From town go S on Hwy. 61, go E on Warren Barrett Dr. (1st road S of Ramada Inn); at 2nd bridge follow signs S to inn.
Restrictions No smoking. No children under 12.
Credit cards MC, Visa.
Rates B&B, $67–107 double. Extra person, $20. Tipping encouraged. 2-night holiday minimum.

KANSAS CITY

Located close to the geographic center of the continental U.S., Kansas City has long been a favorite of convention planners. Lesser known is the fact that it is a pleasant city, with lots of parks and open spaces, several museums of note, including the Nelson Gallery of Art, with world-class collections, and the Liberty Memorial, with museums dedicated to World War I artifacts. Although it has several major shopping and restaurant plazas of note, serious shoppers will want to pay homage (and probably more) at the many fine shops of Country Club Plaza, with its Spanish towers and Moorish tiled fountains—probably the country's first suburban-style shopping mall, built in the 1920s. Kansas City is located in western Missouri, straddling the Kansas border.

Reader tips: "Cafe Allegro is absolutely wonderful and has an excellent wine list; excellent meal at Venue, too." *(LI)* "As in any large city, not all areas are appropriate for strolling alone, especially at night. Ask your innkeeper for advice." *(GO)*

Also recommended: Built in 1907, the **The Doanleigh Inn** (217 East 37th Street, 64111; 816–753–2667) has been handsomely restored and decorated with American and European antiques and quality reproductions. Owners Terry Maturo and Cynthia Brogdon are dedicated to pampering their guests, making service their top priority. The five guest rooms (each with private bath) rent for $90–150 double, including breakfasts of home-baked muffins, homemade granola, plus such menus as a Santa Fe casserole with eggs, cheese, and chilis, served with herbed potatoes, baked blueberries, butterscotch oatmeal bread, and the inn's own blend of gourmet coffee. The inn is located between Country Club Plaza and the Hallmark Crown Center. "Our room had a four-poster bed, fireplace, entertainment center with a large TV/VCR, and a plate of just-baked cookies. We were welcomed with wine and hors d'oeuvres; delicious early-morning coffee was followed by an excellent breakfast." *(Sandra Alt)*

Originally built as an apartment house, the **Raphael** (325 Ward Parkway, 64112; 816–756–3800 or 800–821–5343) was converted to a hotel in the late 1970s. The lobby is paneled in beautiful woods, with traditional furnishings; guest rooms are warm and comfortable, and most have been updated with classic reproduction decor. Double rates for the 123 guest rooms (72 are suites) range from $110–180. "Excellent location, close to Country Club Plaza. Wonderful staff who make a point of addressing guests by name." *(BJ Hensley)* "Spacious suites, small baths; well-run hotel with a good restaurant, elegant lobby. Continental breakfast delivered to the door with the morning paper. Convenient parking." *(Russ Stratton)* "Beautifully managed small hotel in a great location. Our suite was comfortable, the bathroom well supplied. The living room had a refrigerator, large TV, welcoming note, and bottle of wine." *(Ruthie Tilsley)*

A wonderful choice is the **Ritz-Carlton** (401 Ward Parkway, 64112; 816–756–1500 or 800–241–3333) with 373 guest rooms. This 14-story arc-shaped hotel, with its waterfall, sculptures, and wrought-iron balconies, reflects the Moorish influence of neighboring Country Club Plaza. Rates range from $129–275. "Guest rooms are done with flair and luxury. Surprisingly warm and friendly staff. Superb location." *(Tina Kirkpatrick)* "The weekend room rate for the deluxe plaza view room was excellent, the room spacious and comfortable, with a good sitting area, refrigerator, desk, and robes. A special treat during the Christmas season." *(LI)* "Delightfully friendly staff. Enjoyed cocktails in the lounge overlooking the hotel terrace and country Club Plaza." *(Carol Worth)*

Information please: A recently restored historic treasure is the **Hotel Savoy** (219 West Ninth Street, 64105; 816–842–3575 or 800–728–6922), built in 1888, and remodeled with many Art Nouveau features in 1903, when the famous Savoy Grill opened. Renovation of the hotel began in 1985, and 22 of its rooms have been restored, decorated in Victorian furnishings, many original to the hotel. B&B double rates are $89, with suites at $120, including your choice of a continental breakfast or a hearty meal of omelets, roast beef hash, kippers with scrambled eggs, and much more. "Wonderful dinner in the historic restaurant, once a favorite of Harry Truman. Would love to return for an overnight stay." *(Ginny Watkins)*

Southmoreland on the Plaza Inn ♿

116 East 46th Street, 64112

Tel: 816–531–7979
Fax: 816–531–2407

Kansas City was ahead of most of the country when it launched its first planned community in 1922, complete with high-rise apartments, private homes, and shopping enclave. Now the cultural, shopping, and entertainment heart of the city, this well-manicured district, known as Country Club Plaza, is home to an urban inn, the Southmoreland, restored in 1990 by Susan Moehl and Penni Johnson.

This classic Colonial Revival–style New England home has a cheery solarium furnished in white wicker with an Amish rag rug, and a convivial living room decorated with antiques and reproductions, accented with brass sconces and collectibles. Guest rooms are decorated in the spirit of twelve Kansas City notables, and are supplied with sherry, fresh fruit and flowers, down comforters and pillows (hypoallergenic on request), and Caswell-Massey toiletries. Wine and cheese is served every afternoon from 4:30 to 6 P.M. In the morning, breakfast is served in the dining room, in the sunny, enclosed veranda, or in the open-air courtyard. A typical meal might include hot peach/pear crisp, shirred eggs with sausage, sweet peppers, basil, and Monterey Jack cheese, served with twice-baked potatoes and lemon-yogurt bread; or banana-apricot frappes, French toast stuffed with Swiss cheese and ham, and chocolate-zucchini bread. A special Saturday morning summer treat are the inn's breakfast barbecues, with margarita frappes, eggs, and seared Texas toast, pork chops, ribs, or perhaps sausage kabobs, grilled in the courtyard limestone barbecue pit.

"Wonderful hospitality, excellent service. Free use of an excellent nearby fitness center an extra plus." *(Ginny Watkins)* "As a business traveler, it's a real treat to stay where you're greeted by name, with genuine caring. Susan, Penni, and the staff make you feel almost as though you were coming home; Susan's breakfasts are better than at home. Baby the cat also lends a homey touch." *(Molly Long, also William McGuire)* "The delicious evening wine and hors d'oeuvres are a wonderful time to meet the other guests." *(Trudy Hill)* "Great location in the heart of the city, right by the Plaza." *(Ernest E. Allen)*

"Professional staff who are sensitive to the needs of both business and vacation travelers. Meticulously clean; inviting common areas; attractive neighborhood." *(Donna Kmetz)* "Homey charm is perfectly balanced with modern plumbing, windows that really open, and doors that don't stick. Careful attention to detail." *(Tina Kirkpatrick)* "The Ella and Jacob Loose Room has a delightful New England nautical theme and a private balcony. Excellent breakfasts. Easy walking distance to the Plaza, the Nelson Art Gallery, fine shops and restaurants." *(Marilyn Boling)* "Well-run inn; early morning preflight breakfasts no problem." *(CDS)* "Spotless. Delicious breakfast, friendly staff and hosts made our visit a delight." *(Rita Zizak)*

Open All year.

Rooms 12 doubles—all with full private bath, telephone, desk, air-conditioning, clock. 8 with deck or balcony, 3 with fireplace or woodstove, 2 with double Jacuzzi tub.

Facilities Dining room with fireplace, living room with fireplace, wet bar, TV/VCR; study with fireplace, solarium, enclosed dining veranda with fireplace; video library. Deck with grill. Courtyard with waterfall, croquet lawn. Fax, modem connections, copier. Membership privileges at Plaza Athletic club. Off-street parking.

Location 1½ blocks E of Country Club Plaza.

Restrictions No smoking. No children under 13.

Credit cards Amex, MC, Visa.

Rates B&B, $115–170 double, $95–150 single. Midweek business rate (single), $95–125. No tipping.

Extras Wheelchair access; 1 room equipped for disabled.

ST. LOUIS

Long known as the Gateway to the West, St. Louis is located in eastern Missouri, at the Illinois border. Although the Gateway Arch remains its premier tourist attraction, there's lots else to keep you busy. The once-decaying downtown area has been transformed in recent years by several major restoration projects. The once-proud Union Station has been restored to its original glory and now functions as a shopping, entertainment, and hotel complex. The U.S.S. *Admiral* is now permanently moored on the Mississippi as an entertainment complex, and Laclede's Landing has been transformed from an abandoned warehouse district into a 19th-century river town. The St. Louis Science Center offers lots of hands-on exhibits, while the free tours (and samples) available at the Anheuser-Busch plant provide hands-on experiences of a totally different kind.

Reader tips: "The Plaza Frontenac is a shopping oasis—parquet floors, stone walls, pianist not Muzak, not one screaming child. Cafe Zoe is very hip—everyone dresses in black. Cardwells' has fabulous food in a corporate atmosphere. Our favorite restaurant is Balaban's, a foodie's paradise; we also enjoy Bar Italia and Duff's. Lots of great antique shops in the Central West End neighborhood. The elaborate, iron-gated 'Public Place' blocks are great fun to walk as cars are banned on boulevard streets; diverse area near Forest Park." *(SW)*

Also recommended: The Winter House (3522 Arsenal Street, 63118; 314–664–4399; kmwinter@swbell.net) is a century-old Victorian house.

B&B double rates for the three guest rooms, each with private bath, range from $85–100, including a full breakfast (continental before A.M.). "Sarah and Ken Winter are gracious hosts, with friendly but unobtrusive pet cats and dog. Their home is in one of the beautiful old row houses in the Tower Grove East neighborhood, close to bus lines and a block from Tower Grove Park. The Alma Culp room has a beautiful queen-size pineapple four-poster bed and a private hall bath, plus fresh flowers, fruit, and bedtime chocolates. Delicious baked apples and French toast for breakfast, accompanied one morning on the piano by a local musician." *(Janet Collinge)*

Another option just 25 minutes north of St. Louis is the **Boone's Lick Trail Inn** (1000 South Main Street, St. Charles, 63301; 314–947–7000), built as an inn in 1840. The five guest rooms are decorated with regional antiques, folk art, a duck decoy collection, fresh flowers, old quilts, lace curtains, late 19th-century beds, and have yellow pine floors. A breakfast of fresh fruit, freshly baked rolls and breads, homemade jams and jellies, along with a hot entree, is served in the dining room on Haviland china and fine silver. B&B rates are $85–175.

Information please: In the heart of historic South Grand neighborhood is the **Fleur-de-Lys Inn—Mansion at the Park** (3500 Russell at Grand, St. Louis, 63104; 314–773–3500 or 888–969–3500; www.fleurdelys.com), a 1913 Tudor-style home restored as a B&B in 1996. B&B double rates range from $90–125 for the three double rooms, $150–210 for the suite, and include a full breakfast. In addition to the antique furnishings, whirlpool tubs, fine linens and down comforters, and king- and queen-sized beds that will delight any guest, business travelers will be especially pleased to find a working desk, in-room phones with voice mail plus two lines for fax and computer use, and remote-control color cable TV.

Important Note on Area Codes

Telephone area codes are changing faster than a two-year-old's attention span. Although we've tried to incorporate all the new ones in our listings, many numbers were still in the "to be decided" state at press time. *If you dial a number listed here and get an announcement that it's not in service, we urge you to call the information operator and see if that region has been assigned a new area code.* Please forgive the inconvenience!

Montana

Bad Rock Country B&B, Columbia Falls

Fourth-largest state in the country and 44th in population, Montana's majestic landscapes put people in their place. With 10 national forests, a national park, and innumerable state parks, Montana appeals to the hardy who can backpack into spectacular country. Don't miss Glacier National Park with its accessible glaciers and glacier-carved valleys, sparkling lakes, and boundless variety of mammals, birds, and wildflowers.

Other high points include Route 93, which passes through a spectacular valley south of Missoula to the Idaho border; Virginia City, a well-restored mining town best visited in spring or fall; Bannock State Park; a haunting ghost town 17 miles west of Dillon; and Helena, a friendly little capital city. For curiosity's sake, visit the site of a major 1959 earthquake, which moved streams and mountains—a visitor's interpretive center is located on Route 287, 22 miles north of West Yellowstone.

Perfectly flat eastern Montana offers little to interest visitors, except for Pompey's Pillar on I-94, 23 miles northeast of Billings. Named after Pomp, the son of Lewis and Clark's guide Sacajawea, travelers can see where Clark carved his name on this sandstone monolith in 1806.

Reader tips: "Take the time to explore Montana's river valleys, the most beautiful we've seen anywhere: drive Highway 89 along the Yellowstone River through Pleasant Valley between Livingston and Yellowstone; Highway 191 along the Gallatin River between West Yellowstone and Bozeman; and the Bitterroot Valley on Highway 93 between the Idaho border and Missoula. Stop to picnic and watch the rafters and kayakers. We also enjoyed taking the back roads to Virginia City and Nevada City. If you're hungry, stop at the Star Bakery in Nevada City; we enjoyed a terrific breakfast and had fun looking at pictures from the local filming of *Missouri Breaks* with Jack Nicholson and *Little Big Man* with Dustin Hoffman." *(Carol Moritz)*

BIGFORK

On the northeast shores of Flathead Lake (the largest natural fresh-water lake west of the Mississippi) in northwestern Montana, the Swiss-style village of Bigfork has a reputation as an artists' colony, in addition to offering a full range of water sports, nearly 30 golf courses, and other types of outdoor recreation. Bigfork is located in northwestern Montana, 17 miles southeast of Kalispell, and about 50 miles south of Glacier National Park.

Reader tip: "At first, Bigfork seems like a sleepy, picturesque village. Upon closer look, however, we found it most appealing, with numerous art galleries featuring local artists, and mercifully devoid of fast food chains. In addition to the Swan River Inn [see below], we enjoyed the Wild Mile gourmet deli where we bought huge lunches for hikes in Jewel Basin and Glacier Park. The local rep theater, now in its 38th year, offers first-class performances. We enjoyed the Broadway musical, *Sugar*, a reprise of the old Tony Curtis movie, *Some Like it Hot*." *(Maggie Sievers)*

Also recommended: In downtown Bigfork is the **The Swan River Inn** (360 Grand Avenue, 59911; 406–837–2220) combining European charm with a casual Montana atmosphere. Its cafè and restaurant serves three meals daily; accommodations are available in three well-equipped and spacious suites, at rates ranging from $150–200. "Swiss-born Margaret Matter and her sister Elsworth have transformed this restaurant into the best in town. Each suite is individually decorated with exquisite and expensive antique furniture, handmade down comforters, and hand-painted bathroom and kitchen tiles. The Victorian Suite features an antique French hand-carved cherry-wood bed and armoire, a small kitchen with brass chandelier, and a large beautifully appointed bath with a wheelchair accessible shower. The setting is serenely peaceful, overlooking the bay, with spectacular sunset views. We were served lunch on the patio, surrounded by perennial gardens and fresh herbs. Guests order breakfast from the cafè menu and may eat privately in their suite, in the restaurant, or on the deck overlooking Big Fork Bay with the mountain backdrop. We feasted on German apple pancakes, fresh fruit, and muffins." *(Maggie Sievers)*

For an additional area inn, see **Somers**.

Burggraf's Countrylane B&B
Rainbow Drive on Swan Lake, 59911

Tel: 406–837–4608
800–525–3344
Fax: 406–837–2468
E-mail: burggraf@digisys.net

Set on the shores of Swan Lake, this contemporary log home offers magnificent lake and mountain views through the floor-to-ceiling windows. Natalie and R.J. Burggraf offer guests breakfast at 8:30 A.M., plus a welcoming tray of fruit, cheese, and wine.

"The house is nicely constructed to take advantage of the scenery; from the wraparound porch you can see the distant mountains. Our large room had knotty pine walls, with king-size bed, comfortable furnishings, little knick-knacks, a large closet, brass hat stand with padded hangers, a light on each side of the bed, and lots of windows. Outside are inviting lounge chairs, and a rocky path takes you to a picturesque small bay where the Burggrafs keep a canoe and other boats for guest use. Breakfast was served at two tables set with wildflowers and a variety of brightly colored pottery." *(SC)* "Down a country lane, surrounded by beautiful grounds. Guest rooms have reading lamps and bedside tables, antique jewelry boxes filled with candy, and dozens of books; beds are turned down at night. Immaculate bathrooms with plenty of soft towels; an ample supply of soaps, lotions, and shampoo. Heavenly breakfasts of eggs Benedict, homemade breads and preserves, fresh fruit, soufflés, French toast, bacon, sausage. We went canoeing on the lake, rented one of R.J.'s motor boats, and played croquet." *(Jill Botha)* "Friendly, fun, hospitable owners. Spectacular lake and mountain views from their living room and dining area. Generous, varied homemade breakfasts, plus afternoon snacks and wine." *(Beverly Blair, and others)* "Loved all the animals—the Burggrafs' cats and dogs, as well as the hummingbirds and chipmunks outside." *(Joyce Zahlocki)* "Wonderful innkeepers; relaxed, casual, homey atmosphere. Good conversation with guests from all over the U.S." *(Priscilla Cotton)*

Open May through Sept.
Rooms 5 doubles—all with private bath and/or shower, TV. 1 with Jacuzzi tub.
Facilities Living room, breakfast room, guest refrigerator, wraparound porch. 7 acres with beach, free canoes. Fishing boat rentals.
Location NW MT. 47 m E of Glacier Park. Take Hwy. 93 to Mile Marker 81. Go W on Ferndale Dr., go 1 m, cross wooden bridge. Turn S on Rainbow Dr. Go 2⁴⁄₁₀ m to group of mailboxes. Stay right, go ⁷⁄₁₀ m more to B&B.
Restrictions Smoking restricted. Children over 12.
Credit cards MC, Visa.
Rates B&B, $95–130 double. Extra person, $25. 4-night discount.

BOZEMAN

Home of Montana State University and close to lots of cross-country skiing and two downhill ski resorts (Bridger Bowl and Big Sky), Bozeman is located in Gallatin County in the northern Rockies of southwestern Montana, approximately 90 miles north of Yellowstone National Park and 95 miles southeast of Helena. Summer activities include trout fishing in the Madison, Gallatin, and Yellowstone River, and hiking in the Bridger Range; the museum of the Rockies is well worth the visit.

Reader tip: "Bozeman is a treat with its storefronts of cohesive Western architecture, trendy shops, and several respectable eateries that serve more than steak, hamburgers, and beer. The excellent Museum of the Rockies with its first-class display of Montana's archaeological dinosaur digs was a delight, and stays open late." *(Mark Mendenhall)*

Voss Inn ¢
319 South Willson, 59715

Tel: 406–587–0982
Fax: 406–585–2964
URL: http://www.wtp.net/go/vossinn

Built in 1883, the elegantly decorated rooms of this Victorian mansion are highlighted by white bedspreads, curtains, and trim, contrasting with handsome dark flowered wallpapers and gleaming hardwood floors. Restored as a B&B in 1984, the inn has been owned by Bruce and Frankee Muller since 1989. Guests have their choice of eating breakfast in their rooms, or family-style in the parlor.

"Gracious innkeepers; comfortable room, good bed. Great breakfast, served hot and ontime." *(SS)* "A charming, clean, and inviting inn with beautifully appointed guest rooms and common areas, located in a quiet neighborhood within walking distance of downtown; easy parking. Breakfast is delicious and graciously presented; guests fill out a form in the evening and are given menu and mealtime options." *(Jean & Bill Wilson)* "Wonderful hospitality, lovely flower gardens." *(Hal & Martha Davis)* "Friendly atmosphere. Our room had a brass and iron queen-size bed with a wonderful mattress, beautiful linens, embroidered pillow cases, and a down comforter with a cutwork design cover. Breakfast is served in your room or in the dining room at 7:30 or 8:30 A.M. and features fresh fruit, cereal, hot egg dish, warm muffins, and good coffee." *(Dorothy McMillan)* "Charming Victorian atmosphere with interesting books and good lights for reading. Rooms are immaculate, requests are honored, and attention to detail is impressive." *(Barbara Hylton)* "Special touches included bath salts for the tub, evening sherry and chocolates, afternoon tea and cakes." *(Jenny Magro)*

"We have traveled in Africa, and enjoyed talking with the Mullers, who used to live there." *(Phyllis Salesky)* "Robert's Roost is done in forest greens with white eyelet bedspread and window flounces, antique white wicker table and chairs, and a brass bed." *(Patricia Newton)* "The surrounding neighborhood is a great place to walk, and downtown and the Montana State campus are close by. The hosts see to guests' needs in a friendly way, yet stay quietly in the background." *(Bob & Nan Huddleston)* "We were warmly greeted and helped to settle in." *(Martha Davis)*

Open All year.
Rooms 6 doubles—all with full bath, telephone, radio, table, fan. Some with desk, air-conditioning.
Facilities Parlor with TV, piano, books, games, porch, off street parking. 10 m to trout streams, 5 m to cross-country skiing, 15 m to downhill, 1 m to Museum of the Rockies.
Location SW MT. 12 blocks from MSU, 3 blocks from downtown,1 mile to Museum of the Rockies. Bozeman exit off I-90 to Main St.; S on Willson Ave.
Restrictions No smoking. Limited early morning weekday traffic in front rooms.
Credit cards Amex, MC, Visa.
Rates B&B, $85–95 double, $75–85 single. Extra person, $10.
Extras Airport/station pickup. Fluent Spanish, some Dutch, Portuguese, Italian spoken.